Informatik – Fachberichte

Band 1: Programmiersprachen. GI-Fachtagung 1976. Herausgegeben von H.-J. Schneider und M. Nagl. VI, 270 Seiten. 1976

Band 2: Betrieb von Rechenzentren. Workshop der Gesellschaft für Informatik 1975. Herausgegeben von A. Schreiner. VII, 283 Seiten. 1976

Band 3: Rechnernetze und Datenfernverarbeitung. Fachtagung der GI und NTG 1976. Herausgegeben von D. Haupt und H. Petersen. VI, 309 Seiten. 1976

Band 4: Computer Architecture. Workshop of the Gesellschaft für Informatik 1975. Edited by W. Händler. VIII, 382 pages. 1976

Band 5: GI – 6. Jahrestagung. Proceedings 1976. Herausgegeben von E. J. Neuhold. X, 474 Seiten. 1976.

Informatik-Fachberichte

Herausgegeben von W. Brauer
im Auftrag der Gesellschaft für Informatik (GI)

5

GI – 6. Jahrestagung
Stuttgart, 29. Sept. – 1. Okt. 1976

Herausgegeben von E. J. Neuhold

Springer-Verlag
Berlin Heidelberg New York 1976

Herausgeber

Prof. Erich J. Neuhold
Institut für Informatik
Universität Stuttgart
Herdweg 51
D – 7000 Stuttgart 1

AMS Subject Classifications (1970): 68-XX,02B10,02C99,02F10,18B20,
60K30,60K35,90B,94A10,94A20,94A25,94A30,

CR Subject Classifications (1974): 2.1,3.7,4.,5.2,5.5,6.,8.1

ISBN-13: 978-3-540-07912-5   e-ISBN-13: 978-3-642-95289-0
DOI: 10.1007/978-3-642-95289-0

<u>PREFACE / VORWORT</u>

The 6th annual congress of the Gesellschaft für Informatik
was intended
- to convey the current state of the art in various areas
  of Computer Science; a number of well-known experts were
  invited for that purpose,
- to publish original scientific papers from all fields of
  Computer Science, and
- to inform about ongoing projects, (partial-) results,
  special activities e.t.c.

The members of the Program Committee

       E.J. Neuhold (Chairman), Stuttgart

       A. Blaser, Heidelberg

       R. Dierstein, Oberpfaffenhofen

       A. Endres, Sindelfingen

       L. Hieber, Stuttgart

       H. Maurer, Karlsruhe

       H.H. Nagel, Hamburg

       H.J. Schneider, Erlangen

       N. Szyperski, Köln

       E. Vöge, Wolfsburg

with the extremely valuable help of the referees listed below
have tried to select from the many papers submitted to the
conference those which contain the most interesting and important
results. Special emphasis was to be given to the papers on development experience and use of application systems. Unfortunately in these areas only very few papers have been submitted
and as a consequence the longe range goal of the Gesellschaft
für Informatik to attract application oriented persons has not
been achieved.

In addition to the scientific papers there were many submissions
of short papers. For space allocation reasons the Program Committee was only able to accept 60 of these papers. They will be
published as a separate volume and will be distributed to the
conference participants only.

Outside of the scientific section of the conference, presentations by hardware and software industry will be given to inform the conference participants about recent developments in the computer market.

I want to express my thanks to everybody who has contributed to the success of the 6th Annual Congress of the Gesellschaft für Informatik, especially
- the Bundesministerium für Forschung und Technik;
- the University of Stuttgart;
- the Organizing Committee with its chairman R. Gunzenhäuser;
- the referees;
- our invited speakers;
- all other speakers of the conference;
- and the Springer Verlag for publishing the proceedings of this conference

For her help in organizing matters of the Program Committee and in publishing the proceedings I want to thank my secretary Miss U. Günthör.

Stuttgart, July 1976   Erich J. Neuhold

<u>Organizing Committee:</u>

        R. Gunzenhäuser (Chairman), Stuttgart
        W. Glatthaar, Stuttgart
        W. Knödel, Stuttgart
        R. Rühle, Stuttgart
        H.A. Schmid, Stuttgart
        I. Stahn, Stuttgart

<u>Referees:</u>

K. Alber, Braunschweig	H. Bekič, Wien
W. Bibel, München	K.H. Böhling, Bonn
S. Braun, München	P. Deussen, Karlsruhe
H. Donner, München	T. Einsele, München
J. Encarnacao, Darmstadt	G. Goos, Karlsruhe
P. Gorny, Oldenburg	D. Gries, München
V. Haase, Karlsruhe	K. Hanakata, Stuttgart
R. Hansen, Duisburg	U. Herzog, Erlangen
H.-J. Hoffmann, Darmstadt	F. Hofmann, Erlangen
E. Holler, Karlsruhe	P. Hoschka, St. Augustin
G. Hotz, Saarbrücken	K. Indermark, Aachen
H. Kazmierczak, Karlsruhe	G. Krüger, Karlsruhe
P. Kühn, Stuttgart	D. Kurpiun, Köln
K. Lagally, Stuttgart	H. Langmaack, Kiel
D. Lattermann, Heidelberg	R. Lauber, Stuttgart
J. Laubsch, Stuttgart	P. Lockemann, Karlsruhe
O. Mayer, Kaiserslautern	K. Mehlhorn, Saarbrücken
W. Menzel, Karlsruhe	P. Mertens, Nürnberg
G. Meyer-Brötz, Ulm	J. Mühlbacher, Dortmund
P. Namneck, Hamburg	J. Nehmer, Karlsruhe
B. Neumann, Hamburg	H. Niemann, Erlangen
TH. Ottmann, Karlsruhe	D.L. Parnas, Darmstadt
M. Paul, München	D. Pressmar, Hamburg
E. Raubold, Darmstadt	G. Rozenberg, Wilrijk
H. Rzehak, Neubiberg	K. Sauter, Hannover
D. Seitzer, Erlangen	P.P. Spies, Bonn
J. Swoboda, Ulm	H. Scheidig, Saarbrücken
A. Schief, Karlsruhe	S. Schindler, Berlin
G. Schlageter, Karlsruhe	A. Schmitt, Karlsruhe
H. Schmutz, Heidelberg	H.-J. Schneider, Berlin
C.P. Schnorr, Frankfurt	J. Schürmann, Ulm
P. Stahlknecht, Hannover	W. Stucky, Karlsruhe

M. Tasto, Hamburg

H. Trauboth, Karlsruhe

H. Walter, Darmstadt

H.R. Wiehle, Neubiberg

V. ter Meulen, Würzburg

K. Voss, St. Augustin

K. Weihrauch, Bonn

H. Zima, Bonn

This conference was supported by

Stadt Stuttgart

IBM Deutschland GmbH, Stuttgart

Siemens AG, München

Computer Gesellschaft Konstanz mbH, Konstanz

Wandel und Goltermann, Eningen/Württ.

Buchhandlung Messerschmidt, Stuttgart

Standard Elektrik Lorenz AG, Stuttgart

Energie-Versorgung Schwaben AG, Stuttgart

Neckarwerke, Elektrizitätsversorgung-AG,

Esslingen am Neckar

Digital Equipment GmbH, München

Kurtz & Puchner, Endlosdruckerei, Ostfildern

Papierfabrik Scheufelen, Oberlenningen/Württ.

AEG-Telefunken, Seligenstadt

Plessey Deutschland GmbH, München

CONTENTS

MAIN LECTURES

FORMAL LANGUAGES, SYNTACTIC ANALYSIS, SEMANTIC, LANGUAGE MODELS

----

*) This paper was not received in time for publication.

AN EVALUATION OF SEVERAL SYSTEM PROTECTION STRATEGIES

George Radin
IBM Thomas J. Watson Research Center
P. O. Box 218
Yorktown Heights, N. Y. 10598/USA

Let me begin by calling your attention to an excellent discussion of
the general subject of protection in Computer Systems in a paper by
J. Saltzer and M. Schroeder in the September, 1975 IEEE Proceedings (5).
My talk will be confined to protection at the low level of machine
addressing. I will describe some of the more common current approaches
and then discuss some interesting alternatives.

In most systems there is the need to prevent certain types of access
to some system facilities by some program executions. For instance,
a user is normally to be prevented from storing into another user's
data area; only the supervisor is to be allowed to change the authority
state of the system; a device such as a printer is to be accessed by
only one (system) program.

Since this access is accomplished at the machine level by the attempt
to execute a particular instruction with a particular set of operands,
protection requires the system's absolute ability to prevent unauthorized
executions. But in a Von Neumann machine, any string of bits can be
generated and asserted to represent an instruction and operands. A program can then attempt to execute this asserted instruction. Thus, the
earliest time that authority checking can be performed is at each
attempted execution of an instruction which can possibly be illegal.

In System/370 (3), and similarly in most general purpose systems, protection is achieved as follows (see Figure 1):

- The authority state of the CPU at any instant of time is represented by a string of bits, not stored in normally-addressable
  memory. This authority state (the PSW), describes which instructions can be executed, and which areas of memory can be stored
  into.

- Instructions are divided into privileged and nonprivileged categories. Among the privileged instructions is the one that can
  change this authority state (LOAD PSW) and the one that can initiate input/output (SIO).

- Associated with every 2K bytes of addressable memory is a Storage
  Protect Key, which can take values 0 through 15. The PSW also
  contains a key with the same set of permissible values. For
  every operand which names a data area to be stored into, the key
  in the PSW is matched against the key associated with the data
  area. Only if the PSW key is zero, or if the two keys have identical values is the store allowed to execute.

- If a program requires access to a facility which its PSW does not
  allow, it must appeal to an authorized program for help. It does
  this by executing the instruction SVC (Service Call). SVC is nonprivileged and it does change the PSW to a new authority state.
  It is, however, perfectly safe because (unlike LOAD PSW and
  Branch), it does not name a bit string as the new contents of the
  PSW, and it does not name an address in memory as the location of
  the next instruction to be executed. The operand is, instead
  "symbolic" (in this case an integer between 0 and 255). The
  table which associates the new PSW and the branch target with the
  symbol is accessible only to the supervisor (i.e., it is stored
  under key zero). This table is unknown and unavailable to users
  except through its symbolic interface. We will henceforth call
  such an object <u>encapsulated</u>.

- Now the authorized program which has been invoked is requested
  to perform a service on some object via an argument list (called
  a Control Block in OS/370). But this argument list itself is a
  bit string in addressable memory, hence must be checked. This
  checking is accomplished by software using one or both of the
  same strategies which the machine employed. Namely, a software
  analogue of the PSW which represents the user's authority is
  compared against the request, or the request is named symbolically
  and translated via an encapsulated table. For instance, a device
  address may be presented, and checked against the set of devices
  owned by this user. Or the user might have been given a symbolic
  name for this device earlier (e.g., at job creation time) and
  the encapsulated table created then.

  (Notice that, if the machine is enabled for interrupts while this
  service is being performed, the service program must first move
  the arguments into a private data area to prevent another process
  from changing the arguments immediately after they have been
  certified to be correct but before they are used).

The advantages of this type of access-time protection are primarily
with respect to reliability. The amount of hardware logic or software
which must work correctly is small - it is not inconceivable to contem-
plate that its logical correctness can be proven. The damage caused by
a transient error is small in many cases. Primitive facilities like
the S/370 PSW are not expensive or slow but they often do not suffice
to provide the patterns of protection and sharing required by many
installations. An example of the limitations of the S/370 storage protect key facility is the observation that many service programs, which
must access the data areas of different users, are required to run with
PSW key equal zero - hence the integrity of the system depends on their
being correct.

The two strategies just described are commonly used in many systems.
They are not mutually exclusive. The first ensures that the requestor
has the proper authority. The second translates the request into one
which is guaranteed to be safe no matter who the requestor is. A frequently used combination associates a different encapsulated table with
a set of requestors (e.g., a User set accessing a library of files).

The most common example of such a combined strategy is in virtual memory
facilities (see Figure 2). Segment tables and page tables are encapsulated objects which are used to make the addresses generated by programs
symbolic instead of real. A different set of tables is used for each
"virtual machine". If this level of protection were sufficient (as it
is in some minicomputers) then storage protect keys would be unnecessary.

Unfortunately, a 16 megabyte unit of protection is generally too large
to be sufficient without some intra-virtual memory protection as well.
This is primarily due to the fact that, inter-virtual memory communications being slow and awkward, much of the supervisor and many service
programs will reside in the user's virtual memory. The page tables
provide an alternate place to keep storage protect keys, provided no
programs which require protection run real.

The chief advantages of virtual memory addressing are ease of programming
and compatibility. In System/370 old programs, written to address
real memory, can run correctly and utilize large memories more efficiently. In some minicomputers programs written to run in 64K Bytes
of real memory (i.e., with 16 bit addresses) can still run correctly
on models that offer larger real memories. Protection is a side effect
of relocation, not a prime objective. As such its usefulness is often
not great.

Let us next consider an interested variant of virtual addressing which has some cost performance and flexibility advantages over segment/page table approaches.

Taking System/370 addressing as reasonably typical we observe that an effective address is obtained by adding the contents of one general purpose register which acts as the Base Register (B) to another register which acts as the Index Register (X), and finally adding a 12 bit displacement from the instruction (D). B+X+D is interpreted as a 24 bit memory address. Conventional protection strategies, using storage protect keys or relocate, begin with this effective address. But one can observe that loading a Base register is an explicit action to establish addressability to some area. Then, if checking can be accomplished at Load time, it need not be done at every use of that register as a base.

If protection areas are constrained to powers of 2 and suitably aligned (on boundaries consistent with their size) then B can be decomposed into two fields where the left-most field names the protection area. For instance, suppose the protection area is 64K bytes. Then B can be decomposed into one byte Protection Area Name (PAN), and a 2 byte Offset (see Figure 3). Since B can be loaded with any bit string, it must be interpreted as a symbolic name relative to an encapsulated table. But with our constraints it suffices that only the one byte PAN can be symbolic. Then, logically, this byte is used to index the encapsulated table on every use of the register as a base. If, in the effective address calculation, the sum of D+X+Offset overflows 16 bits an exception is raised.

So far this approach would seem to offer no cost/performance advantages over going to a relocate table or to storage protect keys, since it is done for every effective address. But we observe that, once checked, a valid PAN remains valid for a particular mode of use every time it is used as a Base. Thus, we can associate with each general purpose register a "shadow field" which is not observable by software (except as cache memory or relocate table look-aside buffers are observable). This shadow field contains:

- a flag to indicate whether it is still valid:
- an access mask to describe allowable uses of this area to this user;
- a PAN length field if variable.

The machine would monitor all changes to the PAN field of a register.
When it changed, the flag in the shadow field would be set invalid.
Subsequently, on first use of this register as a Base, the encapsulated
table would be accessed and the access mask set. Henceforth, until the
next modification of this PAN, the access mask is in the shadow field
and can be quickly found. As CPU's become faster the penalty for going
to memory becomes more severe and look-aside schemes such as this become
increasingly attractive. (Note that a relocate value could also be
stored in the shadow field if the unit of protection were equal to the
unit of relocation).

It is interesting to observe that, while most existing machines adopt
protection strategies based upon the restrictions of Von Neumann architecture, most programs which run on these machines are written to a
quite different and inherently safer set of architectures - namely high
level languages. It is clearly not possible to write a program, in any
of the widely used high level languages, which creates a bit string and
asks the machine to execute it as an instruction. In languages like RPG
it is not even possible to store into a data area which is unauthorized.

In languages, like ALGOL or FORTRAN, the compiler can take care not to
generate code which can exceed the range of a data area, (e.g., by an
incorrect subscript) or can compile run-time checks when analysis is
inadequate. In languages which allow addresses as data types (such
as POINTERS in PL/1) similar checks can be generated if the pointers are
explicitly associated with AREA's. These latter strategies again impose
a size and performance penalty at run-time.

The advantages of compiler inserted checks are that they are introduced
only where address references can possibly be illegal - a very small
percent of all storage references, given reasonable compile-time
analysis. The flexibility of the resulting protection is far greater
than what a S/370-like machine can provide. For instance, the same
mechanism that checks that a reference is within this user's area can,
at little additional cost, check that each array index is within the
range declared for that dimension of that array.

The chief disadvantages of this approach are:

     - The integrity of the system depends on the correctness of one
or more compilers, or interpreters. Our experience with these large
complex programs is that they continue to contain bugs for years.

- When a check is made at compile-time and thus not compiled into
the running code, the system is more vulnerable to severe damage due to
hardware failure. For instance, suppose the compiler sees:

```
         DCL A (100);
   L:DO    I = 1 to 10;
         A(I) = expression;
```

The compiler may decide that all A(I) references are certainly safe and
thus not generate any run-time range checks. If ever, when this program
runs, the location in which the constant 10 is stored malfunctions, the
entire system can be brought down.

- Since, in most systems, high-level language programs are not
adequate (due to performance or function limitations) for all the software on the system, the hardware cost required to protect assembly
language programs may be required anyway.

We have been describing various strategies for protection, all of which
imply an association of user authority with a requested access. All
schemes, with the exception of high level language systems, assumed that
addresses were strings of bits. Therefore, either the address was considered to be symbolic (i.e., an index to some encapsulated table) or its
use was checked at every access.

One can consider an entirely different strategy for protection. Namely,
we can undertake to protect the creation, copying and distribution of
addresses. If we succeed we can check authorization only when an address
is created. Subsequently possession of an address will absolutely imply
authority to use it. (This approach requires that an address contains not
only a means of locating the object named, but also a description of the
capabilities allowed the user of the address with respect to the object.
Hence it is often called a <u>Capability</u> Architecture approach (1,2,4,6).

The remainder of this paper will describe the protected addressing
aspects of one particular capability architecture which has been defined
in detail in an exploratory project within IBM. It will then attempt to
evaluate its advantages and problems.

Consider a system which is architecturally defined as a collection of
objects which reside in storage and are uniquely named. These names
serve completely to locate the objects. There is no underlying notion
of addresses. The naming strategy employed is strictly one-to-one.
That is, a name, once used, is never reassigned to another object, even

after the first has been destroyed. This results in eliminating the need for scope considerations. (The name generator probably reads a Date-Time clock.) Conversely, an object, once named, is never given a different name; thus aliasing problems are also eliminated.

Objects in this system are of different types (e.g., data segments, processes, queues, modules), and each type is defined to contain different components. One component found in several objects is a data space (i.e., a contiguous string of bits). With the exception of the data space component all components of all objects are encapsulated, (i.e., their internal bit string representations are unknowable to users of the system). Thus special instructions are defined to access and modify these components. For instance:

> - ENQUEUE a message
> - SUSPEND a process
> - INQUIRE about the size of a data space.

An object is normally created by execution of a CREATE instruction and destroyed by execution of a DESTROY instruction. During its lifetime an object (and its components) are addressed by a new type of data called a <u>Pointer</u>. The pointer contains the name of the object or of a component of the object, and a field describing the authority which any holder of the pointer has with respect to this object (see Figure 4). We will explain this more fully later.

In all of the systems we discussed previously, addresses were simply strings of bits. They could be created and modified by computational programs. Therefore, they could not be trusted as evidence of access authority. This authority was either checked at each access, or its addresses were considered to be symbolic references to a table. Unlike these addresses, pointers cannot be arbitrarily created or modified. When an object is created a pointer is given to the creator in a register which can only contain pointers. By execution of specific instructions a pointer which is in such a register can:

> - be copied into another pointer register,
> - have its authority reduced, but never enhanced,
> - be copied into a data space.

When a pointer is copied into a data space the system explicitly tags that string of bits as containing a pointer. Any attempt to modify this string will be executed normally, <u>but the tag will be turned off</u>.

A pointer can be loaded into a pointer register by execution of a LOAD instruction. In this case, however, only bit strings which are tagged as pointers will be loaded. Other attempts will result in a program exception. (See Figure 5).

Thus no program can generate addressability out of a bit string or enhance the authority in a pointer. Since this is the case it is possible to consider protection strategies in which the possession of a pointer constitutes authority to access an object consistent with the constraints in the pointer's authority field.

One limitation that arises immediately when one considers such a strategy is the inability to withdraw addressability or authority once a pointer has been generated. Three features of the architecture address this problem.

1) The shared state between users (e.g., shared data segments, message queues) provide a potential means of pointers proliferating uncontrollably. If user A creates an object and can possibly store a pointer to it in a data space which is shared with user B, then simply suspending and even destroying user A will not absolutely ensure that the object is not accessed. The Architecture defines two bits in the authority field of a data space pointer (and a message pointer). One bit prevents (or allows) storing a pointer in the addressed data space; the other bit similarly controls reading a pointer from the addressed data space. With this feature two users can share data but addressability can be contained.

2) Even for a single user it is often necessary to withdraw (or suspend) addressability. For instance, if a user has addressability to a file of pure data, the data base manager may wish to temporarily keep him from accessing it while an update is occurring so that his view of each record is consistent. To provide this function an object is defined called a <u>Switch</u> <u>Set</u>. (See Figure 6). Each entry in a Switch Set is a direct pointer to some data. He can use this switch pointer just like it pointed directly to the file but in fact every reference goes indirectly through the entry. Thus by turning off the switch, the data base manager can temporarily block accesses to the file. Subsequent attempts to access the file through the switch cause a program exception.

3)   Suppose an installation wished to give authority to user A, via a pointer. User A wishes to pass this authority to selected programs which it invokes, but not to others. But the path between authorized programs includes unauthorized programs. A switch will not work, nor will restricted storing of pointers. The architecture defines a special pointer, called an <u>Extended System Object</u> pointer (named because of an interesting other application). (See Figure 7). This pointer addresses an area in a data space containing two contiguous pointers. The first is used as a password. The second contains the authority which user A wants to pass out selectively. He gives the password only to those programs which he wants to have the second pointer. He then passes the ESO pointer freely. To obtain the second (authority) pointer a program must execute the instruction LOAD ESO USER POINTER. This instruction has three operands. The first is the ESO pointer, the second the password pointer. If the password pointer matches the first (password) pointer addressed by the ESO pointer the system loads the second (authority) pointer into the third operand.

There are seven different types of pointers in this architecture, each having a 16 byte length. The first field, the T field, consists of 4 bits which identify the pointer type. The next 4 bits are called the A (authority) field and are used to control the capability given by this pointer. The meaning of the A bits varies with different pointer types. They are set to all ones at object creation time. Henceforth, each bit may be independently set to zero by the LIMIT AUTHORITY instruction, but, once zero, an A bit in a pointer can never be set to one.

Examples of settings of the A bits are:

- A_0 in a Data Space pointer must be one if a pointer can be written into this Data Space.
- A_2 in a Data Space pointer must be one if a pointer can be read from this Data Space.
- A_1 and A_3 similarly control the writing and reading of data into and out of a Data Space.
- A_1 in a System Object pointer is for authority to destroy the object pointed to.
- A_0 in a System Object pointer allows the holder to listen for certain actions concerning the object (e.g., to listen for attempts to destroy the object, or to write into it).

The seven types of pointers are:

1) <u>Empty pointer</u> (all zeros)
   This is used as an invalid pointer, say, in partially filled control blocks.

2) <u>Token pointer</u>
   A token does not point to an object. It is a protected, guaranteed unique password.

3) <u>Null pointer</u>
   A null pointer is used to specify default operations.

4) <u>Direct Data-Space pointer</u> (See Figure 6)
   These are the most frequently used pointers. They point to a contiguous string of bytes in a Data Space. 32 bit Upper bound and Lower bound fields in the pointer guarantee that the pointer can be used only to address data within these bounds. These bounds can be collapsed from either end by the instructions:

   LOAD POINTER WITH ADDRESS (like S/370 Load Address) and
   DEVELOP SUBSET

5) <u>Indirect Data Space pointer</u> (See Figure 6)
   This is a pointer to a Switch, which we discussed earlier.

6) <u>Extended System Object pointer</u> (See Figure 7)
   This pointer allows passing authority between two end points where the intermediary programs cannot use the authority, which we also discussed earlier.

7) <u>System Object pointer</u>
   These are used to address system objects such as Processes, Queues, Data Segments, Switch Sets.

An Architecture based upon this strategy of protected pointers has many potential advantages and disadvantages. The main ones are:

- In a total system sense it can possibly provide a very efficient mechanism for supporting controlled sharing and privacy at a granularity much finer than any previous hardware schemes. In fact it may approach the functions achievable with high level language interfaces - and for languages which allow computed addresses it can do this more efficiently.

- In a local sense its cost and performance may be more than in conventional systems. Pointers are bigger than addresses. Tagged

memory adds several bits per 16 bytes and requires checking logic. When
X and D are added to the pointer to compute an effective address the
system must check that the reference still falls within the data space.
Local cost/performance is easier to measure than potential system-wide
efficiencies even though the latter may in fact be more important.

   - This strategy, being similar to the high-level language approach
has the same fundamental reliability problem. Whenever you succeed
in logically factoring back checking to some earlier time (compile-time,
pointer creation-time) a malfunction in the system after this time can
have severe consequences. If ever a pointer becomes incorrect the system
may never be able to recover. This problem becomes even more serious in
an architecture which does not support renaming.

What appears to me at present to be an attractive system approach, is an
attempt to develop early checking strategies (via compiler or hardware),
but to back this up by redundantly protecting the critical parts of the
system so that some orderly recovery scheme can be implemented.

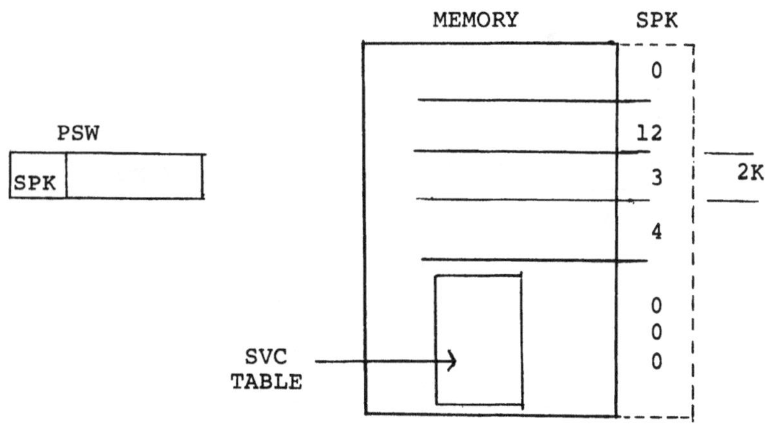

Figure 1.

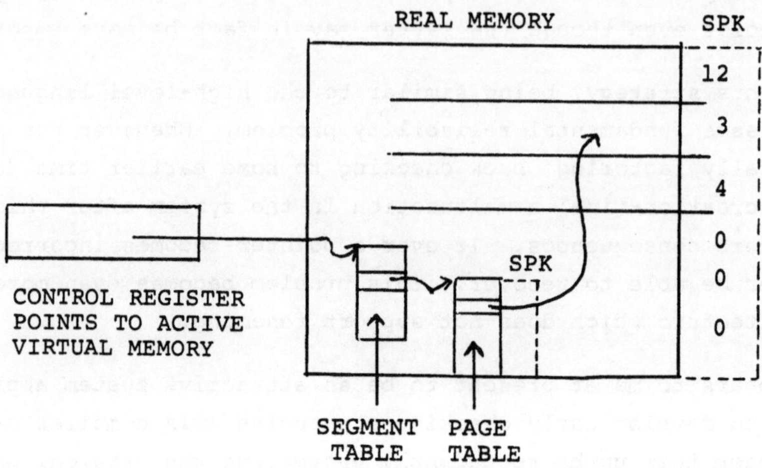

Figure 2.

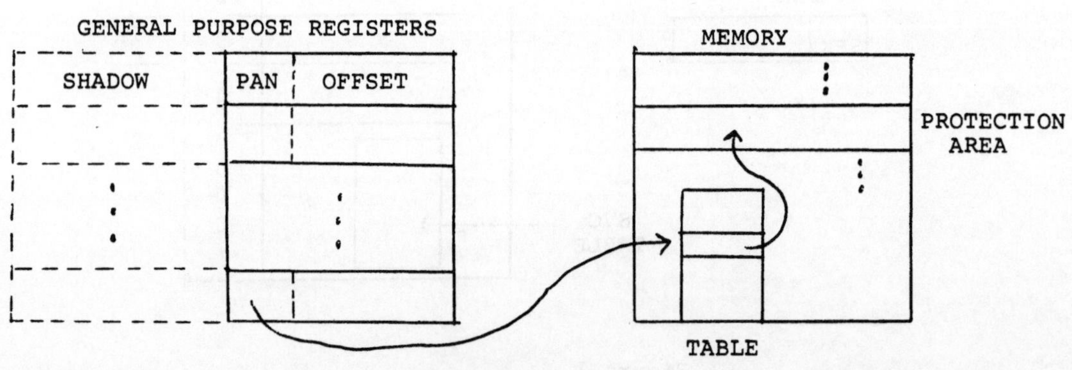

Figure 3.

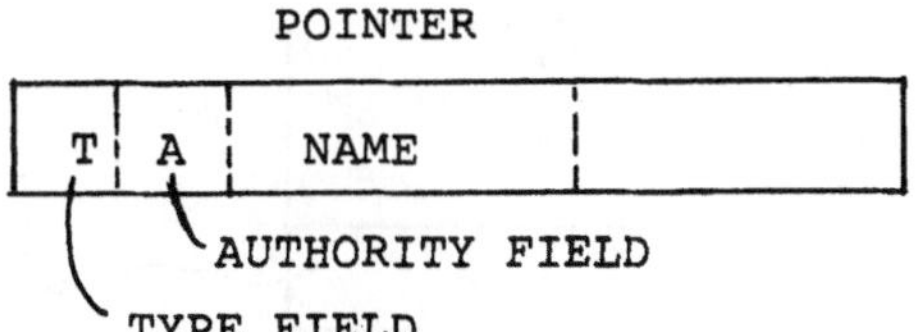

Figure 4.

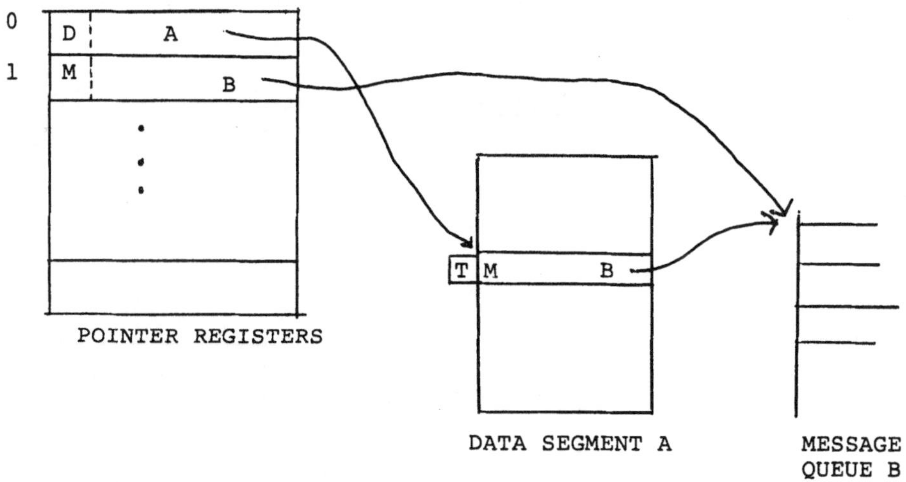

PTR IN REG 0 IS USED TO ADDRESS
POINTER IN SEGMENT A AND LOAD IT
INTO REG 1.   (TAG IS CHECKED ON
LOAD).

Figure 5.

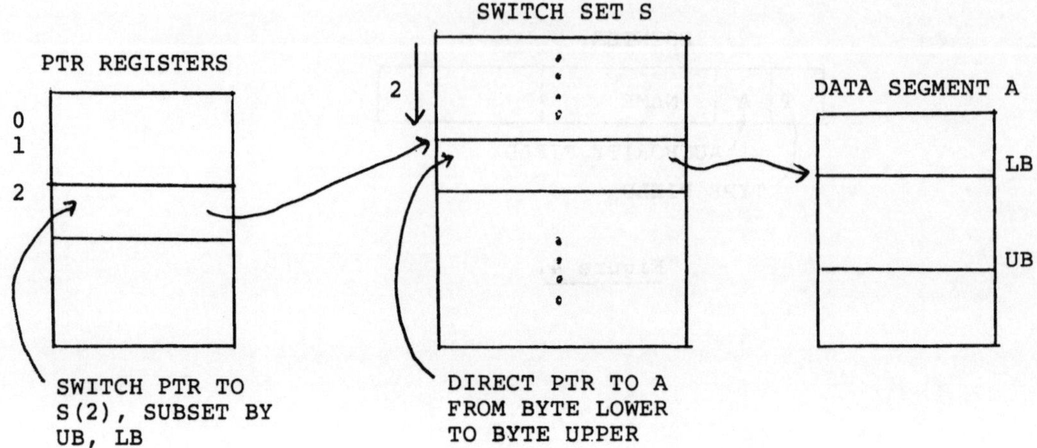

PTR REGISTER 2 ALLOWS ACCESS TO A FROM
BYTE (LB + LOWER) TO BYTE (UB + LOWER),
CHECKING THAT IT IS LESS THAN UPPER + 1

Figure 6.

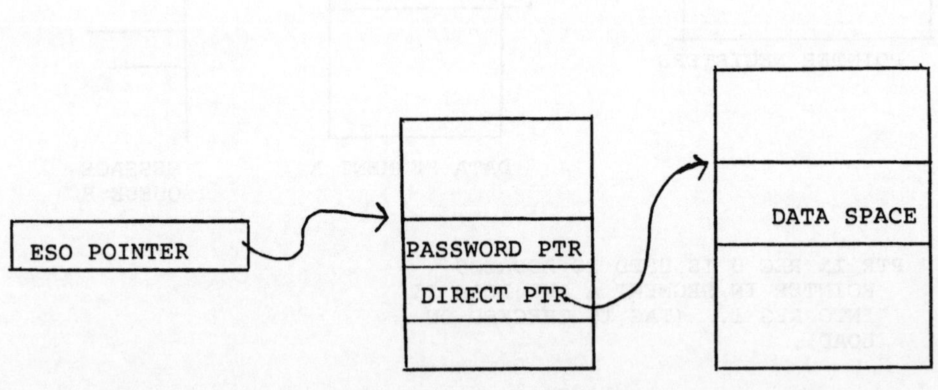

Figure 7.

BIBLIOGRAPHY

1. R. Fabry, "Capability-based addressing", Communications ACM, Vol. 17, pp. 403-412, July 1974.

2. R. Needham, "Protection systems and protection implementations" in 1972 FJCC, AFIPS Conf. Proc., Vol. 41, Pt I, pp. 571-578.

3. The Architecture of System/370, IBM AR-3799-04, Poughkeepsie, N.Y., 1973.

4. J. H. Saltzer, "Protection and control of information sharing in Multics", Communications ACM, Vol. 17, pp. 388-402, July 1974.

5. J. H. Saltzer and M. D. Schroeder, "The protection of information in computer systems", Proc. of the IEEE, pp. 1278-1307, Sept. 1975.

6. W. Wulf et al, "HYDRA: The kernel of a multiprocessor operating system", Communications ACM, Vol. 17, pp. 337-345, June 1974.

DISTRIBUTED CONGESTION CONTROL IN A PACKET NETWORK :
THE CHANNEL LOAD LIMITER

Louis Pouzin

Institut de Recherche d'Informatique et d'Automatique (IRIA)

78150 Rocquencourt, France

ABSTRACT

Congestion control in packet networks has been commonly associated with buffer management. While buffers are indeed an essential resource, they should cause no concern
as long as line load remains within preset limits. Simple analysis and simulation performed on the CIGALE network show that the most critical resource is line bandwidth,
not buffers. Based on this observation, a simple method called channel load limiter
(CLL) has been devised. Load factors (green, yellow, red) are propagated throughout
the network as an adjunction to adaptive routing. Counter measures include sending
signaling packets to offending sources, and traffic deviation on less loaded routes.
The limits and possible improvements to the CLL scheme are also mentioned.

CONGESTION SPOTS

Congestion in a packet switching network (PSN) is a pathological condition in which
traffic throughput tends to fall more or less abruptly, when offered input reaches
a critical threshold. This situation may result from several factors :
a - the receiver does not accept traffic to be delivered and the PSN does not throw
    away waiting packets,
b - lack of buffers to store packets in transit,
c - switching nodes are CPU bound,
d - transmission lines are overloaded,
e - an artificial resource (e.g. virtual circuit table) is running out,
f - delays in distributed resource management create apparent shortage.
In a simple datagram PSN, only b,c and d may occur.

Congestion problems have been identified at an early stage of the emergence of packet
switching[1]. Various methods have been devised[2] and appear to work out satisfactorily
for all practical purposes, although they may induce some traffic limitations beyond
necessity.

This paper describes a simple method being implemented in the CIGALE[3] packet network. Practical results are not yet available. However, it was felt that this method could be of interest for the research community since it can be generalized and applied to a variety of resource management schemes.

CRITICAL RESOURCES

Congestion appears to carry a strong connotation with buffer clogging. Most papers dealing with this subject are concerned with deadlocks, shortage, etc, as if buffers were the sole agent of congestion. Actually, buffer clogging is just a symptom, not a cause, of congestion.

Indeed, with the assumption that both packet arrival and length follow an exponential distribution, simple queue theory shows that the number of packets waiting for output increases drastically when line load exceeds 70 %. As a result, more buffer space is utilized for more time. It is certainly desirable, from the standpoint of cost-effectiveness, to get a high ratio of line utilization. But this conflicts with the objective of shortest transit delay, since queueing and buffering mean increased delay. Therefore, a compromise appears to be necessary between line load and transit delay.

Transit delays are dependent on line speed, packet length, queue length, and number of hops, not to mention transmission error rate. Clearly, queue length is not the only sensitive factor in meeting delay requirements. Assuming that network designers end up with some figures for average and maximum queue length, it is possible to determine from analysis or modeling the average and maximum line load. Or vice versa. Thus, buffer and line utilization are two facets of a single problem : resource management.

Taking into account present technologies, it appears that line bandwidth is scarce, with increasing costs, while buffers may be provided in large enough size, with declining costs. Thus, it is presumably more realistic to determine a bandwidth limit in the first place, and thereafter to derive buffer requirements. Putting more buffers than is actually necessary is a waste of resources, without any improvement in transit delay.

THE CIGALE NETWORK

For a given network such as CIGALE, simulation points out clearly that the primary bottleneck is line capacity[4,5,6], more precisely, the capacity of some particular data link. Past the point where a link load exceeds 80 %, it is obvious that buffer shortage develops. But this appears to be a side effect.

An interesting aspect of CIGALE, from a research point of view, is that it does not contain any intricate flow control machinery. Therefore, congestion may be studied in its primitive form, without being blurred by additional complexity resulting from control mechanisms, such as buffer allocation, fragmentation/reassembly, sequencing, and other incidental functions.

However, CIGALE had to meet the requirements of an operational network. Since the expected traffic was much lower than the theoretical capacity of the net, it was decided to put safeguards intended only for preventing pathological conditions. If a node happens to run out of buffers, it just drops incoming packets, which are acknowledged, until new buffers are released.

This is totally effective in preventing deadlocks, but not satisfactory in terms of quality of service. It would be better not to accept packets when they cannot reach their destination, because they use up some network resources to no avail. Dropped packets have no other consequence, except forcing end-to-end retransmission after a time-out. This is an empirical self tuning way of slowing down sources within the limit of the network bandwidth.

Assumptions about real traffic turned out to be realistic. Simulation studies place the upper throughput limit around 80 to 100 packets/s, while real traffic peaks are about 10 packets/s.

Nonetheless, congestion problems were thought to be an important issue for the future of commercial packet networks. Therefore, simulation studies were carried out in order to analyze sensitive factors, and help the design of simple and effective flow control mechanisms. Results obtained suggested that monitoring line load could be instrumental for a better control of local congestion spots. This method, called channel load limiter (CLL)[7] is described further in this paper.

MEASURING THE CHANNEL LOAD

A channel is 100 % busy when packets are being sent continuously. A criterion is that for a given time the count of transmitted octets is close to the theoretical limit based on channel speed.

By comparing the transmitted octet count with preset values, it is easy to determine straight away a load range, e.g :
- . normal (green)   less than 70 %
- . warning (yellow)   between 70 % and 80 %
- . alarm (red)   more than 80 %

The sampling period should be tuned in relation with the expected traffic arrival,
and the maximum size of the queue allowed on the channel. E.g. if the maximum arrival
rate is A, the channel rate is C, and the maximum queue size is Q, Q/(A-C) is an upper
limit for the sampling period.

If C > A, congestion cannot develop.

The sampling period should anticipate delays introduced in taking counter-actions.

SELECTIVE CHOKE

When a node has determined that some channel load has reached a critical threshold,
an effective but coarse way to bring it back to normal is to block all arriving traffic, including the one which does not contribute to the offending load.

A more satisfactory scheme is to apply selective counter-measures on traffic bound
for the clogged channel.

By looking up the routing tables, all addresses to which the clogged channel is the
best route can be easily identified, and marked.

Later on, routing tables are sent to neighbor nodes, which record the load status for
every marked address. However, if there exists a second best route which has not si-
gnaled clogging, it can be assigned to the traffic arriving subsequently.

Traffic deviation may or may not be desirable, depending on the network topology. If
the alternate route offers a much smaller bandwidth than the normal one, it is predic-
table that subsequent traffic will bring it to a critical threshold almost immediately
without any significant throughput increase. Therefore, traffic deviation should be
considered as an option requiring further investigation.

Routing tables received from a different region are condensed by keeping only one entry for the whole region. Any destination with a warning status places the region in
warning. But the alarm status requires all addresses in alarm.

Thus, by propagation through the network, every node sees a spectrum of load conditions attached to each segment of the visible address space.

When the channel load has been reduced, routing tables are updated, as part of the
normal adaptive routing scheme.

PREVENTIVE ACTIONS

Whenever a packet is received in a node, a routing procedure attempts to place it
onto an outgoing queue. If the corresponding channel is in warning, the following
steps are taken :

> - the packet is queued, as in normal conditions
> - a choke packet is sent back to the source
> - statistics are recorded

If the channel is in alarm, the packet is dropped.
Diagnostics packets are optional, as usual in CIGALE.

HOST ACTIONS

When a host receives a choke packet, it should slow down its traffic for the destination indicated. Otherwise, it runs the risk of having to retransmit dropped packets.

E.g. each choke packet received might induce a pause before another packet is sent to
the choked address. This delay might be in the order of 1/10 the transmission time
of a packet.

FURTHER REFINEMENTS

Before trying to make it more complicated, the CLL scheme should be studied in order
to understand its behavior under adverse conditions.

Possible improvements might be :
a - Include the load factor in a formula giving the best route,
b - When warning occurs, deviate long packets to a second best route,
c - Drop packets selectively, long packets first,
d - Introduce traffic classes in load measurement and routing policies,
e - shut off sources which trigger more than a preset number of packet drops in a
given time period. But this could be under manual control.

A CRITICAL APPRAISAL

The CLL scheme is based on the observation of local conditions. This carries pros
and cons applicable to every similar scheme, i.e. :
> . Mechanisms are simple,
> . Congestion spots are identified as early as desirable,
> . Counter actions are delayed. When they take effect, it may be too late,
>   or the cause may have disappeared,
> . There is no global optimization.

The method assumes also that there is a correlation between present and future traffic. It may be reasonable to consider that packet arrivals and lengths are independent, when traffic interleaving is sufficient. But choke packets would have no effect if sources were distributed at random for each packet. On the other hand, load propagation would still remain effective, since it applies to destinations.

In short, the CLL scheme is presumably effective when traffic does not present large transients. It should be scrutinized for instability when traffic sources may be highly bursty, such as high bandwith I/O devices.

CONCLUSIONS

The CLL scheme is being implemented and simulated, in order to study both its practical and theoretical impacts. A consequence of its simplicity is that its parameters can be adjusted dynamically, if necessary. It can also be turned off in the whole network, or in a subset of nodes. Therefore it will be possible to introduce and observe independently other control mechanisms. This is an important flexibility when several schemes are combined in order to balance one another in various traffic conditions.

REFERENCES

1 - DAVIES D.W. - The control of congestion in packet switched computer networks. IEEE, Transac. on comm. (Jun. 1972), 546-550.

2 - POUZIN L. - Flow control in data networks. Methods and tools. ICCC, Toronto, (Aug. 1976), 8 p.

3 - POUZIN L. - CIGALE, The packet switching machine of the CYCLADES computer network. IFIP Congress, Stockholm, (Aug. 1974), 155-159.

4 - IRLAND M. - Simulation of CIGALE 1974. 4th data communications symp. Quebec, (Oct. 1975), 5.13-5.19.

5 - IRLAND M. - Simulacion of CIGALE. Report on assumptions and results. University of Waterloo. CCNG report E-32, (Jan. 1975), 53 p.

6 - IRLAND M. - Simulation of CIGALE 1975. Progress report : phase I. University of Waterloo. CCNG report (Jul. 1975), 27 p.

7 - POUZIN L. - Congestion control based on channel load. Réseau CYCLADES, MIT 600. (Aug. 1975), 5 p.

ADV-Systementwicklung und Organisation der Aufgabenerfüllung

P. Schmitz

1. Einleitung

Die Entwicklung der automatisierten Datenverarbeitung zeigt ein stän-
diges Nachhinken der Anwendung in Wissenschaft, Wirtschaft und Verwaltung hinter dem technischen Leistungsvermögen der Systeme. Neue Technologien oder neue Nutzungsformen, wie sie etwa durch das Aufkommen
des Massenspeichers mit wahlfreiem Zugriff, durch die Möglichkeiten
des Timesharing, durch neue Sprachen usw. gegeben waren, bedeuteten
jeweils einen sprunghaften Anstieg des Leistungspotentials der Systeme.
Der Anwender mußte sich immer wieder auf diese Neuerungen einstellen,
und es dauerte oft mehrere Jahre, ehe er nach entsprechenden Umstel-
lungsarbeiten in der Lage war, die neuen Möglichkeiten wirtschaftlich
wenigstens teilweise auszuschöpfen.

Es kann davon ausgegangen werden, daß diese Diskrepanz in Zukunft noch
sehr viel stärker werden wird, da einerseits die zu erwartenden Innovationen im Bereich der Technologie und der Nutzungshilfen einen sehr
viel größeren Leistungsanstieg zur Folge haben werden und andererseits
die bisherigen Entwicklungen bei den Anwendern Strukturen geschaffen
haben, die nicht mehr ohne weiteres geändert werden können.

Die zu erwartenden Neuerungen werden einen Einfluß nehmen, nicht nur
auf die Ablauforganisation der Datenverarbeitungsaufgaben im engeren
Sinne, sondern auch auf die Aufbauorganisation und auf das gesamte Kom-
munikationssystem des Anwenders; gleichzeitig wird der Prozeß der An-
passung an diese Neuerungen wichtige soziologische Probleme aufwerfen.

In diesem Beitrag beschränken wir uns auf die Interdependenzen zwischen
der Systementwicklung einerseits und der Organisation der Aufgabenerfüllung in Wirtschaft und Verwaltung andererseits. Nicht betrachtet wird
dagegen die breitere Wirkung der Systementwicklung auf das gesamte Kom-
munikationssystem beim Anwender; hierzu wird zum Beispiel auf Szyperski verwiesen [55]. Ebenfalls ausgeklammert werden spezielle Probleme
der Ein- und Ausgabe, der Einfluß auf die Aufbauorganisation sowie soziologische Probleme, die im Zusammenhang mit der Nutzung der automatisierten Datenverarbeitung stehen; hierzu sei auf entsprechende Arbeiten, die an der Universität Hamburg durchgeführt werden, verwiesen
[26].

Der Grundgedanke dieser Arbeit ist es, Zusammenhänge zwischen den drei
folgenden Komponenten eines ADV-Anwendungssystems aufzuzeigen: Dem
Hardwaresystem auf der einen Seite, dem Aufgabensystem des Anwenders

auf der anderen Seite und den zwischen beiden Komponenten stehenden
Kommunikationshilfen als Gesamtheit von Software, Programmiersprachen
usw. [49, S.3]. Auf Grund der beschränkten zur Verfügung stehenden Zeit
kann dies selbstverständlich nicht erschöpfend geschehen, vielmehr sollen einige wichtige Probleme im Zusammenhang mit der Themenstellung
aufgezeigt werden.

2. Bisherige Entwicklung

Im Bereich der Hardware und der Software läßt sich eine einheitliche
chronologische Entwicklung aufzeigen; dies ist für die Anwendung der
automatisierten Datenverarbeitung in der ganzen Breite einheitlich nicht
möglich [23, S. 18]; es soll daher hier an Hand einiger weniger Aspekte kurz die Anwendungsentwicklung aufgezeigt werden.

Die in einer Stelle als organisatorische Einheit zu erfüllenden Aufgaben waren auf den einzelnen Menschen als Aufgabenträger zugeschnitten.
Die ersten automatisch arbeitenden Anlagen wurden lediglich als ein
Hilfsmittel angesehen, einzelne Funktionen im Rahmen dieser Stellen-
aufgaben zu erfüllen. Ihr Einsatz erforderte die Zergliederung der Aufgaben in - von der Aufgabenstellung her gesehen - unnatürliche Teil-
schritte. Der Grund für das Unvermögen, die Aufgaben geschlossen zu er-
ledigen, lag in der unzureichenden Speicherkapazität der ersten Anlagen.

Insbesondere mit dem Aufkommen von Magnetbändern als Datenspeicher
konnte die Zergliederung der Aufgaben einer Stelle wieder rückgängig
gemacht werden, und darüberhinaus war es im beschränkten Maße möglich,
Aufgabengruppen zu integrieren; damals kam der Begriff der integrierten Datenverarbeitung auf. Eine weitergehende Integration über mehrere
Aufgabenbereiche und damit über mehrere Funktionsbereiche in der Unternehmung war in dieser Phase jedoch nicht gegeben.

Der periphere Massenspeicher mit wahlfreiem Zugriff, wie er Anfang der
60er Jahre herauskam, bot erstmals die Möglichkeit, Aufgabenbereiche
zu integrieren. Damit war gleichzeitig die Möglichkeit gegeben, die ADV
auch für bereichsübergreifende Aufgaben einzusetzen. Insbesondere fallen in diese Zeit die ersten Versuche zur Schaffung von Management-In-
formationssystemen; allerdings führten diese Versuche aus vielerlei
Gründen in den meisten Fällen in eine Sackgasse und machten über Jahre
hinaus einer Resignation des Managements gegenüber solchen Nutzungsformen Platz.

Von der Mitte der 60er Jahre an wurde die Datenfernübertragung für den
Anwender erschlossen. Dadurch konnten bei der Aufgabenstrukturierung
die geographischen Restriktionen zugunsten sachbezogener Gesichtspunk-

te überwunden werden. Mit Hilfe dezentraler Stationen konnte die Kommunikation mit dem zentralen Datenverarbeitungssystem im Hinblick auf Dateneingabe und Datenausgabe wesentlich erleichtert werden.

Einen wesentlichen Einfluß auf die Aufgabenerfüllung der Unternehmung haben die problemorientierten Programmiersprachen, insbesondere COBOL, genommen. Damit war die Möglichkeit gegeben, die Mitarbeiter der Fachabteilungen stärker als bis dahin in den Prozeß der Implementierung von Datenverarbeitungsaufgaben einzubeziehen. Das gleiche gilt für die erst seit den letzten Jahren unter dem Stichwort Softwaretechnologie zur Verfügung stehenden Implementierungshilfen, z.B. die Entscheidungstabellentechnik, die Generatortechnik, moderne Programmierungsmethoden usw.

Der stärkeren Einbeziehung der Endbenutzer der automatisierten Datenverarbeitung, sowohl beim Prozeß der Entwicklung von programmierten Aufgabenlösungen als auch bei der Abwicklung der Aufgaben mit Hilfe der automatisierten Datenverarbeitung kam die Entwicklung der verschiedenen Betriebsarten in Form von Mehrprogrammbetrieb, Dialogbetrieb, Teilnehmerbetrieb usw. entgegen.

Insgesamt läßt sich der derzeitige Stand des Einsatzes der ADV in Wirtschaft und Verwaltung durch eine Zentralisation der folgenden Datenverarbeitungsfunktionen, die auch durch die bisher gültige Kostendegression erzwungen wird, kennzeichnen (in Anlehnung an Johnson [32, S.81]): Bereitstellung und Bereithaltung der Hardware, Systemanalyse, Programmierung, Pflege der Datenbank, wesentliche Mitbestimmung bei der Erstellung neuer Anwendungskonzepte; den Fachabteilungen obliegen die Definition von Aufgabenstellungen, die zu automatisieren sind, und die Mitwirkung bei der Konzipierung von Lösungen und bei deren Implementierung. Bereits jetzt ist abzusehen, daß die Weiterentwicklung wieder in Richtung auf eine stärkere Dezentralisierung der Aufgabenerfüllung geht.

Parallel zur Anwendungsentwicklung von der ursprünglich dezentralen Aufgabenerfüllung zur Zentralisation und nunmehr wieder umgekehrt zur Dezentralisation verlief die ADV-Systementwicklung vom Spezialrechner in den ersten Anfängen zum heutigen Universalrechner. Die Entwicklung läßt erwarten, daß in Zukunft der Spezialrechner wieder stärker in den Vordergrund treten wird.

Was den Einfluß des ADV-Anwenders auf die Hardware/Softwaresystementwicklung angeht, so ist seine Rolle bisher eher rezeptiv: Er stellt sich mit seinen Aufgaben und seiner Organisation auf die auf dem Markt angebotenen Systeme ein. Es wird in der Zukunft notwendig sein, die Erfordernisse der Anwendung bei der Entwicklung von ADV-Systemen sehr viel stärker als bisher zu berücksichtigen.

3. Die Weiterentwicklung der Hardware und Kommunikationshilfen

3.1 Technologie und Architektur der Hardware

Hauptmerkmale der Hardware sind die Geschwindigkeit, der Raumbedarf,
die Kosten, der Energiebedarf und die Zuverlässigkeit; die Betonung
liegt im folgenden auf den drei ersten Merkmalen.

Technologische Komponenten der Hardware sind Schaltkreise und Speicherelemente, aus denen architektonisch Speichersysteme, Prozessoren und
Rechnersysteme aufgebaut werden. Die weitere Entwicklung der Schaltkreise und der Speicherelemente als den bestimmenden Komponenten von Rechensystemen ist für die nächsten Jahre bereits weitgehend vorgezeichnet;
insbesondere sind die Grenzen im Hinblick auf die oben genannten Merkmale abzusehen.

Bezüglich der Verzögerungszeiten von Schaltkreisen sind die Auffassungen in der Literatur nicht ganz einheitlich. Nach Turn [57, S. 153]
werden sich die Verzögerungszeiten von Bipolarhalbleitern von derzeit
etwa 5 ns bis zu etwa 1 ns im Jahre 1990 reduzieren; ein Hersteller
gibt eine Verringerung von 2 ns auf 0,5 ns an [29]; demgegenüber nennt
Einsele [14, S. 13] Zeiten von jetzt 200 ps bzw. 100 ps im Jahre 1990;
dies dürfte dann auch die theoretisch erreichbare Geschwindigkeitsgren-
ze sein.

Im Hinblick auf die Kosten von bipolaren Schaltkreisen rechnet man mit
einer Reduzierung von heute etwa DM 0,60/Gatter auf etwa DM 0,10/Gatter
im Jahre 1990 [57, S. 159], [14, S. 13].

In der Literatur wird einhellig die Auffassung vertreten, daß in abseh-
barer Zeit Speichermedien zur Verfügung stehen, die bezüglich der Zugriffszeit den Bereich bis zu einigen 10 ns abdecken werden (vgl. hierzu und zum folgenden [14, S.12-16], [35], [57, S.177-204]). Den verschiedenen technischen Ausprägungen von Speichern werden wirtschaftliche Zugriffszeitbereiche und Kapazitätsbereiche zugeordnet sein. Damit
wird das gesamte Spektrum von Zugriffszeit und Kapazität lückenlos durch
die verschiedenen Medien abgedeckt sein. Insbesondere wird die bisheri-
ge technologische Lücke in den Zugriffszeiten von 1:10000 zwischen den
als Zentralspeichern realisierten Medien und dem Magnetplattenspeicher
durch verschiedene neue Technologien geschlossen sein.

Bezüglich der Kostenentwicklung wird festgestellt, daß beim Ferrit-Kern-
speicher gegenüber den derzeitigen Kosten von etwa 1 Pf./Bit keine wesentlichen Änderungen mehr zu erwarten sind; beim Halbleiterspeicher
erwartet man dagegen eine Reduzierung der Kosten von derzeit etwa
10 Pf./Bit auf weniger als 0,1 Pf./Bit im Jahre 1990, beim Magnetbla-

senspeicher werden für das Jahr 1990 Kosten in Höhe von 0,01 Pf./Bit
erwartet.

Schünemann stellt die Hypothese auf, daß zwischen dem Logarithmus der
Zugriffszeit einerseits und den Logarithmen der Kosten pro Bit sowie
den wirtschaftlich sinnvollen Speicherkapazitäten andererseits ein linearer Zusammenhang besteht [51].

Aus der Tatsache, daß es auch zukünftig wirtschaftlich nicht vertretbar sein wird, den gesamten hinsichtlich Kapazität und Zugriffszeit für
viele praktische Anwendungen notwendigen Speicherraum durch ein einziges Speichermedium zu realisieren, ergibt sich die Notwendigkeit, unterschiedliche Medien zu Speicherhierarchien in realen Rechensystemen zu
koppeln. Man wird davon ausgehen können, daß in großen Systemen funktionsmäßig und realtechnisch bis zu 6 oder 8 Speicherstufen realisiert
sein werden.

Die erkennbaren und zum Teil bereits vorhandenen Schaltkreisrealisationen ermöglichen Prozessoren von bis vor kurzem nicht vorstellbaren
Leistungen. Bereits heute werden auf dem Markt Mono-Prozessoren mit einer Leistung von mehr als 10 Mio. Instruktionen pro Sekunde angeboten,
entsprechend 10 MIPS; die Entwicklung läßt eine weitere Steigerung auf
100 MIPS erwarten. Dies ist vergleichsweise das 400-fache der Leistung
einer IBM/7090 im Jahre 1960 [57, S.75].

Im Hinblick auf die Kosten wird davon ausgegangen, daß im Jahre 1984
Mono-Prozessoren mittlerer Geschwindigkeit zu Preisen in der Größenordnung von höchstens einem Zehntel heutiger Preise angeboten werden [59,
S.54]. Das reine Preis/Prozessorleistungsverhältnis wird dann um einen
Faktor von 1000 über dem einer IBM/7090 im Jahre 1960 liegen.

Was den Raumbedarf anbetrifft, wird vorausgesagt, daß ein einzelner
Prozessor mit einer Leistung von 10 MIPS auf einem Chip von 1 mm^2 Platz
hat [17, S.558].

Im Hinblick auf ihre Funktion werden die Speicherelemente nicht mehr
ausschließlich in herkömmlicher Weise realisiert, sondern zunehmend
auch als Festspeicher (Read only Memories) zur Aufnahme von im normalen Betrieb unveränderlichen Daten und Programmteilen sowie als Assoziativspeicher für spezielle Suchprozesse. Diese Sonderformen sind dann
Komponenten in einer Speicherhierarchie.

Auf Grund der bereits genannten physikalischen Leistungsgrenzen der
technologischen Komponenten sind den aus diesen Komponenten zusammengesetzten Mono-Prozessoren Geschwindigkeitsgrenzen gesetzt. Eine weitere Leistungssteigerung ist daher nur mehr durch Parallelisierung der

Verarbeitung möglich, wie sie inzwischen bereits in einer Reihe von Rechensystemen realisiert ist. Neben einer Parallelisierung der Eingabe-Ausgabe-Funktionen werden insbesondere die internen Zentralfunktionen von Rechensystemen parallelisiert. Hierbei lassen sich drei ausgeprägte Realisationsformen unterscheiden:

- Pipelining-Prinzip: Als Pipeline wird eine Konfiguration des Rechenwerkes bezeichnet, bei der unabhängige Einheiten jeweils eine bestimmte Teilfunktion von Verarbeitungsschritten übernehmen. Die Daten können so von Einheit zu Einheit weitergegeben werden, und damit ist die parallele Abarbeitung eines einzigen Datenstromes möglich [20], [43].

- Feldrechner-Prinzip: Hierbei arbeiten mehrere Rechenwerke in einer für alle Werke gleichen Folge von Rechenoperationen synchron an den verschiedenen Datenelementen eines Feldes [56].

- Parallelrechner-Prinzip mit unabhängigen Prozessoren: Bei diesem Prinzip, das bereits seit vielen Jahren in einer Reihe von auf dem Markt befindlichen Systemen realisiert ist, arbeiten mehrere Prozessoren mit Zugriff auf einen gemeinsamen Speicher weitgehend unabhängig voneinander an verschiedenen Aufgaben [17].

Typische Vertreter solcher moderner Rechnerarchitekturen, die zum Teil bereits serienmäßig angeboten werden, sind die folgenden (teilweise Kombinationen aus den obigen Prinzipien):

ASC (Advanced Scientific Computer, Texas Instruments) [58],

C.mmp (Multi-Mini-Processor, Carnegie Mellon University) [61],
DAP (Distributed Array Processor, ICL) [45],

HYPERCUBE (IMS-Associates) [52],

ILLIAC IV (University of Illinois) [53],

PEPE (Parallel Element Processing Ensemble, US. Army) [56],

RADCAP (Rome Air Development Center Associative Array Processor) [15],

STAR-100 (String Array Processor, Control Data Corp.) [9, S.13-1], [7],

STARAN (Goodyear Aerospace Corp.) [4].

Als Beispiel für die Leistung solcher Systeme sei der ILLIAC IV genannt, der bei einer Ausstattung mit 64 Prozeßelementen eine Leistungsfähigkeit von 100-200 MIPS erbringt gegenüber der derzeitigen Grenzleistung von ca. 40 MIPS bei einem Mono-Prozessor [53, S.76].

Allerdings steigt die Leistung von Mehrprozessorsystemen wegen der erforderlichen Koordination nicht proportional zu der Anzahl der Prozessoren. Mitchell u.a. haben gezeigt, daß die Gesamtleistung eines Mehrpro-

zessorsystems nur bei einer geringen Anzahl von Prozessoren mit dieser
Zahl linear ansteigt und daß von einer bestimmten, von der Aufgabenstellung nur geringfügig abhängigen Anzahl von Prozessoren ab keine
Leistungssteigerung mehr zu vermerken ist [39, S.400]. Wie Rosenfeld
gezeigt hat, hängt die Leistung eines Mehrprozessorsystems darüberhinaus
auch noch im starken Maße von der Qualität der Programmierung ab [45].

Um die Rechner, die sich auf Grund der Vielzahl von Möglichkeiten aus
den o.g. Funktionstypen kombinieren lassen, einzuordnen, sind eine Reihe von Klassifikationsvorschlägen gemacht worden, die aber alle nur die
internen Prozessorfunktionen, nicht aber die Beziehungen dieser Funktionen zu den Speicherwerken sowie zu den Eingabe- und Ausgabewerken beschreiben und von daher noch nicht voll befriedigen [56, mit einer Vielzahl weiterer Zitate], [24].

Eine wesentliche Voraussetzung für die dezentrale Nutzung von Rechensystemen sowie zum Betrieb von Rechnerverbundsystemen sind leistungsfähige Datenübertragungswege. Derzeit sind diese Voraussetzungen in
Deutschland noch nicht gegeben. Es kann aber davon ausgegangen werden,
daß für diese Zwecke in der Zukunft neue und verbesserte Techniken und
Nutzungsformen zur Verfügung stehen [40]. Wichtige Techniken der Zukunft
sind verbesserte Kabelverbindungen (Koaxial-Kabel anstelle von Adern-
paaren), Funkverbindungen, die in erster Linie für die Satellitenüber-
tragung eingesetzt werden, Hohlleiter, bei denen mit einer Übertragungs-
leistung von 230000 Telefonverbindungen entsprechend etwa 10 Milliar-
den bit/s gerechnet werden kann [38, S.207] sowie in etwas weiterer Zukunft die Laserstrahltechnik über optische Glasfaserleiter [1, S.9].

Diese Techniken werden dem Anwender in verbesserten Wählnetzen, aber
auch in Form überlassener Übertragungswege zur Verfügung stehen. Es ist
zu erwarten, daß sich die Kosten der Datenübertragung für den Anwender
gegenüber dem heutigen Stand wesentlich reduzieren und damit ein ausge-
wogenes Verhältnis zu den Rechnerkosten erreicht werden kann.

Neben dem Einsatz moderner Leitungstechnologien ist im Interesse eines
wirksamen Datenverbundes zu fordern, daß eine Paket-Vermittlung, wie
sie in einigen Ländern bereits besteht, auch in Deutschland ermöglicht
wird. Dies wäre z.B. durch die Ergänzung des EDS-Netzes um einige Spei-
chervermittlungseinheiten möglich [47, S.330].

3.2 Kommunikationshilfen in modernen Rechensystemen

Kommunikationshilfen sind von der Bestimmung her Mittler zwischen Hardware einerseits und Anwendung andererseits. An dieser Stelle sollen diejenigen Hilfen besprochen werden, die eher auf die Hardware ausgerichtet sind und weniger auf eine konkrete Anwendung Bezug nehmen.

Die anteiligen Kosten für die Entwicklung der Software an den gesamten Entwicklungskosten von Hardware/Softwaresystemen, die bereits in der Vergangenheit ständig zugenommen haben, werden weiter ansteigen. Einsele stellt fest, daß bereits jetzt die anteiligen Softwarekosten auf bis zu 80 % angestiegen sind [14, S.11]. Dieser Tendenz kann auf der Ebene der Systemsoftware durch zweierlei Maßnahmen entgegengewirkt werden:

- Auf Grund der Tatsache, daß bei zukünftigen Systemen die Kosten für die Speicherwerke gegenüber dem bisherigen Stand erheblich reduziert werden, wird es nicht mehr notwendig sein, mehrere Betriebssysteme entsprechend den unterschiedlichen Speichergrößen der Systeme einer Universalrechnerfamilie bereitzustellen, sondern man wird für die Systeme einer Rechnerfamilie einheitliche Betriebssysteme entwickeln können [13, Abschnitt 4.2.2].

  Dies wird allerdings voraussetzen, daß die Betriebssysteme stärker modular aufgebaut sind, um so dem Anwender die Möglichkeit zu geben, die für seine Zwecke geeignete Untermenge zu selektieren. Im anderen Fall werden die Systeme zu schwerfällig und stellen, wie gegenwärtige Beispiele zeigen, ihre wirtschaftliche Nutzung in Frage.

- Eine zweite Möglichkeit zur Reduzierung der Entwicklungskosten für Betriebssysteme ist die Verlagerung geeigneter Komponenten in die Hardware. Vielfach werden dabei die betreffenden Funktionen durch Mikroprogrammspeicher realisiert und speziellen Mikroprozessoren zugeordnet [54, S.87]. Beispiele hierfür sind die Look-ahead-Prozessoren, die als Hilfen bei der Parallelverarbeitung sequentieller Programme auf Parallelrechensystemen eingesetzt werden [35] sowie Assoziativprozessoren, die mit einem Assoziativspeicher ausgestattet sind und die Suchprozesse in Datenverarbeitungsaufgaben zeitlich erheblich reduzieren [5].

In Mehrprozessorsystemen, bei denen große Datenbanken in einem zentralen, für alle Prozessoren zugänglichen Speicher geführt werden, hat die Organisation des Speicherzugriffs ein besonderes Gewicht. Schecher hat einen Vorschlag zur Lösung dieses Problems gemacht [48].

Wegen der starken Kostenreduzierung im Hardwarebereich wird es in der Zukunft wirtschaftlich möglich sein, für spezielle Aufgabenklassen Spe-

zialrechner einzusetzen. Für diese werden sich die zugeordneten Betriebssysteme tendenziell vereinfachen, da eine Vielzahl von Betriebssystem-
komponenten eines Universalrechners hier entfällt.

Ein zunehmendes Gewicht gewinnen die Komponenten, die zur Realisierung
der Datenfernübertragung notwendig sind. Es kann davon ausgegangen werden, daß die erforderlichen Funktionen in das Hardware-Softwaresystem
integriert werden und dem Anwender für diese Zwecke geeignete geschlos-
sene Systeme zur Verfügung gestellt werden [22].

Die Nutzung von parallelarbeitenden Systemen macht es erforderlich, die
in Programmiersprachen formulierten Prozeduren für die parallele Abwicklung aufzubereiten. Hierzu sind grundsätzlich 3 Wege möglich: Erstens
die Entwicklung neuer speziell auf die Möglichkeiten der Parallelverarbeitung ausgerichteter Sprachen, zweitens die Erweiterung bestehender
Programmiersprachen und drittens die automatische Übertragung (etwa
durch den Übersetzer) von in den herkömmlichen Sprachen sequentiell
formulierten Prozeduren. Baer und Russel berichten über die wichtigsten
Forschungen auf diesem Gebiet [3]. Lösungen für das Problem, in herkömmlichen Programmiersprachen als sequentielle Prozesse formulierte Prozeduren automatisch in die Parallelverarbeitung zu übertragen, sind zum
Beispiel von Baer [2] und von Parchmann und Sedello [41] angegeben worden. In der Literatur wird dagegen überwiegend die Auffassung vertreten,
daß es wirtschaftlicher ist, die bestehenden Sprachen im Hinblick auf
die Parallelverarbeitung zu erweitern oder neue Sprachen für diesen
Zweck zu schaffen. Vorschläge für mögliche Spracherweiterungen für den
Einsatz von parallelarbeitenden Systemen wurden u.a. von Hecht und Rzehak [25] und von Irani [31] gemacht. Neue Sprachkonzepte sind u.a. von
Davis [10] und Patterson [42] vorgeschlagen worden.

4. Interdependenzen zwischen ADV-Systementwicklung und Organisation der
   Aufgabenerfüllung

4.1 Art und Umfang der betrieblichen Datenverarbeitungsaufgaben

In mittleren und Großunternehmungen und Verwaltungen sind seit vielen
Jahren ADV-Anlagen eingesetzt. Für den Bereich des Versicherungswesens
sagt eine Studie, daß im Jahre 1971 diejenigen Unternehmungen, die ADV-
Anlagen einsetzten, 92 % des gesamten Beitragsvolumen der Versicherungs-
unternehmungen auf sich vereinigten [6, S.2]. Auf Grund der Wettbewerbs-
situation und wegen der absehbaren technischen Entwicklungen werden in
Zukunft auch kleinere Einheiten in allen Anwendungsbereichen in die Lage versetzt, das Sachmittel ADV zur Abwicklung der betrieblichen Datenverarbeitungsaufgaben einzusetzen.

Im Hinblick auf die Art der zu erfüllenden Datenverarbeitungsaufgaben
unterscheidet man entsprechend den hierarchischen Ebenen zwischen Aufgaben der operationellen, der dispositiven und der strategischen Ebene.
Bei den erfahrenen Anwendern sind die Aufgaben der operationellen Ebene
bereits weitgehend automatisiert. Das Hauptinteresse wendet sich daher
in der Zukunft den Aufgaben der dispositiven und der strategischen Ebene, in denen die ADV im wesentlichen Managementaufgaben zu erfüllen
hat, zu. Ference und Uretsky haben diese Entwicklung durch die folgenden Phasen definiert [16, S.57-59]: Datenmanipulationsaufgaben, Gewin-
nung neuer Informationen, Unternehmungssteuerung, strategische Planung.

Aus der Sicht, wie das ADV-System zur Erfüllung der betrieblichen Aufgaben eingesetzt wird, nennt ein Hersteller von ADV-Systemen als Ent-
wicklungsstufen [9, S.7-1]: Information processing, information storage
and retrieval sowie information movement. Während die ersten beiden
Stufen inzwischen realisiert bzw. in der Planung sind, befindet sich
die dritte erst in der Anfangsphase.

Übereinstimmend mit den o.a. Auffassungen zeichnet sich eine zunehmende
Integration der betrieblichen Datenverarbeitungsaufgaben ab. Hieraus
ergeben sich wichtige Anforderungen an die einzusetzenden ADV-Systeme.
Von daher wird es sinnvoll sein, bezüglich der Art der abzuwickelnden
Aufgaben zwischen den beiden folgenden Typen zu unterscheiden:

- Aufgaben, bei denen während des Erfüllungsprozesses ein ständiger Zugriff auf eine zentrale Datenbank erforderlich ist;

- isolierte Aufgaben, die während des Erfüllungsprozesses keinen perma-
  nenten Zugriff zu einer zentralen Datenbank erforderlich machen.

Nach Schätzungen von Praktikern werden die Aufgaben der ersten Klasse
etwa 90 % aller Aufgaben einer Unternehmung ausmachen. Wegen der sehr
unterschiedlichen Anforderungen beider Aufgabenklassen an die ADV-Systeme wird es notwendig sein, hier genauere Untersuchungen bezüglich der
Zuordnung von Aufgaben zu diesen Klassen anzustellen. Außerdem sollte
festgestellt werden, welche Aufgaben und unter welchen Bedingungen aus
der ersten Klasse von Aufgaben herausgelöst werden können dadurch, daß
für sie ein Zugriff auf die zentrale Datenbank lediglich zu Beginn ihrer Erfüllung und an ihrem Ende notwendig wird.

Was den Umfang der zu erfüllenden Aufgaben anbetrifft, so kann davon
ausgegangen werden, daß in den großen und erfahrenen Betrieben bereits
heute ein sehr großer Teil möglicher Datenverarbeitungsaufgaben automatisch abgewickelt wird bzw. sich in der Planung zur automatischen Erfüllung befindet; auf jeden Fall dürfte die sehr rasche Umfangsentwick-

lung der Vergangenheit zukünftig nicht mehr zu erwarten sein. Praktiker schätzen, daß sich der Umfang der zu automatisierenden Aufgaben in den nächsten Jahren höchstens noch einmal verdoppelt. Es wird notwendig sein, auch hier genauere Untersuchungen durchzuführen; vor allem auch für die Herstellerindustrie dürften diesbezügliche Aussagen von größter Bedeutung sein.

4.2 Die Abwicklung der betrieblichen Datenverarbeitungsaufgaben

Die betrieblichen Datenverarbeitungsaufgaben, die über gemeinsame Daten integriert sind, machen es erforderlich, daß entsprechende Datenbestände zentral in einem ADV-System bereitgestellt werden. Wegen des bereits zuvor angeführten Umfangs dieser Aufgaben am gesamten Aufgabenumfang sind hierfür entsprechend leistungsfähige ADV-Systeme mit großen Speicherwerken bereitzustellen. Diese Zentralisation bei der Aufgabenabwicklung ist bei den isolierten Aufgaben nicht notwendig. Hierfür können insbesondere Spezialrechner dezentral eingesetzt werden. Unterstützt wird diese Dezentralisation der isolierten Aufgaben durch die in der Zukunft zu erwartende Kostenreduktion im Bereich der Spezialrechner. Lediglich für solche isolierten Aufgaben, die besonders hohe Kapazitätsanforderungen an den Speicherumfang stellen, wird nach wie vor die Abwicklung in einem leistungsstarken zentralen System sinnvoll sein. Insgesamt wird also die Tendenz dahingehen, für die über Daten integrierten Aufgaben zentrale ADV-Systeme einzurichten, und die isolierten Aufgaben dezentral abzuwickeln.

Im Hinblick auf die zu erwartenden ADV-Systeme der Zukunft kann man, was die Abwicklung der zentralen Aufgaben angeht, folgendes feststellen:

- Der Mono-Prozessor scheidet für die Aufgabenstellungen der genannten Art aus, da er bei der geschilderten Spezialisierung auf Datenmanipulationen nicht ausgelastet werden könnte und andererseits die sequentielle Verarbeitungskapazität nicht ausreichen würde, um die Vielzahl von Zugriffen auf die Datenbank zu realisieren.

- Der Feldrechner scheidet für diese Aufgabenstellung ebenfalls aus. Er ist konzipiert für solche Aufgaben, bei denen zusammenhängende sequentiell angeordnete Datenbestände simultan verarbeitet werden können. Bei den meisten Aufgabenstellungen, die über eine zentrale Datenbank erledigt werden müssen, handelt es sich dagegen um Einzelzugriffe auf gestreut gespeicherte Datensätze.

- Inwieweit Rechner nach dem Pipeline-Prinzip für diese Zentralaufgaben in Frage kommen, muß noch untersucht werden. Die bisher bekannten Pipeline-Konzepte betonen die Parallelverarbeitung in erster Linie im

Hinblick auf arithmetische Prozeduren.

Erforderlich für die zentralen Aufgaben mit gemeinsamer Datenbank wird wahrscheinlich ein System sein, das aus vielen autonomen Prozessoren, ggf. mit einem beschränkten Befehlsrepertoire, besteht, die unabhängig voneinander auf die gemeinsame Datenbank zugreifen können.

In diesem Zusammenhang treten eine ganze Reihe von ungelösten Problemen auf:

- Wie ist ein solches System zu konzipieren, damit man mit einem minimalen Steuerungsaufwand auskommt ?

- Welches ist das erforderliche Befehlsrepertoire ?

- Wieviele Prozessoren wird man bei einer konkreten Ausgabenstellung in ein solches ADV-System einbeziehen ?

- Wie bereits zuvor ausgeführt, wird man ADV-Systeme für große Datenbestände nicht mit einem einzigen homogenen Speicher realisieren, obwohl dies aus der Aufgabenstellung her durchaus zu begrüßen wäre, sondern wird auf Grund der Kostensituation mit einer Speicherhierarchie zu rechnen haben. Hier werden die bereits zuvor genannten Fragen der optimalen Speicherauslegung besonders im Hinblick auf die Anzahl von Hierarchieebenen von großer Bedeutung sein. Erste Modelle zur Berechnung der optimalen Anzahl von Speicherstufen sind von Schünemann [51] und von Gecsei [19] gegeben worden. Es wird notwendig sein, solche Untersuchungen im Hinblick auf konkrete betriebliche Aufgabenstellungen zu erweitern, im Gegensatz zu den idealisierten Voraussetzungen in den vorgenannten Arbeiten.

- Wenn die Verwaltung der Daten auf ein zentrales System ausgelagert wird, ergibt sich der Anreiz, die Benutzer noch mehr als bisher von der Datenverwaltung zu entlasten und das Datenbankmanagementsystem als Kommunikationshilfe noch leistungsfähiger, flexibler und mehr auf die Benutzerbedürfnisse ausgerichtet zu gestalten. Zum Beispiel wird es notwendig sein, die Managementsysteme so einzurichten, daß nachträglich neue Organisationsstrukturen für die Datenbank definiert werden können, was bei den bisherigen Datenbanksystemen nur unter sehr großen Aufwendungen möglich ist [27], [28]. Ein Modell für ein zukünftiges Datenbankmanagementsystem ist von Withington [59, S.65-66] gegeben worden.

- Ein Aspekt bei großen Datenbanksystemen ist die Frage, inwieweit die Routinen des Datenbankmanagementsystems, die in einer konkreten Anwendung erforderlich sind, beim Binden dem Anwendungsprogramm mitgegeben werden, anstatt das gesamte System speicherresident zu halten und erst zur Laufzeit aufzurufen.

- Was die Wirtschaftlichkeit von Datenbanksystemen und deren Benutzer-
  freundlichkeit angeht, sind bisher nur wenige Untersuchungen realer
  Systeme in Form von Benchmarktests bekannt. Ein Ansatz hierzu ist in
  einer Arbeit von Kaiser [33] gegeben. Es ist sinnvoll, auf dieser Basis weitergehende empirische Untersuchungen anzustellen.

- Insbesondere für die Aufgaben mit zentralen Datenbanken, bei denen
  vielfach auch in großem Umfang Personendaten gespeichert sind, haben
  die Fragen des Datenschutzes und der Datensicherheit eine besondere
  Bedeutung. Bei dezentralen Lösungen ist diese Problematik nicht so
  gravierend wie bei großen, schwer zu übersehenden zentralisierten
  Systemen. Das Datenschutzgesetz für die Bundesrepublik Deutschland
  ist vor kurzem im Bundestag verabschiedet worden[1]. Ganz sicher wird
  es notwendig sein, noch Ausführungsrichtlinien zu erarbeiten, um das
  Gesetz praktikabel zu machen.

- Ein weiteres Problem in diesem Zusammenhang ist die Frage, wie es mit
  dem Aufwand zur Realisierung von Datenschutz und Datensicherheit steht,
  der von der Systemgröße abhängen wird. Die Hilfsmittel zur Realisierung von Datenschutz und Datensicherheit sind um so umfangreicher und
  leistungsfähiger, je größer das System ist. Andererseits sinkt mit der
  Größe des Systems die eng mit Datenschutz und Datensicherheit zusammenhängende Überschaubarkeit der Systeme.

- Eine Alternative zur ausschließlich zentralen Datenhaltung mit Einzel-
  zugriffen auf die Datenbank je Arbeitsschritt ist die Möglichkeit, aus
  der zentralen Datenbank in Zeitabständen (etwa stundenweise oder tage-
  weise) schubweise entsprechende Untermengen an dezentrale Stellen zur
  Verarbeitung abzugeben und nach der Verarbeitung wieder in die zentrale Bank zu integrieren. Die besonders hohen Geschwindigkeitsanforde-
  rungen an die Datenübertragung für diese Alternative werden in der Zukunft erfüllt werden können. Ein positiver Aspekt dieser Alternative
  sind auch die besseren Realisierungsmöglichkeiten von Datenschutz und
  Datensicherheit.

Wie bereits ausgeführt wurde, können die isolierten Aufgaben, die keine
zentrale Datenbank erfordern, sofern sie nicht spezielle Kapazitätsanforderungen stellen, auf Spezialrechnern dezentral durchgeführt werden.
Die zu erwartenden neuen Parallelrechnerkonzepte erschließen hier ein
weites Feld für Aufgaben, die bisher nicht oder nur unzureichend erle-

______

[1] Den Bundesrat hatte das Gesetz bei Redaktionsschluß noch nicht pas-
    siert.

digt werden konnten. Eine typische Klasse von Aufgaben in diesem Bereich sind solche, die von der Aufgabenstellung her bereits durch simultane Prozesse beschrieben werden können. Neben den reinen Feldaufgaben gehören hierhin z.B. Simulationsaufgaben etwa im Fertigungsbereich. Hier wird es möglich sein, das reale Nebeneinander eines Prozesses in einem parallelarbeitenden Mehrprozessorsystem auch simultan durchzuführen.

Simultan arbeitende Mehrprozessorsysteme bieten ebenfalls wirkungsvollere Lösungsmöglichkeiten z.B. bei der Branch and Bound-Methode; hier brauchen die einzelnen Zweige nicht mehr nacheinander bis zum Abbruchkriterium durchgerechnet zu werden, sondern man kann sie simultan behandeln, so daß ein Abbruch nicht in Frage kommender Lösungswege sofort beim Auftreten einer besseren Lösung in einem anderen Zweig erfolgen kann.

Im Zusammenhang mit parallelarbeitenden Systemen wird es für den Anwender notwendig sein, sich von der bisher geübten sequentiellen auf eine simultane Denkweise zur Lösung von Datenverarbeitungsaufgaben einzustellen [44, S.65].

Im Hinblick auf den Einsatz von modernen Rechnerkonzepten wie zum Beispiel Feldrechner und Pipeline-Rechner ist festzustellen, daß diese nur dann wirtschaftlich arbeiten, wenn die Aufgabenstellung genau auf die Möglichkeiten des Rechners zugeschnitten ist. Für den Feldrechner bedeutet das, daß die Dimension von Aufgabenstellung und Rechnersystem genau zueinander passen müssen. Von Thurber und Wald [56] sind die Ergebnisse von Untersuchungen für eine Reihe von modernen Rechnerkonzepten publiziert worden. Scrupski [52, S.68] zitiert eine Äußerung von Amdahl, wonach die Leistung von 64 parallelen Prozessoren auf das Niveau von 15 unabhängigen Prozessoren absinkt, wenn nur 5 % der Instruktionen sequentiell abzuwickeln sind. Auch Withington [59, S.54] stellt die Wirtschaftlichkeit solcher parallelarbeitender Systeme für eine Vielzahl von Anwendungen in Frage. Graham [20] führt aus, daß der hohe technische Aufwand für einen Pipeline-Rechner nur dann gerechtfertigt ist, wenn das System durch die Aufgabe über die gesamte Verarbeitungszeit ausgelastet ist. Es muß daher aus der Sicht des Anwenders untersucht werden, welche betrieblichen Aufgaben wirtschaftlich auf solchen Systemen abgewickelt werden können.

Für die isolierten Aufgaben bietet sich als Alternative an, hierzu auch Service-Rechenzentren in Anspruch zu nehmen. Dies wird vor allen Dingen dann von Nutzen sein, wenn auf diese Weise von speziellen Programmsystemen und von überbetrieblichen Datenbanken Gebrauch gemacht werden kann. Ein Beispiel für den letzten Aspekt ist das System Technotec von CDC.

Im Rahmen dieses Systems, das eingebettet ist in das Verbundsystem CY-
BERNET, werden Beschreibungen über neue technologische Konzepte bereit-
gehalten. Ein an der Lösung eines technologischen Problems Interessier-
ter erfährt nach Eingabe seiner Problemstellung in das Verbundsystem, ob
innerhalb Technotec evtl. eine Hilfe existiert, und es werden nach den
erforderlichen Rücksprachen die entsprechenden Partner kurzgeschlossen
[8].

4.3 Planung und Implementierung der betrieblichen Datenverarbeitungsaufgaben

Die Notwendigkeit zur fachgerechten und wirtschaftlichen Nutzung der
ADV wird im wesentlichen durch zwei Aspekte, die insbesondere innerhalb
der Planung und Implementierung von Datenverarbeitungsaufgaben Bedeutung
haben, bestimmt:

- Der durch die modernen Technologien gegebene Trend zur Dezentralisierung der Datenverarbeitung,

- die zunehmenden Personalaufwendungen im Bereich der Datenverarbeitung.

Hieraus ergeben sich im einzelnen die folgenden Forderungen an die Planung und Implementierung:

- Ermittlung der Zuständigkeiten zwischen den dezentralen Fachabteilungen als Endbenutzern der Datenverarbeitung und der im allgemeinen zentralen Datenverarbeitungsstellen,

- verstärkter Ausbau softwaretechnologischer Methoden,

- Einsatz von Standardanwendungssoftware,

- Normung entsprechender Elemente im Gesamtsystem.

Im Gegensatz zum bisherigen Stand der administrativen Datenverarbeitung
in den Unternehmungen und Verwaltungen,bei dem die zentrale Datenverarbeitungsstelle die entscheidenden Kompetenzen nicht nur bei der Abwicklung der Datenverarbeitung sondern auch bei ihrer Planung und Implementierung hatte, wird die Zukunft zu einer verstärkten Mitwirkung der Fachabteilungen am gesamten Datenverarbeitungsprozeß führen. Den Fachabteilungen werden - auch bei den zentral abzuwickelnden Aufgaben - mehr und
mehr die Funktionen der Problemdefinition, der Konzeption des Lösungs-
verfahrens und die anwendungsorientierte Programmierung zukommen, woge-
gen die Zuständigkeit der zentralen Datenverarbeitungsstelle bei den
maschinennahen Aufgaben, wie Systemprogrammierung und Datenbankpflege
liegt. Nach Diebold [12] folgt die Notwendigkeit für die stärkere Einbeziehung der Fachabteilungen auch aus der Tatsache, daß der Nutzen des

ADV-Einsatzes und damit dessen Wirtschaftlichkeit nur von den Fachabteilungen beurteilt werden kann. Eine detaillierte Beschreibung der zukünftigen Funktionen von Datenverarbeitungsstelle und Fachabteilungen gibt Johnson [32] u.a. für die beiden Zeitstufen 1975-1985 und 1985-1995. Bei einem deutschen Anwender wird erwartet, daß sich das Verhältnis von zentralem Personal zu ADV-orientiertem Fachabteilungspersonal von derzeit 1:1 auf 1:10 verändern wird.

Die Regelung der Zuständigkeiten stellt in der Praxis eine sehr schwierige Aufgabe dar, da die durch die bisherigen Entwicklungen vielfach festgefahrenen Strukturen im Bereich der Datenverarbeitung nur sehr schwer modifiziert werden können.

Insbesondere die Personalkostenentwicklung erfordert die Verbesserung und Weiterentwicklung softwaretechnologischer Methoden und die Intensivierung ihres Einsatzes. Nach Diebold [11, S.8-9] werden im Jahre 1978 nur 20-40 % der Datenverarbeitungsanwender, die eigene Rechner betreiben, systematisch softwaretechnologische Methoden einsetzen. Als Gründe für die geringe Verbreitung sind mehrere Faktoren verantwortlich: Die unzureichende Markttransparenz, die hohen Kosten der Methoden, die geringe Überschaubarkeit des Nutzens, fehlende man-power für die Methodenauswahl, unzureichende Methodenbeschreibungen und geringe Portabilität der Methoden.

Schramm und Dörfel haben eine Bewertung softwaretechnologischer Methoden für die späten 70er Jahre gegeben [50]. Danach sind am vordringlichsten solche Methoden, die die Schwachstellenanalyse, den Systementwurf und die Systemimplementierung unterstützen. Ein Aspekt, der in der Literatur nicht festgestellt wurde, ist die Forderung, bei der Gestaltung von softwaretechnologischen Methoden auch die Erfordernisse der Revision einzubeziehen.

Das wichtigste Instrument der Softwaretechnologie sind die Programmiersprachen. Auf einen Aspekt, der stärker auf die Hardware bezogen ist, wurde bereits hingewiesen: Die Einbeziehung von solchen Sprachelementen, mit deren Hilfe die Parallelität bei Einsatz von parallelarbeitenden Systemen ausgedrückt werden kann, Aus der Tatsache, daß zunehmend auch Endbenutzer, also durchweg Nicht-DV-Spezialisten, mit der Programmierung betraut werden, ergeben sich nach Sammet u.a. folgende Tendenzen [46]: Sprachen, die durch den Benutzer definiert und auf diese Weise an dessen spezielle Bedürfnisse und Interessen angepaßt werden können; Ausrichtung auf Problembeschreibungssprachen, bei deren Verwendung die erforderlichen Prozeduren automatisch durch das ADV-System aus einem Vorrat alternativer Prozeduren ausgewählt werden. Lockemann stellt fest, daß, ent-

gegen der bisherigen Entwicklung, bei der man die Programmiersprachen
an den Gegebenheiten der zu benutzenden Anlagen bzw. an den Anwendungs-
gebieten orientiert hat, in der Zukunft die Programmiersprachen die
Erfordernisse des strukturierten Programmierens berücksichtigen und bessere Korrektheitsprüfungen in einfacher Weise ermöglichen sollten [37].
Die gleiche Auffassung vertritt auch Withington [59], der diese Anforderungen in Dialekten von APL, PL/1, COBOL, FORTRAN realisiert sehen will.

Alle bisher bekannten softwaretechnologischen Methoden unterstellen, daß
die zu implementierenden Problemstellungen gegeben sind. Praktiker weisen darauf hin, daß es demgegenüber notwendig sein wird, auch Instrumente zu entwickeln, die es möglich machen, aus Planungen, die die Primär-
aufgaben der Betriebseinheiten betreffen, etwa aus Vorstellungen über
die zukünftigen Produktplanungen einer Fertigungsunternehmung, zukünfti-
ge Problemstellungen für die ADV abzuleiten. Ohne ein solches Instrument
bestehe die Gefahr einer Fehlentwicklung der ADV im Anwendungsbereich.

Eines der wichtigsten Instrumente, die ADV wirtschaftlich zu nutzen,
ist der Einsatz von mehrfach verwendbarer Anwendungssoftware (Standardanwendungssoftware). Die Attraktivität der Entwicklung von Standardanwendungssoftware ergibt sich aus der Tatsache, daß eine Vielzahl von
Problemstellungen für die verschiedensten Anwendungsbereiche existieren;
alleine für den Bereich der Lohn- und Gehaltsprogramme stellt Granholm
fest, daß in den USA mehr solche Programme existierten, als Rechenanlagen installiert waren [21]. Die derzeitige Situation auf dem Markt für
diese Software wird in einer Studie von Infratest und MBP wie folgt dargestellt [30]: Obwohl derzeit etwa 250 Hardwarehersteller und Software-
häuser Standardsoftware anbieten, wird in der Praxis, insbesondere bei
den universellen Großrechenanlagen, nur im geringen Teil von diesen Möglichkeiten Gebrauch gemacht; etwa 79 % der Programme in der Großrechner-
anwendung sind eigenerstellte Programme; ein wichtiges Hindernis für den
Einsatz solcher Programmsysteme ist das Fehlen geeigneter Methoden zur
Beurteilung und zur Auswahl solcher Systeme. Frank [18] hat in einer Arbeit einen systematischen Ansatz gegeben, der es dem Anwender erlaubt,
unter Berücksichtigung der bei ihm gegebenen Umstände zu einer optimalen
Entscheidung zu gelangen.

Die ständig steigende Anzahl von Hardware- und Softwaresystemen, die auf
Grund der Dezentralisierung in einer Unternehmung oder Verwaltungsein-
heit die unterschiedlichsten Systeme zum Einsatz kommen, zwingt zu einer
zunehmenden Normung im Bereich der ADV. Der Normungszweck ist einerseits
die Portabilität von Programmen; hier sind die Programmiersprachen und
die Betriebssprachen Gegenstände der Normung. Andererseits sollen die

Realisierung von Verbundsystemen, die aus unterschiedlichen Hardware-Softwaresystemen komponiert werden, und die Benutzung von Service-Rechenzentren über Fernleitung erleichtert werden; Gegenstand der Normung sind hier die Schnittstellen zwischen den verschiedenen Systemkomponenten.

Obwohl inzwischen eine Vielzahl entsprechender Normen bereits festgelegt sind, ist doch festzustellen, daß aus den verschiedensten Gründen in der Praxis noch erhebliche Abweichungen von diesen Normen gegeben sind. Es wird notwendig sein, von Anwenderseite stärker auf die Festlegung von Normen zu dringen und gegenüber den Hardware- und Softwareherstellern die Einhaltung dieser Normen zu fordern.

5. Zusammenfassung

Die in der Zukunft zu erwartenden Innovationen im Hardware/Softwarebereich ermöglichen völlig neue Konzeptionen für eine wirtschaftliche Erfüllung der Datenverarbeitungsaufgaben in Wirtschaft und Verwaltung. Dem Trend vom Universalrechner zum Spezialrechner auf der einen Seite steht auf der Seite der ADV-Anwendung die Rückentwicklung von der Zentralisation zur Dezentralisation gegenüber. Wenn aus diesen Entwicklungen für den Einsatz der ADV Nutzen gezogen werden soll, so erfordert dies eine bessere Abstimmung zwischen den Herstellern von Hardware/Softwaresystemen und den Anwendern dieser Systeme. Dies bedeutet einerseits, daß sich die Anwender mehr als bisher mit den zu erwartenden technologischen Innovationen auseinandersetzen müssen, und daß andererseits die Hardware/Softwaresystementwicklung stärker auf die Bedürfnisse der Praxis ausgerichtet werden muß.

Literatur

[1] d'Agapeyeff, A.: The impending revolution in business data processing. In: Computer Bulletin, Serie 2, Nr. 6, Dez. 1975, S.8-10

[2] Baer, J.L.: A Survey of Some Theoretical Aspects of Multiprocessing. In: Computing Surveys, Vol 5, No. 1, March 1973, S.31-80

[3] Baer, J.L.; Russel, E.C.: Preparation and Evaluation of Computer Programs for Parallel Processing Systems. In: Hobbs, L.C. (Hrsg.): Parallel Processor Systems, Technologies and Applications. New York, Washington 1970, S.375-415

[4] Batcher, E.: STARAN parallel processor system hardware. In: National Computer Conference, 1974, S.405-410

[5] Berra, P.B.: Some problems in associative processor applications
      to data base management. In: National Computer Conference, 1974,
      S.1-5

[6] Betriebswirtschaftliches Institut der Versicherungswirtschaft:
      EDV-Anlagen, EDV-Anwendungen, EDV-Personal in Unternehmen der
      Individualversicherung. Köln 1975

[7] CDC: Control Data STAR-100 Computer. Features Manual. Control
      Data Corp., o.O. 1975

[8] CDC: Technotec/Worldtech. A global marketing system for the ex-
      change of technology. Control Data Corp., o.O. 1975

[9] CDC: Trends in Large-Scale Computing. Control Data Corp., Minne-
      apolis, Minn. 1975

[1o] Davis, E.W.: STARAN parallel processor system software. In: Nati-
      onal Computer Conference, 1974, S.17-22

[11] Diebold Deutschland GmbH: Der Bedarf an ADV-Fachkräften bis 1978.
      Band 2: Entwicklung des Arbeitsmarktes für ADV-Fachkräfte bis
      1978. Bundesministerium für Forschung und Technologie, Forschungs-
      bericht DV 74-02, o.O. 1974

[12] Diebold Deutschland GmbH: Einsatzmöglichkeiten softwaretechnolo-
      gischer Methoden mit Normungseffekt, Studie im Auftrag des Bun-
      desministers für Forschung und Technologie, April 1976

[13] Drittes Datenverarbeitungsprogramm der Bundesregierung, 1976-
      1979, Bonn 1976

[14] Einsele, T.: Entwicklungstendenzen der Rechnertechnologie und
      Rechnerstruktur. In: Nagel, K. (Hrsg.): DV-Aktuell 1976, Stutt-
      gart 1976, S.11-21

[15] Feldmann, J.; Fulmer, L.C.: RADCAP - An operational parallel pro-
      cessing facility. In: National Computer Conference, 1974, S.7-15

[16] Ference, T.P.; Uretsky, M.: Computers in management: Some in-
      sights into the state of the revolution. In: Management Datama-
      tics, Vol. 5, No. 2, 1976, S.55-63

[17] Foster, C.C.: A View of Computer Architecture. In: Communications
      of the ACM, Vol 15, No. 7, July 1972, S.557-565

[18] Frank, J.: Selektion von Standard-Software. Kriterien und Metho-
      den zur Beurteilung und Auswahl von Software-Produkten. Diss.
      Köln 1976

[19] Gecsei, J.; Lukes, J.A.: A model for the evaluation of storage
      hierarchies. In: IBM Systems Journal, No. 2, 1974, S.163-179

[20] Graham, W.R.: The Parallel and the Pipeline Computers. In: Data-
      mation, Vol. 16, No. 4, April 1970, S.68-71

[21] Granholm, J.W.: Parfait Payroll. In: Datamation, Vol. 17, No. 8,
      April 1971, S.37-38

[22] Gray, J.P.; Blair, C.R.: IBM's Systems Network Architecture. In:
      Datamation, Vol. 21, No. 4, April 1975, S.51-56

[23] Grochla, E.; Meller, F.: Datenverarbeitung in der Unternehmung.
      Teil 1: Grundlagen. Reinbek bei Hamburg 1974

[24] Händler, W.: On Classification Schemes for Computer Systems in
      the Post-von-Neumann-Era. In: Siefkes, D. (Hrsg.): GI-4. Jahres-
      tagung Berlin 1974, Lecture Notes in Computer Science, Band 26,
      Berlin, Heidelberg, New York 1975, S.439-452

[25]   Hecht, V., Rzehak, H.: Languages and translation techniques for
        extensive use of parallel operations. In: Computing, Vol. 14, No.
        1-2, 1975, S.15-17

[26]   Heiby, H.W.; u.a.: Auswirkungen der Datenverarbeitung auf den
        einzelnen Anwender und Organisationen, die die DV anwenden. Uni-
        versität Hamburg, Mitteilung Nr. 20, 1975

[27]   Hoffmann, M.: MIS und Software. Bemerkungen über die Software zum
        Aufbau eines MIS. In: Grochla, E.; Szyperski, N. (Hrsg.): Manage-
        ment-Informationssysteme. Eine Herausforderung an Forschung und
        Entwicklung. Wiesbaden 1971, S.221-233

[28]   ICL: And the shape of things to come ... In: ICL News, Febr. 1976,
        S.7

[29]   ICL: Präsentation von Entwicklungstendenzen im Hardwarebereich.
        West Gorton, 24. Febr. 1976 (unveröffentlicht)

[30]   Infratest Wirtschaftsforschung GmbH und Mathematischer Beratungs-
        und Programmierungsdienst GmbH: Stand und Entwicklung des Marktes
        für mehrfach verwendbare Anwendungssoftware in der gewerblichen
        Wirtschaft. Veröffentlichg.durch das Bundesministerium für For-
        schung und Technologie in Vorbereitung.

[31]   Irani, K.B.: A proposal for a programming language for parallel
        processing environments. Michigan University, AD-AOO9641/2,
        Febr. 1975

[32]   Johnson, J.P.: The changing DP organization. In: Datamation, Vol.
        21, No. 1, Jan. 1975, S.81, 83

[33]   Kaiser, E.-V.: Zur Auswahl und Optimierung von Datenbank-Manage-
        ment-Systemen (DBMS). - Untersuchung mit Hilfe von Benchmark-
        Tests -. BIFOA Arbeitsbericht Nr. 73/2, Köln 1974

[34]   Keller, R.M.: Look-Ahead Processors. In: Computing Surveys, Vol.
        7, No. 4, Dec. 1975, S.177-195

[35]   Köhler, R.: Speicher für die Computer der Zukunft. Die Technolo-
        gien künftiger Speichermedien. In: Bürotechnik, Heft 2, 1976,
        S.34-41

[36]   Kuck, D.J.: Supercomputers for ordinary users. Proceedings 1972
        Fall Joint Computer Conference, S.213-220

[37]   Lockemann,P.C: Systeme, Abläufe, Daten. In: Gebhardt, F. (Hrsg.):
        Tagung Informatik und Informationswissenschaft am 13. und 14.
        April 1976 in der GMD, St. Augustin 1976 (unveröffentlicht)

[38]   Martin, J.: Future Developments in Telecommunications. Englewood
        Cliffs, N.J. 1971

[39]   Mitchell, J.; Knadler, C.; Lunsford, G.; Yang, S.: Multiprocessor
        performance analysis. In: National Computer Conference, 1974,
        S.399-403

[40]   Nolle, F.: Entwicklungstendenzen in Fernmeldenetzen. In: Hassel-
        meier, H.; Spruth, W.G. (Hrsg.): Rechnerstrukturen. Vorträge des
        Informatik-Symposiums der IBM Deutschland, Wildbad 1973. München,
        Wien 1974, S.395-410

[41]   Parchmann, R.; Sedello, M.: Syntaxgesteuerte Programmerzeugung
        zur Parallelverarbeitung arithmetischer Ausdrücke. Veröffentli-
        chung in Kürze in: Angewandte Informatik

[42]   Patterson, W.W.: Some thoughts on associative processing langua-
        ges. In: National Computer Conference, 1974, S.23-26

[43] Ramamoorthy, C.V.; Kim, K.H.: Pipelining - The generalized concept and sequencing strategies. In: National Computer Conference, 1974, S.289-297

[44] Reddaway, S.F.: DAP - a distributed array processor. In: 1st annual Symposium on Computer Architecture, Florida 1973, S.61-65

[45] Rosenfeld, J.L.: A case study in programming for parallel-processors. In: Communications of the ACM, Vol. 12, No. 12, Dec. 1969, S.645-655

[46] Sammet, J.E.: Programming Languages: History and Future. In: Communications of the ACM, Vol. 15, No. 7, July 1972, S.601-610

[47] Sarbinowski, H.: EURONET - mehr als ein 'weiteres' Netz. In: Online, 14 Jg., Heft 5, Mai 1976, S.328-33o

[48] Schecher, H.: Vorschläge für die Organisation einer flexiblen Multiprozessoranlage. In: Fachtagung Struktur und Betrieb von Rechensystemen, Braunschweig 1974, Lecture Notes in Computer Science, Band 8, Berlin, Heidelberg, New York 1974, S.64-78

[49] Schmitz, P.; Seibt, D.: Einführung in die anwendungsorientierte Informatik. München 1975

[50] Schramm, H.W.; Dörfel, H.-J.: Methoden und Werkzeuge der Anwender-Software-Entwicklung. In: Computerwoche, 27. Febr. 1976, S.4

[51] Schünemann, C.: Grundlegendes zur Speicherhierarchie. In: Spruth, W.G. (Hrsg.): Data Base Systems. Proceedings, 5th Informatik Symposium, IBM Germany, Bad Homburg v.d.H. 1975, Lecture Notes in Computer Science, Band 39, Berlin, Heidelberg, New York 1976, S.114-138

[52] Scrupski, S.E.: Coming: cheap, powerful computers. In: Electronics, Dec. 1975, S.67-68

[53] Slotnick, D.L.: The fastest computer. In: Scientific American, Vol. 224, 1971, S.76-87

[54] Syrbe, M.: Die Rechenmaschinen der Zukunft. In: Graef, M. (Hrsg.): 350 Jahre Rechenmaschinen. München 1973, S.80-89

[55] Szyperski, N.: Die büroorientierte Integration der DV-Nachrichten- und Textverarbeitungstechniken. In: DV-Einsatz in der Büroautomation. Fachtagung im Informatikkolleg der GMD 1975, Schloß Birlinghoven, S.225-232

[56] Thurber, K.J.; Wald, L.D.: Associative and Parallel Processors. In: Computing Surveys, Vol. 7, No. 4, Dec. 1975, S.215-255

[57] Turn, R.: Computers in the 1980s. New York, London 1974

[58] Watson, W.J.; Carr, H.M.: Operational experiences with the TI Advanced Scientific Computer. In: National Computer Conference 1974, S.389-397

[59] Withington, F.G.: Beyond 1984: A Technology Forecast. In: Datamation, Vol. 21, No. 1, Jan. 1975, S.54-73

[60] Wolf, G.: Assoziative Speicher und Prozessoren. In: Elektronische Rechenanlagen, 17. Jg., Heft 6, 1975, S.264-271

[61] Wulf, W.A.; Bell, C.G.: C.mmp - A Multi-Mini-Processor. In: Proceedings 1972 Fall Joint Computer Conference, S.765-777.

ANWENDUNGEN DER GRAPHISCHEN DATENVERARBEITUNG

- Konzepte, Systeme, Wirtschaftlichkeit -

von

J. Encarnação
Technische Hochschule Darmstadt
Fachbereich Informatik

Zusammenfassung: Nach der Einführung einiger Grundbegriffe der graphischen Datenverarbeitung, wird die Grundstruktur heutiger graphischer Systeme insbesondere unter dem Aspekt der Geräteunabhängigkeit erläutert.
Dann werden graphische Anwendungssysteme funktionell betrachtet
und das Konzept eines integrierten graphischen Informationssystems
eingeführt. Dieses wird am Beispiel des an der TH Darmstadt realisierten GRIFO-Systems näher erläutert. Abschließend werden einige
Verfahren angegeben, mit denen die Wirtschaftlichkeit des Einsatzes
graphischer Systeme, insbesondere unter Berücksichtigung der Kosteneffektivität und der Kostenreduzierung, analysiert werden kann.

Schlüsselwörter: Graphische Grundbegriffe; Geräteunabhängigkeit, Schnittstellen,
logische E/A-Geräte, graphische Formate; Relationen, "Bedeutung"
des Bildinhaltes; Anwendungssysteme, Anwendungsprogramm, graphisches
Informationssystem; Kosteneffektivität, Kostennutzen, Leistungs-
kennwert, Kostenreduzierung.

Survey report - Übersichtsvortrag
für die 6. Jahrestagung der Gesellschaft für Informatik
28.o9.1976 - ol.10.1976, Stuttgart, W.-Germany

Inhaltsverzeichnis

<u>Einleitung</u>

Auf dem Gebiet der graphischen Datenverarbeitung herrscht bis heute ein terminologischer Wirrwarr. Die rasante technologische Entwicklung und Verbreitung in die verschiedensten Anwendungsrichtungen hatte zur Folge, daß für dieselben Tatbestände in verschiedenen Bereichen der graphischen Datenverarbeitung verschiedene Bezeichnungen und umgekehrt zu finden sind; dies erschwerte u.a. sehr die Kommunikation zwischen den Fachleuten und insbesondere auch den Dialog mit und unter den Anwendern. Als Grundlage für alle weiteren Ausführungen seien hier daher zunächst einige Grundbegriffe eingeführt und kurz erläutert /1,2,3/:

<u>Begriff 1</u>: COMPUTER GRAPHICS

> That branch of data processing concerned with methods and techniques for converting any form of information to or from <u>graphic display</u> via computers.

<u>Begriff 2</u>: GRAPHIC DISPLAY

> A visual representation of data built up from a finite set of graphic elements.

Diese Begriffe sind sehr allgemein und haben als Einschränkung nur, daß die Verarbeitung durch den Rechner möglich sein muß. Dadurch schließen diese Definitionen die Bereiche der Bildanalyse und der Bildverarbeitung nicht aus. Dies wird auch konsequent durch die folgende Definition weiterverfolgt:

<u>Begriff 3</u>: DISPLAY ELEMENT

> An element such as a point, a line segment, or a <u>graphic</u> which may produced by the <u>display writer</u> to construct a <u>display image</u>.

Unter "graphic" versteht man allgemeine Grapheme oder graphische Primärelemente. Hier wird nun eingeschränkt in·dem verlangt wird, daß diese Elemente von einem Teil (display writer) eines Ausgabegerätes sichtbar dargestellt (ausgegeben) werden. Die Fläche auf der diese Darstellung vorgenommen wird, nennt man, <u>"display surface"</u>.

Die Möglichkeit der Strukturierung ist gegeben durch die Zusammenfassung (Kollektion) von DISPLAY ELEMENTS nach den folgenden Definitionen.

<u>Begriff 4</u>: DISPLAY GROUP

> A collection of <u>display elements</u> that can be manipulated as a unit and that can be further combined to form larger groups.

<u>Begriff 5</u>: DISPLAY IMAGE

> A collection of <u>display elements</u>, <u>display groups</u> that are visually represented together at amy one time on a <u>display surface</u>.

Bei graphishen Systemen wird unterschieden zwischen denen die keine Möglichkeit der on-line Benutzerinteraktion haben und die, die den Mensch-Maschine-Dialog als zentralen Bestandteil beinhalten.

<u>Begriff 6</u>: PASSIVE GRAPHICS

> The use of a <u>display device</u> in the <u>passive mode</u>.
> NOTE: Usually passive graphics is associated with plotters and <u>microfilm</u>
> recorders.

<u>Begriff 7</u>: INTERACTIVE GRAPHICS

> Computer graphics where the result of human use of a <u>display console</u> causes
> changes to occur in the status of the <u>display image</u> as fast, or faster than
> the human reaction rate.
> NOTE: This is commonly accomplished by entering data and directing the
> course of the program.

Die angegebenen Begriffe haben eine zentrale Bedeutung und sind ein wichtiger Ausgangspunkt für die anschließenden Ausführungen.

1. Das graphische System

Wir wollen nun vier Typen von graphischen Systemen unterscheiden /4/:

1) Terminalsysteme — diese waren in Hardware und Software her-
stellerspezifische Systeme (IBM 2250,
CDC 1700-Digigraphics, Adage, Vector Generol,
etc.). Sie sind insbesondere für Anwender
aus dem Militärbereich, von der Auto- Flug-
zeugindustrie, etc. entwickelt und z.T. auch
von dort finanziert worden.

2) Typenspezifische Systeme — diese waren meist für spezielle Geräte-Kombi-
nationen (Plotter/Tektronix) konzipiert und
insbesondere im Rechenzentrumsbetrieb zu finden. Die Frage der Ausgabe war generell gelöst. Für die Eingabe gab es nur spezielle
Lösungen, da in den Systemen keine komfor-
table Struktur vorhanden war. Diese Systeme
waren in einer höheren Sprache eingebettet
(meistens FORTRAN); Beispiele hierfür sind
GINO-F und DISSPLA /5/.

3) Anwenderspezifische Systeme — diese Systeme waren für eine spezielle Anwendung, und dort möglichst optimal konzi-
piert. Bei auch nur geringfügigen Änderungen
der Anwendung oder der zugrundeliegenden
Techniken war man auf die Herstellerfirma
angewiesen, da die Systeme selbst für die
Anwender nicht transparent waren. Beispiel
hierfür ist COMPUTERVISION.

4) Geräteunabhängige Systeme   -   sind die neueren Systeme die diesen Problemkreis mit Hilfe eines stufenweisen Auf-
baues zu lösen versuchen. Beispiele sind
GMB /6/, GPGS /7/, UGP /8,9/ etc..

Wenn heute von graphischen Systemen die Rede ist, dann meint man hauptsächlich den angegebenen Typ 4. Unter Geräteunabhängigkeit verstehen wir die Unabhängigkeit der Schnittstelle zu dem Anwender des graphischen Systems hinsichtlich Funktion und Syntax derverfügbaren Peripheriehardware. Der Grundgedanke eines <u>geräteunabhängigen graphischen Systems</u> besteht darin, daß man das Gesamtsystem in einen geräteunabhängigenund einen geräteabhängigen Teil aufspaltet und die graphische Aus- und Eingabe vollkommen vom Anwenderprogramm trennt.

Will man also ein graphisches Anwenderprogramm an verschiedenartige Aus- und Eingabegeräte anpassen, so braucht man dadurch nur die Programmteile neu zu schreiben, die den Aus- und Eingabeprozeß durchführen. In Bild 1 ist dieses (in Anlehnung an /10/) Grundprinzip der Geräteunabhängigkeit dargestellt (Trennung vom Anwenderprogramm und Ausgabe- sowie Eingabeprozessor). Die interessanten Schnittstellen sind:

1. <u>Schnittstelle zum Anwender</u>
   In einem allgemeinen System muß diese Schnittstelle völlig anwendungsunabhängig sein.

2. <u>Codegeneratorschnittstelle</u>
   Dies ist die Schnittstelle zwischen Vorprozessor und Ausgabeprozessor. Der Vorprozessor interpretiert die im Anwenderprogramm in einer höheren Notation enthaltenen, graphischen Ausgabefunktionen und generiert geräteunabhängige Daten die vom Ausgabeprozessor in eine geräteabhängige Form übersetzt werden. Der Vorprozessor hat bezüglich der Ausgabe Bildcompilereigenschaften, der Ausgabeprozessor Bildassemblereigenschaften.

3. <u>Logische Eingabeschnittstelle (nur bei interaktiver Graphik)</u>
   Dies ist die Schnittstelle zwischen Eingabe- und Vorprozessor. Der Eingabeprozessor verarbeitet physikalische Eingabeereignisse und teilt dem Vorprozessor logische Eingabeergebnisse mit.

Da man eine Software haben will, die für die unterschiedlichsten Geräte Anwendung finden soll, muß man nach Gemeinsamkeiten suchen, Geräte mit ähnlichen Eigenschaften in Gruppen zusammenfassen und darauf achten, daß diese Gruppeneigenschaften aufwärtskompatibel sind. Das heißt die Eigenschaften der niedrigsten Gerätegruppe müssen in der nächst höheren Gruppe voll enthalten sein /11,12/.

<u>Klassifizierende Elemente für die Ausgabe sind:</u>

Klasse 1:   1 Zeichen
Klasse 2:   Zeichen, Punkt, Linie, (Kreis und Kreissegment)

Klasse 3: Segment

Klasse 4: Gerichteter Graph

Ein Segment ist eine lineare Liste aus graphischen Grundelementen und stellt den einfachsten graphischen Operanden (display group) dar, der sich aus Grundelementen zusammensetzt und als eine Einheit manipuliert werden und der benutzt werden kann, um größere Einheiten zu bilden. Eine Kollektion ist dann eine lineare Liste aus Segmenten. Ein Segment ist klassifizierend für Geräteklasse 3, weil das Gerätemerkmal die selektive Bildmanipulation ist. Ein Bild, das nach diesen Gesichtspunkten aufgebaut ist, hat ein Format das segmentiert genannt wird. Zu Klasse 4 ist das klassifizierende Element ein gerichteter Graph.

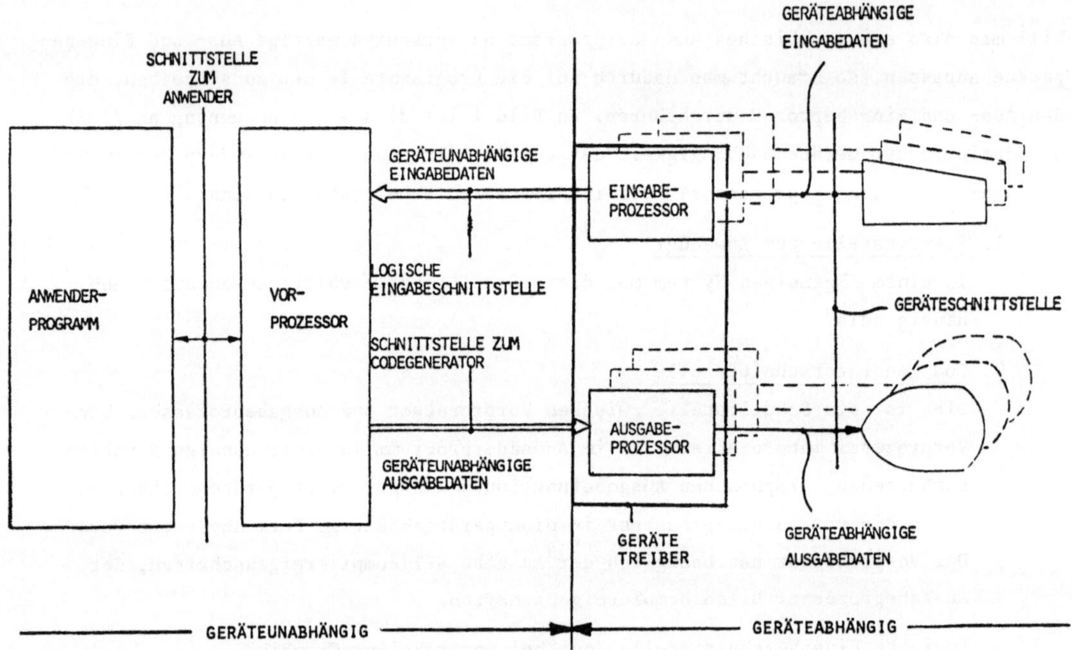

BILD 1: TRENNUNG VON ANWENDERPROGRAMM UND GRAPHISCHER EIN/AUSGABE

Peripherieunabhängige graphische Software darf nicht Sprachelemente oder Unterprogrammaufrufe enthalten, in denen Eingaben mittels physikalischer Eingabegeräte initialisiert werden. Es müssen vielmehr logische Eingabegeräte definiert werden, denen physikalische zugeordnet werden können. Logische Eingabegeräte sind solche, die eine bestimmte interaktive Tätigkeit erlauben. Logische Eingabegeräte können z.B. sein

- Pick device   Identifizieren eines Objektes
- Locator device   Anzeige einer Position
- Button device   1:N Auswahl (Funktionstastatur)
- Valuator device Eingabe von skalaren, kontinuierlichen Größen

Die entsprechenden physikalischen Eingabegeräte sind:

- Light pen
- Tablet
- Keyboard, Light pen switch ...
- Potentiometer

Darüber hinaus können Eingabegeräten Pseudoeingabegeräte zugewiesen werden, die ein funktionelles Äquivalent zum betreffenden logischen Eingabegerät darstellen.

2. Anwendungen der graphischen Datenverarbeitung

Betrachten wir nun die heutigen Anwendungen graphischer Systeme. Die graphische Datenverarbeitung ist praktisch überall dort zu finden, wo Rechner eingesetzt werden. J. Crestin und M. Lucas in /13/ geben dafür die folgende Aufzählung

- Animation: Unterrichtsfilmen, Simulation
- Architektur: Gebäude-Entwurf, Zeichnungs-Layout
- Bauingenieurwesen: Straßenentwurf, Strukturentwurf
- Chemie: Forschung der Protein-Strukturen, X-Strahl-Kristallographie, Chemische Dokumentation
- Elektronik: Schaltungsentwurf, Schaltungs-Layout
- Flächenentwurf: Schiffsbau, Automobilbau
- Kartographie: Automatische Digitalisierung von Landkarten, Analyse von Geodaten, Thematische Karten
- Kunst: Bild-Kunst, Moden-Entwurf, Coreography
- Management information systems
- Mathematik: Numerische Analyse, Operations research
- Mechanik: Numerische Steuerung, Automatischer Zeichnungsentwurf
- Medizin: EEG-Analyse in real-time, Analyse des cardiovascularen Transportphänomenen
- Prozeßsteuerung
- Rechner-gestützter-Unterricht
- Textverarbeitung: Zeitungs-Layout, on-line Texteditierung
  etc., etc..

Man unterscheidet zwischen drei Arten von Personen, die bei allen graphischen Anwendungssystemen sich mit den graphischen Programmen beschäftigen:

(1) Benutzer des Anwendungsprogrammes
(2) Programmierer des Anwendungsprogrammes
(3) Entwerfer des graphischen Systems

Das Anwendungsprogramm greift über ein Abbildungsprogramm in das graphische System ein (Bild 2). Die Art und Weise, wie die Anforderungen des Anwendungsprogrammes im graphischenSystem erfüllt werden, wird vom Operateur gesteuert.

Die Schnittstelle zwischen Anwendungs- und Abbildungsprogramm ist die _logische_ oder
funktionelle oder _virtuelle Schnittstelle_, in der die in Kapitel 1 aufgeführten E/A-
Eingabeklassen verwendet werden; die Schnittstelle zwischen dem Abbildungsprogramm
und dem graphischen System ist durch die _physikalischen E/A-Geräte_ gegeben.

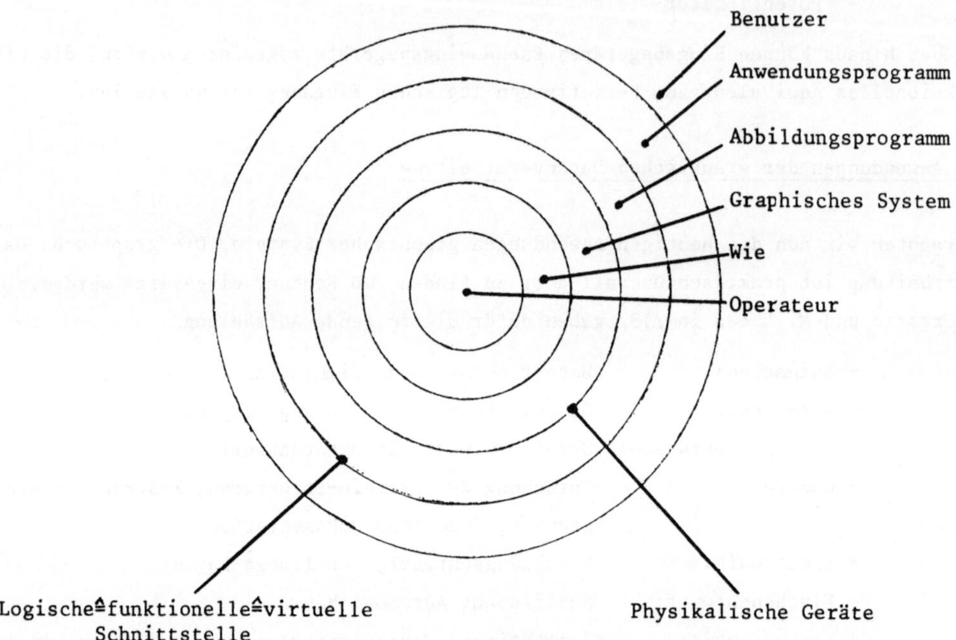

__Bild 2:__ Konzeptioneller Mechanismus eines Anwendungsprogrammes

In vielen Fällen werden die Funktionen vom "Benutzer" und "Operateur" durch dieselbe
Person ausgeführt. In Teilnehmer- oder in Teilhabersystemen sind diese zwei Funktionen personell getrennt. In einigen Fällen können einzelne Schichten, so z.B. das Abbildungsprogramm, wegfallen.

3. Konzept der integrierten graphischen Informationssysteme

Die meisten Anwendungen der graphischen Datenverarbeitung sind dadurch charakterisiert,
daß erstens die Graphik selbst nur ein, wenn auch wesentlicher Teil des Anwendungsprogrammes ist und zweitens für die Anwendung nicht nur die geometrische Information, sondern auch die _Bedeutung eines Bildes_ von Relevanz ist. Dies muß in Zukunft dazu führen,
bei einem graphischen Anwendungssystem die Datenbank in den Mittelpunkt des Systems
zu setzen. Das Anwendungsprogramm selbst sollte eingehend aus Standard-Bausteinen zusammengesetzt werden, die ihm in einer Methodenbank zur Verfügung stehen. R. Noppen
schlägt in /14/ für CAD-Anwendungssysteme die in Bild 3 angegebene Konfiguration vor,
in der der Kommunikationsteil, Verarbeitungsteil und Datenspeicherung entkoppelt ver-
wirklicht werden.

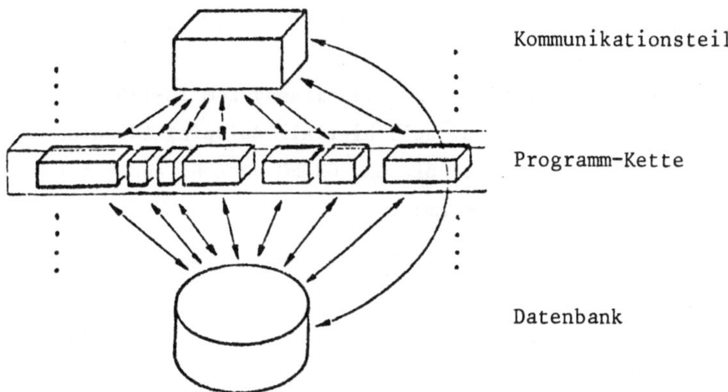

<u>Bild 3</u>: Beziehungen zwischen Kommunikationsteil, Verarbeitungsteil und Datenorgani-
sation in einer CAD-Programmkette

Diese Konzeption kann verallgemeinert werden. Das graphische System besteht dann aus
den folgenden <u>Grundfunktionen</u>

    (1) Anfragesystem (Querry-Schnittstelle)

    (2) Anwendungsprogramm (Problem-Schnittstelle)

    (3) A/N-Dialog (für Entwurf, Entscheidung und Steuerung)

    (4) Graphische Ein- und Ausgabe

und wird als <u>integriertes graphisches Informationssystem</u> aufgebaut. Da es nun schwer
möglich ist eine allgemeine Strukturierung für alle Anwendungsdaten zu wählen (finden), sollte dem Benutzer die Möglichkeit gegeben werden eine eigene, für seine Anwendung gewünschte Datenstrukturierung zu formulieren und im System zu verwenden.
Diese "seine" Datenstruktur muß dann in einer system-internen, allen Funktionen und
Programmen im System gemeinsamen, Datenstruktur übersetzt werden. Ein Beispiel für
die Realisierung eines solchen allgemeinen graphischen Anwendungssystemes wird im
nächsten Kapitel gegeben. Die einzelnen Grundfunktionen sind in Bild 4 verdeutlicht.

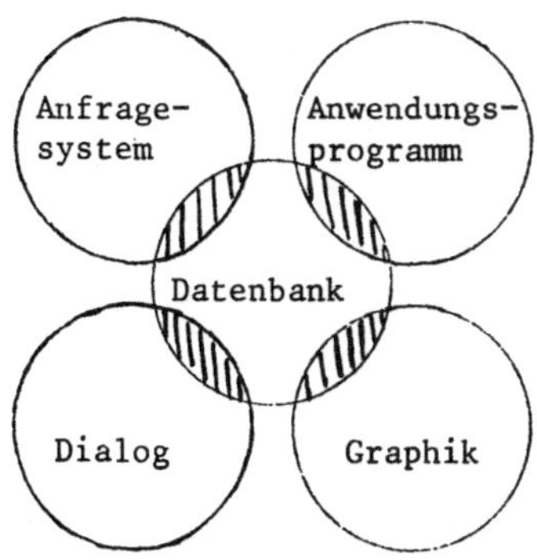

<u>Bild 4</u>: Grundfunktionen eines graphischen Informationssystems

4. GRIFO - Ein Beispiel für ein graphisches Informationssystem

Das hier zu beschreibende graphische Informationssystem (GRIFO) ist an der TH Darmstadt implementiert worden /15/ und soll hier als Beispiel für eine Realisierung der
in Kapitel 3 angegebenen Konzeption dienen. GRIFO besteht aus den folgenden miteinander kommunizierenden Programmsystemen:

  a) einem Datenerfassungs- und -überprüfungssystem, im Folgenden als
     DE-System bezeichnet;

  b) einer assoziativen Datenstruktur als Zentralbaustein (DATAS);

  c) einem interaktiven graphischen System.

DATAS (DATen in Assoziativer Speicherung) ist ein System zur schnellen und bequemen
Arbeit mit beliebigen, assoziativ verknüpften Datenmengen. Diese Arbeit umfaßt Ein-
und Ausgabe, Veränderung, Löschen und Suchen von Daten, die bekannt oder mit bekannten
Daten assoziiert sein müssen. Die verschiedenen in DATAS möglichen Assoziationen werden in den folgenden Abschnitten kurz charakterisiert; für eine ausführliche Beschreibung muß auf den vollständigen Bericht über die Implementierung von DATAS hingewiesen
werden/16,17/.

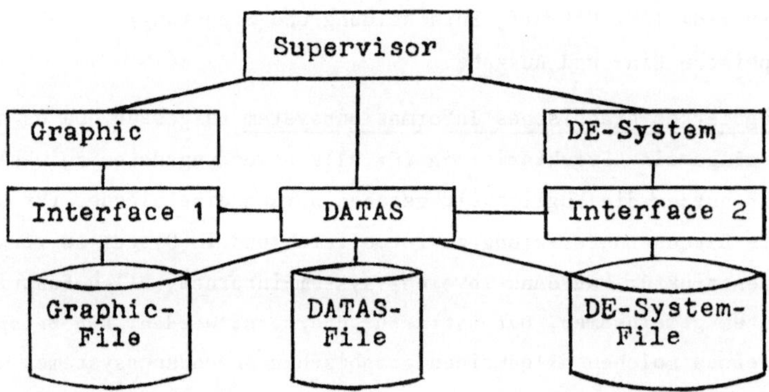

Bild 5: GRIFO-Aufbau

Die Grundelemente von DATAS sind:

  Namen

  Entities

  Triaden .

Dabei werden unter Entities die kleinsten adressierbaren Informationseinheiten in
DATAS verstanden. Vom Benutzer aus werden sie durch Namen adressiert; jede Entity
darf mehrere Namen haben, die dann als Synonyme bezeichnet werden, sowie beliebige
Daten enthalten. Triaden sind Tripel von Verweisen auf Entities; sie beschreiben die
Assoziationen zwischen diesen.

DATAS kennt drei Klassen von Entities:

       Klasse 1 - Relation-Entities

       Klasse 2 - Single-Value-Entities

       Klasse 3 - Multi-Value-Entities

<u>Relation-Entities</u> repräsentieren Assoziationen zwischen Entities; diese Assoziationen werden durch Triaden dargestellt. <u>Single-Value-Entities</u> enthalten nur vom Benutzer definierte Daten oder überhaupt keine Daten; sie können durch Komponenten von Triaden oder als Elemente von Mengen referiert werden. <u>Multi-Value-Entities</u> stellen Mengen dar und enthalten als Daten Zeiger auf die Elemente.

Der DATAS zur Verfügung stehende Speicherraum wird in drei Bereiche aufgeteilt:

       Namenspeicher (Zuordnung von Entities zu Namen)

       Triadenspeicher (Darstellung von Assoziationen durch Triaden)

       Datenspeicher (enthält die Daten der Entities).

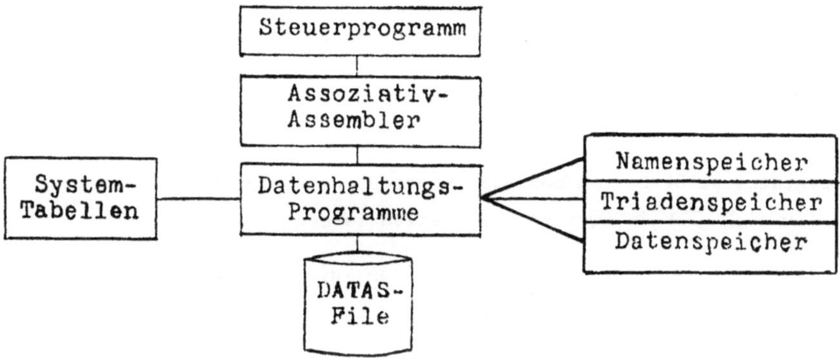

<u>Bild 6</u>: Die Datenspeicherung im GRIFO-System

Alle graphischen Daten werden in einen Display-File eingetragen, der über systemeigene FORTRAN-Unterprogramme verwaltet wird. Er enthält alle sichtbaren graphischen Elemente. Diese werden in Entities eingeteilt, die als Ganzes oder in ihren Einzelteilen manipuliert sind. Jede Entity kann jede Art graphischer Daten enthalten. Als graphische Daten gelten Punkte, (Blank-) Vektoren, A/N-Zeichen, Kreise, und alle Mode-Befehle, die den Display-Prozessor steuern.

Das DE/System ermöglicht einem weiten Kreis von Benutzern, einen rechnergesteuerten on-line Datenverkehr. Dabei kann der einzelne Benutzer - seinen speziellen Anforderungen entsprechend - Formulare oder Tabellen aufbauen und sie, mit aktueller Information versehen, an den Rechner senden. Um sicherzustellen, daß nur fehlerlose Daten zur Speicherung oder weiteren Verarbeitung in den Rechner gelangen, wird die eingegebene Information auf Syntax und Plausibilität geprüft. Die Prüfvorschriften für die einzel-

nen Formularfelder teilt der Benutzer dem System in Form einfacher Anweisung mit.
Bei der Syntaxprüfung wird die eingegebene Information auf formale Richtigkeit überprüft. Die Plausibilitätsprüfung dagegen untersucht die Daten auf logische Richtigkeit. Beim Auftreten von Syntax- oder Plausibilitätsfehle fordert das System bei
gleichzeitiger Fehlererkennung eine erneute Eingabe an.

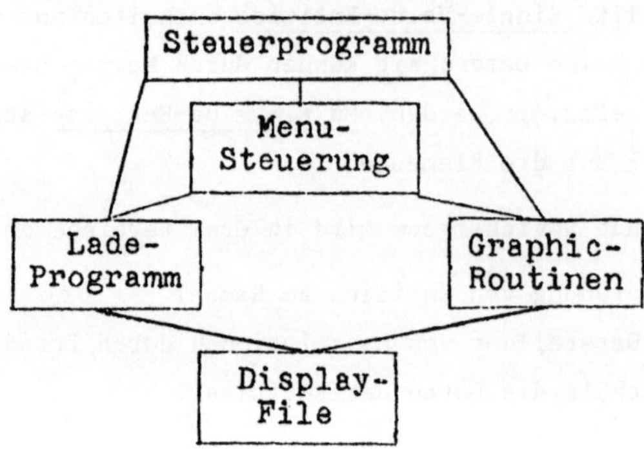

<u>Bild 7:</u> Die Graphik des GRIFO-Systems

Das hier vorgestellte DE-System muß somit verschiedene Gruppen von Arbeitsgängen ermöglichen, die sich grob in zwei Modi einteilen lassen:

   1. System-Modus: umfaßt alle Tätigkeiten, die eine Organisation des
      on-line Datenverkehrs bewirken:
      - Formular-Analyse
      - Syntax-Analyse mit Erstellung eines Syntax-Prüfprogrammes
      - eventuelle Korrektur- und Änderungsdienste hierzu

   2. Daten-Modus: steuert die eigentliche Datenerfassung mittels der im
      System-Modus erzeugten Strukturen.

Sowohl das DE-System als auch das Graphic-System erfordern die Möglichkeiten, Daten
abzuspeichern, aus dem Speicher zu laden, im Speicher zu löschen und im Speicher
auf verschiedene Arten zueinander in Beziehung zu setzen. Dabei sollen die genannten
Operationen vom Benutzer so durchzuführen sein, daß er sich um die Organisation des
Speichers nicht zu kümmern braucht. Diese Nebenbedingung wird im hier beschriebenen
System dadurch erfüllt, daß die Datenorganisation von DATAS übernommen wird. Dabei
werden alle Datenblöcke, gleich von welchem der drei Systeme sie kommen, in DATAS als
Entities abgespeichert, so daß sie immer unter einem oder mehreren alphanumerischen
Namen ansprechbar sind.

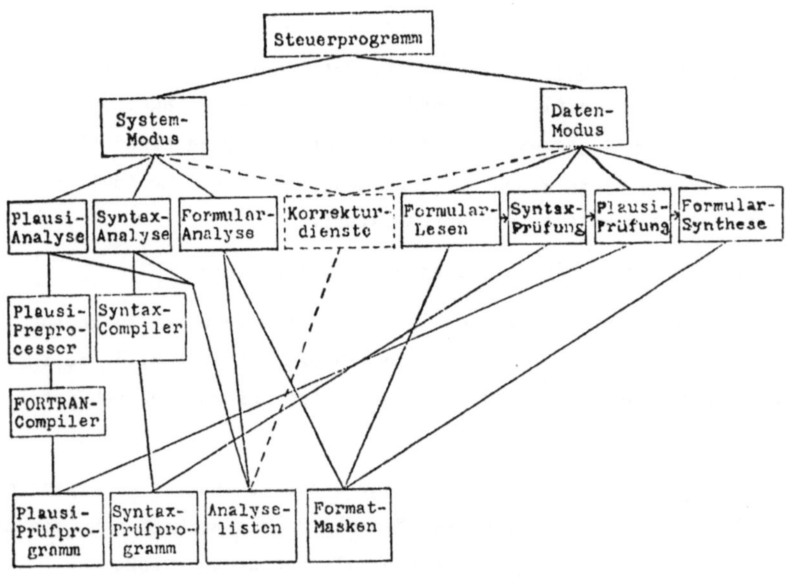

<u>Bild 8</u>: Das DE-System in GRIFO

Die Strukturierung der Daten wird dann nur noch innerhalb von DATAS durchgeführt; so werden zum Beispiel alle aus der Graphic kommenden Datenblöcke in DATAS als Elemente bestimmter Mengen (oder Mengen aller Bilder, der Menge aller abgeschlossenen Teil-bilder usw.) abgespeichert; diese Mengen stellen vom Benutzer nicht löschbare System-Entities dar. Eine weitere Strukturierung der Daten kann durch weitere Interface-Funk-tionen von Graphic und vom DE-System aus angesteuert und spezifiziert werden. So können etwa die Datenblöcke, die ein Formular, seine Analyse-Listen, seine Format-Masken, seine Prüfprogramme und die zugehörigen aktuellen Informationen darstellen, durch Triaden in DATAS assoziiert werden. Auf der Seite der Graphic besteht eine ent-sprechende Möglichkeit für die logische Organisation des Bildes.
Der Benutzer hat die Möglichkeit, graphische Daten in DATAS als Datenbank zu archi-vieren. Er kann dies für ein ganzes Bild bzw. für einzelne Entities tun. Ein ganzes Bild wird unter einem vom Benutzer wählbaren Namen auf einem externen File von DATAS abgelegt; die Namen aller archivierten Bilder sind durch Auflisten zu erfahren. Wird ein archiviertes Bild gelesen, so wird zunächst das aktuelle Bild gelöscht, anschlies-send wird der Display-File mit den neuen Daten überschrieben.

Entities werden vom Benutzer mittels Lichtgriffel ausgewählt und unter einem frei wählbaren Namen als echte Daten in DATAS abgelegt. Wird eine archivierte Entity ge-lesen, so wird im Display-File eine neue Entity erzeugt, in die dann die gelesenen Daten eingetragen werden.

Wird das Graphic-System verlassen so wird der letzte Bildinhalt gesondert auf einem externen File gespeichert; er ist wie ein normales Bild unter einem speziellen Menu-punkt wieder abzurufen.

Auf Wunsch des Benutzers erzeugt das System eine Datenstruktur in DATAS, die den <u>Bild-inhalt mit seinen Bedeutungen</u> widerspiegelt. Der Benutzer gibt hierbei jeweils vor, wie tief die Bildstruktur aufgesplittert werden soll. Die Möglichkeiten reichen von einfacher Namensgebung an ein ganzes Bild bis hin zur Erzeugung eines Bildstrukturbaumes, dessen Blätter die einzelnen graphischen Elemente sind. Bei Manipulationen des Bildinhaltes wird dieser Baum automatisch aktualisiert.

Der Baum enthält drei verschiedene Arten von Informationen:

1) <u>Die Struktur der Graphic</u>: es werden in Triadenform Verweise aufgebaut, die die einzelnen Elemente und Entities hierarchisch in das aktuelle Bild und in die Gesamtheit aller Bilder einordnen. Hierzu werden vom System aus automatisch interne Namen generiert.

2) <u>Namen und Bedeutungen</u>: auf Wunsch kann der Benutzer zusätzlich eigene Namen für jeden Teil der Graphic eingeben. Diese können z.B. als Etiketten an den Baumzweigen aufgefaßt werden, was eine Interpretation als Bedeutung zuläßt.

3) <u>Beschreibungen</u>: das System generiert automatisch für jedes gespeicherte Element einen Datensatz, der eine kurze verbale Beschreibung sowie die Angabe von z.B. Koordinaten oder Radien enthält.

Die gesamte Struktur ist von DATAS aus voll transparent und manipulierbar. Von der graphischen Seite aus können lediglich mit bestimmten Elementen und Entities assoziierte Informationen gelesen werden. Umgekehrt sind die in DATAS vorhandenen System-Entities die diejenigen Informationen enthalten, über die man auf den Baum zugreifen kann, in DATAS so geschützt, daß der Benutzer nicht die Struktur zerstören kann, indem er sie löscht oder umbenennt.

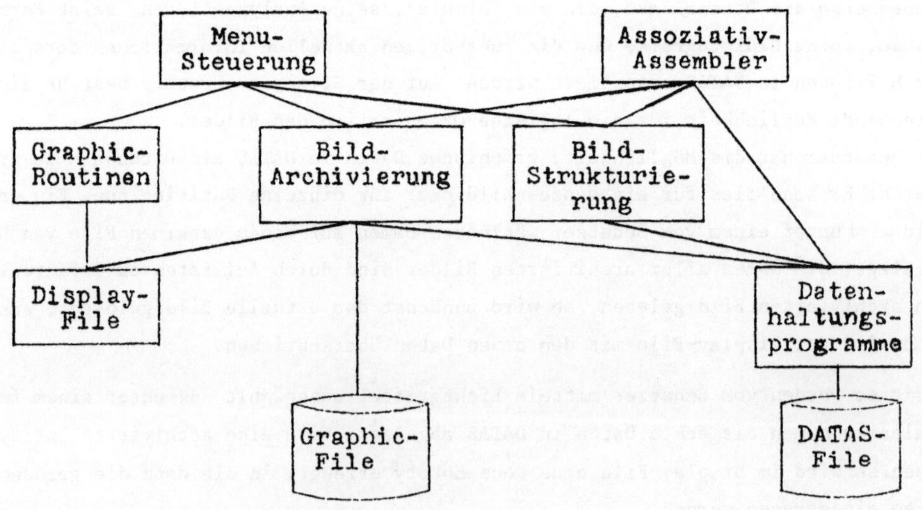

<u>Bild 9:</u> Abspeicherung des Bildinhaltes mit seinen Bedeutungen im GRIFO-System

5. Abschätzung der Wirtschaftlichkeit graphischer Systeme

Nachdem ein allgemeines Konzept für ein graphisches Informationssystem eingeführt wurde, müssen wir nun untersuchen wann und unter welchen Bedingungen es wirtschaftlich sinnvoll ist, die graphische Datenverarbeitung für eine gegebene Anwendung einzusetzen.

Bezüglich der Wirtschaftlichkeit graphischer Systeme kann man grundsätzlich unterscheiden zwischen

    (1) Analyse der Kosteneffektivität und

    (2) Analyse des Kostennutzens

Bei der Analyse der Kosteneffektivität will man die Leistungsfähigkeit des Systems unter Berücksichtigung bestimmter Kriterien und bis zu einer vorgegebenen Investitionshöhe optimieren. Bei der Analyse des Kostennutzens geht es um die Beantwortung von Fragen wie "Ist der Gesamtnutzen vom Einsatz des Systems bei einem vorgegebenen Leistungsgrad größer als die dafür notwendige Investition?" oder "Welches ist die optimale Investitionshöhe um den Nettonutzen zu maximieren?". Die Frage der Kosteneffektivität ist daher sehr wesentlich für die Gültigkeit der Ergebnisse der Analyse des Kostennutzens.

Nach R. Dunn /18,19/ kann man für den <u>Leistungskennwert über der Kostenfunktion</u> die folgende Beziehung verwenden:

$$A = \frac{d_1 \cdot P \cdot (d_2 \cdot IQ + d_3 \cdot GC)}{d_4 \cdot K/C}$$

Die Faktoren d_1 bis d_4 sind vom Benutzer zu wählende Gewichtsfaktoren für das jeweilige System. P gibt die Produktivität im Sinne einer Beschleunigung der Ausgabe durch das graphische System an. Das Verhältnis der Mächtigkeit des vorhandenen graphischen Systems zu dem Gebrauch, der bei der Anwendung davon gemacht wird, wird durch den Interaktivitätsquotient IQ gegeben. Ein Maß für die vorhandene Hardware ist GC (graphics capacity). C gibt die Anzahl der im System konkurrierenden Bildschirmgeräte an. Durch K werden die Kosten des gesamten Systems berücksichtigt. Das Ergebnis A ist dann der Verstärkungsfaktor, d.h. ein Maß für die Änderung der Ausgabe-Produktivität (in Kosten des gesamten Systems) gegeben in den direkten Kosten pro aktives Bildschirmgerät.

Das Ergebnis bei der <u>Analyse der Kosteneffektivität</u> muß nach I. Cotton /20/ eine Effiziensgrenze von Systemen sein, die optimiert sind für die Kosten (C), als Funktion der Leistung (P) und umgekehrt auch für die Leistung als Funktion der Kosten, also

$$C = f_1(P)$$

$$P = f_2(C)$$

mit P ... Leistung

    C ... Kosten.

Sei der maximal mögliche Nutzen

$$B = f_3(P).$$

Das Problem liegt dann also in der Maximierung von

$$NB = B - C = f_3(P) - f_1(P)$$

Typische Kurven hierfür sind aus /20/ entnommen in Bild 10 angegeben.

Die Nutzenfunktion B muß irgendwo höher liegen als die Kostenfunktion C, sonst ist das System unbrauchbar.

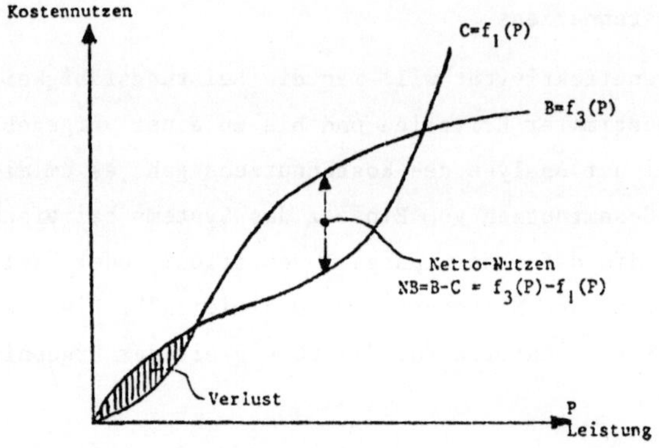

<u>Bild 10:</u> Graphische Darstellung der Kostennutzengleichung

<u>Analytische Lösung:</u> Das gewünschte Maximum liegt vor, wenn die erste Ableitung der Netto-Nutzenfunktion gleich Null ist

$$\frac{d\,(NB)}{dP} = \frac{d}{dP}\,f_3(P) - \frac{d}{dP}\,f_1(P) = 0$$

für NB >0.

Zu einem genaueren Ansatz berücksichtigt man als weiteren Parameter den Benutzungsgrad U:

$$C = f_1(P,U)$$
$$B = f_3(P,U)$$

Die gewünschte analytische Lösung hierzu lautet dann:

$$\frac{\partial}{\partial P}\,(NB) = \frac{\partial}{\partial P}\left[f_1(P,U)\right]$$

$$\frac{\partial}{\partial P}\,(NB) = \frac{\partial}{\partial P}\left[f_3(P,U)\right]$$

für NB >0.

Wir wollen nun ein Verfahren zur <u>Bestimmung der Kostenreduzierung</u> nach S.H. Chasen /21/ kurz beschreiben. Es seien T_1 die Gesamtkosten für eine spezielle Anwendung bei Verwendung der üblichen Technologie ohne graphische Datenverarbeitung. T_1 setzt sich zusammen aus:

A_1 = Planung und Terminplanung

B_1 = Ansatz

C_1 = Kartenlochung und Datenvorbereitung

D_1 = Ausführung

E_1 = Datenanalyse und Bewertung

F_1 = Dokumentation und Verwaltung

G_1 = Korrelierte Funktion, die von der Einführung der graphischen
Datenverarbeitung unabhängig ist.

T_2 gibt die Gesamtkosten nach der Einführung der graphischen Datenverarbeitung an; A_2, B_2, ..., G_2 sind die zugehörigen Teilkosten (Bild 11, /21/).

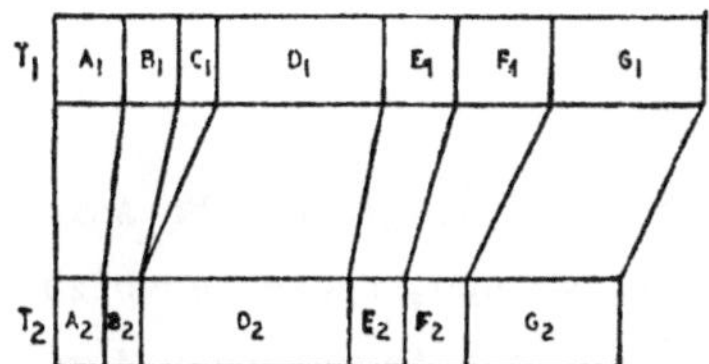

Bild 11: Teilkosten vor und nach der Einführung der graphischen Datenverarbeitung
für eine gegebene Anwendung

Die Kostenreduzierung ist demnach gegeben durch:

$$\Delta T = T_1 - T_2 = (A_1 - A_2) + (B_1 - B_2) + (C_1 - C_2) + (D_1 - D_2) + (E_1 - E_2) + (F_1 - F_2)$$

mit

$$G_1 - G_2 = 0$$

ΔT ist abhängig vom Stundendurchschnitt pro Mann und graphisches Gerät und vom Stundenpreis für die Verwendung des graphischen Systems:

$$\Delta T = f(R_M, R_C)$$

R_M = Stundendurchschnitt pro Mann und pro graphisches Gerät

R_C = Stundenpreis pro graphisches Gerät

daraus folgt:

$$\Delta T = K + R_M (H_1 - H_2) - R_M H_3 - R_C H_3$$

mit

K = Vom graphischen System unabhängige, aber durch die Einführung von
graphischer Datenverarbeitung entstandene akkumulative Kosten
(Gewinne und/oder Verluste)

H_1 = Benutzerzeit vor der Einführung von graphischer Datenverarbeitung

H_2 = Benutzerzeit nach der Einführung von graphischer Datenverarbeitung

H_3 = Benutzerzeit am graphischen Gerät

oder

$$\Delta T = K + (H_1 - H_2 - H_3) \cdot R_M - H_3 \cdot R_C \qquad \text{(siehe Bild 12, /21/).}$$

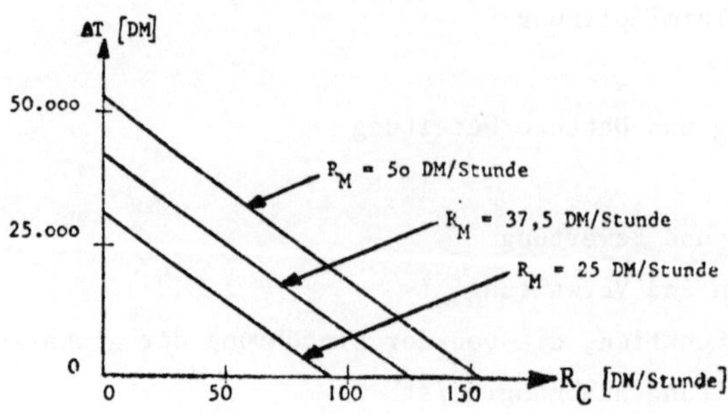

Bild 12: Beispiel für die Kostenreduzierung

6. Schlußbemerkungen

In diesem Aufsatz ist absichtlich nicht auf einzelne graphische Anwendungssysteme eingegangen, sondern es ist vielmehr versucht worden, Konzepte vorzustellen und zu erläutern, die sich aus den mit den verschiedensten Anwendungen der graphischen Datenverarbeitung in den letzten 10 Jahren gewonnenen Erfahrungen heraus entwickelt haben.

Heutige graphische Systeme müssen weitgehend anwendungs- und geräteunabhängig sein. Es ist deswegen die Grundstruktur eines geräteunabhängigen graphischen Systems mit funktioneller Beschreibung der Ein- und Ausgabe diskutiert worden. Eine relative Anwendungsunabhängigkeit kann man nur erreichen, wenn die Datenbank als zentrale Bestandteil des Systems betrachtet wird. Auf der Grundlage dieses Konzepts ist ein graphisches Informationssystem durch seine Grundfunktionen schrittweise beschrieben und anhand eines realisierten Systemes – GRIFO – näher erläutert worden. Wesentlich ist, daß mit diesem System nicht nur mit der geometrischen Information der Bilder sondern auch mit "Bedeutungen" im Bild gearbeitet werden kann.

Schließlich sind für die Analyse der Wirtschaftlichkeit des Einsatzes graphischer Systeme drei Verfahren angegeben worden, die insbesondere die Kosteneffektivität und die Kostenreduzierung analysieren.

Literaturverzeichnis

/ 1 /   ISO/TC 97/SC 1 37
         "Vocabulary", Section 13

/ 2 /   J. Encarnacao
         Computer Graphics – Programmierung und Anwendung
         von graphischen Systemen
         Verfahren der Datenverarbeitung
         R. Oldenbourg Verlag; München, Wien, 1975

/ 3 /   J. Encarnacao und R. Eckert
             Bemühungen und Möglichkeiten bei der Begriffsbildung
             und Normung graphischer Systeme
             Lecture Notes of the German Chapter of the ACM
             "Interaktives Programmieren", 11.3.1976, Erlangen

/ 4 /   J. Encarnacao, B. Fink, E. Hörbst, R. Konkart,
             G. Nees, D. Parnas and E.G. Schlechtendahl
             A recommendation on methodology in Computer Graphics
             Unpublished Position paper for the IFIP Graphics Workshop
             Chateau de Seillac, France, May 23-26, 1976

/ 5 /   GINO-F Users Manual
             Computer Aided Design Centre
             Cambridge

/ 6 /   E. Hörbst, G. Geitz and M. Gonauser
             An integrated System which provides the use of
             various graphic terminals
             Interactive Systems, London, 1975, pp. 45-56

/ 7 /   GPGS Reference Manual
             RC-GFX-75002-0
             Rekencentrum, Technische Hogeschool, Delft

/ 8 /   J. Encarnacao and J. Hunger
             UGP - The Universal Graphical Package
             Definition and Survey of a concept for the ESRO Graphic System
             Final Report, Berlin/Saarbrücken, May 1974

/ 9 /   Programmers' Reference Manual for the
             Universal Graphical Package UGP II
             Christian Rovsing A/S, 273o Herlev, Danmark

/10/   I.W. Cotton
             Network graphic attention handling
             Online 72 Conference Proceedings, pp. 465-490

/11/   J.D. Foley
             Picture naming and modification; an overview
             Computer Graphics, Vol.10, No.1, Spring 1976
             ACM-SIGGRAPH, pp.49-53

/12/   V.L. Wallace
             The semantics of graphic input devices
             Computer Graphics, Vol.10, No.1, Spring 1976
             ACM-SIGGRAPH, pp. 61-65

/13/   J.P. Crestin and M. Lucas
             What might be Computer Graphics?
             Unpublished Position paper for the IFIP Graphics Workshop
             Chateau de Seilaac, France, May 23-26, 1976

/14/   R. Noppen
             Möglichkeiten und Probleme des rechnereinsatzes bei der
             Entwicklung und Konstruktion technischer Objekte
             Vortrag am 28.o7.1975 im Rahmen des
             Informatik-Kolloquium der Universität Erlangen-Nürnberg

/15/   G. Weck, K. Fischer, W. Klos, N. Cullmann und R. Eckert
            GRIFO (Integriertes graphisches Informationssystem)
            Forschungsbericht Nr. GDV 76 - 1
            Forschungsgruppe Graphische Datenverarbeitung
            Technische Hochschule Darmstadt
            Fachbereich Informatik

/16/   J. Encarnacao und G. Weck
            Eine Implementierung von DATAS - Daten-
            strukturen in assoziativer Speicherung
            Institut für Angewandte Mathematik und Informatik
            der Universität des Saarlandes
            Bericht Nr. A 74-1, Januar 1974

/17/   G. Weck
            SAD - Ein Modell einer Strukturunabhängigen
            Assoziativen Datenstruktur
            Dissertation, Mathematisch-Naturwissenschaft-
            liche Fakultät der Universität des Saarlandes, 1974

/18/   R. M. Dunn
            Graphics, problem solving and virtual systems;
            AFIPS Conference Proceedings;
            Vol.42, National Computer Conference 1973, N.Y.,
            June 4-8, 1973; pp. 23-30

/19/   R.M. Dunn
            Computer Graphics: Capabilities
            Costs and Usefulness; Report of
            SIGGRAPH-ACM; Vol. 7, No.1, Spring 1973, pp. 1-29

/20/   I.W. Cotton
            Methodologies for the cost - benefit
            analysis of computer graphics systems
            Computer & Graphics, Vol. 1, pp. 33-43; Pergamon Press 1975

/21/   S.H. Chasen
            Economic principles for interactive graphic applications
            Proceedings of the National Computer Conference
            1975, pp. 613-620

SOME ASPECTS OF RANDOM
CONTEXT GRAMMARS

G.Rozenberg
University of Antwerp, UIA
Universiteitsplein 1
2610 Wilrijk Belgium

S.H. von Solms
Department of Computer Science
Rand Afrikaans University
JOHANNESBURG 2000
South Africa

ABSTRACT

Two generalizations of the notion of a random context grammar are considered. The first one equips a random context grammar with a possibility of a (limited) counting of a number of occurrences of the symbol to be rewritten. The second one applies productions in parallel (as in L systems). It is proved that these two generalizations do not increase the language generating power of the class of random context grammars. Also some normal form theorems are proved.

1. INTRODUCTION

Random context grammars were introduced by van der Walt, see [8] . A typical random context production is of the form

$$A \to \alpha \ , \ (Y \ ; \ N)$$

where A is a nonterminal, α is an arbitrary word and Y,N are disjoint subsets of nonterminals. Y is called the permitting and N the forbidding context of the production. The idea is that A can be replaced in the string $x_1 A x_2$, yielding $x_1 \alpha x_2$, if every element of Y appears in $x_1 x_2$ and no element of N appears in $x_1 x_2$.

In this paper we consider two generalizations of the notion of a random context grammar.

The first one equips a random context grammar with a facility to check that the symbol A to be rewritten appears a minimum number of times in the string under rewriting. This generalization comes naturally when one compares the van der Walt notion af a random context grammar with its Russian variations (see, e.g.,[2]). We show that the class of languages generated by such counting random context grammars coincides with the class of languages generated by random context grammars.

The second generalization we consider is introducing parallel rewriting into random context grammars. It was noticed already before (see [4] ,[5] and [9]) that random context grammars are really suitable to characterize the class of ETOL languages. Now we go a step further and we require that a random context grammar rewrites simultaneously all the symbols in a sentential string. We show that the class of languages generated by the so obtained systems coincides with the class of random context languages. We also show that one can restrict oneself to consider such L random context systems with forbidding fields only, or L random context systems with permitting fields only. These normal forms are inherent to parallel rewriting, because it is known that the analogous results are not true for random context grammars with sequential rewriting. It is worthwhile to notice here that L random context systems are interesting from a biological point of view. This is discussed further in Section 3.

We assume the reader to be familiar with rudiments of formal language theory (see, e.g., [6]).

2. COUNTING RANDOM CONTEXT GRAMMARS

Random context grammars were introduced by van der Walt (see [8]   ) but they were also intensively studied in the Russian literature (see, e.g., [2]   ). However there is a slight definitional difference in random context grammars as introduced by van der Walt and as studied by the Russians. It goes as follows. Let $A \to \alpha$, $(Y ; N)$ be a random context production. To apply it to a word $x_1 A x_2$, to obtain $x_1 \alpha x_2$, van der Walt requires that $x_1 x_2$ contains all elements from Y and none from N; the Russians require that $x_1 A x_2$ contains all elements from Y and none from N. Now suppose that Y contains A. In the van der Walt interpretation it would mean that $A \to \alpha$ can be applied to A providing it is not the only occurrence of A in the string; in the Russian interpretation it is superfluous. Thus using the van der Walt interpretation we get a possibility of (limited) counting of number of occurrences of the letter to be rewritten. This consideration leads to the following generalization of the notion of a random context grammar. (We use min (x) to denote the set of all and only these symbols that occur in x).

Definition 2.1. An n <u>counting random context grammar</u> (an RC^n grammar), $n \geqslant 0$, is a construct $G = (V_N, V_T, P, S)$, where V_N is a finite nonempty set (of <u>non-terminals</u>), V_T is a finite nonempty set (of terminals) disjoint with V_N, $S \in V_N$ (the <u>axiom</u> of G), and
P is a finite nonempty set of productions of the form $A \to \alpha$, $(j ; Y ; N)$ where $A \in V_N$, $\alpha \in (V_N \cup V_T)^*$, $Y \subset V_N \setminus \{A\}$, $N \subseteq V_N$, $Y \cap N = \phi$ and $0 \leqslant j \leqslant n$. We also assume that $A \in N$ if and only if $j = 0$.

Definition 2.2. Let $G = (V_N, V_T, P, S)$ be an RC^n grammar, let x be in $(V_N \cup V_T)^*$ and let π be a production from P of the form $A \to \alpha$, $(j ; Y ; N)$. Let O_A be an occurrence of A in x, thus $x = x_1 O_A x_2$. We say that π is O_A-<u>applicable to</u> x if
(i) $Y \subseteq \min (x_1 x_2)$,
(ii) $N \cap \min (x_1 x_2) = \phi$, and
(iii)   A appears <u>at least</u> j times in $x_1 x_2$.

<u>Definition 2.3.</u>   Let $G = (V_N, V_T, P, S)$ be an RC^n grammar.

(1) Let $x, y \in (V_N \cup V_T)^*$. We say that x <u>directly derives</u> y (<u>in</u> G), denoted as $x \underset{G}{\Rightarrow} y$, if P contains a production π of the form $A \to \alpha$, $(j\,;Y\,;N)$, x contains an occurrence 0_A of A such that $x = x_1\, 0_A\, x_2$, π is 0_A-applicable to x and $y = x_1\, \alpha\, x_2$.

(2) Let $\overset{*}{\Rightarrow}$ denotes the reflexive and   transitive closure of the relation $\underset{G}{\Rightarrow}$. If $x \underset{G}{\overset{*}{\Rightarrow}} y$ then we say that x <u>derives</u> y <u>in</u> G.

(3) The <u>language of</u> G, denoted as $L(G)$, is defined by

$$L(G) = \{x \in V_T^* : S \underset{G}{\overset{*}{\Rightarrow}} x\}$$

We refer to $L(G)$ as an RC^n <u>language</u> and we use $\mathcal{L}(RC^n)$ to denote the class of all RC^n languages.

Sometimes we will assume that productions from P are uniquely labeled. In this way we will have productions of the form

(i) $A \to \alpha$, $(j\,;Y\,;N)$ and we will refer to such a production through its label.

<u>Example 2.1.</u>   Let $G = (V_N, V_T, P, S)$ be an RC^o grammar where

$V_N = \{S, A, B, C, X, Y, Z\}$

$V_T = \{a, b, c\}$,

and P consists of the following productions :

$S \to ABC$, $(0\,;\phi\,;\phi)$,

$A \to X$, $(0\,;\{B,C\}\,;\{Y,Z\})$,

$B \to Y$, $(0\,;\{X,C\}\,;\{A,Z\})$,

$C \to Z$, $(0\,;\{X,Y\}\,;\{A,B\})$,

$X \to aA$, $(0\,;\{Y,Z\}\,;\{B,C\})$,

$Y \to bB$, $(0\,;\{A,Z\}\,;\{X,C\})$,

$Z \to cC$, $(0\,;\{A,B\}\,;\{X,Y\})$,

$X \to a$, $(0\,;\{Y,Z\}\,;\{B,C\})$,

$Y \to b$, $(0\,;\{Z\}\,;\{A,X,C\})$,

$Z \to c$, $(0\,;\phi\,;\{A,B,C,X,Y,Z\})$

Then $L(G) = \{a^m b^m c^m : m \geqslant 1\}$.

We will prove now that providing a counting facility for RC grammars does not increase their language generating power.

<u>Lemma 2.1.</u>   For every $n \geqslant 0$, $\mathcal{L}(RC^n) = \mathcal{L}(RC^o)$.

<u>Proof.</u>

Obviously $\mathcal{L}(RC^o) \subseteq \mathcal{L}(RC^n)$.

Thus it is enough to prove that $\mathcal{L}(RC^n) \subseteq \mathcal{L}(RC^o)$.

Let $G = (V_N, V_T, P, S)$ be an RC^n grammar with productions from P numbered uniquely by $1,\ldots,r$. For a production (j) $A \to \alpha$, $(k\,;Y\,;N)$ with $k \geqslant 1$ we define $M_j = \{A_j^{(1)}, A_j^{(2)}, \ldots, A_j^{(k)}\}$. Let $M = \underset{1 \leqslant j \leqslant r}{\cup} M_j$ and let $Q = \{X^{(j)} : 1 \leqslant j \leqslant r\}$.

Let $G' = (V_N \cup M \cup Q, V_T, P', S)$ be an RC^o grammar where P' consists of the following productions :

(1) For every production (j) $A \to \alpha$, $(k ; Y ; N)$, with $k \geqslant 1$, from P put the following productions in P' :

$A \to A_j^{(1)}$, $(0 ; \phi ; Q \cup M)$,

$A \to A_j^{(2)}$, $(0 ; \{A_j^{(1)}\} ; Q \cup M \setminus \{A_j^{(1)}\})$,

$A \to A_j^{(3)}$, $(0 ; \{A_j^{(1)}, A_j^{(2)}\} ; Q \cup M \setminus \{A_j^{(1)}, A_j^{(2)}\})$,

$\vdots \qquad\qquad\qquad \vdots$

$A \to A_j^{(k)}$, $(0 ; \{A_j^{(1)}, A_j^{(2)}, \ldots, A_j^{(k-1)}\} ; Q \cup M \setminus \{A_j^{(1)}, A_j^{(2)}, \ldots, A_j^{(k-1)}\})$,

$A \to X^{(j)}$, $(0 ; M_j \cup Y ; N \cup Q \cup M \setminus M_j)$,

for every i in $\{1, \ldots, k\}$, $A_j^{(i)} \to A, (0 ; \{X^{(j)}\} ; Q \setminus \{X^j\} \cup M \setminus M_j)$, $X^{(j)} \to \alpha$,

$(0 ; \phi ; Q \cup M)$.

(2) For every production (j) $A \to \alpha$, $(0 ; Y ; N)$ from P put

$A \to \alpha$, $(0 ; Y ; N \cup M \cup Q)$ in P'.

The reader should easily see that $L(G) = L(G')$.

Thus the lemma holds.

In the rest of this paper a <u>random context grammar</u> (an RC <u>grammar</u>) will mean an RC^o grammar and a random context language will mean an element of $\mathcal{L}(RC^o)$. Thus $\mathcal{L}(RC) \equiv \mathcal{L}(RC^o)$.

We call an RC^n grammar propagating (or Λ-free) if it does not contain an erasing production and in analogy with the usual notation for L systems we will use the letter P to denote the propagating restriction. Thuw we use PRC^n to denote a propagating RC^n grammar.

Combining our Lemma 2.1. (and its proof) with the known results about $\mathcal{L}(PRC)$ and $\mathcal{L}(RC)$ ([3] and [8]) we get the following result :

<u>Theorem 2.1.</u> For every $n \geqslant 0$,
$$\mathcal{L}(PRC) = \mathcal{L}(PRC^n) = \mathcal{L}(CFP) \subsetneqq \mathcal{L}(RC) = \mathcal{L}(RC^n) = \mathcal{L}^\Lambda(CFP) = \mathcal{L}(RE),$$
where $\mathcal{L}(CFP)$ denotes the class of Λ-free context free programmed languages, $\mathcal{L}^\Lambda(CFP)$ denotes the class of context free programmed languages and $\mathcal{L}(RE)$ denotes the class of recursively enumerable languages.

3. PARALLEL RANDOM CONTEXT SYSTEMS

In this section we consider random context systems modified in such a way that at each derivation step all occurrences of all symbols in a string under rewriting are replaced. In other words we merge L systems with random context systems. In view of recent interest in parallel rewriting systems (see, e.g., Salomaa [7]) such a generalization is quite natural from the formal language theory point of view.

Because of the biological relevance of L systems (see, e.g., [1]) we would like to point out that parallel random context systems encompass ideas which are biologically quite feasible. The following can often be observed in biological development. At some stage of development a cell or a group of cells can appear which then produces a substance that spreads rapidly through the organism. The effect of this substance is that certain processes can be initiated in many of other cells. As a matter of fact developmental "organizers" are supposed to be this kind of substances. Clearly at the same way a substance can be produced that inhibits particular cell transitions. To simulate such a situation one can make use of permitting and forbidding fields of a production.

Here comes the formal definition.

Definition 3.1. An L <u>system with random context and</u> n <u>counting</u> (abbreviated as an LRC^n <u>system</u>) is a construct $G = (\Sigma, P, \omega, \Delta)$, where Σ is a finite nonempty set (the <u>alphabet of</u> G),

$\Delta \subseteq \Sigma$ (the <u>terminal alphabet</u> of G),

$\omega \in \Sigma^*$ (the <u>axiom of</u> G), and

P is a finite set of productions of the form

$$A \to \alpha, \quad (j\,;Y\,;N), \text{ where}$$

$A \in V_N, \alpha \in (V_N \cup V_T)^*,\ Y \subseteq V_N \setminus \{A\},\ N \subseteq V_N,\ Y \cap N = \phi \quad \text{and } 0 \leqslant j \leqslant n.$

As in the case of RC systems we will often assume that productions in an LRC^n system are preceded by a (unique) label which makes a reference to a production much easier.

Definition 3.2. Let $G = (\Sigma, P, \omega, \Delta)$ be an LRC^n system. Let x be in Σ^*, 0_A be an occurrence of the symbol A in x and let

(i) $A \to \alpha$, $(j\,;Y\,;N)$ be a production in P. We say that this production is 0_A-<u>applicable</u> to x if the following holds :

  (i) $x = x_1 0_A x_2$ with x_1, x_2 in Σ^*,

  (ii) $\min (x_1 x_2) \cap N = \phi$,

  (iii) $Y \subseteq \min (x_1 x_2)$,

  (iv) A occurs <u>at least</u> j times in $x_1 x_2$.

Please note that we are really interested in an application of a production to a given occurrence of a letter. To avoid a cumbersome notation in the sequel, we shall not use distinct symbols for a symbol and its occurrence. This however should not lead to a confusion.

Definition 3.3.

(1) Let $G = (\Sigma, P, \omega, \Delta)$ be an LRC^n system and let $x = A_1 \ldots A_m$ with $A_1, \ldots, A_m$ in Σ. Let $y = \alpha_1 \ldots \alpha_m$ with $\alpha_1, \ldots, \alpha_m \in \Sigma^*$. We say that x <u>directly derives</u> y <u>in</u> G (denoted as $x \underset{G}{\Rightarrow} y$) if, for every i in $\{1, \ldots, m\}$,

$$\alpha_i = \begin{cases} \beta_i & \text{if P contains a production } A_i \to \beta_i, (j\ ;\ Y_i\ ;\ N_i) \\ & \text{which is } A_i\text{-applicable to x,} \\[2ex] A_i & \text{if no production in P is } A_i\text{-applicable to x.} \end{cases}$$

(2) Let $\overset{*}{\underset{G}{\Rightarrow}}$ denotes the reflexive and the transitive closure of the relation $\underset{G}{\Rightarrow}$. If $x \overset{*}{\underset{G}{\Rightarrow}} y$ then we say that x <u>derives</u> y <u>in</u> G.

(3) The <u>language of</u> G, denoted as L(G), is defined by $L(G) = \{x \in \Delta^* : \omega \overset{*}{\underset{G}{\Rightarrow}} x\}$.

We refer to L(G) as an LRC^n <u>language</u> and we let $\mathcal{L}(LRC^n)$ denote the class of all LRC^n languages.

<u>REMARK.</u> It is important to notice that the usual completeness condition is satisfied in an LRC^n system. This is assured in such a way that if $x = x_1 A x_2$ and no production is A-applicable to x then A is rewritten by itself.

<u>Example 3.1.</u> Let $G = (\Sigma, P, \omega, \Delta)$ be an LRC^o system, where
$\Sigma = \{S,A,B,C,X,Y,Z,U,V,W,a,b,c\}$,
$\Delta = \{a,b,c\}$,
$\omega = S$, and
P consists of the following productions :
$S \to ABC$, $(0\ ;\ \phi\ ;\ \phi)$,
$A \to X$, $(0\ ;\ \{B,C\};\ \{X,Y,Z,U,V,W\})$,
$B \to Y$, $(0\ ;\ \{A,C\};\{X,Y,Z,U,V,W\})$,
$C \to Z$, $(0\ ;\ \{A,B\};\{X,Y,Z,U,V,W\})$,
$X \to aA$, $(0\ ;\ \{Y,Z\}\ ;\ \{A,B,C,U,V,W\})$,
$Y \to b$, $(0\ ;\ \{X,Z\}\ ;\ \{A,B,C,U,V,W\})$,
$Z \to cC$, $(0\ ;\ \{X,Y\}\ ;\ \{A,B,C,U,V,W\})$,
$X \to U$, $(0\ ;\ \{Y,Z\}\ ;\ \{A,B,C,U,V,W\})$,
$Y \to V$, $(0\ ;\ \{X,Z\}\ ;\ \{A,B,C,U,V,W\})$,
$Z \to W$, $(0\ ;\ \{X,Y\}\ ;\ \{A,B,C,U,V,W\})$,
$U \to a$, $(0\ ;\ \{V,W\}\ ;\ \{A,B,C,X,Y,Z\})$,
$V \to b$, $(0\ ;\ \{U,W\}\ ;\ \{A,B,C,X,Y,Z\})$,
$W \to c$, $(0\ ;\ \{U,V\}\ ;\ \{A,B,C,X,Y,Z\})$.
Then $L(G) = \{a^n b^n c^n : n \geqslant 1\}$

Now we proceed to investigate the language generative power of LRC^n systems.

<u>Lemma 3.1.</u> $\mathcal{L}(LRC^n) \subseteq \mathcal{L}(CFP)$.

<u>Proof.</u>

Instead of giving a formal proof (which would be rather long and tedious) we will provide an intuitive discussion on basis of which the reader can, if necessary, provide a formal proof of this result.

Given an LRC^n system, the context free programmed grammar simulating it will be gathering the information about a sentential string, such as the specific symbols appearing in the string and the desired number of times that a certain symbol occurs in the string. Note that because we are concerned with an n-counting LRC system, the maximum number of occurrences of a single symbol we need to count is $n+1$. On basis of this information it can be decided precisely which productions can be applied. Control will therefore be transferred to a block of productions consisting exactly of those productions which can be applied under the present circumstances. After the appropriate productions had been applied, control will again be transferred to the "information-gathering" productions.

<u>Lemma 3.2.</u> $\mathcal{L}(RC) \subseteq \mathcal{L}(LRC^o)$.

<u>Proof.</u>

Let $G = (V_N, V_T, P, S)$ be an RC grammar.

Let $Q = \{X^{(i)} : i$ is a label of production in $P\}$ where $Q \cap (V_N \cup V_T) = \phi$.

Now, let $G' = (\Sigma, P', S, \Delta)$ be an LRC^o system where $\Sigma = V_N \cup V_T \cup Q, \Delta = V_T$ and P' consists of the following productions :

(1) for every M in $(V_N \cup V_T)$, $M \rightarrow M$ is in P' ,

(2) for every (i) $A \rightarrow \alpha$, $(0 ; Y_i ; N_i)$ in P, both

$A \rightarrow X^{(i)}$, $(0 ; Y_i ; N_i \cup Q)$ and $X^{(i)} \rightarrow \alpha$, $(0 ; \phi ; Q)$ are in P'.

Note that the production $A \rightarrow X^{(i)}$ can only be applied if no element of Q appears in the sentential string. If more than one element of Q is introduced at the same time, then the sentential string becomes "blocked", because an element of Q can only be replaced if no other element of Q appears in the string.

From the above it is clear that indeed $L(G) = L(G')$.

Thus the lemma holds.

From the above two lemmas and from Theorem 2.1. it follows in particular that, for every n, $\mathcal{L}(LRC^o) = \mathcal{L}(LRC^n)$. For this reason, in the sequel of this paper an L <u>system with random context</u> (an LRC <u>system</u>) will mean an LRC^o system. Consequently an LRC <u>language</u> will mean an element of $\mathcal{L}(LRC^o)$. Thus $\mathcal{L}(LRC) = \mathcal{L}(LRC^o)$.

Now we proceed to investigate two important subclasses of LRC systems.

<u>Definition 3.4.</u> An L system with random context $G = (\Sigma, P, \omega, \Delta)$ is called an L <u>system with forbidding context</u> (an LRC_f system) if for every production $A \rightarrow \alpha$, $(0 ; Y ; N)$ in P we have $Y = \phi$.

We let $\mathcal{L}(LRC_f)$ to denote the class of languages generated by LRC_f systems (LRC_f languages).

<u>Definition 3.5.</u> An LRC^n system $G = (\Sigma, P, \omega, \Delta)$ is called an L <u>system with</u> <u>permitting context and</u> n <u>counting</u> (an LRC_p^n <u>system</u>) if for every production $A \rightarrow \alpha$, $(j ; Y ; N)$ in P we have $N = \phi$.

We let $\mathcal{L}(LRC_p^n)$ to denote the class of languages generated by LRC_p^n systems (LRC_p^n <u>languages</u>).

We will show now that, unlike in the case of RC grammars, restriction to permitting fields only or to forbidding fields only in parallel RC systems do not decrease their language generative power.

<u>Lemma 3.3.</u>　$\mathcal{L}(RC) \subseteq \mathcal{L}(LRC_p^1)$.

<u>Proof.</u>

Let $G = (V_N, V_T, P, S)$ be an RC grammar with its productions labeled uniquely by $1,\ldots,r$. Let

$Q = \{X^{(i)} : 1 \leqslant i \leqslant r\}$,

for i in $\{1,\ldots,r\}$, $M_i = \{\mathscr{B}_{i_1},\ldots,\mathscr{B}_{i_{k+2}} : (i)\ A \to \alpha, (0;Y;\{F_1,\ldots,F_k\})$ is in $P\}$,

$M = \bigcup_{i=1}^{r} M_i$, and

$\Sigma = M \cup Q \cup V_N \cup V_T \cup \{\mathscr{B}, D\}$.

Let $G' = (\Sigma, P', S, V_T)$ be an LRC_p^1 system where P' consists of the following productions :

(1) For every production of the form $S \to \alpha$, $(0;\phi;\phi)$ in P, put $S \to \alpha\, \mathscr{B}_{\ell_1}, (0;\phi;\phi)$ in P' for every ℓ in $\{1,\ldots,r\}$. Clearly we can assume that the only productions in P in which S appears are productions of the form $S \to \alpha$, $(0;\phi;\phi)$ and moreover α does not contain an occurrence of S.

(2) For every production (i) $A \to \alpha$, $(0;Y;\{F_1,\ldots,F_k\})$ in P with $A \neq S$ put the following productions in P' :

$i_1)$ $A \to X^{(i)}, (0;Y \cup \{\mathscr{B}_{i_1}\};\phi)$,

$i_2)$ $\mathscr{B}_{i_1} \to \mathscr{B}_{i_2}, (0;\phi;\phi)$,

$i_3)$ $X^{(i)} \to D, (1;\{\mathscr{B}_{i_2}\};\phi)$,

$i_4)$ $\mathscr{B}_{i_2} \to \mathscr{B}_{i_3}, (0;\phi;\phi)$

$i_5)$ $X^{(i)} \to D, (0;\{\mathscr{B}_{i_3}, F_1\};\phi)$,

$i_6)$ $\mathscr{B}_{i_3} \to \mathscr{B}_{i_4}, (0;\phi;\phi)$,

$i_7)$ $X^{(i)} \to D, (0;\{\mathscr{B}_{i_4}, F_2\};\phi)$

$\vdots$

$i_{2k+3})$ $X^{(i)} \to D, (0;\{\mathscr{B}_{i_{k+2}}, F_k\}, \phi)$,

$i_{2k+4})$ $\mathscr{B}_{i_{k+2}} \to \mathscr{B}, (0;\phi;\phi)$,

$i_{2k+5})$ $X^{(i)} \to \alpha, (0;\{\mathscr{B}\};\phi)$,

$i_{2k+6})\ \$ \to \$_{\ell_1}$, $(0 ; \phi ; \phi)$, for every ℓ in $\{1,\ldots,r\}$, and

$i_{2k+7})\ \$ \to \Lambda$, $(0 ; \phi ; \phi)$.

(3) For every M in $V_N \cup V_T$, put $M \to M$ in P'.

The following remarks should clarify how G' simulates G.

In production i_1 we check the permitting context of the given production. Note that this production can only be applied if the correct marker symbol is present. The i subscript of the marker denotes that we are simulating production i of the given grammar.

In production i_3 we check that production i_1 had only been applied once. If production i_1 had been applied more than once, more than one $X^{(i)}$ symbol will appear in the sentential string. Production i_3 will therefore introduce a D symbol, which is not a terminal, and which can never be replaced. If production i_1 had been applied precisely once, then production i_3 will not be $X^{(i)}$ - applicable to the sentential string, and $X^{(i)}$ will remain unchanged.

From production i_5 to i_{2k+3}, we check the forbidding context of the given production. If a symbol from the forbidding context appears (one of the F_i symbols), we introduce a D symbol. This will imply that we had chosen an illegal production to simulate.

The reader should note that the inherent part of the proof is the fact that if no production is applicable to a spesific symbol, then the symbol remains unchanged. For example, if an $X^{(i)}$ symbol appears in a sentential string together with an $\$_{i_4}$ symbol, we know that no F_1 symbol appears in the string,

i.e. $\quad \ldots\ldots X^{(i)} \ldots\ldots \$_{i_3} \Rightarrow \ldots\ldots X^{(i)} \ldots\ldots \$_{i_4}$

if and only if no F_1 appears. If a F_1 had appeared in the first sentential string, then

$$\ldots\ldots X^{(i)} \ldots\ldots F_1 \ldots\ldots \$_{i_3} \Rightarrow \ldots\ldots D \ldots\ldots F_1 \ldots\ldots \$_{i_4} \ ,$$

under production i_5.

When we reach production i_{2k+5}, we have checked that no forbidding symbol appears, and the given production can be applied. Production i_{2k+6} may now choose nondeterministically, to initiate any other production, or to disappear. If the marker disappears prematurely, then the sentential string will never change again.

It should be clear to the reader that we can do without the marker symbol, by carrying the relevant information on a symbol within the sentential string. The marker symbol is used just to simplify the proof.

Thus $L(G) = L(G')$ and the lemma holds.

<u>Lemma 3.4.</u> $\mathcal{L}(RC) \subseteq \mathcal{L}(LRC_f)$.

<u>Proof.</u>

Let $G = (V_N, V_T, P, S)$ be an RC grammar with its productions uniquely numbered by $1,\ldots,r$. Let

$$M_1 = \{\$_i : 1 \leq i \leq r\},$$

$$M_2 = \{\$_i^C : C \in V_N \text{ and } C \text{ appears in the permitting context of production } i\},$$

$$M_3 = \{X^{(i)} : 1 \leq i \leq r\},$$

$$M_4 = \{\overline{\$}_i : \$_i \in M_1\},$$

$$M_5 = \{Y^{(i)} : 1 \leq i \leq r\},$$

$$M_6 = \{\$_i' : \$_i \in M_1\},$$

$$M = \bigcup_{i=1}^{6} M_i, \text{ and}$$

$$\Sigma = M \cup V_N \cup V_T \cup \{D\}.$$

Now let $G' = (\Sigma, P', S, V_T)$ be an LRC_f system where P' consists of the following productions :

(1) For every production $S \to \alpha$, $(0 ; \phi ; \phi)$ in P, put, for every $\$_i$ in M_1, $S \to \alpha\,\$_i$, $(0 ; \phi ; \phi)$ in P'. Clearly we can assume that the only productions in P in which S appears are productions of the form $S \to \alpha$, $(0 ; \phi ; \phi)$ and moreover α does not contain an occurrence of S.

(2) For every production (i) $A \to \alpha$, $(0 ; \{Z_1,\ldots,Z_t\} ; N)$ in P with $A \neq S$ put the following productions in P' :

$i_1)$ $A \to X^{(i)}$, $(0 ; \phi ; M_3 \cup N \cup M_1 \setminus \{\$_i\})$,

$i_2)$ $\$_i \to \overline{\$}_i$, $(0 ; \phi ; \phi)$,

$i_3)$ $X^{(i)} \to Y^{(i)}$, $(0 ; \phi ; M_3 \cup M_5 \cup M_1 \cup M_2 \cup M_4 \setminus \{\overline{\$}_i\})$,

$i_4)$ $\overline{\$}_i \to \$_i^{Z_1}$, $(0 ; \phi ; \phi)$,

$i_5)$ $Y^{(i)} \to D$, $(0 ; \phi ; \{Z_1\} \cup M_2 \setminus \{\$_i^{Z_1}\})$,

$i_6)$ $\$^{Z_1} \to \$^{Z_2}$, $(0 ; \phi ; \phi)$,

$i_7)$ $Y^{(i)} \to D$, $(0 ; \phi ; \{Z_2\} \cup M_2 \setminus \{\$_i^{Z_2}\})$,

$i_8)$ $\$_i^{Z_2} \to \$_i^{Z_3}$, $(0 ; \phi ; \phi)$,

$$\vdots \qquad\qquad \vdots$$

$$\vdots \qquad \vdots$$

$i_{2t+2})\ \$_i^{Z_{t-1}} \to \$_i^{Z_t},\ (0;\phi;\phi),$

$i_{2t+3})\ Y^{(i)} \to D,(0\ ;\phi;\{Z_t\}\cup M_2\setminus\{\$_i^{Z_t}\}),$

$i_{2t+4})\ \$_i^{Z_t} \to \$_i',\ (0\ ;\phi\ ;\ M_3),$

$i_{2t+5})\ Y^{(i)} \to \alpha,\ (0\ ;\phi;\ M_1\cup M_2\cup M_3\cup M_4\cup M_6\setminus\{\$_i'\}),$

$i_{2t+6})\ \$_i' \to \$_j,\ (0\ ;\phi;M\setminus\{Y^{(i)}\}),$ for every j in $\{1,\dots,r\}$, and

$i_{2t+7})\ \$_i' \to \Lambda,\ (0\ ;\phi;\ \Sigma\setminus V_T).$

(3) For every M in $(V_N\cup V_T)$ put $M\to M$ in P'.

The main idea behind the simulation of G by G' is very much the same as in the construction of G' in the proof of Lemma 3.3.

Observe that there can always be at most one marker (the symbol $\$$ with subscripts and/or superscripts) present in a sentential string. The subscript of the marker indicates the production from G that is simulated.

In productions i_1 to i_4 we replace A by $X^{(i)}$ if $\$_i$ is present and we ensure that one and only one occurrence of A is replaced by $X^{(i)}$.

In productions i_5 to i_{2t+3} we check the permitting context of the given production. If the specific permitting symbol is not present we introduce D. If the symbol is present, no production is applicable to $Y^{(i)}$ and so $Y^{(i)}$ remains unchanged.

When we reach production i_{2t+5} we can apply the given random context production because this production can be reached only if <u>all</u> permitting symbols are present.

In the group of productions i_{2t+6} we can choose the next production from P to be simulated. The marker symbol can disappear by production i_{2t+7} and moreover this can happen only if the sentential string contains the terminal symbols only.

From the above it should be clear that $L(G) = L(G')$ and so the lemma holds.

Given an LRC^n system we call it a <u>propogating</u> LRC^n <u>system</u> if it does not contain an erasing production. We will use the letter P to denote the propagating restriction. In this way we speak of $PLRC^n$ systems, $PLRC_f$ systems, etc.

From the results of this section, Theorem 2.1. and the obvious definitional inclusions we have the following result.

<u>Theorem 3.1.</u>

For every $n\geqslant 1$, $\mathcal{L}(LRC^0) = \mathcal{L}(LRC^n) = \mathcal{L}(LRC_p^1) = \mathcal{L}(LRC_p^n) = \mathcal{L}(LRC_f)$, and $\mathcal{L}(PLRC^0) = \mathcal{L}(PLRC^n) = \mathcal{L}(PLRC_p^1) = \mathcal{L}(PLRC_p^n) = \mathcal{L}(PLRC_f).$

Then Theorem 2.1. together with Theorem 3.1. give the following result.

$\underline{\text{Corollary 3.1.}}$ For every $n \geqslant 1$,

$$\mathcal{L}(\text{CFP}) = \mathcal{L}(\text{PRC}) = \mathcal{L}(\text{PRC}^n) = \mathcal{L}(\text{PLRC}^n) = \mathcal{L}(\text{PLRC}^O) =$$

$$\mathcal{L}(\text{PLRC}_p^1) = \mathcal{L}(\text{PLRC}_p^n) = \mathcal{L}(\text{PLRC}_f) \subsetneqq$$

$$\mathcal{L}(\text{RE}) = \mathcal{L}(\text{RC}) = \mathcal{L}(\text{RC}^n) = \mathcal{L}(\text{LRC}^n) = \mathcal{L}(\text{LRC}^O) =$$

$$\mathcal{L}(\text{LRC}_p^1) = \mathcal{L}(\text{LRC}_p^n) = \mathcal{L}(\text{LRC}_f).$$

4.   CONCLUDING REMARKS

We have considered two generalizations of the notion of a random context grammar. It turned out that both of them, a counting facility and a parallel rewriting facility, do not increase the generating power of the class of random context grammars.

To get the full picture of the situation one should try to settle several open problems.

1. As in the case of LRC^n systems one can talk about the "forbidding" and the "permitting" subclasses of the class of RC^n systems. It is known from the literature that $\mathcal{L}(\text{RC}_f)$ and $\mathcal{L}(\text{RC}_p)$ are strict subclasses of $\mathcal{L}(\text{RC})$. However the relationship between $\mathcal{L}(\text{RC}_f)$ and $\mathcal{L}(\text{RC}_p)$ is not known.
   Also we do not know whether for every $n \geqslant 1$
   $$\mathcal{L}(\text{RC}_p^n) = \mathcal{L}(\text{RC}_p^{n-1}).$$

2. Is it true that $\mathcal{L}(\text{LRC}_p^1) = \mathcal{L}(\text{LRC}_p^O)$?   We conjecture that $\mathcal{L}(\text{LRC}_p^O) \subsetneqq \mathcal{L}(\text{LRC}_p^1)$. Note that in the proof of Lemma 3.3. we essentially use a production of the form $A \rightarrow \alpha,\ (1\,;Y\,;\phi)$

3. Clearly, in the case of RC grammars one can restrict oneself to productions of the form $A \rightarrow \alpha,\ (O\,;Y\,;N)$ with $A \notin N$. Is it true in the case of LRC systems ?

REFERENCES

1. A. Lindenmayer, 1975, Developmental systems and languages in their biological context, contribution to G.T. Herman and G.Rozenberg, _Developmental systems and languages_, North-Holland Publ. Comp., Amsterdam

2. A.N. Maslov and E.D. Stocki, 1975, On some classes of formal grammars (in Russian), _Probability theory. Mathematical statistics. Theoretical cybernetics._ v. 12, 155-187.

3. O.Mayer, 1972, Some restrictive devices for context free grammars, _Information and Control_, v. 20, 69-92.

4. M. Penttonen, 1975, ETOL grammars and N grammars, _Information Processing Letters_, v. 4, 11-13.

5. G. Rozenberg, 1975, More on a connection between ETOL systems and random context grammars, Dept. of Mathematics, University of Antwerp, Technical report No.75/15.

6. A. Salomaa, 1973, Formal languages, Academic Press, New York.

7. A. Salomaa, 1974, Parallelism in rewriting systems, Lecture Notes in Computer Science, v. 14,

8. Van der Walt, 1971, Random context languages, Proceedings of the IFIP-Congress 1971, 66-68.

9. Von Solms, 1975, On TOL languages over terminals, Information Processing Letters, v. 3, 69-70.

ZUR ANALYSENKOMPLEXITAET VON GRAMMATIKEN UND
PUSHDOWN-AKZEPTOREN,DIE HILFSZAEHLER VERWENDEN

J. Albert, W. Erni

Inst. f. Angew. Informatik   Inst. f. Angew. Mathematik
Universität Karlsruhe   Universität Heidelberg

I. Zusammenfassung

In dieser Arbeit werden zwei Beispiele der Verwendung von Hilfszählern
zur Verallgemeinerung der kontextfreien Sprachen angegeben, bei denen
die polynomielle Analysenkomplexität erhalten bleibt. Zuerst werden die
Sprachen betrachtet, die von Quasi-Realzeit Pushdown-Akzeptoren mit k
Zählern erkannt werden. Diese bilden eine principal AFL, welche die m-
Stapel-Zählersprachen für $m \leq k/2$ echt enthält und eine Analysenkomplexität der Ordnung $n^{4 \cdot (k+1)}$ hat. Danach werden 1-indizierte Sprachen definiert. Sie bilden eine Super-AFL, die die EOL-Sprachen echt enthält
und selbst in den indizierten Sprachen echt enthalten ist. Hier läßt
sich eine Analysenkomplexität der Ordnung n^5 nachweisen.

II. Einleitung

Es ist wohlbekannt, daß für jede kontextfreie Sprache $L \subset \Sigma_1^*$ ein Verfah-
ren existiert, das für ein $w \in \Sigma_1^*$, $|w| = n \geq 1$, nach höchstens
$\text{const} \cdot n^3$ Rechenschritten entscheidet, ob $w \in L$ oder $w \notin L$. [2] In letzter
Zeit wurden die Verallgemeinerungen der kontextfreien Sprachen danach
untersucht, ob diese ebenfalls eine Analysenkomplexität der Ordnung n^k,
für eine Konstante k, haben. Es zeigt sich nun z.B. für die indizierten
und die scattered context Sprachen, daß "keine Hoffnung" besteht, ein
solches polynomielles Analyseverfahren zu finden. [16],[11]. Deshalb
ist es naheliegend, echte Teilmengen der obengenannten Sprachklassen zu
untersuchen.
Wir beginnen nun mit einem Überblick über neuere Ergebnisse der Analysenkomplexität verschiedener Sprachklassen. Bezeichnungen und Begriffe, die
im folgenden verwendet werden, aber nicht explicit angegeben sind, findet man bei Ginsburg, S. [10].

Definition

Sei $L \subset \Sigma_1^*$ und A ein (nicht) deterministischer Turingakzeptor, der zu einem nichtleeren Eingabewort $w \in \Sigma_1^*$, $|w| = n$, nach höchstens $c \cdot n^k$, mit $c, k \in N$, Rechenschritten entscheidet, ob $w \in L$ oder $w \notin L$. Dann sagt man, L hat eine (nichtdeterministische) <u>Analysenkomplexität der Ordnung</u> n^k oder L hat eine <u>polynomielle</u> (nichtdeterministische) Analysenkomplexität, kurz $L \in \mathscr{L}_{PZEIT}$ ($L \in \mathscr{L}_{NPZEIT}$). Weiter sagt man für eine Sprachfamilie $\mathscr{L}$ mit $\mathscr{L} \subset \mathscr{L}_{PZEIT}$ ($\mathscr{L} \subset \mathscr{L}_{NPZEIT}$), $\mathscr{L}$ hat eine (nichtdeterministische) polynomielle Analysenkomplexität [2].

In der obigen Definition darf man anstelle des Begriffs Turingakzeptor auch den Begriff Random Access Machine [2] setzen. $\mathscr{L}_{PZEIT}$ und $\mathscr{L}_{NPZEIT}$ werden dadurch nicht verändert.

Folgende Sprachklassen sind in $\mathscr{L}_{PZEIT}$ enthalten: Die EOL-Sprachen und die RMOL-Sprachen [15]. Für die Sprachen der "state grammars of finite degree k" wurde unabhängig von [19] die Ordnung $n^{8 \cdot k}$ nachgewiesen [8]. Die Sprachen der ε-freien ungeordneten Vektorgrammatiken [19]. Die Sprachen der "in-side-out" Makrogrammatiken [13]. Für die Sprachen der "simple matrix grammars of degree k" wurde unabhängig von [19] die Ordnung $n^{4 \cdot k}$ nachgewiesen [8]. Die Sprachen der ultralinearen Grammatiken mit kontextfreier Steuersprache [8],[9].

Nach [6],[2] läßt sich $\mathscr{L}_{PZEIT}$ durch den Automatentyp des k-Kopf zwei-Weg-Pushdown-Akzeptors, kurz k-PDA, charakterisieren. Wie ein gewöhnlicher nichtdeterministischer Pushdown-Akzeptor verfügt ein k-PDA über ein Eingabeband mit Begrenzungszeichen, eine endliche Kontrolle und ein Pushdownband. Das Lesen des Eingabewortes erfolgt jedoch durch $k \geq 1$ (unabhängige) off-line Leseköpfe. Das Akzeptieren eines Eingabewortes geschieht in analoger Weise wie bei gewöhnlichen Pushdown-Akzeptoren.

Satz

(1) Wenn $L \in \mathscr{L}_{PZEIT}$, dann gibt es eine natürliche Zahl k und einen k-PDA M mit $L = L(M)$.

(2) Wenn $L = L(M)$ für einen k-PDA M, dann hat L eine Analysenkomplexität der Ordnung $n^{4 \cdot k}$.

Den Beweis findet man bei Cook, S. [6].

Man kann auch eine Charakterisierung derjenigen Sprachen angeben, für
die die "Hoffnung", eine polynomielle Analysenkomplexität zu finden, als
sehr gering angesehen werden muß [16].

Definition

(1) Man betrachte die Menge der erfüllbaren Booleschen Ausdrücke in kon-
    junktiver Normalform. Sei $C_3(1)$ diejenige Teilmenge, die aus Aus-
    drücken der Form $C_1 \wedge \ldots \wedge C_i \wedge \ldots \wedge C_m$, $m \geq 1$, wobei jedes C_i höch-
    stens 3 Variable enthält, besteht. Variable werden dabei als Ele-
    mente von $\{1\}^+$ dargestellt.
(2) Eine Sprachfamilie $\mathscr{L}$ mit $C_3(1) \in \mathscr{L}$ nennen wir polynomiell hart,
    kurz <u>p-hart.</u>

Man zeigt leicht, daß $\mathscr{L}_{NPZEIT}$ p-hart ist. Weiter kann man zeigen [16],
[2] daß für eine p-harte Sprachfamilie $\mathscr{L}$ die Aussage $\mathscr{L} \subset \mathscr{L}_{PZEIT}$ die
Aussage $\mathscr{L}_{PZEIT} = \mathscr{L}_{NPZEIT}$ nach sich zieht. Manche Autoren benutzen anstelle von $C_3(1)$ eine andere Sprache, um den Begriff p-hart zu definie-
ren. [11]
Folgende Sprachklassen sind p-hart:
Die ETOL-Sprachen [14], die indizierten Sprachen [16], die Sprachen der
programmierten Grammatiken mit ε-freiem kontextfreiem Kern [18], die
Sprachen der "checking automata" [18], die Sprachen der "scattered context" Grammatiken [11],[12].

III. Quasi-Realzeit Pushdown-Akzeptoren mit Zählern

Definition

Für $m \geq 1$ und beliebige Sprachfamilien $\mathscr{L}_1, \ldots, \mathscr{L}_m$ sei

(1) $\mathscr{L}_1 \wedge \ldots \wedge \mathscr{L}_m := \{L_1 \cap \ldots \cap L_m \mid L_i \in \mathscr{L}_i, 1 \leq i \leq m\}$

(2) $\mathscr{H}(\mathscr{L}_1 \wedge \ldots \wedge \mathscr{L}_m) := \{h(L) \mid L \in \mathscr{L}_1 \wedge \ldots \wedge \mathscr{L}_m,\ h\ \varepsilon\text{-freier Homomorphis-}$
$\text{mus}\}$

(3) $\hat{\mathscr{H}}(\mathscr{L}_1 \wedge \ldots \wedge \mathscr{L}_m) := \{h(L) \mid L \in \mathscr{L}_1 \wedge \ldots \wedge \mathscr{L}_m,\ h\ \text{beliebiger Homomorphis-}$
$\text{mus}\}$

Es ist bekannt [10], daß für die Familie der 1-Zählersprachen $\mathscr{L}_C$ gilt:
$\mathscr{L}_{RE} = \hat{\mathscr{H}}(\mathscr{L}_C \wedge \mathscr{L}_C)$.

Wir interessieren uns im folgenden für die Sprachfamilien

$$\mathscr{L}_{CF\text{-}k} := \mathscr{H}(\mathscr{L}_{CF} \wedge \underbrace{\mathscr{L}_C \wedge \ldots \wedge \mathscr{L}_C}_{k\text{-mal}}), \quad k \geqq 1, \quad \text{und} \quad \mathscr{L}_{CF\text{-}0} := \mathscr{L}_{CF}.$$

Mit Hilfe der Methoden der AFL-Theorie [10] läßt sich jedes $L \in \mathscr{L}_{CF\text{-}k}$ durch einen <u>Quasi-Realzeit Pushdown-Akzeptor</u> mit k Zählern charakterisieren. Dies wird später noch genauer erläutert werden.

<u>Abschlußeigenschaften</u>

<u>Satz</u>

(1) $\mathscr{L}_{CF\text{-}k}$ ist für jedes $k \geqq 1$ eine unter Wortspiegelung abgeschlossene principal AFL.

(2) $\mathscr{L}_{CF\text{-}k}$ ist für jedes $k \geqq 1$ bzgl. beliebiger Homomorphismen nicht abgeschlossen.

Zum Beweis vgl. [10] und den folgenden Satz.

<u>Lage von $\mathscr{L}_{CF\text{-}k}$ in der Chomsky-Hierarchie</u>

<u>Satz</u>

(1) $\mathscr{L}_{CF} \subsetneqq \mathscr{L}_{CF\text{-}k} \subset \mathscr{H}(\mathscr{L}_{CF} \wedge \mathscr{L}_{CF} \wedge \mathscr{L}_{CF}) \subset \mathscr{L}_{SCC}$, für alle $k \geqq 1$.

Dabei ist $\mathscr{L}_{SCC}$ die Familie der "scattered context" Sprachen.

(2) Zu jedem $L' \in \mathscr{L}_{RE}$ gibt es ein $L \in \mathscr{L}_{CF\text{-}1}$ und ein $e \in \Sigma_L$, so daß

$L' = h(L)$, wobei h ein Homomorphismus mit $h(e) = \varepsilon$, $h(a) = a$, für

alle $a \in \Sigma_L - \{e\}$, ist.

<u>Beweis</u>

(1) Man zeigt leicht (sh. [10] Example 3.6.1), daß

$\{a^{(2i+2)^2} \mid i \in N\} \notin \mathscr{L}_{CF}$ in $\mathscr{L}_{CF\text{-}1} \subset \mathscr{L}_{CF\text{-}k}$ liegt. Aus der AFL-Theorie

ist bekannt [10], daß $\mathscr{H}(\underbrace{\mathscr{L}_{CF} \wedge \ldots \wedge \mathscr{L}_{CF}}_{j\text{-mal}, \; j \geq 3}) = \mathscr{H}(\mathscr{L}_{CF} \wedge \mathscr{L}_{CF} \wedge \mathscr{L}_{CF}) \subset \mathscr{L}_{SCC}$.

(2) Dies folgt aus $\mathscr{L}_{RE} = \hat{\mathscr{H}}(\mathscr{L}_C \wedge \mathscr{L}_C) = \hat{\mathscr{H}}(\mathscr{L}_{CF} \wedge \mathscr{L}_C)$ und den Methoden der

AFL-Theorie [10]. $\square$

Wegen $\mathscr{L}_{RE} = \hat{\mathscr{H}}(\mathscr{L}_{CF} \wedge \mathscr{L}_C)$ ist das Leerheitsproblem für $\mathscr{L}_{CF} \wedge \mathscr{L}_C$ und

somit auch für $\mathscr{L}_{CF\text{-}1} = \mathscr{H}(\mathscr{L}_{CF} \wedge \mathscr{L}_C)$ nicht entscheidbar.

Analysenkomplexität

Sei $\mathcal{D}_{PDA}$ die AFA-Formalisierung der Familie der gewöhnlichen Pushdown-Akzeptoren [10]. AFA steht für: abstrakte Familie von Akzeptoren. Man sagt, ein Pushdown-Akzeptor $D \in \mathcal{D}_{PDA}$ arbeitet in Quasi-Realzeit, wenn eine Schranke $k \in N$ existiert, so daß D beim Lesen des Eingabebandes seinen Lesekopf höchstens k Rechenschritte auf einem Eingabezeichen "stehenlassen" darf. Mit $\mathcal{L}^t(\mathcal{D}_{PDA})$ bezeichnet man dann die Menge derjenigen Sprachen, die von Quasi-Realzeit Pushdown-Akzeptoren akzeptiert werden. Bekanntlich [10] gilt $\mathcal{L}_{CF} = \mathcal{L}^t(\mathcal{D}_{PDA})$.

Eine analoge Betrachtung läßt sich auch für die Familie der 1-Zähler-Akzeptoren $\mathcal{D}_C$ und die Familie der 1-Zählersprachen $\mathcal{L}_C$ durchführen, dh. es gilt $\mathcal{L}_C = \mathcal{L}^t(\mathcal{D}_C)$.

Wir wissen, daß $\mathcal{L}_{CF-k} = \mathcal{H}(\mathcal{L}_{CF} \wedge \mathcal{L}_C \wedge \ldots \wedge \mathcal{L}_C)$. Dann folgt nach dem eben Gesagten und der AFL-Theorie:

$$\mathcal{L}_{CF-k} = \mathcal{H}(\mathcal{L}^t(\mathcal{D}_{PDA}) \wedge \mathcal{L}^t(\mathcal{D}_C) \wedge \ldots \wedge \mathcal{L}^t(\mathcal{D}_C)) = \mathcal{L}^t(\mathcal{D}_{PDAC-k}),$$ wobei $\mathcal{D}_{PDAC-k}$

die zugehörige Mehrband-AFA ist [10]. Mit anderen Worten, jedes $L \in \mathcal{L}_{CF-k}$ läßt sich durch einen in <u>Quasi-Realzeit</u> arbeitenden <u>Pushdown-Akzeptor</u> <u>mit k Zählern</u> $D \in \mathcal{D}_{PDAC-k}$ akzeptieren.

Satz

Sei $L \in \mathcal{L}_{CF-k}$ für ein $k \in N$. Dann hat L eine Analysenkomplexität der Ordnung $n^{4 \cdot (k+1)}$.

Beweis (Skizze)

Sie $L \in \mathcal{L}_{CF-k}$. Dann gibt es nach dem oben Erläuterten einen Quasi-Realzeit Pushdown-Akzeptor mit k Zählern $D \in \mathcal{D}_{PDAC-k}$, der L akzeptiert. Sei wie in [10] $D = (K_1, \Sigma_1, \delta, q_o, F)$ mit der Zustandsmenge K_1, dem Eingabealphabet Σ_1, der Überführungsfunktion δ, dem Startzustand q_o und der Endzustandsmenge F. Mit Hilfe der Überführungsfunktion δ seien die Relationen $\vdash_D$, genannt "Rechenschritt", und $\vdash_D^*$ wie üblich [10] definiert. Die Quasi-Realzeit-Bedingung gewährleistet nun die Existenz einer Konstanten $c \in N$, so daß für jedes Wort w aus der von D akzeptierten Sprache L mit $|w| = n \geq 1$ aus

$(q_o, w, (\varepsilon, \varepsilon, \ldots, \varepsilon)) \vdash_D^* (p, v, (\gamma_0, \gamma_1, \ldots, \gamma_k))$ die Ungleichungen $|\gamma_1|, \ldots, |\gamma_k| \leq c \cdot n$ folgen; dabei ist $w = uv$ für ein $u \in \Sigma_1^*$ und $\gamma_1, \ldots, \gamma_k \in \{Z\}^*$. M.a.W. die Länge der k Zähler von D ist linear beschränkt bzgl. $|w| = n$. Diese Tatsache weist uns nun den Weg, wie man D

durch einen (k+1)-PDA M simulieren kann. Der erste Kopf von M simuliert
in Verbindung mit dem Pushdownband das Lesen des Eingabewortes w gemäß D. Die restlichen k Köpfe arbeiten als "Hilfszähler". Dabei simuliert der i-te Kopf, $2 \leq i \leq k+1$, in Verbindung mit $q_1,\ldots,q_c$ "Hilfs-
zählzuständen" in der endlichen Kontrolle von M, in leicht einsehbarer
Weise den i-ten Zähler von D. □

Anwendung

Sei $\mathscr{F}_1$ die Familie der Stapel-Zählersprachen [10]. Die AFL
$\mathscr{H}(\underbrace{\mathscr{F}_1 \wedge \ldots \wedge \mathscr{F}_1}_{\text{k-mal}})$, $k \geq 1$, wurde in [5] unter dem Namen <u>k-Stapel-Zählerspra-</u>
<u>chen</u> untersucht. Da man weiß [10], daß

$$\mathscr{H}(\underbrace{\mathscr{F}_1 \quad \ldots \quad \mathscr{F}_1}_{\text{k-mal}}) \subset \mathscr{H}(\underbrace{\mathscr{L}_C \wedge \ldots\ldots\ldots\ldots \wedge \mathscr{L}_C}_{\text{2k-mal}})$$

folgt aus dem vorigen Satz: $\mathscr{H}(\mathscr{F}_1 \wedge \ldots \wedge \mathscr{F}_1) \subset \mathscr{L}_{\text{PZEIT}}$.

Kuriosum

$\mathscr{H}(\mathscr{L}_{CF} \wedge \mathscr{L}_{LIN})$ ist p-hart [4]. Aber $\mathscr{H}(\mathscr{L}_{CF} \wedge \mathscr{L}_C) \subset \mathscr{L}_{\text{PZEIT}}$.

IV. 1-indizierte Grammatiken

Die indizierten Sprachen von Aho bilden bekanntlich eine Hyper-AFL, die
echt zwischen der kontextfreien und der kontextsensitiven Sprachklasse
liegt. [1], [17].
Die 1-indizierten Grammatiken verallgemeinern die kontextfreien in ähnlicher Weise wie die indizierten Grammatiken von Aho. Statt indizierter
Variablen $A\zeta$ werden jedoch Variable mit Hilfszählern der Form A[j],
$j \geq 0$, verwendet, die man immer als indizierte Variable der Gestalt
$Af^j g$ interpretieren kann.
Man kann nun zeigen, daß die Familie der 1-indizierten Sprachen eine
Super-AFL ist, die echt zwischen $(\mathscr{L}_{CF})^{(1)}_{\text{iter}}$ und der Klasse der indizierten Sprachen liegt und eine Analysenkomplexität der Ordnung n^5 hat.

Definition

Ein 4-Tupel G = (V,T,P,S[0]) heißt <u>1-indizierte Grammatik</u>, wenn gilt:
V ist ein endliches Alphabet von <u>Variablen</u>.
$\bar{V} := \{A[i] \mid A \in V, i \in \mathbb{N}\}$ ist die Menge der <u>1-indizierten Variablen</u>.

T ist ein endliches Alphabet von <u>Terminalen</u> mit $\overline{V} \cap T = \emptyset$.

Sei $t \geq 0$ und $A_\nu \in V$, $x_\nu \in T^*$, $c_\nu \in \{0,1\}$, $d_\nu \in N$ für $\nu = 0(1)t$.

Eine Teilmenge von $\overline{V} \times (\overline{V} \cup T)^*$ der Gestalt

$$\{A_0[c_0 \cdot i + d_0] \to x_0 A_1[c_1 \cdot i + d_1]x_1 \ldots x_{t-1}A_t[c_t \cdot i + d_t]x_t \mid i \in N\}$$

heißt <u>Regelschar</u>. P ist eine Vereinigung endlich vieler Regelscharen und heißt <u>Regelmenge</u> von G.

$S[0] \in \overline{V}$ ist die <u>Startvariable</u>.

Analog wie bei kontextfreien Grammatiken wird nun die Ableitbarkeit in G erklärt:

Definition

$G = (V,T,P,S[0])$ sei eine 1-indizierte Grammatik und

$u \in (\overline{V} \cup T)^* \overline{V} (\overline{V} \cup T)^*$, $v \in (\overline{V} \cup T)^*$.

Es ist <u>v in G aus u ableitbar</u>, $u \vdash_G v$, wenn gilt:

$u = XA[i]Y$ für ein $A[i] \in \overline{V}$, $A[i] \to W \in P$ und $v = XWY$.

Die Relation "$\vdash_G^*$" sei der reflexive und transitive Abschluß der Relation "$\vdash_G$".

$L(G) := \{x \in T^* \mid S[0] \vdash_G^* x\}$ heißt <u>die von G erzeugte Sprache</u>.

Beispiel

$G = (\{S,A,B\}, \{0,1,H,a\}, P,S[0])$ sei eine 1-indizierte Grammatik mit den folgenden Regelscharen in P:

$\{S[0] \to 1A[i]B[i] \mid i \in N\}$, $\{S[0] \to 0H\}$,

$\{A[i+1] \to 1A[i]B[i] \mid i \in N\}$,

$\{A[i+1] \to 0A[i] \mid i \in N\}$, $\{A[0] \to H\}$,

$\{B[i+1] \to B[i]B[i] \mid i \in N\}$, $\{B[0] \to a\}$.

Es gibt nun z.B. die folgende Ableitung in G:

$$S[0] \vdash_G 1A[1]B[1] \vdash_G 10A[0]B[1] \vdash_G 10HB[1] \vdash_G 10HB[0]B[0] \vdash_G$$

$$\vdash_G 10HaB[0] \vdash_G 10Haa.$$

Man zeigt leicht durch vollständige Induktion:

$L(G) = \{nHa^n \mid n \in N, n \text{ in binärer Darstellung}\}$.

Die Worte in L(G) haben die Struktur der Hollerithfelder in FORTRAN.

Seien $\mathscr{L}_F$, $\mathscr{L}_{1-IND}$ und $\mathscr{L}_{IND}$ die Bezeichnungen für die Familien der endlichen, der 1-indizierten bzw. der indizierten Sprachen.
Man kann nun analog wie für $\mathscr{L}_{CF}$ zeigen, daß $\mathscr{L}_{1-IND}$ eine Super-AFL bildet, die auch unter Wortspiegelung aber nicht unter iterierter Substi-
tution abgeschlossen ist. [3]
In der Theorie der Lindenmayer-Systeme und der iterierten Substitution
spielen die Iterations-Grammatiken von Rozenberg und Salomaa eine bedeu-
tende Rolle.
So gilt z.B.: $(\mathscr{L}_F)^{(1)}_{iter} = \mathscr{L}_{EOL}$ und $(\mathscr{L}_F)_{iter} = \mathscr{L}_{ETOL}$ [17]

Die Familie der 1-indizierten Sprachen kann man folgendermaßen einordnen:
$$(\mathscr{L}_{CF})^{(1)}_{iter} \subsetneqq \mathscr{L}_{1-IND} \subsetneqq \mathscr{L}_{IND},$$
vgl. [3] und zur Inklusion $(\mathscr{L}_{CF})^{(1)}_{iter} \subsetneqq \mathscr{L}_{1-IND}$ auch [8].

Der folgende Hilfssatz ermöglicht nun die Angabe eines einfachen Syntax-
analyse-Algorithmus', der in Polynomzeit arbeitet.

<u>Hilfssatz</u>

Zu jeder 1-indizierten Grammatik $G = (V,T,P,S[0])$ gibt es eine Konstante
$k = k(G)$ mit der Eigenschaft:
Ist $w \in L(G)$ und $|w| = n \geq 1$, so existiert eine Ableitung $S[0] \overset{*}{\underset{G}{\vdash}} w$,
in der für alle verwendeten 1-indizierten Variablen $A[i]$ gilt: $i < k \cdot n$.

Der nicht einfache Beweis hierzu ist in [3] zu finden.

<u>Satz</u>

Sei $G = (V,T,P,S[0])$ eine 1-indizierte Grammatik und $w \in T^*$ mit
$|w| = n \geq 1$.
Dann gibt es eine Konstante $c = c(G)$, so daß in höchstens $c \cdot n^5$ Schritten
entscheidbar ist, ob $w \in L(G)$ gilt oder nicht.

<u>Beweis</u>

Zur 1-indizierten Grammatik $G = (V,T,P,S[0])$ definiert man eine kontextfreie Grammatik $G_n = (V_n,T,P_n,S[0])$ durch:
$V_n := \{A[i] \mid A \in V, 0 \leq i < k \cdot n\}$;
dabei sei k die Konstante aus dem obigen Hilfssatz und
$P_n := P \cap (V_n \times (V_n \cup T)^*)$.

Offensichtlich gilt dann für ein $w \in T^*$ mit $|w| = n \geq 1$ nach dem obigen Hilfssatz:

$w \in L(G_n)$ genau dann, wenn $w \in L(G)$.

Für w und die kontextfreie Grammatik G_n verwendet man den üblichen Earleyschen Algorithmus [7] und erhält somit für den Zeitbedarf t die Abschätzung:

$$t(n) \leq c_1 \cdot (\mathrm{card}\ P_n)^2 \cdot n^3 \leq c_1 \cdot (c_2 \cdot k \cdot n)^2 \cdot n^3 \leq c \cdot n^5.$$

Literaturverzeichnis

[1] <u>Aho,A.</u>, Indexed Grammars - An Extension of Context-Free Grammars, Journal of the ACM, vol. 15, 1968, pp. 647-671.

[2] <u>Aho,A., Hopcroft,J.,Ullmann,J.</u>, The Design and Analysis of Computer Algorithms, Addison-Wesley, 1974.

[3] <u>Albert,J.</u>, Über indizierte und m-Block-indizierte Grammatiken, Dissertation am Inst. f. Angew. Informatik, Universität Karlsruhe, 1976.

[4] <u>Baker,B. and Book,R.</u>, Reversal-Bounded Multi-Pushdown Machines, Journal of Computer and System Sciences, vol. 8, 1974, pp. 315-332.

[5] <u>Book,R. and Ginsburg,S.</u>, Multi-Stack-Counter Languages, Mathematical Systems Theory, vol. 4, 1970, pp. 97-111.

[6] <u>Cook,S.</u>, Characterizations of Pushdown Machines in Terms of Time-Bounded Computers, Journal of the ACM 18, 1971, pp. 4-18.

[7] <u>Earley,J.</u>, An Efficient Contextfree Parsing Algorithm, Ph.D. Thesis, Carnegie Mellon-University, 1968.

[8] <u>Erni,W.</u>, Complexity of Recognition for Some Language Families Between Contextfree and Contextsensitive, ersch. demnächst als Forschungsbericht des Inst. f. Angew. Informatik, Universität Karlsruhe.

[9] <u>Fleck,A.</u>, An Analysis of Grammars by Their Derivation Sets, Information and Control 24, 1974, pp. 389-398.

[10] <u>Ginsburg,S.</u>, Formal Languages, American Elsevier, 1975.

[11] <u>Greibach,S.</u>, Jump PDAs, Deterministic Contextfree Languages, Principal AFDLs and Polynomial Time Recognition, 5th ACM-Symposium on Theory of Computing, 1973.

[12] Greibach,S. and Hopcroft,J., Scattered Context Grammars, Journal
     of Computer and System Sciences, vol. 3, 1969, pp. 233-247.

[13] Hunt,H., Computational Parallels Between the Regular and Context-
     free Languages, 6th ACM Symposium on Theory of Computing, 1974.

[14] Leeuwen,J.van,The Membership Question for ETOL-Languages is Poly-
     nomially Complete, Inf. Proc. Letters 3, 1975, pp. 138-143.

[15] Opatrný,J. and Culik,K.II, Time Complexity of Recognition and
     Parsing of EOL-Languages, Department of Computer Science, Univer-
     sity of Waterloo, Waterloo, Ontario, Canada, 1974.

[16] Rounds,W., Complexity of Recognition in Intermediate Level Langu-
     ages, IEEE 14th Symposium on Switching Automata Theory, 1973.

[17] Rozenberg,G., Salomaa,A., L Systems, Lecture Notes in Computer
     Science 15, Springer Verlag.

[18] Shamir,E. and Beeri,C., Checking Stacks and Context-Free Programmed
     Grammars Accept p-complete Languages, Lecture Notes of Computer
     Science 14, 1974, pp. 27-33.

[19] Sudborough,I.H., On Languages Log-Tape Reducible to Contextfree
     Languages, Manuskript für einen Vortrag bei der J. Hopkins Kon-
     ferenz, 1976.

CANONICAL BOTTOM-UP PARSING

O. MAYER

UNIVERSITY OF KAISERSLAUTERN, GERMANY

Abstract:

A general theory of canonical bottom-up analysis is presented; it includes the familiar types of deterministic bottom-up parsing methods (e.g. precedence, bounded right context, LR, and LR-regular) as special cases. Among the results obtained are sufficient conditions on the means of construction to guarantee the resulting bottom-up-parsing method being deterministic.

1. Introduction

Several types of deterministic bottom-up analysis methods are known (various kinds of precedence, bounded right context, LR et al.) which all us a shift-reduce mechanism and usually are based on various different construction ideas. The present paper presents a uniform way to describe and to construct deterministic bottom-up parsing methods for unambiguous context-free grammars.

The basic definitions which are required are now presented; familiarity with basic language theory [6,7] is assumed.

Definition: Let a context-free grammar (cfg) be given as a 4-tuple $G=(N,T,P,S)$ where N,T and P are the finite sets of nonterminals, terminals, and productions respectively, and S is the start nonterminal.

For each production $A \to a$ in P let

$$R_{A \to a} = \{(la,r) \mid S \overset{*}{\underset{r}{\Rightarrow}} lAr \underset{r}{\Rightarrow} lar\} \quad ^{1)} \qquad \text{and}$$

$$R_{Shift} = \left\{(la_1,a) \middle| \begin{array}{l} S \overset{*}{\underset{r}{\Rightarrow}} lAr \underset{r}{\Rightarrow} la_1a_2r \overset{*}{\underset{r}{\Rightarrow}} la_1a, \ a \text{ in } T^*, \\[4pt] \qquad\qquad a_2 \neq \varepsilon, \\[4pt] \text{there is no } B \text{ such that } a_2r \overset{*}{\underset{r}{\Rightarrow}} Ba \underset{r}{\Rightarrow} a \end{array}\right\}$$

$R_{A \to a}$ is called the reduction class of the production $A \to a$;

R_{Shift} is called the shift class.
The following proposition is obvious:

---

1) $x \underset{r}{\Rightarrow} y$ means that y results from x by rewriting the rightmost nonterminal in x according to a production in P

<u>Proposition 1</u>:A cfg $G=(N,T,P,S)$ which contains no useless nonterminal is unambiguous if and only if

(i) there is no derivation $S \overset{+}{\Rightarrow} S$

(ii) the classes R_p, p in P $\cup$ {shift}, are pairwise disjoint.

<u>Proof</u>: Suppose G is unambiguous. Clearly, there is no derivation $S \overset{+}{\Rightarrow} S$; if there are different elements p and p' in P such that R_p and $R_{p'}$ have an element, say $(l\alpha,r)$, in common, then each terminal word which is derivable from $l\alpha r$ has different derivation trees which contradicts the unambiguity of G.

Conversely, suppose there is no derivation $S \overset{+}{\Rightarrow} S$ and the classes R_p, p in P$\cup$ {shift},are pairwise disjoint. Assume, G is ambiguous, then there exists at least one sentential form which is generated by different right-most derivations. Let s be the minimal such form in the sense of having rightmost derivations with the minimal total number of derivation steps. In case s equals the startsymbol S we have also $S \overset{+}{\Rightarrow} S$; therefore this case can be excluded.But now, $S \overset{+}{\underset{r}{\Rightarrow}} u \underset{r}{\Rightarrow} s$ and $S \overset{+}{\underset{r}{\Rightarrow}} v \underset{r}{\Rightarrow} s$ with $u \neq v$ and s has at least one decomposition $s=s_1 s_2$ such that (s_1,s_2) is in different classes R_p and $R_{p'}$.

<u>Remark</u>: It may happen, that a grammar G has pairwise disjoint classes R_p, p in P $\cup$ {shift}, and is ambiguous. In this case the ambiguity is caused by a derivation $S \overset{+}{\Rightarrow} S$; further each word in L(G) has a rightmost derivation where no production is used which contains S on the right side, otherwise the classes R_p could not be disjoint. Therefore, the ambiguity can be removed by deleting just all productions where S occurs on the right side. Consequently there is no loss of generality in assuming that the underlying grammar does not allow derivations $S \overset{+}{\Rightarrow} S$.

2. <u>Deterministic Shift-Reduce-Parsing</u>

We are interested in general methods and conditions which allow the construction of deterministic shift-reduce-parsers for a context-free grammar G. In [4] and in essence in [9] the following idea was presented which is the starting point of our considerations.

One tries to find supersets

$$O_p \supseteq R_p \quad , \qquad p \text{ in } P \cup \{shift\},$$

such that (i) it is decidable to determine for an arbitrary cfg whether these supersets are pairwise disjoint or not

(ii) it is decidable to determine for an arbitrary pair of strings and each p in P $\cup$ {shift} whether the pair is contained in O_p or not.

Now, supersets O_p of the classes R_p, p in $P\cup\{shift\}$, having the above properties (i) and (ii) give rise to a deterministic parsing procedure M which works for each cfg G for which the sets O_p, p in $P\cup\{shift\}$, are pairwise disjoint. This parsing procedure M may be described as follows:

<u>Parsing procedure M:</u>
Let w in T^*be the word to be analyzed.

1) Begin with the <u>a</u>ctual <u>p</u>air ap= (ε,w) [2];
2) Check whether ap is in any O_p, p in $P\cup\{shift\}$;
21) If ap is not contained in any O_p,
    then stop with an error message: w is not in L(G).
22) If ap is in $O_{A\to a}$ for a production $A\to a$ or in O_{shift}
    then the new ap is obtained from the previous one by performing the
    corresponding reduction (of the suffix a of the first component to A)
    or a shift (of the leftmost symbol of the second component to the
                right end of the first component)
3) If ap = (S,ε) then stop with a success message:
    w is in L(G) and the reductions performed so far describe the in-
    verse of a rightmost derivation of w.
4) If ap $\neq$ (S,ε) then goto 2).
end of procedure M.

Intuitively, the action to be performed for each actual pair is determined by the superset containing it.

<u>Remark:</u> If the supersets O_p, p in $P\cup\{shift\}$, are disjoint a possible ambiguity of G caused by a derivation $S \xRightarrow{+} S$ does not really touch the effectiveness of the parsing procedure M. On the other hand by the above remark this kind of ambiguity is easily removed.
We mention that in this framework the LR(k)-method is based on the super-
sets

$$O_p^k = \left\{ (x,\bar{y}) \;\middle|\; \begin{array}{l} (x,y) \text{ in } R_p \text{ for some } y, \\ first_k\,(\bar{y})= first_k\,(y) \end{array} \right\} \text{ [3]} \quad , \text{ p in } P\cup\{shift\},$$

where a grammar G is LR(k)-grammar [5,8]
iff (i) there is no derivation $S \xRightarrow{+} S$ in G and
    (ii) the sets O_p^k, p in $P\cup\{shift\}$, are pairwise disjoint.

---

2) ε denotes the empty word
3) $first_k(x)$ denotes the word u where x=uv for some v and $|u| = k$
                                    or $|u|<k$ and x=u

The following Theorem describes the effectiveness of M:

__Theorem 2:__   Let $G=(N,T,P,S)$ be a cfg; which contains no useless non-terminals; assume there is no derivation $S \overset{+}{\Rightarrow} S$ and there are pairwise disjoint supersets $O_p \supseteq R_p$, p in P $\cup$ {shift}, such that it is decidable to determine for each p in P $\cup$ {shift} and each pair (x,y) of strings, x and y in $(N \cup T)^*$ whether (x,y) is in O_p or not.

a) If w is in $L(G)$ then M constructs the inverse of a rightmost
                            derivation of w.
b) If w is not in $L(G)$ then M stops with an error message or may
                            run forever.

__Proof:__   a) We first show that each actual pair which occurs during the execution of M for a word w in $L(G)$ is contained in exactly one R_p for some p in P $\cup$ {shift}. This is true for the initial pair (ε,w). Regard now an actual pair ap which is obtained after one or more reduction and shifts; assume ap is in R_p for some p in P $\cup$ {shift}, then it is also in the superset O_p and there is no $O_{p'}$, $p' \neq p$, which contains ap, too. The action to be performed – a reduction by p if p is in P or a shift – is the same as that "required" by R_p; therefore it leads to an actual pair which is also in some $R_{\bar{p}}$, $\bar{p}$ in P $\cup$ {shift}. Clearly, each reduction performed by M is a reduction step in a right reduction of w and the number of reductions and shifts to be performed equals the length of the rightmost derivation of w plus the number of symbols in w.
b) An example will be given where M does not stop but performs reduction by ε-productions forever. Regard the grammar $G=$ ({S,A,B,C}, {a,b}, P,S) with $P=$ {S $\to$ AB, S $\to$ C, A $\to$ a, B $\to$ b, C $\to$ ε}.
The reduction classes are easily obtained; we have

$$R_{S \to AB} = \{(AB,\varepsilon)\},$$

$$R_{S \to C} = \{(C,\varepsilon)\},$$

$$R_{A \to a} = \{(a,b)\},$$

$$R_{B \to b} = \{(AB,\varepsilon)\},$$

$$R_{C \to \varepsilon} = \{(\varepsilon,\varepsilon)\},$$

$$R_{shift} = \{(\varepsilon,ab), (A,b)\}.$$

Take pairwise disjoint supersets O_p as follows:

$$O_{S \to AB} = R_{S \to AB} , \qquad O_{S \to C} = R_{S \to C}$$

$$O_{A \to a} = R_{A \to a} , \qquad O_{B \to b} = R_{B \to b}$$

$$O_{C \to \varepsilon} = R_{C \to \varepsilon} \cup \{(bC^n, \varepsilon) \mid n \geq 0\}$$

$$O_{shift} = R_{shift} \cup \{(\varepsilon, b)\}.$$

Clearly, $L(G) = \{ab, \varepsilon\}$. Now, apply M with the above supersets to the word b which is not in $L(G)$. Then the following actual pairs are obtained:
$(\varepsilon, b) \vdash (b, \varepsilon) \vdash (bC, \varepsilon) \vdash \ldots (bC^n, \varepsilon) \vdash \ldots$.
Clearly, M performs now reduction by the production $C \to \varepsilon$ forever.

Part b) of Theorem 2 is rather unsatisfactory; we are therefore interested in supplementary conditions on G and or the supersets O_p which imply that M stops for each input word. Since the non-stop-behaviour in the above example was caused by ε-productions, we first regard a restriction to ε-free grammars; under this condition M stops for each input word:

<u>Theorem 2'</u>: Let $G=(N,T,P,S)$ be an ε-free cfg which contains no useless nonterminals; assume, there is no derivation $S \overset{+}{\Rightarrow} S$ and there are pairwise disjoint supersets $O_p \supseteq R_p$, p in $P \cup \{shift\}$, such that it is decidable to determine for each p in $P \cup \{shift\}$ and each pair (x,y) of strings, x and y in $(N \cup T)^*$ whether (x,y) is in O_p or not.

a) If w is in $L(G)$ then M constructs the inverse of a rightmost
derivation of w.

b) If w is not in $L(G)$ then M stops eventually with an error message.

<u>Proof</u>: As a) is covered by Theorem 2 only b) has to be proved.
Assume M does not stop for some input word w.
Clearly, the number of possible shifts is bounded by $|w|$; therefore eventually no further shift operations are performed. Let (α_1, β) be an actual pair such that no shift is performed during the further execution of M and let (α_2, β), (α_3, β), $\ldots$ be the succeeding actual pairs; then

$|\alpha_i| \geq |\alpha_{i+1}|$ and $|\alpha_i| \geq 1$ for all $i \geq 1$.
Since M does not stop there exist l and k, $1 \leq l < k$ such that $(\alpha_1, \beta) = (\alpha_k, \beta)$. This implies that $|\alpha_i| = |\alpha_{i+1}|$ for $1 \leq i < k$ where each reduction of α_i to α_{i+1} comes from productions of the form $A \to B$ where B is a nonterminal. Let C be the rightmost symbol in $a_1 = \alpha_k$ then $C \overset{+}{\Rightarrow} C$, which is a contradiction to the unambiguity of G.

We mention that the restriction to ε-free grammars as in Theorem 2' is typical for all precedence parsing methods.

3. The main result

We are now interested in conditions on the supersets O_p which allow us
to drop the restriction to ε-free grammars. Indeed, there is yet the
LR-parsing method as a famous example for a very general method which is
not restricted to ε-free grammars [8]. We will obtain a consistency
condition such that pairwise disjoint supersets meeting this condition
give rise to a parsing method M which stops for each input.
We need the following auxiliary definition.

__Definition:__ Let $G = (N,T,P,S)$ be a cfg;
supersets $O_p \supseteq R_p$, p in $P \cup \{shift\}$, are called __exact__ (with respect to
the first component) if for each p in P and each pair $(\bar{x}, \bar{y})$ in O_p there
is some (x,y) in R_p such that $\bar{x} = x$.

We ask whether disjoint supersets which are exact with respect to the
first component give rise to a parsing method M which stops for each input
word. The answer is given by a counterexample:

Regard the grammar $G=(\{S,A\}, \{a,b\}, P,S)$ with $P=\{S \to ASa, S \to b, A \to \varepsilon\}$.
The reduction classes are

$$R_{S \to ASa} = \{ (A^{n+1}Sa, a^n) \mid 0 \leq n\}$$

$$R_{S \to b} = \{ (A^n b, a^n) \mid 0 \leq n\}$$

$$R_{A \to \varepsilon} = \{ (A^n, ba^m) \mid 0 \leq n < m\}$$

$$R_{shift} = \{ (A^{n+1}S, a^{n+1}), (A^n, ba^n) \mid 0 \leq n\}.$$

Take pairwise disjoint supersets O_p as follows:

$$O_p = R_p \quad \text{for p in } \{S \to ASa, S \to b, shift\} \text{ and}$$

$$O_{A \to \varepsilon} = R_{A \to \varepsilon} \cup \{ (A^n, bb) \mid 0 \leq n\}.$$

Now apply M based on the above supersets to the word bb which is not in
$L(G)$. Then by turns the following actual pairs are obtained:

$$(\varepsilon,bb) \vdash (A,bb) \vdash (A^2, bb) \vdash \ldots (A^i, bb) \vdash \ldots$$

Clearly, reductions by the production $A \to \varepsilon$ are performed forever.

The above example shows that even disjoint supersets which are exact with
respect to the first component do not give rise to a parsing method which
stops for each input word. Therefore we are now looking for conditions on

the second component, too which imply that the obtained parsing method
stops for each input. Such a condition is described in the following definition.

<u>Definition</u>: Let $G = (N,T,P,S)$ be a cfg.
Exact supersets $O_p \supseteq R_p$, p in P $\cup$ {shift}, are called <u>consistent</u> (with
respect to the second component)

if $\qquad (x,y)$ in R_p
$\qquad\qquad (x,\bar{y})$ in O_p
$\qquad\qquad (u,y)$ in $R_{p'}$
$\qquad\qquad$ for arbitrary p,p' in P

implies $\qquad (u,\bar{y})$ is in $O_{p'}$.

Consistency means that the second components of the pairs in exact supersets are obtained from those in the reduction classes in a uniform way:
If for one pair (x,y) in some reduction class R_p a substitution of the
second component y by some $\bar{y}$ does not lead out of the corresponding superclass O_p then the same substitution of a second component does for no
reduction class $R_{p'}$ lead out of the corresponding superclass $O_{p'}$.
We are now able to obtain the main result:

<u>Theorem 3</u>: Let $G=(N,T,P,S)$ be a cfg such that there is no derivation
$S \overset{+}{\Longrightarrow} S$; let $O_p \supseteq R_p$, p in P $\cup$ {shift}, be consistent and pairwise disjoint
supersets, then the parsing procedure M stops for each input w in T and
outputs if w is in L(G) a rightmost derivation of w and if w is not in
L(G) an error message.

<u>Proof</u>: Assume there is a word w such that M does not stop for input w.
The number of possible shift operations is bounded by $|w|$; therefore M
performs eventually just reductions. Let (u_o,v) be an actual pair with
the property that the succeeding actions are all reductions and let (u_1,v),
(u_2,v), ... be the succeeding actual pairs.
The second component in (u_o,v) is a suffix of w; assume $w = \bar{u}v$ with $\bar{u}$ in T^*.
Let O_p be the superset containing (u_1,v) then p is in P. By the exactness
of the supersets there is a

$\qquad \bar{v}$ in T^* such that $(u_1, \bar{v})$ is in R_p. This implies
that $\bar{u}\bar{v}$ is in L(G).
Regard the simultaneous application of M to the input words $\bar{u}v$ and $\bar{u}v$
Starting from actual pairs $(\varepsilon, \bar{u}\,\bar{v})$ and $(\varepsilon,\bar{u}v)$, M performs the same moves
to reach $(u_1, \bar{v})$ and (u_1,v), respectively, since these actions describe
the unique right reduction of $\bar{u}$ to u_1. In the further elaboration the both
cases diverge:

For input $\bar{u}\bar{v}$ which is in L(G) M passes $(u_0, \bar{v})$, then $(u_1, \bar{v})$ and stops after a finite number of moves with a rightmost derivation for $\bar{u}\bar{v}$. For input $w=\bar{u}v$ which is not in L(G) M passes (u_0,v), then (u_1,v) and does not stop by hypothesis but performs reductions forever. Therefore there is an integer $l\geq1$ such that $(u_j, \bar{v})$ and (u_j,v) are in the same superset O_{p_j} for $0\leq j<l$ but $(u_l, \bar{v})$ and (u_l,v) are in supersets O_{p_l} and $O_{p_l'}$, respectively, with $p_l \neq p_l'$. Note, that for $0\leq j\leq l$ the pair $(u_j,\bar{v})$ is also in the reduction class R_{p_j} since M determines the right reduction of $\bar{u}\bar{v}$; but (u_j,v) is in the corresponding superclass Op_j only for $0\leq j\leq l-1$ where as $(u_l, \bar{v})$ is not in O_{pj}; this contradicts the consistency of the reduction classes.

We mention that if the LR parsing method (including the SLR and LALR cases [3] and the LR-regular parsing method [2] are based on supersets as described here then these supersets meet our consistency condition. The author does not know a deterministic canonical bottom-up parsing method which is not restricted to ε-free grammars and does not meet our consistency condition. We close with a remark concerning the time requirements of M. The number of moves (i.e. reductions and shift operations) which are performed in course of parsing a word w is linearly bounded by the length of w. The author has the feeling that the number of elementary steps to determine such a move cannot be generally bounded by a constant (as for LR parsing [8] and LR-regular parsing [2])without further restrictions on the supersets O_p. This is not surprising; indeed, such a general constant bound would bring us rather near to a deterministic parsing method which works for each unambiguous grammar in linear time.

References

[1]   Aho, V.A., and Ullmann, J.D. (1972), _The Theory of Parsing,_
        Translation and Compiling, Prentice Hall, Engle-
        wood Cliffs, N.J.

[2]   Culik II, K. and Cohen,R. (1973), LR-Regular Grammars
        - an Extension of LR(k)-Grammars, _JCSS_ 7, 66-96.

[3]   De Remer,F.L.(1971), Simple LR(k)-Grammars _CACM_ 14, 453-46o.

[4]   Eickel, J. (1972), Methoden der Syntaktischen Analyse bei
        Formalen Sprachen, _Lecture Notes in Economics_
        and Mathematical Systems, Springer, Vol. 78, 37-53.

[5]   Geller, M.M., and Harrison, M.A. (1973), Characterizations
        of LR(o) Languages, _Proceedings of Symposium_
        on Switching and Automata Theory 1973, 1o3-1o8.

[6]   Ginsburg, S. (1966), _The Mathematical Theory of Context-free_
        Languages, Mc Graw-Hill, New York.

[7]   Hopcroft, J.E., and Ullman, J.D. (1969), _Formal Languages_
        and their relation to Automata, Addison Wesley,
        Reading, Mass.

[8]   Knuth, D.E. (1965), On the translation of languages from left
        to right, _JC_ 8, 6o7-639.

[9]   Langmaack, H. (1971), Application of Regular Canonical Systems
        to Grammars Translatable from Left to Right, _Acta_
        Informatica 1, 111-114.

<u>TOP DOWN PARSING OF</u>

<u>MACRO GRAMMARS</u>

(Preliminary Report)

Manfred Heydthausen and Kurt Mehlhorn

Fachbereich Angewandte
Mathematik und Informatik
Universität des Saarlandes
D-6600 Saarbrücken

Recursive descent is for its ease of description and for its transparency one of the popular parsing methods [Gries, Knuth]. The class
of languages, for which recursive descent works as a parsing method,
is known as the LL-languages; their properties were studied by Lewis &
Stearns, Rosenkranz & Stearns and many others (see [Aho & Ullman] for
complete references).

In the late 60's several extensions of context-free languages were proposed in order to cope with the non context-free features of programming
languages (e.g. applied and defining occurences of identifiers). Two
remarkable examples are the macro languages of Fischer [Fischer] and the
indexed languages of Aho [Aho 68]. Because of the lack of efficient
parsing methods for these classes of grammars, they were never used in
actual programming language design.

Weiß [Weiß] proposed a top down parsing scheme for indexed languages.
He introduced the notion of indexed LL grammars and showed that ε-free
indexed LL grammars can be parsed efficiently (time $O(n^2)$). His work
and work by Bertsch [Bertsch] were the starting point for this paper.

In section I we introduce macro grammars and formulate the LL property
for macro grammars. In section II we give first evidence for the power
of MLL languages: every deterministic context-free language is generated
by an MLL grammar. In section III we show that transformation to standard form can be done whilst preserving the LL property. In section IV
we show that it is decidable whether an arbitrary macro-grammar is MLL(k)
for a fixed k. Our decision procedure has time complexity $O(2^{(1+\varepsilon)n^2})$
and space complexity $O(2^{(1+\varepsilon)n})$ for some $\varepsilon > 0$ where n is the size of

the grammar. We also show that $c^n(n^{2-\varepsilon})$ for some constant $c > 1$ is a lower bound for the time (space) complexity of MLL(1) testing. In section V we review Weiß's definitions of indexed LL grammars, and show that our concept of MLL grammar is equivalent to one of his notions of ILL grammar. This notion was introduced by him, but only a simpler was studied. In section VI we give an automata-theoretic characterization of the class of MLL languages and show that MLL languages can be parsed in time $O(n^2)$ and space $O(n)$ where n is the length of the input. Finally we give some examples of MLL grammars.

I. Macro grammars, LL property

A macro grammar [Fischer] is a 6-tuple $(\Sigma, \mathcal{F}, \mathcal{V}, \mathcal{S}, S, P)$ where:

Σ is a finite set of terminal symbols;

$\mathcal{F}$ is a finite set of non-terminal or function symbols;

$\mathcal{V}$ is a finite set of argument or variable symbols;

$\mathcal{S}$ is a function from $\mathcal{F}$ into nonnegative integers ($\mathcal{S}(F)$ is the number of arguments which F takes);

$S \in F$ is the start symbol, $\mathcal{S}(S) = 0$;

P is a finite set of productions of the form

$F(x_1,\ldots,x_{\mathcal{S}(F)}) \to \tau$ where $F \in \mathcal{F}$, $x_1,\ldots,x_{\mathcal{S}(F)}$ are

distinct members of $\mathcal{V}$, and τ is a term over Σ, $\{x_1,\ldots,x_{\mathcal{S}(F)}\}$, $\mathcal{F}, \mathcal{S}$.

The set of terms over $\Sigma, \mathcal{V}, \mathcal{F}, \mathcal{S}$ is defined inductively

a) ε is a term,
   a is a term for every $a \in \Sigma$.
   x is a term for every $x \in \mathcal{V}$.

b) if τ_1 and τ_2 are terms then $\tau_1 \cdot \tau_2$ is a term

c) if $F \in \mathcal{F}$ and $\tau_1,\ldots,\tau_{\mathcal{S}(F)}$ are terms, then $F(\sigma_1,\ldots,\sigma_{\mathcal{S}(F)})$ is a term.

We consider macro grammars with the outside-in (OI) mode of derivation [Fischer, Nivat] , i.e. only top-level occurrences of function symbols can be rewritten at every step. Instead of giving a formal definition of this mode of derivation, we give an example.

<u>Example:</u> A macro grammar generating $\{a^n b^n c^n; n\ 0\}$

$$\begin{aligned}
S &\to F(\varepsilon,\varepsilon) \\
F(x,y) &\to A\ F(xB,yC)
\end{aligned}$$

```
F(x,y)  →  xy
A       →  a
B       →  b
C       →  c
```

F is a function symbol of arity 2 and S,A,B,C are function symbols of arity O. A sample derivation is

$$S \to F(\varepsilon,\varepsilon) \to A\ F(B,C) \to A\ A\ F(BB,CC)$$
$$\downarrow \qquad\qquad \downarrow$$
$$a\ F(B,C) \qquad AA\ BB\ CC$$
$$\downarrow \qquad\qquad \downarrow$$
$$aA\ F(BB,CC) \to aA\ BB\ CC$$
$$\downarrow *$$
$$a^2\ b^2\ c^2$$

Note that we had the choice of rewritting either A or F in the sentential form A F(B,C). We could not have rewritten B or C since they do occur at the top-level but rather within a parameter list. Rewriting A in A F(B,C) corresponds to a left-most derivation.

The macro grammar given above suggests a top-down parsing algorithm (recursive descent) for the language $\{a^n b^n c^n; n \geq 0\}$

<u>procedure</u> S; call $F(\varepsilon,\varepsilon)$ <u>end</u>;

<u>procedure</u> F(x,y);

  <u>begin</u> <u>case</u> next-symbol <u>in</u>

    a: <u>call</u> A; <u>call</u> F(xB,yC);

    b, eof: write xy as $\tau_1 \cdot \tau_2 \ldots \tau_k$

      where τ_i is a term starting with a function symbol;

      <u>for</u> i <u>from</u> 1 <u>to</u> k <u>do</u> <u>call</u> τ_i;

    c: Error

  <u>end</u>;

<u>procedure</u> A;

  <u>begin</u> <u>case</u> next-symbol <u>in</u>

    a: advance reading head by one and read the next symbol;
    b,c: Error

  <u>end</u>;

 .
 .
 .

The parse is performed in a single left to right scan of the input string. Next-symbol always contains the symbol of the input string which

is presently scanned. (end-of-file (eof) designates the end of the input string). Within each procedure we branch on the symbol under the
reading head and call the appropiate production.
This strategy is possible whenever the decision between the different
alternatives for a function symbol can be made on the bases of knowing
the next (the next k for some fixed k) input symbol. This leads to the
following definition.

Definition:

a) Let $r = F(x_1, \ldots, x_{\rho(F)}) \to \tau$ be a rule of a macro-grammar and let k
be an integer. Then

$$\text{First}_k(r) = \{u;\ S \overset{*}{\underset{lm}{\Rightarrow}} w\, F(\tau_1, \ldots, \tau_{\rho(F)})\, \tau' \underset{lm}{\Rightarrow}$$

$$w\ \tau[\,{}^{\tau_1}\!/_{x_1}, \ldots, {}^{\tau_{\rho(F)}}\!/_{x_{\rho(F)}}\,]\,\tau'$$

$$\overset{*}{\underset{lm}{\Rightarrow}} w\, u\, v\ ;\ w, u, v \in \Sigma^*, \tau', \tau_1, \ldots, \tau_{\rho(F)} \quad \text{are}$$

$$\text{terms},\quad |u| = k \text{ or } |u| < k \text{ and } v = \varepsilon\}$$

$\tau[\,{}^{\tau_1}\!/_{x_1}, \ldots, {}^{\tau_{\rho(F)}}\!/_{x_{\rho(F)}}\,]$ is the term obtained by replacing x_i by

τ_i, $1 \le i \le \rho(F)$, in τ .

b) A macro-grammar has the LL(k) property if for every pair r_1, r_2 of
distinct rules having the same left hand side:

$$\text{First}_k(r_1) \cap \text{First}_k(r_2) = \emptyset .$$

In this case we will say that the grammar is MLL(k) (is a MLL(k)
grammar).
Our example grammar is MLL(1).

II. The power of MLL grammars

In this section we show that MLL-grammars generate a proper superset
of the deterministic context-free languages.

<u>Thm. 1:</u> Given any deterministic pushdown automaton A, we can find an
equivalent MLL grammar G, i.e. $L(A) \dashv = L(G)$, where $\dashv$ is the end marker.

<u>Proof:</u> Let $A = (S, \Sigma, \Gamma, q_0, Z_0, F)$ be a deterministic pushdown automaton
(accepting by final state). $S = \{q_0, \ldots, q_n\}$ is the set of states,

Σ the input alphabet, Γ the stack alphabet, q_0 the start state, Z_0 the symbol initially placed at the bottom of the pushdown store and F is the set of final states. We may assume w.l.o.g. that A writes at most two symbols onto the stack in a single move.

The macro grammar G has function symbols $S \times \Gamma \cup \{START\}$; START has arity 0, all other function symbols have arity $|S|$. The rules are:

(1) $START \rightarrow [q_0,Z_0] \underbrace{(\epsilon,\epsilon,\dots,\epsilon)}_{|S|\text{-times}}$

(2) for $a \in \Sigma \cup \{\epsilon\}$ and $\delta(q,a,A) = (q_i,\epsilon)$

$[q,A] \; (x_0,\dots,x_n) \rightarrow a x_i$

(3) for $a \in \Sigma \cup \{\epsilon\}$ and $\delta(q,a,A) = (q_i,B)$

$[q,A] \; (x_0,\dots,x_n) \rightarrow a[q_i,B] \; (x_0,\dots,x_n)$

(4) for $a \in \Sigma \cup \{\epsilon\}$ and $\delta(q,a,A) = (q_i,BC)$

$[q,A] \; (x_0,\dots,x_n) \rightarrow$

$a[q_i,B]([q_0,C](x_0,\dots,x_n),[q_1,C](x_0,\dots,x_n),\dots,[q_n,C](x_0,\dots,x_n))$

(5) for all $q \in F$ and $A \in \Gamma$

$[q,A](x_0,\dots,x_n) \rightarrow \; \dashv$

The correctness of the construction follows from the following claim which is proved by induction on the length of the computation (derivation).

<u>Claim:</u> Let $x_1,\dots,x_n \in \Sigma$, $z_0,z_1,\dots,z_j \in \Gamma$ and $q \in S$.

Then $(q_0,x_1,\dots,x_n,Z_0) \overset{*}{\vdash} (q,\epsilon,z_j \dots z_1)$

iff $START \overset{*}{\rightarrow} x_1 \dots x_n[q,z_j]$ (expansion of $z_{j-1} \dots z_1$)

where expansion of $\epsilon = \underbrace{(\epsilon,\epsilon,\dots,\epsilon)}_{|S|\text{-times}}$

and expansion of $Z\alpha = ([q_0,Z] \text{ expansion of } \alpha,\dots,[q_n,Z] \text{ exp. of } \alpha)$

The macro grammar G is MLL(1) since A is deterministic.

<u>Corollary:</u> The class of MLL(1) languages properly contains the deterministic context-free languages.

III. Transformation to Standard Form

A macro grammar is in <u>standard form</u> if every one of its rules is in one of the following four forms

(1) $F(x_1,\dots,x_n) \rightarrow G(H_1(x_1,\dots,x_n),\dots,H_m(x_1,\dots,x_n))$ with $n,m \geq 0$

(2) $F(x_1,\dots,x_n) \rightarrow x_1 \dots x_n, \; n \geq 0;$

(3) $F(x_1, \ldots, x_n) \rightarrow x_i$, $n \geq 0$, $1 \leq i \leq n$;

(4) $F(x_1, \ldots, x_n) \rightarrow a$ for $a \in \Sigma \cup \{\epsilon\}$, $n \geq 0$

Fischer showed that every macro grammar has an equivalent standard form grammar. We observe that this transformation preserves the MLL(k) property for every k.

We illustrate the technique by way of example. Consider the rule $F(x,y) \rightarrow AF(xB,yC)$ which is not in standard form. Write the right-hand side as a tree

introduce a new 2-ary function symbol for each edge of the tree (e.g. $H_1, H_2, H_3, H_4, H_5, H_6, H_7, H_8$) and introduce a new function symbol for every node labelled by a dot whose arity is equal to the number of descendants of that node. (e.g. C_1, C_2, C_3). Replace the rule $F(x,y) \rightarrow$ $AF(xB,yC)$ by the set of rules

$$
\begin{aligned}
F(x,y) &\rightarrow C_1(H_1(x,y), H_2(x,y)) \\
H_1(x,y) &\rightarrow A \\
H_2(x,y) &\rightarrow F(H_3(x,y), H_4(x,y)) \\
H_3(x,y) &\rightarrow C_2(H_5(x,y), H_6(x,y)) \\
H_5(x,y) &\rightarrow x \\
H_6(x,y) &\rightarrow B \\
H_4(x,y) &\rightarrow C_3(H_7(x,y), H_8(x,y)) \\
H_7(x,y) &\rightarrow y \\
H_8(x.y) &\rightarrow C \\
C_1(x,y) &\rightarrow xy \\
C_2(x,y) &\rightarrow xy \\
C_3(x,y) &\rightarrow xy
\end{aligned}
$$

Note that the number of new function symbols is proportional to the length of the right hand side of the rule. Hence the number of rules of the transformed grammar is bounded above by the total number of symbols (= size) in the description of the old grammar. A careful analysis is done in the full paper.

IV. Testing for the LL(k) property

In this section we will show that it is decidable if an arbitrary macro
grammar is MLL(k) . We assume w.l.o.g. that all macro grammars are in
standard form.

Given a macro grammar G (in standard form) and a rule $r=F(x_1,\ldots,x_n)\to\tau$
of this grammar we want to compute $First_k(r)$. We proceed in two steps:

(1) Let Σ be the terminal alphabet of G. Then the language L_r over
$\Sigma \cup \{\bar{a};a \in \Sigma\}$ is a macro language where

$$L_r = \{a_1\ldots a_m\bar{a}_{m+1}\ldots\bar{a}_n; S \xrightarrow{*} a_1\ldots a_m F(\tau_1,\ldots,\tau_p)\tau'$$
$$\to a_1\ldots a_m\tau[{}^{\tau_1}/_{x_1},\ldots,{}^{\tau_p}/_{x_p}]\tau'$$
$$\xrightarrow{*} a_1\ldots a_m a_{m+1}\ldots a_n \in L(G)\}$$

(2) For any $x \in \Sigma^*$;

if $|x| < k$ then $x \in First_k(r)$ iff $(L_r \cap \Sigma^* \bar{x}) \neq \emptyset$

if $|x| = k$ then $x \in First_k(r)$ iff $(L_r \cap \Sigma^* \bar{x}\bar{\Sigma}^*) \neq \emptyset$

Since the class of macro languages is closed under intersection with
regular sets and their emptiness problem is decidable [Fischer] this
implies the decidability of the MLL(k) property. Fischer showed the
decidability of the emptiness problem by reducing it to the emptiness
problem for indexed languages and appealing to a result of Aho.
We give a direct proof here; this will provide us with a tighter time
bound.

<u>Lemma 1:</u> Given a macro-grammar G and a production r we can find a macro-
grammar G_r generating L_r.

<u>Proof:</u> For every function symbol F in G there are function symbols
$F^\Sigma, F^{\bar{\Sigma}}$ and F^{mixed} in G_r having arity $\varrho(F)$, $\varrho(F)$ and $3\cdot\varrho(F)$ respectively.
F^Σ generates strings in Σ^*, $F^{\bar{\Sigma}}$ strings in $\bar{\Sigma}$ and F_{mixed} strings in $\Sigma^*\bar{\Sigma}^*$.
For every rule in G the following rules are in G_r:

(1) if the rule is of the form $F(x_1,\ldots,x_n) \to$
   $H(H_1(x_1,\ldots,x_n),\ldots,H_k(x_1,\ldots,x_n))$ then

   $F^\Sigma(\ ) \to H^\Sigma(H_1^\Sigma(\ ),\ldots,H_k^\Sigma(\ ))$

   $F^{\bar{\Sigma}}(\ ) \to H^{\bar{\Sigma}}(H_1^{\bar{\Sigma}}(\ ),\ldots,H_k^{\bar{\Sigma}}(\ ))$

   $F^{mixed}(x_1^\Sigma,x_1^{\bar{\Sigma}},x_1^{mixed},\ldots,x_n^\Sigma, x_n^{\bar{\Sigma}}, x_n^{mixed})$

   $\to H^{mixed}(H_1^\Sigma(x_1^\Sigma,\ldots,x_n^\Sigma),H_1^{\bar{\Sigma}}(x_1^{\bar{\Sigma}},\ldots,x_n^{\bar{\Sigma}}),H_1^{mixed}(x_1^\Sigma,x_1^{\bar{\Sigma}},x^{mixed},\ldots,)\ldots)$

(2) if the rule is of the form $F(x_1,\ldots,x_n) \to x_1\ldots x_n$ then

$$F^{\Sigma}(x_1,\ldots,x_n) \rightarrow x_1 \ldots x_n$$
$$F^{\overline{\Sigma}}(x_1,\ldots,x_n) \rightarrow x_1 \ldots x_n$$
$$F^{\text{mixed}}(x_1^{\Sigma},x_1^{\overline{\Sigma}},x_1^{\text{mixed}},\ldots) \rightarrow x_1^{\Sigma} \ldots x_{i-1}^{\Sigma} \; x_i^{\text{mixed}} \; x_{i+1}^{\overline{\Sigma}} \ldots x_n^{\overline{\Sigma}}$$

for every i with $1 \leq i \leq n$

(3) if the rule is of the form $F(x_1,\ldots,x_n) \rightarrow x_i$ then

$$F^{\Sigma}(x_1,\ldots,x_n) \rightarrow x_i$$
$$F^{\overline{\Sigma}}(x_1,\ldots,x_n) \rightarrow x_i$$
$$F^{\text{mixed}}(x_1^{\Sigma},x_1^{\overline{\Sigma}},x^{\text{mixed}},\ldots) \rightarrow x_i^{\text{mixed}}$$

(4) if the rule is of the form $F(x_1,\ldots,x_n) \rightarrow a$ for $a \in \Sigma \cup \{\epsilon\}$ then

$$F^{\Sigma}(x_1,\ldots,x_n) \rightarrow a$$
$$F^{\overline{\Sigma}}(x_1,\ldots,x_n) \rightarrow \overline{a}$$

(5) and finally if $F(x_1,\ldots,x_n) \rightarrow \tau$ is the rule r we add

$$F^{\text{mixed}}(x_1^{\Sigma},x_1^{\overline{\Sigma}},x_1^{\text{mixed}},\ldots,) \rightarrow \overline{\tau}$$

where $\overline{\tau}$ is obtained from τ by adding the superscript $\overline{\Sigma}$ to all symbols.

The start symbol of G' is S^{mixed}.

Note that only function symbols of the form F^{Σ} and $F^{\overline{\Sigma}}$ have terminal rules and that rule (5) is the only rule with a function symbol F^{mixed} on the left hand side and no "mixed" symbol on the right hand side. Therefore rule (5) has to be used to get rid off the mixed function symbols.

Assume now, that we want to decide if $x \in \text{First}_k(r)$ where $|x| = k$. By our preliminary considerations this is equivalent to $L_r \cap \Sigma^* \overline{x} \overline{\Sigma}^* \neq \emptyset$, We first construct a finite automaton recognizing $\Sigma^* \overline{x} \; \overline{\Sigma}^*$. Such an automaton has $k+1$ states. Then we construct from G_r a macro grammar for $L_r \cap \Sigma^* \overline{x} \overline{\Sigma}^*$. The construction is similar to the proof of lemma 1. Then we have to decide emptiness of this grammar.

<u>Lemma 2:</u> Given any macro grammar G, we can decide $L(G) \neq \emptyset$

<u>Proof:</u> We proceed in three steps

(1) Replace all rules of the form $F(x_1,\ldots,x_n) \rightarrow a$ for $a \in \Sigma$ by $F(x_1,\ldots,x_n) \rightarrow \epsilon$. Then $L(G) \neq \emptyset$ iff the new grammar generates the empty string.

(2) Eliminate ϵ-rules by the following process:

    <u>while</u> there is a rule of the form $F(x_1,\ldots,x_n) \rightarrow \epsilon$ with F not being the start symbol

> <u>do</u> apply the rule $F(x_1,\ldots,x_n) \to \varepsilon$ to the right hand sides of all
> productions in G (even if the occurrence of F is not at the
> top-level) and delete all rules having F( ) as their left-hand
> side.

We are now left with a grammar G' all of whose rules are of the form:
$S \to \varepsilon$, where S is the start symbol;
$F(x_1,\ldots,x_n) \to H(\tau_1,\ldots,\tau_k)$ with $\tau_i = \varepsilon$ or $\tau_i = H_i(x_1,\ldots,x_n)$
$F(x_1,\ldots,x_n) \to x_1 \ldots x_n$
$F(x_1,\ldots,x_n) \to x_i$

Apparently $\varepsilon \in L(G')$ iff $\varepsilon \in L(G)$. If $S \to \varepsilon$ is a rule of G' then
$L(G') \neq \emptyset$. Otherwise we go to step (3).

(3) At this point an example might be useful. We apply step (1) and (2)
to the standard form grammar of section 3. In step (1) we replace the
rules $A \to a$, $B \to b$ and $C \to c$ by $A \to \varepsilon$, $B \to \varepsilon$, $C \to \varepsilon$, and in step (2)
we get the rules
$S \to F(\varepsilon,\varepsilon)$
$F(x,y) \qquad \to \text{Conc}(\varepsilon,H_2(x,y))$
$F(x,y) \qquad \to xy$
$H_2(x,y) \quad \to F(H_4(x,y),H_5(x,y))$
$H_4(x,y) \quad \to \text{Conc}(H_6(x,y),\varepsilon)$
$H_6(x,y) \quad \to x$
$H_5(x,y) \quad \to \text{Conc}(H_8(x,y),\varepsilon)$
$H_8(x,y) \quad \to y$
$\text{Conc}(x,y) \to x \cdot y$
A sample derivation $S \overset{*}{\to} \varepsilon$ is:
$S \to F(\varepsilon,\varepsilon) \to \varepsilon \cdot \varepsilon$

In order to detect derivations of this form we have to determine for
every function symbol $F(x_1,\ldots,x_n)$ all subsets
$J \subseteq \{1,\ldots,n\}$ with $F(x_1,\ldots,x_n) \overset{*}{\to} x_{i_1} \ldots x_{i_m}$ and $J = \cup \{i_l\}$. To do so

we consider the pairs (F,J) for $F \in \mathcal{F}$ and $J \subseteq \{1,\ldots,\varrho(F)\}$. We mark these
pairs in an iterative process: The pairs (F,J) will be marked if and
only if $F(x_1,\ldots,x_{\varrho(F)}) \overset{*}{\to} x_{i_1} \ldots x_{i_m}$ with $J = \cup\{i_l\}$; then $\varepsilon \in L(G)$ iff
$(S,\emptyset)$ is marked upon termination of the algorithm.

<u>for</u> all rules of the form $F( ) \to \tau$ where τ does not contain any function
symbol
<u>do</u> mark (F,J) where $J = \bigcup_{x_i \in \tau} \{i\}$;

<u>while</u> there is a production $F(x_1,\ldots,x_n) \to H_0(\tau_1,\ldots,\tau_k)$ with

(1) (H_0, J_0) is marked,

(2) $J = \bigcup_{i \in J_0} J_i$ where either $\tau_i = H_i(x_1, \ldots, x_n)$ and (H_i, J_i) is marked

$$\text{or} \quad \tau_i = \epsilon \quad \text{and} \quad J_i = \emptyset$$

(3) (F, J) is unmarked

<u>do</u> mark (F, J).

<u>Claim:</u> (F, J) is marked during this process iff $F(x_1, \ldots, x_n) \overset{*}{\to} x_{i_1} \ldots x_{i_m}$ with $J = \bigcup \{i_1\}$.

<u>Proof:</u> The proof is similar to the proof of the corresponding claim in [Aho 68] and therefore left to the reader.

We execute the algorithm on our example grammar. In the initialisation phase the pairs $(F, \{1,2\})$, $(H_6, \{1\})$ $(H_8, \{2\})$ and $(Conc, \{1,2\})$ are marked. During execution of the while-loop the following pairs are labelled in some order: $(S, \emptyset)$, $(H_4, \{1\})$, $(H_5, \{2\})$, $(H_2, \{1,2\})$.

<u>Thm.:</u> Given any macro grammar G and integer k we can test if G is MLL(k) in time $O(2^{(9+\epsilon)} k^4 size^2(G))$ and space $O(2^{(9+\epsilon)} k^2 size(G))$ where size (G) is the length of the description of grammar G and $\epsilon > 0$ is arbitrary.

<u>Proof:</u> By a careful analysis of the decision procedure outlined above.

<u>Corollary:</u> Given an arbitrary macro grammar G, we can test if G is MLL(1) in time $O(2^{(9+)} size^2(G))$ for every $\epsilon > 0$.

The running time of our decision procedure is exponential. We will show next that this inefficiency is inherent to our problem.

<u>Thm.:</u> Every algorithm which tests if an arbitrary macro grammar is MLL(1) takes time $c^{size(G)}$ for some constant c and space $size(G)^{2-\epsilon}$ for every $\epsilon > 0$ infinitely often.

<u>Proof:</u> We use the following fact from [Hunt & Rosenkrantz].

<u>Fact:</u> Every algorithm which decides $L(G) = \emptyset$ for arbitrary macro-grammars G takes time $c^{size(G)}$ for some constant c and space $size(G)^{2-\epsilon}$ for every $\epsilon > 0$ infinitely often.

We reduce the emptiness problem to MLL(1) testing. The following trivial macro grammar generates Σ^* $\qquad S_0 \to \epsilon \mid a\, S_0 \mid b\, S_0 \mid \ldots$

Let $G = (\Sigma, \mathcal{F}, \mathcal{U}, \mathcal{G}, S, P)$ be a macro grammar with $S_0, S' \notin \mathcal{F}$. Consider $G' = (\Sigma, \mathcal{F}', \mathcal{U}, \mathcal{G}', S', P')$ with $\mathcal{F}' = \mathcal{F} \cup \{S_0, S'\}$

$$\mathcal{G}'(F) = \begin{cases} \mathcal{G}(F) & \text{if } F \in \mathcal{F} \\ o & \text{if } F = S_0 \text{ or } F = S' \end{cases}$$

$P' = P \cup \{S' \to S_0 \mid S\} \cup \{S_0 \to \epsilon \mid a S_0 \; ; \; a \in \Sigma\}$

Then G' is MLL(1) if and only if $L(G) = \emptyset$. Furthermore size (G') = size(G) + $O(|\Sigma|)$ = O(size(G)). Since $L(G) = \emptyset$ may be tested by constructing G' and testing it for the MLL(1) property, MLL(1) testing takes time $c^{size(G)}$ and space $size(G)^{2-\varepsilon}$ for some c and every $\varepsilon > 0$ infinitely often.

V. Macro Grammars and Indexed Grammars
==

Weiß [Weiß] introduced in this theses three notions of indexed LL-grammars: α-, β- and γ-ILL grammars. The γ-condition puts a very severe restriction of the form of the grammar and even excludes some context-free LL grammars. Weiß intensively studied the class of γ-ILL grammars. The β-ILL class of grammars is a proper extension of the class of context-free LL grammars. We give his definition.

<u>Definition:</u> Let G = (V,F,Σ,S,P) be an indexed grammar. Let r be any rule in P.

a) if $r = [A \to \alpha] \in f$ is an index rule then

$\quad First_k(r) = \{x \in \Sigma^* \; ; \; \exists \, u \in \Sigma^* , \delta \in (V \cup F)^*, w \in \Sigma^*$ with

$\qquad\qquad\qquad$ (1) $S \overset{*}{\to} uAf\delta \to u\alpha\delta \overset{*}{\to} uxw$

$\qquad\qquad\qquad$ (2) $|x| < k \Rightarrow w = \varepsilon$

$\qquad\qquad\qquad$ (3) $|x| \leq k \qquad\qquad \}$

$\quad$ if $r = A \to \alpha \in P \qquad\qquad$ then

$\quad First_k(r) = \{x \in \Sigma^*; \exists u \in \Sigma^*, \delta \in (V \cup F)^*, w \in \Sigma^*$ with

$\qquad\qquad\qquad$ (1) $S \overset{*}{\to} uA\delta \to u\alpha\delta \overset{*}{\to} uxw$

$\qquad\qquad\qquad$ (2) $|x| < k \Rightarrow w = \varepsilon$

$\qquad\qquad\qquad$ (3) $|x| \leq k \qquad\qquad \}$

b) An indexed grammar is ILL(k) if for every pair r,r' of distinct rules having the same left hand side:

$\quad First_k(r) \cap First_k(r') = \emptyset$.

<u>Thm.:</u> Given any MLL(k) grammar G, we can effectively find an equivalent ILL(k) grammar G' and vice versa.

VI. MLL languages and restricted nested stack automata
==

In this section we give an "automata-theoretic" definition of ILL (and hence MLL) languages. In [Aho 69] Aho introduced one-way deterministic nested stack automata. The storage structure of such an automata is a nested stack. It operates in one of four modes:

Pushdown mode: read and write at the top of one of the nested stacks

stack reading mode: read and move up and down within a stack
stack creating mode: create a new stack
stack destruction mode: destroy an empty stack

A downward reading nested stack automaton is a nesa with the following restriction placed on the behaviour in the stack reading mode. In the stack reading mode a downward reading nesa can only move down. If it hits the bottom of the outermost stack in this mode then the machine is put in a special state and the storage tape head is placed at the top of the right most stack.

<u>Thm.:</u> A language L is ILL (and hence MLL) if and only if there is a 1-way deterministic downward reading nesa accepting L.

<u>Proof:</u> Inspect the equivalence proof of nesa and indexed grammars in [Aho 69] closely.

We are now able to describe a parsing algorithm for MLL languages. Weiß showed that (his version of) ε-free ILL grammars can be parsed in time $O(n^2)$. He constructs an equivalent nesa and computes its running time. This construction also works for our version of ILL grammars. We obtain

<u>Thm.:</u> Let G be a ε-free MLL grammar. Then there is a recognizer for L(G) working in time $O(n^2)$ and space $O(n)$.

In section 2 we constructed an MLL grammar for every deterministic context-free language. The nesa corresponding to these grammars is essentially a deterministic pushdown automata and works in linear time.

<u>Open Problem:</u> Find a class of MLL languages which properly includes the deterministic context-free languages but can still be parsed in linear time.

VII. An Example
=================

The following rules are part of the ALGOL 60 syntax for assignment statements.

```
<assignment>    →   <Var>  ←   <Expression>
<Expression>    →   <Var>   |    (<Var> + <Expression>)
<Var>           →    A|B|C|...
```

Some of the strings which can be derived from this grammar are not legal
ALGOL 68 assignment statements: if the variable on the left hand side
is of type integer then the expression on the right hand side should
better yield a value of type integer. This restriction is part of the
semantics of the assignment statement.

In ALGOL W this restriction is made part of the syntax

<assignment> → <integer assignment> |

           <real assignment>

<integer assignment> → <integer var> ← <integer expr>

$$\vdots$$

<integer var> ← A|B|C

<real var> ← X|Y|Z

by explicitly listing a set of the ALGOL 60 rules for every type. In
the presence of infinitely many modes the explicite listing does not
suffice. In ALGOL 68 an implicite listing is achieved by means of two
level grammars. The goal can also be reached using macro grammars.

Suppose that we have the modes $\underline{int}$, $\underline{long}$ $\underline{int}$,$\underline{long}$ $\underline{long}$ $\underline{int}$,...; $\underline{int}$
means single precision, $\underline{long}$ $\underline{int}$ means double precision,... . We also
want to include a simple form of coercion: widening.
A value of type $\underline{long}^{i}\underline{int}$ is also a value of type $\underline{long}^{i+k}\underline{int}$ for all
$k \geqslant 0$. The following macro grammar generates the set of legal assign-
ment statements.

<assignment> → F($\underline{int}$<var>, $\underline{int}$)

F(x,y) → F($\underline{long}$ x, Ay) | x ← Expression(y)

Expression(y) ← y<Var> | (y<Var> + Expression(y))

A → $\underline{long}$ | ε

This grammar is not MLL(k) for any k due to the "left recursion" in the
rules for F( ). However a trick similar to the one used in the context-
free case will remove left recursion:

<assignment> → G(ε)

G(y) → $\underline{long}$ G(Ay) | $\underline{int}$<var> ← Expression(y)

Expression(y) → y $\underline{int}$<var> | (y $\underline{int}$<Var> + Expression(y))

A → $\underline{long}$ | ε

Bibliography

Aho, A.V. [1968]. Indexed grammars - an extension of context-free grammars. J. ACM 15:4, 647-671.

Aho, A.V. [1969]. Nested Stack Automata, JACM, 16:3, 383-406

Aho, A.V. & Ullman, J.D. [1972]. The Theory of Parsing, Translation and Compiling, Prentice Hall, Series in Automatic Computation.

Bertsch, E., Two Thoughts on Fast Recognition of Indexed Languages, Information & Control, 29:4, Dec. 1975

Fischer, M., Grammars with Macro-Like Instructions, 9th SWAT Conference 1968

Gries, D., Compiler Construction for Digital Computers, Addison Wesley

Heydthausen, M. & Mehlhorn, K., Parsing Macro Grammars Top-Down, Technischer Bericht A 76/3, Fachbereich 10, Univ. d. Saarlandes 1976

Knuth, D.E. [1967]. Top-down syntax analysis. Lecture Notes. International Summer School on Computer Programming, Copenhagen, Denmark

Lewis, P.M.II, & Stearns, R.E. [1968]. Syntax directed transduction J. ACM 15:3, 464-488.

Nivat, M., On the Interpretation of Recursive Program Schemes, IRIA Rapport Laboria 84, 1974

Rosenkrantz, D.J. & Stearns, R.E. [1970]. Properties of deterministic top-down grammars. Information and Control 17:3, 226-256

Weiß, K., Deterministische indizierte Grammatiken, 2tes Kolloquium über Automatentheorie und formale Sprache, Kaiserslautern, 1975 u. Doktorarbeit, TH Karlsruhe, Januar 1976

HOW PROGRAM STATEMENTS TRANSFORM PREDICATES

L. Ammeraal

Mathematisch Centrum

Amsterdam

ABSTRACT

This paper deals with relationships between conditions that hold before the initiation of a statement and on its completion. Statements are semantically defined by statement functions which map states to states. Statement functions induce predicate transformers which map state-space subsets to state-space subsets. The predicate transformers and their inverses are explicitly given for some well-known constructs including the conditional statement and the while statement. A number of examples illustrate how predicate transformers can be used.

INTRODUCTION

Sequences of the form

$$\{X\} \ S \ \{Y\}$$

are frequently found in papers on program correctness. Usually X and Y are assertions or conditions which hold before initiation of a statement S and on its completion, respectively. Since X and Y are comments, they are not very precisely defined and anything that improves program readability will do. However, X, Y and S are not mutually independent. It would be nice if two of them determined the third, like the sides of a right-angled triangle. Unfortunately we have not yet discovered a relationship between X, Y and S which is as elegant as Pythagoras' theorem. In cases like

$$\{x > 0\} \ x := x + 1 \ \{x > 1\}$$

this relationship is intuitively clear without precise definitions or any other mathematical equipment, but in general it is not evident how one unknown in the triple (X,S,Y) can be derived from the other two items. It is not difficult to realize that

$$\{X\} \ \underline{\text{while}} \ B \ \underline{\text{do}} \ S \ \underline{\text{od}} \ \{X \wedge \neg B\}$$

is a consequence of

$$\{X \wedge B\} \ S \ \{X\},$$

but it is less well known how Y in

$$\{X\} \ \underline{\text{while}} \ B \ \underline{\text{do}} \ S \ \underline{\text{od}} \ \{Y\}$$

can be expressed as a function of X if Y' is given as a function of X' in

$$\{X'\}\ S\ \{Y'\}.$$

Such functions and their inverses are discussed in this paper. Because functions have unique values we will only accept the strongest Y or X that follows from a given X or Y. If we would tolerate information to be lost then, e.g., $1 + 1 = 2$ could serve as a Y for any X and S.

In this paper we will avail ourselves of the conventional notation of elementary set theory. This has two pleasant aspects. First, anyone who is not altogether unfamiliar with modern mathematics understands it. Secondly, useful theorems from set theory can immediately be applied.

The idea of viewing predicates as sets is also briefly mentioned by DIJKSTRA [3]. His predicate transformers derive predicates in the backward direction, i.e. X is derived from Y in $\{X\}\ S\ \{Y\}$. We will call them "inverse predicate transformers" and pay at least as much attention to (forward) predicate transformers that yield Y when X is given.

STATES AND PREDICATES

There are two distinct ways of writing things down, viz. either in mathematical or in symbolic notation. E.g. $x := x + 1$ is in symbolic notation. In mathematics we would write something like $x' = x + 1$. Objects in symbolic notation can be discussed with the aid of mathematical notation. In the program

(1) $\underline{\text{begin}}\ \underline{\text{real}}\ x,\ y;\ \underline{\text{int}}\ i,\ j;\ \underline{\text{bool}}\ b;$

$$S_1\ ;\ldots;\ S_m$$

$\underline{\text{end}},$

where $S_1,\ldots,S_m$ stand for statements, the symbols x, y, i, j, b are usually called "variables". This is not a deifnition. The term "variable" is a source of trouble when we use both notations at the same time. We will therefore neither define this term nor use it. This is possible if we replace program (1) by

(2) $\underline{\text{begin}}\ \underline{\text{real}}\ x_1,\ x_2;\ \underline{\text{int}}\ x_3,\ x_4;\ \underline{\text{bool}}\ x_5;$

$$S_1;\ldots;S_m$$

$\underline{\text{end}}.$

If R is the set of real numbers and Z is the set of all integers, we will say that the set

$$V = R \times R \times Z \times Z \times \{\underline{\text{true}},\ \underline{\text{false}}\}$$

is the state space of program (2). It is the set of all 5-tuples $(\xi_1,\xi_2,\xi_3,\xi_4,\xi_5)$, where

$$\xi_1, \xi_2 \in R$$

$$\xi_3, \xi_4 \in Z$$

$$\xi_5 \in \{\underline{true}, \underline{false}\}.$$

Greek letters ξ_i were written here to emphasize that mathematical notation was used. When this is clear from the context we can safely use x_i instead of ξ_i. We will do so and keep in mind that such an x_i is just an element of some set, say R. The resemblance of x_3 in $x_3 \in Z$ and in program (2) is pure accident. The example leads to the following definitions.

A __state space__ is a Cartesian product

$$V = V_1 \times V_2 \times \ldots \times V_n.$$

The sets $V_1, \ldots, V_n$ are sometimes called __types__. The elements $\underline{x} = (x_1, x_2, \ldots, x_n)$ of V are called __states__.

If now, for instance, the statement

$$(3) \qquad x_3 := 50$$

is chosen for S_1 in program (2), its effect (semantics) can be described in terms of the state space: any state $(x_1, x_2, x_3, x_4, x_5)$ is mapped to the state $(x_1, x_2, 50, x_4, x_5)$. We will write this as

$$\forall \, \underline{x} = (x_1, x_2, x_3, x_4, x_5) \in V : f(\underline{x}) = (x_1, x_2, 50, x_4, x_5)$$

or simply as

$$(4) \qquad f(x_1, x_2, x_3, x_4, x_5) = (x_1, x_2, 50, x_4, x_5),$$

when it is clear that f is defined for all $\underline{x} \in V$.

In the context of program (2) we regard (3) as just a symbolic notation for (4). The subset

$$Y = \{\underline{x} \in V \mid \underline{x} = (x_1, x_2, 50, x_4, x_5)\}$$

of V is the mathematical equivalent of the symbolically written condition $x_3 = 50$ that could be inserted as a comment after S_1 in program (2). Thus subsets of the state space V are equivalent to "restrictions" or "conditions" imposed on V. We will use the term __predicate__ for a subset of V when we think of the corresponding condition at the same time. We should be aware of the following correspondence between conditions (Boolean expressions) and set expressions.

Boolean expression	set expression
$A \lor B$	$A \cup B$
$A \land B$	$A \cap B$
$\neg A$	$\overline{A}$ (=V−A; A's complement)
$A \Rightarrow B$	$A \subset B$
$\underline{true}$	V
$\underline{false}$	$\emptyset$

STATEMENT FUNCTIONS AND PREDICATE TRANSFORMERS

Program statements are strings of symbols composed according to syntactic rules. Thus $x_3 := 50$ and $x_3 := 5 * 10$ are different statements. Their effects on a state space V, however, are the same and can be described by a so-called "statement function"

$$f: W \to V,$$

defined on some domain $W \subset V$. ($W = V$ is assumed if W is not specified).

EXAMPLE 1. Let $V = R^2$, i.e. the program has the form

> $\underline{begin}$ $\underline{real}$ $x_1, x_2;$
>
> $\underline{end}.$

We consider the statement

$$S: x_1 := sqrt(x_1 + x_2).$$

Then

$$f(x_1, x_2) = (\sqrt{x_1 + x_2}, x_2).$$

The domain of f is

$$W = \{(x_1, x_2) \in V \mid x_1 + x_2 \geq 0\}.$$

We are interested in mappings not only from states to states but also from predicates to predicates. Predicates are considered to be subsets of the state space V. For the powerset (i.e. the set of all subsets) of A we write $P(A)$. As before, W denotes the domain of the statement function f. Then f induces a function from $P(W)$ to $P(V)$. The latter function is also written as f and is given by

$$f(X) = \{f(\underline{x}) \in V \mid \underline{x} \in X\} \quad \text{for all } X \in P(W).$$

This new function f will be called *predicate transformer*.

EXAMPLE 2.
$$V = R^2$$
$$X = \{(x_1, x_2) \in V \mid x_1 > 0\}$$
$$S: x_1 := x_1 + 1.$$

Then

$$f(x_1, x_2) = (x_1 + 1, x_2),$$
$$f(X) = \{(x_1, x_2) \in V \mid x_1 > 1 .$$

In the next section some general rules to find $f(X)$ will be given. In this and some other examples x_2 seems superfluous. Its only purpose is to prevent us from identifying state spaces with the set of real numbers, which would be highly unrealistic. Set theory (cf.[7]) provides many interesting properties of mappings which we may use for our purposes by virtue of our definition of predicate transformers. For a given statement function f with domain W we define the *inverse predicate transformer* f^{-1} as the function from $P(V)$ to $P(W)$ given by

$$f^{-1}(Y) = \{\underline{x} \in W \mid f(\underline{x}) \in Y\} \quad \text{for any } Y \subset V.$$

Then for any X, X_1, $X_2 \subset W$ and Y, Y_1, $Y_2 \subset V$ we mention the following properties, which are easy to prove.

(5) $\qquad f(X_1 \cup X_2) = f(X_1) \cup f(X_2)$

(6) $\qquad f(X_1 \cap X_2) \subset f(X_1) \cap f(X_2)$

(7) $\qquad X_1 \subset X_2$ implies $f(X_1) \subset f(X_2)$

(8) $\qquad f^{-1}(Y_1 \cup Y_2) = f^{-1}(Y_1) \cup f^{-1}(Y_2)$

(9) $\qquad f^{-1}(Y_1 \cap Y_2) = f^{-1}(Y_1) \cap f^{-1}(Y_2)$

(10) $\qquad Y_1 \subset Y_2$ implies $f^{-1}(Y_1) \subset f^{-1}(Y_2)$

(11) $\qquad f(X) = \emptyset$ if and only if $X = \emptyset$

(12) $\qquad f(f^{-1}(Y)) \subset Y$

(13) $\qquad X \subset f^{-1}(f(X))$

(14) $\qquad f^{-1}(V-Y) = W - f^{-1}(Y)$

If the statement function f maps W <u>onto</u> V, i.e. $f(W) = V$, then

(15) $\qquad f(f^{-1}(Y)) = Y.$

If f is one-to-one, i.e. $\underline{x}_1 = \underline{x}_2$ whenever $f(\underline{x}_1) = f(\underline{x}_2)$, then

(16) $\qquad f^{-1}(f(X)) = X,$

(17) $\qquad f(X_1 \cap X_2) = f(X_1) \cap f(X_2).$

Often $W = V$, as in the following examples.

<u>EXAMPLE 3.</u>
$$V = R^2$$
$$X = \{(x_1, x_2) \in V \mid x_1 > 3\}$$
$$S: x_1 := x_1 * x_1.$$

Then

$$f(x_1, x_2) = (x_1^2, x_2),$$
$$f(X) = \{(x_1, x_2) \in V \mid x_1 > 9\},$$
$$f^{-1}(f(X)) = \{(x_1, x_2) \in V \mid x_1 < -3 \lor x_1 > +3\}.$$

This example illustrates (13). Since f is not one-to-one, (16) does not apply here.

<u>EXAMPLE 4</u>.

$$V = R^2$$

$$Y = \{(x_1, x_2) \in V \mid x_1 > -2\}$$

$$S: \quad x_1 := x_1 * x_1$$

Then

$$f^{-1}(Y) = V,$$

$$f(f^{-1}(Y)) = \{(x_1, x_2) \in V \mid x_1 \geq 0\}.$$

Here (12) applies, but (15) does not, because f does not map V <u>onto</u> V.

PREDICATE TRANSFORMERS FOR SOME STATEMENTS

Each program statement has the statement function as its semantic definition. The predicate transformer and its inverse are then determined. In other words, $f(\underline{x})$ is given by definition; $f(X)$ and $f^{-1}(Y)$ by theorems. They will be presented in this section for

    a. the dummy statement,

    b. the assignment statement,

    c. the compound statement,

    d. the conditional statement,

    e. the while statement.

The given expressions for $f(X)$ and $f^{-1}(Y)$ are rather obvious, so we will omit their proofs but insert some elementary examples.

    a. <u>The dummy statement</u>.

The semantics of the dummy statement are defined by $f(\underline{x}) = \underline{x}$ for all $\underline{x} \in V$. We denote this statement by the symbol <u>skip</u>. Clearly, $f(X) = X$ and $f^{-1}(X) = X$ for all $X \subset V$.

    b. <u>The assignment statement</u>

Let the state space be $V = V_1 \times V_2 \times \ldots \times V_n$, and, for some i $(1 \leq i \leq n)$ let a function

$$\phi: W \to V_i \qquad (W \subset V)$$

be given. Then the statement function f with domain W and given by

$$\begin{cases} f(\underline{x}) = (x_1, \ldots, x_{i-1}, \phi(\underline{x}), x_{i+1}, \ldots, x_n) \\ \underline{x} = (x_1, \ldots, x_i, \ldots, x_n) \end{cases}$$

defines the semantics of the assignment statement symbolically denoted by

$$x_i := \phi(\underline{x}).$$

It then follows that, for all $X \subset W$ and $Y \subset V$,

$$(18) \quad f(X) = \{(x_1,\ldots,x_i,\ldots,x_n) \in V \mid$$
$$\exists \overset{o}{x_i} : \underline{x}^{o} = (x_1,\ldots,x_{i-1}, \overset{o}{x_i}, x_{i+1},\ldots,x_n) \in X \wedge x_i = \phi(\underline{x}^{o})\}$$

$$(19) \quad f^{-1}(Y) = \{\underline{x} \in W \mid \underline{x} = (x_1,\ldots,x_n) \wedge (x_1,\ldots,x_{i-1}, \phi(\underline{x}), x_{i+1},\ldots,x_n) \in Y\}.$$

EXAMPLE 5.

$$V = R^2$$
$$X = \{(x_1,x_2) \mid x_1 + x_2 > 0\}$$
$$S: \quad x_1 := x_1 - x_2.$$

Then

$$f(x_1,x_2) = (x_1 - x_2, x_2),$$
$$f(X) = \{(x_1,x_2) \mid \exists \overset{o}{x_1} : (\overset{o}{x_1},x_2) \in X \wedge x_1 = \overset{o}{x_1} - x_2\}$$
$$= \{(x_1,x_2) \mid \exists \overset{o}{x_1} : \overset{o}{x_1} + x_2 > 0 \wedge x_1 = \overset{o}{x_1} - x_2\}$$
$$= \{(x_1,x_2) \mid x_1 + 2x_2 > 0\}.$$

The last step consisted of eliminating $\overset{o}{x_1}$.

We now take $Y = f(X)$ and apply (19):

$$f^{-1}(Y) = \{(x_1,x_2) \mid (x_1 - x_2, x_2) \in Y\}$$
$$= \{(x_1,x_2) \mid (x_1 - x_2) + 2x_2 > 0\}$$
$$= \{(x_1,x_2) \mid x_1 + x_2 > 0\} = X.$$

Because f is one-to-one, we could have predicted this by using (16).

Remark on the symbolic notation of statements.

We have used the symbol S for statements and f for the corresponding statement functions. When several statements are involved, it is more convenient to denote them by
capital letters F, G,..., and their statement functions by the corresponding small
letters f, g,... .

    c. The compound statement

    The sequence G;H is considered to be a new statement F, semantically defined
by

$$f(\underline{x}) = h(g(\underline{x})) \quad \text{for all } \underline{x} \in g^{-1}(h^{-1}(V)).$$

Then

$$f(X) = h(g(X)) \quad \text{for all } X \subset g^{-1}(h^{-1}(V)),$$
$$f^{-1}(Y) = g^{-1}(h^{-1}(Y)) \quad \text{for all } Y \subset V.$$

    d. The conditional statement

    For any predicate $B \subset V$ the sequence

      if B then G else H fi

is called a *conditional statement* F, semantically defined by

$$(20) \qquad f(x) = \begin{cases} g(x) & \text{if } \underline{x} \in B \cap g^{-1}(V), \\[2ex] h(x) & \text{if } \underline{x} \in \bar{B} \cap h^{-1}(V). \end{cases}$$

Here $\bar{B} = V - B$, the complement of B. Clearly the domain of f is $[B \cap g^{-1}(V)] \cup [\bar{B} \cap h^{-1}(V)]$.

For all subsets X of this domain and for all $Y \subset V$:

$$(21) \qquad f(X) = g(B \cap X) \cup h(\bar{B} \cap X)$$

$$(22) \qquad f^{-1}(Y) = [B \cap g^{-1}(Y)] \cup [\bar{B} \cap h^{-1}(Y)].$$

<u>EXAMPLE 6.</u>

$$V = R^2$$
$$X = \{(x,y) \mid x + y > 1\}$$

(For convenience we write (x,y) instead of (x_1,x_2).)

F: <u>if</u> $x < y$ <u>then</u> $x := x + y$ <u>else</u> $y := x + y$ <u>fi</u>

Consequently

$$B = \{(x,y) \in V \mid x < y\}$$
$$G : \quad x := x + y$$
$$H : \quad y := x + y \ .$$

Then

$$g(x,y) = (x+y,y),$$
$$h(x,y) = (x,x+y).$$

Our goal is to find $f(X)$ by using (21).

$$B \cap X = \{(x,y) \mid x < y \wedge x + y > 1\}$$
$$\bar{B} \cap X = \{(x,y) \mid x \geq y \wedge x + y > 1\}.$$

We apply (18):

$$\begin{aligned} g(B \cap X) &= \{(x,y) \in V \mid \exists x^\circ : (x^\circ,y) \in B \cap X \wedge x = x^\circ + y\} \\ &= \{(x,y) \in V \mid (x-y,y) \in B \cap X\} \\ &= \{(x,y) \in V \mid x-y < y \wedge (x-y)+y > 1\} \\ &= \{(x,y) \in V \mid 1 < x < 2y\}. \end{aligned}$$

We can find $h(\bar{B} \cap X) = \{(x,y) \in V \mid 1 < y \leq 2x\}$ in a similar way. Then (21) yields

$$f(X) = \{(x,y) \in V \mid 1 < x < 2y \vee 1 < y \leq 2x\}.$$

<u>EXAMPLE 7.</u>

$$V = R^2$$
$$Y = \{(x,y) \mid y = 2\}$$

F: <u>if</u> $x > 0$ <u>then</u> $y := x + 1$ <u>else</u> <u>skip</u> <u>fi</u>.

Thus

$$B = \{(x,y) \mid x > 0\}$$
$$G: y := x + 1$$
$$H: \underline{\text{skip}}.$$

Then we find by using (22):

$$
\begin{aligned}
f^{-1}(Y) &= [B \cap \{(x,y) \mid (x,x+1) \in Y\}] \cup \\
&\quad [\bar{B} \cap \{(x,y) \mid y = 2\}] \\
&= [\{(x,y) \mid x > 0\} \cap \{(x,y) \mid x + 1 = 2\}] \cup \\
&\quad [\{(x,y) \mid x \leq 0\} \cap \{(x,y) \mid y = 2\}] \\
&= \{(x,y) \mid x = 1 \vee (x \leq 0 \wedge y = 2)\}.
\end{aligned}
$$

    e. <u>The while statement</u>

We will adopt the obvious notation

$$
g^{-k}(Y) = \begin{cases}
Y & \text{if} \quad k = 0, \\[2ex]
g^{-1}(g^{-k+1}(Y)) & \text{if } k > 0.
\end{cases}
$$

The sequence

(23)   <u>while</u> B <u>do</u> G <u>od</u>

is called a *while statement* F. We will define its statement function f in terms of
statement G (with statement function g) and predicate $B \subset V$. The domain of f is

(24) $W = \bigcup\limits_{k=0}^{\infty} g^{-k}(\bar{B})$.

Intuitively, W is the set of all states $\underline{x} \in V$ which have the property that repeated
application of g eventually results in a state $\underline{x}' \in \bar{B}$. Then the statement function for
(23) is

(25) $f(\underline{x}) = \begin{cases}
f(g(\underline{x})) & \text{if } \underline{x} \in B \cap W, \\[2ex]
\underline{x} & \text{if } \underline{x} \in \bar{B} \cap W \quad \text{(i.e. } x \in \bar{B}).
\end{cases}$

(The domain W is closely related to the recursive nature of this definition. A (not
allowed) attempt to find $f(\underline{x})$ for some $\underline{x} \in V - W$ may result not only in an undefined
$g(\underline{x})$, as in Example 1, but also in an infinite process.)
The predicate transformer and its inverse are

(26) $f(X) = \bar{B} \cap \bigcup\limits_{k=0}^{\infty} T_k$ for any $X \subset W$,

where

$$
\begin{cases}
T_0 = X, \\[2ex]
T_{k+1} = g(B \cap T_k) & (k=0,1,2,\ldots),
\end{cases}
$$

and

(27) $f^{-1}(Y) = \bigcup\limits_{k=0}^{\infty} S_k$ for any $Y \subset V$,

where

$$\begin{cases} S_0 = \bar{B} \cap Y \\ S_{k+1} = B \cap g^{-1}(S_k) \quad (k=0,1,2,\ldots). \end{cases}$$

EXAMPLE 8.

$V = Z$ (the set of all integers)

$X = \{x \in Z \mid x > 0 \wedge x \text{ even}\}$

F: $\underline{while}$ $x \le 10 \vee (x{\ge}20 \wedge x{\le}30)$ $\underline{do}$ $x:= 2 * x + 1$ $\underline{od}$.

Then

$B = \{x \in Z \mid x \le 10 \vee 20 \le x \le 30\}$,

$\bar{B} = \{x \in Z \mid 10 < x < 20 \vee x > 30\}$,

$T_0 = X = \{2,4,6,\ldots\}$, $B \cap T_0 = \{2,4,6,8,10,20,22,24,26,28,30\}$,

$T_1 = g(B{\cap}T_0) = \{5,9,13,17,21,41,45,49,53,57,61\}$, $B \cap T_1 = \{5,9,21\}$,

$T_2 = g(B{\cap}T_1) = \{11,19,43\}$, $B \cap T_2 = \emptyset$,

$T_3 = g(B{\cap}T_2) = \emptyset$, etc.,

$f(X) = \bar{B} \cap (T_0{\cup}T_1{\cup}T_2) =$

$\{11,12,13,14,16,17,18,19,41,43,45,49,53,57,61\} \cup \{32,34,36,\ldots\}$.

Here X satisfies $X \subset W$, because $W = \bigcup\limits_{k=0}^{\infty} g^{-k}(\bar{B}) = \{x \in Z \mid x \ge 0\}$.

EXAMPLE 9.

$V = Z$

$Y = \{x \in Z \mid x \text{ even}\}$

F: $\underline{while}$ $x \le 10$ $\underline{do}$ $x := x + 3$ $\underline{od}$.

Then

$B = \{x \in Z \mid x \le 10\}$,

$S_0 = \bar{B} \cap Y = \{12,14,16,\ldots\}$,

$S_1 = B \cap g^{-1}(S_0) = B \cap \{9,11,13,\ldots\} = \{9\}$,

$S_2 = B \cap g^{-1}(S_1) = B \cap \{6\} = \{6\}$,

$S_3 = B \cap g^{-1}(S_2) = B \cap \{3\} = \{3\}$,

etc.,

$f^{-1}(Y) = S_0 \cup S_1 \cup S_2 \cup \ldots$

$\qquad = \{\ldots,-6,-3,0,3,6,9,12,14,16,\ldots\}$.

We will now mention some properties that can be derived from (25), (26) and (27). First, the equivalence of

$\underline{while}$ B $\underline{do}$ G $\underline{od}$

and

$\underline{if}$ B $\quad\underline{then}$ G; $\underline{while}$ B $\underline{do}$ G $\underline{od}$

$\qquad\underline{else}$ $\underline{skip}$

$\underline{fi}$

follows immediately if we formulate the statement function of the latter conditional statement. If we write the predicate transformer and its inverse for this conditional statement, we find the recurrence relations

$$f(X) = f(g(B \cap X)) \cup [\bar{B} \cap X],$$
$$f^{-1}(Y) = [B \cap g^{-1}(f^{-1}(Y))] \cup [\bar{B} \cap Y].$$

Some less general but more practical results than (26) and (27) can be derived from our predicate transformer. For example, Hoare's "Rule of Iteration" (cf. [2]):

if $\vdash P \wedge B \ \{S\} \ P$ then $\vdash P \ \{\underline{while} \ B \ \underline{do} \ S\} \ \neg B \wedge P$

is written in our notation as :

if $g(X \cap B) \subset X$ then $f(X) \subset \bar{B} \cap X$, where

F: $\underline{while}$ B $\underline{do}$ G $\underline{od}$.

It is proved as follows. It follows from (26) that $f(X) \subset \bar{B}$.
Furthermore

$$g(X \cap B) \subset X \overset{(\alpha)}{\Rightarrow} T_k \subset X \ (k=0,1,\ldots) \Rightarrow \overset{\infty}{\underset{k=0}{\cup}} T_k \subset X \Rightarrow f(X) \subset X.$$

(α) is proved by induction:

   i. $T_0 = X$, thus $T_0 \subset X$.

   ii. Suppose $T_k \subset X$. Then $B \cap T_k \subset B \cap X \Rightarrow$

       $g(B \cap T_k) \subset g(B \cap X) \Rightarrow T_{k+1} \subset g(B \cap X)$.

       It is given that $g(B \cap X) \subset X$; thus $T_{k+1} \subset X$.

Thus $g(X \cap B) \subset X$ implies $f(X) \subset \bar{B} \cap X$.

We conclude with a rule for the while statement mentioned in DE BAKKER [5] and written there as

W5: $\forall \ u,v \ [\exists \ w[u \subseteq w, w; \ p; \ S \subseteq S; \ w, w; \ \bar{p} \subseteq v] \Rightarrow u; \ p \ast S \subseteq p \ast S; \ v]$

In a less sophisticated notation this theorem applied to our while statement

      F: $\underline{while}$ B $\underline{do}$ G $\underline{od}$

reads as follows.

For all predicates X and Y, it is true that $f(X) \subset Y$ if there is a predicate W satisfying the three conditions:

(28) $X \subset W$

(29) $g(W \cap B) \subset W$

(30) $W \cap \bar{B} \subset Y$.

PROOF. We take W for X in our last example. This gives:

      if $g(W \cap B) \subset W$ then $f(W) \subset \bar{B} \cap W$.

Thus $f(W) \subset \bar{B} \cap W$, since (29) is given. Combining this with (30) yields $f(W) \subset Y$. From

(28) it follows that $f(X) \subset f(W)$. Thus $f(X) \subset Y$. $\square$

REFERENCES

[1] FLOYD, R.W., *Assigning Meanings to Programs*, Proc. Symp., Appl. Math. 19, American
    Math. Soc. (1967) 19-32.

[2] HOARE, C.A.R., *An axiomatic Basis of Computer Programming*, CACM, Vol. 12. No. 10
    (October 1969), 576-580.

[3] DIJKSTRA, E.W., *A Simple Axiomatic Basis for Programming Language Constructs*, Proc.
    Kon. Ned. Akad., Ser. A, 77 (or Indagationes Math., $\underline{36}$), 1-15 (1974).

[4] MANNA, Z. & A. PNUELI, *Axiomatic Approach to Total Correctness of Programs*, Report
    STAN-CS-73-382, Stanford University (1973).

[5] DE BAKKER, J.W., *Flow of control in the proof theory of structured programming*,
    Proc. 16th IEEE Symp. on Foundations of Computer Science (1975).

[6] MILLS, H.D., *The New Math of Computer Programming*, CACM, Vol. 18, No. 1 (January
    1975), 43-48.

[7] HALMOS, P.R., *Naive Set Theory*, D. van Nostrand Company (1969).

<u>PROGRAM PROVING : EXIT AND RETURN JUMPS</u>

<u>IN STRUCTURED PROGRAMS</u>

G. De Michelis , G.A. Lanzarone , C. Simone

Gruppo di Elettronica e Cibernetica
Istituto di Fisica - Università di Milano
Via Viotti 5 - Milano   Italy

<u>Abstract</u>

The inadequacy of <u>goto</u>-free programming languages to express algorithms
has clearly been shown in the literature. On the other hand, the axiomatic definition of jumps is rather complex, and there aren't complete or
efficient proposals for it.
On the basis of Clint and Hoare's semantical analysis of jump occurrences
in structured programs, which leads to the distinction between return and
exit jumps, a twofold solution to the above problem is presented in the
present paper.
On the one hand, to express return jumps (considered as belonging to the
normal computation flow of the algotithm), iterative one-level exit
constructs wider than the simple iteration (<u>do-while</u> like) statement
are considered, and the related correctness rules are given. On the
other hand, a limited form of <u>goto</u> statement is introduced, with which
an explicit definition of the jump condition is associated, restricted to
deal with the case of exit jump only (considered as expressing exceptions
in the program)
The jump condition is then used to prove the ' almost everywhere correctness ' of the normal computation flow of the program, ignoring the exit
jumps, whose correctness can be dealt with separately.
Examples of the above constructs and correctness rules and of an ' almost
everywhere correctness ' proof, are given.

<u>Introduction : the role of jumps in structured programs</u>

Dijkstra's letter [4] began in 1968 a critical analysis of the use of
jumps in program construction, observing that the readability and quality of a program decrease with the increasing number of jump instructions
it contains. This letter gave rise to many papers in which the autors
explained their motivations for preserving or avoiding such jumps (see
the ' goto controversy ' [6] , [9] , [13] and, more recently, [8] and
 [11]).
On the one hand, it was argued that <u>goto</u>-free programs are more readable
and easier to prove correct, and emphasis was given to the one-entry,
one-exit basic control structures (such as composition, <u>if</u>...<u>then</u>...<u>else</u>,
<u>while</u>...<u>do</u> and <u>repeat</u>...<u>until</u> statements included for instance in the new
programming language PASCAL [10]). On the other hand, <u>goto</u>-less programming was considerd as often inefficient and not suitable to express
all the situations occurring in program design.   Therefore, several kinds
of limited jumps were considered, such as the simple (one-level) <u>exit</u>
statement (proposed by Wirth and reported in [7]), or labelled (multi-level) <u>exit</u> statements like the BLISS [12], [13] <u>leave</u> L statement.
Several attempts have been made to understand the basic control structures limitations. Some of these have been identified in the inability
to express loops with one, or more, exits in the middle; for instance,
the ' loop which is performed n and a half times '(as Knuth [8] calls
it in Dijkstra's words) typical of the backtracking problem, or the
two-exit iteration typical of the table search routine (both discussed
in [7]). Others are due to non iterative decision situations more
complex than binary selection, for which statements like <u>case</u> in PASCAL,
<u>select</u> in BLISS and the non iterative ' event indicator ' statement [8]
 [14] have been introduced, in order to avoid the node-splitting problem (but the iterative cases are the most significant, and we will be
concerned with them only).
A semantical analysis of the different kinds of jumps and the corresponding programming situations has been carried out by Clint and Hoare [2] ,
who introduced the important distinction between exit jumps and return
jumps.
Exit jumps occur when at a certain point of the program some conditions
are no longer satisfied and the computation cannot continue correctly.
The control must abandon the current state and jump to the appropriate
procedure or program component which possibly handles   this abnormal
situation.   The most natural example of this kinds of jumps are error
situations : the program must abandon the current environment and, possibly trying to make some modifications, must terminate or continue with
the component prepared to handle the error.
Return jumps are characterized by the fact that the solution of the problem is reached before executing all the statements of a certain environment. The control flow must go where the solution of the problem is
requested and continue from this point on. In such cases in general
two kinds of jumps are present in an iterative block : the one for the
normal termination, for example when the predicate of a <u>while</u> statement
becomes false, and the other for the early termination during the execution of the body of the iterative construct.
Essentially the same distinction results in a paper by Zahn [14] , where

it is shown _that, besides the above mentioned situations ,jumps are
especially needed in connection with the error handling probem, where
they are of the multi-level exit type.   In fact, when a program reaches
an error, the control flow must break away, at whatever point (possibly
inside a set of nested environments) the error occurs.
In addition, special attention is dedicated by Zahn to statement orienta-
tion towards the top-down program construction method, in proposing his
iterative ' event indicator ' statement (which we will consider in the
following).
In this paper we will present some correctness rules corresponding to
control constructs suitable for top-down developed structured programs,
based   upon the above results.   The basic idea is that, if return
jumps are considered as belonging to the normal computation flow, and
exit jumps are devoted to describe exceptional situations only, then it
is possible to take advantage of treating them separately both in program construction and in correctness verification (the above two situations will be considered in the next two paragraphs respectively).

Axiomatization of one-level exits iterative constructs

Leaving aside the need of multi-level exits, it is possible to provide
within a programming language control constructs more ' powerful ' (in
a   sense that is precisely specified in $[3]$, and is related to the
capability of expressing classes of algorithms), than _do-while_ like
statements, but such as to still allow (as opposed to the use of _goto_)
the structuring of programs.   More specifically, these are iterative
one-level exit constructs, retaining the one-entry, one-exit property
of blocks.
Two principal types of such constructs can be considered.   The first
type corresponds to a specific computation model, consisting of an iteration whose body is a succession of predicative and functional blocks.
The truth of any one of the predicates during execution leads to (execution of an associated functional block and) termination of the loop.
These structures (called Ω_n by Böhm and Jacopini $[1]$) may be expressed for instance with the following iterative compound statement :

      loop ;
      S_0 ;
      when p_1 _do_ S_{n+1} _and_ _exitloop_ ;
      S_1 ;
      when p_2 _do_ S_{n+2} _and_ _exitloop_ ;
      ....
      S_{n-1} ;
      when p_n _do_ S_{2n} _and_ _exitloop_ ;
      S_n ;
      endloop ;

where p_i ($1 \leq i \leq n$) are predicates ans S_j ($0 \leq j \leq 2n$) are groups of
statements.   Any number of _when_ clauses may appear between _loop_ and
endloop ; some of the S_k ($0 \leq k \leq n$) blocks may be empty and so may be
the S_{n+i} ($1 \leq i \leq n$) blocks (the clause _do_ S_{n+i} _and_ is optional).
It is easy to see that the above statement can express all the loops with
exits in the middle recalled in the introduction.
The second type of iterative construct corresponds to a computation model which is not predefined but has to be specified case by case. It
can be represented for instance by the following compound statement :
      repeat ⟨ body ⟩ _end_
(reported in $[7]$) where ⟨ body ⟩ is a group which contains one or more
exit statements (appearing inside conditional statements) .
Another interesting version of this construct is Zahn's ' event indicator ' $[14]$; as revised by Knuth $[8]$, it is the following :
      loop until ⟨ event ⟩$_1$ _or_ ...._or_ ⟨ event ⟩$_n$:
        ⟨ statement list ⟩$_0$
      repeat ;
      then ⟨ event ⟩$_1$ ⟹ ⟨ statement list ⟩$_1$;
      ....
      ⟨ event ⟩$_n$ ⟹ ⟨ statement list ⟩$_n$;
      end ;

Its semantics is as follows . The ⟨ statement list ⟩$_0$ is executed itera-
tively until one of the event identifiers declared at the beginnig is
reached.   In this case, the control passes to the statement identified

by that event in the <u>then</u> part of the statement. No other termination
of the ⟨statement list⟩ $_0$ is allowed.
Since the events occurrences show explicitly where the execution of the
iteration body must be interrupted and what must be done before abando-
ning the whole environment, clearly separating the two parts, it is a
nice statement for top-down program construction.
As presented by the author, however, this statement implements an iterative construct with multi-level exits. Since we want one-level construct,
we impose an additional syntactic constraint, i. e. that inside an event
indicator statement only the event identifiers declared at his head can
occur.
The eliminability of return jumps by using iterative one-level constructs,
such as those considered above, is not completely demonstrated by the
previous considerations ; however, in almost all the examples in the literature in which jumps of the return type occur, their presence is due
either to the poverty of the <u>do-while</u> like statements (which is overcome
when the above constructs are considered) or by yhe need for simulating
symmetrically interacting processes (algorithm components), for which
other control mechanisms such as coroutines seem to be most appropriate
[8] (which we will not consider in the present paper).
Thus, the sufficency of one-level iterative constructs for expressing
all algorithms not containing exceptional conditions may be assumed as
a reasonable working hypothesis, particularly indicated in the top-down
program construction methodology, where algorithm decomposability into
one-entry, one-exit components (except for errors) is one of the foun-
damental requirements.
Indeed, program readability and ease of top-down construction are not
the only requirements for a good programming language. Another important characteristic, emphasized by many authors, is the possibility of
proving program properties like correctness.
Hoare [5] has given an axiomatization for proving the correctness of programs built up with assignment, conditional, composition and simple iteration.
If this set of statements is exstended to include those presented above,
Hoare's axiomatic basis can correspondingly be extended with very little
difficulty, i. e. simple correctness rules correspond to the above iterative constructs (what constitutes another indication about their sui-
tability).
These rules given in Hoare's calculus (but using braces around the assertions, not around the statements) are shown below.
For the <u>loop</u>...<u>when</u>...<u>endloop</u> statement the rule (we will call it the
Ω_n rule) is as follows :

$$\frac{\begin{array}{lll} \{I\} & S_0 & \{Q_0\} \\ \{R_i\} & S_i & \{Q_i\} \qquad \forall i \quad (1 \le i \le 2n) \\ \{Q_{i-1}\} & p_i & \{R_i\} \quad \forall i \quad (1 \le i \le n) \\ \{Q_{i-1}\} & p_i & \{R_{n+i}\} \, \forall i \quad (1 \le i \le n) \\ \{Q_n\} & \supset & \{I\} \\ \{Q_i\} & \supset & \{Q\} \end{array}}{\{I\} \ \underline{loop} \ S_0 \ ; \ \underline{when} \ p_1 \ \underline{do} \ S_{n+1} \ \underline{and} \ \underline{exitloop} \ ; \ S_1 \ ; \ \dots \quad \underline{endloop} \ \{Q\}}$$

The rule for the <u>repeat</u>...<u>end</u> statement is :

$$\frac{\{Q\} \quad \underline{exit} \ \{\underline{false}\} \vdash \{I\} \ S \ \{I'\} \qquad \{I'\} \supset \{I\}}{\{I\} \quad \underline{repeat} \quad S \ \underline{end} \quad \{Q\}}$$

The rule for the event indicator statement is :

$$\frac{\{R_i\} \ ev_i \ \{\underline{false}\} \vdash \{I\} \ S_o \ \{I'\} \ \forall i \ (\ 1 \le i \le n) \qquad \{I'\} \supset \{I\} \qquad \{R_i\} \ S_i \ \{Q\}}{\{I\} \ \underline{loop} \ \underline{until} \ \cdots \ S_o \ \underline{repeat} \ ; \ \underline{then} \ \cdots \cdots \ \underline{end} \quad \{Q\}}$$

In the above rules, I is the invariant associated with the loop.
These rules, added to Hoare's axiomatic system, allow one to prove the
partial correctness of any program built ut with structured statements
that avoid the need for jumps of the return type.
In the last paragraph, examples of applications of the above statements
and rules are given.

Exit jumps : the notion of almost everywhere correctness of structured programs

The considerations developed in the previous paragraphs tend to indicate that the need for <u>goto</u> statements remains only for dealing with exit
jumps.   In this case, the <u>goto</u> statement is, indeed, more adequate
than the <u>exit</u> or <u>leave</u> statements to emphasize the break of the normal
computation due to the occurrence of an exceptional condition.
For specializing the <u>goto</u> statement to express exit jumps, thus introducing this semantic constraint into the language itself, we propose a
syntactic form like the following :

<u>on</u> 〈 condition 〉 <u>goto</u> 〈 label 〉

This statement emphasizes not only that control breaks away, under some
circumstances, from the normal flow, but also the condition under which
this case occurs, since such a condition appears explicitly in the statement.
If this condition is tought of as an exceptional condition (tipically,
an error condition), then the above restricted form of <u>goto</u> statement
plays a considerable role in imposing a correct and coherent expansion
of a block in the top-down program construction : the occurrence_ of
this condition must appear in the functional specification of the block
to be expanded.   Thus, the programmer is induded to have an early knowledge of the jump that will appear in the expansion, as an exceptional
interruption of the normal flow of the computation of the block that he
is going to implement.
The problem of proving correct a program in which a <u>goto</u> occurs, is there
fore 'semantically' restricted to the problem of proving correct a program in which an exit jump occurs, and in which the jump condition is
explicitly defined.
Let B be a component of a structured program in which a <u>goto</u> occurs, that
breaks away from B itself; if we assume the negation of the jump condition
as a precondition of block B, (or better as a part of the invariant of
the iterative statement in which the <u>goto</u> occurs) we can reduce ourselves to deal with B, except for <u>goto</u>'s; that is,the problem is reduced to
proving the normal computation case, and, possibly, the jump case, one
separately from the other.
It is important to remark that we can separate the two cases not only because we can substitute the block invariant condition I with the disjunc-
tive expression ($I \wedge \neg p) \vee (I \wedge p$), where p is the exit condition, but
also because the jump we are speaking about is an exit jump and therefore
we can assume that if the jump condition is true we don't need anymore
to reenter the normal flow of the algorithm. By such a method we isolate
the exceptional case and we prove the program in the normal case.
A program whose correctness has been proved but for <u>goto</u>'s , can be called an ' almost everywhere correct ' program.
Clint and Hoare had already attempted the axiomatization of jumps [2] .
They addressed their attention to jumps which cannot enter inside compound and conditional statements, but can go backward and downward, and
gave the following correctness rule :

$$\frac{\{Q\} \ \underline{goto} \ K \ \{\underline{false}\} \ \vdash \ \{P\} \ S_1 \ \{Q\} \qquad \{Q\} \ \underline{goto} \ K \ \{\underline{false}\} \ \vdash \ \{Q\} \ S_2 \ \{R\}}{\{P\} \ S_1 \ ; \ K : S_2 \qquad \{R\}}$$

where S_1 and S_2 are supposed to be two consecutive compound statements,
the latter labelled by K, each of which may contain statements <u>goto</u> K.
Label K is supposed to be the only one local to this part of the program, and Q is a condition which describes the state of the execution
at that point (Q must be true before any jump to K).
The authors themselves discussed the limitations of their rule,that is:
it can only deal with blocks containing a single label; it becomes cumbersome to be applied particularly if the jumps go backward;and,overall,
it leaves open the problem of identifying a precondition Q meaningful
enough to allow carrying on the proof.
In our approach, which is a particular case of that considered by Clint
and Hoare, the semantic limitation imposed on the <u>goto</u> statement,carried
over into its syntactic form, simplifies the proof. In fact, the precondition associated with the jump appears right inside the statement, and
the proof of the blocks containing the <u>gotos</u> is carried on not by formally imposing the condition <u>false</u> after the jumps, but by ignoring the
presence itself of the statement <u>on</u> p <u>goto</u>..., which is excluded by as-
sociating p with the invariant in the loop.
In the second example of the next paragraph we give a proof of the 'almost everywhere correctness' of a program.

Examples

As the first example we give the correctness proof of a program which uses Zahn's event indicator, limited as previously indicated.

Let us consider the well known "tree search and insertion" problem, where "a binary search tree is being represented by three arrays: $A(i)$ denotes the information stored at node number i, and $L(i)$, $R(i)$ are the respective node numbers for the roots of that node's left and right subtrees; empty subtrees are represented by zero. The program searches down the tree until finding an empty subtree where x can be inserted; and variable j points to an appropriate place to do the insertion. For convenience, we assume in this example that x is not already present in the search tree" [8] . The related program is the following:

```
loop until left leaf hit  or  right leaf hit :
     if A(i) < x
     then if L(i)≠ 0   then i:= L(i) else  left leaf hit
     else if R(i)≠ 0   then i:= R(i) else right leaf hit ;
repeat ;
then    left leaf hit  => L(i):= j ;
        right leaf hit  => R(i):= j ;
end ;
A(j):=x ; L(j):= 0 ; R(j):= 0 ; j:= j+1 ;
```

In order to construct the logical assertions, let us introduce the following notation :

$\text{Different}(A) \equiv \forall 1,k \left[1 \neq 0 \wedge k \neq 0 \wedge k \neq 1 \supset L(k) \neq R(1) \wedge L(k) \neq L(1) \wedge R(k) \neq L(1) \wedge R(k) \neq R(1) \right]$
        means that all the node numbers are different;

$\text{Ordered}(A) \equiv \forall k \left[L(k) \neq 0 \supset A(L(k)) > A(k) \wedge R(k) \neq 0 \supset A(R(k)) \leq A(k) \right]$

$\text{NO-J}(A) \equiv \forall k \left[L(k) < j \wedge R(k) < j \right]$
        means that the node number j has not yet been introduced in the tree ;

$\text{ONE-J}(A) \equiv \exists k' \left[\forall k \left[k \neq k' \supset \left[\left[L(k) < j \wedge L(k')=j \right] \vee \left[R(k) < j \wedge R(k')=j \right] \right] \right] \right]$
        means that the node number j has been introduced.

Thus, the initial assertion, which is the invariant too, is :
  $\text{Invariant} \equiv \text{Different}(A) \wedge \text{Ordered}(A) \wedge \text{NO-J}(A).$

The final assertion is :
  $\text{Final}(A) \equiv \exists k \left[\left[L(k)=j-1 \vee R(k)=j-1 \right] \wedge A(j-1)=x \wedge L(j-1)=0 \wedge R(j-1)=0 \right]$

The proof steps are the following :

1. $\{\text{Invariant}\}$ left leaf hit $\{\underline{\text{false}}\}$ $\wedge$
   $\{\text{Invariant}\}$ right leaf hit $\{\underline{\text{false}}\}$ $\vdash$
   $\{\text{Invariant}\}$ if $A(i) < x$ then ... else .... $\quad \{\text{Invariant}\}$
because of 2. , 3. and the conditional rule .

2. $\{\text{Invariant} \wedge A(i) < x \wedge L(i) \neq 0\}$ i:= L(i) $\{\text{Invariant}\}$ (assignment)

3. $\{\text{Invariant} \wedge A(i) \not> x \wedge R(i) \neq 0\}$ i:= R(i) $\{\text{Invariant}\}$ (assignment)

since the hypotheses of 1. , which hold for the 2. and 3. too, prevent the execution of the event statements.

4. $\{\text{Invariant}\}$ L(i):= j $\{\text{ONE-J}(A)\}$ (assignment)

5. $\{\text{Invariant}\}$ R(i):= j $\{\text{ONR-J}(A)\}$ (assignment)

From 1. ,4. and 5., by applying the event indicator rule, it follows :

6. $\{\text{Invariant}\}$ loop until .... repeat ... end $\{\text{ONE-J}(A)\}$

7. $\{\text{ONE-J}(A)\}$ A(j):= x ; L(j):=0 ; R(j)=0 ; j:= j+1 ; $\{\text{Final}(A)\}$
                                (assignment)

The proof is completed, by applying the composition rule to 6. and 7.

As the second example we give the correctness proof of a program realizing the "table search" algorithm : "find the first occurrence of x in a sequential table A and increment a counter v ariable associated with the matching table entry. If no match exists a new table entry is created for x and the associated counter variable initialized to 1 ". [14] Further, it is supposed that x belongs to an input file X. This program contains an exit jump, with the condition that the index n, which is the lenght of table A, is equal to a fixed index nmax. The program, using the previously given instructions <u>loop</u>...<u>when</u>...<u>endloop</u> and <u>on</u> ... <u>goto</u> , is the following :

```
    begin
    "Initialize table A" ;
    loop  x:= "read X" ;
       when EOFX  exitloop ;
       begin  i:= 1 ;
              loop
              when  A(i)= x  do  begin  m:= i ; B(m):= B(m)+1  end
              and  exitloop ;
              i:= i+1 ;
              when i > n do begin on n=nmax goto overflow; n:=n+1;
                                  A(n):=x; B(n):=1 end  and exitloop;
              endloop ;
       end
    endloop ;
    "Print complete table A"
    end ;
    ..........
  overflow :   "Print partial table A"
```

Since no explicit hypothesis is made on the table A and the file X , we indicate it with Table(A) and File(X) respectively, supposing that the elements of X may be added to the table A .   At the beginning, table B is supposed to have the same number of elements as table A and all set to 0.

Hence, the precondition of the whole program is :

$$\text{Precondition} \equiv \text{Table(A)} \land \text{File(X)} \land \text{Null Integer Table(B)} \land$$
$$\text{Card(A)} = \text{Card(B)}$$

where Card(A) is the number of elements of the table A .

The final condition is (indicating the number of occurrences of an element x in X as : Occ(x,X)) :

$$\text{Postcondition} \equiv (\forall x \in X)(\exists i)\,[A(i){=}x \land [(\forall k < i)\, A(k) \neq x] \land B(i)= Occ(x,X)]$$

We need further the loops invariants.

The invariant related to the external loop is :

$$I1 \equiv (\forall x \in X' \subseteq X)(\exists i)\,[A(i){=}x \land [(\forall k < i)\, A(k) \neq x] \land B(i){=}Occ(x,X') \land n \leq nmax]$$

The second invariant is :

$$I2 \equiv [x \in X' \subset X] \land (\forall k)\,[k < i \leq n \land A(i) \neq x]$$

In the proof the condition $n < nmax$, which is . the negation of the condition causing the exit jump , is always associated with the invariant I2 . The proof is thus " but for <u>goto</u> " and is carried on with the following steps :

1. $\{$ Precondition $\}$ "Initialize table A" $\{$ I1 $\}$ (since X' is empty)

2. $\{$ I1 $\wedge \neg$ EOFX $\}$ i:= 1 $\{$ I2 $\}$ (assignment : since i=1 implies that X' is empty)

3. $\{$ I2 $\wedge$ n < nmax $\wedge$ A(i)=x $\}$ <u>begin</u> m:=i ; B(m):= B(m)+1 <u>end</u> $\{$ I1 $\}$ (assignment and composition)

4. $\{$ I2 $\wedge$ n < nmax $\wedge$ A(i)$\neq$x $\}$ i:= i+1 $\{$ I2 $\wedge$ n < nmax $\}$ (assignment)

5. $\{$ I2 $\wedge$ n < nmax $\wedge$ i > n $\}$ <u>begin</u> <u>on</u> n=nmax <u>goto</u> overflow ; n:= n+1 ; A(n):=x ; B(n):= 1 <u>end</u> $\{$ I1 $\}$ (assignment and composition : since the n < nmax hypothesis prevents the execution of <u>goto</u>)

From 3. ,4. and 5. we have :

6. $\{$ I2 $\wedge$ n < nmax $\}$ <u>loop</u> <u>when</u> ..... <u>endloop</u> $\{$ I1 $\}$ (Ω_n rule)

From 2. and 6. we have :

7. $\{$ I1 $\wedge \neg$ EOFX $\}$ <u>begin</u> i:= 1; <u>loop</u> <u>when</u> ..... <u>endloop</u> $\{$ I1 $\}$ (composition)

From 7 , using the Ω_n rule we have :

8. $\{$ I1 $\}$ <u>loop</u> x:= "read X"... <u>begin</u> .... <u>end</u> <u>endloop</u> $\{$ I1 $\wedge$ EOFX $\}$ (assignment)

9. $\{$ I1 $\wedge$ EOFX $\} \supset \{$ Postcondition $\}$ (since EOFX implies X' $\equiv$ X)

From 1. and 9. we have :

10. $\{$ Precondition $\}$ <u>begin</u> "Initialize table A" ; <u>loop</u> ... <u>endloop</u> <u>end</u> $\{$ Postcondition $\}$ (composition)

References

[1] Böhm C., Jacopini G.:"Flow diagrams, Turing machines and languages
                with only two formation rules" CACM 9,5 1966
[2] Clint M., Hoare C.A.R.:"Program proving: jumps and functions"
                Acta Informatica 1   1972
[3] De Michelis G., Simone C.:"Well formed programs optimal with respect
                to structural complexity" Proc. GI-75 Conf.
                Springer Lecture Notes in Computer Science
[4] Dijkstra E.W.:"Goto statement considered harmful" CACM 11,3   1968
[5] Hoare C.A.R.:"An axiomatic basis for computer programming"
                CACM   12,10   1969
[6] Hopkins M.:"A case for the goto" SIGPLAN Not. 7,11   1972
[7] Knuth D.E.,Floyd R.V.:"Notes on avoiding goto statements" IPL 1,1
                1971
[8] Knuth D.E.:"Structured programming with goto statements"
                Comp. Surveys 6,4   1974
[9] Leavenworth B.M.:"Programming with(out) the goto" SIGPLAN Not.
                7,11   1972
[10] Wirth N.:"The programming language Pascal" Acta Informatica 1   1971
[11] Wirth N.:"On the composition of well structured programs"
                Comp. Surveys 6,4   1974
[12] Wulf W.A.:"Programming without the goto" in Information Processing
                71, North Holland , Amsterdam,   1972
[13] Wulf W.A.:"A case against the goto" SIGPLAN Not. 7,11   1972
[14] Zahn C.T.:"A control statement for natural top-down structured
                programming" Symp. Progr. Languages,
                Springer Lecture Notes in Computer Science
                1974

This research has been sponsored by HISI and by CNR (Progetto speciale
per l'Informatica).

LANGUAGE REPRESENTATION BASED ON ABSTRACT SYTAX

By H. Diel, IBM Labor Boeblingen

Introduction

For most of the traditional programming languages, the concept of
(concrete) syntax has been the only conceptual framework that relates
to the external representation of those languages. Nowadays, more and
more people realize that also such language features as extendability,
subsetting, and defaulting, which also deal with the external representation of the language need unique concepts. Moreover, more and more
people become aware that it is just as important to have these concepts
consistently integrated.

This paper proposes a method which provides a consistently integrated framework for all such languages features, including sematic prompting, that is, prompting without relation to the syntax of the language,
which up to now has not found much attention in programming literature.
This method is based on the concept of abstract syntax.

Section 1. Abstract Syntax

The concept of abstract syntax was introduced by Mc Carthy in 1962
[3,4] . The Vienna Definition Language (VDL) [1,2,5] incorporated
this concept into their language description method. Generally speaking, the abstract syntax of a language describes only information that
is essential for programs written in that language.

Example 1, which is written in VDL notation, shows the abstract
syntax for a given programming language X. The example assumes that
for this language the following information must be supplied with a
program:

- the user's name
- the program name
- one or more commands with name(s), attribute(s),
  or expression(s) depending on the type of command.

For the purpose of this paper a restriction is established for the
definition of a predicate (such as is-X-Program or is-attribute) in VDL
notation. The predicate must be defined in either of the following forms:

```
Form-1
    is-pred = is-pred-1 v ..... v is-pred-n


Form-2
    is-pred = ( <s-sel-1:is-pred-1> , ...
                <s-sel-n:is-pred-n> )
```

Example 1. Abstract syntax of language X

```
is-X-Program              = ( <s-user-name:is-USER-NAME> ,
                              <s-progr-name:is-PROGR-NAME> ,
                              <s-body:is-command-list> )

is-command                = is-declare-command v is-set-command

is-declare-command        = ( <s-name:is-NAME> ,
                              <s-attribute:is-attribute> )

is-attribute              = is-BINARY v is-DECIMAL

is-set-command            = ( <s-lhs-name:is-LHS-NAME > ,
                              <s-rhs-expression:is-RHS-EXPRESSION> )
```

Note: The meaning of underlining is-BINARY and is-DECIMAL is explained
         later.

An abstract syntax defined as shown in Example 1 can also be represented
as AND/OR graph, where the OR nodes refer to alternatives (see predicate
definition Form-1 above) and the AND nodes refer to the object composition (see predicate definition Form-2 above).

Example 2 shows an AND/OR graph representing the abstract syntax of
language X as defined in Example 1.

AND nodes are shown as $\bigwedge$.

OR nodes are shown as $\bigvee$.

Example 2.   Abstract syntax of language X as an AND/OR graph

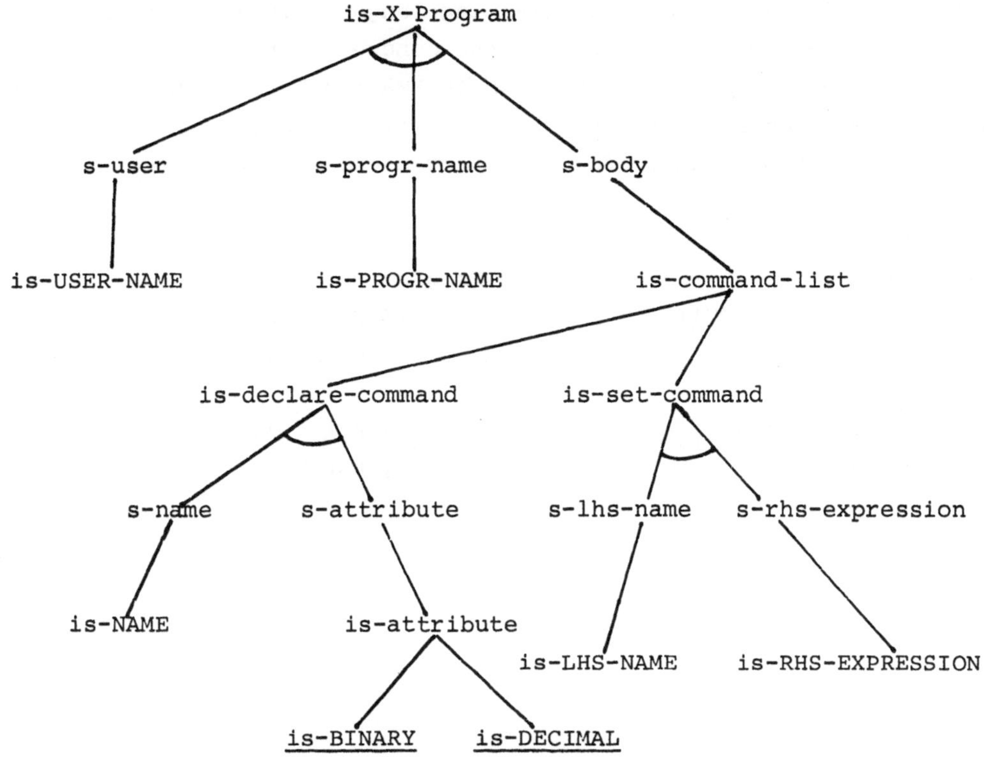

For the purpose of this paper the terminal nodes of an AND/OR graph representing the abstract syntax of a language are grouped into basic and non-basic ones.

A basic terminal node is a node for which a specific value must be provided in the actual program to indicate that this node is to be selected. The above example has two basic terminal nodes: is-BINARY and is-DECIMAL. These nodes are undersccored to differentiate them from the other, non-basic terminal nodes.

A non-basic terminal node is a node for which additional information must be supplied in the actual program. The node is-USER-NAME in Example 2 is a non-basic terminal node; in the actual program a character string representing the user's name must be provided. The remaining non-basic terminal nodes in Example 2 are: is-PROGR-NAME, is-NAME, is-LHS-NAME, is-RHS-EXPRESSION.

Admittedly, defining a node such as is-RHS-EXPRESSION as a terminal node is arbitrary. However, this decision has no bearing on the discussion in this paper.

Section 2. Association of concrete syntax to abstract syntax

Once the abstract syntax for a programming language is defined, there is still much freedom with respect to the concrete syntax for that language. For the abstract syntax shown in Example 1, for instance, the following three programs describe the same information, but all three (program A through program C) follow different concrete syntax.

```
Program A                              Program B
    PROG1: BEGIN USER (U1),            // START PRNAME = PROG1
           DCL A BIN,                  // DV A, BIN
           SET A = 1,                  // S A, 1
           SET A = A+1,                // S A, A+1
           END,                        /& USER = U1
```

```
Program C
    BEGIN OF PROG1 FOR USER U1.
    DECLARE A AS BINARY.
    SET A TO 1.
    SET A TO A+1.
```

These three examples show the flexibility of abstract syntax. The abstract syntax for a language can be considered as the common image of several concrete syntax representations. Although this allows much freedom in selecting a certain concrete syntax, any concrete syntax that is mapped onto an abstract syntax must meet the following requirements:

. It must contain all the information that is also contained in the abstract syntax.
. Its structure must correspond to the structure of the abstract syntax.

Suppose that for a specific term -- an attribute, for example -- the abstract syntax distinguishes between several cases such as binary and decimal. According to the requirements stated above, the concrete syntax must also distinguish those cases. Should the abstract syntax call for additional information for any such case, then the concrete syntax must also express a requirement for the same additional information.

Obviously, the abstract syntax concept allows enough freedom in selecting a concrete syntax to offer programming languages which may have different external representations. For example, one standard concrete syntax could be provided and users could define additional personal (concrete syntax) representations.

Before the above requirements can be cast in a set of rules, the notation used in this paper to describe concrete syntax should be introduced.

Notation for Concrete syntax

The notation used in this paper to describe concrete syntax is an extended and modified BNF notation. The extensions and modifications are as follows:

- The syntax description for a specific term is initiated by
  syntax (term)::=
- Non-terminal symbols are written in angular brackets (e.g. ⟨set-command⟩). If a non-terminal symbol corresponds to the same term in a Form-1 abstract syntax description, then it carries the abstract syntax selector as a label in the concrete syntax description. Example:

  ⟨s-attribute:attribute⟩

  where s-attribute is the label.

  This extension was made for ease of association of concrete syntax items with abstract syntax items.
- Terminal symbols are any characters (or character strings) except ⟨, ⟩, v, and lower case letters. However, complex syntactical terms such as expressions and identifiers can be defined as so called non-basic terminal symbols. Those are written like non-terminal symbols, however, the name of the symbol is given in upper case letters. Example:

  ⟨s-user-name:is-USER-NAME⟩
- Lists of non-terminal symbols are indicated by the suffix -list. This list notation is not provided for any other case.
- The end of a syntax description is indicated by an underscored dot (.).

  Note that alternatives are written as usual, i. e. separated by v.

Furthermore, it is a requirement, that the syntax description be written in a kind of canonical form, that is, each definition should have either of the following forms:

Form-1:
    syntax (term)::= list of terminal and/or
                            non-terminal symbols

Form-2:
    syntax (term)::= list of alternatives

Example 3. Concrete syntax for Program A, above.

syntax (is-X-Program)::=
    ⟨s-progr-name:is=PROGR-NAME ⟩:BEGIN USER (
    ⟨s-user name: is-USER-NAME ⟩),
    ⟨s-body:is-command-list ⟩ END,.

syntax (is-command)::= ⟨is-decl-command⟩ v
                    ⟨is-set-command⟩.

syntax (is-decl-command)::=
    DCL ⟨s-name:is-NAME⟩
        ⟨s-attribute:is-attribute⟩ ,.

syntax (is-attribute)::= ⟨is-decimal⟩ v
                    ⟨is-binary ⟩.

syntax (is-decimal)::=DEC v DECIMAL.

syntax (is-binary) ::=BIN.

syntax (is-set-command)::=
    SET ⟨s-lhs-name:is-LHS-NAME⟩
    = ⟨s-rhs-expression:is-RHS-EXPRESSION⟩ ,.

Rules for associating concrete syntax with abstract syntax

These rules are given and discussed below; they show how an abstract
syntax can be extracted from a concrete syntax. If the abstract syntax
so generated is equivalent to the abstract syntax of the language under
consideration, then that concrete syntax is associable with the abstract
syntax. This means that the concrete syntax and the abstract syntax can
be considered as representing the same language.

The rules for generating an abstract syntax from a concrete syntax are
as follows:

1. If the concrete syntax definition for the considered term contains
    non-terminal or non-basic terminal symbols, then:
    a. A Form-1 concrete syntax definition is changed to a Form-1
        abstract syntax definition by eliminating all basic terminal
        symbols and by some minor editorial changes such as separating
        the elements by comma; deleting the word 'syntax (' or symbols
        such as') ', ':=', and '.'.
    b. A Form-2 concrete syntax definition is changed to a Form-2
        abstract syntax definition by some minor editorial changes such
        as explained under a, above, and by eliminating the angle
        brackets (< >).

2. If the concrete syntax definition does not contain a non-terminal
    or non-basic terminal symbol, no abstract syntax definition is
    generated for that term. Instead within the whole abstract syntax
    definition of the considered language, the appearance of that term
    is changed to a basic terminal node; that is the lower case letters
    are changed to upper case letters and the entire symbol is under-
    scored.

    Obviously, the above rules when applied to Example 3 result in an
    abstract syntax as shown in Example 1, except that the two elements
      <s-progr-name:is-PROGR-NAME>
      <s-user-name:is-USER-NAME>
    appear in reverse order. According to VDL, however, this does not
    change the equivalence relation between two abstract syntaxes.

Section 3. Language Extensions

This section discusses how the concept of an abstract syntax can be used (1) as a basis for the definition of language extensions and (2) to define the extensions themselves.

Using an abstract syntax as basis for extensions

When a language is to be extended, it is important to know where, in the language structure, extensions are allowed. The approaches vary. Examples of various approaches are:

1. Extensions are allowed only for certain terms (e.g. ALGOL 68).
2. Extensions are allowed for any concrete syntax non-terminal
    (e.g. Gallers ALGOL D).
3. Extensions are allowed for any portion of the source text
    (e.g. macro facilities).

In this section it is proposed to consider extensions as additions of alternatives to existing alternative lists (OR nodes) of the abstract syntax. This sounds very similar to item 2 above. However, it provides two distinct advantages over the extension schemes for item 2, and these advantages are discussed below.

First advantage: The extensions are independent of the concrete syntax of the language. As has been shown in section 2, it might be useful to offer programming languages with different external representations. If then an extension is required, it is reasonable to associate this extension with a specific term of the abstract syntax rather than of the concrete syntax. Of course either the concrete syntax of the extension must be compatible with the concrete syntax of the different representations in which the extension is used or it must be possible to define a different concrete syntax of the extension for the various representations. However, this does not eliminate the requirement that the location where an extension applies to must be independent of the different external representations.

Second advantage: The extensions apply automatically also to other concepts of language representations such as prompting, defaulting and subsetting. Assuming that the implementation of those features be done by use of the concepts described in the following sections, this would allow to incorporate them into language extensions.

Using abstract syntax to define extensions

For existing extension schemes the following kind of information has to
be supplied with an extension definition:
1. Definition of the invocation. In many cases this is mainly a speci-
    fication of the parameters for the extension.
2. Definition of the expansion, i.e., of the text that will replace
    the original text on invocation.

For the extension scheme proposed here, essentially the same kind
of information has to be supplied, plus some additional information
needed to control the defaulting, subsetting, and prompting facilities.
Thus the following has to be specified for an extension:
1. General information (for example: name of the extension, term in
    abstract syntax to which extension applies).
2. Parameters of the extension, that is, essential information that
    must be supplied by the user when using the extension.
3. Invocation specification.
4. Expansion specification.
5. Prompting specification.
6. Defaulting specification.
7. Subsetting specification.

For our discussion, items 2. through 4 are the most interesting
ones. Looking at these items more closely as they are discussed below,
we can find that item 3, the invocation specification, relates to item 2,
the parameter specification, like a concrete syntax definition to a
pertinent abstract syntax. Conversely, the parameter specification relates to item 4, the expansion specification, like the abstract syntax
of a language definition to the corresponding concrete syntax definition.
In summary, the parameters can be viewed as an abstract syntax (AND/OR
graph) while the invocation specification and the expansion specification
each describe a concrete syntax that can be associated to this abstract
syntax.

The foregoing shows that extension definitions can be written using
the method suggested in this paper, Example 4, shows how items 2 through
4 might look like in an actual extension definition. The example uses
some notation that has not been defined in this paper, but is considered
self-explantory.

Considering the expansion definition as a concrete syntax which can
be associated to the (parameters) abstract syntax requires a minor addition to the rules for extracting an abstract syntax from a concrete
syntax. As Example 4 shows, it is reasonable to allow the multiple

appearance of a certain selector (e.g., s-name) in the concrete syntax. On the other hand, of course, this selector must not appear more than once in the extracted abstract syntax. Hence the following additional rule applies: multiple use of a specific selector in a concrete syntax definition for a single term results in only one appearance of that selector in the extracted abstract syntax definition.

It is worth noting here that the parameter specification part is redundant in an extension definition since, as shown previously, this information can also be extracted from the invocation specification and/ or expansion specification.

Example 4. Extension definition for language X.

```
EXTENSION DEFINTION FOR 'COMMAND'
        NAME = 'INITAL-COMMAND'


PARAMETER SPECIFICATION:/*ABSTRACT SYNTAX*/
        Initial-command=
                ( ⟨s-name:is-NAME⟩ ,
                  ⟨s-attribute:is-attribute⟩ ,
                  ⟨s-rhs-expression:is-RHS-EXPRESSION⟩ )


INVOCATION SPECIFICATION: /*CONCRETE SYNTAX (1)*/
        syntax (Initial-command)::=
        DEFINE  ⟨s-name:is-NAME⟩
          AS    ⟨s-attribute:is-attribute⟩
        INITIALIZE TO   ⟨s-rhs-expression:is-RHS-EXPRESSION⟩ ,


EXPANSION SPECIFICATION: /*CONCRETE SYNTAX (2)*/
        syntax (Initial-command)::=
                DCL   ⟨s-name:is-NAME⟩
                      ⟨s-attribute:is-attribute⟩ ,
                SET   ⟨s-name:is-NAME⟩
                =     ⟨s-rhs-expression:is-RHS-EXPRESSION⟩ ,
```

Example 4 would result in the following: Suppose the string
        DEFINE X AS BIN INITIALIZE TO 10,
is written in an actual program at a location where the syntax allows for commands. This string would then be translated to the string
        DCL X BIN, SET X = 10,

Section 4. Prompting

Two kinds of prompting can be distinguished:

1. Syntactic Prompting: The user must supply his program in the correct
    concrete syntax of the language used. However, the user gets guid-
    ance from the sytem in building his input.

2. Semantic Prompting: The user does not need to know the concrete
    syntax. Instead the system obtains from him all relevant information
    in a question and answer process.

    Since syntactic prompting is more or less an implementation
consideration this section addresses aspects only of sematic prompting.

Associating semantic prompting information with abstract syntax

In semantic prompting, the system asks the user appropriate questions
to obtain all the relevant information. But, what type of information
comprises information relevant to the system? What is the essential
information of a program? What are the decisions the user has to make
and what is the information he must supply? The abstract syntax, per
definition, describes this information.

Now, in order to support semantic prompting for a language with a
given abstract syntax, it is only necessary to associate prompting
information with the nodes of the AND/OR tree for the abstract syntax.
Specifically, the following information is required:

1. For each OR node:
    .   The text to be displayed
    .   For each alternatives, the string that the user must provide
        when he selects an alternative.
2. For each non-basic terminal node:
    .   The text to be displayed.
3. For each node denoting a list:
    .   The text to be displayed.
    .   Two strings, one indicating continuation of the list and one
        indicating the end of the list.

No information is required for any of the remaining nodes.

    Example 5 shows the specification of prompting information for
language X (compare this with Example 1). Most of the notation used in
the example is self-explanatory. However, the prompting information for
a specific term (or node) is identified by

        prompt-inf (term)::=

followed by the character string to be displayed and, optionally, a set
of alternate reply specifications.

Example 5. Specification of prompting information for language X

```
prompt-inf (is-USER-NAME)::=          'TYPE YOUR NAME';

prompt-inf (is-PROGR-NAME)::=         'TYPE NAME OF PROGRAM';

prompt-inf (is-command)::=            'WHICH COMMAND?
                                      D    DECLARE COMMAND
                                      S    SET COMMAND'
reply (is-declare-command) = 'D',
reply (is-set-command) = 'S';


prompt-inf (is-command-list)::=       'FURTHER COMMANDS?
                                      Y    YES
                                      N    NO'
reply (continue) = 'Y',
reply (no-continue) = 'N';


prompt-inf (is-NAME)::=               'TYPE NAME';

prompt-inf (is-attribute)::=          'WHICH ATTRIBUTE?
                                      B    BINARY
                                      D    DECIMAL'
reply (is-BINARY) = 'B',
reply (is-DECIMAL) = 'D'


prompt-inf (is-LHS-NAME)::=           'TYPE NAME OF TARGET VARIABLE';

prompt-inf (is-RHS-EXPRESSION)::=     'TYPE EXPRESSION';
```

Output of Semantic Prompter

The output of a semantic prompter could be either of the following:

- One of the external representations of the program, (possibly in
  stylised format).
- Exactly the same as that which would have been produced by a syntax
  input translator had the program been specified by the user in the
  correct concrete syntax of the language used.

Relatively simple algorithms can be shown for prompters generating
either kind of output.

Example 6, illustrates the prompting sequence for part of the program
A (or B, or C) as shown in Section 2.

System message	Users reply
TYPE NAME	
	A

WHICH ATTRIBUTE?
    B BINARY
    D DECIMAL	

	B

FURTHER COMMANDS?
    Y YES
    N NO	

	Y

WHICH COMMAND?
    D DECLARE
    S SET COMMAND	

	S
TYPE NAME OF TARGET VARIABLE	
	A
TYPE EXPRESSION	
	1

FURTHER COMMANDS?
    Y YES
    N NO	

	Y

WHICH COMMAND?
    D DECLARE
    S SET COMMAND	

	S
TYPE NAME OF TARGET VARIABLE	
	A
TYPE EXPRESSION	
	A+1

FURTHER COMMANDS?
    Y YES
    N NO	

	N

Application of extensions to prompting

Earlier in this section, it was shown how information can be associated
to the abstract syntax allowing semantic prompting for that program.
Since an extension definition contains also the extension's abstract
syntax (=parameter specification), prompting information can easily be
associated also with extensions. Thus by making the prompting specification a mandatory part of an extension definition, the function of
semantic prompting can be readily applied also to extensions.

Section 5. Possible further applications of abstract syntax language
representation.

The concept of abstract syntax can be applied to allmost any feature
which usually is considered in terms of the concrete syntax only. Two
more examples of such a features are subsetting and defaulting. From
these two features only the latter is discussed below in little more
details.

In most programming languages there exist areas where default values
are taken if no value is specified by the user. There are also some
languages where the user can specify his own default values for parameters being defaultable. The concept of abstract syntax allows defaultable areas to be specified and provides for default values to apply
automatically also to semantic prompting. The method proposed considers
each OR node as a potential candidate with which default values can be
associated. A default value represents an instance for the whole subtree of the corresponding OR node.

Since default values should automatically apply to both the concrete
syntax of all representations and to the semantic prompting the default
value must be stored in the internal form chosen by the implementation
(this internal form may be considered as an instance of the abstract
syntax).

The example below illustrates the specification of a defaultable
area and an associated default value for a given language. For this
example, assume that the language designer (or user) would like to define
a default attribute. This could be done in two steps, that is, in two
statements as follows:

```
DEFAULTABLE_AREA=is-attribute;
DEFAULT_VALUE (is attribute)=is-BINARY;
```

Note: Although so far defaulting has been defined without relation to
concrete syntax, the decision to apply default values must be made, of
course, on the basis of the user's (concrete syntax or prompting) input
text.

Obviously, default values can be indicated in two ways: 1.by a
special character (string) or 2. by omission of a pertinent input
specification. Of course, each of the two possibilities effects the
concrete syntax of the language. However, these effects are not subject of discussion here.

SUMMARY

Extendability, prompting and other features that are related to the representation of a programming language can be effectively formulated, handled and controlled by defining them in terms of an abstract syntax. Relation of these features to the common abstract syntax provides, in addition, a consistently integrated frame for them.

To keep this paper reasonably compact many a topic has only be sketched. Certain restrictions (e.g. for the syntax notation) were made for better comprehension of the subjects. Should the concepts discussed in this paper be implemented, most of these restrictions could be removed entirely or in part.

Discussion and examples presented in this paper show that the proposed concepts can be applied to the definition of any programming language which has a natural relation between its concrete syntax and its abstract syntax. As a matter of fact, these concepts were applied even to language definitions whose concrete syntaxes did not have an apparent relation with the corresponding abstract syntax.

REFERENCES

(1) LUCAS, P., LAUER, P., STIGLEITNER, H. - Method and Notation for the Formal Definition of Programming Languages.
IBM Laboratory Vienna, Techn. Report TR 25.087, 28. June 1968, revised 1 July 1970.

(2) LUCAS, P., WALK. - On the Formal Description of PL/I. Annual Review of Automatic Programming, 6 Part 3, 1970, p. 105.

(3) McCARTHY, J. - Towards a Mathematical Science of Computation.
In: Information Processing 1962 (C.M.POPPLEWELL, Ed.) North-Holland Publ. Comp., Amsterdam 1963, pp. 21-28.

(4) McCARTY, J. - A Formal Description of a Subset of ALGOL.
In: Formal Language Description Languages (T.B. STEEL Jr., Ed.), Proc. IFIP Working Conference, Vienna 1964;
North-Holland Publ. Comp., Amsterdam 1965 1965, pp. 1-12.

(5) WALK, K., ALBER, K. FLECK, M., GOLDMANN, H., MOSER, E., OLIVA, P., STIGLEITNER, H., ZEISEL, G.
Abstract Syntax and Interpretation of PL/I.
IBM Laboratory VIENNA, Techn. Report TR 25.098, 30 June 1969.

ON THE COMPLEXITY OF DECISION PROBLEMS

FOR CLASSES OF SIMPLE PROGRAMS ON STRINGS

G.Ausiello - M.Moscarini

Istituto di Automatica, Centro di Studio
dei Sistemi di Controllo e Calcolo Automa
tici del C.N.R., Via Eudossiana,18 - Roma

SUMMARY

1. Motivation and relation to other work

2. Definitions and basic properties

3. Classes of simple programs on strings

4. Decidability properties for simple programs on strings

5. An undecidability result

6. References

ABSTRACT

Classes of simple programs operating on strings are considered.
Their power as acceptors and their power as generation devices are compared and consequences on upper bounds and lower bounds for several decision problems are derived. It is shown that even for such a small
class of programs some problems are undecidable.

1. MOTIVATION AND RELATION TO OTHER WORK

The interest for studying the properties of small classes of programs comes from different areas of Computer science. The first reason
(at least from a historical point of view) is to characterize the computational power achieved by using particular data structures, particular primitives, particular control structures. Some relevant work in
this direction has been done by Meyer and Ritchie (1967) with the intro
duction of the so-called LOOP programs and of the hierarchy of classes
of programs L_n defined by depth of nesting of LOOP instructions.

Strictly related to the syntactic characterization of classes of
programs is the complexity of their decision problems. Like the problem
of equivalence of regular expressions has been shown to become harder
and harder as long as new, more powerful operators (squaring, intersection, complement) are allowed (see Meyer and Stockmeyer (1972) and Meyer

and Stockmeyer (1973)), the same can be expected for equivalence in small classes of programs: by adding new features to a programming language which either increase the power of the language or allow to write more succint programs, the properties of the programs become harder to decide. In this direction the work of Jones and Muchnick (1975) deals exhaustively with the class of programs (FMP: Finite memory programs) which compute exactly the finite state mappings. Several problems, which are shown to be exactly of linear nondeterministic space complexity, become quadratic or even exponential when a variable word size or subscripted identifiers are allowed.

Another reason for exploring this research area comes from the point of view of the semantics of programs. Since we know what are the theoretical and practical difficulties of automatically proving properties of programs it would be reasonable to look for small classes of programs which correspond to non trivial classes of functions, but whose properties are decidable. An example of such classes is the class L_1^+ (Cherniavsky (1974)) which gives an exact realization of the theory of integer addition (Presburger arithmetic): given any relation $R(x_1, \ldots \ldots, x_n)$ described by a formula $R[x_1, \ldots, x_n]$ in the language of the theo$\underline{\text{o}}$ ry there is a program π in the programming language L_1^+ such that $\pi(a_1, \ldots, a_n)$ halts iff $R[a_1, \ldots, a_n]$ is valid (also a notion of functional realization of Presburger arithmetic is given, and it is satisfied by the same programming language) and viceversa.

Unfortunately even if, in all cases, the semantics of the classes of programs is very restricted, the properties are already intractably hard (for example, in the last case, the equivalence requires at least exponential time).

A different approach has been followed by Cook (1975) whose aim is to characterize the class E_2^Σ of feasibly (polynomial time) computable functions by providing a logical theory whose formulas are equations of the form $t = u$ (where t and u are terms built out of variables, constants and function symbol ranging over E_2^Σ) and whose theorems are conjectured to be exactly the formulas which have a polynomially long verification (that is the number of steps for verifying an instance $t(x) = =u(x)$ is uniformly polynomially bounded in $|x|$. An interpretation of

Cook's results in term of properties of programs, though, is not possi
ble because no definition is known of a programming language which allows to define programs for exactly the functions in E_2^Σ and, besides,
some relevant properties such as equivalence are already undecidable
at this level.

In this paper we carry on the exploration of the properties of
small classes of programs by considering how these properties are affec
ted by a change of the data structures on which the programs operate.
For this purpose, first of all, we present an extension of LOOP programs
from integer to string manipulation. This extension is achieved by introducing, together with the new date structure, also new primitive o-
perations and new interpretations of the LOOP control structure. The na
turality of this extension of the LOOP programming language is shown by
the first results in §2.

Classes of "simple" LOOP programs on strings with only one loop
level are then considered (§3) and their power as language acceptors
is shown.   Finally (§4) we state upper bounds and lower bounds
for decision problems an classes of simple programs on strings and
(§5) we show that already for classes of programs with such a particular control structure some problems become undercidable.

2. DEFINITIONS AND BASIC PROPERTIES

In this paragraph we will give the definitions of classes of programs for manipulating strings, based on the LOOP control structure
(Meyer and Ritchie (1967)).

In order to express the operational semantics of LOOP programs on
strings we have to think of each identifier as being the name of a register which contains an arbitrary word in Σ^*. Then the statements have the following meaning:

a) $\langle id_1 \rangle = \varepsilon$:   clear register $\langle id_1 \rangle$;

b) $\langle id_1 \rangle = \langle id_2 \rangle$:   transfer the content of $\langle id_2 \rangle$ in regi-
                             ster $\langle id_1 \rangle$;

c) $\langle id_1 \rangle = \sigma_j - \text{SUCC} \ \langle id_1 \rangle$:   compute the σ_j right (left) successor of
                                    the word which is in $\langle id_1 \rangle$ and put the
                                    result in $\langle id_1 \rangle$;

Let $\Sigma = \{\sigma_1, \ldots, \sigma_n\}$ be a finite alphabet. Let us define   the fol-

151

lowing classes of programs (LOOP programs on strings)

DEFINITION 1. A program π is in the class L_o^Σ of *LOOP-programs on strings* if it is a finite sequence of statements of the form a), b),c) where $\langle id_1 \rangle$, $\langle id_2 \rangle$ are identifiers out of a countably infinite set of identifiers. A program π is in the class L_{i+1}^Σ $(i \geq 0)$ if

    i) π is in L_i^Σ

    ii) π is of the form   LOOP $\langle id_1 \rangle$ $\sigma_1 : \pi_1 ; \ldots ; \sigma_n : \pi_n$ END

         where $\pi_1, \ldots, \pi_n$ are in L_i^Σ

    iii) π is the concatenation of two programs in L_{i+1}^Σ

The LOOP control structure is interpreted by the following informal program:

- transfer the content of $\langle id_1 \rangle$ in the register $\langle control \rangle$;
- while $\langle control \rangle \neq \varepsilon$ execute

    π_i if the leftmost (rightmost) character of $\langle control \rangle$ is σ_i;

    erase the leftmost (rightmost) character of $\langle control \rangle$.

As we can see, every LOOP program on strings can be interpreted in four possible ways.

Accordingly we have the following definitions:

DEFINITION 2. i) A *LOOP program on strings is in the class* $L_i^{LR,\Sigma}$ if it is in the class L_i^Σ and the successor is a left successor (denoted $\langle id \rangle \circ \sigma_j \rangle$) and the LOOP instruction requires the rightward scanning of the content of $\langle id \rangle$ (denoted R LOOP $\langle id \rangle$). Analogously are defined the classes $L_i^{LL,\Sigma}$, $L_i^{RR,\Sigma}$, $L_i^{RL,\Sigma}$.

    ii) *A function* $f : (\Sigma^*)^m \to \Sigma^*$ *is said to be in the class* $L_i^{LL,\Sigma}$ (resp. $L_i^{LR,\Sigma}$, $L_i^{RR,\Sigma}$, $L_i^{RL,\Sigma}$) if there is a program π in $L_i^{LL,\Sigma}$ (resp. $L_i^{LR,\Sigma}$, $L_i^{RR,\Sigma}$, $L_i^{RL,\Sigma}$) such that if it is started with $x_1, \ldots, x_m$ in m specified input registers (*) it terminates with y in a specified output register if and only if $f(x_1, \ldots, x_n) = y$.

In future we will allow the notation X=f(Z,Y) to stand for the program which computes the function f of the content of registers Z and Y and puts the result in X: for example X=reverse (X), X=conc(Y,Z),etc.

The following basic properties are immediate consequences of the definitions and of results of Henke, Indermark and Weihrauch (1972):

(*) All other registers are initialized to ε

152

Basic properties

i)   For $|\Sigma|=1$, $L_i^{LL,\Sigma}=L_n^{LR,\Sigma}=L_n^{RR,\Sigma}=L_n^{RL,\Sigma}$ for all $n\geq 0$ and f L_n iff

$\lambda x_1 \ldots \lambda x_m [\sigma_1^{f(|x_1|,\ldots,|x_m|)}] \in L_n$ (all LOOP programs on one letter

strings correspond exactly to LOOP programs on integers).

ii)   For all Σ and all n the LL(RR) LOOP classes coincide with the clas-

ses of functions defined by depth of nesting of simultaneous pri-

mitive left (resp. right) recursion on notation with the left

(resp.right) successor as basic function, introduced in $[14]$.

For example, let $f_1,\ldots,f_m$ be defined as follows

$$f_i(\bar{x},\varepsilon) = g_i(\bar{x}) \qquad\qquad i=1,\ldots,m; \quad j=1,\ldots,n$$

$$f_i(\bar{x},\,w\sigma_j) = h_{ij}(\bar{x},w,f_1(\bar{x},w),\ldots,f_m(\bar{x},w))$$

then the function f_i is computed by the following program:

```
            IN{X̄, W}; OUT F_i      (*)
            F 1 = g_1(X̄)
            ...
            F m = g_m(X̄)
            Y = ε
            RLOOP W
            ...
            σ_j : F 1 = h_1j(X̄,Y, F 1 ,...,F m)
            ...
                  F m = h_mj(X̄, Y, F1,...,Fm)
                  Y = Y o σ_j
            ...
            END
```

iii) For all Σ, $n\geq 2$ $L_n^{LL,\Sigma}=L_n^{LR,\Sigma}=L_n^{RR,\Sigma}=L_n^{RL,\Sigma}=E_{n+1}^{\Sigma}$ (from the second LOOP

level, analogously to what happens for LOOP programs integers,

(see Meyer and Ritchie (1967) and Grzegorczyk (1953)) the LOOP hie-

rarchy and the Grzegorczyk - like hierarchy on strings coincide).

(*) In the first statement the input variables and the output variable are declared.

3. CLASSES OF SIMPLE PROGRAMS ON STRINGS

In what follows we will concentrate on the classes of functions computable with only one LOOP level. In the case of LOOP programs on integers Tsichritzis (1970) characterizes the one LOOP level class of functions in terms of basic functions and closure under composition ("simple functions") and from this characterization he derives decidability properties for the class of programs L_1 ("simple programs"). In order to establish decidability results for the programs in the classes L_1^Σ we examine more carefully some of their properties. Let $|\Sigma| \geq 2$

FACT 1   i) $L_o^{\Sigma,RR} \equiv L_o^{\Sigma,RL}$ and $L_o^{\Sigma,LL} \equiv L_o^{\Sigma,LR}$

            ii) $L_o^{\Sigma,RR} \not\equiv L_o^{\Sigma,LL}$

PROOF   i) obvious

          ii) $f_R(x) = x \circ w$ is in $L_o^{\Sigma,RR}$ and not in $L_o^{\Sigma,LL}$ while $f_L(x) = w \circ x$ is in $L_o^{\Sigma,LL}$ and not in $L_o^{\Sigma,RR}$

$$Q\,E\,D$$

FACT 2 $L_o^{\Sigma,RR} \cup L_o^{\Sigma,LL} \subsetneq L_1^{\Sigma,RR} \cap L_1^{\Sigma,LL}$

PROOF   The containment is immediately proved. The fact that it is proper derives from the fact that the concatenation is in any of L_1^Σ but in nome of L_o^Σ

$$Q\,E\,D$$

The relative properties of the classes defined by one LOOP level programs are summarized in the following result:

THEOREM 3.   i) $L_1^{\Sigma,RR} \subsetneq L_1^{\Sigma,RL}$; $L_1^{\Sigma,LL} \subsetneq L_1^{\Sigma,LR}$

            ii) $f \in L_1^{\Sigma,RR}$ iff $\tilde{f} \in L_1^{\Sigma,LL}$ where

$$\tilde{f}(x_1,\ldots,x_n) = \widetilde{f(\tilde{x}_1,\ldots,\tilde{x}_n)} \qquad (*)$$

            iii) $L_1^{\Sigma,RL} \equiv L_1^{\Sigma,LR}$

PROOF   i) The "reverse" function is in both $L_1^{\Sigma,RL}$ and $L_1^{\Sigma,LR}$ but in none of $L_1^{\Sigma,LL}$ and $L_1^{\Sigma,RR}$. On the other side any func̲tion in $L_1^{\Sigma,RR}(L_1^{\Sigma,LL})$ is computable by RL(LR) programs

---

(*) With the notation $\tilde{x}$ we denote the string x reversed

because the sequence

R LOOP X

π

END

can be realized by

y = reverse (X)

L LOOP Y

π

END

ii) We will prove that $f \in L_1^{\Sigma,RR}$ implies $\tilde{f} \in L_1^{\Sigma,LL}$ (the other part of the statement has a symmetrical proof).

In order to prove the result we show the following *Claim:* given any program π in $L_1^{\Sigma,RR}$ there is a program $\tilde{\pi}$ in $L_1^{\Sigma,LL}$ such that if at the beginning of the execution of π the content of all registers is $x_1,\ldots,x_n$ and at the end of the execution of π the content of all registers is $z_1,\ldots,z_n$, then when the registers of $\tilde{\pi}$ are initiali zed to $\tilde{x}_1,\ldots,\tilde{x}_n$, the content of the registers at the end of the execution of $\tilde{\pi}$ is $\tilde{z}_1,\ldots,\tilde{z}_n$.

The claim can be proved by induction on the structure of the definition of a program in $L_1^{RR,\Sigma}$. The only non trivial case is when π is of the form

R LOOP X ... ; $\sigma_i : \pi_i$; ... END

Let $\tilde{\pi}$ be the following program:

L LOOP X ...; $\sigma_i : \tilde{\pi}_i$; ... END

where any $\tilde{\pi}_i$ is the program in $L_o^{\Sigma,LL}$ obtained by replacing right successors with left successors in π_i. Without loss of generality we may assume that X does not oc cur in the LOOP body and we may prove the claim by induction on the length of the content of the word x contained in X.

iii) The proof is very similar to the proof of part ii).First it can be proved that f is in $L_1^{\Sigma,RL}$ iff $\tilde{f}$ is in $L_1^{\Sigma,LR}$. Then it can be observed that f is in $L_1^{\Sigma,RL}(L_1^{\Sigma,LR})$ iff $\tilde{f}$ is in $L_1^{\Sigma,RL}(L_1^{\Sigma,LR})$ because the reversal can be defined in $L_1^{\Sigma,RL}(L_1^{\Sigma,LR})$.

$$Q\,E\,D$$

For what it concerns the relation among the L_1^Σ classes and other known classes of string functions and transductions, the following facts hold:

FACT 4   i) $L_1^{\Sigma,RL} \asymp E_o^\Sigma$

  ii) $L_1^{\Sigma,RL} \subsetneq E_1^\Sigma$

PROOF   i) Concatenation is in $L_1^{\Sigma,RL}$ but not in E_o^Σ. On the other side Rose and Weihrauch (1973) show that if f is in $L_1^{\Sigma,LL}$ then there exists a k such that for all $z \in$ range (f) $\exists\, x_1,\ldots,x_n$ such that $f(x_1,\ldots,x_n)=z$ and $\Sigma|x_i|\leq k(|z|+1)$. The same can be easily seen to hold for $L_1^{\Sigma,RL}$.

Since the function sqrt such that for all x

$$|\mathrm{sqrt}(x)| = \lfloor\sqrt{|x|}\rfloor$$

is definable in E_o^Σ and is not in $L_1^{\Sigma,RL}$ the proof is completed.

  ii) For all functions f in $L_1^{\Sigma,RL}$ it can be shown that there are constants $c_1,\ldots,c_n$ such that

$$|f(x_1,\ldots,x_n)| \leq \Sigma c_i|x_i|$$

Hence all functions in $L_1^{\Sigma,RL}$ can be defined in E_1^Σ by primitive recursion on notation limited by concatenation. On the other side fact 4 i) implies proper containment.

Q E D

DEFINITION 4. A *generalized sequential machine* is a 6-tuple $M = \,=\langle K,\Sigma,\Delta,\delta,\lambda,q_o\rangle$ where K is the finite set of states, Σ is the input alphabet, Δ is the output alphabet, $\delta{:}K \times (\Sigma\cup\{\cent\})\to K$ is the state transition function, $\lambda{:}K \times (\Sigma\cup\{\cent\})\to\Delta^*$ is the output function, q_o is the initial state.

DEFINITION 5. Let M be a generalized sequential machine; let $\bar\lambda$; $\bar\delta$ be the output function and the state transition function extended to Σ^+. Then we denote by g_M the mapping defined by $g_M(x) = \bar\lambda(q_o,x)$ for every $x\in\Sigma^*$. G is the class of *mappings defined by generalized sequential machines*.

THEOREM 5. (Rose and Weihrauch (1973)) $G \subsetneq L_1^{\Sigma,LL}$.

THEOREM 6. $G \subsetneq L_1^{\Sigma,LL} \cap L_1^{\Sigma,RR}$

PROOF. If $g \in G$ then λx [reverse (g (reverse (x)))] $\in G$. Hence, by theorem 3 ii) and theorem 5, $G \subsetneq L_1^{\Sigma,RR}$. On the other side the mapping from Σ^* into $\{a^n b^n | n \geq 0\}$ can be defined both in $L_1^{\Sigma,LL}$ and $L_1^{\Sigma,RR}$

Q E D

In the next pages we will consider L_1^{Σ} programs as acceptors. Here we consider two simple basic properties of ranges of L_1^{Σ} functions:

FACT 7   i) If $|\Sigma| \geq 2$ there is a function f in $L_1^{\Sigma,LL}$ such that range(f) is not a bounded language.

         ii) For all Σ, for all $f \in L_1^{\Sigma,RL}$, range (f) is a context sensitive language

PROOF   i) For $|\Sigma| \geq 2$ Σ^* is not a bounded language.

         ii) any program in $L_1^{\Sigma,RL}$ can be simulated in linear space by a deterministic Turing machine and, hence $z \in$ range (f) for $f \in L_1^{\Sigma,RL}$ can be recognized by simulating the program for all inputs $x_1,\ldots,x_n$ which satisfy $\Sigma_i |x_i| \leq k(|z|+1)$ (see proof of fact 4 i)) and this can be done in deterministic linear space.   Q E D

REMARK. Fact 7 i) is particularly interesting since the graphs of L_1^{Σ} functions on one letter alphabets are bounded c.f languages (D. Tsichritzis (1970)) and from this fact decidability of equivalences of programs and its complexity can be derived.

An interesting property of L_1^{Σ} programs is that while they are very powerful as transducers, their power as acceptors is much weaker.

DEFINITION 6. Let π be a program in L_1^{Σ} and let X, Y be two registers. We define $L(\pi,X,Y)$ to be the *language accepted by program π i.e.* $L(\pi,X,Y)=\{x \in \Sigma^* | f(x) \neq \varepsilon$ where f is the function computed by π with input in X and output in Y$\}$. When X and Y are fixed we will write $L(\pi)$.

DEFINITION 7. *Simple languages* are the languages accepted by programs in $L_1^{\Sigma,RR}$; we will denote the class of simple languages by S^{Σ}.

In [2] it is proved that L_1^{Σ} programs can be simulated by a two-way finite state transducer and as a consequence we have the following RESULT (Chytil (1976)). Simple languages are exactly the regular languages.

A consequence of this fact will be that problems about languages accepted by simple programs are indeed easier than problems about functions computed by simple programs.

4. DECIDABILITY PROPERTIES FOR SIMPLE PROGRAMS ON STRINGS

Our main goal will be to establish decidability properties for programs in $L_1^{\Sigma,RR}$. In order to do so and to establish lower and upper bounds for the complexity of decidable properties we will relate sets of programs in the following way:

DEFINITION 8. i) Let A and B be two languages over a given alphabet Γ, we say that A is log-linearly reducible to B if there exists a function $f : A \to B$ such that for every $x \in \Gamma^*$

- $x \in A$ iff $f(x) \in B$

- $|f(x)| \leq c|x|$

- f is Turing computable within log space

ii) $A \equiv B$ if $A \leq B$ and $B \leq A$.

Let us now consider the following sets of programs (or pairs of programs) in $L_1^{\Sigma,RR}$.

DEFINITION 9. $\quad ACC\emptyset = \{\pi \mid L(\pi) \text{ is empty}\}$

$$ACCEPT = \overline{ACC\emptyset} = \{\pi \mid (\exists x)\, [\pi \text{ accepts } x]\}$$

$$EQACC = \{<\pi_1,\pi_2> \mid L(\pi_1) = (\pi_2)\}$$

$$INEQACC = \overline{EQACC} = \{<\pi_1,\pi_2> \mid L(\pi_1) \neq L(\pi_2)\}$$

$$EQUIV = \{<\pi_1,\pi_2> \mid (\forall x_1,\ldots,x_n)\, [f_{\pi_1}(x_1,\ldots,x_n) =$$
$$= f_{\pi_2}(x_1,\ldots,x_n)]$$

$$INEQUIV = \overline{EQUIV} = \{<\pi_1,\pi_2> \mid (\exists x_1,\ldots,x_n)\, [f_{\pi_1}(x_1,\ldots$$
$$\ldots,x_n) \neq f_{\pi_2}(x_1,\ldots,x_n)]$$

$$RINT = \{<\pi_1,\pi_2> \mid range(f_{\pi_1}) \cap range(f_{\pi_2}) \neq \emptyset\}$$

$$GRINT = \{<\pi_1,\pi_2> \mid graph(f_{\pi_1}) \cap graph(f_{\pi_2}) \neq \emptyset\}$$

Besides we will use the following languages:

DEFINITION 10. CNF = {satisfiable formulas of propositional calculus in conjunctive normal form}

PCP = Post's correspondence problem =

$$= \{<<u_1,\ldots,u_n>\, <v_1,\ldots,v_n>> \mid u_i, v_i \in \Sigma^+,$$

$$|\Sigma| \geq 2 (\exists i_1,\ldots,i_k \leq n)\, [u_{i_1} \ldots u_{i_k} = v_{i_1} \ldots v_{i_k}]\}$$

The following reductions are consequences of properties of $L_1^{\Sigma,RR}$ programs established in the preceding paragraphs.

THEOREM 7.   i) ACC$\emptyset$ = EQACC

          ii) ACC$\emptyset$ $\leq$ EQUIV

PROOF.   i) ACC$\emptyset$ $\leq$ EQACC

Let $\pi_\emptyset$ be the program which accepts the empty set π;

ACC$\emptyset$ iff $\langle \pi, \pi_\emptyset \rangle \in$ EQACC.

EQACC $\leq$ ACC$\emptyset$

$\langle \pi_1, \pi_2 \rangle \in$ EQACC iff $L(\pi_1) \equiv L(\pi_2)$ iff $(\overline{L(\pi_1)} \cap L(\pi_2)) \cup (\overline{L(\pi_2)} \cap L(\pi_1)) =$

    $= \emptyset$ iff $\pi' \in$ ACC$\emptyset$

where π' is the program such that

$L(\pi') = (\overline{L(\pi_1)} \cap L(\pi_2)) \cup (\overline{L(\pi_2)} \cap L(\pi_1))$.

It is easy to see that also in this case $|\pi'| \leq c(|\pi_1| + |\pi_2|)$ and the function mapping $\langle \pi_1, \pi_2 \rangle$ into π' does not require more than log n space to take care of renamings.

         ii) ACC$\emptyset$ $\leq$ EQUIV

Let π_o be the program which gives constant output 0 and let π_c the program which computes the characteristic function of $L(\pi)$. Then

$$\pi \in \text{ACC}\emptyset \text{ iff } \langle \pi_c, \pi_o \rangle \in \text{EQUIV} \qquad\qquad \text{Q E D}$$

In a similarly straightforward manner we can prove

THEOREM 8.   i) ACCEPT $\equiv$ INEQACC

        ii) ACCEPT $\leq$ INEQUIV

PROOF.   i) $\pi \in$ ACCEPT iff the complement of $L(\pi)$ is not Σ^*;

        on the other side $L(\pi_1) \neq L(\pi_2)$ iff $(\overline{L(\pi_1)} \cap L(\pi_2)) \cup$

        $\cup (\overline{L(\pi_2)} \cap L(\pi_1))$ is not empty

        ii) $\pi \in$ ACCEPT iff the characteristic program of $L(\pi)$

        is not equivalent to the characteristic program

        which outputs the constant 0.

                                            Q E D

Because of the result of Chytil (1976) the set EQACC is obviously decidable. The dollowing theorems characterize the complexity of the decision problem.

THEOREM 9. The decision procedure for INEQACC requires at most nondeterministic polynomial time.

PROOF. Let π_1 and π_2 be two programs in L_1^Σ of length $\leq n$. Since L_1^Σ acceptors are closed under complement and union, we can construct a program π_3 in the same class, whose length is linear in n (say c n) and such that

$$L(\pi_3) = (\overline{L(\pi_1)} \cap L(\pi_2)) \cup (\overline{L(\pi_2)} \cap L(\pi_1))$$

Then the problem of whether π_1 and π_2 are equivalent as acceptors is reduced to see whether π_3 ever gives output $\neq \varepsilon$. Now we can use the following lemma:

LEMMA. Given any program π in $L_1^{\Sigma,RR}$ of length n if $L(\pi) \neq \emptyset$ then there is a string $x \in L(\pi)$ such that $|x| \leq n$

Sketch of the proof. Without loss of generality we restrict ourselves to consider programs of the following form:

```
IN{x}; OUT Y

π₁                  where every         ⎧  π̄ᵢₒ
                    πᵢ is the           ⎪  RL OOP Xᵢ
π₂                  program             ⎨  σ₁ : π̄ᵢ₁
 .                                      ⎪   .
 .                                      ⎪   .
 .                                      ⎪  σₘ : π̄ᵢₘ
πₖ                                      ⎩  END
```

and where $\overline{\pi}_{ij} \in L_o^{\Sigma,RR}$ ($1 \leq i \leq K$, $1 \leq j \leq m$).

Now let K=1. In this case the following situations may arise:

- $X_1 = w$ (w is a constant independent from X and $|w| \leq |\overline{\pi}_{10}|$)

- $X_1 = x \circ w$ (where x is the content of X)

The only interesting case is the second. Let us denote $\tilde{y}_i$ the content of register Y_i after the execution of $\overline{\pi}_{10}$. At the end of the execution of π_1 the content of Y may be $\neq \varepsilon$ only in the following cases:

- one of the programs $\overline{\pi}_{1j}$ inserts a string $w_j \neq \varepsilon$ in Y
- the content of another non empty register is transferred into Y either directly or through a series of assignments.

Hence the shortest x_1 such that $Y \neq \varepsilon$ at the end of π_1 is the shortest string $\sigma_{j_h} \ldots \sigma_{j_1}$ $(j_1, \ldots, j_h = 1, \ldots, m)$ such that we have

$\overline{\pi}_{1j_1}$ computes $Y = \overline{Y}_{i_1}, \ldots, \overline{\pi}_{1j_h}$ computes $\overline{\overline{y}}_{i_{h-1}} = w_{j_h}$ and $w_{j_h} \neq \varepsilon$ or

$\overline{\overline{y}}_{i_{h-1}} = \overline{y}_{i_h}$ w_{i_h} and $w_{j_h} \neq \varepsilon$ or $\overline{\overline{y}}_{i_{h-1}} = \overline{y}_{i_h}$ and $\tilde{y}_{i_h} \neq \varepsilon$

where $\overline{y}_i$ and $\overline{\overline{y}}_i$ are the contents of register Y_i respectively before and after the execution of a program $\overline{\pi}_{ij}$ and all i_s are different.

Since every $\overline{\pi}_{1j}$ needs at least one step to perform the corresponding computation we have $h \leq n - |\bar{\pi}_{10}|$ and, hence, $|x| \leq n$.

In the general case, let us consider the program

$$\pi_2$$
$$\vdots$$
$$\pi_K$$

by inductive hypothesis, if we may have output $\neq \varepsilon$ this case be achieved by patting in some input register Z a string z of length $\leq \sum_{i=2}^{K} |\pi_i|$. Since by a program of length ℓ we can shorten a string of at most ℓ characters, this implies that the input register X at the beginning of the execution of program π must contain a string x of length at most $\sum_{i=1}^{K} |\pi_i|$. $\qquad$ Q E D

Coming back to the main theorem, in order to decide whether program π_3 ever gives output $\neq \varepsilon$ we may simulate π_3 an a nondeterministic Turing machine for all inputs of length $\leq cn$. This solution will take time polynomial in n. $\qquad$ Q E D

THEOREM 10. CNF $\leq$ IN EQACC

PROOF. The proof can be given essentially by using a result of Constable, Hunt and Sahni (1974) who prove that CNF is reducible to the inequivalence of simple programs on integers. This would imply the reducibility of CNF to INEQUIV. By a slight modification we obtain the desired result. The direct proof can be found in Ausiello (1975). $\qquad$ Q E D

COROLLARY. INEQACC is NP-complete.

It is an interesting fact that if we add a statement of the type $X = Y \underline{x} Z$ (which is interpreted X contains ε if both Y and Z contain ε, σ_1 otherwise) to the language of the LOOP programs on strings the decision problem of equivalence of simple acceptors becomes much harder.

DEFINITION 11. A *simple program with weak sum* is a program in $L_1^{\Sigma, RR}$ where also the basic instruction $\langle id_1 \rangle = \langle id_2 \rangle \underline{x} \langle id_3 \rangle$ is allowed.

By a result of Chytil (1976) the class of languages accepted by simple programs with weak sum is exactly the class of regular languages.

In the following theorem we show how nondeterministic automata can be succinctly simulated by programs of this type and from this fact a result on the complexity of the equivalence problem is derived.

THEOREM 11. Let $A_N = \langle \Sigma, K, \delta_N, F, Q_0 \rangle$ be a nondeterministic finite automaton. We can define a program π which accepts the same language as

A_N.

PROOF. Let $K = \{q_1,\ldots,q_n\}$ and $\Sigma=\{\sigma_1,\ldots,\sigma_m\}$.

The program π makes use of the registers $X,Y,Q_1,\ldots,Q_n$ and is defined as follows:

π_{INIZ}

RLOOP X

...

$\sigma_j : \pi_j$

...

END

π_{FIN}

$\left\{\begin{array}{l} \pi_{INIZ} \text{ puts 1 in all } Q_i \text{ such that } q_i \in Q_o \\[1em] \pi_j \text{ puts in } Q_k \left\{\begin{array}{l} \varepsilon \text{ if for no } q_i \quad q_k \in \delta_N\,(q_i,\sigma_j) \\ \underline{X}\,Q_i \;(*) \text{ for all } q_i \text{ such that } q_k \in \delta_N(q_i,\delta_j) \end{array}\right. \\[2em] \pi_{FIN} \text{ puts in Y the weak sum of all registers corresponding to final states} \end{array}\right.$

QED

COROLLARY. The equivalence of simple acceptors with weak sum is PTAPE hard.

PROOF. For any regular expression of length n there is a NDFA with $K \leq 2n$ states and for any such NDFA there is a program of length $\ell \leq 2K(c+1)$ where c is the max indegree of a state, that is $\ell = 0(n^2)$. Since the problem of the equivalence of regular expressions is PTAPE complete this is the lower bound for the complexity of the problem of the equivalence of simple programs with weak sum.

QED

5. AN UNDECIDABILITY RESULT

As we have noticed before, the power of $L_1^{\Sigma,RR}$ programs as generators is much stronger than their power as recognizers.

This results in a greater complexity of problems about ranges of simple functions on strings than of problems about sets recognized by simple programs.

THEOREM 12. i) For $|\Sigma| \geq 2$, PCP $\leq$ GRINT

ii) For $|\Sigma| \geq 2$, PCP $\leq$ RINT

PROOF. i) Let $u_1,\ldots,u_n$ and $v_1,\ldots,v_n$ be given words an $\Sigma=\{0,\ 1\}$. Then we may construct two programs π_u and π_v in the following way:

(*) Weak sum over all Q_i $(1 \leq i \leq n)$

```
IN{X}; OUT Y₁                         IN{X}; OUT Y₁
RLOOP  X                              RLOOP  X

     0 : Y₁ = Y₁ o u₁                      0 : Y₁ = Y₁ o v₁
           ...                                    ...
         Yₙ = Yₙ o uₙ                          Yₙ = Yₙ o vₙ

     1 : Z = Yₙ                            1 : Z = Yₙ

         yₙ = Yₙ₋₁                            Yₙ = Yₙ₋₁
           ...                                    ...

         Y₂ = Y₁                              Y₂ = Y₁

         Y₁ = Z                               Y₁ = Z

END                                   END
```

π_u and π_v give the same output for same input string x if and only if there is a sequence $i_1,\ldots,i_k$ such that $u_{i_1},\ldots,u_{i_k} = v_{i_1},\ldots,v_{i_k}$. The details of the proof are given in Ausiello (1975).

ii) Let π_1, π_2 be as in part i). Let π_i' (i=1,2) be the following programs on $\Sigma \cup \{\not\subset\}$ (output in Y_1'):

$$\pi_i$$
$$Y_1' = X \circ \not\subset \circ Y_1$$

Then $<<u_1,\ldots,u_n><v_1,\ldots,v_n>> \in$ PCP iff $<\pi_1,\pi_2> \in$ GRINT iff $<\pi_1',\pi_2'>$ $\in$ RINT. Let τ be the following homomorphism: $\tau(0)=101$, $\tau(1)=10^2 1$, $\tau(\not\subset)=10^3 1$; we can define π_i'' on Σ in the following way:

$$\pi_i$$
$$Y_1'' = \tau(X) \circ 10^3 1 \circ \tau(Y_1)$$

Hence $<\pi_1',\pi_2'> \in$ RINT iff $<\pi_1'',\pi_2''> \in$ RINT.

Q E D

COROLLARY. i) The graph intersection of simple functions is unde-
cidable for $|\Sigma| \geq 2$.

ii) The range intersection of simple functions is unde-
cidable for $|\Sigma| \geq 2$.

REMARK. The intersection problem for simple programs on integers is decidable. This shows that the extension of LOOP programs from integers to strings is not trivial.

REFERENCES

[1] AUSIELLO G.(1975). *Simple programs on strings and their decision problems*. Istituto di Automatica, R.75-15, Roma.

[2] CHERNIAVSKY J(1974). *A notion of realizability for decidable logi̱cal theories*. SUNY at Stony Brook, Dept. of C.S.

[3] CHYTIL M.P.(1976). *A note on simple programs and 2-way finite state transducers* (in preparation).

[4] CONSTABLE R.L., H.B. HUNT III, S.SAHNI (1974). *On the computational complexity of scheme equivalence*. Dept. C.S.-TR 74-201, Cornell University.

[5] COOK S.(1975). *Feasibly constructive proofs and the propositional calculus*. Proceedings of VII ACM Symposium on Theory of Computing, Albuqyerque, N.M.

[6] GRZEGORCZYK A.(1953). *Some classes of recursive functions*. Rozprawy Matematyczne, 4.

[7] HENKE F.W., K.INDERMARK, K.WEIHRAUCH (1972). *Hierarchies of primi̱tive recursive word functions and transductions defined by automa̱ta*. Automata,Languages and Programming,Nivat Ed. North Holland.

[8] JONES N.D.,Y.E.LIEN,W.T.LAASER (1975). *New problems complete for nondeterministic log space*.(S-TR-75) University of Kansas.

[9] JONES N.D.,S.MUCHNICK (1975). *Even simple programs are hard to ana̱lyse*. To be published in JACM.

[10] MEYER A.R., D.M.RITCHIE (1967). *Computational complexity and program structure*. IBM Research RC-1817.

[11] MEYER A.R., L.J.STOCKMEYER (1972). *The equivalence problem for re̱gular expressions with squaring requires exponential space*. XIII Symposium on Switching and Automata Theory.

[12] MEYER A.R., L.U.STOCKMEYER (1973). *Word problems requiring exponential time*. Proceedings of the Fifth Annual ACM Symposium on Theory of Computing, Austin, Texas.

[13] ROSE G., K.WEIHRAUCH (1973). *Eine charackterisierung der klassen L, und R, primitiv-rekursiver Wortfunktionen*. GMD - Bericht 63.

[14] TSICHRITZIS D. (1970). *The equivalence problem of simple programs*. JACM 17,4.

[15] WEIHRAUCH K.(1974). *Teilklassen primitiv-rekursiver Wortfunktionen*. BMFT - GMD - 91.

<u>DEVELOPMENTS IN COMPILER WRITING SYSTEMS</u>

Kari-Jouko Räihä and Mikko Saarinen
Department of Computer Science, University of Helsinki
Töölönkatu 11, SF-00100 Helsinki 10, Finland

1. INTRODUCTION

Compiler writing systems have been a popular research topic within the field of programming languages ever since the pioneering work of Brooker and Morris ([8],[9]) in the early 1960's. By 1967 several different systems had evolved. The characteristics of these systems were excellently expounded in the state-of-the-art survey by Feldman and Gries [20], which is still a must for anyone interested in compiler writing systems.

Since 1968, however, theoretical research on formal languages has developed many new grammatical forms that have been used in specifying the source language for compiler writing systems. In this paper we give an explanatory introduction to the characteristics of recent systems. Other general introductions can be found in [27] and [58].

We approach the subject by dividing the systems into several logically distinct phases. For each phase the methods used in both 'traditional' and more recent compiler writing systems are outlined and analyzed. The analysis is mainly based on the understandability and usability of the methods, although implementation considerations are also briefly discussed.

2. BASIC CONCEPTS

Figure 1 illustrates the input-output relations of an idealized compiler writing system (which we shall synonymously call a compiler-compiler). No existing system fulfills this ideal scheme, the main shortcoming being that the implementation language (I) can not be specified. Rather, the compilers that the system produces are written in a fixed language. This departure from the ideal structure is not serious, since the system can exist in several versions, each producing compilers written in a different language [39,p.385]. Even if this possibility is not usable, one can employ the compiler writing system a second time as indicated in Figure 2 to change the implementation language of the compiler.

Another common deviation from the ideal scheme is that a separate description of the object language is neither needed nor allowed. Instead, in most systems the only input is a description of a compiler from the source language to the object language.

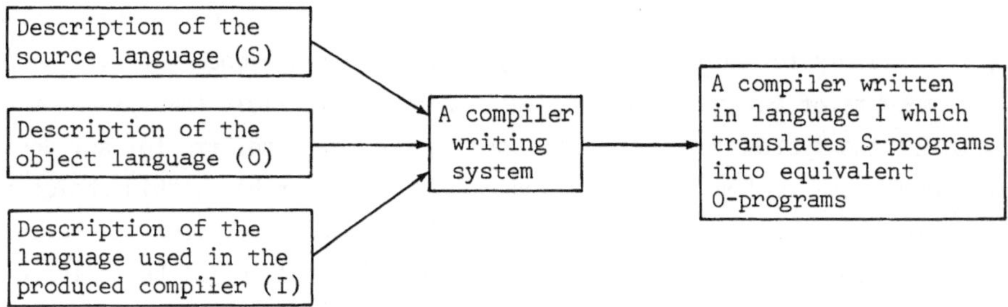

Figure 1. An ideal compiler writing system.

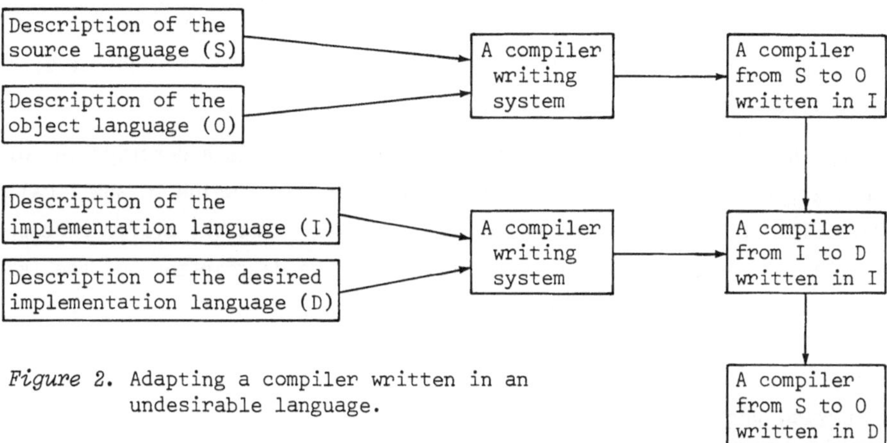

Figure 2. Adapting a compiler written in an
undesirable language.

This is undesirable, since it is reasonable to believe that a formal semantic definition would be simpler and more comprehensible than a description of the compilation methods employed. Of course, it is much easier to construct the compiler from a
complete description than to automatically derive that program only from its input
and output specifications.

The compiler description leaves still a lot of room for variations. First, the system may allow only the use of a fixed object language, which in most cases is an intermediate language of relatively high level in order to hide the annoying details
of actual machines and to ease the description. If efficiency considerations are of
primary importance, the language may be machine oriented [26]. On the other hand, if
portability is more important, the language should be machine independent so that
the same compiler description can be used to produce compilers for several machines.
In any case, the apparent extra compilation from the intermediate language to the
final machine language is not necessary, since the system can automatically replace
the statements generating intermediate language instructions by statements which directly generate the final object code ([19],[16],[64]). Explicit generation of the
intermediate language program is mainly used for special reasons, such as exhaustive
optimization ([17],[43]).

The alternative to the use of a fixed object language is to leave the choice of object language entirely to the user ([39],[59]). This approach does not tie the user down to the concepts of any specific language, nor does it limit the system to any set of machines: the system can readily be used to produce compilers for any desired machine supporting the implementation language. On the other hand, this choice burdens the task of the user, since he has to describe the compiler from the beginning to the end. A feasible combination of the above two approaches might be to leave the decision about the object language to the user and to provide supporting software for some intermediate language.

The approach presented in Figure 1, i.e. the use of a separate description of the object language, remains as the most elegant solution. Although there have been a few proposals for methods to be used in the description of the object language ([53],[22],[54]), they have not yet gained especial popularity.

Thus usually the only input to a compiler writing system is a description of the source language. This description is given using a language, which we shall call the metalanguage. It reflects the structure of the compilers that the system produces in the sense that it contains different features for the description of the lexical analysis, syntactic analysis, and semantic processing. In the following sections we will discuss the properties of various systems in these three areas.

3. COMPILER-COMPILERS AND LEXICAL ANALYSIS

Lexical analysis has in the past attracted little attention in compiler-compilers, although there are good reasons ([25,p.50],[35]) for separating the lexical aspects of the source language from the syntactic definition. Using the syntax to describe also the lexical structure is tolerable only, if the lexical analyzer is automatically separated from the parser ([41],[49]).

Some systems (e.g. [19],[64],[18]) use a standard analyzer to perform the lexical analysis. This imposes a fixed format for all source language programs, unless some kind of a preprocessor is used to convert the input string to the form expected by the system (cf. [43]).

A slightly less restrictive means of describing the lexical aspects of the source language is to allow the user to parameterize the standard analyzer [44]. Typical examples of parameters are the maximum length of identifiers and the form of comments. However, this approach is suitable only as long as a certain class of source languages is considered. Should the user wish to implement a language whose textual appearance is different from the one that the constructor of the compiler-compiler had in mind, then parameterization does not provide much assistance.

If one does not wish to restrict the application domain of the compiler-compiler, then the only (truly) usable way of handling the lexical aspects of the source

language is to provide adequate tools for their description. Since lexical tokens
can be considered to be elements of regular sets, regular expressions are an appropriate form for their description ([35],[12],[57],[45],[60],[46]). From this input
data the compiler writing system automatically constructs a finite transducer, which
performs the lexical analysis.

As an illustration of a flexible formalism consider Figure 3, which describes the
lexical aspects of a simple example language using the notation of [60]. At the
lexical level our example language comprises only identifiers, integers, two re-
served words IF and FI and simple %-comments. Identifiers and numbers must be separated from each other by at least one space or comment.

```
         LEXICAL DESCRIPTION example_language
         CHARACTER SETS
             letter            = 'ABCDEFGHIJKLMNOPQRSTUVWXYZ' ;
             digit             = '0123456789' ;
         END OF CHARACTER SETS
         TOKEN CLASSES
             identifier        = letter (letter|digit|'_')* [64] ;
             % identifiers may contain at most 64 characters
             integer           = digit+ ; % means the same as  digit digit*
             spaces            = ' '+ ;
             comment           = '%' ANY* ENDOFLINE ;
             % character set ANY contains all characters
         END OF TOKEN CLASSES
      A: BEGIN
             identifier [B] => IDENTIFIER | 'IF' | 'FI' ;
             integer    [B] => UNSIGNED_INTEGER ;
             spaces     [A] => ; % spacestrings and comments are deleted
             comment    [A] => ;
         END OF A
      B: BEGIN
             spaces     [A] => ;
             comment    [A] => ;
         END OF B
         END OF LEXICAL DESCRIPTION example_language.
```

Figure 3. Lexical description of the example language.

Scanning begins in block A, where the lexical analyzer can isolate tokens belonging
to four distinct token classes. Suppose that the scanned token is an identifier. If
it happens to be IF or FI then the parser is given the internal representation of
the corresponding keyword, otherwise the parser gets a token belonging to the token
class IDENTIFIER. This separative process is called screening (cf. [12]). After this
control is transferred to block B, where only a comment or a spacestring is possible. In the screening process they are both deleted.

It is a debatable point whether the lexical structures of different source languages
really should differ to the degree of making an explicit description necessary. If
we wish to apply the compiler-compiler in the implementation of special-purpose languages, then the need for such a description is obvious, since specialized languages
often make use of some rather unusual notation. On the other hand, if we are willing

to concentrate only on general-purpose algorithmic languages, then it would seem possible to develop a uniform lexical structure for all languages in that class. The differences found in existing languages often seem rather casual.

4. COMPILER-COMPILERS AND SYNTACTIC ANALYSIS

There are many ways to construct a syntactic analyzer from the specification of the syntax of the source language. In this section we shall consider only those aspects of the construction which directly affect the user. From our point of view, the user is either a person who constructs or maintains compilers or one who uses them. First we shall treat various grammatical forms used in specifying the syntax of the source language.

One such notation is the Floyd-Evans production language used in several traditional compiler-compilers ([19],[16],[26]) developed in the sixties. The inconvenience of writing and modifying the production language program (which essentially describes a parser instead of the syntax) and the introduction of more advanced parsing methods are the main reasons for the lessened use of this notation.

Another formalism is van Wijngaarden's notation which is used in Koster's CDL [39]. As an example let us consider the syntax of binary numbers

```
binary number:        sign, rest.
sign:                 plus; minus; .
rest:                 bit, tail: (bit, :tail; ).
```

where binary number, sign, etc. are called predicates instead of nonterminals. Successive predicates are separated by ',' and different alternatives by ';'. The definition can also contain labels (tail:) and jumps to these labels (:tail).

In the evergreen Backus-Naur-form (BNF) the same syntax can be written

```
<binary number>   ::= <sign> <rest>
<sign>            ::= + | - | <empty>
<rest>            ::= <bit> <tail>
<tail>            ::= <bit> <tail> | <empty>
```

where the nonterminal <tail> is preserved for clarity only. Nowadays BNF or some modification of it is by far the most popular notation used in compiler-compilers ([64],[43],[34],[11],[46],[50],[15],[62]). In one popular modification ([15],[62]) our example goes

```
binary_number     = sign rest ;
sign              = '+' | '-' | ;
rest              = bit tail ;
tail              = bit tail | ;
```

where instead of bracketing nonterminals, terminals are surrounded with single quotes. We prefer this notation to BNF, because it allows the use of metacharacters within terminals (the only exception being quote).

A way of improving BNF is to use a regular expression as the right part of a production ([15],[6]). In this case our example goes

        binary_number   = (|'+'|'-') bit bit* ;

which admittedly is a concise description. The notations we have treated so far have much in common: they are all linear specifications and are a suitable input for the parser generator.

Although BNF is very popular, it has been criticized because "people can be trained to read BNF, but it is not an easy notation to use, or to understand" [4,p.17]. The proposed remedy is to use syntax charts by which the syntax of binary numbers can be depicted as follows:

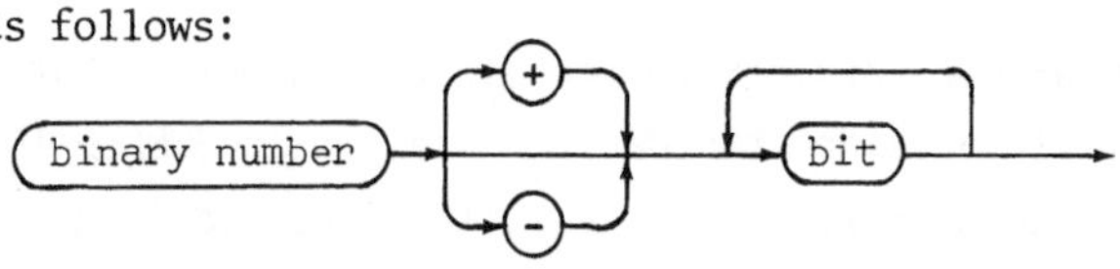

The correct binary numbers are those which can be obtained by following the arrows. Obviously, this is difficult to use as an input format. One solution is to use two grammars: a reference grammar and an implementation grammar. The former could well be represented by a syntax chart. But there is one requirement: if we have different grammars for the same language intended for different purposes, there must be a way to automatically show their equivalence. DeRemer [14] has described a procedure for printing a syntax chart from BNF notation with regular expressions. He even states that "every translator writing system and compiler writing shop should have a syntax charter" [14,p.21].

Nowadays there are two kinds of methods by which the parsers usually work, namely deterministic top-down and bottom-up techniques. Top-down parsers are normally restricted to LL(1)-grammars and are used relatively seldom in parser generators (cf. CDL [39], which is, however, able to use some backtracking), although they are popular in hand-written parsers. Bottom-up parsers can be subdivided into three classes: those which employ Floyd-Evans productions ([19],[16],[26],[50],[11]), those which employ precedence techniques ([51],[64],[52]) and finally those which employ LR-techniques ([42],[3],[34],[15],[46],[62]) and the like ([40],[18]). A thorough introduction to various parsing methods can be found in [2].

One frequently stated objection to the use of compiler-compilers is that the compilers produced tend to be uneconomical. Surely, this is not true of parsers generated by LL-, LR- or precedence techniques (cf. [28],[13],[42],[3],[55],[52]). These results seem to favor LR-methods when compared to precedence techniques. However, considering that the parser is only a small part of a compiler and its usage of time is quite modest, all previously mentioned parsing methods are acceptable as regards both space and time.

The next important criterion of the usability of a parsing method is the width of
the class of languages that it will parse. Fortunately, theory and practice has
shown [30,p.105] that we do not sacrifice any important, deterministically parsable
languages if we use the techniques mentioned above. However, we must also take into
account how naturally we can build a grammar for the source language to suit a particular parsing method.

It is well known that finding an LR-grammar for a given language is relatively easy,
whereas this does not hold for LL-grammars. Even for the conditional statements,
where the then-part may again be a conditional statement, it is impossible to find
an LL(k)-grammar, though an extended LL(1)-grammar does exist [1,p.206]. Fortunately
methods exist by which one can often transform a grammar into LL(1)-form (e.g. [28],
[47],[63]).

The same problem arises when we use precedence techniques, namely that grammars
written by the user tend to fall outside the desired class. In JOSSLE [64] this
problem is solved in the following manner: "If however, the language is unacceptable
or a simpler parser is possible, information indicating various syntactic changes
that will yield an acceptable language, or a simpler parser, is fed back to the
user." This is a fairly good procedure, the only nuisance being that the user is responsible for inserting the semantics into the transformed grammar. This could turn
out to be difficult.

Perhaps only the LR-parser generators, many of which are nowadays based on LALR(1)-
techniques ([42],[34],[46],[62]), permit a class of natural grammars so wide that
there is no urgent need for transformations. At Purdue University [52] they have
even developed a system, which first transforms any LR(k)-grammar into a grammar acceptable to the parser generator. What is more, semantics is transformed at the same
time. When the transformation is done in this way there can be no complaint. An
analogous transformation effort is made by Bochmann [6].

However, although the grammars accepted by LR-systems are less restricted than those
accepted by other methods, they are usually not the best possible for the reader.
The main obstacle is that the syntax must be unambiguous. This fact is taken into
account in some systems (e.g. [18],[34],[3]) by allowing ambiguities, which are
solved either by syntactic and semantic interaction or alternatively by syntactic
directives or default rules.

The handling of syntax errors is an important as well as a subtle problem to solve
successfully. The reason for difficulties in a compiler-compiler environment is that
the handling should be as automated as possible and yet work adequately. Ideally,
the parser should report all syntax errors and no nonexistent errors. The error
message should be understandable. The method should have no substantial effect on
parsing correct portions of the program and it should be rather independent of the
form of the input grammar. Moreover, interaction between the syntactic and semantic

parts of a compiler assists in handling the semantic processing adequately in error situations. The work along these lines has resulted in many promising applications within parser generators ([24],[34],[10],[21],[61] and [62]). A more detailed discussion can be found in [31].

5. COMPILER-COMPILERS AND SEMANTIC PROCESSING

In the 1970's the development of compiler writing systems has probably been greatest in the capabilities to describe the semantics of the source language. In this area a clear distinction can be seen between the traditional genre (e.g. [19],[16],[26], [64]) and most of the recent compiler-compilers. The former systems generally use a language with Algol-like control structures for describing the semantics. Such a language usually contains convenient data types (e.g. strings, bitstrings, pointers and descriptors) and a few data structures (e.g. stacks and records) that have proved useful in the construction of existing compilers.

As an example, consider the description of the translation of conditional statements in Figure 4. The example (adapted from [64]) is given in the JOSSLE language [64], which is used in one of the most recent traditional systems and is perhaps the best structured semantic metalanguage of its kind.

A JOSSLE program consists of type definitions, variable declarations, and semantic routines. A program has at most one semantic routine for each syntactic rule. After the parser finds the appropriate reduction it passes control to the semantic part, which executes the corresponding routine. The routine has access to the semantic stack, which is a parallel structure to the parse stack. The top of the parse stack contains the symbols of the right hand side of the production to be used in the reduction. The top symbols of the semantic stack are labeled SEM1, SEM2 etc. For example, SEM1 denotes the semantic description of the rightmost symbol of the right hand side of the production. After the routine has been executed, control returns to the parser, which finally performs the reduction by adjusting the stacks. In other respects we hope that the example is self-explanatory.

```
PROGRAM SEMANT;
   DEFINE
      SYMBOL_TABLE_ENTRY = NEWTYPE
         NAME: INTEGER;
         TYPE: INTEGER;
         DESC: DESCRIPTOR;
      END NEWTYPE;
   END DEFINE;
   DECLARE
      TOP_SYMBOL_TABLE INTEGER;
      L DESCRIPTOR;
      SYMBOL_TABLE LINLIST(50) OF SYMBOL_TABLE_ENTRY;
   END DECLARE;

   /* Semantic routines */
   CASE RULE# OF
```

```
/* Rule 0, Initialization */
TOP_SYMBOL_TABLE <- 0;

/* Rule 1, IF_CLAUSE -> IF BOOLEAN_EXPRESSION */
BEGIN
    /* Allocate run-time label. */
    L <- ALLOCATE_RTL;
    /* Generate a conditional branch  around the statement  following THEN.  A de-
        scription  of the value of the condition  is found in a symbol table entry,
        which was created  by the rules for  BOOLEAN_EXPRESSION.  The index  of the
        entry is given by SEM1. */
    CODE(IF ¬(SYMBOL_TABLE(SEM1).DESC) THEN L);
    /* Set SEM(IF_CLAUSE) =  destination of branch around UNCONDITIONAL_STATEMENT.
        After this routine,  SEM1  is connected with IF_CLAUSE,  and a reference to
        the properties of  BOOLEAN_EXPRESSION  through SEM1 is no more possible. */
    SYMBOL_TABLE(SEM1).DESC <- L;
END;

/* Rule 2, IF_STATEMENT -> IF_CLAUSE THEN UNCONDITIONAL_STATEMENT */
    /* Make the description of IF_STATEMENT equal to the description of
        IF_CLAUSE. */
    SEM1 <- SEM3;

/* Rule 3, IF_THEN_ELSE -> IF_STATEMENT ELSE */
BEGIN
    /* Generate a branch around BASIC_STATEMENT following ELSE. */
    L <- ALLOCATE_RTL;
    CODE(GOTO L);
    /* Define the destination of the branch generated in routine 1. */
    CODE(SYMBOL_TABLE(SEM2).DESC: );
    /* Set SEM(IF_THEN_ELSE) = destination of branch around BASIC_STATEMENT
        following ELSE. */
    SEM1 <- SEM2;
    SYMBOL_TABLE(SEM1).DESC <- L;
END;

/* Rule 4, CONDITIONAL_STATEMENT -> IF_STATEMENT */
BEGIN
    /* Define branch around UNCONDITIONAL_STATEMENT. */
    CODE(SYMBOL_TABLE(SEM1).DESC: );
    /* Pop temporary entry from symbol table. The entry was created in the routine
        for BOOLEAN_EXPRESSION, which we shall omit. */
    TOP_SYMBOL_TABLE <- TOP_SYMBOL_TABLE - 1;
END;

/* Rule 5, CONDITIONAL_STATEMENT -> IF_THEN_ELSE BASIC_STATEMENT */
BEGIN
    /* Define branch around BASIC_STATEMENT. */
    CODE(SYMBOL_TABLE(SEM1).DESC: );
    TOP_SYMBOL_TABLE <- TOP_SYMBOL_TABLE - 1;
END;

END CASE;
END PROGRAM;
```

Figure 4. Translation of conditional statements in JOSSLE.

Many recent compiler-compilers ([18],[44],[48],[23],[15],[59],[46]) are based on the
use of attribute grammars, which were presented by Knuth in 1968 [38]. In an attribute grammar each nonterminal symbol of the grammar has an associated set of attributes, each of which describes some property of the nonterminal. An attribute whose
value depends on the values of attributes of descendants of the corresponding node

is said to be synthesized. Alternatively an attribute can be inherited, in which
case it depends on the values of the attributes that are attached to the ancestor
and siblings of the node in the parse tree. The values of attributes are given by
semantic rules, which are associated with the syntactic productions. Each rule specifies the value of one attribute, and may depend only on values of the other attributes attached to the nonterminals of the same production.

As an example, Figure 5 contains a description of the translation of the same conditional statements as in Figure 4. Each nonterminal has two synthesized attributes,
code and *follow*, and one inherited attribute, *start*. The *code* attribute contains the
code generated for each nonterminal symbol. The code begins from memory location
start and the last location it occupies is *follow*-1. In addition, the attribute
otheralternate is associated with the nonterminal conditional_head. The value of
otheralternate is either the start address of the <u>else</u>-part or the address of the
following statement, depending on whether the <u>else</u>-part is present in the
conditional_statement or not. Subscripts are used to associate attributes with nonterminals. The line transfer operator is denoted by '&'.

```
conditional_statement₀ = conditional_head₁ ;
    code₀ ← code₁ ;
    follow₀ ← follow₁ ;
        start₁ ← start₀ ;
        otheralternate₁ ← follow₁ ;

conditional_statement₀ = conditional_head₁ 'else' basic_statement₂ ;
    code₀ ← code₁ & "Branch" follow₀ & code₂ ;
    follow₀ ← follow₂ ;
        start₁ ← start₀ ;
        start₂ ← follow₁ + 1 ;
        otheralternate₁ ← start₂ ;

conditional_head₀ = if_clause₁ unconditional_statement₂ ;
    code₀ ← code₁ & "Branch on false" otheralternate₀ & code₂ ;
    follow₀ ← follow₂ ;
        start₁ ← start₀ ;
        start₂ ← follow₁ + 1 ;

if_clause₀ = 'if' boolean_expression₁ 'then' ;
    code₀ ← code₁ ;
    follow₀ ← follow₁ ;
        start₁ ← start₀ ;

basic_statement₀ = conditional_statement₁ ;
    code₀ ← code₁ ;
    follow₀ ← follow₁ ;
        start₁ ← start₀ ;
```

Figure 5. An attribute grammar for conditional statements.

One of the most important differences between attribute grammars and traditional
methods is that the order of evaluation of the semantic rules is in no way visible
in an attribute grammar; in particular, it does not depend on the parsing method, as
in Figure 4. In general terms, a metalanguage based on attribute grammars can be
called declarative, whereas languages like JOSSLE can be called algorithmic.

In principle, the execution of semantic rules of an attribute grammar can proceed by traversing the parse tree in any desired manner. At each node, the values of all attributes are evaluated, whose semantic rules depend only on attributes that have already been evaluated. This nondeterministic tree traversal is continued until all attributes have been evaluated. The synthesized attributes of the root represent the translation of the source program to the equivalent object program.

The efficiency of the nondeterministic method of evaluation tends to be relatively poor. Better results have been achieved by placing more or less severe restrictions on the form of semantic rules in order to make deterministic attribute evaluation possible. The trade-off between efficient evaluation and the expressive power of semantic rules is very subtle, and there has been no proper investigation of the kind of restrictions that would be tolerable in practical language implementation situations.

In the example of Figure 5, the evaluation can proceed by traversing the tree twice in the order "visit the root, visit the sons from left to right, visit the root". During the first traversal, the value of the *start* attribute can be evaluated on the first visit to each node, while the value of *follow* must be evaluated on the second visit. The second traversal consists of evaluating *otheralternate* on the first visit to each node labeled `conditional_head` and finally evaluating the *code* attribute at the second visit to each node.

One should not draw too far-reaching conclusions from Figures 4 and 5, since the former is an example of a real metalanguage, while the latter only illustrates a principle that can be found in many recent compiler-compilers. The notation of Figure 5 might have been less transparent, had we used the metalanguage of some particular system. However, one should note the locality of the semantic description in Figure 5, which is a result of the declarative nature of the definition. Even the method of Figure 4 could be considered to be based on an attribute grammar, in which each symbol has only one synthesized attribute; this principle was suggested already in [32]. The result of this is that the single attribute must denote different things at different nodes. This makes the semantic rules inherently dependent on each other, since one has to recall what the single attribute describes in each specific situation, when he wishes to alter or merely understand the rules. In a true attribute grammar the use of several attributes removes this problem, provided that the names of the attributes are chosen descriptively.

The differences between 'traditional' metalanguages and languages based on attribute grammars are largely the same as those between general algorithmic languages and declarative languages, which have been thoroughly discussed by Hammer [29]. Our small example seems to support Hammer's opinion that declarative languages are more understandable than algorithmic languages, since part of the problem solving methodology has been embedded in the language, thus relieving the task of the user of the

language. On the other hand, in a compiler construction environment efficiency is a
crucial factor in the assessment of a language and in this area algorithmic languages have so far been superior to declarative languages, mainly because their efficient implementation is much easier. However, researchers are actively developing
new methods for the realization of attribute grammars (e.g. [33],[37],[36]), and it
seems likely that declarative languages will in future be more competitive with
algorithmic languages also as regards efficiency.

Attribute grammars are certainly not the only declarative form of metalanguages used
in compiler-compilers. Koster's CDL [39] is based on affix grammars, which resemble
attribute grammars in many respects. However, the evaluation of affixes in CDL is
performed by macro statements, and this gives it a special flavour when compared to
attribute grammars. ALEPH [7] is another system employing affix grammars.

Attribute grammars have proved to be a convenient tool in the description of semantic analysis, but for other areas other grammatical methods have been proposed. For
code generation the translation grammars [47], which contain output actions inter-
leaved with the symbols on the right hand side of a production, are a useful tool.
The output actions write the generated code to the desired file, which is probably
more practical than collecting the possibly large fragments of code into attributes.
Another useful tool is the transformation grammar [15], which maps trees into trees
or strings. It has found many applications within compiler-compilers from lexical
analysis to code generation. Both of these grammars have also been augmented with
semantic attributes; the results have been called attributed translations [47] and
attributed transformations [65].

A useful form of compiler-compilers that does not fit either of our two classes of
declarative and algorithmic languages is the system developed at Purdue University
([43],[52]). The system is based on a large set of uniform code generation routines.
When the user wishes to implement a language, he only has to write the syntax and
place the calls of code generation routines in the proper places within the syntactic rules. Thus the system can be viewed as a realization of a translation grammar,
where the system provides the user with a large set of ready-to-use output actions.
This kind of approach seems to work well in the implementation of a language that
belongs to the class for which the code generation routines have been designed.
However, the user can anticipate difficulties, if he wishes to implement a language
whose primitives were not taken into consideration in the preparation of the standard set of code generation routines.

6. CONCLUDING REMARKS

In the past, compiler-compilers have stimulated a remarkable amount of research in
formal language theory. So far the results of this research have mainly benefited
parser generating systems by introducing advanced parsing methods. In future the

main emphasis should be on the efficient implementation of grammatical forms that can be used in the description of semantics.

A compiler writing system can be an important tool for a language designer, because with its help he can easily realize the effects of different possibilities. However, this goal requires increased attention on the usability aspects of compiler-compilers. Even a person who is going to implement an existing language is likely to think twice before using a compiler writing system, even if he had one available.

The reason for this reluctance can be understood in the light of the trouble of having to learn a new language (i.e. the metalanguage), which in many cases looks cumbersome. Furthermore, the manuals available for these languages are often poor, and assume that the reader is familiar with compiler writing technology. This is unfortunate, since compiler writing systems have found applications in many other areas, notably symbolic and algebraic manipulation ([20],[56]). However, the increasing interest in compiler-compilers makes it plausible to believe that the removal of unnecessary practical limitations will gradually lift compiler writing systems to truly usable aids in software production.

ACKNOWLEDGMENT. This work was supported by a research project investigating translator writing systems. The project is led by professor Martti Tienari and sponsored by the Academy of Finland.

REFERENCES

[1] Aho,A.V.: Language theory in compiler design. In *Applied computation theory: analysis, design, modeling* (ed R.T.Yeh), Prentice-Hall, Inc., Englewood Cliffs, N.J., 1976, pp.185-249.

[2] Aho,A.V. & J.D.Ullman: *The theory of parsing, translation and compiling. Vol.1: Parsing.* Prentice-Hall, Inc., Englewood Cliffs, N.J., 1972.

[3] Anderson,T., J.Eve & J.J.Horning: Efficient LR(1) parsers. *Acta Informatica* 2,1 (1973), 12-39.

[4] Barnard,D.T.: *Automatic generation of syntax-repairing and paragraphing parsers.* University of Toronto, Computer Systems Research Group, Technical Report CSRG-52, April 1975.

[5] Bauer,F.L. & J.Eickel (eds): *Compiler construction: an advanced cource.* Springer-Verlag, Berlin - Heidelberg - New York, 1974.

[6] Bochmann,G.V.: *Semantic attributes for grammars with regular expressions.* Université de Montréal, Département d'Informatique, Publication 195, 1975.

[7] Bosch,R., D.Grune & L.Meertens: ALEPH, a language encouraging program hierarchy. *International Computing Symposium 1973* (eds A.Günther, B.Levrat & H.Lipps), North-Holland Publ. Co., Amsterdam - London, 1974, pp.73-79.

[8] Brooker,R.A., J.R.MacCallum, D.Morris & J.S.Rohl: The compiler compiler. *Annual Review in Automatic Programming,* vol.3, 1963, pp.229-275.

[9] Brooker,R.A. & D.Morris: A general translation program for phrase structure languages. *J. ACM* 9,1 (January 1962), 1-10.

[10] Ciesinger,J.: Generating error recovery in a compiler generating system. *GI - 4.Fachtagung über Programmiersprachen,* Springer-Verlag, Berlin - Heidelberg - New York, 1976, pp.185-193.

[11] Cohen,J.: Experience with a conversational parser generating system. *Software - Practice & Experience* 5,2 (April - June 1975), 169-180.

[12] DeRemer,F.L.: Lexical analysis. In [5], pp.109-120.

[13] DeRemer,F.L.: Simple LR(k) grammars. *Comm. ACM* 14,7 (July 1971), 453-460.

[14] DeRemer,F.L.: *Syntax charts constructed automatically.* University of California, Santa Cruz, 1975.

[15] DeRemer,F.L.: Transformational grammars. In [5], pp.121-145.

[16] Dove,R.K.: Design highlights of CABAL - a compiler-compiler. *Proc. AFIPS 1968 Fall Joint Computer Conference*, vol.33, part two, pp.1321-1328.

[17] Ershov,A.P.: Problems in many-language systems. *International Summer School on Language Hierarchies and Interfaces*, Munich, July 1975.

[18] Fang,I.: *FOLDS, a declarative formal language definition system.* Stanford University, Computer Science Department, STAN-CS-72-329, December 1972.

[19] Feldman,J.A.: A formal semantics for computer languages and its application in a compiler-compiler. *Comm. ACM* 9,1 (January 1966), 3-9.

[20] Feldman,J.A. & D.Gries: Translator writing systems. *Comm. ACM* 11,2 (February 1968), 77-113.

[21] Feyock,S. & P.Lazarus: Syntax-directed correction of syntax errors. *Software - Practice & Experience* 6,2 (April - June 1976), 207-219.

[22] Frommwieser,H.: *Implementierung eines Minimalsystems zur maschinenunabhängigen Codeerzeugung.* Technische Universität München, Abteilung Mathematik, Diplomarbeit, Juli 1974.

[23] Ganzinger,H.: *Modifizierte attributierte Grammatiken.* Technische Universität München, Abteilung Mathematik, Bericht Nr. 7420, November 1974.

[24] Graham,S.L. & S.P.Rhodes: Practical syntactic error recovery. *Comm. ACM* 18,11 (November 1975), 639-650.

[25] Gries,D.: *Compiler construction for digital computers.* John Wiley & Sons, Inc., New York, 1971.

[26] Gries,D.: *CIL - a compiler implementation language.* Stanford University, Stanford Linear Accelerator Center, SLAC-102, March 1969.

[27] Griffiths,M.: Introduction to compiler-compilers. In [5], pp.356-365.

[28] Griffiths,M.: LL(1) grammars and analysers. In [5], pp.57-84.

[29] Hammer,M.: The design of usable programming languages. *Proc. ACM 1975 Annual Conference*, October 1975, pp.225-229.

[30] Horning,J.J.: LR grammars and analyzers. In [5], pp.85-108.

[31] Horning,J.J.: What the compiler should tell the user. In [5], pp.525-548.

[32] Irons,E.T.: A syntax directed compiler for Algol 60. *Comm. ACM* 4,1 (January 1961), 51-55.

[33] Jazayeri,M. & K.G.Walter: Alternating semantic evaluator. *Proc. ACM 1975 Annual Conference*, October 1975, pp.230-234.

[34] Johnson,S.C.: *YACC - yet another compiler-compiler.* Bell Laboratories, Computing Science Technical Report 32, July 1975.

[35] Johnson,W.L., J.H.Porter, S.I.Ackley & D.T.Ross: Automatic generation of efficient lexical processors using finite state techniques. *Comm. ACM* 11,12 (December 1968), 805-813.

[36] Kastens,U.: Systematische Analyse semantischer Abhaengigkeiten. *GI - 4.Fachtagung über Programmiersprachen*, Springer-Verlag, Berlin - Heidelberg - New York, 1976, pp.19-32.

[37] Kennedy,K. & S.K.Warren: Automatic generation of efficient evaluators for attribute grammars. *Proc. Third ACM Symposium on Principles of Programming Languages*, January 1976, pp.32-49.

[38] Knuth,D.E.: Semantics of context-free languages. *Math. Systems Theory* 2,2 (1968), 127-145.

[39] Koster,C.H.A.: Using the CDL compiler-compiler. In [5], pp.366-426.

[40] Kron,H.H., H-J.Hoffmann & G.Winkler: On a SLR(k)-based parser system which accepts non-LR(k) grammars. *GI - 4.Jahrestagung* (ed D.Siefkes), Springer-Verlag, Berlin - Heidelberg - New York, 1975, pp.214-223.

[41] Krzemien,R. & A.Łukasiewicz: Automatic generation of lexical analyzers in a compiler-compiler. *Information Processing Letters* 4,6 (March 1976), 165-168.

[42] Lalonde,W.R., E.S.Lee & J.J.Horning: An LALR(k) parser generator. *Proc. IFIP 1971 Congress*, North-Holland Publ. Co., Amsterdam - London, 1972, pp.513-518.

[43] Lancaster,R.L. & V.B.Schneider: Quick compiler construction using uniform code generators. *Software - Practice & Experience* 6,1 (January - March 1976), 83-91.

[44] Lecarme,O.L. & G.V.Bochmann: A (truly) usable and portable compiler writing system. *Proc. IFIP 1974 Congress*, North-Holland Publ. Co., Amsterdam - London, 1974, pp.218-221.

[45] Lesk,M.E.:   *Lex - a lexical analyzer generator.* Bell Laboratories, Computing Science Technical Report 39, October 1975.

[46] Lewi,J., K.DeVlaminck, J.Huens & P.Mertens: SLS/1: a translator writing system. *GI - 5.Jahrestagung* (ed J.Mühlbacher), Springer-Verlag, Berlin - Heidelberg - New York, 1975, pp.627-641.

[47] Lewis,P.M., D.J.Rosenkrantz & R.E.Stearns: *Compiler design theory.*   Addison-Wesley Publ. Co., Reading, Mass., 1976.

[48] Lorho,B.: *De la définition à la traduction des langages de programmation: méthode des attributs sémantiques.* Université Paul Sabatier, Toulouse, Thèse d'Etat, 1974.

[49] Lynch,W.C. & H.L.Pierson: A finite state transducer model for compiler lexical scanners. *Proc. IFIP 1968 Congress.* North-Holland Publ. Co., Amsterdam, 1969, pp.448-455.

[50] Machado,N.C.: *ISL - a semantic language for a translator writing system.* University of Illinois at Urbana-Champaign, Department of Computer Science, Report No. 367, December 1969.

[51] McKeeman,W.M., J.J.Horning & D.B.Wortman: *A compiler generator.* Prentice-Hall, Inc., Englewood Cliffs, N.J., 1970.

[52] Mickunas,M.D. & V.B.Schneider: A parser generating system for constructing compressed compilers. *Comm. ACM* 16,11 (November 1973), 669-674.

[53] Miller,P.L.: *Automatic creation of a code generator from a machine description.* Massachusetts Institute of Technology, Project MAC, TR-85, May 1971.

[54] Newcomer,J.M.: *Machine-independent generation of optimal local code.* Carnegie-Mellon University, Department of Computer Science, May 1975.

[55] Pager,D.: On eliminating unit productions from LR(k) parsers. *Second Colloquium on Automata, Languages and Programming* (ed J.Loeckx), Springer-Verlag, Berlin - Heidelberg - New York, 1974, pp.242-254.

[56] Petrick,S.R.: On the use of syntax-based translators for symbolic and algebraic manipulation.   *Proc. Second Symposium on Symbolic and Algebraic Manipulation,* March 1971, pp.224-237.

[57] Ripken,K.:   *Ein Programmsystem zur automatischen Erzeugung von Leseprogrammen.* Technische Universität München, Abteilung Mathematik, Bericht 7417, September 1974.

[58] Räihä,K-J.: On compiler writing systems. *Proc. NordDATA 76 Conference,* Finnish Data Processing Association, June 1976, pp.668-679.

[59] Räihä,K-J.:   *Design of the semantic phase of a compiler writing system*   (in Finnish). University of Helsinki, Department of Computer Science, series C, number 1976/24, January 1976.

[60] Saarinen,M.: *Design of the lexical analyzer of a compiler writing system* (in Finnish). University of Helsinki, Department of Computer Science, series C, number 1976/23, January 1976.

[61] Sippu,S.S.: *Error recovery in LR-parsing* (in Finnish). University of Helsinki, Department of Computer Science, series C, number 1976/22, February 1976.

[62] Soisalon-Soininen,E.: *Design of an automatic constructor of LR-parsers* (in Finnish). University of Helsinki, Department of Computer Science, series C, number 1976/27, January 1976.

[63] Soisalon-Soininen,E. & E.Ukkonen: A characterization of LL(k) languages. *Third Colloquium on Automata, Languages and Programming,* Edinburgh, July 1976.

[64] White,J.R. & L.Presser: A structured language for translator construction. *Computer J.* 18,1 (February 1975), 34-42.

[65] Wilhelm,R.: Code-Optimierung mittels attributierter Transformationsgrammatiken. *GI - 4.Jahrestagung* (ed D.Siefkes), Springer-Verlag, Berlin - Heidelberg - New York, 1975, pp.257-266.

STRUCTURED DEVELOPMENT OF THE COMPUTER AIDED DESIGN SYSTEM IOD

by E. Kantorowitz
IBM Heidelberg Scientific Center
Tiergartenstrasse 15, D-69 Heidelberg
On sabbatical leave from Technion
Israel Institute of Technology, Haifa, Israel

Abstract

A CAD system emphasizing creative development of new design ideas is discussed. The system assumes no computer knowledge. Beside the use of menus and prompts, the user has only to learn a mini programming language for formulation of arithmetic and boolean expressions. The system utilizes a data management system fitted for engineering design. With the retrieved data the user constructs, through menu guidance, a constrained non-linear model of his design. Interactive optimization of the model facilitates introduction of useful trade offs.

The structured development of the CAD system is discussed. First an unsophisticated prototype was implemented. The insight gained form this implementation enabled significant improvements that could not have been suggested without this insight. This technique involves however a repeated implementation of sizable parts of the system. The costs of these repeated implementations were reduced by employing principles of having code for a certain activity only one place in the program, and of accessing complex data structures only through special functions.

The APL language proved very useful for the project. An analysis is made of the properties that made APL so useful in spite of its poor program structuring facilities.

1. Introduction

The subject of this paper is an experimental system for studying computer aided design (CAD) emphasizing designer creativity. In the first part of the paper the system will be discussed from the point of view of a user. In the second part of the paper the techniques employed for the structured development of the large system will be analyzed.

One of the objectives of the system was to facilitate the utilization of the insight gained by the designer through the process. An example is the engineer, who through the process of designing a new machine learns that some of the original specifications involve very high costs. He will then analyze these specifications and may decide to change them. Another example is when the insight gained through the design process inspires the designer to employ new principles, whereby advantages that have not been foreseen at the beginning of the design process, are achieved. It was felt that such a system should

1. Support the psychological learning process through which the designer gains an understanding of the properties of his design, e.g. through display of graphs that illustrate these properties.

2. Be handled in a simple and obvious way such that the designer can invest the most of his mental resources in the design process.

3. Provide a data base from which data needed for the design may be retrieved in a convenient way.

4. Provide computational capabilities, e.g. for statistics, that may be used with a minimum of knowledge in mathematics and computers.

5. Provide a methods data base enabling a convenient search of procedures that may be of use to solve problems encountered through the design process.

This paper discusses the IOD (Interactive Optimum Design) system which attempts to meet the above requirements. The data base and the method data base systems to be used are described in (10) and (8) respectively. A program called INTERFACE that interfaces the IOD system with the terminal and with subroutines written in other languages, e.g. FORTRAN was written by M. Bergen (4) . It is intended to evaluate the IOD system by using it for ship design, an area familiar to the author. It is thus planned to study the use of the system by shipbuilding students in an experimental laboratory. The conduction of experiments with experienced engineers is also considered, although this involves high costs. Since the prime purpose is the study of computer aided problem solving by non computer specialists, the IOD system need not be a full CAD (Computer Aided Design) system in the sense described by Lang (15). There will thus be no aids for manufacturing the designed ships. The experiments planned will only cover the preliminary ship design. The IOD system has some common goals with ship CAD systems which are currently being developed at some universities (6) (11) (22). The use of interactive optimization procedures for ship design is discussed in a number of papers (5) (1) (9) (13) (16) (17) (18). The emphasis in the IOD system is, however, on the study of computer techniques for non computer specialists using ship design as a case.

2. The designers view of the IOD system

In this section the system as seen by its user (the designer) will be discussed. It was attempted to design the system such that the user will only have to learn few and simple concepts in order to use it. Beside the assumption that the designer (the user) has no computer knowledge it was also necessary to assume that he has only a minimal knowledge of operations research techniques and of numerical methods. It was therefore necessary to base the system on few numerically robust methods that may be used in a wide range of cases. The search for optimal solution is based on a non-linear optimization model with constraints because this model has proved useful for solving many ship design problems (19).

The data needed for the construction of the optimization model of the ship may either be supplied directly by the designer or retrieved from the underlying data base using a quite simple query language EXTENDED QUERY BY EXAMPLE (EQBE) which is described by U. Schauer in (20). It is a further development of Zloof's system (21). Say for instance that in an optimization model of a tanker the weight of the steel hull is needed as function of the displacement (total weight) of the ship. The user enters the string HULL, which is the name of the table in the data base that contains the required data. The structure of this table will now appear on the screen

SHIP #	SHIP-TYPE	DISPLACEMENT	STEEL-WEIGHT

The user may then specify the retrieval by typing

	z	oX	oY

z = TANKER

Two arrays X and Y will hereafter be generated containing the values of the displacements and steel weight of all ships in the table, where the SHIP-TYPE column contains the word TANKER. The retrieved data may now be displayed on the screen (Y over X), and will show some scatter because of differences in the structure of the different tankers. The user may therefore invoke a facility for approximation and fit a polynominal to the data in the least squares sense. The graphical representation of the polynominal will appear on the screen. If the designer feels the approximation is acceptable he may use the polynominal in the optimization model as a representation for the STEEL-WEIGHT(DISPLACEMENT) function. If the approximation is not satisfactory the designer may try another type of approximation. The handling of the approximation facility is menu driven, so the designer need not learn a special language in order to use it.

The optimization model is based on few concepts:

Model - a set of data which represent the model. Three kinds of data are provided.

Independent variables x_i - e.g. the length of the ship, the price of fuel.

Dependent variables $y_i = y_j(y_i, x_{i+j})$ - are normally used to define the properties of the model ("figures of merits"), e.g. the costs of transporting 1 ton 1 mile with the designed ship, the probability that the ship will sink if a collision causes a damage of a specified size. As appears from these examples the figures of merits may represent quite complex functions.

Constraints - e.g. the draught of the ship must be small enough to permit it to enter a particular harbour. Each constraint is defined by an expression $g(x_i, y_j)$ such that

$$g_u(x_i, y_j) \geqq 0$$

for all permissible (feasible) designs.

Constants -   Any independent variable may at any stage of the
optimization process be converted into a constant. By converting a
variable into a constant the number of optimization variables is
reduced by one and the processing speed is increased. It is
likewise possible to convert a constant into an independent
variable, such that the optimal value of this variable will be
computed.   This involves   however   a   prolongation of   the
computations.

The construction of the model is menu driven, so the user need no
programming language. An exception are the arithmetic expressions for
the dependent variables and for the constraints, which must be entered
in a formal language (APL in the current version).

When the model has been constructed the designer selects one of the
dependent variables, e.g. the costs for transporting 1 ton cargo 1 mile
with the designed ship, as the objective function to be minimized. The
optimum solution is normally found on one of the constraint surfaces,

$$g_u(x_i, y_j) = 0$$

which bound the feasible domain (the solution space). By relaxing the
constraint (moving the constraint surface) a lower minimum may often be
found. Such a relaxation of a constraint typically represents a
modification of a design requirement.
 This kind of trade off may be profitable and is therefore facilitated
in the IOD system by an interactive optimization procedure.   The
Hilleary tangent search method (12) employed for the search of the
minimum has thus been modified, such that a message is displayed
whenever a new constraint surface is encountered. The designer may then
study the case, and move the encountered constraint surface.

In spite of the very complex services provided by the IOD system, the
handling of the system is expected to be easy .
 This is due to the few principles employed for handling the system.
The basic view is that the designer controls the design process and the
IOD system is his tool. Whenever the designer needs a service form the
system, e.g. for converting a model variable to a constant. The IOD
function that provide this service (CONSTANT) is selcted from the IOD
function menu which is always available on the right most part of the

screen (Fig. 1). The list of IOD functions is given in Table 1. After the selection of a IOD function the user is asked to supply the data needed for execution of the IOD functon selected. These data are supplied through prompts and menus in the central and left part of the screen (the work area in Fig. 1).

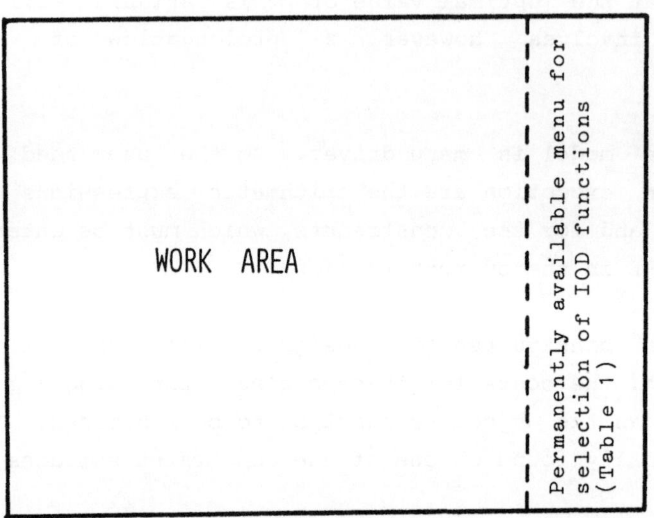

FIG 1   Arrangement of Displays on the Screen

If the purpose of such a menu is not clear to the user, he may invoke the IOD function EXPLANATION. An explanation to a prompt request is achieved by pressing the "?" key. The use of these two different explanation mechanisms is unfortunate, but it was enforced by a hardware limitation in the TEKTRONIX 4015 used.

3. Programmer View of the IOD System

The structured programming approach (7) has been employed in the development of the IOD system. Since the literature on structured programming is mostly based on small examples, the experience with the use of the approach in the development of the large IOD system will be discussed in some detail. The IOD system was implemented in APL (2) because it had to interface with other programs in this language. The author has most of his previous programming experience with various ALGOL like language (including PL/1) and had therefore some hesitation in using APL, whose only control structure is GOTO, which has no

Menu item	Purpose on explanation	
CREATE MODIFY DELETE	Kind of activity: Example: Deletion of dependent variables is accomplished by selection of DELETE followed selection of DEP_VAR, thereafter the names of the variables to be deleted are selected	Model generation activities
MODEL IND_VAR DEP_VAR CONSTRAINT CONSTANT	Type of data: Model of an entire ship Independent variable X_i Dependent variable Y_j. It is at the same time a definition of an equation $Y_j=Y_j(Y_t,X_i)$ to be satisfied by the solution Constraint to be met by the solution A variable may be converted into a constant and vice versa	
GET_MODEL STORE_MODEL DISPLAY_MODEL APPROX OPTIMIZE DATA_BASE METHODS EXPLANATION	Get a previously stored model Store a model for later use Fit a mathematical function selected from a menu to data which are either provided by the user or retrieved from the data base Search a min for the objective function to be selected by the user Data retrieval using EQBE Search of method from method data base Display an explanation for the current activity	

Table 1:   Menu for selection of IOD functions

blocks and whose procedures ("defined functions" in APL terminology) may not contain local procedures. However, APL has other advantages and eventually proved to be very adequate for the project.

This confirmed the general principle that the usefulness of a programming system is due to the entire combination of facilities it provides, and cannot be assessed on the basis of the absence or presence of a particular facility. This point will be further illustrated by various examples in the discussion of the implementation (the reader is not assumed to know APL).

3.1 Structure of the IOD System

When a user selects an IOD function through the IOD menu an APL function having the same name is executed (Fig. 2). During the execution of this function other functions may be called, so actually a whole subprogram is executed. Fig. 3 shows an example of such a subprogram. The development of a subprogram followed basically the structured programming approach as illustrated for instance in (3) and (21). The segmentation of the subprogram into functions was based on two principles.

1. Each function solves logically similar problems at same "level of abstraction". The function OPTIMIZE (Fig. 3) initializes the variables needed in the optimization process and calls OPTIMIZATION_MAIN. The initializations are regarded to be logically similar while the optimization is another kind of activity, and is therefore pushed to another APL function (OPRIMIZATION_MAIN) representing another level of abstraction. The function OPTIMIZATION_MAIN selects the successive directions along which the minimum of the objective function is searched. The details of the search along a selected direction are pushed to a lower level of abstraction in the function PATTERN_MOVE called from OPTIMIZATION_MAIN.

2. A function must be so small that it may be thoroughly analyzed by the programmer. The previous requirement that a function contains only logically similar activities obviously enhances the programmers ability to analyze the function. A further enhancement is achieved by emphasizing a clear coding style (14) The requirement that functions be so small that a programmer may analyze them thoroughly

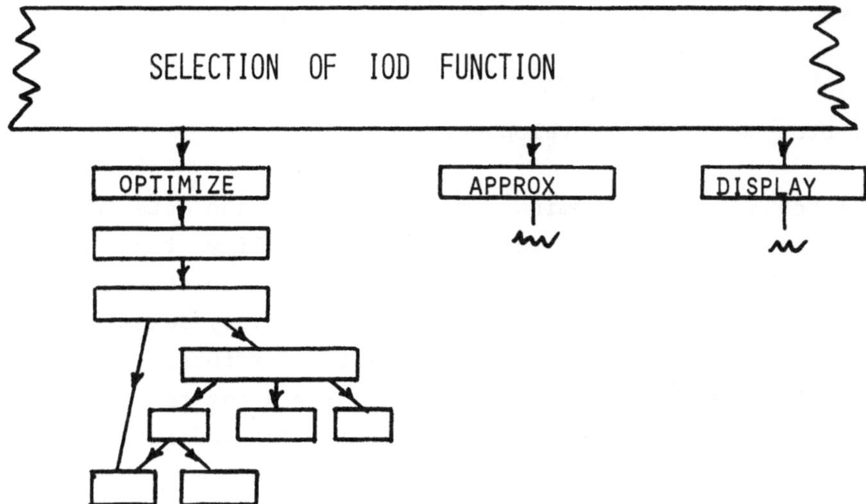

FIG. 2   Structure of the IOD system. A list of the IOD functions
is given in Table 1. Each IOD function is implemented
as a subprogram (a module). Every box represents an
APL function and the arrows show the direction of the
function calls. An example of such a module is shown
in Fig. 2.

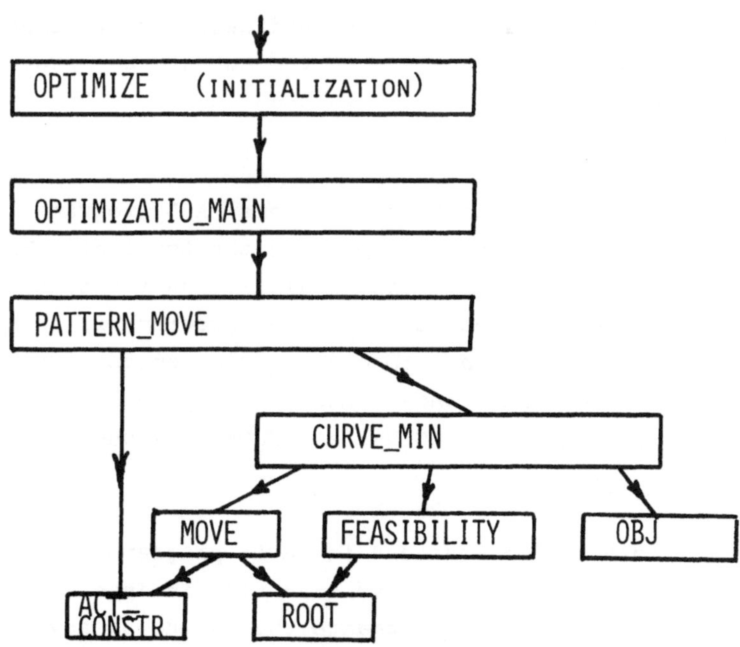

FIG. 3   The organization of the implementation of the IOD
function OPTIMIZE. Each box represents an APL function.
The arrows show the direction of function calls.

resulted in short functions, typcially 5-10 statements.

3.2 The prototype program development techniques.

Many text books in programming advise careful and detailed program planning before coding. This reduces the probability for ill designed programs that have to be recoded at high cost. If, however, the problem area is not well understood the investment in a very detailed planning and coding may prove to be an enormous waste of efforts. It is in such cases probably most economical first to develop a not too sophisticated and relatively inexpensive prototype program. The understanding of the problems gained through the development and use of the prototype program is then utilized for a gradual program improvement. If the principles underlying the prototype program are not appropriate the gradual improvement process may result in a "patched" and inefficient program. It is in such a case advantageous to discard the prototype system and design a new one. Coding is thus a frequent recurring activity in the prototype methodology, and it is therefore essential to employ a programming system where the costs of program writing and testing are low. The APL system proved very useful for the gradual improvement techniques because the costs of coding and testing with this interactive system were significally lower than with the batch oriented ALGOL like systems that the author has previously used. Some of the reasons for the usefulness of the APL system will be discussed.

Due to the powerful primitive functions APL programs tend to be short, which reduces the amount of typing at the terminal. With the extremely simple language structure, the possibilities for syntax errors are few, and they are all corrected while the program is entered There is no possiblity for forgetting to close a program comment, because like in FORTRAN, a new line ends automatically a comment. There is no possiblity for missing BEGINs and ENDs, because the language has no blocks.

A major cost saving factor in APL programming are the excellent debugging aids. When a program execution is interrupted by a bug, the programmer may inspect and change the value of any program variable, explore the nature of the bug through test calculations using any of the functions of the program. When the bug is detected the program is corrected and the execution is continued (no compilation is required because the APL system is interpretative). Many bugs may thus be corrected in a single session. Similar debugging aids are found in other interpretative systems.

3.3 Code for same activitiy only once in the program

Program modification may be facilitated by adhering to the principle:

A piece of code for an activity needed at different places in the program appears only in one place.

This principle may be implemented by putting the code for such an activity in a separate APL function , and has the advantages that a single program modification involves only one function. Let us illustrate this principle with a simple case. All the I/O of the IOD system are made through three functions:

1) SELECTOR ← SELECTION_IN MENU
   The line above is the first line of the definition of the function SELECTION_IN. This function displays the character matrix supplied by the argument MENU and assigns to the variable SELECTOR the number of the row (line) that the light pen or (cursor) point at. Note,by the way, the clarity by which the first line of this APL function definition conveys the purpose of the function.

2) DISPLAY MESSAGE
   The function DISPLAY displays the character matrix supplied by the argument MESSAGE.

3) INPUT ← EXPLANATION PROMPT PROMPT_REQUEST
   The function PROMPT displays the character matrix supplied by the argument PROMPT_REQUEST, and assigns to INPUT the character string entered by the user at the terminal. If the user types a sole "?" the character string EXPLANATION is displayed.

In accordance with the principle of having a piece of code only once in the program, the functions SELECTION_IN and PROMPT call DISPLAY for displays. An improvement of the DISPLAY function will thus automatically be useful for all the many functions which call SELECTION_IN and PROMPT. A further advantage is that a bug in the display process has only to be searched and corrected in one place in the program, i.e. in DISPLAY.

The principle of having the code for a given activity only once in the program was implemented in the IOD system with no hesitation; even when it involved the definition of very short functions of say 3 statements. The reason is that the costs involved in the call of an APL function are for most purposes negligible. This is among other reasons due to the very simple argument transfer mechanism in APL with no check of the types of the arguments at the function call time. The costs of procedure calls in an ALGOL like language is on the other hand high. Many programmers are therefore reluctant to use procedure calls intensively (they should however only be hesitant with procedure calls in the body of loops that may be frequently repeated).

3.4 Clear programming style

The syntax of the APL statement enables often a very clear programming style. One example is the statement

$$SELECTOR \leftarrow SELECTION\_IN\ MENU$$

discussed in section 3.3. It is seen that by employing long self explaining identifiers, e.g. SELECTION_IN, the need for program comments is avoided. This is a good strategy since programmers often forget to update the comments when they modify their program.

The underscore symbol proved useful for identifiers composed of a number of words, e.g. SELECTION_IN, and it is therefore difficult to understand why it is not accepted in some APL implementations. Short identifiers, e.g. of one character, were only employed for frequently appearing variables or for auxiliary variables of local nature.

Loops and conditionals (IF-THEN-ELSE-FI) may in APL only be coded with GOTOs, and as pointed out by Dijsktra (7) and others this reduces the clarity of the program. The negative effects of the use of the GOTO were reduced by

1. Employing self explanatory labels.
2. The scope of GOTO in APL is limited to the function in which it appears. For the reasons given in section 3.2, the functions were generally small (5-10 statements) and had a very simple flow structure with few GOTOs.
3. Loops are relatively seldom in APL, because the language has many functions that operate on entire arrays.

The author has in the entire IOD project only observed a single bug due to the GOTOs so they have not been specially harmful.

Two restrictions of the APL language are generally quite irritating:

1. A function may at the most have two arguments. Globals must therefore often be used for transmission of arguments.

2. There is no way of limiting the scope of function names. Merging of programs produced by different programmers may therefore involve name collision problems.

4. Conclusions

4.1 A powerful, general and nevertheless handy CAD system

The power of the IOD system is due to its many functions (Table 1). The handling of the system is nevertheless simple, because the same simple operation rules are employed for all the functions . The user need not learn an elaborate programming language because most communication is through prompts and menus. The exception is the subset of APL required for writing of arithmetic and boolean expressions. However since the potential users are engineers, it is anticipated that only a relatively modest effort is needed for training.

A number of sophisticated menu driven CAD systems have been used for a number of years. These are mostly systems taylored to a special trade. Compared to such systems the IOD system may be regarded as a general purpose system. Adaptation of the IOD system to a particular area of engineering involves only the creation of a data base for this particular area. The user of the system may thereafter use EQBE for a convenient retrieval of data within a wide space of search criteria. With these data complex non-linear models with constraints may be constructed and optimized. The creative designer is thus expected to have a flexible tool for developing and checking his ideas. Experiments are planned to check to what extent the expectations to the system are met.

4.2 The programming techniques employed and the use of APL

The described project was developed and implemented by the author in one year. Beside system development a considerable effort was required in search of a suitable optimization model and a numerically robust optimization method. There was a considerable number of open problems at the beginning of the project, and the insight gained through the development and use of the first crude system helped in clarifying these problems. In the successive system improvements that followed, considerable parts of the program were recoded. The effort required for recoding with the programming techniques employed proved,however, to be modest. So the author did not hesitate to improve unsatisfactory program segments. Program modification was facilitated by well established techniques such an extreme emphasize on the the clarity of the programming style, and a logical segmentation of the program into APL functions that are so small, that each of them may be thoroughly analyzed. Furthermore the principles that code for any given activity appears only once in the program, and that operation on a complex data structure is allways done through a single special function. These principles ensure that a single program modification may always be accomplished by changes in a single code segment.

The use of APL seemingly reduced the effort for program development as compared to what the author would expect with the ALGOL-like batch systems that he has used previously. As illustrated, APL syntax is useful for writing clear programs. It is recommended that all APL implementations permit this use of underscores in identifiers. This will enable identifiers composed of more than one word and further facilitate writing of self explanatory programs. The useful set of primitive functions for array handling makes APL programs short and easy to type. APL's primitive program structures reduce the possibilities for syntax error, but make modular programming more difficult. APL's interactive debugging aids result in a very sizeable saving of programmer time. The ease by which the APL system is handled, the reliability of the APL implementation as well as the simple and logical structure of the language produce a system that it is a pleasure to work with.

References

(1)   K. Aihara, N. Sugawara, An Interactive Real Time Procedure in Ship
      Initial Design, Proceedings of ICCAS, Tokyo, August 1973,
      reprinted in Computer Applications in Shipping and Shipbuilding,
      vol. 2, North Holland Publishing Company, Amsterdam, 1974,
      425-434.

(2)   APL Language, Order no. GC26-3847-0, IBM, 1975.

(3)   Amman, U., The Method of Structured Programming Applied to the
      Development of a Compiler, Proceedings of ACM International
      Computing Symposium Davos 1973, North Holland Publishing Company,
      Amsterdam 1974.

(4)   Bergen, M., Interface Manual, IBM Heidelberg Scientific Center,
      1976, (unpublished).

(5)   Beier, K. P., Nowacki, H., Schubert, C., Weichbrodt, A., A General
      Purpose Software System for Optimization, International Conference
      on Computer Applications in the Automation of Shipyard Operation
      and Ship Design, Gothenburg 1976, North Holland Publishing
      Company, Amsterdam 1976, 111-116.

(6)   Chryssostomidis, C., Computer Aided Ship Design Education at the
      Massachusetts Institute of Technology, International Conference on
      Computer Applications in the Automation of Shipyard Operation and
      Ship Design, Gothenburg 1976, North Holland Publishing Company,
      Amsterdam, 1976.

(7)   Dahl, O. J., Dijkstra, E. W., Hoare, C. A., Structured
      Programming, Academic Press, London, 1972.

(8)   Erbe, R., Walch, G., Ein Dialogsystem zur Methodensuche, GI-5.
      Jahrestagung, Lecture Notes in Computer Science, 34, 133-148,
      Springer Verlag, 1975.

(9)   Gallin, C., Which Way Computer-Aided Preliminary Ship Design and
      Optimization, Proceedings of ICCAS, Tokyo, August 1973, reprinted
      in Computer Applications in Shipping and Shipbuilding, vol. 2,
      North Holland Publishing Company, Amsterdam, 1974, 393-403.

(10) Hartwig, R., Interactive Storing ,Retrieval, Transformation and
      Evaluation of Scientific Data with an Experimental System,
      GI-6.Jahrestagung, Springer Verlag,Heidelberg, 1976.

(11) Herzog, B., A Transportable FORTRAN Based Executive System for
      Computer Aided Ship Design Education, International Conference on
      Computer Applications in the Automation of Shipyard Operation and
      Ship Design, Gothenburg 1976, North Holland Publishing Company,
      Amsterdam, 1976, 79-90.

(12) Hilleary, R.R., The Tangent Search Method for Constraint
      Minimization, U.S. Naval Postgraduate School Technical
      Report/Research Paper No. 59, March 1966.

(13) Johnson, R. S. et al, Man-Computer Graphics in Preliminary Ship
      Design, Joint AIAA/SNAME Meeting, Annapolis, July 1972.

(14) Kernigham, B. W., Plauger, P. J., Programming Style, Examples and
      Counterexamples, Computing Surveys, 6, 1974, 303-319.

(15) Lang, C. A., Achievements in Computer Aided Design, IFIP   74,

758-767, North Holland, Amsterdam, 1974.

(16) Matsuka, H., Kavai, T., Fujisaki, T., Interactive Ship Design System, Proceedings of ICCAS, Tokyo, August 1975, reprinted in Computer Applications in Shipping and Shipbuilding, vol. 2, North Holland, Amsterdam, 1974,417-424.

(17) Miura, H., Kavlie, J., Moe, J., Interactive Optimum Design of Tanker Structures, Proceedings of ICCAS, Tokyo, August 1973, reprinted in Computer Applications in Shipping and Shipbuilding, vol. 2, North Holland, Amsterdam, 1974, 349-361.

(18) Nowacki, H., Optimization in Pre-Contract Ship Design, Proceedings of ICCAS, Tokyo, August 1973, reprinted in Computer Applications in Shipping and Shipbuilding, vol. 2, North Holland, Amsterdam, 1974, 327-338.

(19) Parson, G. M., Optimization Methods for Use in Computer Aided Ship Design, STAR Symposium Society of Naval Architects and Marine Engineers, 1975.

(20) Schauer, U., Ein System zur interaktiven Bearbeitung umfangreicher Messdaten, Lecture Notes in Computer Science, 39, 213-231, Springer Verlang, 1975.

(21) Wirth, N., On Composition of Well-Structured Programs, ACM Computing Surveys, 6, Dec. 1974, 247-260.

(22) Woodward, J. B., Computer Aided Ship Design Education at the University of Michigan, International Conference on Computer Applications in the Automation of Shipyard Operation and Ship Design, Gothenburg, 1976, North Holland Publishing Company, Amsterdam, 1976, 73-78.

(22) Zloof, M., Query by Example, NCC 75, 431-438.

ÄNDERUNGSFREUNDLICHKEIT KOMMERZIELLER ANWENDUNGSPROGRAMME

Hubert Österle

am Lehrstuhl für Betriebsinformatik

Universität Dortmund, Postfach 500500, 4600 Dortmund 50

Gliederung

1. Vorbemerkung

Rechnet man die Weiterentwicklung einer EDV-Anwendung zur Anwendungsentwicklung, so
können rund 50 Prozent der Entwicklungskosten einer betrieblichen Anwendung der Änderung von Programmen zugeordnet werden[1]. Damit erlangt unter den Anforderungen, die
man an die Programmentwicklung stellen muß[2], die Änderungsfreundlichkeit eines Programmes eine besondere Bedeutung.

Unter **Programmentwicklung** verstehen wir in diesem Zusammenhang die Umsetzung einer Programmvorgabe in ein Rechnerprogramm. **Die Programmvorgabe** besteht aus der Festlegung von
Eingabe, Ausgabe und Funktion eines Programmes. Im Gegensatz zum technisch-wissenschaftlichen Bereich liegen Programmvorgaben in der betrieblichen Datenverarbeitung
gewöhnlich nicht formal exakt beschrieben vor[3]. Der Programmierer ist jedoch dank
seines Kontextes im Anwendungsgebiet meist in der Lage, eine grobe Aufgabenbeschrei-
bung zu konkretisieren.

Mit der <u>Änderungsfreundlichkeit</u> eines Programmes wird ausgedrückt, wie hoch der erwartete Aufwand einer Programmänderung ist.

In der Folge stellen wir einige Charakteristika von Änderungen heraus. Darauf aufbauend untersuchen wir, welche Eigenschaften eines Programmes den Änderungsaufwand bestimmen und mit welchen Methoden bei der Programmentwicklung diese erreicht werden.

2. Charakteristik der Änderungen

<u>Programmänderungen</u> sind Anpassungen der Leistung eines bestehenden Programmes an davon abweichende Anforderungen der Programmvorgabe.

2.1. Ursachen

Für die Abweichung von Leistung und Aufgabe eines Programmes können primär folgende Ursachen genannt werden:

- Fehler in der Programmentwicklung

  Ein sehr häufiger Grund sind inhaltliche Fehler im Umsetzen einer Programmvorgabe in ein Rechnerprogramm. Die Anzahl dieser Fehler kann zwar durch die Anwendung verschiedener Techniken[4] reduziert werden, ist aber vor allem bei umfangreichen Problemstellungen immer noch hoch. Dies resultiert im Bereich betrieblicher Anwendungen zum Teil auch daraus, daß dem Programmierer die Aufgabe der Konkretisierung grob vorgegebener Aufgaben zukommt.

- Änderung im Programmumfeld

  Häufige Ursache für Änderungen in laufenden Programmen ist eine Änderung in der Umgebung des Programmes. Ist beispielsweise eine Debitorenbuchhaltung als Offene-Posten-Buchhaltung organisiert und wird als neue Anwendung ein automatisiertes Mahnwesen entwickelt, so kann es notwendig werden, in die Offene-Posten-Datei pro Satz einen Hinweis auf bereits erfolgte Mahnungen aufzunehmen. Dies hat aber zur Folge, daß alle Programme, die bisher diese Datei verwendet haben, geändert werden müssen. Als weiteres Beispiel sei die Umstellung auf neue Hardware und Basissoftware (Betriebssysteme etc.) erwähnt.

- Fehler in der Programmvorgabe

  Entspricht die organisatorische Konzeption einer Anwendung und damit die Programmvorgabe nicht den betrieblichen Anforderungen, so wird dies spätestens im Betrieb der Anwendung deutlich. Es folgt daraus eine Konzeptions- und Programmänderung. Als Beispiel dafür sei ein Programmsystem zur Auftragsüberwachung angenommen, in dem eine Funktion "Stornierung eines Auftrages" vorkommt. Darin sollen Kundenaufträge und Aufträge von Außenlagern gleich behandelt werden. Bei dieser Vorgabe sei allerdings übersehen worden, daß ein Kundenauftrag nur innerhalb einer gewissen Frist nach Erteilung zurückgezogen werden kann, während Aufträge von Außenlagern jederzeit rückgängig gemacht werden können. Derartige Fehler treten bei der Übernahme manueller

Verarbeitungen auf den Rechner häufig auf, da eine vollständige Erfassung auch von
so einfachen Entscheidungsabläufen äußerst schwierig ist.

- <u>Änderungen im organisatorischen Umfeld</u>

Das organisatorische Umfeld einer Anwendung wird durch das Anwendungsgebiet (beispielsweise eine Lohnabrechnung) und die Gesellschaft (vor allem in Form von Gesetzen)
gebildet. Diese Bereiche unterliegen einerseits einem stetigen organisatorischen
Wandel, durch den Änderungen bestehender Programmteile notwendig werden; andererseits
entstehen in ihnen laufend neue Anforderungen an EDV-Anwendungen. Als Beispiel sei
hier auf die sich laufend ändernden gesetzlichen Bestimmungen zur Lohn- und Gehalts-
abrechnung oder auf die zunehmende Umstellung von off line- auf on line-Anwendungen
hingewiesen.

2.2. Auswirkungen

Änderungen aufgrund von Fehlern in der Programmvorgabe und in der Programmentwicklung
werden zum überwiegenden Teil im Modultest bzw. Systemtest entdeckt und beseitigt. Sie
sind die Hauptursache für den hohen Testaufwand, der mit 20 Prozent des Gesamtaufwandes
der Anwendungsentwicklung angegeben wird[1].

Änderungen in der Umgebung des Programmes sowie dem organisatorischen Umfeld der Anwendung treten überwiegend nach der Übergabe des Programmes in den Routinebetrieb auf. Sie
verursachen zusammen mit den oben genannten Änderungsgründen einen Wartungsaufwand, der
derzeit auf ca. 30 bis 40 Prozent der gesamten Anwendungsentwicklung geschätzt wird[1].

2.3. Arten

Neben den Ursachen von Änderungen und deren Auswirkungen auf die Entwicklungskosten ist
hier vor allem die Art der Änderungen in einem Programm interessant.
Eine Änderungsart, die meist mit geringem Aufwand verbunden ist, stellt die Modifikation
von Größen dar, die als Parameter des Programmsystems aufgefaßt werden können. Sie betrifft Angaben wie beispielsweise die Anzahl von Verarbeitungssätzen und damit die Bedingung zur Terminierung iterativer Operationen. Ein Beispiel dafür ist die Anzahl der
Kostenstellen, für die ein Betriebsabrechnungsbogen erstellt werden soll.

Bei Änderungen, welche die auszuführenden Operationen betreffen, können wir unterscheiden, ob davon die der Verarbeitung zugrunde liegenden Datenstrukturen berührt werden
oder nicht. Wir betrachten hier nicht die Datenstruktur im Sinne der Datenorganisation,
sondern jene Struktur der Daten, die sich ergibt, wenn die Elemente einer Datenmenge
entsprechend ihrer unterschiedlichen Verarbeitung klassifiziert werden[5]. Durch die
Klassifikation nach der Verarbeitung kann man eine Datenmenge hierarchisch strukturie-
ren, wie dies zum Beispiel in Abb. 1 (siehe nächste Seite) zum Ausdruck kommt.
Wird beispielsweise ein Algorithmus zur Provisionsabrechnung umgestellt und verwendet
er dieselben Daten wie zuvor, so bleiben die Datenstrukturen unverändert. Es ändern
sich lediglich die auf sie angewandten Operationen. Eine Änderung der Datenstruktur

liegt beispielsweise vor, wenn ein Datenerfassungsprotokoll, in dem alle Sätze der
Dateneingabe ausgegeben wurden, nun Kopf- und Abschlußzeilen erhalten soll.

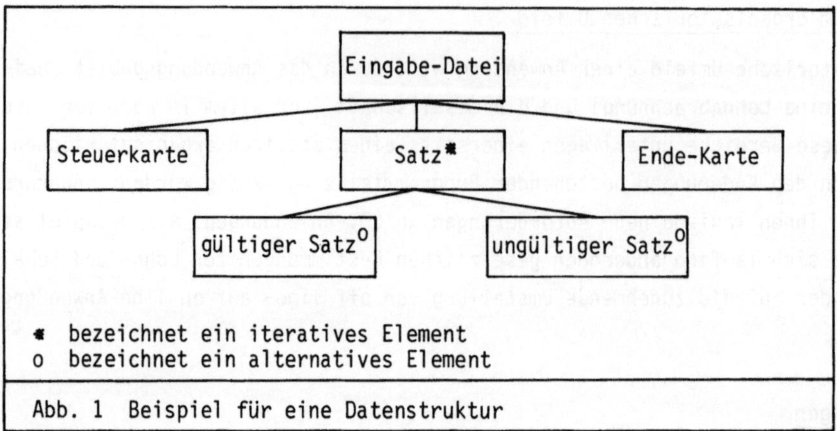

Abb. 1 Beispiel für eine Datenstruktur

2.4. Ablauf

Eine Programmänderung läuft in allgemeiner Form in folgenden Schritten ab:

- Suchen der zu ändernden Stellen im Programm,
- Erfassen von deren logischer Umgebung,
- Ausführung der direkten und indirekten Änderungen und
- Kontrolle des Erfolges der Änderung (Test).

Ist eine Änderung nicht erfolgreich (laut einer Untersuchung der RAND Corporation jede
zweite Änderung[6]), so ist eine erneute Änderung notwendig: die vier Schritte werden
wiederholt durchlaufen. Am folgenden Beispiel seien die Änderungsschritte kurz erläutert.

Durch Verschiebung des Produktspektrums reicht die in einem Fakturierungsprogramm vorhandene dreistellige Dezimalgröße für den Preis nicht mehr aus. Nun muß zunächst gesucht werden, an welchen Stellen im Programm die Variable für den Preis festgelegt ist.
Danach beginnt das Erfassen der logischen Umgebung, d.h. es muß einerseits untersucht
werden, ob sich bei der Verwendung dieser Variablen (z.B. bei Multiplikationen) Änderungen ergeben, andererseits muß für Variable, deren Wert durch Verknüpfung mit dem
Preis zustande kommt (z.B. Zeilen- und Totalbeträge, Mehrwertsteuerbeträge), dieselbe
Prüfung angestellt werden. Die Auswirkungen der Änderung können so weit gehen, daß dadurch auch andere Programme betroffen werden. So erstellt beispielsweise das Fakturier-
programm Sätze für die Finanzbuchhaltung, in denen unter anderem der Fakturabetrag und
der Mehrwertsteuerbetrag vorkommen.

Sind alle Änderungsstellen aufgefunden, muß die Änderung im Programm ausgeführt werden.
Da dieser Prozeß aber mit Unsicherheiten belastet ist, muß das modifizierte Programm
getestet werden. Werden dabei Fehler sichtbar, so folgt daraus eine neue Änderung.

Aus den Ursachen für Programmänderungen geht hervor, daß zwar ein gewisser Teil des

sehr hohen Änderungsaufwandes durch die Korrektheit der Programmentwicklung beeinflußt
werden kann, ein anderer Teil davon unberührt bestehen bleibt. Die Ursachen für diese
Änderungen tauchen erst nach Abschluß der Programmentwicklung auf. Die Änderungsfreundlichkeit eines Programmes ist daher auch für vollständig korrekte Programme von Bedeutung. Sie hängt davon ab, welcher Aufwand bei den verschiedenen Änderungsarten innerhalb der einzelnen Änderungsschritte anfällt. Die Programmeigenschaften, die diesen
Aufwand beeinflussen, werden im folgenden untersucht.

3. Einfluß der Programmeigenschaften auf die Änderungsfreundlichkeit

3.1. Anzahl der zu ändernden Programmteile

Zunächst ist die Frage interessant, wieviele Programmteile von einer Änderung betroffen
sind. Als <u>Programmteil</u> verstehen wir hier den Abschnitt eines Programmes, der die
logisch nächste Umgebung der Änderung bildet. Bei einem modularen Programmaufbau ist
dies ein Modul. Die Anzahl der zu ändernden Programmteile beeinflußt den Änderungsaufwand in mehrfacher Weise: sie bestimmt die Zeit, die zum Suchen der Änderungsstellen
notwendig ist, beeinflußt die Wahrscheinlichkeit, mit der alle zu modifizierenden
Stellen gefunden werden, legt fest, wie oft der Aufwand zur Ausführung von Änderungen
anfällt und wirkt sich auf den Umfang der Programmtests aus.

Bei der oben zuerst genannten Änderungsart, der Modifikation von "Systemparametern",
wird besonders deutlich, welchen Einfluß die Programmgestaltung auf den Änderungsaufwand besitzt. Wird beispielsweise in einem Programm mehrmals auf eine Zeichenketten-
variable zugegriffen, so kann die Zeichenkettenlänge (z.B. 80 Zeichen, wenn die Variable
einen Eingabesatz von einer Lochkarte erhält) an mehreren Stellen im Programm als Konstante, die die Systemauslegung definiert, enthalten sein. Sie kann aber auch in einer
Variablen gespeichert werden, auf die sich alle Stellen im Programm beziehen, die die
Zeichenkettenlänge benötigen. Fällt eine Änderung des Eingabesatzes und damit der
Zeichenkettenvariablen (z.B. durch Umsteigen auf on line-Eingabe) an, muß bei der
ersten Alternative zur Festlegung der Zeichenkettenlänge an mehreren Stellen geändert
werden, während bei der zweiten die Änderung auf genau eine Stelle im Programm abgrenz-
bar ist.

Wir können als in diesem Zusammenhang wichtige Eigenschaft eines Programmes die Anzahl
der Stellen im Programm festhalten, an denen dieselbe Größe (Systemkonstante) als konstanter Wert verwendet wird.

Ähnliche Überlegungen kann man anstellen, wenn dieselbe Funktion in einem Programm
mehrfach benötigt wird. Ein Beispiel dafür könnte die Funktion "Suche in einem sequentiellen File einen Satz mit dem Kennzeichen X" sein. Wird diese Funktion in einem allgemein verwendbaren "Such"-Operator realisiert, so schlägt sich eine eventuell notwendige Änderung in einem einzigen, genau definierten Programmabschnitt nieder.

Als weitere für die Änderungsfreundlichkeit wichtige Programmeigenschaft können wir somit die Anzahl der Stellen, an denen dieselbe Funktion ausgeführt wird, festhalten.

In gleicher Weise hängt die Anzahl der von einer Änderung betroffenen Programmteile vom Programmaufbau ab, wenn sich die Datenstruktur ändert. Eine Änderung, die sich auf eine bestimmte Datenstruktur bezieht, muß an all jenen Stellen in einem Programm ausgeführt werden, an denen die Datenstruktur in der Steuerungslogik fixiert ist. Enthält beispielsweise eine sequentiell verarbeitete Eingabedatei zwei Satzarten und wird die Unterscheidung zwischen den beiden Satzarten an mehreren Stellen vorgenommen, so ist die Einführung einer dritten Satzart mit einem hohen Änderungsaufwand verbunden.

Somit kann man feststellen, daß der Änderungsaufwand von der Anzahl der Stellen abhängt, an denen dieselbe Entscheidung (Unterscheidung nach Datenelementen) getroffen wird.

3.2. Umgebung der zu ändernden Programmteile

Sind die Stellen, an denen ein Programm geändert werden muß, festgestellt, so muß für jede überprüft werden, welche Auswirkungen von der Änderung auf das restliche Programm ausgehen. Der Aufwand dafür hängt von folgenden Faktoren ab:

3.2.1. Steuerungsschnittstelle

Die Größe der Umgebung, die von einer Änderung betroffen ist, wird durch die Steuerungsschnittstelle des zu ändernden Programmteiles mit dem Rest des Programmes wesentlich beeinflußt. Besitzt ein Programmteil mehrere Ein- und Ausgänge und kann zu ihm von mehreren Stellen bzw. von ihm zu mehreren Stellen verzweigt werden (typisch für monolithisch organisierte Programme[7]), so muß bei einer Änderung eine Vielzahl von Beziehungen geprüft werden. Die Problematik derartiger Programmstrukturen wird besonders offenkundig, wenn beispielsweise Files verarbeitet werden, die an mehreren Stellen geöffnet und geschlossen werden.

Besitzt dagegen ein Programmteil nur einen einzigen Eingang und einen einzigen Ausgang und wird zu ihm nur von einer einzigen Stelle verzweigt (typisch für baumstrukturierte Programme[8]), so ist die Anzahl der Beziehungen, die bei einer Änderung im Auge behalten werden muß, sehr gering. Die Wahrscheinlichkeit, daß Auswirkungen einer Änderung nicht beachtet werden, ist klein.

Der Aufwand von Änderungen ist daher dann am geringsten, wenn der Umfang der Steuerungsschnittstelle am kleinsten ist.

3.2.2. Datenschnittstelle

Für die Datenschnittstelle gelten ähnliche Überlegungen wie für die Steuerungsschnittstelle: Die Auswirkungen von Änderungen sind erst dann überprüfbar, wenn die Benutzung von Größen, die von der Änderung betroffen sind, in anderen Programmteilen geklärt ist. Bei der Datenschnittstelle muß daher die Betrachtung auf andere Pro-

gramme ausgedehnt werden. Dabei ist zwischen einer internen und einer externen Datenkommunikation zu unterscheiden.

Eine Änderung, bei der beispielsweise ein neues Datenelement in einen Satz einer
externen Datei aufgenommen werden muß, wirkt sich auf den externen Datenaustausch
mit anderen Programmen aus. Ebenso hat eine Änderung in den Ausprägungen einer Steue-
rungsvariablen über die interne Datenkommunikation unter Umständen weitverzweigte
Folgen.

In Analogie zur Steuerungsschnittstelle kann für die Datenschnittstelle festgestellt
werden, daß der Änderungsaufwand von ihrem Umfang, also der Anzahl der intern und
extern ausgetauschten Datenelemente, abhängt.

3.3. Klarheit der zu ändernden Programmteile

Sind die Stellen, an denen ein Programm geändert werden muß, gefunden und ist deren
Umgebung erfaßt, so muß die Änderung in den so abgegrenzten Programmteilen vorgenommen werden. Dazu müssen diese vollständig überblickt werden können.

3.3.1. Größe

Die Größe des Programmteiles beeinflußt in erster Linie die Verständlichkeit. Aus
diesem Grunde werden vereinzelt Begrenzungen für die Modulgröße gefordert. Eine gute
Lesbarkeit eines Programmteiles wird angenommen, wenn dieser einen Umfang von ca.
30 Statements[9] nicht überschreitet. Ein anderer, weit verbreiteter Wert ist eine
Seite Programmcode[10].

Auch wenn derartige Angaben als allgemeine Richtlinien durchaus verwendbar sind, so
treffen sie keineswegs in jedem Falle zu (z.B. große lineare Sequenz oder große Zahl
gleichartiger Verzweigungen). Sie müssen immer im Zusammenhang mit der Steuerungslogik
und den Operatoren der Zielsprache gesehen werden. Ein Programm, das aus einer Reihe
sehr komplexer Operatoren zusammengesetzt ist, ist schwieriger zu überblicken als eines,
das aus derselben Anzahl weniger mächtiger Operatoren besteht. Die Funktionsbreite
und damit aber auch der Informationswert seiner Operatoren ist höher.

3.3.2. Struktur

Für die Überschaubarkeit eines Programmteiles ist - wie schon für die anderen Faktoren
der Änderungsfreundlichkeit - die Anzahl der gleichzeitig zu beachtenden Elemente des
Programmes wichtig. Kann man sich auf wenige Elemente konzentrieren, ohne stets die
gesamte Umgebung im Auge behalten zu müssen, so ist der Aufwand der Änderung geringer
und die Wahrscheinlichkeit ihres Erfolges höher. Ein klarer Kontrollfluß kann dafür
sorgen, daß jeweils nur ein abgeschlossener Teil betrachtet werden muß. Die Anzahl
der Sprünge, die den sequentiellen Ablauf eines Programmes unterbrechen, beeinflussen
die Lesbarkeit eines Programmteiles wesentlich.

Ein weiterer Faktor, der die Klarheit eines Programmes bestimmt, sind die Elemente
der Zielsprache. Einerseits können die Steuerungselemente die Struktur eines Programmes deutlich machen, andererseits bestimmen die Mächtigkeit und die Problemnähe der
Operatoren den Umfang eines Programmteiles. Der Umfang des Programmcodes, der bei
einer Änderung gelesen und überblickt werden muß, ist beispielsweise bei Verwendung
einer Planungssprache wesentlich geringer als in einer allgemeinen Programmiersprache.

Faßt man die Eigenschaften von Programmen zusammen, die für die Änderungsfreundlichkeit von Bedeutung sind, so kann man sie auf die allgemeine Programmeigenschaft "Lokalität" reduzieren. Wir sprechen hier in Analogie zum Programmverhalten bezüglich Verarbeitung in einem Rechnersystem[11] von Lokalität bezüglich Änderungen.

Mit Lokalität bezeichnen wir die Eigenschaft eines Programmes, welche die Anzahl und
die Distanz der Programmelemente bestimmt, auf die eine Änderung Bezug nimmt.

4. Entwicklung von Programmen mit hoher Lokalität

Aus der Literatur und aus der Praxis sind verschiedene Ansätze der Programmentwicklung bekannt[12]. Diese sind geschaffen worden, um die zunehmende Komplexität der Anwendungen in den Griff zu bekommen. Wir untersuchen hier, wie eine hohe Lokalität von
Programmen erreichbar ist. Dabei werden mehrere Verfahren zur Programmentwicklung
kombiniert und um einige Aspekte ergänzt.

Da die Techniken sich häufig auf einer unterschiedlichen Detailebene in der Programmentwicklung bewegen, scheint es angebracht, hier eine Unterscheidung zwischen Programmentwurf und Programmierung vorzunehmen. Mit Programmentwurf bezeichnen wir alle
Aktivitäten, die auf den globalen Aufbau eines Programmes (z.B. die Modulstruktur) bezogen sind. In ihm wird bestimmt, welche Funktionen in einem Programm enthalten sind
und welche Abhängigkeit zwischen ihnen besteht. In der Programmierung dagegen wird
festgelegt, wie die Funktionen realisiert werden.

4.1. Programmentwurf

4.1.1. Basisentwurfstechnik

Die Schrittweise Verfeinerung (stepwise refinement)[13] ist die Basis vieler Entwurfstechniken, die vor allem für die kommerzielle Anwendungsprogrammierung geschaffen worden sind. Sie läßt sich wie folgt allgemein darstellen:

- Die Funktion eines Programmes wird so in Teilfunktionen zerlegt, daß sie in diesen
  vollständig repräsentiert wird. Diese können dann auch als Operatoren einer virtuellen Maschine, die bestimmte Objekte manipulieren, betrachtet[14] werden.

- Jede der so entstehenden Teilfunktionen wird in gleicher Weise wieder zerlegt. Dieser Vorgang wiederholt sich so lange, bis die Operatoren der "Anwendungsmaschine"
  mit den Operatoren der Zielsprache (z.B. PL/I-Maschine) dargestellt werden können.

Die Schrittweise Verfeinerung wird in der Literatur an vielen Stellen beschrieben[15].
Die Darstellungen unterscheiden sich oft nur in sekundären Aspekten. Wir beziehen uns
hier in erster Linie auf die Beschreibungen von Wirth[16] und Ledgard[17]. Letzterer
hat versucht, mehrere Ansätze zusammenzufassen.

Analysiert man die Beispiele, die zur Illustration dieser Entwurfstechnik in der Literatur ausgeführt werden, so stellt man fest, daß meist über die grundsätzliche Vorgehensweise der Schrittweisen Verfeinerung hinaus noch zusätzliche allgemeingültige
Überlegungen in den Programmentwurf eingeflossen sind. Teilweise wird auf diese "Re-
geln" des Entwurfes explizit hingewiesen, ein großer Teil wird jedoch nicht in allgemeiner Form beschrieben.

Will man im Bereich kommerzieller Rechneranwendungen zu einer Erhöhung der Änderungsfreundlichkeit kommen, so muß man alle Elemente der Entwurfstechnik, die zu einer
höheren Lokalität führen und sich allgemein verwenden lassen, explizit formulieren.
Wir definieren diese als Erweiterungen der Schrittweisen Verfeinerung.

4.1.2. Erweiterungen

4.1.2.1. Definition von Moduln

Die oben gegebene Beschreibung der Schrittweisen Verfeinerung enthält keinen expliziten Hinweis darauf, daß Teilfunktionen aus der übergeordneten Funktion im Quelltext
eines Programmes ausgegliedert werden sollen. In den Beispielen zur Methode der Schrittweisen Verfeinerung werden als Funktionen definierte Programmteile jedoch in den meisten Fällen als Moduln dargestellt. Diese Vorgehensweise entspricht auch dem praktischen Einsatz dieser Methode. Sie reduziert den Umfang des Programmteiles, der bei
einer Änderung betrachtet werden muß, d.h. sie erhöht die Lokalität. Würden die Teilfunktionen nicht als selbständige Programmteile konzipiert, sondern unmittelbar an der
Stelle kodiert, an der sie definiert werden, so würden nicht unterteilte Programme
entstehen, bei denen sich eine Laufschleife beispielsweise über mehrere Seiten der
Programmliste erstrecken kann[18]. Diese könnte nicht mehr überlickt werden.

4.1.2.2. Kombination mit bottom up-Entwurf

Die Schrittweise Verfeinerung ist grundsätzlich eine top down-Technik. Im Einsatz dieser Methode findet aber eine gewisse Synthese mit der bottom up-Methode statt. Funktionen, die man an mehreren Stellen im Programm benötigt, werden als allgemeine Operatoren definiert.

4.1.2.3. Entwurfskriterien

Ein von den Anwendern oft kritisierter Mangel der Schrittweisen Verfeinerung ist das
Fehlen expliziter Kriterien, nach denen die Aufgliederung von Funktionen erfolgt[19].
Dies kommt auch darin zum Ausdruck, daß bei den Beschreibungen dieser Methode oft der
Hinweis zu finden ist, daß der Entwurfsprozeß iterativ abläuft: Wird auf einer Detail-

lierungsstufe festgestellt, daß eine auf höherer Hierarchieebene getroffene Entwurfs-
entscheidung ungünstig ist, wird der Entwurf ab dieser Stelle revidiert.

Dieser Mangel macht sich auch bezüglich der Änderungsfreundlichkeit bemerkbar. Die
Einführung der folgenden Kriterien kann die Lokalität von Programmen erhöhen:

- <u>Orientierung an der Datenstruktur</u>

  Der Programmaufbau soll die Datenstruktur, die der Verarbeitung zugrunde liegt,
  widerspiegeln[20]. Die Datenstruktur kommt - wie in Abschnitt 2 erläutert - durch
  eine Klassifikation nach der Verarbeitung zustande. Damit wird letztlich wieder
  nach funktionalen Gesichtspunkten gegliedert: Datenstruktur und die auf sie angewandten Algorithmen können nicht unabhängig voneinander betrachtet werden[21].

  Programme, die primär unter Beachtung der Funktionen erstellt werden, weichen daher
  meist nicht wesentlich von solchen ab, bei denen zuerst auf die Datenstruktur ge-
  achtet wird. Diese Feststellung kann auch durch Vergleiche von Programmgliederungen,
  die wir an mehreren Programmen vorgenommen haben, bekräftigt werden. Allerdings
  konnte festgestellt werden, daß es bei einer Orientierung des Entwurfes an der Datenstruktur wahrscheinlicher ist, daß für Entscheidungen über unterschiedliche Ver-
  arbeitungsfälle eine hohe Lokalität erreicht wird.

- <u>Verwendung allgemein einsetzbarer Operatoren</u>

  Funktionen, die in einem Programm an mehreren Stellen benötigt werden, sollen als
  allgemeine Operatoren definiert werden, die von mehreren Moduln verwendet werden
  können[22]. Änderungen, die diese Funktionen betreffen, beziehen sich dann nur auf
  diese Operatoren, also auf einen einzigen Programmteil. Wird beispielsweise ein Pro-
  gnoseverfahren, das in einem Lagerhaltungsmodell zur Vorhersage mehrerer Größen benutzt wird, als "Prognose"-Operator definiert, so bezieht sich eine Änderung im Verfahren auf genau eine Stelle im Programm.

- <u>Schnittstelle zur Umgebung des Programmes</u>

  Der Bezug auf die externe Datenorganisation und Datendarstellung soll auf einen
  oder wenige Moduln reduziert werden [23]. Eine Änderung beispielsweise eines Satz-
  aufbaues betrifft dann nur jeweils jene Stelle in allen berührten Programmen, die
  auf diesen Satz zugreift.

- <u>Verwendung eines Initialisierungsmoduls für Systemparameter</u>

  Konstante Größen sollen bei der Definition von Funktionen vermieden werden. Sie
  sollen als Systemparameter benutzt werden, denen in einem eigenen Initialisierungsmodul Werte zugewiesen werden[24]. Ob diese Werte dabei jeweils beispielsweise von
  Vorlaufkarten eingelesen oder im Initialisierungsmodul durch Ergibtanweisungen zugewiesen werden, hängt von der Änderungshäufigkeit und dem gewünschten Komfort der
  Benutzung ab.

  Dieses Entwurfs-Kriterium hängt teilweise mit dem zuvor genannten zusammen, enthält aber Aspekte, die von jenem nicht berührt werden (und umgekehrt).

- <u>Größe der Moduln</u>

Die Größe der Moduln soll 30 Statements oder zumindest die einer Seite der Programmliste nicht überschreiten[22]. Dabei soll aber auch die Mächtigkeit der Zielsprache
berücksichtigt werden.

- <u>Umfang der Datenschnittstelle zwischen Moduln</u>

Der Umfang von Datenschnittstellen soll möglichst gering gehalten werden. Dadurch
nimmt die Wahrscheinlichkeit, daß von einer Änderung mehrere Moduln betroffen sind,
ab. Ist die Datenschnittstelle sehr umfangreich, so ist dies zudem unter Umständen
ein Hinweis darauf, daß in einem Modul mehr als eine Funktion enthalten ist.

- <u>Verwendung von Steuerungsvariablen</u>

Steuerungsvariable können zwar nicht vollständig vermieden, ihre Verwendung soll aber
minimiert werden. Werden sie benutzt, so sollen sie nur im Sinne von Statusvariablen
eingesetzt werden, die dem rufenden (hierarchisch übergeordneten) Modul keine "Hand-
lungsalternativen (z.B. in Form von Markenvariablen)" vorschreiben.

Die beschriebene Vorgehensweise beim Programmentwurf führt zusammen mit den Entwurfs-
kriterien zu einer hohen Lokalität der Programme. Die resultierenden Programmeigenschaften wirken sich auf den Änderungsaufwand aber erst dann günstig aus, wenn der
Programmentwurf ausreichend dokumentiert ist. Die Programmliste allein kann diese
Funktion nicht erfüllen, es sei denn durch Übernahme der Dokumentation als Programm-
kommentar.

4.1.3. Darstellung des Programmentwurfes

- <u>Programmaufbau</u>

Über die Dokumentation des Programmentwurfes wird bei der Behandlung der Methode
der Schrittweisen Verfeinerung meist nichts ausgesagt. Sie beschränkt sich gewöhnlich auf den Programmtext, wobei dafür oft ein Pseudocode[25] gewählt wird (Formulierung des Programmes in der Muttersprache).

Soll eine bestimmte Funktion in einem Programm gefunden werden, so wird dies durch
die Beschreibung der Programmsteuerung, die in diesem Zusammenhang zunächst nicht
interessant ist, erschwert. Dasselbe gilt in abgeschwächter Form auch dann, wenn
anstelle des Pseudocodes ein Programmablaufplan[26] oder ein Struktogramm[27] tritt.
Eine einfachere Auffindbarkeit von Funktionen erlaubt dagegen das Moduldiagramm[28]
(vgl. Abb. 2), in dem weitgehend auf die Darstellung der Ablaufsteuerung verzichtet
wird.

Es wird sinnvollerweise durch eine sehr allgemein gehaltene Funktionsbeschreibung
der Moduln ergänzt.

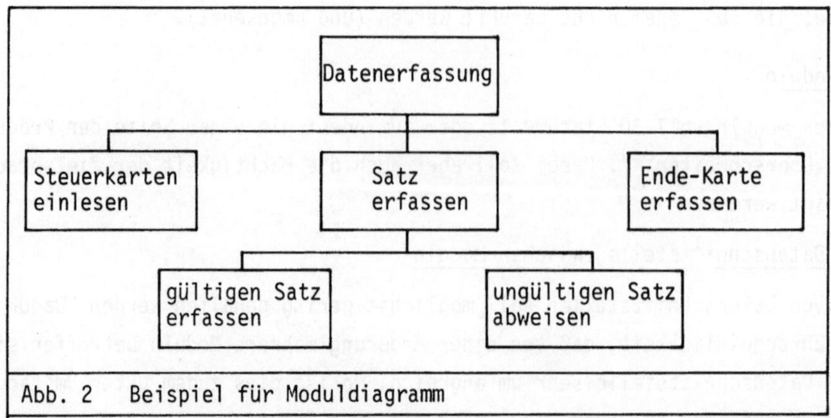

Abb. 2   Beispiel für Moduldiagramm

Diese Darstellungstechnik wirkt sich besonders bei großen Programmen vorteilhaft aus, da sie den Programmaufbau auf sehr kleinem Raum beschreibt.

- Datenkommunikation

Die im kommerziellen Bereich üblichen Programmiersprachen führen nicht automatisch zu einer Beschreibung der Datenschnittstelle pro Modul, die nach Eingabe und Ausgabe differenziert. Weiter kann die Kommunikation mit externen Dateien nur aus den Lese- und Schreibbefehlen abgeleitet werden. In jedem Fall ist es notwendig, zur Bestimmung der Datenschnittstelle den Programmcode zu analysieren. Eine übersichtliche Darstellung aller Aspekte bietet eine Datenkommunikationstabelle[29], in der Eingabe- und Ausgabegrößen eines Moduls unterteilt nach externen und internen Beständen aufgeführt sind.
Sie reicht allein jedoch noch nicht aus. Aus ihr geht nicht hervor, welchen Wertebereich und welche inhaltliche Bedeutung eine Variable besitzt. Erst durch diese Informationen ist es aber möglich, die Betrachtung weitestgehend auf einen einzelnen Modul zu begrenzen. Da dieselben Variablen aber in mehreren Datenschnittstellen enthalten sein können, bietet es sich an, getrennt von der Datenkommunikationstabelle auch eine Variablenliste zu führen, in der Variablenname, inhaltliche Bedeutung, Wertebereich und Speicherungsform aufgeführt sind.

Die hier beschriebenen Darstellungsmittel sind die Voraussetzung dafür, daß die Lokalität eines Programmes zum Änderungszeitpunkt nutzbar wird.

4.2. Programmierung

Während mit den Methoden des Programmentwurfes aus der Sicht der Änderung vor allen die Anzahl der zu ändernden Programmteile sowie deren Umgebung und Größe beeinflußt werden, legt die Programmierung die Struktur innerhalb der zu ändernden Programmteile fest.

Die Vorgehensweise, die Ablaufsteuerung eines Programmes ausschließlich aus strukturierten Anweisungen wie zusammengesetzte, bedingte und repetierende Anweisung zu er-

stellen, brachte eine wesentliche Verbesserung in der klarheit gegenüber "unstruktu-
rierten" Programmen. Ihr Vorteil liegt in der Möglichkeit, alle für einen speziellen
Verarbeitungsfall zutreffenden Statements unabhängig von bestimmten Datenwerten in
ihrer Verarbeitungsreihenfolge lesen zu können.

Darin besteht eine grundsätzlich hohe Lokalität der Strukturierten Programmierung.
Enthält eine Verarbeitung eine große Anzahl von Entscheidungen, so ist es jedoch möglich, daß die für einen bestimmten Verarbeitungsfall vorausgesetzten Bedingungen einen
großen Umfang annehmen und dadurch ihre Lesbarkeit vermindert wird. Eine Erhöhung der
Lokalität ist in diesen Fällen durch die Benutzung von Entscheidungstabellen möglich.
In diesen kann eine Vielzahl von Bedingungen und alternativen Aktionen übersichtlich
auf kleinem Raum dargestellt werden.

Die Moduln sind wegen ihres geringen Umfanges meist bereits durch die Programmlisten
ausreichend dokumentiert. Wo diese zum leichten Verständnis nicht ausreicht, kann sie
um Kommentare und/oder einen Programmablaufplan ergänzt werden.

4.3. Implementationsmittel

Neben den Entwurfs- und Programmiermethoden ist im Zusammenhang mit der Programmentwicklung auch das Implementationsmittel von Bedeutung. Sowohl Entwurf als auch Programmierung werden durch dieses geprägt.

Die Leistungsfähigkeit des Implementationsmittels beeinflußt den Umfang und die Lesbarkeit des Quelltextes sowie den Änderungsumfang. Grundsätzlich kann festgestellt
werden, daß ein sehr leistungsfähiges Implementationsmittel (z.B. ein Berichts-Genera-
tor oder eine Planungssprache) zu leicht änderbaren Programmen führt. Diese Aussage muß
aber unter dem Aspekt der Transparenz[30] eingeschränkt werden. Sehr oft ist beispielsweise in einer Planungssprache eine bestimmte Struktur einer Problemklasse abgebildet.
Wird durch eine Änderung von dieser abgewichen, so kann diese unter Umständen nicht
oder nur sehr schwer ausgeführt werden.

Werden allgemeine Programmiersprachen als Implementationsmittel eingesetzt, so ergeben sich auch aus den darin verfügbaren Steuerungsanweisungen sowie deren Möglichkeiten zur Definition von selbständigen Programmteilen (z.B. das Prozeduren-Konzept)
Rückwirkungen auf Entwurf und Programmierung und dadurch auch auf die Änderungsfreundlichkeit. So ist es beispielsweise wesentlich einfacher, in PL/I strukturiert zu programmieren, als dies in FORTRAN der Fall ist.

5. Zusammenfassung

Die Untersuchung hat gezeigt, daß ein großer Teil der Änderungen auch durch die Entwicklung korrekter Programme nicht vermieden werden kann. Der Änderungsaufwand kann
aber durch Techniken zur Programmentwicklung, die eine hohe Lokalität der Programme
bezüglich Änderungen bewirken, reduziert werden. Die Basis dazu bietet die Schritt-

weise Verfeinerung. Sie muß jedoch um einige Verfahrens- und Darstellungsdetails erweitert werden, um bei der Erstellung kommerzieller Anwendungsprogramme die geforderten Programmeigenschaften zu erreichen. Die Änderungsfreundlichkeit innerhalb von Moduln kann durch die Verwendung von strukturierten Anweisungen bzw. von Entscheidungstabellen gefördert werden. Bei allen Überlegungen zur Programmentwicklung muß aber auch das Implementationsmittel beachtet werden, da auch von diesem die Änderungsfreundlichkeit beeinflußt wird.

Literaturverzeichnis

1) Diese Aussage ist aus folgenden Literaturstellen abgeleitet worden:
   Boehm, B.W., The High Cost of Software, Software World 6 (1975) 1, S. 3 f.,
   Davoren, A.G., Effective Programming, The Australian Computer Journal 4 (1972) 3,
       S. 113 f.
   Schuchmann, H.R., Strukturierte Programmierung - ein pragmatischer Ansatz für
       eine umfassende Software-Technologie, Elektronische Rechenanlagen 17 (1975)1,
       S. 35 sowie
   o.V., Leistungsbeurteilung ist fragwürdig, Computerwoche (1975) 44, S. 11.
       (In diesem Beitrag wird eine Studie von Infratest bei 135 Programmierabtei-
       lungen erläutert.)

2) Vgl. z.B. Sherman, P.M., Techniques in Computer Programming, Englewood Cliffs
       1970, S. 320 ff.

3) Diese Feststellung treffen ohne Einschränkung auf kommerzielle Anwendungen

   Conway, R., Gries, D., An Introduction to Programming, Cambridge 1975 (2. Aufl.),
       S. 5.

4) IBM (Hrsg.), Improved Programming Technologies, IBM GE 19-5085-0, Zoetermeer 1975.

5) Vgl. dazu Jackson, M.A., Principles of Program Design, London u.a. 1975, S. 26 ff.

6) Auf diese Untersuchung wird Bezug genommen in:
   Davoren, A.G., a.a.O., S. 114.

7) Maynard, J., Modular Programming, London 1972, S. 1 f.

8) Vgl. dazu auch Dahl, O.J., Hoare, C.A.R., Hierachical Program Structures, in:
       Dahl, O.J., Dijkstra, E.W., Hoare, C.A.R., Structured Programming, London
       und New York 1972, S. 176.

9) Stevens, W.P., Myers, G.J., Constantine, L.L., Structured Design, IBM Systems
       Journal 13 (1974) 2, S. 133.

10) Mills,H., Top Down Programming in Large Systems, in:
       Rustin, R. (Hrsg.), Debugging Techniques in Large Systems, Englewood Cliffs
       and New Jersey, 1971, S. 48.

11) Denning, P.J., The Developing Theory of Operating Systems, in:
       Boon, C. (Hrsg.), Operating Systems, Infotech State of the Art Report, No.14,
       Maidenhead u.a., S. 390.

12) Vgl. z.B. Freeman, P., Functional Programming, in:
       Hetzel, W.C., Program Test Methods, Englewood Cliffs 1972, S. 50 oder
       Sherman, P.M., a.a.O.

13) Dijkstra, E.W., Notes on Structured Programming, in:
       Dahl, O.J., Dijkstra, E.W., Hoare, C.A.R.,a.a.O., S. 1 ff.

14) Zum Konzept der virtuellen Maschinen vgl.
   Wegner, P., Programming Languages, Information Structures and Machine Organization,
       New York 1971.

15) Aus den zahlreichen Beiträgen sei hier besonders auf folgende hingewiesen:

   Dijkstra, E.W., a.a.O.,
   Freeman, P., a.a.O.,
   Mills, H., a.a.O.,
   Wirth, N., Systematisches Programmieren, Stuttgart 1975.
   Ledgard, H.F., The Case for Structured Programming, BIT 14 (1974), S. 45 ff.

16) Wirth, N., a.a.O., S. 120 f.

17) Ledgard, H.F., a.a.O., S. 46 f.

18) Vgl. Mills, H., a.a.O., S. 48.

19) Vgl. Jackson, M.a., a.a.O., S. 4 sowie

Parnas, D.L., On the Criteria To Be Used in Decomposing Systems into Modules, Communications of the ACM, 5 (1972) 12, S. 1053

20) Jackson, M.A., a.a.O., S. 11 ff.

21) Vgl. Wirth, N., Algorithmen und Datenstrukturen, Stuttgart 1975, S. 7.

22) Vgl. Stevens, W.P., Myers, G.J., Constantine, L.L., a.a.O., S. 133.

23) Vgl. ebenda, S. 134 und
Parnas, D.L., a.a.O., S. 1056.

24) Ebenda, S. 1056.

25) IBM (Hrsg.), a.a.O., S. 7.

26) Schrieber, T.J., Fundamentals of Flowcharting, New York u.a. 1969.

27) Nassi, I., Schneiderman, B., Flowchart Techniques for Structured Programming, SIGPLAN Notices 8 (1973) 8, S. 12 ff.

28) Vgl. Stevens, W.P., Myers, G.J., Constantine, L.L., a.a.O., S. 126.

29) Ein ähnlicher Ansatz findet sich
ebenda, S. 128.

30) Parnas, D.L., Use of the Concept of Transparency in the Design of Hierarchically Structured Systems, Communications of the ACM 18 (1975) 7, S. 401 ff.

<u>An Optimal Evaluation of Boolean
Expressions in an On-Line Query System</u>

Michael Z. Hanani

Ben-Gurion University of the Negev
Beer-Sheva, Israel

<u>Abstract</u>

A method is given for a fast evaluation of a Boolean expression of attributes against
a record of a file, and it thus enables a faster response to general queries for·reports
from a data bank stored as a file. In this method, the time it takes to test a particular attribute in a record and the probability that the attribute is possessed by a
record are taken into account to produce an evaluation algorithm for which the expected
time of evaluation of the Boolean expression for a record is minimal.

Key Words and Phrases: query, Boolean expression, information retrieval,
                        file organization.

CR Categories: 3.5   3.70   3.74

Introduction

In this paper we consider the problem of retrieving records from a very large file, containing hundreds of thousands of records. Each record consists of a list of attributes and values. The selection of the subset of records from the file is in response to a Boolean expression which specifies a combination of desired values of certain attributes and values. The Boolean expression is communicated to the system by the user as a query, typed in on a low speed remote terminal. As a response to the query, the entire file has to be searched, and the Boolean expression is evaluated for each record. The method presented here improves the performance of such a system by speeding up the process of computing the truth value of a Boolean expression for an individual record. This is done by evaluating the expression based on the values of just a part of its components.

The idea of evaluating a Boolean expression based on the values of a selected subset of its components is in itself not new. An early paper that presents that approach is (1). However, our approach to the problem differs in that we do not consider the individual components of the expression as being comparable in the effort it takes to compute their individual Boolean values, but rather we do take into account a measure of that effort, and select the subset of components to be evaluated so that the "expected effort" of evaluating the entire expression is minimal.

The problem of easy and fast access to large data banks is today's one of the most important topics in data processing, and is dealt with by the modern methods that are being developed under the general title of "database" (see, for example, (7)). In particular, the idea of organising the data in formats that enable easy access such as tree formats ((2), (10), (12)) and more general approaches such as Codd's ((4), (5), (6)) have been researched. However, the problem that we have been confronted with, and which is not an atypical one, is making a very large data bank stored as a file available to a quick response reporting system, flexible enough to respond to very general queries. Changes in the structure of the data bank would be very expensive to implement, and the requirement regarding the generality of the queries made the desired structure of the database unclear. Consequently we have directed our efforts towards minimizing the time of negotiating the existing file rather than change its structure.

In the presentation that follows we first define the set of Boolean expressions that are being dealt with in this paper as a context free language. We then describe a particular tree representation of an expression. The terminal nodes I_i $(i = 1,...,n)$ of the tree represent the attributes and values of the expression, and with each of them we assiciate two numbers $t(i)$ and $p(i)$ that are properties of the file and of the attribute. We then associate two numbers t and p , which are, in a way,

generalizations of t(i) and p(i) , with every node of the tree. Two theorems are
then given which enable one to compute the number t for a node in a straightforward
fashion (p is easy enough to compute from its definition). Finally, an algorithm is
given that computes the value of the Boolean expression so that the expected time of
evaluation is minimal.

The Boolean expressions

The set of Boolean expressions that is dealt with in this paper is the language generated from the context free grammer whose production rules are,

$$\langle BE \rangle \quad ::= \quad \langle BT \rangle \mid \langle BE \rangle \vee \langle BT \rangle$$
$$\langle BT \rangle \quad ::= \quad \langle BF \rangle \mid \langle BT \rangle \wedge \langle BF \rangle$$
$$\langle BF \rangle \quad ::= \quad \langle BP \rangle \mid \neg \langle BP \rangle$$
$$\langle BP \rangle \quad ::= \quad I \mid (\langle BE \rangle)$$

The terminal symbol I represents the set of attributes and values (T, F) (see, for
example, (3)). In the following we add subindices to I whenever the difference among
individual attributes and values is important.

A Boolean expression is representable as a tree where,
1. every node that is a terminal node of the tree has a label I ,
2. every node that is not a terminal node has a label from the set $\{\wedge, \vee\}$,
3. the nodes that are descendants of a node whose label is $\wedge$ are labelled with either
   I or V , and the nodes that are descendants of a node whose label is V are labelled
   with either I or $\wedge$.

For example, the tree representation of the expression

$$I_1 \vee I_2 \vee I_3 \vee \neg (I_4 \wedge I_5 \wedge I_6) \wedge I_7$$

is

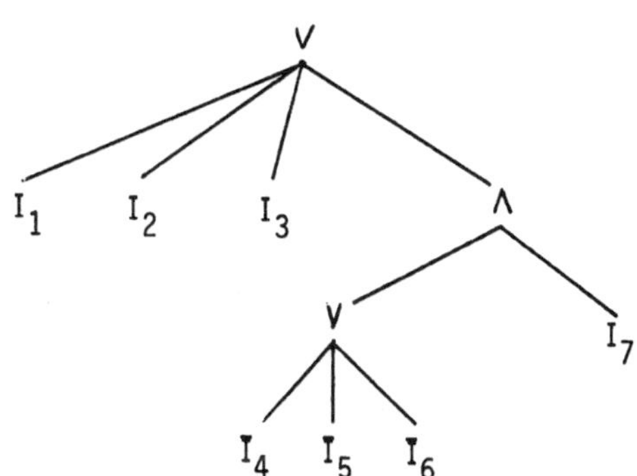

($\bar{I}$ is the logical complement of the attribute or value that is represented by I).
An algorithm that constructs the tree representation of a Boolean expression is a
slight modification of the well-known algorithm to construct the binary tree representation of an expression (see, for example, (8)), combined with applications of the
de-Morgan laws to eliminate the negation operator

The evaluation of a Boolean expression for a record of the file involves testing, for
every attribute of the expression, whether the record possesses that attribute, replacing the attributes that are possessed by the record with the value T (TRUE), and
the others with F (FALSE), and computing the resulting expression. However, it is
not always necessary to test all the attributes of the expression. For example consider the expression $I_1 \wedge I_2 \wedge I_3$, where an F value for one of the attributes ren-
ders the testing of the others unnecessary. In the following we expand on this consideration and give a systematic way of selecting the attributes to be tested so that
the expected time of evaluating the entire expression is minimal.

Definitions

We assume that for every terminal symbol I_i of the expression (i.e. for every attribute and value) two numbers, $t(I_i)$ and $p(I_i)$, are associated, where

$t(I_i)$ is the time it takes to check if attribute I_i is possessed by a record of the
        file, and
$p(I_i)$ is the probability that attribute I_i is possessed by a record.

(If I_i is a value, the numerical values of $t(I_i)$ and $p(I_i)$ are obvious). In
practice we have used the number of assembly language commands that are required to
check attribute I_i as $t(I_i)$, and the frequency of the records that possess attribute
I_i in the file as $p(I_i)$.

The number p is defined for a node in the tree representation of a Boolean expression
as follows: if the node is a terminal node I_i , $p = p(I_i)$. For an $\wedge$ ($\vee$) node
W with descendants $W_1 , \ldots , W_n$ with corresponding numbers $p_1 , \ldots , p_n$, p is
defined as:

$$p = p_1 \ldots p_n \qquad (p = 1 - q_1 \ldots q_n \text{ where } q_i = 1 - p_i , \quad i = 1, \ldots , n).$$

p is, thus, the probability that the value of the subexpression that is represented
by the subtree whose root is that particular node, turns out to be T (TRUE) for a
record of the file.

The minimal expected time of evaluation, t, of a node in the tree representation of a Boolean expression is defined as follows: if the node is a terminal node I_i, $t = t(I_i)$. For an $\wedge$ ($\vee$) node W, with descendants W_1, ..., W_n with corresponding minimal expected times of evaluation t_1, ..., t_n, and for a particular ordering s of the descendants: W_{i_1}, ..., W_{i_n}, we define the expected time of evaluation $ET(\wedge,s)$ $(ET(\vee,s))$ as:

$$ET(\wedge,s) = t_{i_1} + p_{i_1} t_{i_2} + \ldots + p_{i_1} \ldots p_{i_{n-1}} t_{i_n}$$

$$(ET(\vee,s) = t_{i_1} + q_{i_1} t_{i_2} + \ldots + q_{i_1} \ldots q_{i_{n-1}} t_{i_n}).$$

The minimal expected time of evaluation t for the node W is the expected time of evaluation with the ordering s of the descendants such that the value of $ET(\wedge,s)$ $(ET(\vee,s))$ is minimal.

For example consider the expression $I_1 \wedge I_2$ where,

$$t(I_1) = 10, \quad t(I_2) = 90, \quad p(I_1) = 0.95, \quad p(I_2) = 0.2$$
$$t_1 = 10, \qquad t_2 = 90, \qquad p_1 = 0.95, \qquad p_2 = 0.2$$

Let the ordering s_1 be I_1, I_2 and the ordering s_2 be I_2, I_1.

$$ET(\wedge,s_1) = t_1 + p_1 t_2 = 10 + 0.95 \times 90 = 95.5$$

$$ET(\wedge,s_2) = t_2 + p_2 t_1 = 90 + 0.2 \times 10 = 92$$

Thus, the minimal expected time of evaluation, t, for the node is 92.

Ordering theorems

In this section we prove two theorems that give practical ways to ordering the descendants of a node so that the minimal expected time of evaluation of that node is achieved.

Lemma

Given a finite sequence of elements, $(a_1, \ldots, a_n)$. Every permutation of that sequence can be constructed from it by a finite series of consecutive steps, whereby in each step two adjacent elements $a_i a_j$, such that $i < j$, are interchanged.

Proof

The proof is by induction on the number of elements in the sequence. When the number of elements is 2 the assertion is obvious. We now assume it to be true for a sequence of $n-1$ elements and prove it to be true for a sequqnce of n elements.

Let the original sequence be $(a_1 , \ldots , a_n)$. For any k , $1 \le k \le n$, all the permutations in which a_k is the first element can be constructed from the original sequence in the following way: a_k changes places with a_{k-1} , then it changes places with a_{k-2} and so on, until a_k reaches the first place. The rest of the elements follow a_k in the order: $(a_1 , \ldots , a_{k-1} , a_{k+1} , \ldots , a_n)$, and according to the induction hypothesis, every permutation of this sequence can be constructed from it by a finite series of steps each of which is a change of places of two adjacent elements $a_i a_j$ such that $i < j$.

QED

Theorem 1

Let W be an $\wedge$ node in a tree representation of a Boolean expression. The expected time of evaluation, t , of W is minimal when the ordering of the descendants is: $W_1 , \ldots , W_n$ such that

$$\frac{t_1}{q_1} \le \frac{t_2}{q_2} \le \cdots \le \frac{t_n}{q_n}$$

where $q_i = 1 - p_i$ $(i = 1 , \ldots, n)$, $t_1 , \ldots , t_n$ are the respective minimal expected times of evaluation of the descendants, and $p_1 , \ldots , p_n$ are the respective numbers p.

Proof

We have to show that any rearrangement of the descendants does not decrease the expected time of evaluation of W . According to the lemma, any rearrangement of the descendants can be constructed by a series of interchanging of adjacent descendants $W_i W_j$ such that $i < j$. It is enough, therefore, to prove that any such change of places does not decrease the expected time of evaluation of W .

Let there be given an arbitrary ordering of the descendants of W :

$$(1) \qquad W_{i_1} , \ldots , W_{i_k} , W_{i_{k+1}} , \ldots , W_{i_n}$$

such that $i_k < i_{k+1}$. Interchange W_{i_k} and $W_{i_{k+1}}$,

$$(2) \qquad W_{i_1} , \ldots , W_{i_{k-1}} , W_{i_{k+1}} , W_{i_k} , W_{i_{k+2}} , \ldots , W_{i_n} .$$

The expected time of evaluation of W with ordering (1), $ET(\wedge ,1)$ is:

$$(3) \quad ET(\wedge,1) = t_{i_1} + p_{i_1} t_{i_2} + \ldots + p_{i_1} \ldots p_{i_{k-1}} t_{i_k} + p_{i_1} \ldots p_{i_k} t_{i_{k+1}} + \ldots +$$

$$+ p_{i_1} \ldots p_{i_{n-1}} \cdot t_{i_n}$$

The expected time of evaluation of W with ordering (2), $ET(\wedge,2)$ is computed by an expression similar to (3) except that instead of

$$p_{i_1} \ldots p_{i_{k-1}} t_{i_k} + p_{i_1} \ldots p_{i_k} t_{i_{k+1}}$$

in (3) we write

$$p_{i_1} \ldots p_{i_{k-1}} t_{i_{k+1}} + p_{i_1} \ldots p_{i_{k-1}} p_{i_{k+1}} t_{i_k}$$

Hence,

$$ET(\wedge,2) - ET(\wedge,1) = p_{i_1} \ldots p_{i_{k-1}} (t_{i_{k+1}} + p_{i_{k+1}} t_{i_k} - t_{i_k} - p_{i_k} t_{i_{k+1}})$$

$$= p_{i_1} \ldots p_{i_{k-1}} q_{i_k} q_{i_{k+1}} \left(\frac{t_{i_{k+1}}}{q_{i_{k+1}}} - \frac{t_{i_k}}{q_{i_k}} \right) \geqslant 0$$

(The expression in the parentheses is nonnegative considering the assumption of the theorem, and that $i_{k+1} > i_k$).

QED

Theorem 2

Let W be an $\vee$ node in a tree representation of a Boolean expression. The expected time of evaluation, t, of W is minimal when the ordering of the descendants is: W_1 , $\ldots$, W_n such that

$$\frac{t_1}{p_1} \leqslant \frac{t_2}{p_2} \leqslant \ldots \leqslant \frac{t_n}{p_n}$$

where t_1 , $\ldots$, t_n are the respective minimal expected times of evaluation of the descendants, and p_1 , $\ldots$, p_n are the respective numbers p .

Proof

By resons that are similar to those given in the proof of Theorem 1, we consider an arbitrary ordering of the descendants of W ((1) in the proof of Theorem 1) and another ordering ((2) there) that differ from the first by interchanging W_{i_k} and $W_{i_{k+1}}$.

The expected time of evaluation of W with ordering (1), $ET(V,1)$ is:

$$(3') \quad ET(V,1) = t_{i_1} + q_{i_1} t_{i_2} + \ldots + q_{i_1} \ldots q_{i_{k-1}} t_{i_k} + q_{i_1} \ldots q_{i_k} t_{i_{k+1}} + \ldots +$$

$$+ q_{i_1} \ldots q_{i_{n-1}} t_{i_n}$$

The expected time of evaluation of W with ordering (2), $ET(V,2)$ is computed by an expression similar to (3') except that instead of

$$q_{i_1} \ldots q_{i_{k-1}} t_{i_k} + q_{i_1} \ldots q_{i_k} t_{i_{k+1}}$$

in (3') we write

$$q_{i_1} \ldots q_{i_{k-1}} t_{i_{k+1}} + q_{i_1} \ldots q_{i_{k-1}} q_{i_{k+1}} t_{i_k}$$

Hence,

$$ET(V,2) - ET(V,1) = q_{i_1} \ldots q_{i_{k-1}} (t_{i_{k+1}} + q_{i_{k+1}} t_{i_k} - t_{i_k} - q_{i_k} t_{i_{k+1}})$$

$$= q_{i_1} \ldots q_{i_{k-1}} p_{i_k} p_{i_{k+1}} \left(\frac{t_{i_{k+1}}}{p_{i_{k+1}}} - \frac{t_{i_k}}{p_{i_k}} \right) \geqslant 0$$

(The expression in the parentheses is nonnegative considering the assumption of the theorem and that $i_{k+1} > i_k$).

QED

The evaluation algorithm

The tree that represents the Boolean expression can now be restructured so that the descendants of every node are ordered as is specified in theorems 1 and 2. Based on that tree we now give an algorithm that evaluates any node, in particular the root, so that the expected time of evaluation is minimal. The algorithm is presented in the form of a recursive function, using Zahn's control structure (see (9), p. 275). It is to be stressed, though, that this algorithm will be performed many times since it evaluates the expression for every record of the file, and it is therefore advisable to give high priority to efficiency considerations when programming it.

```
Boolean function value (node);
    if node = terminal node then value := value of the variable, or constant, that is
        represented by that node else
        if node's label is ∧ then
            loop until all descendants are marked or value is false:
                lm := leftmost unmarked descendant;
                if value(lm) = F then value is false else mark descendant;
            repeat;
            then all descendants are marked ⟶ value := T;
                value is false ⟹ value := F;
            fi;
    else comment node's label is ∨ ;
        loop until all descendants are marked or value is true:
            lm := leftmost unmarked descendant;
            if value(lm) = T then value is true else mark descendant;
        repeat;
        then all descendants are marked ⟶ value := F;
            value is true ⟹ value := T;
        fi;
```

Conclusion

The discussion in this paper centers around the handling of a single query, and results
in an optimal technique for a response to it. In practice, however, queries arrive in
streams from many remote terminals and into the central computer system. In order to
have our response system function more efficiently in that environment, we accumulate
incoming queries and handle them in groups. Namely, we prepare the record negotiating
algorithm described above for each query, and then apply the group of individual algorithms to every record of the file. Thus, with one search of the file we respond to a
number of queries.

The method described in this paper is applicable in other contexts as well. For example,
in the evaluation of a regular Boolean expression, when all the components I_i are
assumed to have equal values of $t(I_i)$ and $p(I_i)$, or in the analysis of problem solving techniques such as is described in (11), chapter 4. There a use is made of AND/OR
graphs which resemble our tree structure, and the property of a node being "solved"
there is similar to a node having a value T here.

References

(1) Arden, B.W., Galler, B.A., and Graham, R.M., An algorithm for translating Boolean expressions. J. Assoc. Comput. Mach. 9 (1962) 222-239.

(2) Casey, R.G., Design of tree structures for efficient quering. Comm. ACM 16,9 (Sept. 1973) 549-556.

(3) Cheatham, T.E., and Sattley, K., Syntax directed compiling. In Programming Systems and Languages, edited by Saul Rosen, McGraw-Hill 1967.

(4) Codd, E.F., A relational model of data for large shared data banks. Comm. ACM 13,6 (June 1970) 377-387.

(5) Codd, E.F., Further normalization of the data base relational model. In Data Base Systems, edited by R. Rustin, Prentice Hall (Courant Computer Science Symposium 6, 1971).

(6) Codd, E.F., Relational completeness of data base sublanguages. (Same book as (5)).

(7) Date, D.J., An Introduction to Database Systems. Addison Wesley 1975.

(8) Knuth, D.E., The Art of Computer Programming, vol. 1, ch. 2. Addison Wesley.

(9) Knuth, D.E., Structured programming with goto statements. Comput. Surveys 6,4 (Dec. 1974) 261-301.

(10)Nievergelt, J., Binary search trees and file organization. Comput. Surveys 6,3 (Sept. 1974) 195-207.

(11)Nilsson, N.J., Problem Solving Methods in Artificial Intelligence, McGraw-Hill 1971.

(12)Severance, D.G., Identifier search mechanism: a survey and generalized model. Comput. Surveys 6,3 (Sept. 1974) 175-194.

THE USER SPECIALTY LANGUAGES SYSTEM

R. Kogon, D. Lattermann, H. Lehmann, N. Ott, M. Zoeppritz

IBM Deutschland GmbH
Wissenschaftliches Zentrum Heidelberg

ABSTRACT

An interactive system is introduced, designed for non-programmers in problem solving and decision making environments, by providing access to a data base for query, data analysis, and data entry in a natural-like language. The system is built on a relational view of data. It makes use of the conventions of natural language German for requesting and giving information and converts expressions into function calls for executing relational operations on the data base.

1 Introduction

The need to access data in different, sometimes unanticipated ways brought about new kinds of data base systems as well as new kinds of data manipulation languages.

The use of natural language as a data manipulation language or - more generally - as a means of communication with the computer has been challenging many - but it also seems to have caused skepticism in others. A number of experimental systems have been developed, and many different aspects of the problem have been addressed. When designing the USL-system, the objectives were different in many respects from the experimental systems (a comparison with twelve of them is given below).

The first objective for the USL-system was to use an independent data base management system (DBMS), and thus to translate input sentences to the formal data manipulation language of the DBMS (a similar approach is also taken in the TORUS project [15]). Hence the main work to be done for the design and implementation of the present system was in writing a grammar for German that could be recognised by the parser (a modified form of Martin Kay's parser [8] also used in the REL-system [20] and in the project at the TH Karlsruhe [9]), and in developing suitable interpretation routines to perform the mapping from German to the data manipulation language.

The second objective was to restrict the language of the USL-system in such a way that everything that can reasonably be interpreted within the scope of the system would be interpreted, and also that as many reasonable formulations as possible that a user might choose would be allowed. Artificial restrictions in the use of the language had to be avoided, because a language that looks natural in some respects, but behaves differently in others, will be bound to confuse the user, and may be more difficult to learn than a formal language. So the only solution could be to move the boundaries of the language of the USL-system so far out that a user would hardly notice they existed, i.e. that the user would have the illusion that nearly the full power of German was at his disposal.

It was not attempted to build deductive capabilities into the system although many scholars are fascinated by such facilities, and although obviously they would be useful provided they worked reliably and did not produce misleading results. It was felt, however, that more urgent problems had to be solved first, and also that much work would still be required to implement deductive algorithms that work in a safe and economic way.

Clarifying dialogue as proposed by Codd [3] and others was not implemented in the USL-system, because there are two kinds of unsolved problems: Firstly, one should have fairly clear ideas on the purposes of clarifying dialogue to avoid developing talkative or nagging systems. Secondly, there are technical problems concerning the generation of sentences from a semantic representation, and little work has been done on this. Moreover, in many cases the system would have to make sense of input it cannot completely understand to be able to generate an appropriate question.

One point where it was felt indeed that restatement of queries was desirable, was in the case of ambiguous requests. But the problem here is that the system would have to find unambiguous paraphrases of the input sentence which do not necessarily exist. So it may be a way out to restate the sentence in a formal or semiformal language, provided this language were evident to the user. The present conclusion is that this problem still requires thorough investigation in the future.

The preceding paragraphs gave an account of what is and what is not in the USL-system, it now remains to describe what is new or different from other comparable systems. Maybe the most important point is that, although the most serious problems to be solved were problems of language, the main goal of the system is not the enhancement of the understanding of language but the attempt to find ways to bridge the gap between people and the computer, where people are above all professionals whose interest is in their problems and not in the problems of electronic data processing.

This main goal affects the manner in which language analysis can be done in the system, because it implies that linguistic information requested from the user when he defines a new word for example must be kept to a minimum. For the USL-system this means that e.g. declension classes of nouns are not available, and it turned out that no serious problems arose from this restriction.

Concerning the semantics of natural language, there are several respects where the USL-system uses a new or better solution. The range of temporal expressions that can be interpreted is much wider than in the CHRONOS-system [2] which was specifically designed for that purpose. Notoriously, the interpretation of quantifiers is a big problem in question answering systems, especially, when more than one quantifier as well as negation are to be considered. For the purposes of the USL-system, a thorough analysis of the scope of quantifiers in German sentences was done and an appropriate algorithm was implemented. The interpretation of coordinate noun phrases is an important problem, and it is also implemented in the system. Here, too, empirical investigations specific to German were necessary to be able to derive the required algorithm.

As it stands now, the USL-system is ready to be evaluated in a real world environment, i.e. several applications have already been developed using it, and others will be. The feedback from the users working with the system will be used to improve it and also to develop more precise requirements for future projects.

A comparison of the USL system with other systems has a variety of aspects to it.   Below only a comparison with natural language information systems is given although a comparison with information systems that offer a formal data language would also be interesting. Natural language information systems (or question answering systems) fall into two major groups - English based and German based.

English based systems are:

CHRONOS (Bruce [2]), ENGOLISH (Isner [7]), LSNLIS (Woods &al [23]), REL/ENGLISH (Thompson &al [19]), REQUEST (Plath &al [17]), SHRDLU (Winograd [22]) SQAP (Palme &al [16]), TORUS (Mylopoulos &al [15]).

German based systems are:

ISLIB (IDS [25]), LIANA (Batori &al [1]), PLIDIS (IDS [26]), TH Karlsruhe (Kraegeloh &al [9]), USL (WZH).

Clearly, although English and German are related languages, may phenomena of syntax and semantics are different and require different solutions.   But there are also many points where one can apply a solution for one language to another one. This is especially true for the basic semantics.

The point to be discussed is then, what the systems cited offer in terms of generally applicable solutions, where different approaches are to be taken, and in what areas nothing is offered at all. This is rather cumbersome to assess as most authors do not tell in their documentation how generally applicable their solutions are, nor what exactly they have accomplished, nor what they would have liked to have accomplished. The following table tries to present the results of our study of the literature, and it must be noted that generally the authors' claims were taken at face value, and in many cases, capabilities had to be extrapolated from examples. The table hence does not tell much about the quality of the solutions offered by the respective systems.   The table does show, however, that all question answering systems that claim to handle natural language are at best able to handle fragments of it, and not all systems could make the claim to handle even its most fundamental structures.

Comparison of question answering systems

Property	CHRONOS	ENGOLISH	LSNLIS	REL	REQUEST	SHRDLU	SQAP	TORUS	ISLIB	LIANA	PLIDIS	THK	USL
I. System aspects													
DBMS	–	L	L	O	O	L	O	I	O	–	O	O	I
Non-NL input req	–	–	–	+	–	–	+	–	–	–	–	+	–
Vocab update	–	A	A	+	–	+	?	?	–	–	?	+	P
Diagnostics	–	?	C	M	CD	C	?	Q	?	M	CD	?	M
NL generation	–	+	–	–	–	+	–	P	–	–	P	–	–
Output	S	S	T	TU	T	S	?	TU	?	T	?	TU	TU
Applications	N	R	R	RI	R	N	?	NI	N	N	NI	RI	RI
Inference	+	+	?	–	–	+	+	P	P	–	P	–	–
Consist check	–	–	–	–	–	?	–	–	–	–	P	–	–
II. Linguistic Coverage													
Complement qu	+	+	+	+	+	+	–	P	+	+	?	+	+
Appositions	–	–	+	–	+	?	?	P	–	–	?	+	+
Negation	–	–	+	+	+	+	–	–	SN	+	?	+	+
Comparative	–	–	+	G	G	+	–	P	+	–	?	G	G
Passive	–	–	+	–	+	+	+	P	+	–	?	–	–
Relative clause	–	–	+	+	+	+	SU	P	P	–	?	+	+
Quantification	–	?	1	1	P	1	1	P	–	PS	P	1	+
Coordination	–	–	+	–	+	+	&	P	–	–	?	–	&
Time handling	+	–	–	+	+	+	+	?	t	–	?	+	+
Anaph reference	–	–	+	–	+	+	+	P	–	+	?	–	–
continuous texts	–	–	+	–	–	+	+	–	–	+	P	–	–
Ordinals	–	–	+	–	+	–	–	P	–	–	?	–	–
Mass nouns	–	–	+	–	–	–	–	–	–	–	?	–	–
Nominalisations	–	–	+	–	+	–	–	P	–	–	?	–	–
Infinit clause	–	–	–	–	–	–	–	P	–	–	?	–	–
That-clause	–	–	+	–	–	+	?	P	–	–	?	–	–
Modality	–	–	–	–	–	+	–	P	–	–	P	–	–
Reasons	–	+	–	–	–	+	–	–	–	–	–	–	–

Legend:

L LISP data storing capabilities, O own DBMS, I interface to
independent DBMS, A almost (vocabulary update without linguistic
training), P planned, C request to correct input, D display of
ambiguous readings for user disambiguation, Q NL questions produced by
the system, M messages (specificity varies considerably), S sentence
(generated or previously stored), T table, U user influence, N no real
application (model only), R real application (outside data and users),
RI real application and applications independence, NI no real
application but applications independence, SN sentence negation only,
G greater/smaller only, SU relative pronoun in subject of clause only,
1 one quantifier per sentence, PS pseudo quantification,
& and-coordination only, t tense.

2 System Structure

The USL system consists of

- a set of language rules (grammar)
- a syntax processor
- an input analyzer (parser)
- an interpreter providing an interface to a data base
  management system (DBMS)
- processing routines for the manipulation of data.

In the USL system, data are viewed as relations. Relations are tables
that are built in a standardized way. Every relation has a name to
refer to it, and it consists of columns and rows (tuples). The columns
can be referred to by names (selectors). A statement in the language
can be represented as a tuple of a relation.

For example, when the ages of persons are to be recorded, a table with
two columns can be established, one holding persons and the other
years. Data is entered into this table by statements as

        JOHN'S AGE IS 30.
        THE AGE OF MARY IS 25.
or
        JOHN IS 30 YEARS OLD.
        25 IS THE AGE OF MARY.

AGE

        ! PERSON ! YEARS !
        +--------+-------+
        ! JOHN !   30 !
        ! MARY !   25 !
        !   !   !

This table permits to answer questions like

        WHAT IS THE AGE OF JOHN?
or
        WHOSE AGE IS 25?

The syntax of the language supplied in USL describes some of the conventions of German usage, the keywords in the dictionary are connectives and words the meanings of which are constant over applications (English equivalents would be AND, OF, JULY, etc.) and system commands. Names of data elements and of the dependencies between elements differ from application to application and will be selected by the users according to the data and the intended use of this data in the application. These identifier names can be taken from the set of German nouns and verbs (e.g. MASCHINE, NAME). They can also be defined freely (e.g. X1, AVSAL).

The language in USL like a programming language is a set of rules describing syntactic conventions and a set of system defined keywords. A language is defined or extended using the language definition or edit mode. Thus vocabulary items and elements of syntax can be added successively to improve the flexibility of the language.

The language is defined in modified Backus Normal Form (BNF). The set of rules constitutes a formal description of expressions in the language. Expressions are words or strings of words which are combined in different ways to yield different meanings. For a detailed description of the language and its grammar see [10], [11], [13], and [14].

Each rule specifies a syntactic configuration to which the rule is applicable and specifies an output category that is to result after application of the rule. Associated with the rules are function calls representing the semantics of a given syntactic configuration with input elements as parameters. A set of rules - a grammar - is given as data in BNF to the syntax processor, which converts the grammar into the format used by the parser and makes the language available for further use. This permits specification of user specialty languages and extensions to languages provided.

Input by a user is first analyzed by the parser, which builds up a tree structure that represents the functional dependencies of the elements in the input string. For ambiguous input all possible representations are built in parallel.

The tree structure built by the parser is passed to the interpreter which executes the function calls which are associated with each node of the tree. The functions successively build a sequence of calls to the DBMS with the appropriate parameters representing the meaning of the input string: Data retrieval, selection, comparison, or entry. Accordingly, the DBMS yields an answer to a query or performs an update function. A detailed description of the interpretation functions is given in [12].

Answers to queries may be subject to further processing, for instance statistical functions may be applied to them.

Finally, the output is formatted and displayed.

3 User View

The USL system provides an application independent natural-like extensible language and a set of functions which map expressions in that language into a relational view of data for query, entry, and manipulation in a data base.

Data entry statements are informal when they concern relations that are already defined.

    MUELLER WOHNT IN MAINZ.
    MAYER WOHNT IN KOELN.

The words related to new concepts in the data base must be defined for the language. If the user does not want to become involved with the formal definition mechanism, a help routine prompts the necessary information and converts user answers to rule format for language extension. These words can then be used for data entry in language mode.

Data entry in language mode makes it possible for individuals or small user groups to create small data bases for their purposes. Occasionally assistance from the computing department may be needed to add functions not already supplied by USL.

For users not authorized to enter or update data, language mode permits queries of the data base. Simple questions require data to be listed as stored in the data base, as for example the query:

        WER WOHNT IN KOELN?

More complex questions require data to be compared and selected
according to criteria supplied by the query as well as arithmetic
operations on data.

        WAS IST DER DURCHSCHNITT DER GEHAELTER DER MITARBEITER, DIE IN
            KOELN WOHNEN ?

Results of a query can be assigned to a variable for further
reference.

        AVSAL = DER DURCHSCHNITT DER GEHAELTER DER MITARBEITER, DIE IN
            KOELN WOHNEN

USL permits bulkloading of data from a file. Single items can be
entered directly in language mode. To make these data accessible
through USL, the concepts used are defined for the language formally in
edit mode or through a prompting routine in language mode.

Data can also be entered or accessed through a command-type language.
Certain functions like displaying the names of all relations currently
in the data base can also be called in this way. The advantages are
conciseness and quick response, but queries involving several
operations require experience in using this language.

The command-type language is intended for users whose responsibility is
the creation and maintenance of larger data bases according to end user
requirements and the coordination of their requests to preserve data
base integrity. These users will be soon familiar with the formal
mechanism and probably prefer it.

Function extension is necessary where a desired operation on data is
not provided in the system. Such function processor extensions are
written in a programming language and then linked into the system.
They can then be specified in a syntax rule and will be invoked as the
rule applies to input in the language.

A word not known to the language implemented is assumed to be a name.
If the use of the word in the input string is consistent with that
assumption, the system will look for the required information and
return an answer if the word is indeed a name and known in the data

base, or it will signal that the information is not available.
Otherwise, the system will signal that the input is not understood.
The user may then use the definition facility to enter the word in the
dictionary or repeat input if the word was misspelled. User errors are
indicated by a set of diagnostic messages.

4 Applications

USL is designed as a problem solving system. In this context, problem
solving means the creative process of performing non-routine,
non-repetitive operations to solve a problem. The solution criteria of
such problems are often incompletely defined, therefore many solution
methods are possible.

The operations in this process involve
    - Data retrieval based on search criteria
    - data analysis (numeric and non-numeric)
    - Data entry and update

Problem solvers are professionals in their field of specialty. Often
they have insufficient data processing knowledge to use the computer
directly as a problem solving tool. USL permits access and manipulation
of computer-stored data in user terminology, eliminating the need for
formal data processing education:

    - Managers make decisions with greater confidence based on
      information they selected personally concentrating on problems
      not possible to delegate.
    - Professionals (e.g. administrators, planners, technicians,
      scientists, ...) reach problem solutions faster because
      intermediaries are eliminated.

USL does not address processing standard jobs requiring large
transaction volumes. Formal programming facilities are adequate and
well established for these applications.

USL can serve in administration, management, and science for fact
finding, decision making, planning (what if-questions) and analysis.
Data is accessible when required. Assistance of a programming
specialist is not mandatory.

It can be easier for planners and decision makers to evaluate alternative solutions to a given problem and to understand consequences of decisions before they are implemented. Scientists can make use of USL to explore dependencies among data and to test hypotheses. This will not necessarily reduce the time needed for problem solution, but it can reduce the time spent adjusting the solution to facts that seemed unrelated at first.

In administration, files are maintained containing data on personnel, customers, inventory etc. Often, these files are accessed by clerks or secretaries to satisfy requests on single items. DP training for such use is unrealistic. This points out the need for a system that permits data access without knowledge of a formal query language. USL users will have no difficulty formulating queries because of extensive rules permitting flexible input.

Legislative changes affecting administrative data processing require expensive program modifications. Consequences are difficult to assess effectively on a timely basis. USL permits to simulate the effect of legislative changes.

Exploration and exploitation of natural resources is an application using geographic, geological, atmospheric, and agricultural data. The task includes examining locations of resources and determining exploitation profitability. The latter depends on many factors: availability of manpower, transportation cost, cost of refinement of raw materials etc. USL contributes to solve these problems by providing the capabilities required to query data accumulated according to varying criteria and to evaluate different possible solutions.

In manufacturing product planning requires repeated data analysis in the areas of
- product forcasting
- inventory control
- planning the production process

Many of these are applications known in advance and can be preprogrammed. Unanticipated or unusual decision situations like raw material shortage problems or impact of customer bankruptcy proceedings must be handled in a more dynamic and flexible manner. USL permits the person who has the responsibility and who usually will not be a DP professional to directly access the data and get the information he needs for making a decision, without having to ask a specialist to write a program for him.

Empirical research in industry or universities involves varying amounts of data depending on the project and the size of the group participating in the project. Aside from repetitive, routine operations, processing of these data is poorly supported.

Studies in the humanities, for example in sociology and psychology often require data collection from questionaires. Processing them using unanticipated evaluation criteria is difficult without programming assistance.

In all these situations, solutions are supported by USL, eliminating manual processing or need for programmer assistance.

5 Examples

The following sample session shows some of the flexibility that USL offers for querying data. The questions reference data in a pseudo personnel data base.

```
USLDEMO --- VERSION:  20. MAI 1976
?
welcher erfahrene mitarbeiter, der kein manager ist, wohnt in heidelberg?
 GESUCHTES OBJEKT NICHT VORHANDEN
?
welche erfahrenen mitarbeiter wohnen wo?
 PERSON              ORT
 ------------------------------------------
 KOCH                BEI HEIDELBERG
 SCHULZ              IN WIESENBACH
?
ist koch kein manager?
 DOCH

?
```

```
was verdient welcher erfahrene mitarbeiter?
 PERSON              DM
 ------------------------------------------
 KOCH                        4100
 SCHULZ                      3820
?
wer ist der manager von schulz?
 MANAGER
 ---------------------
 MEIER
?
welche mitarbeiter hat meier?
 MITARBEITER
 ---------------------
 SCHULZ
?
was ist das alter und das gehalt des mitarbeiters, der in -
:
sandhausen wohnt ?
 ALTER              GEHALT              PERSON
 ------------------------------------------------------------
      27                  2500              KUEBLER
 ?
welcher mitarbeiter vertritt die manager von von bauer und von meier?
 PERSON
 ---------------------
 FRITZ
?
was ist die summe der gehaelter ?
     11550
 ?
dg=(summe der gehaelter) / anzahl der gehaelter
 ?
y=(gehalt - dg)**2
 ?
vg=(summe von y) / ((anzahl der gehaelter) - 1)
 ?
was ist vg**0,5 ?
       863,163947
 ?
ende
```

6 References

[1] Batori, S., et al.: 'LIANA - Ein deutschsprachiges
     Frage-Antwort-System', 1975.
[2] Bruce, B. C.: 'A Model for Temporal References and Its Application
     in a Question Answering Program', Artificial Intelligence
     vol. 3, 1, spring 1972.
[3] Codd, E. F.: 'Seven Steps to Rendezvous with the Casual User', IBM
     Research Report RJ 1333 (Nr. 20842), January 1974.
[4] Dostert, B. H., F. B. Thompson: 'The syntax of REL English, REL
     Report No. 1, California Institute of Technology, Pasadena,
     1971.
[5] Dostert, B. H., F. B. Thompson: 'Verbal semantics in a relational
     data base system', California Institute of Technology,
     Pasadena, 1973.
[6] Helbig, G., J. Buscha: Deutsche Grammatik, Ein Handbuch fuer den
     Auslaenderunterricht, VEB Verlag Enzyklopaedie, Leipzig,
     1974.
[7] Isner, D.W.: 'An inferential processor for interacting with
     biomedical data using restricted natural language.' AFIPS
     Vol.40, Sprg 1972.
[8] Kay, M.: 'Experiments with a powerful parser', Second
     International Conference on Computational Linguistics,
     Grenoble, August 1967.
[9] Kraegeloh, K.-D., P. C. Lockemann: 'Hierarchies of Data Base
     Systems: An Example', Information Systems vol. 1, 1975.
[10] Lehmann, H., M. Zoeppritz: 'Language facilities of USL/German',
     Version II, Heidelberg Scientific Center, TN 75.01.
[11] Lehmann, H., M. Zoeppritz: 'Grammar rules for German', Version II,
     Heidelberg Scientific Center, TN 75.02.
[12] Lehmann, H., N. Ott: 'Interpretation routines for German grammar
     rules', Heidelberg Scientific Center, TN 75.03.
[13] Lehmann, H., M. Zoeppritz: 'Partition of German grammar',
     Heidelberg Scientific Center, TN 75.05.
[14] Lehmann, H., M. Zoeppritz: 'Grammar rules with examples',
     Heidelberg Scientific Center, TN 75.06.
[15] Mylopoulos, J., et al.: 'TORUS - A natural Language Understanding
     System for Data Management', Proc. 4th Int. Joint Conf. on
     Art. Intelligence, September 1975.
[16] Palme, J.: 'Making computers understand natural language', FOAP
     Rapport C 8257-11(64), Stockholm, July 1970.
[17] Plath, W.J.: 'Transformational grammar and transformational

parsing in the REQUEST system. Proc. 1973 Intern. Conf. on Comp. Linguistics. Pisa, 1973.

[18] Simmons, R. F.: 'Natural Language Question-Answering Systems', CACM 13 (1), 15, 1970.

[19] Sparck Jones, K., M. Kay: Linguistics and Information Science. New York, 1973.

[20] Thompson, F. B., P. C. Lockemann, B. H. Dostert, R. S. Deverill: 'REL: A rapidly extensible language system', Proc. 24th National ACM Conference, New York, August 1969.

[21] Walker, D. E.: 'Automated language processing'. Annual Review of Information Science and Technology, vol.8, Carlos A. Cuadra (ed.), AFIPS, Washington, 1973.

[22] Winograd, T.: 'Procedures as a representation for data in a computer program for understanding natural language'. MIT, Cambridge, Mass., 1971.

[23] Woods, W.A.: 'Semantics for a question-answering system'. The AIKEN Computation Laboratory, Harvard Univ., Cambridge, Mass., 1967.

[24] Woods, W.A. &al.: 'The lunar sciences natural language information system: final report'. BB&N, Cambridge, Mass., 1972.

[25] Wulz, Hanno: 'ISLIB - Ein Informationssystem auf linguistischer Basis', Institut fuer Deutsche Sprache, mimeographed, 1975.

[26] (without author): 'Vorhabenbeschreibung zum Vorhaben Problemloesendes Informationssystem mit Deutsch als Interaktionssprache (PLIDIS)'. Institut fuer Deutsche Sprache, mimeographed, August 1975.

<u>DIE BESTIMMUNG OPTIMALER OPERATIONSFOLGEN ZUR KONVERSION</u>

<u>VON DATEIEN MIT MEHRFACH VORHANDENEN DATENELEMENTEN</u>

M. Deck   Siemens AG Mannheim
T. Härder TH Darmstadt FB Informatik
J. Reus   Siemens AG Frankfurt

1. Einleitung

Mit dem verstärkten Übergang von individuellen Dateisystemen zu standardisierten
Datenbanksystemen und der Notwendigkeit, Dateien für Anwendungen (Planungsdaten,
Datenverbund) auf verschiedenen Rechnersystemen extrahieren und austauschen zu
müssen, wächst der Bedarf, Daten zu übersetzen oder zu konvertieren. Vergleichsweise
einfache Konversionsprobleme sind dabei die Änderung des Datentyps von Attributen,
die Reihenfolge von Attributen innerhalb eines Satzes oder der Wechsel der internen
Darstellung vom ASCII-Code zum EBCDIC-Code. Werden dagegen Änderungen in der Datenstruktur notwendig, ergeben sich im allgemeinen Fall recht komplexe Problemlösungen.

In dieser Arbeit wird der für praktische Anwendungen wichtige Fall diskutiert, wie
aus einer Reihe von vorhandenen Dateien (Quelldateien), die redundante Daten be-
sitzen können, eine Zieldatei auf zeitoptimale Weise zu erstellen ist.

Gegenwärtig ist für jede Umstrukturierung von Daten, die beispielsweise zur Beseiti-
gung der Speicherredundanz oder beim Übergang zu einem Datenbanksystem erforderlich
wird, ein spezielles Programm zu schreiben, was zu einem unerträglichen Gesamtauf-
wand führt. Deshalb ist es Ziel verschiedener Arbeiten, das Problem der Datenübersetzung in allgemeiner Weise zu lösen (Fr 72, Sh 75, Si 73, Sm 72). Mit Hilfe einer
Datendefinitionssprache beschreibt der Benutzer die Daten der vorhandenen Quelldateien und der gewünschten Zieldatei auf verschiedenen Darstellungsebenen. Neben
Angaben zur logischen Datenstruktur und zu existierenden Zugriffspfaden sind Informationen zu den Speicherungsstrukturen und deren Zuordnung auf den physischen Speichermedien notwendig. Mit einer Datenübersetzungssprache, die nur deskriptive Sprachelemente besitzt, gibt der Anwender eine Operationenfolge an, nach der aus den Quelldateien die Zieldatei generiert werden kann. Da zur Erstellung der Zieldatei oft
mehrere Lösungswege möglich sind und außerdem die Reihenfolge der einzelnen Operationen den gesamten Zeitaufwand wesentlich bestimmen, liegt die Verantwortung für
die Wirksamkeit der Konversion allein beim Benutzer. Für die zeitoptimale Lösung ist
eine große Anzahl von Detailinformationen auf allen Beschreibungsebenen zu berücksichtigen, deren Einfluß auf das Zeitverhalten der Datenübersetzung für den Benutzer
nicht zu übersehen ist. Außerdem erfolgt keine semantische Prüfung der Zulässigkeit
der Zieldatei. Der Anwender kann deshalb semantisch unsinnige Daten erzeugen, wenn
er beispielsweise in seiner Operationenfolge einen Verbund (Co 70) über zwei Nicht-
Schlüssel-Attribute angibt.

Im Gegensatz zur expliziten Festlegung der Operationenfolge durch eine Datenübersetzungssprache wird in unserem Ansatz versucht, diese Aufgabe einem Programmsystem
zu übertragen. Dazu ist die Beschreibung der logischen Datenstrukturen von Quell-
und Zieldateien durch Elementare Funktionalrelationen (EFR, (De 73)) nötig. Durch
einen Algorithmus werden alle möglichen Wege zur Erzeugung der Zieldatei abgeleitet.
Die Beschreibungen der Zugriffspfad- und Speicherungsstrukturen werden zusammen mit
den Angaben über die verwendeten physischen Speichermedien (physische Datenbeschrei-
bung) dazu benutzt, den optimalen Lösungsweg auszuwählen und die günstigste Operationsfolge festzulegen. Als Operationen sind auf der logischen Beschreibungsebene
Relationenoperationen (Projektion, Verbund und Restriktion) und Mengenoperationen
(Mischen) zugelassen (We 74). Für die tatsächliche Ausführung dieser Operationen
auf der physischen Ebene ist vor allem die Ausnutzung einer vorhandenen Sortierordnung oder die explizite Ausführung von Sortierungen von großer Wichtigkeit.

Das folgende Funktionendiagramm veranschaulicht das prinzipielle Lösungsschema:

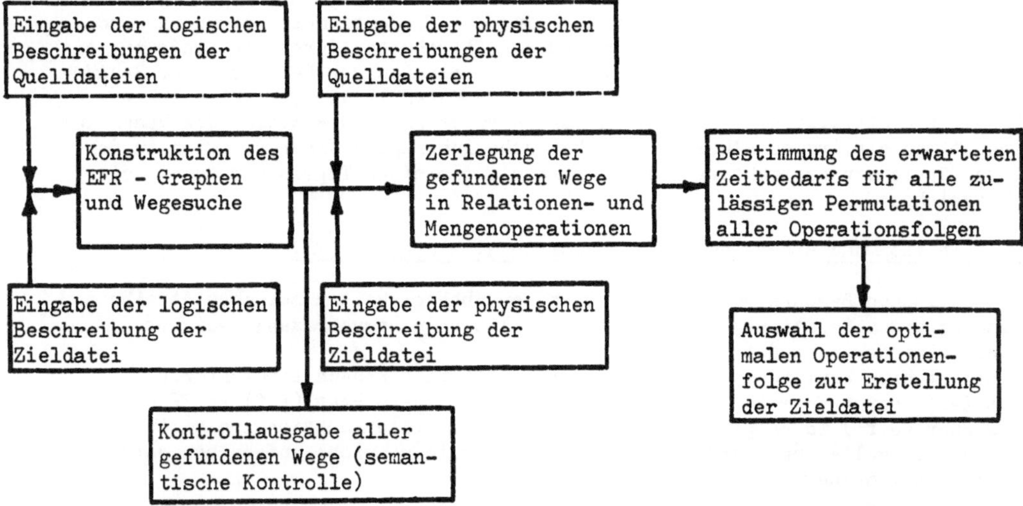

Mit diesem Ansatz kann sicherlich nicht jede Zieldatei im Sinne der Auswahlfähigkeit des Prädikatenkalküls erster Ordnung erzeugt werden, da beispielsweise kein ALL-Quantor eingesetzt wird. Doch lassen sich damit eine Vielzahl von Aufgaben des praktischen Einsatzes lösen. Auch wird dabei eine semantische Prüfung bei der Ableitung der Zieldatei durchgeführt, soweit diese mit Hilfe des "syntaktischen" EFR-Beschreibungskonzeptes möglich ist. Gegebenenfalls wird angezeigt, daß eine gewünschte Zieldatei unter Einhaltung semantischer Restriktionen (z.B. kein Verbund über Nicht-Schlüssel-Attribute) nicht erstellt werden kann. Das EFR-Konzept gewährleistet, daß jede Ausprägung einer Attributgruppe Z in der Zieldatei mit einer eindeutigen Ausprägung einer Attributgruppe Q in den Quelldateien korrespondiert und somit nur bedeutungsvolle Zieldateien abgeleitet werden. Zur Kontrolle werden alle gefundenen Wege ausgegeben, damit der Benutzer entscheiden kann, welche Ableitungsfolgen zu semantisch korrekten Zieldateien (Sm 75) führen.

Das entwickelte Programmsystem läßt sich als Optimierungshilfe für einen Datei-Übersetzer heranziehen. Wie das Anwendungsbeispiel in Abschnitt 4 zeigt, ergeben sich bei Konversionsaufgaben mit mehreren Dateien große Zeitunterschiede für die möglichen Lösungswege und Operationenfolgen, so daß durch die optimale Reihenfolge der Operationen des zeitgünstigsten Weges die Wirksamkeit der Datei-Übersetzung beträchtlich gesteigert werden kann.

2. Lösungsmodell

2.1 Grundlagen

2.1.1 Normalisierte Relationen

Zur Beschreibung der an der Konversion beteiligten Daten ziehen wir das Relationenmodell nach E.F. Codd heran (Co 70), durch das sich logische Datenstrukturen einer Datenbank darstellen lassen. Danach ist eine n-stellige normalisierte Relation $R(A_1, A_2, \ldots, A_n)$ als Untermenge des Cartesischen Produktes über ihre Definitionsbereiche A_i definiert:

$$R(A_1, A_2, \ldots, A_n) \subseteq A_1 \times A_2 \times \ldots \times A_n$$

Die Mengen $A_1, A_2, \ldots, A_n$ müssen nicht notwendigerweise disjunkt sein.

Die Namen der Mengen sind Attributnamen und deren Elemente Attribut-Werte. Eine
n-stellige Relation heißt normalisiert, wenn alle Bereiche der Relation einfach sind,
d.h., wenn keiner ihrer Bereiche wiederum eine Relation ist. Eine n-stellige Relation läßt sich als eine Menge von n-Tupeln, für die Eindeutigkeit gefordert wird,
darstellen. Attribute oder minimale Gruppen von Attributen, durch die Eindeutigkeit
der Tupeln gewährleistet wird, heißen Schlüsselkandidaten der Relation. Der Schlüsselkandidat, der zur Identifizierung der Tupeln ausgewählt wird, heißt Primärschlüssel. Ein Attribut einer Relation, das in einer anderen Relation Schlüssel ist,
bezeichnet man als Fremdschlüssel. Die physische Ausprägung einer Relation in der
Ebene der Speicherungsstrukturen wird als Datei, die eines Tupels als Satz fester
Länge bezeichnet.

2.1.2 Definition und Eigenschaften von Funktionalrelationen (FR)

Zur syntaktischen Beschreibung der funktionalen Abhängigkeiten zwischen Attributen
in normalisierten Relationen sind Funktionalrelationen hervorragend geeignet.
Sie sind folgendermaßen definiert:
Es existiert eine Funktionalrelation von einem Attribut E nach einem Attribut F
- dargestellt durch $E \longrightarrow F$ -, wenn es für jedes geordnete Paar (e,f) in EF kein
anderes Paar (e,f') in EF gibt, so daß $f \neq f'$ gilt. Diese Funktionalrelation muß
zeitunabhängig gelten und darf durch den Änderungsdienst nicht aufgehoben werden.
E ist das bestimmende und F das abhängige Attribut.

Die Definition der Funktionalrelationen kann folgendermaßen erweitert werden:

E und F seien zwei bestimmte zusammengesetzte Attribute mit $E = \{E_1, E_2, \ldots, E_n\}$
und $F = \{F_1, F_2, \ldots, F_m\}$. Für eine Funktionalrelation zwischen diesen zusammengesetzten Attributen schreibt man

$$E \longrightarrow F \quad \text{oder} \quad E_1, E_2, \ldots, E_n \longrightarrow F_1, F_2, \ldots, F_m \ .$$

Wenn zwischen E und F eine FR besteht und außerdem für jede Untermenge $E' \subset E$ die
funktionale Beziehung $E' \longrightarrow F$ nicht gilt, dann bezeichnet man $E \longrightarrow F$ als eine elementare Funktionalrelation (EFR). Wenn zwei Attribute in einem 1:1 Zusammenhang
stehen, läßt sich diese Beziehung durch Funktionalrelationen in beiden Richtungen
$E \longrightarrow F$ und $F \longrightarrow E$ ausdrücken.

Folgende Eigenschaften gelten für Funktionalrelationen (De 73):

a) Transitivität: wenn $E \longrightarrow F$ und $F \longrightarrow G$, dann $E \longrightarrow G$;
b) Reflexivität : $E \longrightarrow E$;
c) Trivialität : wenn $E \subset F$, dann $F \longrightarrow E$; ($F \longrightarrow E$ kann in diesem Fall keine EFR sein).
d) Additivität : F,G seien ein zusammengesetztes Attribut als Vereinigung der
   Komponenten F und G;
   dann folgt: wenn $E \longrightarrow F$ und $E \longrightarrow G$, dann $E \longrightarrow F,G$;
e) Pseudotransitivität: wenn $E \longrightarrow F$ und $F,G \longrightarrow H$, dann $E,G \longrightarrow H$;
f) Erweiterung : wenn $E \longrightarrow G$, dann $E,F \longrightarrow G$. F ist dabei irgendein anderes Attribut.

2.2 Konstruktion des EFR-Graphen

In unserem Lösungsmodell ist für die Darstellung der Dateien eine logische und eine
physische Beschreibungsebene erforderlich.
In der logischen Beschreibung werden die funktionalen Abhängigkeiten zwischen den
Attributen mit Hilfe von elementaren Funktionalrelationen ausgedrückt. Die physische
Beschreibung der Dateien enthält Angaben über Speicherungsstrukturen (SAM, ISAM),
Satz- und Attributanzahlen, Schlüssel, Sortierung u.a.

Die eingegebenen funktionalen Abhängigkeiten zwischen den Attributen der Quelldateien
dienen dazu, einen gerichteten EFR-Graphen aufzubauen. Besteht beispielsweise zwischen
den Attributen PERS# (# bedeutet Nummer) und NAME die EFR PERS# $\longrightarrow$ NAME, erhält der
Graph eine gerichtete Verbindung von PERS# nach NAME. Die funktionalen Abhängigkeiten
bilden die Kanten, die Attribute oder Attributgruppen die Knoten im Graph. Gleiche
EFR's, die in verschiedenen Dateien vorkommen, erscheinen nur einmal im Graph.

Beispiel 1:

EFR-Graph
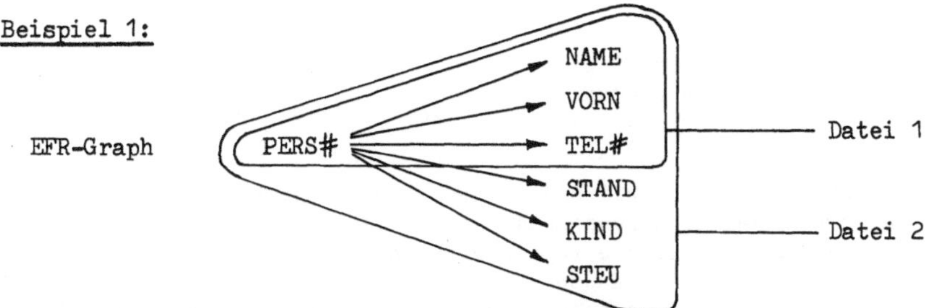

Im Beispiel erkennt man, daß die EFR's PERS#→NAME, PERS#→VORN und PERS#→TEL#
in den Dateien 1 und 2 vorkommen, jedoch im Graph nur einmal auftreten.

Der EFR-Graph soll nur die Suche nach verschiedenen Lösungswegen veranschaulichen.
Er enthält alle eingegebenen EFR's, mit denen die logischen Datenstrukturen der
einzelnen Dateien beschrieben werden. Die transitive Hülle aller ableitbaren EFR's
wird nicht konstruiert, da dadurch nicht direkt in den physischen Dateien vorhandene
EFR's eingeführt werden. Solche EFR's müssen über einen zu findenden Lösungsweg abgeleitet werden. Die minimale Überdeckung des Graphen wird ebenfalls nicht erzeugt,
da dadurch wegen der physischen Redundanz der Daten direkt vorhandene Lösungswege
verloren gehen können. Zum Auffinden aller Wege erweist es sich als notwendig, neben
den elementaren Funktionalrelationen auch triviale funktionale Abhängigkeiten (TFR's)
(Co 71) einzuführen. Diese entsprechen der Trivialität, wie sie Delobel und Casey
(De 73) als Eigenschaft von Funktionalrelationen abgeleitet haben.

Neben den TFR-Beziehungen werden auch alle additiven Beziehungen im Graph eingetragen.
Die Kanten des daraus resultierenden endlichen und schlichten Graphen sind unbewertet
und gerichtet.

Für die Zieldatei sind ebenfalls die funktionalen Abhängigkeiten zwischen den Attributen anzugeben. Für alle elementaren Funktionalrelationen der Zieldatei werden Wege
im Graph gesucht, die zusammen Lösungswege für die Zieldatei ergeben.

2.3 Algorithmus zur Wegsuche

Der EFR-Graph dient ausschließlich zur Wegsuche, die zur Ableitung einer Operationenfolge zur Erstellung der gewünschten Zieldatei führt. Für jede EFR der logischen
Zieldateibeschreibung wird ein Weg im Graph vom bestimmenden Attribut (Attributgruppe)
zum abhängigen Attribut gesucht. Existiert für eine EFR kein Weg, ist die Zieldatei
nicht abzuleiten. Die EFR's der Quelldateien bilden entweder keinen zusammenhängenden
Graphen oder es wird versucht, eine semantisch unsinnige Zieldatei zu erstellen, d.h.
in der Zieldatei werden nicht existierende EFR's angegeben.

Der Algorithmus zur Wegsuche muß in dem gerichteten Graphen alle Wege zwischen
2 Knoten finden. Die Suche aller Wege ist nötig, da der erste gefundene Weg nicht
notwendigerweise der optimale ist. Der im Hinblick auf die Konversion günstigste Weg
läßt sich erst nach den Zeitberechnungen zur Ermittlung der optimalen Operationenfolge feststellen. Für diese Aufgabe wurde ein Algorithmus entwickelt, der auf der
Methode des Durchsuchens mit Rückverfolgen (Backtracking-Verfahren) basiert.

2.4 Erstellen der Operationenfolgen

Es ist nicht möglich, sofort aus allen Lösungswegen die zeitoptimale Operationenfolge
zu konstruieren. Deshalb ist für jeden Weg eine Operationenfolge abzuleiten, für deren
Erstellen auch die physischen Dateibeschreibungen heranzuziehen sind. Es können die
Operationen Projektion, Restriktion, Verbund und Mischen auftreten.

Projektion

Mit Hilfe der Projektion lassen sich aus einer Relation R bestimmte Spalten (Attribute)
auswählen. Die übrigen Spalten sind zu streichen und aus der neu gewonnenen Relation R'
die doppelten Tupeln zu entfernen. Deshalb ist die Mächtigkeit von R' gleich oder
kleiner der Mächtigkeit von R. Eine Projektion bewirkt also, daß aus einer Datei nur
die Attribute gewonnen werden, die zum Aufbau der Zieldatei notwendig sind.

Restriktion

Durch die Restriktion wird die Anzahl der Tupeln einer Relation durch boolesche
Operatoren oder Vergleichsoperatoren eingeschränkt.

Verbund

Durch die Operation Verbund lassen sich zwei Relationen über ein gemeinsames Attribut
(Attributgruppe) zu einer neuen Relation zusammenfassen. Beim Gleichverbund werden im
Gegensatz zu anderen Verbundarten nur solche Tupeln verknüpft, in denen das Verbundattribut den gleichen Wert hat. Wir beschränken uns auf diesen praktisch relevanten
Fall, den wir kurz Verbund nennen. Eine Verbundoperation ist notwendig, wenn in aufeinanderfolgenden EFR's, die in einem Weg zur Erstellung der Zieldatei vorkommen,
eine Dateigrenze überschritten wird.

Ein Verbund zwischen zwei Relationen ist auf vier Arten möglich:

Verbundattribut ist in der EFR der 2. Relation	Verbundattribut ist in der EFR der 1. Relation
bestimmendes Attribut	abhängiges Attribut
bestimmendes Attribut	bestimmendes Attribut
abhängiges Attribut	abhängiges Attribut
Teil der bestimmenden Attributgruppe	abhängiges Attribut

Sind beide Relationen in dritter Normalform, so ist das bestimmende Attribut jeweils
Schlüsselkandidat und das abhängige Attribut Fremdschlüssel, wenn der Verbund möglich ist.

Mischen

Eine Mischoperation wird durchgeführt, um Daten aus redundanten Dateien zu vereinigen.
Das Mischen von Relationen (Dateien) kann eine größere Mächtigkeit und/oder einen
größeren Grad der Ergebnisrelation bewirken, wenn undefinierte Attributwerte zugelassen sind. Kommt ein Attribut in mehreren Dateien vor, und ist dieses Attribut in
der Zieldatei Schlüsselattribut, so muß gemischt werden.

Im Beispiel 1 werden für eine Zieldatei die EFR's PERS#→NAME, PERS#→VORN und
PERS#→STEU verlangt, wobei PERS# das Schlüsselattribut sein soll. Es wird ein
Mischen zwischen den Dateien 1 und 2 abgeleitet, da im allgemeinen nicht angenommen
werden kann, daß die Attributwerte von PERS# in Datei 1 und 2 übereinstimmen.
Im folgenden Beispiel wird ebenfalls ein Mischen abgeleitet.

Beispiel 2:

EFR-Graph

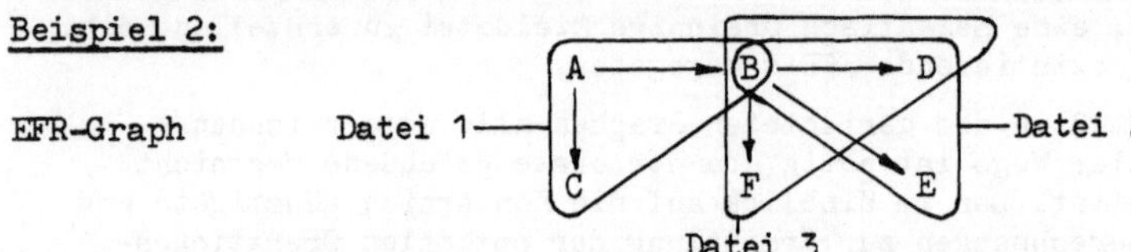

Die EFR B→D kann in den Dateien 2 und 3 teilweise unterschiedliche Attributwerte
enthalten. In der Zieldatei sei die EFR A→D verlangt, wobei Attribut A das
Schlüsselattribut sein soll. Es wird der Weg A→B, B→D abgeleitet. Wird der Verbund über Attribut B zwischen Datei 1 und 2 oder Datei 1 und 3 ausgeführt, ohne vorher die Dateien 2 und 3 zu mischen, so können Informationen verloren gehen. Dies
läßt sich vermeiden, wenn man erst die Dateien 2 und 3 mischt und danach den Verbund
über Attribut B durchführt.

3. Bestimmung des erwarteten Zeitbedarfs zur Durchführung der Konversion

Durch Zeitbetrachtungen für das Verarbeiten von Dateien werden die Ausführungszeiten
der abgeleiteten Operationen bestimmt. Die Auswertung der Operationen mit Hilfe von
Zugriffszeitbeziehungen unter Variation ihrer Reihenfolge ermöglicht die Festlegung
der optimalen Folge für die verschiedenen Lösungswege.

3.1 Physische Dateibeschreibungen

Um möglichst genaue Zeit- und Mengenberechnungen durchführen zu können, sind vom Benutzer für jede Quelldatei detaillierte Angaben notwendig.

Die Kopfzeilen enthalten Angaben, die die gesamte Datei betreffen:

```
DNR          - Fortlaufende Nummer zur Identifizierung der Dateibeschreibungen
DATEINAME    - Bezeichnung der Datei
SATZANZAHL   - Anzahl der logischen Sätze der Datei  (N   )
                                                        REC
SATZLAENGE   - Länge eines logischen Satzes in Bytes
BLOCKUNG     - Anzahl von logischen Sätzen in einem Block
ORGANIS      - Organisationsform der Datei         S - sequentiell organisiert
                                                   I - indexsequentiell organisiert
PAD-FAKTOR   - gibt bei Dateien an, wieviel Prozent eines Blockes nicht belegt werden,
               damit bei Änderungen neue Sätze eingefügt werden können.
GERAET       - Datenträger der Datei               P - Magnetplatte
                                                   B - Magnetband
```

Die Rumpfzeilen enthalten Werte über die Attribute einer Datei:

```
ATTRNAME   - Attributbezeichnung
LAENGE     - größte Länge eines Attributes in Bytes
ANZAHL     - Anzahl der unterschiedlichen Attributwerte
WIE        - Die Angabe im Feld WIE entspricht dem Auflösungsfaktor
             (Resolutionsfaktor) nach C.P. WANG (Hä 75)
             mit j als Anzahl der Attributwerte eines Attributes
SI         - Ist eine "1" gesetzt, so ist für das zugehörige Attribut
             ein sekundärer Index vorhanden.
KEY        - Indentifizierender Schlüssel. Eine "1" besagt, daß das entsprechende
             Attribut zum Schlüssel der Datei gehört (zusammengesetzte Schlüssel
             sind begrenzt auf 3 Attribute).
FOR-KEY    - Fremdschlüssel (foreign key)
             Stellt das Verbindungsattribut zwischen zwei Dateien dar (Verbund).
CAND-KEY   - Schlüsselkandidat (candidate key)
SORT       - Sortierordnung (Reihenfolge der Sortierattribute)
```

$$R = \frac{N_{REC}}{j}$$

Für die physische Beschreibung der Zieldatei kann der Benutzer in der Kopfzeile die Organisation, das Gerät sowie die Blockung bestimmen. In den Rumpfzeilen muß er lediglich die Namen der gewünschten Attribute, sowie die Sortierordnung und den Schlüssel angeben. Das Programm berechnet während des Laufs die Satzanzahl und die Satzlänge in der Kopfzeile, sowie die fehlenden Angaben in den Rumpfzeilen. Restriktionen für Attribute müssen gesondert durch Angaben zur Mengenberechnung beschrieben werden.

3.2 Beschreibung der Anlagenkonfiguration

Die Zeitbeziehungen können nicht ohne eine bestimmte Systemumgebung betrachtet werden. Daher wird im folgenden die der Bestimmung der Zugriffszeit zugrunde liegende Anlagenkonfiguration erläutert.

Die Quelldateien sind auf externen Speichern (Band, Platte) abgespeichert. Der Hauptanteil der Verweilzeit wird durch die Ein/Ausgabezeiten der Daten zwischen der Zentraleinheit und den externen Speichermedien bestimmt. Es wird dabei unterstellt, daß die Ein/Ausgabe der Daten über Wechselpuffer stattfindet und die interne Verarbeitungszeit gegenüber der Ein/Ausgabezeit vernachlässigt werden kann.

Bei allen Berechnungen wird vorausgesetzt, daß die verwendete DV-Anlage im Einzelprogrammbetrieb arbeitet.

Für Zeitabschätzungen zum Lesen oder Schreiben von Daten auf Magnetband oder -platte, ist es notwendig, auf die technischen Daten von bestehenden Geräten Bezug zu nehmen. Die Gerätedaten finden sich in (SIEM) und (Hä 75).

3.3 Funktionelle Beschreibung der verschiedenen Operationsarten

Jede Operation wird in einzelne Schritte (Aktionen) zerlegt. Für die Bestimmung der
Verarbeitungszeiten von Dateien auf externen Speichermedien werden deterministische
worst case Abschätzungen durchgeführt.

Projektion

Bei der Ausführung einer Projektion ist es erforderlich, die zugehörige Datei zu
lesen, die nicht notwendigen Attribute zu löschen (Sätze verkürzen) und den Rest in
eine Datei zurückzuschreiben. Sind für die Zieldatei des Benutzers gleichzeitig noch
andere Operationen (Mischen, Verbund) hergeleitet worden, so erfolgt die Projektion
nicht in der oben beschriebenen Weise, da sie dann gleichzeitig mit anderen Operationen ausgeführt wird.

Restriktion

Mit der Einschränkung lassen sich bestimmte Sätze einer Datei durch vorgegebene
boolsche Operatoren ($\wedge$, $\vee$) und Vergleichsoperatoren ($<$, $\leqslant$, $>$, $\geqslant$, $=$, $\neq$)
auswählen.

Wenn für diese Sätze kein Zugriffspfad existiert, ist die gesamte Datei fortlaufend
zu lesen. Die qualifizierten Sätze werden ausgewählt und zurückgeschrieben. Durch die
Ausnutzung vorhandener Zugriffspfade läßt sich diese Operation beschleunigen. Gegebenenfalls wird sie mit der Ausführung anderer Operationen verknüpft.

Verbund

Ein Verbund kann auf verschiedene Arten durchgeführt werden. Anhand des folgenden
Beispiels werden die notwendigen Aktionen beschrieben.

Beispiel 3:

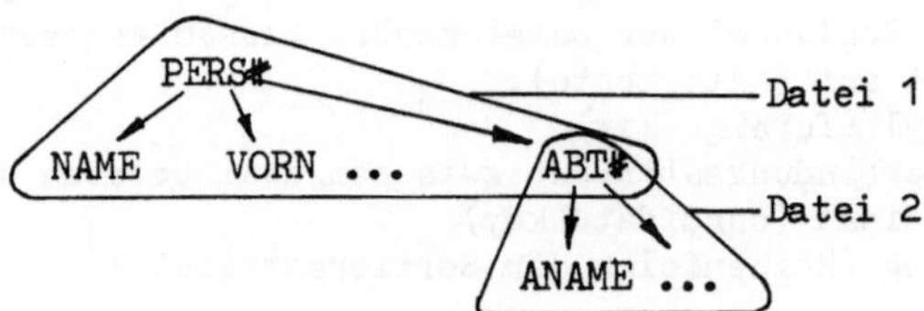

Drei Verbundarten

Bei der ersten Verbundart sind die beiden Dateien gegebenenfalls nach dem Verbundattribut (Attributgruppe) zu sortieren. Danach werden die sortierten Dateien fortlaufend blockweise in den Kernspeicher gelesen. Die Sätze mit gleichem Wert im
Verbundattribut sind zu bilden und in eine Zwischendatei zurückzuschreiben.

Die zweite Verbundart ist nur durchführbar, wenn ein wahlfreier Zugriff auf die
Sätze der Datei 2 möglich ist. Die Datei 1 wird sequentiell gelesen und gleichzeitig
für jeden Satz der zugehörige Satz aus der Datei 2 wahlfrei gelesen. Die verknüpften
Sätze werden in eine Zwischendatei geschrieben. Die Anzahl der wahlfreien Zugriffe
zur Datei 2 wird wesentlich durch die Satzanzahl von Datei 1 bestimmt, die bei dieser
Verbundart nach einem beliebigen Attribut sortiert sein kann.

Bei der dritten Verbundart wird vorausgesetzt, daß die Datei 1 für das Verbundattribut einen sekundären Index besitzt. Aus der Datei 2 wird ein Satz gelesen. Der gefundene Schlüssel ABT# dient jetzt als Suchargument für den sekundären Index der
Datei 1. Die so gefundenen Sätze aus der Datei 1 werden mit dem Satz aus der Datei 2
verknüpft und in eine Zwischendatei ausgeschrieben. Dieser Vorgang wiederholt sich
solange, bis alle Sätze aus der Datei 2 verarbeitet sind. Die Datei 2 kann dabei nach
einem beliebigen Attribut sortiert sein.

Bei jeder abgeleiteten Verbundoperation wird der Zeitbedarf für die 3 Verbundarten
mit Hilfe von detaillierten Zugriffszeitbeziehungen berechnet. Die Verbundart mit
dem geringsten Erwartungswert für die Ausführungszeit wird ausgewählt.

Mischen

Das Mischen kann in einem Durchgang erfolgen, wenn jede Datei nach dem gemeinsamen
Attribut sortiert ist (gegebenenfalls Sortierlauf durchführen). Es genügt ein m-Wege
Mischen (m=Anzahl der zu mischenden Dateien), um eine einzige Datei (Zwischendatei)
zu erhalten. Dabei werden Sätze mit gleichem Satzschlüssel nur einmal übernommen.
Beim Mischen müssen alle beteiligten Dateien in den Kernspeicher übertragen und die
Zwischendatei auf ein externes Speichermedium zurückgeschrieben werden.

Insgesamt sind im Hinblick auf die Schlüsselattribute vier Fälle bei einer Mischoperation zu beachten. Die beiden Schlüsselattribute werden mit A und A' bezeichnet.

Im Fall (1) sind Schlüsselwerte von A' in A enthalten. A' ist eine Teilmenge von A.
Ein Mischen ist überflüssig, da dadurch keine neuen Attributwerte gewonnen werden
(Die Mächtigkeit der Relation vergrößert sich nicht). Für die weiteren Berechnungen
wird die Datei mit dem Schlüsselattribut A ausgewählt und die Mischoperation nicht
ausgeführt. Der Fall (2) verhält sich analog zu Fall (1). Im Fall (3) ist das Mischen
tatsächlich durchzuführen, da das Schlüsselattribut teilweise unterschiedliche Ausprägungen in den verschiedenen Dateien besitzt. Im Grenzfall ist der gemeinsame
Durchschnitt der Schlüsselausprägungen leer. Im Fall (4) sind alle Attributwerte von
A auch in A' vorhanden und umgekehrt, deshalb ist ein Mischen überflüssig. Für die
Weiterverarbeitung wird die Datei ausgewählt, die eine kürzere Verarbeitungszeit erwarten läßt. Als Auswahlkriterien dienen Sortierung, Gerät und Dateiorganisationsform.

Aus den physischen Beschreibungen der Dateien ist nicht eindeutig entscheidbar, um
welchen der 4 Fälle es sich handelt. Deshalb sollte der Benutzer bei einer Mischoperation angeben, welcher Fall bei seiner Anwendung vorliegt, um eine aufwendige,
maschinelle Fallerkennung zu vermeiden.

3.4 Bestimmung der Zugriffszeiten

Die Zugriffszeitbeziehungen für das Verarbeiten von Dateien sind in (Hä 75) und
(Dk 75) ausführlich erläutert. Je nach Speicherzuordnungsstruktur, Gerät und Verar-
beitungszeit der Dateien wird unter Einbeziehung der physischen Dateibeschreibungen
der Erwartungswert für die Ausführungszeit berechnet. Für die genaue Bestimmung der
Sortierzeit sind viele Variablen in Betracht zu ziehen, u.a. Sortieralgorithmus,
Größe des Arbeitsspeichers, technische Daten der verfügbaren Anlage, technische
Charakteristika der Zwischenspeicher und verwendetes Betriebssystem. Daraus folgt,
daß die Sortierzeiten sehr stark von der vorhandenen Anlagenkonfiguration und
Software-Unterstützung abhängen.
Da für die meisten Betriebssysteme ein Sortierdienstprogramm zur Verfügung steht,
ist es einfacher, die zugehörigen, vom Hersteller in umfangreichen Tests erstellten
Sortierkurven heranzuziehen. Durch eine Auswertung der Sortierkurven lassen sich für
die jeweils benutzte Anlagenkonfiguration einfache Näherungsbeziehungen finden, die
im wesentlichen nur noch von der zu sortierenden Datenmenge (Datenmenge = Satzanzahl·
Satzlänge) und dem zugewiesenen Kernspeicherplatz abhängig sind. Wird während der
Abarbeitung einer Operationenfolge festgestellt, daß eine Sortierung für eine Datei
notwendig ist, so wird die dazu erforderliche Zeit durch die abgeleiteten Näherungsbeziehungen bestimmt.

3.5 Ermittlung der physischen Zwischendateibeschreibungen

Beim Abarbeiten einer Operationenfolge sind Zwischendateibeschreibungen aufzustellen,
die in den nachfolgenden Operationen weiterverwendet werden. Dabei müssen für eine
Zwischendatei häufig Satzanzahl, Wiederholungsfaktoren (Auflösungsfaktor) und Anzahl
der Attributwerte mit Hilfe einer Näherungsrechnung bestimmt werden. Dazu ist es notwendig, diese Werte nach jeder Operation zu überprüfen und gegebenenfalls neu zu bearbeiten. Eine ausführliche Diskussion dieser Näherungsrechnung für jede Operation
erfolgt in (Dk 75).

3.6 Variation der Operationenfolge eines Lösungsweges

Da für jeden Lösungsweg nicht nur eine einzige Reihenfolge, in der die dazugehörigen Operationen ablaufen müssen, existiert, ist es von großer Wichtigkeit für die Wirksamkeit der Konversion, die zeitoptimale Operationsfolge zu finden. Dazu bestehen grundsätzlich zwei Möglichkeiten:

(1) Heuristische Entscheidungen für die "beste" Reihenfolge.
   Kriterien für die Entscheidungen sind:
   a) Die Projektions- und Restriktionsoperationen so früh wie möglich auszuführen
   b) Dateien mit kleiner Datenmenge zuerst verarbeiten
   c) Berücksichtigung der Sortierordnung

Diese Möglichkeit ist in dem Ansatz von Smith/Chang (SC 75) aufgezeigt. Es ist im allgemeinen äußerst schwierig, eine Reihenfolge zu finden, in der die Anzahl der Sortierungen minimal ist.

(2) Überprüfung aller Möglichkeiten
   Um tatsächlich die optimale Reihenfolge zu finden, ist es notwendig, die Folgen zu permutieren. Bei größeren Anwendungen müssen aber in der Regel nicht alle permutierten Operationenfolgen berechnet werden, da bestimmte Paare von Operationen nur in einer Reihenfolge ablaufen dürfen. Die Anzahl der zu berechnenden, zulässigen Folgen verringert sich dann erheblich.

4. Anwendungsbeispiel

Für unseren Ansatz zur Datenkonversion geben wir ein ausführliches Beispiel an, für das mit Hilfe des entwickelten Programmsystems die optimale Operationenfolge bestimmt wird. Es bezieht sich auf Daten aus einem Betrieb.

Datei 1 - Personaldaten; Datei 2 - Telefonverzeichnis; Datei 3 - Abteilungen;
Datei 4 - Gebäude; Datei 5 - Personaldaten.

Die Datei 5 enthält nur Attribute, die auch in der Datei 1 vorhanden sind, ist aber im Gegensatz zu Datei 1 auf Band abgespeichert und nach einem anderen Attribut sortiert.
Die nächsten Seiten zeigen die physischen und logischen Beschreibungen der Quelldateien in ausführlicher Form.

LOGISCHE QUELLDATEIBESCHREIBUNGEN

DATEI-NR	ELEMENTARE FUNKTIONALRELATION	DATEI-NR	ELEMENTARE FUNKTIONALRELATION
1	PERS# → NAME	3	ABT# → ANAME
1	PERS# → VORN	3	ABT# → GEB#
1	PERS# → PLZ	3	ABT# → ALEIT
1	PERS# → ORT	3	ABT# → MITAR
1	PERS# → STR	3	ABT# → ETAT
1	PERS# → H-NR	4	GEB# → GNAME
1	PERS# → GEB	4	GNAME → GEB#
1	PERS# → STAND	4	GEB# → BAUJ
1	PERS# → KIND	4	GEB# → RAUM
1	PERS# → BERUF	4	GEB# → LAGE
1	PERS# → ABT#	5	PERS# → NAME
1	PERS# → TEL#	5	PERS# → VORN
1	PERS# → STEU	5	PERS# → PLZ
1	PERS# → GEHAL	5	PERS# → ORT
2	TEL# → NAME	5	PERS# → STR
2	TEL# → VORN	5	PERS# → H-NR
2	TEL# → ANAME	5	PERS# → GEB
2	TEL# → GEB#	5	PERS# → BERUF
2	TEL# → ZI#	5	PERS# → ABT#
		5	PERS# → TEL#

Logische Beziehungen im Anwendungsbeispiel

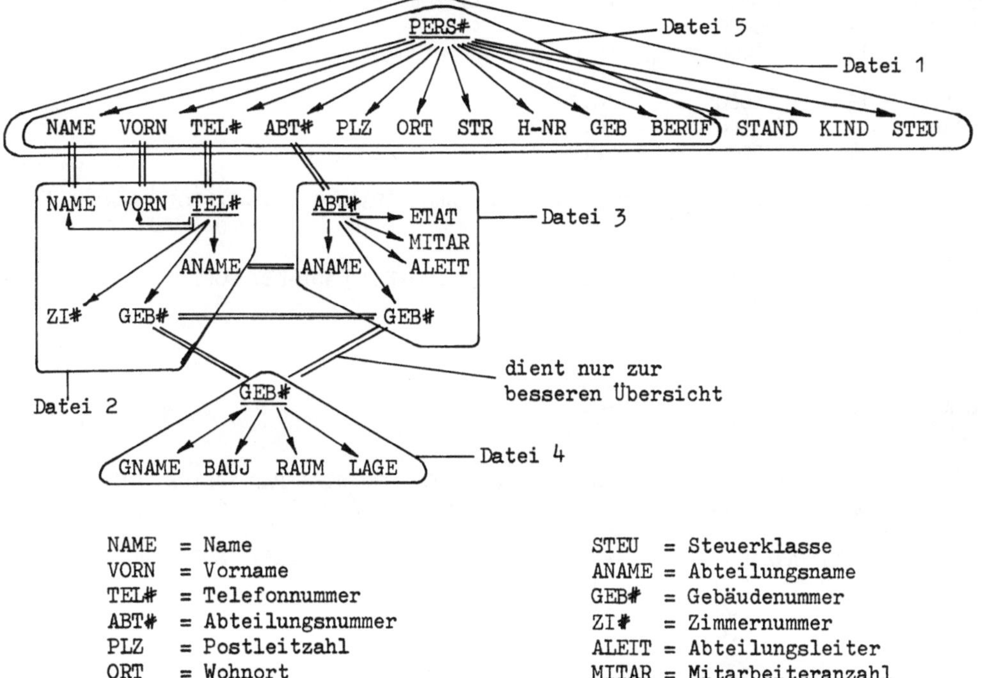

NAME	= Name		STEU	= Steuerklasse
VORN	= Vorname		ANAME	= Abteilungsname
TEL#	= Telefonnummer		GEB#	= Gebäudenummer
ABT#	= Abteilungsnummer		ZI#	= Zimmernummer
PLZ	= Postleitzahl		ALEIT	= Abteilungsleiter
ORT	= Wohnort		MITAR	= Mitarbeiteranzahl
STR	= Straße		ETAT	= Etat
H-NR	= Hausnummer		GNAME	= Gebäudename
GEB	= Geburtsdatum		BAUJ	= Baujahr
BERUF	= Berufsbezeichnung		RAUM	= Größe
STAND	= Familienstand		LAGE	= Lage
KIND	= Kinderzahl			

PHYSISCHE QUELLDATEIBESCHREIBUNGEN

DNR	DATEINAME	SATZANZAHL	SATZLAENGE	BLOCKUNG	ORGANIS	PAD-FAKTOR	GERAET
1	PERSONAL-1	200000	116	17	I	0	P

ATTRNAME	LAENGE	ANZAHL	WIE	SI KEY	FOR-KEY	CAND-KEY	SORT
PERS#	10	200000	1.0	1			1
NAME	15	2000	100.0				
VORN	15	500	400.0				
PLZ	4	50	4000.0				
ORT	15	50	4000.0				
STR	15	500	400.0				
H-NR	4	1000	200.0				
GEB	6	2000	100.0				
STAND	2	4	50000.0				
KIND	2	10	20000.0				
BERUF	15	100	2000.0				
ABT#	2	1000	200.0		1		
TEL#	4	10000	20.0	1	1		
STEU	2	5	40000.0				
GEHAL	5	500	400.0				

DNR	DATEINAME	SATZANZAHL	SATZLAENGE	BLOCKUNG	ORGANIS	PAD-FAKTOR	GERAET
2	TELEFON	10000	55	37	S	0	P

ATTRNAME	LAENGE	ANZAHL	WIE	SI KEY	FOR-KEY	CAND-KEY	SORT
TEL#	4	10000	1.0	1			
NAME	15	1000	10.0				1
VORN	15	250	40.0				2
ANAME	15	1000	10.0				
GEB#	2	500	20.0		1		
ZI#	4	5000	2.0				

DNR	DATEINAME	SATZANZAHL	SATZLAENGE	BLOCKUNG	ORGANIS	PAD-FAKTOR	GERAET
3	ABTEILUNG	1000	47	43	S	0	P

ATTRNAME	LAENGE	ANZAHL	WIE	SI KEY	FOR-KEY	CAND-KEY	SORT
ABT#	2	1000	1.0	1		1	
ANAME	15	1000	1.0				
ALEIT	15	500	2.0				
MITAR	5	50	20.0				
ETAT	8	25	40.0				
GEB#	2	500	2.0		1		

DNR	DATEINAME	SATZANZAHL	SATZLAENGE	BLOCKUNG	ORGANIS	PAD-FAKTOR	GERAET
4	GEBAEUDE	500	37	55	S	0	P

ATTRNAME	LAENGE	ANZAHL	WIE	SI KEY	FOR-KEY	CAND-KEY	SORT
GEB#	2	500	1.0	1			1
GNAME	15	500	1.0			1	
BAUJ	4	100	5.0				
RAUM	8	500	1.0				
LAGE	8	500	1.0				

DNR	DATEINAME	SATZANZAHL	SATZLAENGE	BLOCKUNG	ORGANIS	PAD-FAKTOR	GERAET
5	PERSONAL-2	200000	105	100	S	0	B

ATTRNAME	LAENGE	ANZAHL	WIE	SI KEY	FOR-KEY	CAND-KEY	SORT
PERS#	10	200000	1.0	1			
NAME	15	2000	100.0				
VORN	15	500	400.0				
PLZ	4	50	4000.0				
ORT	15	50	4000.0				
STR	15	500	400.0				
H-NR	4	1000	200.0				
GEB	6	2000	100.0				
BERUF	15	100	2000.0				
ABT#	2	100	2000.0		1	1	
TEL#	4	10000	20.0	1	1		

Für eine neue Anwendung wird eine Zieldatei (sequentiell auf Magnetplatte) mit den Attributen Personalnummer, Name, Abteilungsname und Gebäudename verlangt. Sortiert werden soll nach Abteilungsname, Name, Vorname.

Das Programm findet 4 mögliche Lösungswege zur Erstellung der Zieldatei. Jede Operationenfolge wird in 2 Tabellen dargestellt. In der Projektionstabelle stehen für jede Datei die zur weiteren Verarbeitung benötigten Attribute. Die Misch-Verbund-Tabelle enthält die Attribute und die zugehörigen Dateien, die am Mischen oder Verbund beteiligt sind.

Lösung Nr.	DNR	ATTRIBUTE	OPERATION	ATTRIBUT-NAME	DATEI-NR	
		Projektions-Tabelle		Misch-Verbund-Tabelle		
1	1	PERS# NAME VORN ABT#	M	PERS#	1	5
	3	ABT# ANAME GEB#	V	ABT#	1	3
	4	GEB# GNAME	V	GEB#	3	4
	5	PERS# NAME VORN ABT#				
2	1	PERS# NAME VORN ABT# TEL#	M	PERS#	1	5
	2	TEL# ANAME	V	ABT#	1	3
	3	ABT# GEB#	V	TEL#	1	2
	4	GEB# GNAME	V	GEB#	3	4
	5	PERS# NAME VORN ABT# TEL#				
3	1	PERS# NAME VORN ABT# TEL#	M	PERS#	1	5
	2	TEL# GEB	V	ABT#	1	3
	3	ABT# ANAME	V	TEL#	1	2
	4	GEB# GNAME	V	GEB#	2	4
	5	PERS# NAME VORN ABT# TEL#				
4	1	PERS# NAME VORN TEL#	M	PERS#	1	5
	2	TEL# ANAME GEB#	V	TEL#	1	2
	4	GEB# GNAME	V	GEB#	2	4
	5	PERS# NAME VORN TEL#				

Das Programm bestimmt nun die optimale Operationenfolge. Für jeden Lösungsweg sind alle zulässigen Permutationen für diese Operationenfolge mit der jeweiligen Gesamtausführungszeit aufgelistet. Die Angabe der optimalen Folge mit allen notwendigen Aktionen, sowie den Ausführungszeiten und Zwischendateibeschreibungen bilden den Schluß der Ergebnisse.

Der 1. Weg mit der Permutationsfolge 2   1 ist der zeitschnellste Weg. Die Permutationsfolge gibt die Reihenfolge der Operationen aus der Misch-Verbund-Tabelle an. Die Mischoperation ist nicht notwendig, da redundante Attribute aus den Dateien 1 und 5 verlangt werden. Für jede permutierte Folge wird die Datei ausgewählt, die eine kürzere Verarbeitungszeit ergibt (Fall (4), K.3.3). In diesem Fall wird die Datei 5 ausgewählt, da die Sortierung nach ABT# eine kürzere Verarbeitungszeit erwarten läßt. Es wird zuerst ein Verbund zwischen den Dateien mit den geringsten Datenmengen durchgeführt. Die Zwischendatei wird dann mit der Datei 5 (große Datenmenge) verbunden.

Die umgekehrte Permutationsfolge im 1. Weg ergibt eine um 95 % höhere Gesamtzeit. Bei beiden Verbundoperationen werden große Datenmengen verarbeitet.

Die längste Zeit aus allen Wegen ist sogar 275 % höher als die optimale Zeit.

Das Ergebnis liefert die optimale Folge von Operationen zur Erstellung der gewünschten Zieldatei, sowie den Erwartungswert für die Ausführungszeit.

Weg	Ausführungszeiten	
Nr.	Gesamtzeit (sec)	Permutationsfolge
1	1330.637 681.273	1 2 2 1
2	1942.570 1942.570 2555.916 1893.924 1409.746 1893.924	1 2 3 1 3 2 2 1 3 2 3 1 3 1 2 3 2 1
3	2050.149 1397.997 2414.368 2414.368 1397.997 1920.120	1 2 3 1 3 2 2 1 3 2 3 1 3 1 2 3 2 1
4	1867.352 1243.784	1 2 2 1

Optimale Operationenfolge für den 1. Weg

```
OPERATION   ATTRIBUT      DATEINRN
    V         GEB#          3  4
    V         ABT#          5  3
```

- DATEI 3 SORTIEREN NACH GEB#
- ZEIT (sec) FUER SORT = 0.920

```
DNR   DATEINAME   SATZANZAHL   SATZLAENGE   BLOCKUNG   ORGANIS   PAD-FAKTOR   GERAET
51    ZW03        1000         19           107        S         0            P

ATTRNAME LAENGE   ANZAHL            WIE    SI KEY FOR-KEY CAND-KEY SORT
  ABT#      2     1000             1.0         1
  ANAME    15     1000             1.0
  GEB#      2      500             2.0                        1               1
```

- DIE AM VERBUND BETEILIGTEN DATEIEN SIND SORTIERT NACH GEB#
VERBUND DER DATEIEN 51 04 UEBER DAS(DIE) ATTRIBUT(E) GEB#

- LESEZEITBERECHNUNG FUER DATEI 51 ZEIT (sec) = 0.216
- LESEZEITBERECHNUNG FUER DATEI   4 ZEIT (sec) = 0.216

```
DNR   DATEINAME   SATZANZAHL   SATZLAENGE   BLOCKUNG   ORGANIS   PAD-FAKTOR   GERAET
52    ZW51 04     1000         34           60         S         0            P

ATTRNAME LAENGE   ANZAHL            WIE    SI KEY FOR-KEY CAND-KEY SORT
  ABT#      2     1000             1.0         1
  ANAME    15     1000             1.0
  GEB#      2      500             2.0                        1               1
  GNAME    15      500             2.0
```

- SCHREIBZEITBERECHNUNG FUER DATEI 52 ZEIT (sec) = 0.349

- DATEI 52 SORTIEREN NACH ABT#
- ZEIT (sec) FUER SORT = 1.132

```
DNR   DATEINAME   SATZANZAHL   SATZLAENGE   BLOCKUNG   ORGANIS   PAD-FAKTOR   GERAET
53    ZW52        1000         34           60         S         0            P

ATTRNAME LAENGE   ANZAHL            WIE    SI KEY FOR-KEY CAND-KEY SORT
  ABT#      2     1000             1.0         1                      1
  ANAME    15     1000             1.0
  GEB#      2      500             2.0                 1
  GNAME    15      500             2.0
```

```
VERBUND DER DATEIEN  5  53  UEBER DAS(DIE) ATTRIBUT(E)  ABT#

- LESEZEITBERECHNUNG FUER DATEI  5  ZEIT (sec)  =  185.600
- LESEZEITBERECHNUNG FUER DATEI 53  ZEIT (sec)  =    0.349

   DNR   DATEINAME  SATZANZAHL  SATZLAENGE  BLOCKUNG  ORGANIS  PAD-FAKTOR  GERAET
   54    ZW05 53     200000        74         27        S         0          P

   ATTRNAME LAENGE   ANZAHL         WIE    SI KEY FOR-KEY CAND-KEY SORT
     PERS#    10     200000         1.0        1
     NAME     15       2000       100.0
     VORN     15        500       400.0
     ABT#      2        100      2000.0               1              1
     ANAME    15       1000       200.0
     GEB#      2        500       400.0               1
     GNAME    15        500       400.0

- SCHREIBZEITBERECHNUNG FUER DATEI  54  ZEIT (sec)  = 144.374

- DATEI  54  SORTIEREN NACH  ANAME  NAME  VORN
- ZEIT (sec) FUER SORT  =  492.840

   DNR   DATEINAME  SATZANZAHL  SATZLAENGE  BLOCKUNG  ORGANIS  PAD-FAKTOR  GERAET
    6    ZIELDATEI   200000        70         29        S         0          P

   ATTRNAME LAENGE   ANZAHL         WIE    SI KEY FOR-KEY CAND-KEY SORT
     PERS#    10     200000         1.0        1
     NAME     15       2000       100.0                                  2
     VORN     15        500       400.0                                  3
     ANAME    15       1000       200.0                                  1
     GNAME    15        500       400.0

Gesamtzeit (sec)  =  681.273
```

5. Zusammenfassung

Es wurde ein Verfahren beschrieben, durch das alle Lösungswege bei der Konversion
von redundanten Dateien gefunden und die optimale Reihenfolge der notwendigen Operationen bestimmt werden kann. Mit Hilfe dieser automatischen Optimierungsmöglichkeit
kann dann ein Datei-Übersetzer minimale Ausführungszeiten erzielen. Falls dabei die
erforderliche Beschreibung aller vorhandenen Quelldateien zentral durchgeführt und
gespeichert wird, braucht der Benutzer jeweils nur noch die gewünschte Zieldatei
auf der logischen und physischen Ebene zu spezifizieren.
Mit Hilfe eines Backtracking-Algorithmus werden in einem EFR-Graphen, der aus den
logischen Beschreibungen der Quelldateien erstellt wird, alle möglichen Lösungswege
für die Zieldatei gefunden. Unter Einbeziehung der physischen Dateibeschreibungen
lassen sich diese Lösungswege in Operationenfolgen zerlegen.
Um den minimalen Erwartungswert für die Ausführungszeit einer Datenübersetzung zu
finden, müssen alle zulässigen Permutationen dieser Operationenfolgen berechnet
werden. Übersteigt dieser Aufwand das zulässige Maß, so lassen sich durch heuristische
Auswahlverfahren gute Näherungslösungen finden, indem vor allem Restriktionen so früh
wie möglich durchgeführt und vorhandene Sortieranordnungen nach Möglichkeit ausge-
nutzt werden.
Durch die strikte Trennung von logischer Datenstrukturbeschreibung durch EFR's und
physischer Dateibeschreibung durch Zugriffspfade, Speicherungsstruktur und Parameter
der Speicherzuordnungsstruktur lassen sich bei diesem Verfahren in einfacher Weise
weitere physische Speicherungsstrukturen und Zugriffsmethoden einbeziehen.
Beispielsweise kann die Konversion hierarchischer Datensätze vorgesehen werden,
solange sich diese auf der logischen Beschreibungsebene durch EFR's darstellen
lassen.

Die Autoren danken Herrn D. Hesse für wertvolle Anregungen.

250

6. Literaturverzeichnis

(Co 70) Codd, E.F.: A relational model for large shared data banks, in:
CACM, Vol. 14, 1970, No 6, S. 377 - 387.

(Co 71) Codd, E.F.: Further normalization of the data basa relational model,
Courant Computer Science Symposium "Data Base Systems",
R. Rustin (Hrsg.) Prentice Hall, New York 1971, S. 33 - 64.

(De 73) Delobel, C., Casey, R.G.: Decomposition of a data base and the theory of
boolean switching functions, in: IBM Journal of Research and Development,
Vol. 17, 1973, No 5, S. 374 - 386.

(Dk 75) Deck, M.: Zeit- und Mengenberechnungen zur Erstellung einer Zieldatei aus
mehreren Quelldateien mit redundanten Daten, Diplom-Arbeit an der
TH Darmstadt, Fachbereich Informatik, Dez. 1975.

(Fr 72) Fry, J.P., Smith, D.P., Taylor, R.W.: An Approach to Stored Data
Definition and Translation, in:
ACM SIGFIDET Workshop on Data Description and Access, 1972.

(Hä 75) Härder, T.: Das Zugriffszeitverhalten von relationalen Datenbanksystemen,
Dissertation an der TH Darmstadt, Fachbereich Informatik, 13. Juni 1975.

(Re 75) Reus, J.: Ableitung einer Operationenfolge zur Erstellung einer Zieldatei
aus redundanten Quelldateien, Diplomarbeit an der TH Darmstadt,
Fachbereich Informatik, FG Datenverwaltungssysteme, Dez. 1975.

(Sc 75) Smith, J.M., Chang, P.Y.: Optimizing the Performance of a Relational
Algebra Database Interface, in:
Comm. of the ACM, Vol. 18, No. 10, Oct. 1975, S. 568 - 579.

(Sh 75) Shu, N.C., Housel, B.C., Lum, V.Y.: CONVERT: A high level translation
definition language for data conversion, in: IBM Research Report,
San Jose, RJ1500, January 17, 1975.

(Si 73) Sibley, E.H., Taylor, R.W.: A data definition and mapping language, in:
CACM, Vol. 16, No. 12, Dec. 1973, S. 750 - 759.

(SIEM) Siemens System 4004: Magnetbandgerät 4453, Bedienungsanleitung,
August 1971.

(Sm 72) Smith, D.P.: A Method for Data Translation Using the Stored Data
Definition and Translation Task Group Languages, in:
ACM SIGFIDET Workshop on Data Description and Access, 1972.

(Sm 75) Schmid, H.A., Swenson, J.R.: On the Semantics of the Relational Data
Model, in: Proc. of the ACM SIGMOD Conference, San Jose, May 1975,
S. 211 - 223.

(We 74) Wedekind, H.: Datenbanksysteme I, Reihe Informatik/16,
Bibliographisches Institut, Mannheim 1974.

INTERACTIVE STORING, RETRIEVAL, TRANSFORMATION, AND EVALUATION
OF SCIENTIFIC DATA
WITH AN EXPERIMENTAL SYSTEM

R. Hartwig

Heidelberg Scientific Center

IBM Germany, Tiergartenstrasse 15, D-6900 Heidelberg

Abstract: The user's view of an experimental system under development
and under investigation at the Heidelberg Scientific Center is
described. Its goal is to provide a user oriented problem solving
environment for manipulation and evaluation of "measurement data" in
the widest use of the word.   That means numerical data upon which
analysis and application of algorithms are to be performed acquired by
measurement devices, or from any other source.

The processing of such data is connected with the following items:
large quantities of data; complex algorithms for data evaluation; need
for interaction between human imagination and machine processing.

The main purpose of this research project is to get a better
understanding of the possiblities of interactive processing in this
field of application.

Key-words: APL - data analysis - data base - data description -
guidance system   - interactivity -   measurement data   - method
description - query - sampled function - units of measure -
user-friendlyness.

Acknowledgement

The work described here is due to various former and present members
of a project group: M.Bergen, A.Blaser, H.Eberle, R.Hartwig, P.Pistor,
U.Schauer, H.Schmutz.

1. Introduction

The system introduced here is under development and under investigation at the Heidelberg Scientific Center. This paper can be seen as an extract from a more extensive report (15) which describes the main aspects of the usage and the user's view of this system. The considerations are based on such questions as: Which groups of application specialists might be the potential user; what is their present situation; which main requirements can be recognized in this field; how can these requirements be met by such a system; which experience is expected from the user; what categories of data are covered; how can those data be stored, documented, managed, and evaluated in a user-friendly way; how can the user be guided by such a system; how can he get information from the system about data and methods; and finally how can such a system be evaluated from the aspect of its user-friendlyness.

One essential component is a guidance subsystem which serves for guidance with regard to data as well as to methods. This component is also available as a stand alone system (6,7).

The data types handled in connection with this system are measurement data. In this environment the item "measurement data" is to be seen in the fullest sense of the word. The data may be acquired by measurement devices or may come from any other source. The data need not be measurement data in the usual meaning; all data can be considered upon which analysis and application of algorithms are to be performed.

By this definition the meaning of the item measurement data becomes much wider. In addition to the usual meaning now much more must be seen in this connection, e.g. such data as quotation of shares, marketing data, election results, cost estimation data, planning data, production data, price lists, logistic data, etc.

2. The user

Corresponding to the defintion of the data to be manipulated and analyzed the potential users and first of all the fields of application may be outlined.

The various fields of application can easily be derived from the
meaning of the item measurement data as used here. Several fields can
use and benefit from this system; some of them are:
Engineering - Manufacturing - Geophysics - Mining - Medicine -
Commercial Science - Social Science - Logistics - Education.

The potential users of this system are specialists in their field of
application. They need not have experience in data processing and
moreover they are not expected to be ambitious to gain such
experience. So the main purpose of this experimental system must be to
develop a direct access to data processing without data processing
knowledge in the usual sense.
There is only little knowledge in APL (8) required to begin with. The
application of this system shows that the notation of APL as it is
required to begin with is very simple and quite similar to that
notation the application spcialist is familiar to.

Two statements may characterize this field of application: Normally
the way of solving a problem cannot be described in advance; the
application specialist "has to feel" his way to a solution. Many
problems within these application areas must be considered as "ad hoc
problems".

Independent of the application field the scientific environment of
every application specialist can be illustrated as shown in Fig. 1.

There are four seperate areas around him: measurement data,
algorithms, and descriptions (documentation) for both of them.

Up to now there is no system that can help to cover these
relationships.The application specialist himself has the full
responsibility. Everyone who is familiar with the fields of
application knows questions and problems that arise here: how to
document the measurement data, where to keep the documentation and how
to find it again; how to find an appropriate algorithm for evaluation,
how to use the algorithm, how to specify the data, where to find
criteria for selection of algorithms, and where to write down
information about experience in using certain methods in certain
cases. There are many more such questions and problems and all of them
characterize the poor situation of the specialist in this field at
present.

3. The gross-architecture

Starting from this experience an experimental interactive system is under development for storing, retrieval, transformation and evaluation of measurement data. In particular, this system should be seen as a combination of the following features in an integrated, user-friendly way:

Integration of large quantities of raw measurement data into an interactively manageable data base; support of special data type for this field of application such as vectors, sampled functions, units of measure; a high level data manipulation language as an extension to APL; integration of standard subroutines or special application programs written in PL/1 or FORTRAN to be invoked in a dialogue mode and to run with data in the APL workspace; a subsystem for guiding the user to data and programs; support of various display systems.

Corresponding to the several areas around the user shown in fig. 1, the functional components of this system can be understood as shown in fig. 2 and fig. 3.

The system has to provide communication to all four areas, the two documentation areas as well as the corresponding areas of the problem data on the one side and the methods on the other. In addition to that, the relationships between the several areas must be recognized and managed automatically. The user communicates with the system in a dialogue via terminal and display units. Thus the system supports the interactive problem solving process in several ways: in getting information about data and algorithms; in performing analysis and processing of data by application of algorithms; and in giving user guidance with respect to the information part as well as to the processing part.

As shown already three different groups of data are to be covered: Problem data - Algorithms - Inventory data.
Problem data are all types of raw data and/or extracted and/or evaluated data. They are stored as relations (tables) of n-tuples (rows). Each table as well as each column within that table is adressed by a name, usually one meaningful to the user.
Algorithms are all types of programs: standard program libraries and/or special application programs written in APL, PL/1, FORTRAN (11,12,13,14), or in other program languages. They may be seen from

the view of the user similarly in a tabular form.
Inventory data are all types of descriptive data about problem data as
well as algorithms. They may appear in tabular form, or in a network
form with the ability to guide the user to nodes which contain
information about problem data or algorithms.

All these data are contained in the "data part" of the system, in a
data base and in program libraries respectively.

The "processing part" of the system consists of three main subsystems:
The data management system - The information system - The manipulation
system.

For the management of the data base a low level query language uses
XRM (Extended Relational Memory) (10), written in PL/1 and contained
in the "PL/1 area".
The manipulation system as well as the information system are written
in APL (8) and contained in the "APL area". The manipulation system
communicates with the problem data and with the collection of
algorithms. It is embedded in APL as an interactive host language and
allows for very complex computations within a high level query.

4.   The operation

In general the dialogue with the system has the following goals: To
find out, which information can be obtained from data, and in which
way that can be done; then to describe the way of solving the problem
and finally to start the execution. In detail that includes such
activities as: To define data contained in the data base and to
prepare them for application; to find out appropriate algorithms; to
invoke algorithms to run with selected data; to display the raw or the
evaluated data, to name them, and to store them back into the data
base again.

The operation of this system may be seen in two phases:
The information phase - The manipulation phase.
During the information phase the user communicates with the
information system (see fig. 3) and he can get information from the
inventory part of the data base. This happens in dialogue form and the
user is guided step by step to the data group which may be of interest

for his present problems as well as to algorithms to be applied for
these problems.Finally the user knows which data might be of interest
and the selected relations may be displayed. Figure 4 shows an
example. In addition to names the user can get information about the
type of data and the unit of measure for each column in the relation.
The availability of algorithms may be displayed similarly in tables of
the general form shown in fig. 5.
During the manipulation phase the user specifies the data in a non-
procedural way. That happens by entering "fill-ins" into the table
skeleton; in this way the entered name is "bound" to the values in the
table. In addition to that constraints and other processing
statements are entered in APL-notation. The user has only to describe
how to bind the data, everything else is done by the system
automatically (2,9,10).

5.   Examples of application

Three representative examples will show the actual usage of the
system. The first one shows the evaluation of data from one relation
using only simple ad hoc written statements for selection and
processing. In the second one the data of only one relation are used
, however, in connection with a standard program. The third example
shows how data from different relations (tables) can be used at the
same time and how the units of measure are handled automatically by
the system.

Example 1: A user wishes to select and to process data from the
relation shown in fig. 4. After selection of the relation called
"AUTOMOBILE" he assignes arbitrary names to those columns he wants to
use (T, YOC,...) as shown in fig. 6.
Then he describes the constraints for this data selection in
APL-notation; all of the APL-predicates must evaluate to true for the
resultant data, therefore the sequence in which they are specified has
no meaning.

Example 2: Let us assume that a collection of sampled functions for a
large set of different materials exist in the data base. The usual
representation of that collection named "REFLECTANCE" is shown in
fig. 7.

Now a user wants to select those materials which have a mean reflectance over the range 250 to 300 nm which is greater than 60 (fig. 8).

In this case the user needs an appropriate integration algorithm. Within the information phase the user may have found out that the relation "REFLECTANCE" contains data he can use and after calling for this table (fig. 9) he gets information about the content of that relation (row 1) and about other details (row 2); in this case function limits and resolutions are shown. Now the user wants to select an algorithm for integration.

The information system guides the user to appropriate methods. The final step of such a guidance procedure may be seen as follows: the user has been guided to a node called "INTEGRAL" and after entering this name into a skeleton (fig. 5) the system offers him several programs; one of which is the "SIMPSONRULE" as shown in fig. 10. This point may be seen as the end of the information phase.

The next step may be seen as the beginning of the manipulation phase: by entering the name "SIMPSONRULE" the corresponding skeleton appears as shown in fig. 11. In this stage the skeleton is still empty, i.e. only the header for the table is shown. It has already been mentioned that the skeletons of functions (methods) have the same structure as the skeletons of data tables (fig. 4,9). From the first row the user recognizes which input data are required for this function and which output data will be received; from the second row he sees the units of measure of each column. Now the user defines and enters arbitrary names into the columns (I,CURVE,LB,UB). By entering the corresponding name (CURVE) into the skeleton "REFLECTANCE" (fig.9) the system is informed that the data from that table should be subjected to integration; and by entering "MAT60" (fig.9) the user defines the name for the selected material he is looking for. Finally the predicates (corresponding to fig. 8) have to be entered (fig.11) and in addition to a statement for listing the names and the calculated values of all material that meets the given conditions.

Example 3: This can be seen as an extension of example 2. The user is looking for only those materials which meet the additional conditions: The product of specific weight, specific heat and heat conductivity (values given in certain units) must be greater than 0.5 (fig. 12).

A table "THERMAL PROPERTIES" may contain the values as shown in fig. 13. Names are entered into the skeleton and by using these names the conditions are formulated. So the physical units are written in connection with the names. By this the system recognizes in which units the value is to be calculated and if necessary a conversion of units will be done automatically before calculations.

6. Conclusion

One of the objectives of this research project is to develop a user-friendly system. Everyone has an idea about the meaning of this expression and especially every user will learn after a time what user-friendlyness of such a system may mean for him.

Passing the examples in review it could be worthwile for the evaluation of such a system to study a) what steps have to be done at all by the user for solving his problem and b) which of these steps could furthermore be done automatically by the system. From such abstraction it can be seen in a very distinct form

- that all input has to be written in a notation the user is
  very familiar with, and
- that the input contains only such information which is due
  to personal decisions of the user. Not one of the several
  steps could be left to be done automatically by the system.

Finally one can recognize that in general the whole problem solving process shown in the examples means "REDUCING USER's WORK to only those actions which contribute to the DEFINITION OF A PROBLEM".

LITERATURE

1. P.Pistor, U.Schauer: Summary of a Feasibility Study on
    Measurement Data Base. IBM Germany, Heidelberg Scientific
    Center, Technical Note TN74.05.

2. M.Bergen, R.Erbe, P.Pistor, U.Schauer, G.Walch: An Environment
    for the Interactive Evaluation of Scientific Data and its
    Application in Computer Aided Design. Proc. ACM workshop on data
    bases for interactive design (1975), 26-35.

3. U.Schauer: Ein System zur interaktiven Bearbeitung umfangreicher
    Messdaten. In Lecture Notes in Computer Science No. 39, Springer
    Verlag, 1976, 213-231.

4. H.Schmutz: Overall Design of the Measurement Data Base System.
    IBM Germany, Heidelberg Scientific Center Technical Note
    TN75.04.

5. E.Kantorowitz: A Computer Aided Design Front End for the
    Measurement Data Base. IBM Germany, Heidelberg Scientific
    Center, Technical Note TN 75.07.

6. R.Erbe, G.Walch: An Interactive Guidance System for Method
    Libraries. IBM Germany, Heidelberg Scientific Center, Technical
    Report TR75.04.001.

7. R.Erbe, G.Walch: Ein Dialogsystem zur Methodensuche. GI-5.
    Jahrestagung, Lecture Notes in Computer Science, Springer Verlag,
    1975, 133-147.

8. R.P.Polivka, S.Pakin: APL:The Language and its Usage. Prentice
    Hall, Inc. 1975.

9. U.Schauer: Interactive High Level Data Manipulation. IBM Germany,
    Heidelberg Scientific Center, (Internal).

10. Lorie,R.A.: XRM-An Extended (n-ary) Relational Memory. IBM
    Cambridge Scientific Center, Report G320-2096, 1974.

11. Scientific Subroutine Package (SSP,FORTRAN) Progr. No.
    360A-CM-03X, IBM Form No. 20-0205.

12. Scientific Subroutine Package (SSP, PL/1) Progr. No. 360A-CM-07X,
    IBM Form No. 20-0586.

13. Subroutine Library - Mathematics (SL-Math, FORTRAN) Progr. No.
    5736-XM7, IBM Form No. SH12-5300.

14. Procedure Library - Mathematics (PL-MATH, PL/1) Progr. No.
    5734-XM3 IBM Form No. SH20-0985.

15. R.Hartwig: Interactive Maniplation and Analysis of Scientific
    Data (MESDB). IBM Germany, Heidelberg Scientific Center,
    Technical Report TR76.07.003.

Figure 1 - "The problem": There are four distinct areas at the disposal of the application specialist and there are many relationships between the corresponding subject areas, but up to now there is no system that can help to cover these relationships.

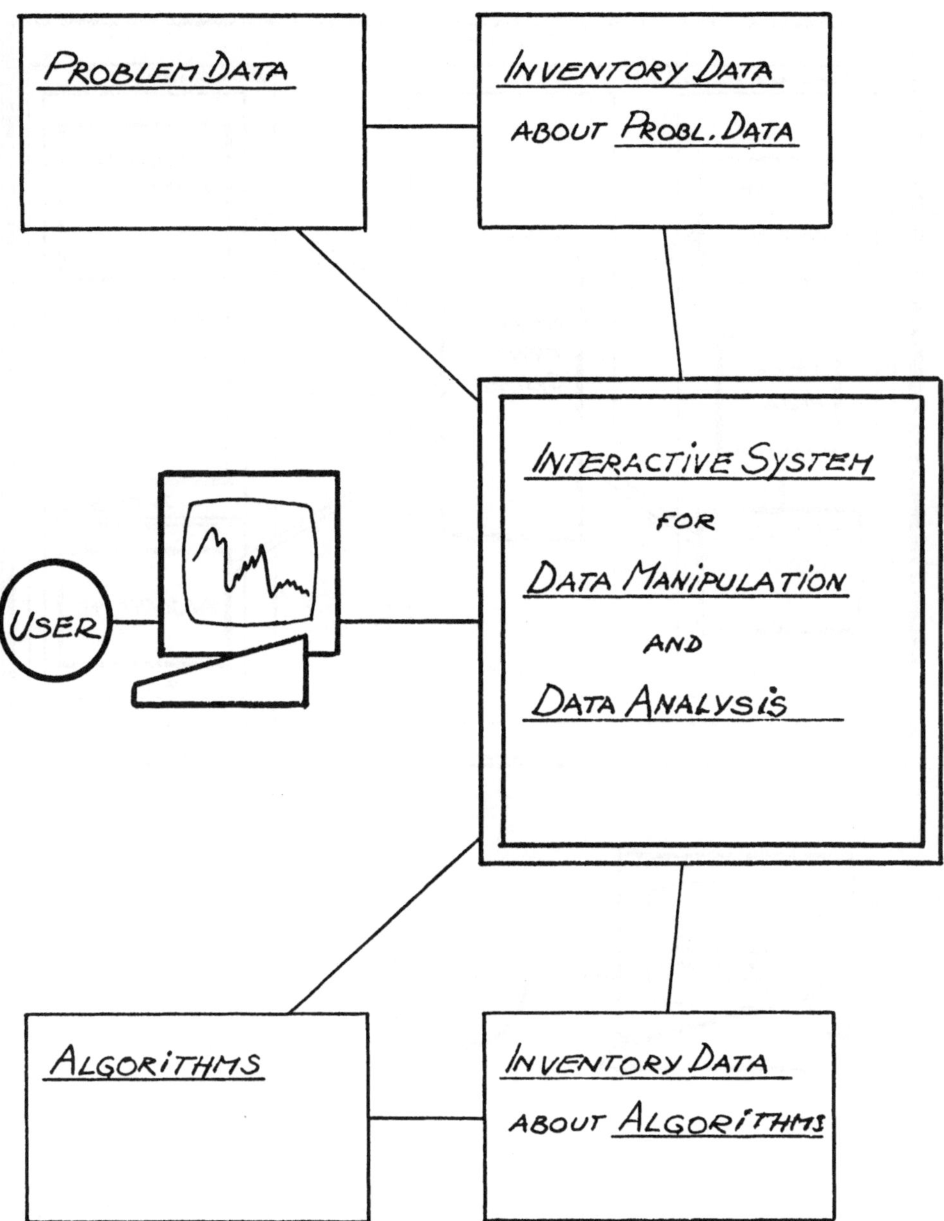

Figure 2 - "The proposed solution": An interactive system provides communication to all four working areas. All relationships between the different working areas are recognized and managed automatically. The user communicates in a dialogue mode via terminals and display units.

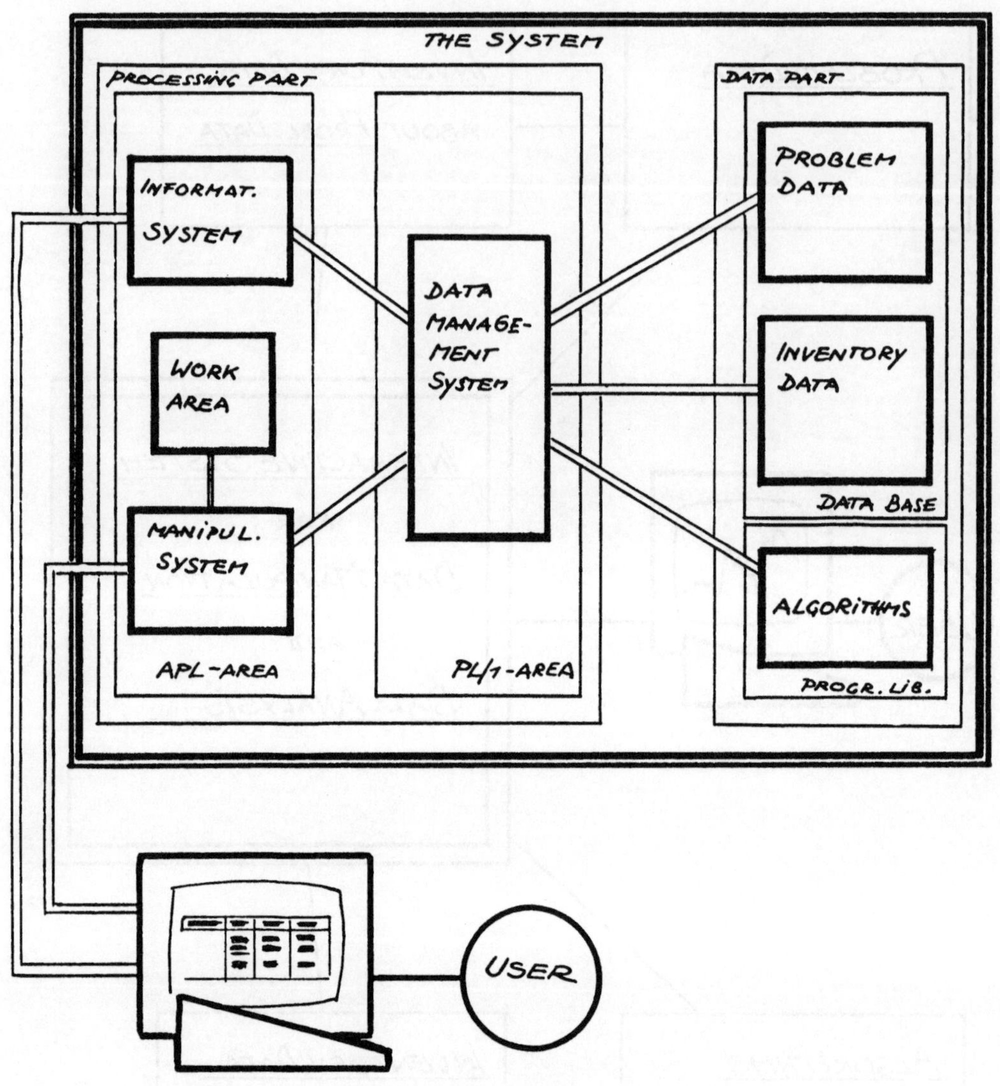

Figure 3 - The functional characteristics of the system. The system supports the interactive problem solving process in several ways: In giving information about data and algorithms, in performing processing and analysis of data by the application of algorithms, and in giving user guidance.

AUTOMOBILE	MANUF.	TYPE	YEAR	CUBIC	POWER	WEIGHT
	—	—	—	cm*3	PS	KP

Figure 4 - The typical form the relations of data are displayed. The user can get out of it information about names and in addition to that - by special request - information about the type of data and/or the units of measure for each column within the relation.

METHODS	METHOD - IDENTIFIC.	PROGRAM - IDENT.

Figure 5 - The available algorithms are displayed very much like the relations of data. The column "Method-Identification" informs about the purpose of a method, e.g. Integration. The column "Program-Identification" informs about names of corresponding programs available.

AUTOMOBILE	MANUF.	TYPE	YEAR	CUBIC	POWER	WEIGHT
	FAB	T	YOC	CC	N	W

$(yoc \geq 1950) \wedge (yoc \leq 1974)$

$N > 60$

$UP = W \div N$

$UP < 15$

$\square \longleftarrow FAB, T, UP$

Figure 6 - After selection of the relation "AUTOMOBILE" the user assignes arbitrary names to those columns he wants to use. Then he describes the constraints in APL notation and enters the request for output (bottom line).

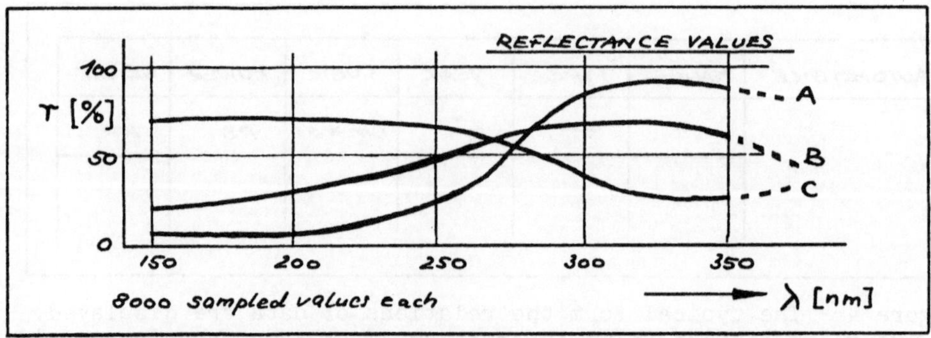

Figure 7 - The usual representation of a collection of functions showing reflectance values of (only three) different materials A,B, and C. The data are available from 15o nm through 35o nm. The materials may be represented as sampled function by 8ooo sampled values each. The name of the collection is "REFLECTANCE".

$$60 < \frac{1}{\lambda_U - \lambda_L} \int_{\lambda_L}^{\lambda_U} r(\lambda)\, d\lambda \qquad \lambda_U = 300 \text{ nm} \qquad \lambda_L = 250 \text{ nm}$$

Figure 8 - The usual form to describe the condition for selection of certain materials.

REFLECTANCE	MATERIALNAME	REFL. - VALUES		
		150NM	8000	350NM
	MAT 60	CURVE		

Figure 9 - By calling for the table "REFLECTANCE" the user gets informed about the content of that relation (row 1) and in addition to that - by special request - about details (row 2) (compare fig.7). Row 3 is still empty, the two names are entered at a later time during the manipulation phase.

METHODS	METHOD - ID.	PROGRAM - ID.
	INTEGRAL	———— ———— ———— SIMPSONRULE ———— ———— ————

Figure 1o - For selecting an appropriate algorithm for integration the user has to enter "INTEGRAL". After that the system offers him several programs available for this purpose; one of which is the "SIMPSONRULE".

SIMPSONRULE	VALUE OF INT.	INTEGRAND	LOW. B.	UP. B.
	D1 x D2	D1	D2	D2
	I	CURVE	LB	UB

60 < MEAN

UB = 300 'NM'

LB = 250 'NM'

MEAN = I ÷ (UB - LB)

☐ ⟵ MAT 60 , MEAN

Figure 11 - After calling for the table "SIMPSONRULE" the user gets informed about the data required for the operation and which output data will be obtained (row 1). By special request the dimensions are shown (row 2). Arbitrary names (row 3), the predicates, and request for output (bottom line) have to be entered.

$$0.5 < \gamma \cdot C \cdot \lambda \left[\frac{kP}{cm^3} \cdot \frac{Cal}{Grad \cdot g} \cdot \frac{Cal}{cm \cdot Grad \cdot sec} \right]$$

Figure 12 - The usual form to describe the condition for selecting certain material.

THERMAL PROP.	MAT. NAME	SPEC. D.	SPEC. H.	HEAT COND
	MAT 60	GAMMA	C	LAMBDA

0.5 < GAMMA 'CM*3 KP*-1' × C 'GRAD G CAL*-1'....

.... × LAMBDA 'CM GRAD SEC CAL *-1'

□ ← MAT 60

Figure 13 - After calling for the relation "THERMAL PROPERTIES" the user gets informed about its content (row 1), after that arbitrary names (row 2), the predicates (corresponding to fig.12), and request for output (bottom line) have to be entered.

A GENERAL APPLICATION GUIDANCE SYSTEM

FOR

THE PROBLEM SOLVER

R. Erbe

G. Walch

IBM Germany
Heidelberg Scientific Center
Tiergartenstr.15
D6900 Heidelberg

1.   INTRODUCTION

When working with to-day's software systems, most users, in particular the casual or unexperienced users, run into problems because
even if the systems are well documented, there is insufficient guidance from a semantic point of view. To enable the problem solver who
is not necessarily a DP-professional, to make extensive use of DP-fa-
cilities he has to be supported in several ways:

1. The user of program libraries has to be assisted in identifying the
   suitable program for a given problem.
2. The user of data bases should be assisted in identifying data with
   a specific semantic meaning.
3. After the identification of the appropriate problem solving method
   or program and the data to be processed, the execution of the program has to be invoked without burdening the user with DP specific
   problems.
4. The user of any system should be guided through the jumble of usage
   rules, e.g. the data base user has to be told intelligibly how to
   set up a query.

In most practical situations these four types of tasks with which
the problem solver is confronted, cannot be handled separately, rather
they must be seen as a unit. To illustrate this statement consider the
situation of a medical researcher who wants to compare some current

biochemical measurements with the respective results of another time period: He has to identify the statistical method delivering the significance of a possible difference between the two measurements, then he has to retrieve the data after having been instructed how to set up the respective data base query, and finally the retrieved data must be processed by the method identified.

To support these manifold user needs, a General Application Guidance System -GAGS- is developed. In its function as a methods dictionary it guides the user from a defined problem to the respective solution method /1,2/. Methods are understood as implemented programs and abstract methods. This idea allows a guidance to a solution even if respective programs do not exist or if the problem is not tailored for a computerized solution.

Just as the system is used as a guide for program retrieval and use, it may also serve as a guide for data retrieval and use, delivering information about the data available in a system, e.g. their meaning, origin, use, format, and relationships, i. e. GAGS may function as a data dictionary.

Beyond the capabilities for information retrieval about programs and data, the system is extended to give interactive support for program execution by prompting the user for the specification of the arguments, and - optionally - by displaying explanations of the meanings of arguments and results. The specification may be done by value, by variable name, or by file name. In the latter case, the file description can be found in the data dictionary and used by system functions to access the data.

Finally, it should be pointed out, that the network concept described in chapter 2 allows to make the GAG-System selfexplanatory: it may contain as one of its applications the structured description of the GAGS usage, or of the usage of any other information retrieval and processing system, to which GAGS may be attached as a kind of man-machine interface.

2. METHODS DICTIONARY

An intermediate version of the methods dictionary component of the GAG-System was already presented on the fifth annual congress GI75 of the Gesellschaft fuer Informatik /2/. Therefore only the basic concepts of the methods dictionary complemented by a new search feature, is summarized in this chapter:

The information about application areas and abstract methods including their prerequisites is separated from the conventional program documentation. It is broken down into small interconnected elements. The resulting structures may be understood as information networks /3,4/ with nodes representing information elements and connecting arcs leading from elements of general information to elements of more detailed information. Each node may have an arbitrary number of incoming and outgoing arcs.

The system offers elements of information in a systematic way such that the user is guided from more general to more specific information. In the most general case this implies a guidance from some application area via specific problems and subproblems to the adequate method and program.

The starting point for a method search depends on the user's knowledge. The user can begin at a node of general information or at a node of relatively specific information.   In principle, every node is a possible entry node. If the user does not know what the content of the system is, he is offered a list of all application areas or problem fields for which documentations exist. But if he has general knowledge and only wants some specific information he can directly identify the respective node.

Based on the information contained in this start-node the user has to decide to which of the successor nodes he wants to proceed. Then the selected successor becomes the current node. From the set of its successors a new current node has to be chosen. This procedure is repeated until an end-node containing the documentation of a method or program is reached.

Complementary to this stepwise guidance, which the user can follow even if he does not know the terms in which to describe his problem, there exists a direct search which allows to enter several keywords, that describe the respective problem. The system then automatically extracts the paths through the network, connecting the corresponding nodes. If there is more than one method found, decision criteria are displayed, and the user can make his selection. This direct search is suitable for the application specialist, who can describe his problem correctly, but does not know the method and program for its solution.

Before the search for methods can be invoked, the respective information network has to be constructed and fed into the system. The structuring of an application area into an information network is a very important task because the efficiency of the method search highly depends on the quality of the network. It has to be performed by the application expert because only he has the knowledge necessary to break down a general application area into information elements (network nodes), to establish links (network arcs) between these elements and to point out relationships between some of the elements established and the methods identified. Input of the network structure and of the network information is also done interactively with the GAG-System.

3. DATA DICTIONARY

3.1. Definition, Justification

Retrieval and housekeeping of data is as tedious as finding the proper evaluation program. Therefore, it seems worthwhile to extend the system by a data dictionary component.

A data dictionary is the collection of all information known about data. It may contain:

1. Information independent from the physical storage, e.g. meaning and source, relationships to other data, relationships to functions. This type of information is intended for the enduser who has to evaluate the data. Therefore it consists mainly of unformatted explanatory text.
2. Information related to data storage, e.g. storage device, file structure, coding. Since this type of information is needed by system functions, e.g. to select the proper functions for data access, conversion, or translation, it consists of formatted data

or at least of semi-formal information to be transformed into strongly formatted data.

Current data base systems lack such information, in particular the representation independent part. Therefore, the addition of such a data dictionary might provide a bridge between the enduser and the DB system. Thus, the data dictionary helps to identify the data semantically before the actual values are retrieved with a query language.

3.2. Network Approach

The data dictionary component is built and accessed for retrieval by the same functions which are used for the methods dictionary.

Descriptions of data elements (files, records, relations, columns, tuples, segments) can be considered as information elements (nodes) in an information network. Common attributes of different elements are described once and linked to the elements by an arc in the network.

In the network approach, data elements can be connected concurrently according to different schemata: a source node may refer to all data of the respective source, a node describing an evaluation method refers to all data suitable for that evaluation or to all data generated by its application.

For a general example, consider figure 1 where the highest classification is according to different application fields. At the next level, one grouping corresponds to different data sources, e.g. the result of 2 different measurement devices, another to different evaluation methods. Then data of source S2 is further subdivided in two groups. From every data type description there is an arc to the corresponding data directory of the original data and one arc to the description of evaluated data. The method M1 is connected to data types T2 and T2.1 for original and evaluated data, respectively. Of course this network design is arbitrary. It is left to the application specialist to design that view of data he wants to see.

The significance of this approach lies in the fact that the structure is not merely a logical view of data, - described formally for system and system administrator use -, rather the structure is realized by nodes of textual information and arcs leading from the de-

scription of more general facts to the description of details. This
description can be accessed and understood by all users.

3.3. Consistency Problems

To achieve consistency between data descriptions in the dictionary,
as far as formal parameters are concerned, and the actual parameters
for data storage, the following rules are established:

1. The data dictionary functions for creation and modification of information are used to enter descriptions of new data, i.e. as a
   high level data definition tool.
2. The formal data description parameters are automatically extracted
   from the data description containing unformatted explanatory text
   as well as strongly formatted information.
3. System functions to write and read data make use of these formal
   parameters.
4. System functions can create new data only if corresponding data
   descriptions are available. (They can create new files, but only
   of a file type already described). Then, the functions also must
   establish the links from the description to the data, or make en-
   tries in directories, which already exist.
5. Modifications of data descriptions which change formal parameters
   are only allowed if no existing data are referred to by that description. Otherwise a new data description is generated or the
   modification is rejected.

4.   EXECUTION OF METHODS

The methods dictionary described in section 2 assists the user in
identifying the appropriate method to solve a given application problem. Once a method is found, it is desirable to be able to apply this
method without being forced to change the environment of the methods
dictionary, i.e. to switch to another system. Sometimes it is even
necessary to apply a method during a method search session to get decision support for the choice of another method suitable for the data
(e.g. the result of a statistical method which tests data on normal
distribution must be known before the t-test for the comparison of
meanvalues can be chosen).

Thus, it is obvious that the method search by means of a method dictionary has to be extended by a feature for the immediate execution of identified methods or programs.

To make immediate execution possible also for the problem solver without DP-knowledge, execution is designed as a system triggered facility: The user is prompted for entering the necessary input values, and the program is executed automatically by the system.

4.1. Program Documentation and Program-Code

The basic information for the system invoked program execution is the program documentation contained in the methods dictionary. The program documentation is set up by the program developer or another authorized person who is prompted by the GAG-System with characteristic keywords such as PROGRAM-NAME, USE, ARGUMENT, REMARKS, LANGUAGE, TYPE. The prompting facility is introduced to guarantee a standardized documentation which in turn is a prerequisite for a sytem triggered program execution.

The program documentation contains two types of information:
1. Unformatted data for verbal explanations of the program or parts of it such as PURPOSE of the program or EPXLANTION of the meanings of parameters
2. Formatted information which is mandatory for program execution such as USE, UPPER INDICES, TYPE, CONSTRAINTS.

A serious problem is the consistency between program-documentation and program-code. In the present version of the GAG-System the program-documentation is entered manually without automatic extraction of information from the program code. It is felt, however, that the interdependence between documentation and code should be more integrated in the GAG-System such that the formal parts of the documentation are directly derived from the code itself and only the semantic explanation has to be added manually. In addition, it should be made sure that relevant changes in program code invoke automatic update of the documentation. As a prerequisite the program code must be accessible by the GAG-System.

4.2.   Dialogue

The program independent execution facility of the GAG-System imbeds every application program in a dialogue environment without modification of the program itself. Program specific characteristics are considered only at execution time when the documentation is used for prompting and checking the user's input.

When, after a successful method search, the interactive execution facility is invoked, the user is prompted for the input values. Program parameters can be entered either by value, by variable name, or by file name.

Once the data are entered, they are checked against the information from the program documentation. If there are contradictions of data types, data dimensions or additional constraints of variables or between variables, the entered data are rejected and the input of new data is prompted. If the data are accepted, the program is executed and the results are displayed and stored.

By entering a '?' the user is offered a display of semantic information about selected input or/and output variables.   An example for dialogue supported execution is given in figure 2.

5.   SYSTEM GUIDANCE

5.1.   General Remarks

The information about the use of a special data retrieval and processing system can also be structured as an information network and fed into this guidance system. Then the network can be used instead of a printed user's manual with several advantages:

1. The newcomer can be offered a systematic walk through the complete
    set of instructions and rules. The information is stored in one
    place and not scattered over several binders.
2. The user who wants one specific information can be served quickly,
    either by following a special path through the network, or by addressing directly the point in question.
3. If the guidance system is connected to the system described by it,

it may be used as a HELP-feature for the latter one.
4. The structure and the content of the guidance system can easily be
   updated in case of changes in the system described by it. There
   is no need to print new user manuals.

This application guidance may best be illustrated by an example,
given in the next section, which is a spooled terminal protocol. The
concept, the rules for use, and the system features are explained for
the GAG-System by GAGS itself.

The descriptions of the features are connected to each other in the
same network structure as the features are linked when GAGS is used.

The use of this GAGS-description is invoked automatically when the
first question at the start: 'DO YOU KNOW HOW TO USE THIS SYSTEM?' is
answered with 'NO'. It can also be accessed by selecting the item
GAGS-DESCRIPTION as start node. Thereafter, the further use is de-
cribed extensively by GAGS itself.

5.2.   Example

Note: For the convenience of the reader, the user input in
the following protocol is marked by a preceding '+'.

+START
 DO YOU KNOW HOW TO USE THIS SYSTEM?
+NO
 THE CURRENT NODE IS: 742 GAGS-DESCRIPTION

 " GAGS-DESCRIPTION "
    HERE THE CONCEPT, THE USAGE RULES, THE SYSTEM FEATURES,
 AND THE FILES FOR 'GAGS' ARE DESCRIBED.
    TO GET MORE INFORMATION, SELECT ONE OF THE ITEMS OF THE
 FOLLOWING LIST BY ENTERING SIMPLY 1, 2, 3, OR 4.

```
SELECT FROM THE SUCCESSORS (?=HELP/' '=ESCAPE/S=STATUS):
   1  743 CONCEPTS
   2  744 USAGE-RULES
   3  745 FEATURES
   4  746 GAGS-FILES
   5  756 END-GUIDANCE
+1
THE CURRENT NODE IS:  743 CONCEPTS
```

" CONCEPTS "

   THE MOST IMPORTANT FACT IN 'GAGS' IS THAT THE INFORMA-
TION IS DIVIDED IN SMALL PARTS. THESE PARTS ARE CONNECTED TO
EACH OTHER, ACCORDING TO THEIR SEMANTICS, IN A NETWORK LIKE
STRUCTURE. THEREFORE THE INFORMATION PARTS ARE CALLED
NODES, THE LINKS ARE CALLED ARCS.
   .....
   TO PROCEED, SELECT ONE OF THE ITEMS OF THE FOLLOWING
LIST BY ENTERING 1, 2, OR 3.

```
SELECT FROM THE SUCCESSORS (?=HELP/' '=ESCAPE/S=STATUS):
   1  744 USAGE-RULES
   2  745 FEATURES
   3  746 GAGS-FILES
   4  756 END-GUIDANCE
+1
THE CURRENT NODE IS:  744 USAGE-RULES
```

" USAGE-RULES "

   HERE, THE IMPORTANT RULES FOR THE BEGINNER ARE GIVEN.
FURTHER DETAILS ARE FOUND IN THE NODES 'DIALOGUE-MODES' AND
'HELP-FUNCTION'.
   .....

```
SELECT FROM THE SUCCESSORS (?=HELP/' '=ESCAPE/S=STATUS):
   1  747 DIALOGUE-MODES
   2  748 HELP-FUNCTION
   3  745 FEATURES
   4  746 GAGS-FILES
   5  756 END-GUIDANCE
+1
THE CURRENT NODE IS:  747 DIALOGUE-MODES
```

" DIALOGUE-MODES "

    THERE ARE TWO DIALOGUE MODES CONCURRENTLY AVAILABLE:
PROMPT-MODE AND COMMAND-MODE.

    THE HINTS, GIVEN IN 'USAGE-RULES' RELATE TO THE PROMPT-
MODE WHERE, IN ADDITION, TWO DIFFERENT LENGTHS OF GAGS-
MESSAGES ARE OFFERED. MOREOVER, DIFFERENT NATURAL LANGUAGES
ARE AVAILABLE, AT PRESENT ENGLISH AND GERMAN.

    IN THE COMMAND-MODE, CONCEIVED FOR THE MORE TRAINED USER
OF GAGS, SYSTEM MESSAGES ARE REPLACED BY USER INPUT OF GAGS-
COMMANDS.

    FURTHER DETAILS ARE FOUND IN THE NODES 'PROMPT-MODE',
'COMMAND-MODE', AND IST SUCCESSORS.

    .....
Note: At this point, the protocol is cut off.

6.   EXPERIMENTAL SYSTEM

Based on the ideas outlined in the chapters 2 to 5, a dialogue system has been implemented using APL/CMS /5/. The choice of APL/CMS as
implementation language offers great advantages for the implementor
due to its nature as a dialogue system and its support for implement-
ing, debugging, and modifying functions, adding new functions, and
thereby extending the system. It does not influence the user's view of
the system, in effect, he is not aware of APL.

The dialogue system is selfexplanatory. Optionally, a description
of system usage is given at start time (see also chapter 5). Further
information may be requested via a help function entering '?' whenever
user input is expected. The help option offers explanations for system
or application oriented keywords if the user is not sure how to proceed. If the user enters a keyword that does not match a keyword
for which an explanation is stored, a search for similar keywords is
performed /6/. In case that no similar keyword is found the keyword
entered is stored to permit the data base administrator to add the
respective explanation.

There exist two complementary versions for the man machine dialogue: the prompting mode and the command mode /7/. In the prompting
mode there is never a need for the user to remember the options which
are available. In each state, all possibilities are made visible in a

multiple choice menu or by a yes/no question.

In the command mode the display of menus and questions is suppressed. The user selects options and answers to anticipated questions by entering commands. In general, a command is the main keyword taken from the dialogue item which it replaces. Only when the user requests prompting by '?' or when he enters an invalid command, the question or menu is displayed. Several commands may be entered in one line. At any time the user can switch between prompting and command mode. Thus, when the casual user develops towards the trained user he can make more efficient use of GAGS.

For the reason of information security, different user classes are introduced. Users with write permission are registered in a directory. Usage of the network construction part is only possible after successful pass-control.

The system is a multi-user system which allows for concurrent retrieval, insertion and update by several users. To provide multi-user access to a consistent version of the latest information, all application dependent information which is subject to updates, e.g. the list of node names, the textual node information, and the binary relation representing the network structure, is stored in files outside the APL workspace.

7.   SUMMARY

The GAG-System described here helps the user in the problem solving environment in four ways: confronted with a specific problem constellation the enduser who is not a DP-professional is supported to find the appropriate solution method(s), to identify the data to be processed by the identified method(s), to execute the methods and finally he is assisted in the use of information processing systems.

The fundamental information structure for the dialogue oriented guidance of the GAG-System is the information network. Both functions, the use of the information networks for the interactive guidance of the enduser as well as the construction of the networks by the respective application experts are integrated in the GAG-System.

The GAG-System is not tailored to a special application. In principle, every application area for which information-networks can be set up, can be fed into the system.

The GAG-System can be employed by users with different levels of experience in GAGS as well as in the application area. GAGS offers menu type dialogue for the beginners and provides command type dialogue for the advanced user. Application oriented information can be requested in two different modes. The beginner is guided through the information network whereas the advanced user can invoke a more direct search by entering problem describing keywords.

8.   REFERENCES

1. R.Erbe, G.Walch: An Interactive Guidance System for Method Libraries, IBM Scient. Cent. TR 75.04.001, Heidelberg, 1975
2. R.Erbe, G.Walch: Ein Dialogsystem zur Methodensuche, Lecture Notes in Computer Science, GI-5. Jahrestagung, Springer Verlag Berlin, Heidelberg, New York, 1975
3. K.Brunnstein, J.W.Schmidt: Structuring and Retrieving Information in Computer Based Learning, Int.J.Computer & Information Sciences, 2 (1973) 89
4. J.D.Wexler: Information Networks in Generative Computer Aided Instruction, IEEE MMS 11 (1970) 181
5. APL/CMS User's Manual, Programming RPQ MF2608, IBM File No.S370.22, Order No. SC20.1846 (1974)
6. R.Erbe, H.J.Schek: Search with Fuzzy Keywords Applied in a Methods Data Base, IBM Scient. Cent. TR 75.05.003, Heidelberg, 1975
7. G.Walch: Dialogue Programming with Easy Transition from Prompting-to Command-Mode, IBM Scient. Cent. TR, Heidelberg, to be published

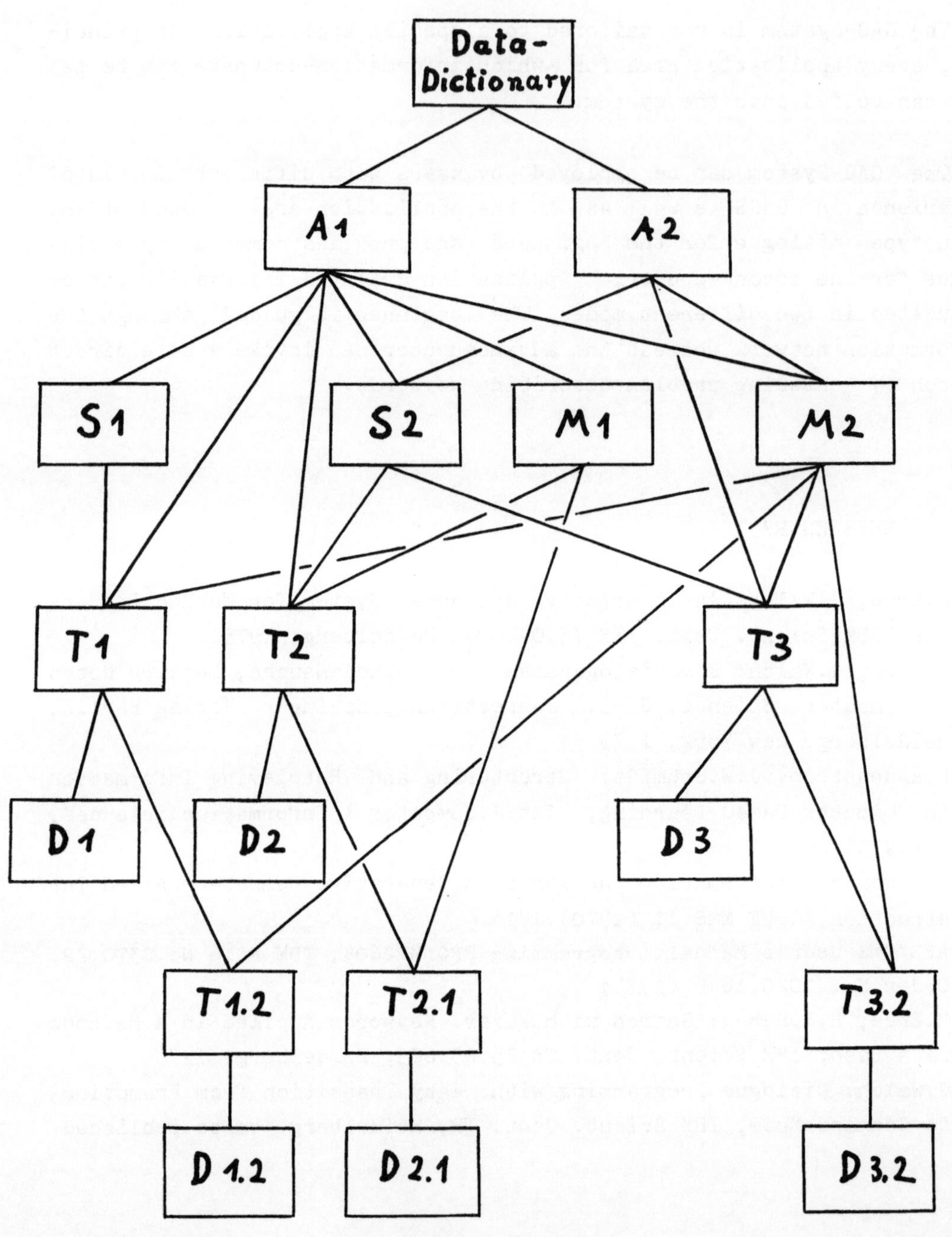

Fig. 1: General Example of a Data Dictionary Network

```
EXEC LIN.REGRESSION

PARAMETER-INPUT :
X ← ?
   EXPLANATION: VALUES OF THE INDEPENDENT VARIABLE
                STORED AS A VECTOR
X ← ι10
Y ← ?
   EXPLANATION: VALUES OF THE DEPENDENT VARIABLE
                STORED AS A VECTOR
Y ← 3 2 4 5 4 7 3 4 9
(ρX)=(ρY)  : CONSTRAINT NOT FULFILLED !

PARAMETER-INPUT :
X ←
Y ← Y,11.2

RESULT :
R ←          0.726          1.227          3.177          8.000          0.050
?
   EXPLANATION: R[1]  REGRESSION-COEFFICIENT OF THE LINE
                      Y = R[1]×X + R[2]
                R[2]  COEFFICIENT OF THE LINE
                      Y = R[1]×X + R[2]
                R[3]  T-VALUE FOR SIGNIFICANCE-TEST (T-TEST)
                      RELATED TO R[1]
                R[4]  NUMBER OF DEGREES OF FREEDOM (T-TEST)
                R[5]  ERROR-PROBABILITY
EXEC

PARAMETER-INPUT :
X ← ι10
Y ← YVALUE
YVALUE : VARIABLE/FILE NOT DEFINED !
Y ← YVALUES

RESULT :
R ←          0.779          11.267          4.815          8.000          0.010

YVALUES
10.1 12.2 15.5 14.3 15.9 18.1 16.7 15.9 18.9 17.9

EXEC

PARAMETER-INPUT :
X ← ι12
Y ← YVALUES,20.1 22.2

RESULT :
R ←          0.848          10.970          7.382          10.000          0.001

END END
```

Fig. 2: Three Examples of the Execution of Linear Regression
        (User Input Underlined)

Die Überprüfung von semantischen Integritätsbedingungen in Relationalen Datenbanksystemen

Hartmut Wedekind, Technische Hochschule Darmstadt

Zusammenfassung:

In einem Datenbanksystem werden semantische Integritätsbedingungen
in einem Subsystem zentral angeordnet und überprüft. Die Prüfungen
der Bedingungen können als Regelprüfungen oder als Sonderprüfungen
durchgeführt werden. Regelprüfungen sind nach Datenänderungen vorzunehmen, während zeitaufwendige Sonderprüfungen besondere Anlässe
voraussetzen. Die Bedingungen werden aus Gründen der Vereinheit-
lichung in der nicht-prozeduralen Sprache SEQUEL formuliert. Be-
rechnungsmethoden für den Zeitbedarf der Prüfungen werden angegeben.

Abstract:

In a database system semantical integrity constraints are assorted
in a subsystem and are enforced by the system itself and not by
application programmers. The verification of integrity constraints
can be accomplished by regular controls in case of data maintenance
or by time consuming special controls for a particular purpose. The
constraints are described in the non-procedural language SEQUEL
in order to look at the user's representation of queries and integrity constraints in a unified way. Outlines are given for
computation of time requirements to check the constraints.

1. Einleitung

Ein Datenbanksystem unterscheidet sich von konventionellen Datenverarbei-
tungssystemen nicht nur durch die zentralisierte Anordnung der Dateien mit
den Möglichkeiten einer zentralen Dateipflege und einer beliebigen Verknüpfung in der Dateiauswertung, sondern auch durch die zentrale Überprüfung von
semantischen Integritätsbedingungen, die vom Datenbanksystem und nicht wie
bisher vom Anwendungsprogrammierer vorgenommen wird. Semantische Integritätsbedingungen sind Vorschriften, um die Vollständigkeit und Korrektheit der
Daten aus der Sicht der Anwendung zu garantieren. Durch die zentrale Überprüfung der Integritätsbedingungen in Datenbanksystemen soll das dezentrale Auffinden einfacher Fehler bei der Datenerfassung nicht eingeschränkt
werden. Kostenkriterien zwingen zu einer Beachtung des Grundsatzes, daß
Fehler möglichst schon an der Datenquelle entdeckt werden sollten.

Semantische Integritätsbedingungen sind Qualitätsbedingungen der Daten und sind
abzugrenzen von den Integritätsbedingungen der Zugriffspfade (eingehaltene
Sortierfolge, korrekte Invertierung etc.) und von den Mechanismen zur Erhaltung
der Datenintegrität bei gleichzeitigen Schreibzugriffen mehrerer Transaktionen
(Zugriffsintegrität und Ablaufintegrität). Die Begriffsbildung stammt von
Eswaran und Chamberlin (9).

Semantische Integritätsbedingungen – und nur diese werden hier behandelt –
können, wenn sie auf den Zustand der Datenbank abheben, nach den Datenobjek-
ten, auf die sie sich beziehen, klassifiziert werden. Wir unterscheiden Bedingungen, die sich auf Felder (Attribute), Sätze (Tupeln), Dateien (Relationen) oder gar mehrere Dateien beziehen. Die einfachen feldorientierten Integritätsbedingungen, die sich in der Regel auf Datentypen, Wertebereiche
und Prüfgleichungen mit Prüfziffern beziehen, werden heute in der Datendeklaration mit Hilfe einer Datenbeschreibungssprache (DDL) formuliert. Abzugrenzen
von den Zustandsbedingungen sind die Übergangsbedingungen. Bei einer Wertän-
derung kann z.B. als Übergangsbedingung gefordert werden, daß ein Wert nur
ansteigen kann.

Von Datenbanksystemen wird eine erhöhte Datenintegrität verlangt, da wegen der
Zentralisation ein Datenfehler schwerwiegendere Folgen hat. Es ist Voraussetzung für Datenbanksysteme, daß auch die schwierig zu implementierenden und
auf mehrere Dateien sich beziehenden Bedingungen überwacht werden müssen. So
muß z.B. für Teile-Nummern einer Auftragsdatei gewährleistet sein, daß sie
eine Untermenge der Teile-Nummern einer Teilestammdatei bilden.

Der Entwurf eines Datenbanksystems ist ein Vorgang, der in mehreren voneinander unabhängigen Ebenen erfolgen soll. Ein vollständiger Entwurfsprozeß auf
vier Ebenen wird von Senko et al. beschrieben(12). Die vier logischen Ebenen sind:

1. Logische Datenstruktur (entity set level),
2. Logische Zugriffspfade (string level),
3. Speicherungsstruktur (encoding level),
4. Abspeicherung auf den Geräten (physical device level).

Semantische Integritätsbedingungen dienen zur Kontrolle auf der Ebene der logischen Datenstrukturen. In (17) wird der Entwurf eines Datenbanksystems ausführlich geschildert. Dabei wird nur auf die Formulierung, nicht aber auf die Einbeziehung semantischer Integritätsbedingungen in den Entwurfsprozeß eingegangen.
Der Gegenstand dieser Arbeit ist es zu zeigen, wie die Integritätsprüfung in
ein relationales Datenbanksystem eingeordnet werden kann.

In konventionellen Systemen werden semantische Integritätsbedingungen entweder
auf prozedurale Art und Weise durch Anwendungsprogramme oder durch das Aus-
werten von Protokollen dezentral überwacht. In relationalen Datenbanksystemen

wird ein zentral angelegtes Subsystem für das Einbringen und für die Kontrolle
der Integritätsbedingungen angestrebt. Die Bedingungen werden in einer nicht-
prozeduralen Sprache, etwa in der Sprache SEQUEL (6), formuliert. Sie gelten
global für die ganze Datenbank. Spezielle Bedingungen, die sich der Benutzer
aus seiner besonderen Anwendungssicht auferlegen will, sind lokal im Anwendungsprogramm zu berücksichtigen. Die Forderung einer Abteilung, daß ein
Lagerbestand niemals unter einen eisernen Bestand sinken darf, könnte z.B.
eine solche lokale Bedingung sein, wenn man sich nicht entschließen kann, sie
global gelten zu lassen.

2. Zustandsänderungen und Zustandsprüfungen in Datenbanksystemen

2.1 Der Begriff "Transaktion"

Die Integrität eines Datenbanksystems ist immer dann in Gefahr, wenn eine Datenänderung vorgenommen werden muß. Ein Lesen der Daten kann die Integrität nicht
beeinträchtigen. Eine Datenänderung ist ein Vorgang, der einen Satz einfügt,
löscht oder in einem Satz einen Wert durch einen anderen ersetzt. Wir definieren
eine verändernde Transaktion oder einfach eine Transaktion als eine Zustandsänderung der Daten, die von einem korrekten Zustand der Daten ausgeht, um die Daten
wieder in einen korrekten Zustand zu überführen (8). Einfügen, Löschen und
Ersetzen sind nur dann zulässige Transaktionen, wenn sie die Datenbank in einem
korrekten Zustand hinterlassen. Es wird im folgenden angenommen, daß die Datenbank sich auf Massenspeichern mit halbdirektem Zugriff befindet.

2.2 Regelprüfungen und Sonderprüfungen

Wir wollen die Prüfungen von Integritätsbedingungen in zwei Klassen zerlegen.
Immer dann, wenn der Prüfungsanlaß eine Zustandsänderung ist, sprechen wir
von einer Regelprüfung.Ist die Prüfung hingegen nicht unmittelbar durch eine Zustandsänderung verursacht, so liegt der Fall einer Sonderprüfung vor, Sonderprüfungen können z.B. durch Beschwerden der Benutzer, durch besonders vorgese-
hene Testläufe oder durch Revisionsabteilungen erforderlich werden. Das Erstellen einer Hintergrundsdatei zur Wiederherstellung zerstörter Dateien ist ebenfalls eine günstige Gelegenheit für eine Sonderprüfung. Bei Sonderprüfungen
stehen auch vorzugsweise Bedingungen zur Debatte, die wegen ihres hohen Prüfauf-
wandes im Normalbetrieb nicht überwacht werden können. Der Prüfaufwand ist dann
von vornherein als hoch anzusehen, wenn durch den Bedingungstyp es unumgänglich
ist, ganze Dateien in den Prüfvorgang einzubeziehen. Die folgenden Bedingungen
erfordern z.B. den Massenspeicherzugriff zu ganzen Dateien: 1. Die Bedingung der
Eindeutigkeit des Schlüssels. 2. Die Bedingung der funktionalen Abhängigkeit von
Attributen und 3. die Bedingung der Vollständigkeit einer Datei.Wir werden im
nachfolgenden Abschnitt eine weitere Klassifizierung der Integritätsbedingungen vornehmen. Es wird angenommen, daß die Regelprüfung einer Transaktion in vier Schritten abläuft:

1. Bereitstellen der neuen Daten
   in einem speziellen, benannten Bereich

2. Einbringen der Transaktion, z.B.
   in der Sprache SEQUEL

} Benutzer-
   verantwortung

---

3. Überprüfung der Integritätsbedingung. (Maßnahmen bei Nichterfüllung)

4. Ausführung der Transaktion und Bei-
   schreibung von Systemdaten

} Systemverant-
   wortung

Eine Sonderprüfung besteht im wesentlichen nur aus dem dritten Schritt. Die
ersten beiden Schritte stehen unter der Verantwortung des Benutzers. Aus
Gründen der einfacheren Darstellung wurde nach dem zweiten Schritt die Übersetzung der Transaktion, die dem Datenverwaltungssystem obliegt, nicht erwähnt. Die neuen Daten, die zu einer Zustandsänderung führen, können entweder in der Datenerfassung gewonnen werden (lokale Daten), oder sie werden
durch eine Retrievaloperation aus der Datenbank extrahiert (globale Daten).

Die Überprüfung sowie die Ausführung und das Beischreiben von Systemdaten
wird in Datenbanken vom System vorgenommen. Systemdaten sind Kataloge für
die Hauptdaten und Kataloge für die Zugriffspfade (17). Zu den Systemdaten
gehören aber auch Kontrollfelder, die der Benutzer nicht sieht, z.B. das
Feld für die Satzzählung, das bei Vollständigkeitsprüfungen von Dateien
herangezogen wird.

Es muß noch erwähnt werden, daß parallel zur Integritätskontrolle im dritten
Schritt auch die Überprüfung der Zugriffsberechtigung des Benutzers durchgeführt wird. Durch die Überwachung der Zugriffsberechtigung wird sichergestellt, daß nur befugte Benutzer Daten in der Datenbank sehen und verändern
dürfen (17), (16).

Zustandsänderung und Zustandsprüfung sollen an einem Beispiel dargestellt
werden. Gegeben sei die folgende Datenbank:

TEIL (TNR, BEZ)

KUNDE (KNR, NAME)

AUFTRAG (TNR, KNR, DATUM, MENGE)

Die Datei(Relation) TEIL enthält als Stammdaten die Teile-Nummer (TNR) und die
Bezeichnung (BEZ). Die Kundenstammdatei KUNDE setzt sich zusammen aus der
Kunden-Nummer (KNR) und dem Kunden-Namen (NAME). Eine Auftragsdatei besteht
neben der Teile-Nummer und der Kunden-Nummer noch aus dem DATUM und der Be-
stellmenge (MENGE). Die Schlüsselattribute sind unterstrichen.

Um den Aufbau einer verändernden Transaktion, das Bereitstellen von neuen
Daten, die von der Transaktion verarbeitet werden sollen, und die Formulie-
rung von Integritätsbedingungen erläutern zu können,nehmen wir an, daß eine
Schar von neuen Aufträgen in die Auftragsdatei eingefügt werden soll. Bis
auf die eigentlichen Integritätsbedingungen, die in der Sprache SEQUEL
schon in (5) formuliert werden, sind alle anderen Sprachelemente für den
Änderungsdienst und das Initialisieren einer Integritätprüfung als eine
Erweiterung dieser Sprache aufzufassen.

Die einzufügenden Sätze werden in einen Bereich, der Puffer genannt werden
soll, eingelesen. Der Bereich ist über den zentral vorgegebenen Namen P ansprechbar und kann wie eine gewöhnliche Relation in der Datenbank behandelt
werden.

```
1:   READ P (TNR, KNR, DATUM,  MENGE)
             1    K5    1.10.73  1000
    z.B.:    6    K10   1.10.73  5000
            20    K10   1.10.73  6000
             .    .     .        .
             .    .     .        .
             .    .     .        .
```

Wenn globale, allen berechtigten Benutzern zur Verfügung stehende Daten in der
Datenbank zur Veränderung bereitgestellt werden sollen, so geschieht die Extrak-
tion aus der Datenbank in SEQUEL durch einen (SELECT..FROM..WHERE..)- Block.
Die vorliegenden Daten werden danach im Bereich P verändert, geprüft und in die
Datenbank zurückgeschrieben.

```
2: BEGIN TRANSACTION.

     INSERT P.TNR, P.KNR, P.DATUM, P.MENGE
     IN AUFTRAG
   END TRANSACTION
   CHECK MODE IS BATCH
```

Vom Anwender, der eine Zustandsänderung in der Datenbank vornimmt, muß der Anfang
und das Ende einer Transaktion angegeben werden. Die Transaktion wird hier als
Tätigkeitsbeschreibung aufgefaßt. Das genaue Festlegen des Anfangs und des Endes
einer Tätigkeit ist auch vor allem für das Sperren und Entsperren beim gleichzeitigen Zugriff mehrerer Transaktionen von großer Wichtigkeit. BEGIN... und END...
sind Klauseln zur Steuerung der Ablaufintegrität des Systems, die den Benutzer
ansonsten nicht tangiert.

Als Erweiterung der zunächst nur als Anfragesprache konzipierten Sprache SEQUEL
(6) sollen hierzu Schreibweisen für Zustandsänderungen ergänzt werden, deren Bedeutung selbsterklärend ist:

INSERT Satz   UPDATE Attributnamen   DELETE Satz
IN Dateiname   IN Dateiname   IN Dateiname
WHERE Bedingung   WHERE Bedingung   WHERE Bedingung

Es ist sinnvoll, ein UPDATE und ein DELETE immer über den Primärschlüsselzugriff vor sich gehen zu lassen. Denn alles, was existiert und vernichtet bzw. verändert werden soll, muß zunächst identifiziert werden. In der "Bedingung" muß somit der Primärschlüssel angesprochen werden, oder es findet durch ein Retrieval zunächst eine Bereitstellung der Primärschlüssel statt.

Mit Hilfe der Klausel CHECK MODE kann der Benutzer durch die Parameter SINGLE oder BATCH bestimmen, ob die Prüfung einzeln erfolgen soll, und zwar sofort, wenn ein Satz bereitgestellt wurde, oder ob ein ganzer Stapel von Sätzen geprüft werden kann. Der Modus SINGLE ist im Realzeitbetrieb mit scharfen Zeitrestriktionen vorzusehen. Im Falle einer Auslassung wird als default-Wert "Batch" angenommen.

Als semantische Integritätsbedingungen soll in unserem Beispiel folgendes gefordert werden, was von der Datenbankverwaltung zu berücksichtigen ist:

X1: In der Datei AUFTRAG dürfen nur KNR enthalten sein, die auch in der Datei KUNDE stehen.

Y1: In einem Auftrag mit TNR = '20' darf für ein Teil die MENGE = '5000' nicht überschritten werden.

Beide Bedingungen sollen für Einfüg- und Änderungsvorgänge geprüft werden. Es ist ein Vorteil der deskriptiven Sprachen, daß die Anfragen des Anwenders, die Sicherheitsbedingungen, die Datendeklarationen und die Integritätsbedingungen in einer Sprache formuliert werden können (4). Für die obigen Bedingungen wird von der Datenbankverwaltung geschrieben:

```
3:   INTEGRITY CONSTRAINT X1:
     IN CASE OF  INSERTION IN AUFTRAG;
     IN CASE OF  UPDATE AUFTRAG.KNR;

         (SELECT KNR FROM P) ⊆ (SELECT KNR FROM KUNDE);;

     INTEGRITY CONSTRAINT Y1:
     IN CASE OF  INSERTION IN AUFTRAG;
     IN CASE OF  UPDATE AUFTRAG.TNR, AUFTRAG.MENGE;

         (SELECT MENGE FROM P WHERE TNR='20') < '5000';;

     INTEGRITY CONSTRAINT Z1:
     IN CASE OF  INSERTION IN AUFTRAG;
             NAUFTRAG = NAUFTRAG + N(P);;
```

<u>INTEGRITY CONSTRAINT</u> Z2:

<u>IN CASE</u> OF <u>DELETION</u> <u>IN</u> AUFTRAG;

              NAUFTRAG = NAUFTRAG - N(P);;

Eine Integritätsbedingung, deren Prüfung durch eine Zustandsänderung initiiert
wird, besteht aus einem deklarativen Teil und einem Handlungsteil. Im deklarativen Teil wird mit Hilfe der Klausel IN CASE OF das auslösende Ereignis beschrieben. Im Handlungsteil steht die Prüfanweisung in der Sprache SEQUEL. Sie
verknüpft im allgemeinen Falle der   Regelprüfung die neuen Daten im Bereitstellungsbereich mit Relationen in der Datenbank.

Die Integritätsbedingung X1 muß selbstverständlich auch für den Fall aufgestellt werden, daß in der Datei KUNDE Löschungen oder Änderungen der Kunden-
nummer vorgenommen werden. Die Bedingung Y1 ist insofern besonders einfach, als
sie ohne Massenspeicherzugriffe zur Datenbank lokal im Bereitstellungsbereich
verifiziert werden kann. Die Bedingungen Z1 und Z2 sind Zusatzbedingungen für
die Datei AUFTRAG. Um Vollständigkeitsprüfungen durchführen zu können, wird
im Falle des Einfügens und Löschens der Satzzähler NAUFTRAG beigeschrieben.
N(P) soll ein vom System bereitgestellter Satzzähler sein. Das Verändern der
anderen Katalogdaten insbesondere der Zugriffspfade für den Primär- und die
Sekundärschlüssel geschieht mit Sprachelementen, die besonders für diese Ebene
zu entwicklen sind (12). Diese Änderungen liegen in relationalen Systemen
außerhalb des Gesichtskreises der Anwendung.

Da es sich bei Integritätsbedingungen um mathematische Bedingungen handelt,
wird die Schreibweise in einer Zeile und nicht die Schreibweise in Blöcken wie
bei den Transaktionen vorgezogen. Allgemeiner kann für eine Integritätsbedingung in einfacher Form geschrieben werden:

(SELECT .. FROM .. WHERE) Θ_i (<u>SELECT</u> .. <u>FROM</u> .. WHERE ..)

mit Θ entweder als elementarer Vergleichsoperator

$$\Theta_1 \; \varepsilon \; \{ \; =, \; \neq, \; <, \; \leq, \; >, \; \geq \}$$

oder mit Θ als Mengenvergleichsoperator

$$\Theta_2 \; \varepsilon \; \{ \; =, \; \neq, \subset, \subseteq, \supset, \supseteq \}.$$

Vorausgesetzt wird, daß die auf der linken und rechten Seite ausgewählten Attribute Θ-vergleichbar sind. Zwei Attribute A und B sind Θ-vergleichbar, wenn AΘB
entweder wahr oder falsch, aber nicht undefiniert ist (7, S. 73). Es wird für
Integritätsbedingungen allgemein vereinbart, daß sie für einige und nicht alle
Tupeln gelten. Die Bedingungen werden quantorenfrei formuliert. Je nachdem, ob
für die Integritätsbedingung in ihrem Handlungsteil auf wahr oder falsch er-

kannt wird, erfolgt eine Annahme oder Ablehnung der Transaktion. Die Frage,
welche Maßnahmen nach einer Ablehnung zu treffen sind, soll hier nicht diskutiert werden. Es wird zwischen einem linken und einem rechten SELECT-Block,
die allgemein Prädikatausdrücke sind, unterschieden. Ein SELECT-Block kann
wie bei der Bedingung Y1 durch eine Konstante oder wie bei Z1 und Z2 durch
einen Ausdruck ersetzt werden. In Sonderfällen besteht eine Seite auch nur aus
einem oder mehreren Attributen.

Die Elementarfunktionen der Sprache SEQUEL wie MIN, MAX, COUNT, AVG, SUM etc.
sind im Hinblick auf die ausgewählten Attributnamen zugelassen. Für die Überprüfung von Bedingungen mit den Funktionen MAX, MIN, AVG, SUM etc., d.h. Bedingungen, die einen Vergleich mit einem Parameter eines Wertekollektivs impli-
zieren, wird im Katalog ein Kontrollfeld angelegt. Auf diese Weise braucht nicht
ein ganzer Datenbestand in die Prüfung einbezogen zu werden. Die Prüfung kann
dann im günstigsten Fall auch ohne Massenspeicherzugriffe durchgeführt werden.
Eine häufig auftretende Bedingung mit der Funktion SUM wird im kaufmännischen
Sprachgebrauch "Abstimmkreis" genannt.

   (SELECT SUM (A) FROM R1) = (SELECT SUM (B) FROM R2)

stellt einen solchen Abstimmkreis dar. Als Beispiel sei erwähnt, daß die Summe
der Tagesforderungen gleich der fakturierten Rechnungssumme sein muß.
Wir wollen im folgenden annehmen, daß die Integritätsbedingungen in einfacher
Form gegeben sind, d.h., es liegen Ausdrücke ohne tiefere Klammerstrukturen vor.

   (SELECT Y FROM A WHERE X = (SELECT X FROM B WHERE Z = '10'))

ist ein Beispiel für einen komplexen Ausdruck, der die linke oder rechte Seite
einer Integritätsbedingung ausmachen kann. Zur Verifizierung eines komplexen
Ausdruckes ist die Operation 'join' erforderlich. Da durch komplexe Ausdrücke
sehr lokale Integritätsforderungen aufgestellt werden, ist es sehr schwer, einen
sinnvollen praktischen Anwendungsfall anzugeben. In einem Datenverwaltungssystem
dürfen jedoch tiefere Klammerstrukturen nicht ausgeschlossen werden. Zum bequemen Einbringen von Übergangsbedingungen schlagen Eswaran und Chamberlin (9)
die Einführung der Sprachelemente OLD und NEW vor. Eine Übergangsbedingung für
nicht fallende Werte kann wie folgt formuliert werden:

OLD (SELECT .. FROM .. WHERE ..) $\leq$ NEW (SELECT .. FROM .. WHERE ..)

Der Name einer Integritätsbedingung ist vor allen Dingen für Katalogisierungs-
zwecke vorgesehen. Ob die Prüfung einer Integritätsbedingung erfolgt oder
nicht, sollte bei Regelprüfungen nicht vom Benutzer bestimmt werden können. Maß-
gebend sind allein die Zustandsänderungen, die eine Regelprüfung automatisch
auslösen. Bei Sonderprüfungen hingegen kann der Benutzer die Prüfungen autonom
durch das Kommando:

ENFORCE Name der Integritätsbedingung

bewirken. Die Integritätsbedingungen, die auf diese Weise angesprochen werden, beziehen sich nicht auf den Bereitstellungsbereich, sondern in allen Teilen global auf die Datenbank. Würde die Bedingung X1 als Sonderprüfbedingung formuliert und aufgerufen werden, so müßte geschrieben werden:

INTEGRITY CONSTRAINT X1:
(SELECT KNR FROM AUFTRAG) ⊆ (SELECT KNR FROM KUNDE)

Das Kommando

ENFORCE X1

zieht dann im Hinblick auf die KNR die Prüfung der gesamten Auftragsdatei gegenüber der gesamten Kundendatei nach sich.

Was die Prüfung von Feldern betrifft, so sind in (17, Band II) spezielle Klauseln vorgeschlagen worden. Es handelt sich um die folgenden reservierten Wörter, deren Bedeutung in Klammern hinzugefügt wird: UNIQUE (Eindeutigkeit eines Schlüssels), CHECK (Prüfziffernkontrolle), BOUND (Wertebereich), TYP (Datentyp), VALUE (diskrete Werte).

Wenn ein klar abgrenzbares Subsystem für die Überprüfung von Integritätsbedingungen angestrebt wird, dann sollten diese Attributmerkmale aus der Datendeklaration herausgelöst und in das Bedingungssystem unter Hinzufügen eines Namens eingebracht werden.

3. Klassifikation der Prüfungen von Integritätsbedingungen

Wir wollen in diesem Abschnitt die Klassifizierung der Überprüfungsvorgänge vervollständigen. Es war im vorhergehenden Abschnitt zwischen Sonder- und Regelprüfungen unterschieden worden. Dabei waren bei Sonderprüfungen eine Vielzahl von Massenspeicherzugriffen erforderlich. Regelprüfungen sind bei Zustandsänderungen durchzuführen. Beide Prüfungen unterscheiden sich auch deutlich durch die Art der Auslösung der Prüfung.

Beim Aufbau einer Datenbank sollten die wesentlichen Integritätsbedingungen aufgelistet werden, und zwar nicht nur für die Zwecke der Überprüfung, sondern auch aus Gründen der Dokumentation. Das Subsystem der Integritätsbedingungen soll in aktive und nicht aktive Bedingungen zerlegbar sein. Für eine nicht aktive Bedingung findet keine Prüfung statt. Die Bedingung wird ignoriert. Ein eventueller Fehler kann zumindest momentan passieren, da angenommen wird, daß er nur unbedeutende Auswirkungen hat. So darf z.B. die Angabe des Wohnortes falsch sein, wenn die Postleitzahl korrekt ist.

Die aktiven Bedingungen, die hier zur Debatte stehen, werden weiter unterteilt, je nachdem, ob ihre Verifizierung in einer Sonderprüfung oder in einer Regelprüfung erfolgt. Auf einer weiteren Stufe soll bei Regelprüfungen unterschieden werden, ob Massenspeicherzugriffe verlangt werden oder nicht. Bei Regelprüfungen ohne Massenspeicherzugriffe beschränkt sich die Prüfung auf den Bereitstellungsbereich. Sie ist rein lokal ohne Bezug zur Datenbank. Die Prüfung ist so einfach, daß zumindest bei lokalen Daten Teile von ihr an die Datenerfassung delegiert werden können. Konventionelle Systeme, die im wesentlichen nur Feld- und Satzprüfungen kennen, beschränken sich auf Regelprüfungen ohne Massenspeicherzugriff. Die Prüfung der Bedingung Y1 im Beispiel des vorhergehenden Abschnitts ist eine Prüfung dieses Typs.

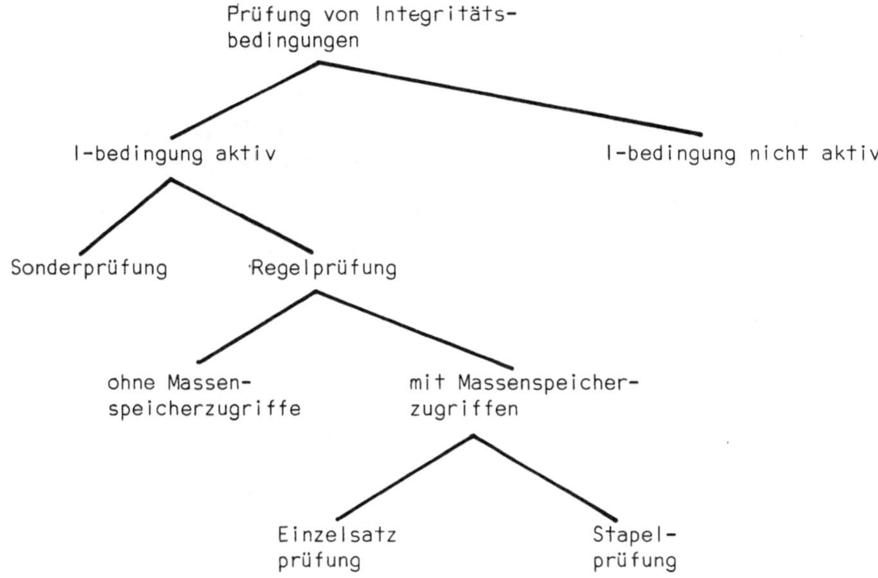

Bild 1: Klassifikation der Integritätsprüfungen

Regelprüfungen mit Massenspeicherzugriffen sind neben den vielfältigen Möglichkeiten, Sonderprüfungen durchzuführen, ein wesentliches Charakteristikum von Datenbanksystemen. Die Bedingung X1 wird auf diese Weise geprüft. Eine wirkungsvolle Durchführung dieser Prüfungen steht im Mittelpunkt des Interesses. Im DBTG-Konzept der CODASYL-Gruppe werden Integritätsbedingungen dieser Art durch Zugriffspfade implementiert. Charakteristisch für eine hierarchische Struktur des DBTG ist eine funktionale Beziehung zwischen Member-Satztyp und OWNER-Satztyp. Mehrere MEMBER-Sätze sind über einen OWNER-Satz zugriffstechnisch zu erreichen. Die Untermengenbedingung bedeutet in der Sprache der DBTG, daß ein MEMBER-Satz nicht ohne einen zugeordneten OWNER-Satz existieren darf. Da der Fremdschlüssel KNR in die Datei AUFTRAG im DBTG-Konzept nicht zwingend eingeführt wird, kann der Zugriffspfad Informationen der Anwendung enthalten, was die hohe

Datenabhängigkeit des DBTG-Ansatzes zur Folge hat. Zugriffspfad und Integritätsbedingung sind beim DBTG-Konzept miteinander vereinigt. Die Integritätsbedingung X1 läßt sich z.B. im DBTG darstellen, indem KUNDE zum OWNER-Satztyp und AUFTRAG zum MEMBER-Satztyp erklärt wird. Der Pfeil vom OWNER-Satztyp
KUNDE zum MEMBER-Satztyp AUFTRAG enthält die Information KUNDE.KNR=AUFTRAG.KNR,
wodurch die Integritätsbedingung X1 sichergestellt wird, wenn sie wie folgt zu
lesen ist: Für alle AUFTRAG.KNR existiert mindestens ein KUNDE, so daß die
Gleichung wahr ist.

In Relationalen Datenbanksystemen werden Zugriffspfade separat in Katalogen
bereitgestellt; sie werden nicht mit Integritätsbedingungen verschmolzen, da
Zugriffspfade methodologisch der darunter liegenden Abstraktionsebene zugeordnet werden. Ob die Prüfung von Integritätsbedingungen der betrachteten Art durch
bereitzustellende Zugriffspfade beschleunigt werden soll oder nicht, ist eine
Frage, die im nächsten Abschnitt angesprochen wird. Sicher ist, daß Zeiger, die
in die Hauptdaten eingebettet werden, gegenüber separat abgespeicherten, in-
vertierten Listen in hohem Maße unvorteilhaft sind (17, Band II)

Regelprüfungen mit Massenspeicherzugriffen werden weiter unterteilt. Wir unterscheiden die Prüfung von einzelnen Sätzen (CHECK MODE SINGLE) und von Mengen
von Sätzen (CHECK MODE BATCH). Beim Prüfen von einzelnen Sätzen würde in unserem Beispiel jeder Auftragssatz einzeln die Verifikation der Integritätsbedingung auslösen. Bei n Auftragssätzen werden die Integritätsbedingungen jeweils
sofort nach der Bereitstellung eines Satzes im Bereich insgesamt n mal aufgerufen.
Der Prüfmodus ist zu wählen, wenn im Realzeitbetrieb scharfe Zeitbeschränkungen
im Hinblick auf die Verarbeitung einer Transaktion herrschen, die sich auf einen Satz bezieht. Bei der Prüfung einer Menge von Sätzen werden die Bedingungen
für einen Stapel nur einmal aufgerufen. Für Regelprüfungen ohne Massenspeicherzugriffe soll die Unterscheidung von Einzelsatz- und Stapelprüfung nicht aus-
drücklich gemacht werden. Wenn Prüfroutinen dieser Art in übersetzter Form
speicherresident gehalten werden, kann in Modellrechnungen angenommen werden, daß
die gesamte Prüfzeit in beiden Fällen gegenüber den anderen Ein- und Ausgabe-
vorgängen vernachlässigbar klein ist. Die Prüfmodi, Einzelsatz- und Stapelprüfung, sind nicht zu verwechseln mit den Betriebsmodi für die verändernden Transaktionen. Hier wird zwischen Einzel- und Stapelverarbeitung unterschieden, um so
auf den Transaktionsumfang abzuheben. Von den vier Kombinationsmöglichkeiten
zwischen Prüf- und Betriebsmodi ist nur die Zuordnung "Einzelsatzprüfung - Stapelverarbeitung" auszuschließen.

4. Der Zeitbedarf für Prüfungsvorgänge

4.1 Zeitbestandteile bei wahlfreien und fortlaufenden Massenspeicherzugriffen

Die Ermittlung des Zeitbedarfs für Prüfungsvorgänge kann im Rahmen dieser Arbeit

knapp beschrieben werden, da die Prüfung von Integritätsbedingungen auf der zweiten, dritten und vierten Entwurfsebene auf bekannte Tatbestände zurückgeführt werden kann. Um die Darstellung abzukürzen, werden die Ausführungen ohne entwurfs-
methodologische Differenzierung unabhängig von der Schichtenbildung gemacht.

Der wesentliche Zeitbestandteil einer Prüfung ist der Zeitbedarf für das Wiederauffinden (Retrieval) der Daten auf den Plattenspeichern. Das Einlesen der übersetzten Prüfbedingung und das eventuelle Bereitstellen von Zugriffspfaden zur Beschleunigung der Retrieval-Operation sind demgegenüber als klein anzusehen. Da
Integritätsbedingungen in SEQUEL formuliert werden, können auch die Implementie-
rungstechniken dieser zunächst nur für Benutzer gedachten Sprache herangezogen
werden. Diese einheitliche Sicht auf Benutzerfragen und Integritätsbedingungen,
die noch um die Komponente "Sicherheitsbedingungen" zu erweitern ist, wurde auch
in das Produkt "System R" eingebracht (2). Das System R ist ein Prototyp eines
Relationalen Datenbanksystems des IBM-Forschungslabors in San José.

Was Berechnungsmodelle für das Zeitverhalten von Retrieval-Operationen und das
Bereitstellen von Zugriffspfaden anbetrifft, so ist in (17) eine ausführliche
Darstellung zu finden. Der Zeitbedarf ist als durchschnittliche Zeit dargestellt.
Falls Abschätzungen zu machen sind, so werden diese im Sinne einer "worst-case"-
Abschätzung durchgeführt. Es wird bei den Massenspeicherzugriffen angenommen, daß
die E/A-Anforderungen vor Plattengeräten und Kanälen keine Warteschlangen bilden
(14, S. 265).

Wir nehmen bei der Behandlung des Zeitbedarfs für die Integritätsprüfungen an, daß
das Entwurfsproblem "Bereitstellen von Zugriffspfaden" für den Primär- und für
die Sekundärschlüssel gelöst ist. Insbesondere wird in (11) ein erweitertes Be-
rechnungsmodell angegeben, um eine kostenoptimale Auswahl von Sekundärindizes
bei Retrieval-, Einfüg-, Lösch- und Veränderungsoperationen vorzunehmen. In
diesem Modell sind die Prüfvorgänge für Integritätsbedingungen als Retrieval-
Operationen einzuordnen. Die bereitzustellenden Indizes sind als Zugriffspfade
von den Überprüfvorgängen zu nutzen. Die Prüfung von Integritätsbedingungen kann
anschaulich interpretiert werden als vorformulierte Retrieval-Operationen eines einzigen Benutzers, der Prüfer genannt wird und eine hervorgehobene Stellung
unter den Benutzern innehat. Es ist die Aufgabe dieses Abschnittes, den Zeitbedarf für diesen Benutzer zu bestimmen, der nur Fragen stellen darf, die dem
System bekannt sind. Ad-hoc-Fragen sind ihm nicht erlaubt. Diese Personifizierung
soll zum leichteren Verständnis beitragen.

Es wurde in den beiden vorangehenden Abschnitten dargetan, daß Regelprüfungen
mit Massenspeicherzugriffen für Datenbanksysteme von besonderer Bedeutung sind.
Auf Prüfungen dieser Art wollen wollen wir uns in diesem Abschnitt konzentrieren.
Die Festlegung des Zeitbedarfs für Regelprüfungen ohne Massenspeicherzugriffe
und für Sonderprüfungen ist demgegenüber sehr einfach. Regelprüfungen ohne Mas-

senspeicherzugriffe können als zeitlos angenommen werden. Für Sonderprüfungen
steht die Berechnung des Zeitbedarfs für fortlaufende Verarbeitung einer Datei in Abhängigkeit von Parametern der physischen Geräte und der Speicherzu-
ordnung (Belegungsdichte, Blockungsfaktor etc.) im Mittelpunkt der Betrachtungen (17, Band II, S. 138 ff.).

Zur Bestimmung des Zeitbedarfs für Regelprüfungen mit Massenspeicherzugriff
soll von einer Anordnung ausgegangen werden, wie sie in Bild 2 dargestellt
wird.

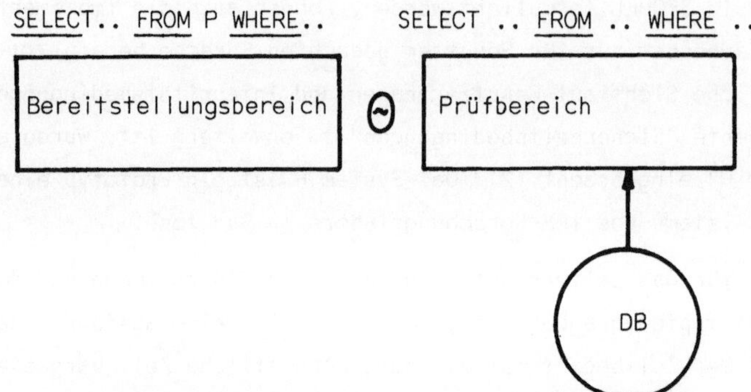

Bild 2: Bereiche zur Überprüfung von Integritätsbedingungen

Aus der Datenbank (DB) werden die durch einen (SELECT .. FROM .. WHERE)-Block
spezifizierten Datentupeln in einen Prüfbereich eingelesen. Dieser Bereich soll
abstrakt ohne Dimensionierung im Hinblick auf Geräte betrachtet werden. Im Sinne
der Relation Θ findet ein Vergleich mit den ausgewählten Daten im Bereitstellungsbereich statt. Es wird angenommen, daß die Bedingung keine tieferen Klammerstrukturen enthält und daß für den Θ-Vergleich der existenzielle Quantor
"für einige" und nicht der universelle Quantor "für alle" gilt. Wären Klammerstrukturen zugelassen, so müßten Aussagen über den Zeitbedarf einer "join"-Ope-
ration gemacht werden, was heute noch nicht mit der erforderlichen Genauigkeit
möglich ist.

Für das Einbringen der sich qualifizierenden Daten in den Prüfbereich sind drei
Zeitkomponenten mit Massenspeicherzugriffen zu betrachten:

1. Die durchschnittliche Zeit zum Einlesen der übersetzten Form der Integritätsbedingung, $\bar{t}_{Bed}$.

2. Die durchschnittliche Zeit, um zu den ausgelagerten Sekundärindizes (inver-
   tierte Datei) zuzugreifen, $\bar{t}_{inv}$.

3. Die durchschnittliche Zeit, um die Zahl N_{qual} qualifizierter Sätze in den
   Prüfbereich einzulesen, $\bar{t}_{TR} = N_{qual} \cdot \bar{t}$. $\bar{t}$ ist die mittlere Zugriffszeit für
   einen Datensatz. Für die Strategie zur Zugriffspfadauswahl ist der Begriff
   "Trefferrate TR" von ausschlaggebender Bedeutung. $TR = N_{qual}/N \cdot 100\,[\%]$. Es

werden die Zahl der qualifizierten Sätze und die Gesamtzahl der Sätze in
einer Datei ins Verhältnis gebracht. Die Liste mit den N_{qual} Primärschlüsseln wird Trefferliste genannt. $\bar{t}$ ist die mittlere Zugriffszeit, die nach Ablauf von $\bar{t}_{Bed}$ und $\bar{t}_{inv}$ beginnt. Es gilt auch:

$$\frac{\bar{t}_{TR}}{N} = \frac{TR}{100} \, \bar{t}.$$

In (17) wird dargestellt, von welchen Parametern $\bar{t}$ abhängt. Es ist eine so große
Vielzahl gerätetechnischer und abspeicherungstechnischer Größen, daß hier nur
auf die Literatur verwiesen werden kann.

Bei der Berechnung der Zeit $\bar{t}_{inv}$ werden in (17) für die Zugriffe zu den Katalogdaten B-Bäume angenommen. B-Bäume, die sehr gute Retrieval- und Änderungseigen-
schaften haben, sind eine Verallgemeinerung der index-sequentiellen Speicherungsstruktur (ISAM-Struktur). Die Katalogdaten sind entsprechend der Aufsuchhierar-
chie in formatierten Dateien (Dateiname/Attributname/Attributwert) dreistufig
angeordnet. Der Katalog der Datei- und Attributnamen kann, durch statische
Daten- und Kontrollfelder ergänzt, im allgemeinen speicherresident gehalten
werden.

Die Speicherungsstruktur zum Auffinden der übersetzten Form der Integritätsbedingungen kann als B-Baum, oder in der Terminologie der IBM Betriebssysteme als
"partioned" angenommen werden. Damit ergeben sich ebenso einfache Berechnungs-
schemata für $\bar{t}_{Bed}$ wie für $\bar{t}_{inv}$. Da $\bar{t}_{Bed}$ wesentlich kleiner als $\bar{t}_{inv}$ anzusehen
ist, kann $\bar{t}_{Bed}$ bei Entwurfsrechnungen auch vernachlässigt werden.

Die Entscheidung, ob eine ganze Datei wie in der Regel bei Sonderprüfungen
fortlaufend zu verarbeiten ist oder ob die durch die Prüfbedingung qualifizierten Sätze wahlfrei eingelesen werden können, hängt in entscheidendem Maße von der
Trefferrate TR ab. Bei hohen Trefferraten ist die fortlaufende Verarbeitung
der wahlfreien Verarbeitung vorzuziehen, da dann keine Sekundärindizes zu
Trefferlisten umgeformt werden müssen und die wahlfreie Verarbeitung über den
Primärschlüssel keine zeitlichen Vorteile bringt. Es existiert eine Grenztrefferrate TR_g, deren Überschreiten eine fortlaufende Verarbeitung zur Folge hat.
$\bar{t}_{min}$ sei die minimale Prüfzeit. Wir schreiben in Anlehnung an (17, S. 364):

$$\bar{t}_{min} \geq \bar{t}_{TR} + \bar{t}_{inv} + \bar{t}_{Bed} \qquad \text{für} \quad TR \leq TR_g$$

$$\bar{t}_{min} \geq \bar{t}_{TR_g} \qquad \qquad \text{für} \quad TR > TR_g$$

Die Grenztrefferrate TR_g, die im Katalog geführt wird, und damit auch $\bar{t}_{TR_g}$

werden über die Bestimmungsgleichung

$$\bar{t}_{TR} + \bar{t}_{Bed} = \bar{t}_{fortl}$$

festgelegt. $\bar{t}_{fortl}$ ist die Zeit für die fortlaufende Verarbeitung der Gesamt-
datei.
Die Ungleichungen werden in Bild 3 durch eine Datenbankkennlinie (17. S. 365)
qualitativ dargestellt.

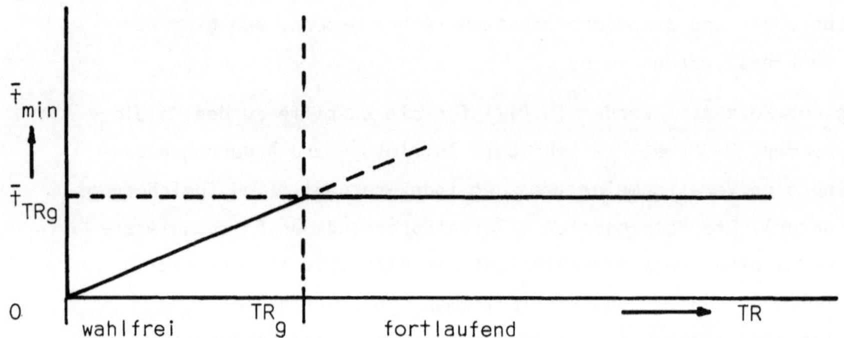

Bild 3: Datenbankkennlinie

Sollte für das Wiederauffinden von Sätzen im Rahmen einer Regelprüfung die
Trefferrate größer als TR_g und somit eine fortlaufende Dateiverarbeitung
günstiger sein, so ist es zweckmäßig, die im Subsystem befindlichen Bedingungen
für Sonderprüfungen gleichzeitig ohne zusätzlichen Aufwand mitzuprüfen. Eine
Sonderprüfung für eine Datei kann dann nicht nur durch ein ENFORCE-Kommando
eines Benutzers (external trigger), sondern auch durch die Bedingung $TR > TR_g$
(internal trigger) ausgelöst werden.

Die in Bild 1 dargestellte Regelprüfung mit Massenspeicherzugriffen kann für die
Einzelsatz- und Stapelprüfung noch weiter zerlegt werden. Wir unterscheiden im
Hinblick auf die Art der Retrieval-Operation zwischen Regelprüfungen über den
Primärschlüssel und Regelprüfungen über Sekundärschlüssel.

4.2 Regelprüfungen über den Primärschlüssel

Diese Prüfungen mit Massenspeicherzugriff sind besonders einfach und auch schnell
durchzuführen. Um die Sätze für den Prüfbereich zu selektieren, ist bei dieser
Prüfart nur der vom Betriebssystem gewährleistete Primärschlüsselzugriff erforderlich. Angeboten werden von Betriebssystemen in der Regel der klassische
ISAM-Zugriff und der Zugriff über Schlüsseltranformationen (hash code). Es
braucht über Zugriffspfade für die Sekundärschlüssel keine Reduktion auf eine
Trefferliste von Primärschlüsseln durchgeführt zu werden. Die Trefferliste
ist schon durch die Primärschlüssel im Bereitstellungsbereich gegeben. Die Zeit

$\bar{t}_{inv}$ entfällt.

Wir verdeutlichen diese Prüfung am Beispiel der Bedingung X1, die als Untermengen-
bedingung für den Fremdschlüssel im Hinblick auf seinen Stammschlüssel in
Relationalen Systemen eine besondere Bedeutung hat. Sie entspricht der MEMBER-
OWNER Relation in hierarchischen Systemen.

(SELECT KNR FROM P) $\subseteq$ (SELECT KNR FROM KUNDE)

Die rechte Seite erfordert Massenspeicherzugriffe über Primärschlüssel,
die durch den Ausdruck auf der linken Seite im Bereitstellungsbereich verfügbar gemacht werden. Da Untermengenbedingungen nicht die Frage einer besonderen
Qualität der Daten aufwerfen, sondern nur die Existenz von Daten sicherstellen
sollen, kann die Prüfung, ob ein Wert von P.KNR in KUNDE.KNR enthalten ist
oder nicht, ausgelagert werden. Ohne Sätze in den Prüfbereich einlesen zu
müssen, wird durch Vergleich am Lese- und Schreibkopf oder in der Steuer-
einheit festgestellt, ob die Werte von P.KNR in KUNDE.KNR vorhanden sind.
Die für Relationale Systeme wichtigen Untermengenbedingungen sind ohne das
Einlesen von Hauptdaten durchführbar. Die Zeiten für Massenspeicherzugriff
werden drastisch reduziert. Dies wird berücksichtigt, indem in den Formeln für
$\bar{t}$ der Übertragungszeitanteil herausgenommen wird. Die Grenztrefferrate
TR_g wird hierdurch beträchtlich erhöht, so daß ein wahlfreier Zugriff häufig
zum Zuge kommt. Eine fortlaufende Verarbeitung zur Prüfung einer Untermengenbedingung bei einer Zustandsänderung kommt praktisch nur dann vor, wenn die
Transaktionen und die Bereitstellung der neuen Daten im Modus einer Stapelverarbeitung ablaufen. Diese Aussage muß als Tendenzaussage aufgefaßt werden.

4.3 Regelprüfungen über Sekundärschlüssel

Die Prüfung der Θ-Beziehungen zwischen der linken und rechten Seite und das
Einbringen der N_{qual} Sätze in den Prüfbereich sind jetzt zwei gegenseitig
abgesetzte Vorgänge. Für die Sätze, die sich mit ihren Attributen im Sinne
eines (SELECT-FROM-WHERE)-Blockes für den Prüfbereich qualifizieren, muß erst
eine Trefferliste ermittelt werden, um dann über Zugriffsmethoden des Betriebs-
systems Daten einlesen zu können. Danach findet die Prüfung der Θ-Beziehung
statt. Als Beispiel für eine Regelprüfung über Sekundärschlüssel sei die Prüfung der folgenden Bedingung angegeben, die z.B. in wirtschaftlichen Krisen-
zeiten von Bedeutung sein kann:

Teile mit der Bezeichnung BEZ = 'Schraube' dürfen nur in Mengen unter 1000
(MENGE $\leq$ 1000) in Auftrag gegeben werden.

(SELECT TNR FROM P WHERE MENGE $>$ '1000') $\neq$
(SELECT TNR FROM TEIL WHERE BEZ = 'SCHRAUBE')

Was die Trefferrate für Retrieval-Bedingungen dieses Typs anbetrifft,
so wird in (17) gezeigt, wie Erwartungswerte zu ermitteln sind. Da es sich jedoch um eine vorformulierte Bedingung handelt, kann die Trefferrate auch bei
der Formulierung der Bedingung unter Berücksichtigung der angelegten Sekundärindizes ausgezählt werden. Auf Grund der bekannten Grenztrefferrate ist dann
zu entscheiden, ob es günstiger ist, zu den Sätzen wahlfrei oder fortlaufend
zuzugreifen.

Es soll hier nur erwähnt werden, daß beim Entwurf die Möglichkeiten des Clustering
der Daten im Sinne der Sekundärschlüssel zu untersuchen ist. Clustering bedeutet, daß eine logische Nachbarschaft in physische Nachbarschaft umgesetzt wird.
Alle Teile mit der Bezeichnung 'Schraube' könnten bei einem Clustering in
einer Plattenspur oder in einer Seite als vorformatiertem Bereich abgespeichert
werden. Belford et.al. (3) sind der Auffassung, daß die Forschungen auf dem
Gebiete des Clusterings zu intensivieren sind, da hier noch Leistungsreserven
zu vermuten seien.

Über Kennlinien kann bei Regelprüfungen über den Primärschlüssel im Falle des
Modus CHECK MODE BATCH die maximale Stapelgröße bestimmt werden, wenn Zeit-
schranken von der Anwendung her vorgegeben werden. Die Gesamtzeit $\bar{t}_{ges}$ setzt
sich zusammen aus Bereitstellungszeit $\bar{t}_{ber}$, Prüfzeit $\bar{t}_{prüf}$ und Ausführungszeit $\bar{t}_{aus}$
der Transaktion, so daß sich für $\bar{t}_{prüf}$ ergibt:

$$\bar{t}_{prüf} = \bar{t}_{ges} - \bar{t}_{ber} - \bar{t}_{aus}$$

$\bar{t}_{ber}$ und $\bar{t}_{aus}$ können abgeschätzt werden, so daß $\bar{t}_{prüf}$ bei vorgegebenem $\bar{t}_{ges}$
errechnet werden kann. Am Schnittpunkt der Linien $\bar{t}_{prüf}$ mit der Kennlinie
liest man dann als Trefferrate die maximale Stapelgröße im Bereitstellungsbereich ab. Da bei Regelprüfungen über Sekundärschlüssel die Trefferrate nicht
durch die Sätze im Bereitstellungsbereich bestimmt wird, sondern von der
Qualifizierung im WHERE-Teil auf der rechten Seite abhängt, ist man bei der Wahl
einer Trefferrate nicht frei. Die Angabe von $\bar{t}_{prüf}$ führt zu einer geschätzten
oder ausgezählten Trefferrate nur zu einer Aussage darüber, ob der Gesamtvor-
gang innerhalb der geforderten Zeit ablaufen kann oder nicht. Eine Verbesserung
des Zeitablaufs ist nur möglich, wenn man bei der Ausführung der Transaktion zu
kleineren Verarbeitungsstapeln oder zum Einzelmodus übergeht.

Beim Entwurf sollte in Abhängigkeit von der Anwendung untersucht werden, ob Regelprüfungen über Sekundärschlüssel wegen ihres beträchtlichen Zeitaufwandes nicht
auch in Form von Sonderprüfungen ablaufen können. Sonderprüfungen sind im Hinblick auf die Berechnung ihres Zeitbedarfs unproblematisch, da für die zu prüfen-
den Dateien in der Regel nur die Zeit $\bar{t}_{fortl}$ in Ansatz gebracht werden muß.

Unabhängig von den gewählten Prüfungsarten sollten alle wesentlichen Merkmale einer Prüfung für technische Belange und für Revisionszwecke protokolliert werden.

Literaturverzeichnis

(1) Astrahan, M.M und Chamberlin, D.D.: Implementation of a Structured English Query Language, in: Comm. of the ACM, Vol. 18 (1975), No. 10, October 1975, S. 580-588..

(2) Astrahan, M.M. et. al.: System R: A Relational Approach to Data Base Management, Part 2: The Relational Data System (unveröffentlichtes Manuskript), erscheint 1976 in den Comm. of the ACM.

(3) Belford, G., Bunch, St. und Day, J.D.: A State-of-the Art Reporter on Network Data Management and Related Technology, Center for Advanced Compution, University of Illinois at Urbana, April 1, 1975.

(4) Boyce, R.F. und Chamberlin, D.D.: Using a Structured English Query Language as a Data Definition Facility, IBM Research Report, RJ 1318, Dec. 10, 1973.

(5) Chamberlin, D.D., Gray, J.N. und Traiger, I.L.: Views, Authorization and Locking in a Relational Data Base System, IBM Research Report, RJ 1486, San José , Dec. 19, 1974.

(6) Chamberlin, D.D., Boyce, R.F.: SEQUEL: A Structured English Query Language, in : Proc of 1974 ACM SIGFIDET Workshop on Data Description, Access and Control, Ann Arbor, Michigan 1974, S. 249-264.

(7) Codd, E.F.: Relational Completeness of Data Base Sublanguages, in: R. Rustin (Hrsg.): Data Base Systems, Prentice-Hall, Englewood Cliffs, 1972, S. 65-98.

(8) Eswaran, K.P., Gray, J.K., Lorie, R.A. und Traiger, I.L.: On the notions of consitency and predicate locks in a data base systems, IBM Research Report, RJ 1487, San José , Dec. 30, 1974.

(9) Eswaran, K.P. und Chamberlin, D.D.: Functional Specifikations of a Subsystem for Data Base Integrity, IBM Research Report, RJ 1601, San José, June 24, 1975.

(10)Gray, J.N., Lorie, R.A., Potzolu, G.R und Traiger, L.L.: Granularity of Locks and Degrees of Consistency in a Shared Data Base, IBM Research Report, RJ 1654, San José, Sept. 19, 1975.

(11)Härder, Th.: Auswahl optimaler Indexmengen, Forschungsbericht DV 75-2, Forschungsgruppe Datenverwaltungssysteme, TH Darmstadt, Sep. 1975.

(12) Senko, M.E., Altmann, E.B., Astrahan, M.M und Fehder, P.L.: Data
      Structures and Accessing in Data Base Systems, in: IBM Systems Journal,
      Vol. 12 (1973), No. 1, S. 30-93.

(13) Stonebraker, M.: Implementation of Integrity Constraints and Views
      by Query Modification, in: ACM SIGMOD, May14-16, 1975, San José,
      S. 65-77.

(14) Wedekind, H.: Systemanalyse - Die Entwicklung von Anwendungssystemen
      für Datenverarbeitungsanlagen, Carl Hanser-Verlag, München 1973.

(15) Wedekind,H.: On the Selection of Access Paths in a Data Base System
      in: J.W. Klimbie u.a. (Hrsg.); Data Base Management, North Holland,
      Amsterdam, 1974, S. 385 - 397.

(16) Wedekind, H.: Datensicherheit in Datenbanksystemen, in:
      G. Goos und J. Hartmanis (Hrsg.) : Data Base Systems, Lecture Notes in
      Computer Science, Springer-Verlag, Berlin-Heidelberg-New-York, 1976,
      S. 315-338.

(17) Wedekind, H.: Datenbanksysteme I, Bibliographisches Institut, Mannheim,
      1974; Wedekind, H. und Härder, Th.: Datenbanksysteme II, Bibliographisches
      Institut, Mannheim, 1976.

Binary Search Trees: Average and
Worst Case Behavior
(Extended Abstract)

by

Reiner Güttler, Kurt Mehlhorn
Wolfgang Schneider, Norbert Wernet
Fachbereich Angewandte
Mathematik und Informatik
Universität des Saarlandes

D-6600 Saarbrücken

Summary

We introduce several rules of thumb for constructing nearly optimal
binary search trees and survey results about the average search time
of the trees yielded. Then we introduce a new point of view: worst case
behavior. We show that the trees produced by the rules of thumb exhibit
good worst case behavior by proving upper and lower bounds for the time
needed to perform a single search. Then we apply the results to digital
search trees. Next we report the findings of an experimental study of
the different approximation rules and discuss worst and average case
running times of different implementations.

The full paper with complete proofs is available as a Technical Report
from the authors.

I. Introduction and Survey of Known Results

"One of the popular methods for retrieving information by its 'name'
is to store the names in a binary tree. We are given n names
$B_1, B_2, \ldots, B_n$ and 2n+1 frequencies $\beta_1, \ldots, \beta_n$, $\alpha_o, \ldots, \alpha_n$ with $\Sigma\beta_i + \Sigma\alpha_j = 1$.
Here β_i is the frequency of encountering name B_i, and α_j is the fre-
quency of encountering a name which lies between B_j and B_{j+1}, α_o and α_n
have obvious interpretations" [Knuth 71].

We may always assume w.l.o.g. that $\beta_i + \alpha_j + \beta_{i+1} \neq o$ for all i. Otherwise, the i-th (or the (i+1)-th) key might as well be removed.

A <u>binary search tree</u> T is a tree with n interior nodes (nodes having
two sons), which we denote by circles, and n+1 leaves, which we denote

by squares. The interior nodes are labelled by the B_i in increasing
order from left to right and the leaves are labelled by the intervals
(B_j, B_{j+1}) in increasing order form left to right. Let b_i be the distance
of interior node B_i from the root and let a_j be the distance of leaf
(B_j, B_{j+1}) from the root. To retrieve a name X, $b_i + 1$ comparisons are
needed if $X = B_i$ and a_j comparisons are required if $B_j < X < B_{j+1}$.
Therefore we define the <u>weighted path length</u> of tree T as:

$$P = \sum_{i=1}^{n} \beta_i (b_i + 1) + \sum_{j=0}^{n} \alpha_j a_j$$

D.E. Knuth [Knuth 71] gives an algorithm for constructing an optimum
binary search tree, i.e. a tree with minimal weighted path length. His
algorithm has $O(n^2)$ time complexity and $O(n^2)$ space complexity. Hu and
Tucker [Hu & Tucker] consider the case that alle names have frequency
zero, i.e. $\beta_i = o$ for $1 \leq i \leq n$. They give an algorithm with $O(n \log n)$
time complexity for this case.

Approximation algorithms were considered early in the game [Bruno &
Coffman, Walker & Gotlieb].

Walker and Gotlieb consider the following rule of thumb:

<u>Rule I (Weight Balancing)</u>: Choose the root so as to equalize the weight
of the left and right subtrees as much as possible, then proceed similarly on the subtrees. (The weight of a subtree is the sum of the frequencies of all nodes and leaves in this subtree.)

They describe an implementation of this rule with time complexity
$O(n \log n)$ and space complexity $O(n)$ and report that the rule tends to
produce trees which are within a few (5) percent of the optimum.

Recently several other rules of thumb were suggested.

<u>Rule II (Min-Max)</u> [Bayer, Schnorr]: Choose the root so as to minimize
the maximum of the weights of the left and right subtree, then proceed
similarly on the subtrees.

We illustrate rule I and II on an example

Consider $n = 5$, $(\alpha_o, \beta_1, \ldots, \beta_5, \alpha_5) = (^1/_6, ^1/_{24}, o, ^1/_8, o, ^1/_8, ^1/_8, o, ^5/_{12})$.

The Min-Max tree is   The weight balanced tree is

Both rules always choose nodes as the root which are close to the center
of the distribution and in subtrees close to the center of the subdistri-
bution as well. We could instead look for a node as root of the left
(right) subtree, which is close to 1/4 (3/4) of the distribution, close
to 1/8, 3/8, 5/8, 7/8 in the subtrees of the next level and so on. This
strategy may be formalized as

RULE III (Bi-section) [Mehlhorn 75b] , which yields the following tree:
we infer the reader to
[Mehlhorn 75b] for an
exact defintion

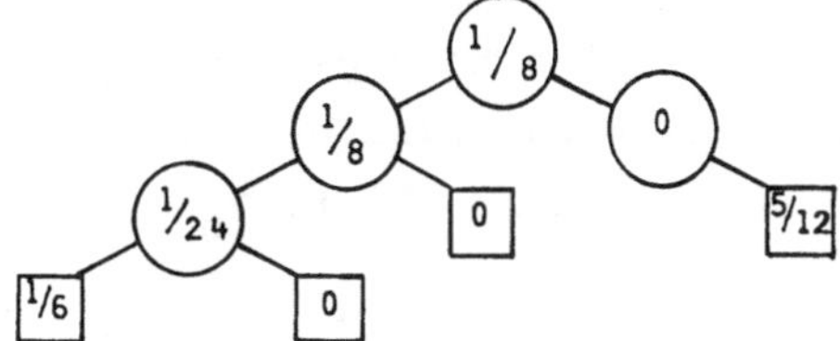

The first theoretical results about the behavior of binary search trees
were obtained by Gilbert and Moore [Gilbert & Moore]. They consider the
case that the weight is concentrated in the leaves, i.e. $\beta_i = o$ for all
i, and showed that in this case $H \leq P_{opt} \leq H+2$ where

$$H = \Sigma \beta_i \log {}^1/_{\beta_i} + \Sigma \alpha_j \log {}^1/_{\alpha_j}$$ is the entropy of the frequency

distribution. Rissanen [Rissanen] later showed $P_{MM} \leq H+2$ in this case.
The general case was first considered by Mehlhorn [Mehlhorn 75a] who

proved ${}^1/_{\log 3} \cdot H \leq P_{opt} \leq P_{WB} \leq 1.44\ H+2$. Bayer [Bayer] improved upon

this. The best bounds presently known are:

$${}^1/_{\log 3} \cdot H \leq P_{opt} \qquad \text{[Mehlhorn 75a]}$$

$$H - \log \log n \leq P_{opt} \qquad \text{[Bayer]}$$

$$P_{WB} \leq H+2 \qquad \text{[Bayer]}$$

$$P_{MM} \leq H+1+\Sigma \alpha_j \qquad \text{[Bayer]}$$

$$P_{BI} \leq H+1+\Sigma \alpha_j \qquad \text{[Mehlhorn 75b]}$$

All bounds are achievable for a wide range of frequency distributions.

These results answer two important questions:
1) They give an a-priori test for the performance of binary search trees,
   i.e. they enclose the average path length in a narrow interval.
2) They prove that the approximation rules described above always produce nearly optimal search trees.

The importance of the approximation rules was increased by a recent result of Fredman [Fredman]. He describes an implementation of the Min-
Max, Weight-Balancing and Bi-section Rules which runs in time O(n).

II. Worst Case Behavior
========================

In the preceding section we surveyed results about the average case behavior of optimal and nearly optimal binary search trees. We pose the
following question.

<u>What can we say about the time needed for a single search</u> (worst case
behavior)?

We give a simple example of a tree performing well on the average, but
exhibiting extremely bad worst case behavior.
Consider $n = 2^k - 1$, $\beta_i = 0$ for all i, $\alpha_o = 2^{-k}$,

$\alpha_1 = \ldots = \alpha_n = \epsilon$, $\alpha_{n+1} = \ldots = \alpha_{2n} = 2^{-k} - \epsilon$ where ϵ is a samll
positive number. Then $H(\alpha_o, \ldots, \alpha_n) \approx \log(n+1)$.

The following tree

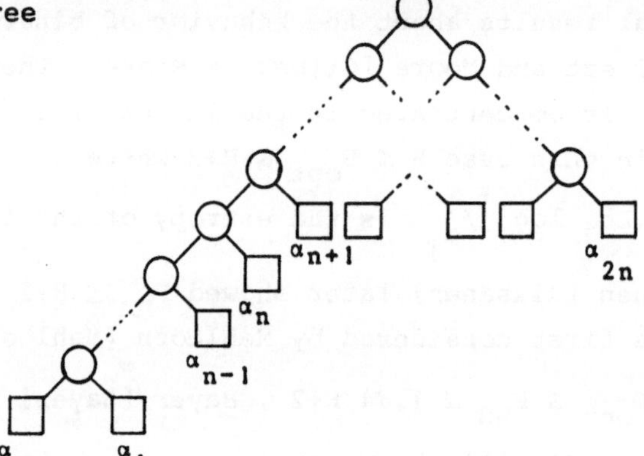

complete binary
tree with n+1
leaves of depth k

has weighted path length
$$P = n \cdot (2^{-k} - \epsilon) \cdot k + \sum_{i=k+1}^{k+n} \epsilon \cdot i + 2^{-k} \cdot (k+n)$$

$\approx \log (n+1) + 1$. The results of Gilbert and Moore tell us that
$P_{opt} \geq H$, i.e. the tree is nearly optimal. However, a search ending in
the left-most leaf takes n+log n steps, i.e. there is a huge discrepancy
between average and worst case behavior: log n vs. n + log n.

This example should make it perfectly clear that concentrating on
average case behavior does not suffice; we should instead try to relate
weight and search time for every single node separately. This was done
already in [Mehlhorn 75a and 75b], however, without noting it.

There are rules for which it is difficult to find an upper bound of the
average search time, i.e. the weighted path length. Then the sum of the
maximal search times (the worst case distances from the root) of all
nodes and leafs delivers a useful (but not very tight) upper bound of the
weighted path length. Together with empirical results the worst case

behavior is also an interesting information of the quality of a construction rule.

We quote :

Let T_R be a search tree constructed according to rule R, let b_i^R be the distance of leaf (B_j, B_{j+1}) from the root, where R can be WB (weight-balanced), BI (Bi-section) and MM (Min-Max). Then [Mehlhorn 75a]

$$b_i^{WB} \leq (\log \delta)^{-1} \cdot \log {}^1/_{\beta_i} + 1$$

$$a_j^{WB} \leq (\log \delta)^{-1} \cdot \log {}^1/_{\alpha_j} + 2$$

and [Mehlhorn 75b]

$$b_i^{BI} \leq \log {}^1/_{\beta_i} + 1$$

$$a_j^{BI} \leq \log {}^1/_{\alpha_j} + 2$$

where $\delta = {}^1/_2 (1 + \sqrt{5})$ is the golden ration. The value of $(\log \delta)^{-1}$ is approximately 1.44.

We add to this list:

<u>Thm.:</u> (Upper Bounds for the Worst Case Behavior of Nearly Optimal Binary Search Trees)

<u>Case 1:</u> The weights concentrated in the nodes, i.e. $\Sigma \alpha_j = 0$

then
$$b_i^{WB} \leq (\log \emptyset)^{-1} \cdot \log {}^1/_{\beta_i} + 0.412 \qquad \emptyset = \frac{2}{\sqrt{17}-3}$$

$$b_i^{MM} \leq \log {}^1/_{\beta_i}$$

$$b_i^{BI} \leq \log {}^1/_{\beta_i} + 1$$

The value of $(\log \emptyset)^{-1}$ is approximately 1.201.

<u>Case 2:</u> The weight is concentrated in the leaves, i.e. $\Sigma \beta_i = 0$

then
$$a_j^{WB} \leq (\log \delta)^{-1} \log {}^1/_{\alpha_j} + 2$$

$$a_j^{MM} \leq (\log \delta)^{-1} \log {}^1/_{\alpha_j} + 2$$

$$a_j^{BI} \leq \log {}^1/_{\alpha_j} + 2$$

<u>Case 3:</u> General case i.e. $\Sigma \alpha_j \geq 0 \quad \Sigma \beta_i \geq 0$

$$b_i^{MM} \leq (\log \delta)^{-1} \log {}^1/_{\beta_j} - 0,2823$$

$$a_j^{MM} \leq (\log \delta)^{-1} \log {}^1/_{\alpha_j} + 2$$

All bounds are achievable (in the limit).

<u>Proof</u>: Constructing "worst-case" trees "bottom-up" one can easily find recursive functions for the lowest weights of the subtrees having a node (leaf) of weight β_i (α_i) at depth b_i (a_i). Using the method of generating functions we solve these recursions receiving expressions of the form $b_i \leq c_1 \cdot \log {}^1/_{\beta_i} + c_2$.

This list together with table 1 and the earlier results suggests to choose different rules depending on the more important request: to receive a good average search time or to bound above the single search time. Here we see that the bisection rule shows good worst-case behavior. Since the upper bounds of the average search time are equal for the bisection and the min-max rule, table 1 suggests to prefer the later. We will now show, that the worst case behavior of a construction rule hardly can be improved; we therefore give some lower bound results which are based on the following lemma.

<u>Lemma</u>: Let T be an arbitrary binary search tree with n interior nodes, let b_i be the depth of node B_i, let a_j be the depth of leaf (B_j, B_{j+1})

Then

1) $\quad \sum_{j=0}^{n} 2^{-a_j} = 1$

2) $\quad \sum_{i=1}^{n} 2^{-b_i} \leq (\log (n+1))$

3) $\quad \sum_{i=1}^{n} 3^{-(b_i+1)} + \sum_{j=0}^{n} 3^{-a_j} = 1$

<u>Proof</u>: A simple induction proof on the height of T.

<u>Theorem 2</u>: (Lower bounds for the worst case behavior of binary search trees)

(a) For $c \in R$ let

$$L_c = \{j;\ a_j \leq \log {}^1/_{\alpha_j} - c\}$$

and

$$N_c = \{i;\ b_i \leq \log {}^1/_{\beta_i} - \log \log (n+1) - c\}$$

Then

$$\sum_{j \in L_c} \alpha_j \leq 2^{-c} \quad \text{and} \quad \sum_{i \in N_c} \beta_i \leq 2^{-c}.$$

(b) For $c \ R$ let

$$L_c = \{j;\ a_j \leq \frac{1}{\log 3} \log {}^1/_{\alpha_j} - c\}$$

and

$$N_c = \{i;\ b_i + 1 \le \frac{1}{\log 3}\ \log\ {}^1/_{\beta_j} - c\ \}$$

Then
$$\sum_{j \in L_c} \alpha_j + \sum_{i \in N_c} \beta_i \le 3^{-c}$$

<u>Proof</u>:

$$1 = \sum_{j=0}^{n} 2^{-a_j} \ge \sum_{j \in L_c} 2^{-a_j} \ge \sum_{j \in L_c} 2^{-(\log\ {}^1/_{\alpha_j} - c)} \ge 2^c \cdot \sum_{j \in L_c} \alpha_j$$

and hence $\sum_{j \in L_c} \alpha_j \le 2^{-c}$

The proofs of the other parts are similar and can be found in [Güttler, Schneider].

An example should clarify this theorem. Consider the case that the weight is concentrated in the leaves, i.e. $\Sigma \beta_i = 0$.

Then rule II (Bisection) yields a tree with the property that the search time for leaf (B_j, B_{j+1}) is bounded above by $\log\ {}^1/_{\alpha_j} + 2$. (Theorem 1).

Theorem 2 tells us that in every tree (especially in the optimal tree) for a set of leaves having weight $\ge {}^1/_2 ({}^3/_4)$, i.e. for 50 (75) % of the searches, the search time will be larger than $\log\ {}^1/_{\alpha_j} - 1$ (resp. $\log\ {}^1/_{\alpha_j} - 2$) : Rule III (as well as the other rules) produces trees whose worst case behavior is close to optimal.

III. Application to digital search trees
===

Quite frequently the "names" B_i will be strings. Instead of basing the search method on comparisons between names, we can make use of the representation as a sequence of characters. A classic example of such a search method is the trie [cf. Knuth 73, Sec 6.3] . Suppose that the names $B_1, \ldots, B_n$ are strings over a k character alphabet Σ. A trie is then a k-ary tree. For each prefix of name B_i there is a node in the tree, the branching is done on the next character.

Different <u>representations</u> of the nodes of a trie were proposed: vectors of length k, linked lists or binary trees. The first alternative minimizes processing time, the two others save memory space.

From now on we restrict ourself to the case that the weight is concentrated in the keys. ($\Sigma \alpha_j = 0$). This restriction simplifies the noation; the general case may be treated analogously [Güttler, Schneider]. Consider a node w of the trie. The branch corresponding to character $a \in \Sigma$

is taken with probability p_{wa}/p_w; for $v \in \Sigma^*$ p_v is the sum of the weights of all names having v as a prefix. Hotz [Hotz] proposed to represent each node by an optimal (or nearly so) binary search tree; he showed that this strategy works well in the case of "uniform distributions". We show that it performs well for all distributions.

Assume that we represent each node of a trie by a binary search tree whose weighted path length is bounded above by $c_1 H + c_2$ where H is the entropy of the associated frequency distribution. Consider a search for $B_i = a_1 a_2 \ldots a_{l_i}$ with $a_j \in \Sigma$, l_i = length of string B_i. We search first for the node a_1 in the top level tree, then for a_2 in the tree T_{a_1}, then for a_3 in the tree $T_{a_1 a_2}$ and so on, finally we search for a_{l_i} in the tree $T_{a_1 a_2 \ldots a_{l_i - 1}}$.

<u>Thm.</u>: Suppose that we represent each node of a trie by a binary search tree whose weighted path length is bounded above by $c_1 H + c_2$, then the average search time is bounded by

$$c_1 H(\beta_1, \ldots, \beta_n) + c_2 \bar{I}$$

where $\bar{I} = \sum_{i=1}^{n} \beta_i \cdot \text{length } (B_i)$ is the average word length of the names B_i.

Consider the case that all names have length m. It is reasonable to assume that the time needed to compare two names of length m takes $O(m)$ units of time. Using binary search trees based on comparison of entire names then results in an average search time of $O(m \cdot (c_1 H + c_2))$. This contrasts sharply to the average search time of $O(c_1 H + c_2 \cdot m)$ achieved by the search method based on comparisons of characters.

We turn now to the worst case behavior.

<u>Thm.</u>: Assume that we represent each node of a trie by a binary search tree whose worst case behavior is bounded above by $c_1 \cdot \log {}^1/_{probalility}$ + c_2, then a search for name B_i of length l_i and frequency β_i takes at most

$$c_1 \cdot \log {}^1/_i + c_2 l_i$$

comparisons between characters.
The remarks following the preceding theorem apply here as well.

IV. Average Case Behavior - experimental results
===

In section I and II we represented theoretical results about the average and worst case behavior of optimal and nearly optimal binary search trees. The results are rather similar for the three approximation rules considered.

Gotlieb & Walker [Gotlieb & Walker] applied rule I (weight balancing) and variants of it (after determining a candidate for the root by rule I they search for a heavy node in the vicinity and take it as the root) to the construction of an author catalog for the University of Toronto library. They took the number of cards containing the name of an author to be the frequency of that author. We refer the reader to [Gotlieb & Walker] for a detailed description of the test data.

Table I shows the results of applying rules I, II and III to their data (See [Wernet] for a detailed description of the programs). Another rule was also included in the empirical study. It is based on information theoretic considerations. A comparison with a name is a decision with three possible outcomes: $<, = , >$. The probabilities of the three outcomes are the weight of the left subtree W_L, the weight of the root W_{ROOT} and the weight of the right subtree W_R respectively, the information gained by this comparison is equal to the entropy $H(W_L, W_{ROOT}, W_R)$.

Rule IV (Entropy): Choose the root so as to maximize the local information gain $H(W_L, W_{ROOT}, W_R)$, then proceed similarly on the subtrees.

	OPT	ENT	MM	WB	BI	
Set 1						
Case 1	4.29	4.45	4.55	4.93	6.09	
2	6.61	6.63	7.02	7.09	7.65	
3	5.87	6.01	6.11	6.12	7.19	
4	6.06	6.17	6.32	6.42	7.17	
5	6.64	6.71	6.79	6.82	7.40	
6	5.96	6.02	6.31	6.59	7.21	
7	5.82	5.92	6.14	6.33	7.21	
8	6.26	6.52	6.72	6.85	7.65	
9	7.08	7.47	7.45	7.44	8.30	*)
10	7.34	7.38	7.51	7.52	7.65	
Set 1						
Case 1	4.63	4.77	5.00	5.66	6.60	
2	7.25	7.30	7.64	7.80	8.06	
3	6.25	6.33	6.68	6.84	7.52	
4	6.39	6.51	6.87	6.88	7.49	
5	7.02	7.09	7.21	7.24	8.03	
6	6.54	6.61	6.88	7.03	7.67	
7	6.45	6.50	6.80	6.99	7.68	
8	6.58	6.95	6.84	6.87	7.82	*)
9	7.12	7.50	7.35	7.32	8.03	*)
10	7.69	7.79	7.87	7.89	8.05	

	OPT	ENT	MM	WB	BI	
Set 3						
Case 1	4.00	4.08	4.23	4.54	6.14	
2	6,42	6.49	6.56	6.99	7.37	
3	5.55	5.69	5.83	5.85	6.63	
4	5.76	5.85	5.98	6.21	6.58	
5	6.22	6.40	6.28	6.37	6.86	*)
6	5.65	5.75	6.02	6.25	7.10	
7	5.59	5.65	5.91	6.02	7.08	
8	6.08	6.38	6.39	6.62	7.65	
9	7.01	7.38	7.22	7.26	8.39	*)
10	6.97	7.05	7.10	7.09	7.32	*)
Set 4						
Case 1	5.03	5.08	5.38	5.88	6.67	
2	7.41	7.50	7.69	7.85	8.05	
3	6.54	6.61	6.81	6.98	7.56	
4	6.65	6.74	7.03	7.18	7.57	
5	7.27	7.35	7.45	7.46	8.02	
6	6.54	6.59	6.87	7.08	7.67	
7	6.75	6.82	7.05	7.18	7.78	
8	6.73	7.05	6.91	6.96	8.02	*)
9	7.11	7.50	7.29	7.31	8.15	*)
10	7.87	7.91	8.02	8.03	8.16	
Set 5						
Case 1	4.13	4.28	4.32	5.32	6.40	
2	5.97	6.05	6.19	6.75	7.32	
3	5.75	5.93	5.95	6.28	7.26	
4	5.99	6.11	6.44	6.51	6.93	
5	6.66	6.79	6.87	6.96	7.65	
6	5.33	5.46	5.61	5.97	7.01	
7	5.41	5.53	5.90	6.37	7.29	
8	5.81	5.97	6.05	6.36	7.14	
9	6.99	7.31	7.22	7.24	8.09	*)
10	7.26	7.32	7.42	7.41	7.63	*)

<u>Table 1:</u> Weighted path length P_{opt}, P_{WB} P_{MM}, P_{BI} and P_{ENT}.

*) Only in these cases

$P_{ENT} < P_{MM} < P_{WB} < P_{BI}$ is not true!

Rule II (Min Max) beats rule I (Weight Balancing) consistently, rule I
in turn always beats rule III (Bisection). Rule IV (Entropy) performs
best in most cases, however, looses to rule II in some cases. Whilst
we expected the excellent behavior of rule II - the proofs of the performance bounds are a little bit simpler and the bounds slighty better-,
we were surprised by the showing of the entropy rule. We are presently
trying to understand its behavior.

V. Implementations

In this section we report on a comparative study of different implementations of the various rules of thumb. The trees are always constructed
in a top-down fashion, the search for the root always requires us to
minimize (or maximize) some functions, e.g. difference in weight or
entropy. In the case of rules I, II, III (WB, MM, BI) this function is
a convex (concave) function of the root. Several strategies for searching for the root come to mind.

1) Searching from both ends in steps of 1
2) Binary search
3) Exponential search [Fredman] ; i.e. search in exponentially increasing steps from both ends and then do a binary search on the so determined interval.

We analysed these strategies both with respect to worst case and
average case behavior. For the average case behavior, we assumed that
all frequency distributions are equally likely to occur.

	Worst Case	Average Case	Running time
Rules I, II, III			
Binary Search	$O(n \log n)$	$O(n)$	
Linear Search	$O(n \log n)$	$O(n \log n)$	
Exponent. Search	$O(n)$	$O(n)$	
Rule IV	$O(n^2)$	$O(n \log n)$	

The details may be found in [Wernet]. There the constants and low order
terms are explicitely computed. The discussion there shows that (as
expected) binary search is always superior to linear search, and that
binary search is best for small n. The cut point (with respect to
worst case behavior) between binary search and exponential search is
fairly small about 40. With respect to average case behavior, binary
search is best.

VI. Conclusion
================

We surveyed known results about the average case behavior of binyry
trees. We then introduced a new point of view: worst case behavior and
gave an example of a tree with good average case but poor worst case
behavior. Next we studied nearly optimal binary search trees with respect to worst case behavior, we proved upper and lower bounds for the
worst case behavior. In section III we applied our results to digital
search trees. Section IV was devoted to a brief sketch of an experimental study and in the last section we compared the worst case and average
case running time of different implementations of different rules of
thumb.

Bibliography
=============

[Ash],   "Information Theory", Interscience Publishers, N.Y. 1965

[Bayer, P.], "Improved Bounds on the Costs of Optimal and Balanced
        Binary Search Trees" , MIT, 1975

[Bruno, J. & Coffman, E.G.],"Nearly Optimal Binary Search Trees"
        Proc. IFIP Congress 1971

[Fredman, M.L.], "Two Applications of a Probabilistic Search Technique
        Sorting X+Y and Building Balanced Search Trees", Proc. 7th
        Annual ACM Symp. 1975

[Gilbert, E.N. & Moore, E.F.],"Variable Length Encodings" Bell System
        Technical Journal, 1971

[Gotlieb, C.C. & Walker, W. A.],"A Top-Down Algorithm for Constructing
        Nearly Optimal Lexicographical Trees"
        Graph Theory and Computing, Academic Press, 1972

[Güttler, R.], "Binäre Suchbäume", Diplomarbeit, FB 10, Universität
        des Saarlandes, 1976

[Hotz, G.],"Schranken für Balanced Trees bei ausgewogenen Verteilungen",
        Universität des Saarlandes, Techn. Bericht, 1975

[Hu, T.C & Tucker, A.C.], "Optimal Computer Serach Trees and Variable
        Length Alphabetic Codes", Siam J. Applied Math. 21, 1971

[Knuth, D.E. 71], "Optimum Binary Search Trees", Acta Informatica I,
        1971

[Knuth, D.E., 73] ,"The Art of Computer Programming", Vol. III,
        Addison-Wesley, 1973

[Mehlhorn, K.   75a] , "Nearly Optimal Binary Search Trees", Acta
        Informatica 5, 1975

[Mehlhorn, K, 75b], "Best Possible Bounds on the Weighted Path Length
        of Optimum Binary Search Trees", GI Fachtagung für Automaten-
        theorie und formale Sprachen, Springer Lecture Notes in
        Computer Science   Vol. 33. 1975

[Rissanen, J.], "Bounds for Weight Balanced Trees", IBM Journal of
        Research and Development, 1973

[Schneider, W.], "Binäre Suchbäume", Diplomarbeit, FB 10
        Universität des Saarlandes, 1976

[Schnorr, C.P.], "Two Algorithms for Nearly Optimal Binary Search
        Trees", Universität Frankfurt, 1974

[Wernet, N.]"Binäre Suchbäume, Diplomarbeit, FB 10, Universität des
        Saarlandes, 1976

Neueintragung in binären Suchbäumen
durch Verdrängung

C. Pokorny, TU Wien

Eine bekannte und viel verwendete Speicherform für die Speicherung von
Datenmengen ist der binäre Suchbaum. Das ist ein Baum, in dessen Knoten
Information und zugehörige Schlüssel gespeichert sind, und zwar so, daß
bei jedem Knoten gilt: Die Schlüssel in seinem linken Unterbaum sind
kleiner als der Schlüssel dieses Knotens und die Schlüssel in seinem
rechten Unterbaum sind größer. In Fällen, in denen die Datei häufigen
Änderungen durch Neueinfügen oder Löschen unterworfen ist, ist der binäre Suchbaum anderen Speicherformen überlegen.

Ein Qualitätskriterium für einen Suchbaum ist die mittlere Zugriffszahl
für das Aufsuchen eines beliebigen Knotens, die im wesentlichen gleich
der mittleren Pfadlänge ist. Letztere hängt von der Form des Suchbaumes
ab. Ist der Suchbaum ausgewogen, d.h.: linker und rechter Unterbaum
enthalten ungefähr gleichviele Knoten und beide sind wieder ausgewogen
usw., dann ist die mittlere Pfadlänge $\approx$ ld N, wobei N die Anzahl der Knoten des Baumes ist. Man spricht von einem entarteten Suchbaum, wenn für
die meisten Knoten gilt: Der linke Unterbaum enthält wesentlich mehr
oder wesentlich weniger Knoten als der rechte. Bei solchen Bäumen ist
die mittlere Pfadlänge viel größer als ld N. Bei einem extrem entarteten
Baum, bei dem in allen Knoten gilt, daß einer der Unterbäume leer ist,
ist sie sogar N/2.

Am meisten ausgewogen und daher in der mittleren Pfadlänge optimal ist
der symmetrische Baum. Das ist ein binärer Baum, bei dem alle Knoten
mit weniger als 2 Nachfolgern sich in 2 benachbarten Ebenen befinden.
Aber von der Verwendung dieses Baumes sieht man fast immer ab, da der
Änderungsdienst (Einfügen eines neuen Knotens oder Löschen eines vorhandenen), also auch der Aufbau durch sukzessives Einfügen von jeweils einem
neuen Knoten, sehr aufwendig ist.

Trifft man beim Ändern bzw. Aufbau des Baumes keinerlei Maßnahmen für
die Ausgewogenheit, so entsteht ein Random-Baum. Dieser kann entartet
sein, wobei allerdings die Wahrscheinlichkeit für eine krasse Entartung,
die die mittlere Pfadlänge proportional N machen würde, bei zufällig
ankommenden, ungeordneten Daten verschwindend gering ist [3]. Die mittlere Pfadlänge des Random-Baumes ist im Mittel von der Ordnung ld N,
allerdings im Durchschnitt um 38% höher als die des symmetrischen
Baumes.

Es sind daher Verfahren entwickelt worden, die beim Ändern, also auch
beim Aufbau, eine mäßige Ausgewogenheit des Baumes erzwingen, aber wesentlich weniger aufwendig sind. Die entstehenden Bäume sind z.B. der
AVL-Baum [1],[3], oder der Tree of Bounded Balance [1],[5], die auch
"balancierte Suchbäume" genannt werden. Der AVL-Baum erreicht mit geringem Aufwand eine mittlere Pfadlänge, die praktisch optimal ist, denn sie
liegt durchschnittlich nur 1 - 2% über dem Optimum. Eine Verbesserung
des Verhältnisses von Aufwand zu Ergebnis scheint kaum möglich. Um so
erstaunlicher ist es, daß es doch ein in dieser Hinsicht noch günstige-
res Verfahren gibt.

Bei der Verwendung eines balancierten Suchbaumes wird eine mittlere
Pfadlänge von der Größenordnung ld N auch in den Fällen garan-
tiert, in denen sich zu den gleichen Daten ein krass entarteter Random-
Baum einstellen würde. Wegen der außerordentlichen Seltenheit solcher
Entartungen bei zufällig ankommenden, ungeordneten Daten, wird im folgenden auf diese "Garantie" verzichtet, die doch einen Großteil des Aufwan-
des für den Änderungsdienst beim balancierten Suchbaum ausmacht. Mit
noch geringerem Aufwand erreicht man eine gute mittlere Pfadlänge, wenn
man mit dem sogenannten Verdrängungsbaum (V-Baum) arbeitet. Das Prinzip
des Änderungsdienstes besteht dabei darin, die Ausgewogenheit des Baumes
nur zu fördern, aber nicht zu erzwingen. Die Pfadlänge des V-Baumes liegt
im Mittel nur wenig höher als beim balancierten Suchbaum, aber viel
niedriger als beim Random-Baum und der Änderungsdienst ist äußerst einfach. Dieser V-Baum wird hier beschrieben und untersucht.

1. Die Verdrängung

Es sollen folgende Bezeichnungen gelten: K ist ein beliebiger Knoten,
L(K) bezeichnet den am weitesten rechts liegenden Knoten im linken
Unterbaum von K, falls dieser Unterbaum existiert, andernfalls ist L(K)
undefiniert. R(K) hat entsprechende Bedeutung. Der Schlüssel von K ist
SK, die Schlüssel von L(K) und R(K) sind SL(K) und SR(K). Beispiel:

Der Schlüssel und die Information eines Knotens werden im folgenden zusammengefaßt und mit Datensatz bezeichnet. Der Schlüssel des neu einzutragenden Datensatzes heißt SNEU, der neu erzeugte Knoten NEUKNO.

1.1. <u>Einfache Verdrängung</u>

Gilt bei einem Knoten K: SL(K)<SNEU<SK, so kann entweder NEUKNO den neuen Datensatz aufnehmen und rechts an L(K) angehängt werden oder der neue Datensatz kann in den Knoten K eingesetzt werden und den dort befindlichen Datensatz verdrängen. Im letzten Fall, der einfache Verdrängung nach rechts heißt, nimmt NEUKNO den verdrängten Datensatz auf und wird entweder links an R(K) oder, wenn R(K) nicht existiert, rechts an K angehängt.
Analog gibt es im Falle SK<SNEU<SR(K) die Möglichkeit einer einfachen Verdrängung nach links. Im folgenden Beispiel sind die Zahlen in den Knoten die Schlüssel.

Gegebener Baum:

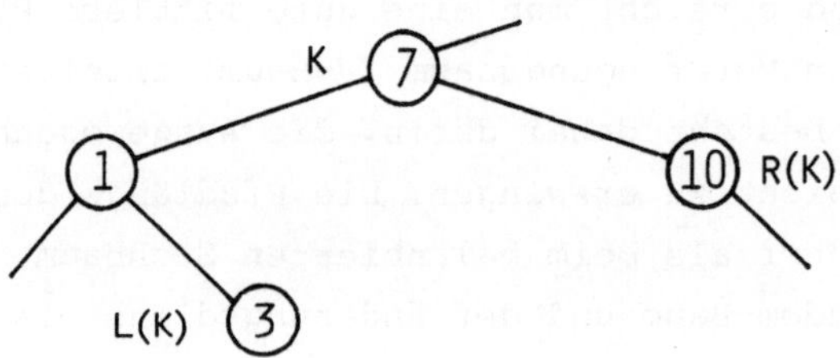

Eingefügt werden soll der Datensatz mit SNEU=5, es gilt SL(K)<SNEU<SK und man erhält

ohne Verdrängen: mit Verdrängen:

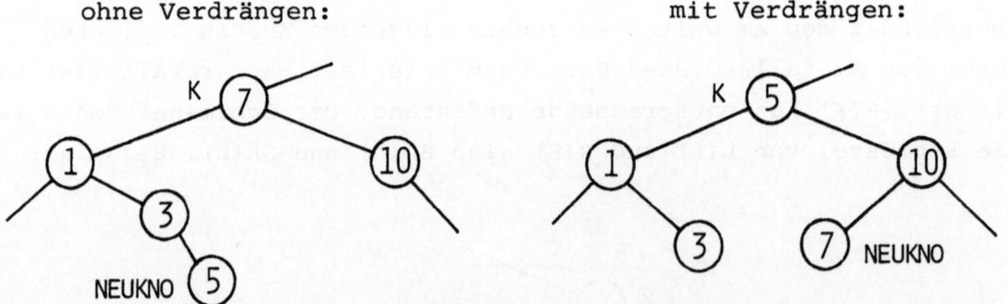

Die Verdrängung bringt also in diesem Fall eine Verringerung der Pfadlänge. Das ist aber nicht bei jeder Verdrängung der Fall. Soll in den gegebenen Baum ein Datensatz mit SNEU=8 eingefügt werden, so gilt SL<SNEU<SR(K) und man erhält

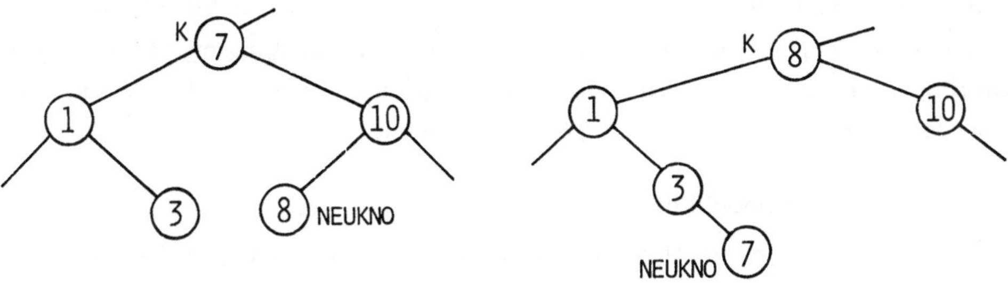

Diese Verdrängung vergrößert also die Pfadlänge.

1.2. Doppelte Verdrängung

Durch doppelte Verdrängung kann man in manchen Fällen, in denen die vorher besprochene einfache Verdrängung keine Verringerung der Pfadlänge bringt, eine solche dennoch erreichen. Soll in den gegebenen Baum ein Datensatz mit SNEU=2 eingefügt werden, dann erhält man ohne Verdrängen:

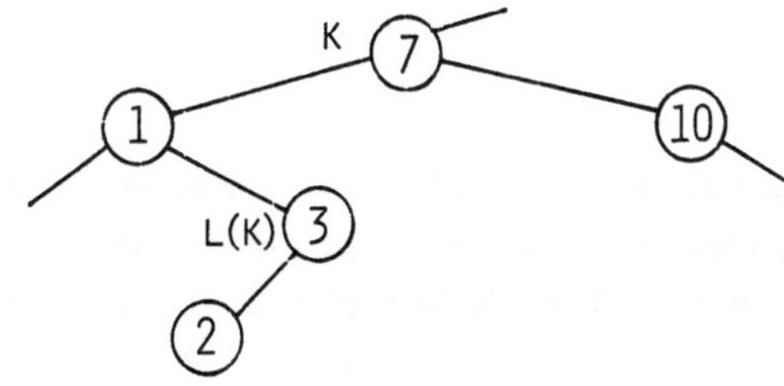

Es kann jedoch zunächst der neue Datensatz den in L(K) nach rechts verdrängen. Diese Verdrängung bringt keine Verringerung der Pfadlänge:

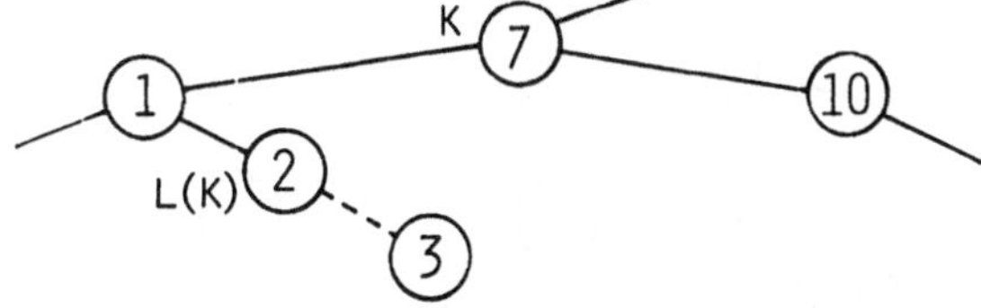

Anschließend kann der verdrängte Datensatz den in K nach rechts verdrängen, was u.U. eine Verringerung bringt:

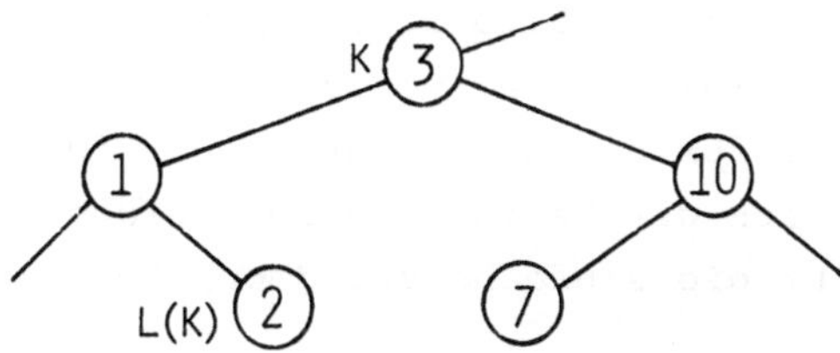

Wendet man bei Neueinfügungen in einem binären Suchbaum die einfache oder doppelte Verdrängung immer dann an, wenn sie eine Verringerung der Pfadlänge bewirkt, so entsteht nach vielen Neueinfügungen im Mittel ein Suchbaum mit erheblich geringerer Pfadlänge als beim Random-Baum. Dieser Baum heiße Verdrängungsbaum, abgekürzt V-Baum.

1.3. Fortgesetzte Verdrängung

Wird eine Verdrängung durchgeführt, so muß der verdrängte Datensatz in den Teilbaum, in den er verdrängt wurde, eingefügt werden. Statt dieser Einfügung kann man wieder eine Verdrängung vornehmen, die aber in dieselbe Richtung wie die vorhergehende gehen muß, denn sonst würde der ursprüngliche Zustand wiederhergestellt. Das kann solange fortgesetzt werden, wie die Verdrängungen eine Verringerung der Pfadlänge bringen. Theoretisch kann man, wenn man geeignet steuert, Entartungen des Baumes verhindern. Bei den für diese Arbeit erzeugten V-Bäumen wurde einfache und doppelte, aber keine fortgesetzte Verdrängung verwendet.

2. Methoden zur Durchführung der Verdrängung

2.1. Gefädelter Baum [4]

Eine Methode besteht darin, einen gefädelten Baum zu verwenden. Im gefädelten Baum zeigt jeder rechte Zeiger, der nicht zu einem Nachfolger zeigt, auf den Knoten mit dem nächstgrößeren Schlüssel und jeder linke Zeiger, der nicht auf einen Nachfolger zeigt, auf den mit dem nächstkleineren. Es muß dann im Knoten bei jedem Zeiger angegeben werden, ob er zu einem Nachfolger zeigt oder nicht. Im letzten Falle heißt der Zeiger Rückwärtszeiger. (Ausnahme: größter und kleinster Knoten im Baum).

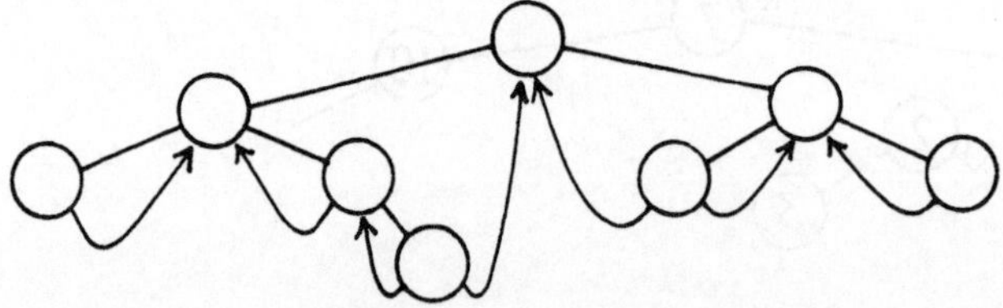

Geht man mit einem neu einzufügenden Datensatz im Baum bis zu dem Knoten, an den er normal angehängt würde, so zeigt der von dort ausgehende Rückwärtszeiger auf den Knoten, dessen Datensatz für eine Verdrängung in Frage kommt. Gehen zwei Rückwärtszeiger von dort aus, so zeigen beide auf solche Knoten, der eine für einfache, der andere für doppelte Verdrängung. Dies ist leicht aus der Definition des gefädelten Baumes und aus den Voraussetzungen für die einfache und doppelte Verdrängung herleitbar.

2.2. Nichtgefädelter Baum

Eine andere Methode ist die folgende: Der Knoten, an den ein neueinge-
fügter Datensatz normal angehängt würde, heiße "letzter Knoten". Wenn
man den Weg von der Wurzel des Baumes bis zum "letzten Knoten" durchgeht
(Suchweg), kann man sich die beiden Knoten merken, die für Verdrängung
nach links oder nach rechts in Frage kommen. Der "letzte linke Vorgänger"
das ist der letzte Knoten auf den Suchweg, bei dem zum rechten Nachfolger weitergegangen wurde, kommt für eine einfache Verdrängung nach
links in Frage, wenn NEUKNO normal linker Nachfolger des "letzten Knotens"
würde. Beispiel:

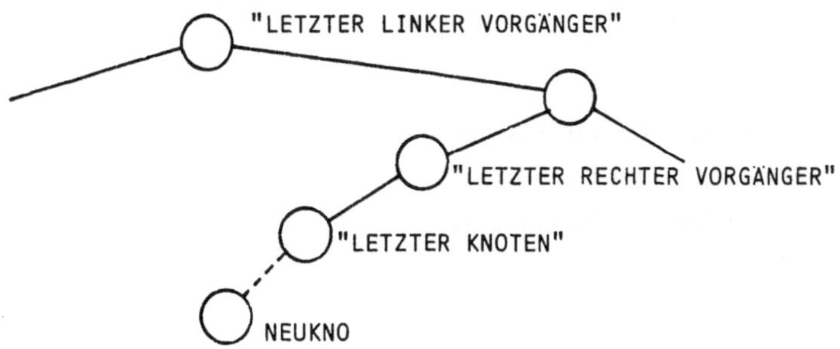

Für Verdrängung nach rechts käme in diesem Fall der Datensatz im "letzten Knoten" selbst in Frage, das würde aber keine Verringerung der Pfadlänge bringen. Hat der "letzte Knoten" keinen Nachfolger und würde NEUKNO
normal rechts angehängt, so wäre die doppelte Verdrängung: Neuer Datensatz → "letzter Knoten" → "letzter linker Vorgänger" möglich. Für den
"letzten rechten Vorgänger" gilt entsprechendes. Diese beiden Knoten
sind also diejenigen, die beim Durchgehen des Suchweges für eine eventuelle Verdrängung gemerkt werden müssen.

Bei beiden Methoden 2.1. und 2.2. muß es eine Möglichkeit geben, zu
erkennen, ob eine Verdrängung eine Verringerung der Pfadlänge bringt,
bevor sie durchgeführt wird. Hierzu wird in jedem Knoten K eine ganze
Zahl gespeichert, die die Differenz zwischen der Weglänge w_r von K zu
R(K) und der Weglänge w_l von K zu L(K) angibt. Beispiel:

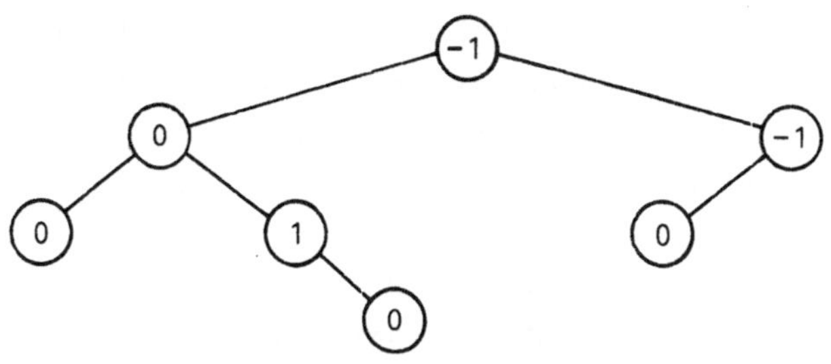

Sei K der Knoten, dessen Datensatz nach rechts verdrängt werden kann
und liege in Ebene x. In einem der Unterbäume von K wird ein neuer
Knoten angehängt und zwar:

ohne Verdrängen im linken, die Pfadlänge wächst um $x + w_l$

mit Verdrängen im rechten, die Pfadlänge wächst um $x + w_r$

(kann nach links verdrängt werden, dann ist es seitenvertauscht).

Die Kenntnis der Differenz $w_r - w_l$ ermöglicht die Entscheidung, ob Verdrängen oder gewöhnliches Anhängen eine geringere Zunahme der Pfadlänge
bewirkt.

3. Aufwand für den Änderungsdienst, Vergleich mit dem AVL-Baum

Bei der Aufwandsuntersuchung sollen folgende Größen berücksichtigt
werden:

> Anzahl der Zugriffe zu Knoten
>
> Anzahl der Umspeicherungen
>
> Anzahl der Differenzänderungen

Dabei werden einige Vernachlässigungen begangen. Diese werden den Vergleich aber kaum stören, da sie bei beiden Aufwandsuntersuchungen dieselben sind. Zumeist wird bei mehreren Aktionen an einem Knoten ein
einziger Zugriff zu diesem Knoten gerechnet. Z.B.: Das Ändern von 2
Komponenten eines Knotens wird praktisch bei allen Implementierungen
in höheren Pogrammiersprachen 2 Speicherzugriffe zu diesem Knoten erfordern. Es ist aber vorstellbar, daß Implementierungen geschaffen werden
können, die etwa einen ganzen Knoten in ein Register holen, alle Aktionen daran ohne weiteren Speicherzugriff an Ort und Stelle durchführen
und den geänderten Knoten wieder einspeichern. Rechnet man dafür einen
Zugriff, so hat man einen Mindestwert zugrundegelegt, der durch keine
Implementierung unterschreitbar ist.

In den meisten Fällen ist es berechtigt, die Umspeicherung eines Datensatzes als gleichaufwendig anzunehmen, wie die Umspeicherung eines
Zeigers (Zeigerumspeicherungen werden beim Änderungsdienst im AVL-Baum
verwendet). Für eine Zeigerumspeicherung ist es am günstigsten, wenn
der Zeiger für sich allein in einem ganzen Kernspeicherwort steht, bzw.
in einer direkt adressierbaren Hardware-Einheit. Leider bringt dies zumeist eine Speicherplatzverschwendung mit sich. Stehen die Zeiger in
irgendeiner platzsparenden Form, dann erfordert die Umspeicherung ein
Packen und Entpacken und wird zeitaufwendiger. - Die bei der Verdrängung
besprochene Umspeicherung betrifft den im Knoten befindlichen Datensatz
(Schlüssel und Information). Befinden sich Schlüssel und Information
in einem einzigen Kernspeicherwort, so ist der Aufwand für eine Daten-

satzumspeicherung genau so groß, wie für die günstigste Zeigerumspeicherung. Befinden sie sich in 2 Kernspeicherworten, dann müssen beide umgespeichert werden. Der Aufwand hierfür dürfte ungefähr dem beim Zeigerumspeichern in gepackter Form entsprechen. Ist die Information sehr lange, so daß sie sich über mehrere Kernspeicherworte erstreckt, dann ist es auf jeden Fall besser, nicht die Information, sondern einen Zeiger auf diese in den Knoten aufzunehmen. Wenn dieser Zeiger mit dem Schlüssel in ein Kernspeicherwort paßt, dann ist die Datensatzumspeicherung wieder die günstigste. Das Suchen ist in dem Fall praktisch nicht aufwendiger, da bei den meisten Implementierungen für die Abfrage des Schlüssels höchstens ein Ausblenden des Zeigers, aber weder Packen noch Entpacken erforderlich ist. Stehen Schlüssel und Zeiger auf die Information in getrennten Kerspeicherworten, dann hat man wieder einen schon oben beschriebenen Fall.

Aufwendig wird die Datensatzumspeicherung nur, wenn der Schlüssel selbst sehr lang ist und sich über mehrere Kernspeicherworte erstreckt. In einem solchen Fall muß einem Verfahren mit Zeigerumspeicherung der Vorzug gegeben werden. Die Datensatzumspeicherung bietet auf jeden Fall den Vorteil, daß man Zeiger immer in gepackter Form verwenden kann.

Zur Simulation der V-Bäume werden ganzzahlige Zufallszahlen im Bereich von 1 bis 2N erzeugt und diese als Schlüssel verwendet. Ist die gerade erzeugte Zufallszahl im Baum nicht vorhanden, dann wird sie eingefügt, andernfalls aus den Baum gelöscht. Dadurch kann das Verhalten der V-Bäume sowohl im Aufbau, als auch bei Nullwachstum (Zustand, in dem Einfügungen und Löschungen sich die Waage halten) getestet werden. Bei Beginn mit einem leeren Baum wächst dieser an, bis sich etwa bei N Knoten das Nullwachstum einstellt.

3.1. Aufbau eines Baumes durch sukzessives Einfügen

V-Baum

Führt man eine Verdrängung nicht durch, so hängt man den neuen Knoten direkt an den "letzten Knoten" an. Der Aufwand ist identisch mit dem für das normale Anhängen. Zusätzlichen Aufwand hat man für die Abfrage der Differenz(en), den wir vernachlässigen, und das Ändern der Differenzen in 2 Knoten. Dies bedingt einen zusätzlichen Zugriff zu einem Knoten.

Führt man die Verdrängung durch, so ist die Länge wl des Weges, den man mit dem verdrängten Datensatz zurücklegen muß, bis man ihn selbst einfügt, gleich der Anzahl der zusätzlichen Zugriffe, also die für den Aufwand interessanteste Größe.

Bei einer einfachen Verdrängung hat man eine Umspeicherung eines Datensatzes, bei einer doppelten deren zwei:

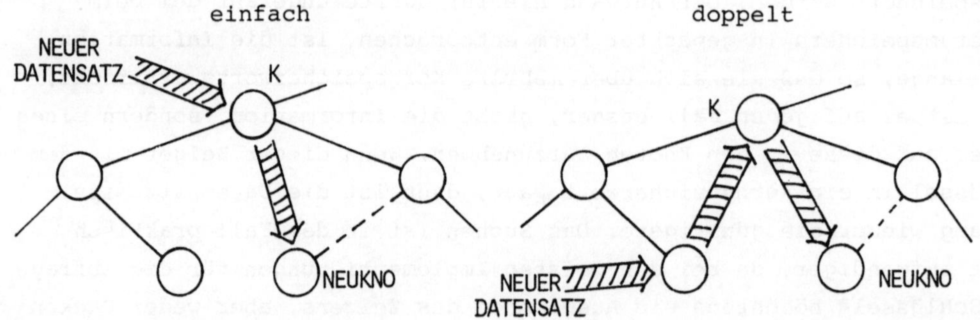

Das Einspeichern des verdrängten Datensatzes in den neuen Knoten erfolgt an Stelle der Einspeicherung des neuen Datensatzes und ist daher kein zusätzlicher Aufwand.

Um den durchschnittlichen Aufwand pro Einfügung feststellen zu können, braucht man folgende Werte:

v = Häufigkeit der Verdrängungen unter allen Einfügungen,

vdop = Anteil der doppelten an allen Verdrängungen,

wl = mittlere Weglänge pro Verdrängung.

Die Simulationen ergeben: v = 0.43   vdop = 0.35   wl = 1

Der letzte Wert ist ein sehr überraschendes Ergebnis.

In der Hälfte aller Verdrängungsfälle ist wl = 0, es wird also NEUKNO direkt an K angehängt und man braucht einen weiteren Zugriff zum vorletzten rechten bzw. linken Vorgänger um dort die Differenz zu ändern. Dies geht mit 0.5 Zugriffen in den Aufwand pro Verdrängung ein. Man hat daher für eine Verdrängung folgenden mittleren Aufwand:

2.5 Zugriffe, 1.35 Umspeicherungen und 2 Differenzänderungen.

Die mittlere Pfadlänge eines Baumes, der mit dieser Methode aus Zufallszahlen aufgebaut wird, ergibt sich zu 5% über dem Optimum, also 3 - 4% über der des AVL-Baumes. Dies ist ein Durchschnittswert, da die mittlere Pfadlänge einer gewissen Streuung unterliegt. Um diese Streuung zu veranschaulichen, wurden 50 Bäume von je 500 Knoten aufgebaut. Ihre mittlere Pfadlänge lag im Durchschnitt 5.4% über dem Optimum. Weiter wurden 30 Bäume von je 1000 Knoten aufgebaut, bei denen obiger Durchschnitt 5.3% über dem Optimum lag. Macht man eine prozentweise Klasseneinteilung von 2% bis 14% und trägt in jede Klasse die Anzahl der Bäume mit der entsprechenden Prozentzahl über dem Optimum ein, so erhält man folgende Aufteilung von diesen 80 Bäumen, die die Streuung und Verteilung der mittleren Pfadlänge solcher Bäume einigermaßen zeigt:

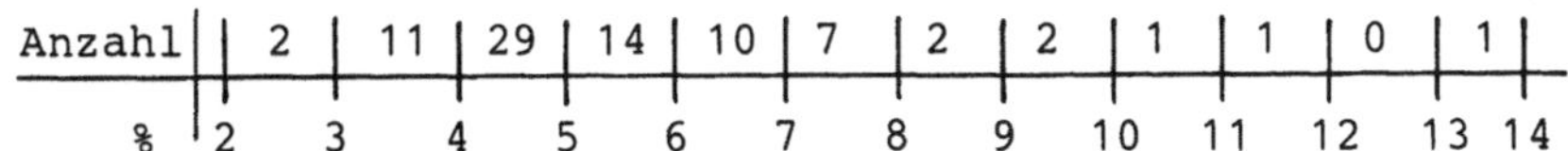

In der folgenden Zeichnung entspricht die Höhe des senkrechten Striches
der Anzahl der Bäume in der betreffenden Klasse.

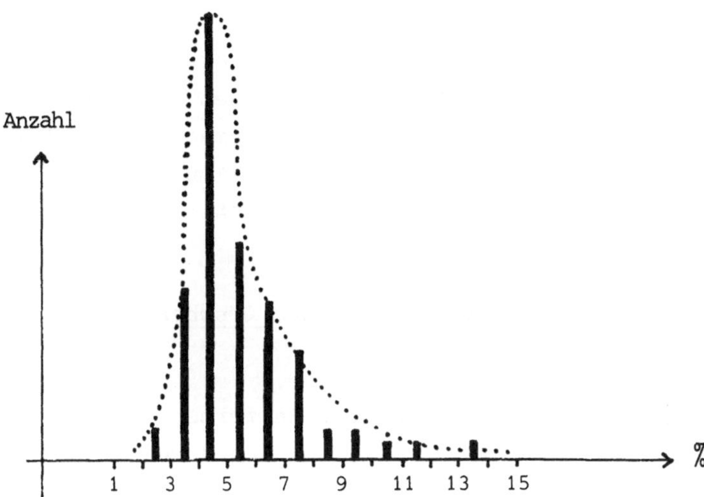

Bei 80% der Bäume liegt die mittlere Pfadlänge weniger als 7% über dem
Optimum.

Ist c_V die mittlere Pfadlänge im V-Baum, so ist der mittlere Aufwand
für eine Einfügung:

c_V + 1.6 Zugriffe, 0.6 Datensatzumspeicherungen
und 2 Differenzänderungen.

<u>AVL-Baum</u> [2]

Hier beträgt der Aufwand für eine einfache Rotation: 3 Zugriffe, 4 Um-
speicherungen und 2 Differenzänderungen, für eine doppelte Rotation:
4 Zugriffe, 6 Umspeicherungen und 3 Differenzänderungen.
Häufigkeit der Rotationen an allen Einfügungen: 0.4
Anteil der doppelten an allen Rotationen beim Einfügen: 0.5
Mittlere Anzahl der beim Kontrollprozeß zu ändernden Differenzen: 2.7
Für diese Differenzänderungen werden 1.7 zusätzliche Zugriffe gerechnet.

Ist c_{AVL} die mittlere Pfadlänge im AVL-Baum, so ist der mittlere
Aufwand für eine Einfügung:
c_{AVL} + 1.4 + 1.7 = c_{AVL} + 3.1 Zugriffe, 2 Zeigerumspeicherungen
und 3.7 Differenzänderungen.

Vergleichstabelle - Einfügen

	AVL-Baum	V-Baum
Zugriffe	c_{AVL}+3.1	c_V+1.6
Umspeichergn.	2	0.6
Diff.-Ändergn.	3.7	2

Nun gilt $c_{AVL} < c_V$ und zwar im Durchschnitt:

$c_{AVL} = c_{OPT}$*1.015 und $c_V = c_{OPT}$*1.055. Es ist denkbar, daß bei größeren Bäumen die Aufwandsersparnis bei den Zugriffen des V-Baumes durch die kürzere mittlere Pfadlänge des AVL-Baumes wettgemacht wird. Die Berechnung von c aus der Gleichung c*1.015 + 3.1 = c*1.055 + 1.6 ergibt für c = 37.5 und zeigt, daß der Ausgleich erst für Bäume ab der Größe 2^{37} Knoten eintritt.

3.2. Nullwachstum des Baumes bei Einfügen und Löschen

V-Baum

Wie beim AVL-Baum ist auch beim V-Baum das Entfernen (Löschen) eines Knotens möglich. Es ist aber nicht nötig, danach durch irgendwelche Reorganisationen wie beim AVL-Baum eine bestimmte Baumstruktur wiederherzustellen, da der V-Baum jede beliebige Form haben kann. Es wird daher beim Löschen auf eine Reorganisation durch Verdrängung, die theoretisch möglich wäre, ganz verzichtet. Nur müssen in 2 Knoten die Differenzen geändert werden und dafür werden 2 Zugriffe gerechnet. Im folgenden bedeutet Änderungsaufwand den mittleren Aufwand über gleichhäufiges Einfügen und Löschen.

Der mittlere Aufwand für eine Löschung ist:

c_V + 2 Zugriffe, 0 Umspeicherungen und 2 Differenzänderungen.

Der mittlere Aufwand für eine Änderung ist daher:

c_V + 1.8 Zugriffe, 0.3 Datensatzumspeicherungen und 2 Differenzänderungen.

Die mittlere Pfadlänge ist bei Nullwachstum noch etwas niedriger. Sie liegt nach einer gewissen Einpendelungszeit durchschnittlich 2 - 3% über dem Optimum.

AVL-Baum [2]

Häufigkeit der Rotationen an allen Löschungen: 0.2
Anteil der doppelten an allen Rotationen beim Löschen: 0.36
mittlere Anzahl der beim Kontrollprozeß zu ändernden Differenzen: 1.9
Für diese Differenzänderungen werden 1.9 Zugriffe gerechnet.
Der mittlere Aufwand für eine Löschung ist:

$c_{AVL} + 1.9 + 0.67 = c_{AVL} + 2.6$ Zugriffe, 0.9 Umspeicherungen
und 2.4 Differenzänderungen.

Der mittlere Aufwand für eine Änderung ist daher:

$c_{AVL} + 2.9$ Zugriffe, 1.5 Zeigerumspeicherungen
und 3.1 Differenzänderungen.

<u>Vergleichstabelle - Einfügen und Löschen</u>

	AVL-Baum	V-Baum
Zugriffe	$c_{AVL}+2.9$	$c_V+1.8$
Umspeichergn.	1.5	0.3
Diff.-Ändergn.	3.1	2

4. <u>Zeitmessungen</u>

Einen wirklichkeitsnahen, aber leider implementierungsabhängigen Auf-
schluß über den Aufwand geben Zeitmessungen. Zu diesem Zweck wurde eine
Folge von 2000 Zufallszahlen, die einen V-Baum mit 5.5% über dem Opti-
mum ergab, gespeichert. Mit dieser Folge wurden verschieden große AVL-
Bäume, V-Bäume und Random-Bäume aufgebaut und die Aufbauzeiten gemessen.
Die Verhältnisse der verbrauchten Zeiten blieben in etwa dieselben.
Bei 2000 Knoten ergab sich:

	Random-Baum	V-Baum	AVL-Baum
Millisekunden	259	342	463

Das folgende Schema soll den Durchschnittsaufwand der 3 Baumtypen zwischen den Extremen "Nur Ändern" (links) und "Nur Suchen" (rechts) zeigen.
Die Zeitmessungen bestätigen die Ergebnisse aus der Aufwandsuntersuchung.

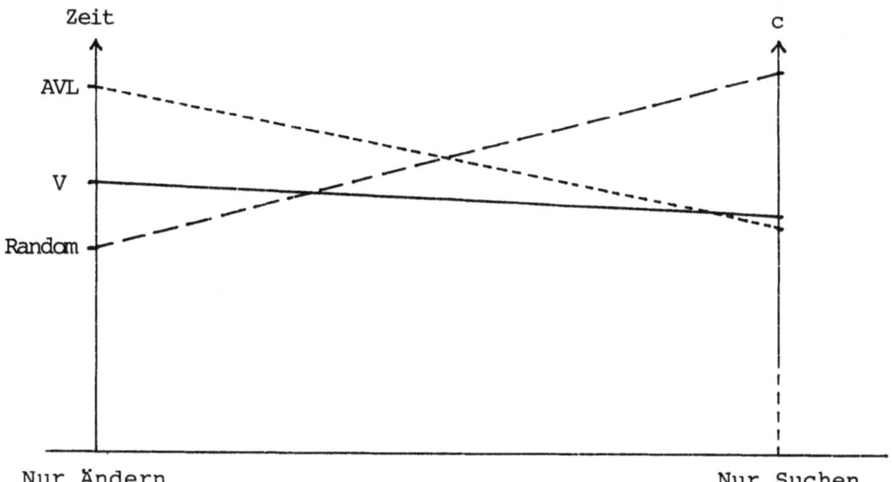

Schlußbemerkung

In allen Fällen erweist sich der V-Baum als weniger aufwendig mit einer fast so guten Pfadlänge wie der AVL-Baum. Es sei aber besonders hervorgehoben, daß der V-Baum diese Eigenschaften nur für zufällig ankommende Daten hat, die in keiner Weise geordnet sind. Liegt irgendeine Art von Ordnung oder Vorsortierung der Daten vor, dann kann der V-Baum wie der Random-Baum entarten (allerdings weniger stark). In solchen Fällen ist der AVL-Baum oder ein verwandtes Prinzip besser geeignet.

Es gibt noch den Einwand, daß der Random-Baum für das reine Ändern im Durchschnitt weniger aufwendig ist als der AVL-Baum, da er gar keine Reorganisation verlangt, was seine schlechte mittlere Pfadlänge wieder ausgleicht [3]. Aus dem Grunde könne man daher gleich einen Random-Baum verwenden, wenn man ganz zufällige Daten hat. Da aber das Suchen und nicht das Ändern bei einem Suchbaum die wichtigere Rolle spielt - siehe hierzu das Schema aus den Zeitmessungen - ist der Random-Baum mit seiner schlechten mittleren Pfadlänge im Nachteil, während diese beim V-Baum sehr nahe beim Optimum liegt.

Literatur

[1] Albrecht W., Die Konstruktion von Binär-Zugriffsbäumen,
        Dissertation, TH Darmstadt 1974.
[2] Karlton P.L., Fuller S.H., Scroggs R.E., Kaehler E.B., Performance
        of Height-Balanced Trees, CACM 19 (1976), S.23 - 28.
[3] Knuth D., Sorting and Searching, Vol.3, Addison-Wesley, 1973.
[4] Maurer H., Datenstrukturen und Programmierverfahren,
        Teubner Studienbücher 1974.
[5] Nievergelt J., Reingold E.M., Binary Search Trees of Bounded
        Balance, SIAM J.Computing 4 (1973), S. 33 - 43.

Zum optimalen Multiprogramming-Grad bei streuender Programm-Größe*

von Bernhard Walke
Mitteilung aus dem AEG-TELEFUNKEN-
Forschungsinstitut, Ulm

Zusammenfassung

Die Arbeit behandelt verkehrstheoretische Modelle einer Rechenanlage
im Stapelbetrieb. Das betrachtete Aufgabenprofil orientiert sich an
Messungen im Rechenzentrumsbetrieb. Mit zunehmender Zahl in einen begrenzt großen Arbeitsspeicher geladener Programme entfällt auf jedes
immer weniger Speicherplatz. Diese Platzbeschränkung verursacht zusätzliche Transporte, so daß Speicherplatz gegen Transportleistung
tauschbar wird. Der Durchsatz wird für den Fall konstanter Programmgröße exakt und bei streuender Größe näherungsweise berechnet. Die
vorgelegten Ergebnisse erlauben die Festlegung der optimalen Zahl
teilweise zu ladender Programme. Sie hängt ab von der Größe des Arbeitsspeichers und der Leistung von Transportkanal und Rechnerkern.
Alle in der Praxis mit virtuellen Speichersystemen und demand paging
gemachten guten und schlechten Erfahrungen werden durch die Rechenergebnisse anschaulich klar.

1. Einleitung

Für Rechenanlagen im Stapelbetrieb ist der Durchsatz (fertiggestellte
Programme pro Zeiteinheit) das allgemein anerkannte Leistungsmaß.
Typisch für solche Anlagen ist, daß der Vorrat an unbearbeiteten Programmen praktisch unbegrenzt ist. Im folgenden werden verkehrstheoretische Modelle betrachtet, in denen nur die Betriebsmittel Rechnerkern, Arbeitsspeicher und Transportkanal zwischen Arbeits- und Hintergrundspeicher enthalten sind. Es wird dabei unterstellt, daß die Programme keinen Ein-/Ausgabeverkehr zur Rechnerperipherie haben. Damit
ist der für technisch-wissenschaftliche Rechenzentren typische Betrieb mit asynchronem E/A-Verkehr (spooling) erfaßt. Jedes Programm
belegt während seiner Bearbeitung nacheinander den Kanal und den
Rechnerkern. Wenn es vollständig geladen ist, dann kann der Ablauf
nach Bild 1a modelliert werden: Nach einer Transportphase mit der

---

*) Die Arbeit ist zu 50 % durch das 2. DV-Programm der Deutschen
   Bundesregierung gefördert worden.

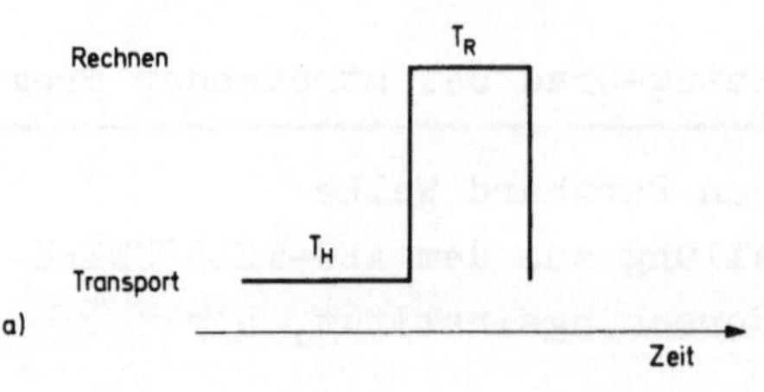

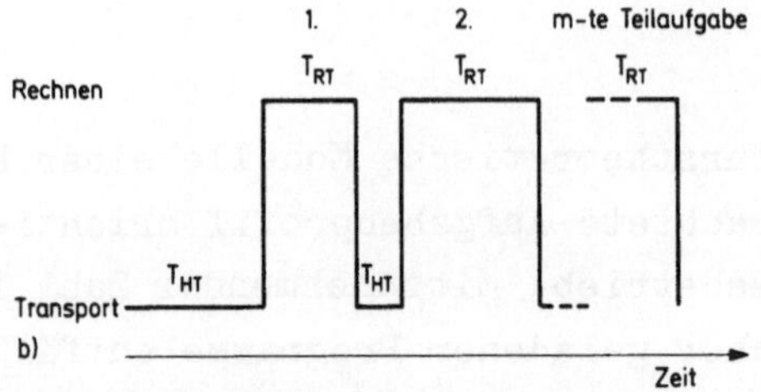

<u>Bild 1</u>: Modell der Programm-Bearbeitung
a) vollständig geladenes Programm: eine Transport- und
eine Rechenphase
b) unvollständig geladenes Programm: es entstehen m Teilaufgaben, jede mit einer Transportzeit T_{HT} und einer
Rechenzeit T_{RT}.

zufälligen Dauer T_H folgt eine Rechenphase der zufälligen Dauer T_R.
Wir sprechen im folgenden von "Programm-Plätzen" im Arbeitsspeicher.
Die Zahl der Plätze ist gleich der Zahl ladbarer Programme. Im Verlauf der Arbeit wird der Platzbedarf eines Programmes stärker spezifiziert werden. Es wird ein Belastungsprofil der Rechenanlage unterstellt, wie es für technisch-wissenschaftliche Rechenzentren typisch
ist. Die Modell-Annahmen stützen sich auf Meßergebnisse für technisch-wissenschaftliche Programme bei Großrechenanlagen, beispielsweise der CGK-TR 440. Damit erhalten die später betrachteten ver-
kehrstheoretischen Rechnermodelle einen unmittelbaren Bezug zur
Praxis.
Der Arbeitsspeicher ist ein entscheidender Kostenfaktor in einer
Rechenanlage. Man versucht deshalb, mit weniger Platz pro Programm
auszukommen, indem man Programme nicht vollständig mit allen Befeh-
len und Daten, sondern nur teilweise in den Arbeitsspeicher lädt.
Voraussetzung dafür ist das heute allgemein angewandte virtuelle
Speicherprinzip, zusammen mit einer demand-paging genannten Technik,
die das automatische Ergänzen teilweise geladener Programme erlaubt
[1]. Damit verspricht man sich eine deutliche Durchsatzverbesserung
durch das Laden von "working sets" verschiedener Programme, und

einen dadurch bei gegebenem Arbeitsspeicher gegenüber dem Laden vollständiger Programme spürbar erhöhten Multiprogramming-Grad. Diese
Hoffnung wird durch die Ergebnisse dieser Arbeit stark eingeschränkt.
Teilt man einem Programm einen kleineren als für den Bearbeitungsab-
lauf nach Bild 1a nötigen Arbeitsspeicher zu, dann zerfällt eine Programmbearbeitung in eine Folge mehrerer Transport- und Rechenphasen
(Bild 1b). Im Unterschied zur Aufgabenbearbeitung (Bild 1a) treten
jetzt Transportzeiten T_{HT} und Rechenzeiten T_{RT} von Teilaufgaben auf.
Nach Bild 1b ist eine Teilaufgabe nicht beendet, wenn der Rechnerkern ihre Bearbeitung vorübergehend unterbricht. Wird ein Programmteil mehrfach durchlaufen, dann hat die Platzbeschränkung im Arbeitsspeicher u.U. zur Folge, daß es mehrmals vom Hintergrundspeicher geladen werden muß - nämlich wenn es inzwischen zugunsten eines anderen
verdrängt worden ist. Dabei erhöht sich mit zunehmender Platzbeschränkung für ein Programm die Zahl der Transporte zwischen Arbeits- und
Hintergrundspeichern.

2. Zyklisches Modell mit n Plätzen im Arbeitsspeicher und genau einer Teilaufgabe pro Aufgabe

Erhält jede Aufgabe einen ihrem Adressenraum im virtuellen Speicher
entsprechenden Platz im Arbeitsspeicher, dann hat sie genau eine Teilaufgabe. Der Arbeitsspeicher muß dann sehr groß sein. Wir modellie-
ren die Programmbearbeitung entsprechend Bild 1a. Die Transportzeit
T_H und die Rechenzeit T_R einer Aufgabe werden als Zufallsvariable
mit bekannten Verteilungsfunktionen betrachtet. Wir setzen eine negativ exponentielle Transportzeitverteilung mit dem Erwartungswert
$E(T_H)$ an

$$P(T_H \leq t) = 1 - e^{-\mu_H t} \quad (2.1), \quad E(T_H) = 1/\mu_H . \quad (2.2)$$

Die Rechenzeiten werden durch eine entartet negativ exponentielle
Verteilung mit dem Erwartungswert $E(T_R)$ beschrieben

$$P(T_R \leq t) = 1-(1-p_g)e^{-\mu_R t} \quad (2.3) \quad E(T_R) = (1-p_g)/\mu_R \quad (2.4)$$

Ihre Streuung ist $\sigma^2(T_R) = (1-p_g^2)/\mu_R^2$.

Bild 2 zeigt ein Meßergebnis für die Summenhäufigkeit der Aufgaben-
rechenzeit mit einer Näherung nach Gl. (2.3) mit gleichem Mittelwert
und gleicher Streuung. Solche Messkurven sind auch aus der Literatur
bekannt. Der Ansatz Gl. (2.3) enthält für p_g = 0 den Spezialfall der

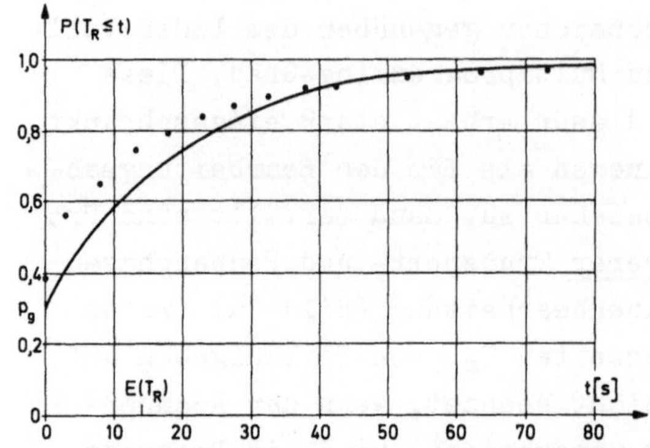

Bild 2:

Summenhäufigkeit von
Aufgaben-Rechenzeiten.
Messung (Punkte);
Näherung (Kurve) Gl.(2.3).

negativ exponentiellen Verteilung . Mit $p_g > 0$ kann die für technisch-
wissenschaftliche Programme festgestellte deutlich größere Streuung be-
friedigend nachgebildet werden. Es wird berücksichtigt, daß ein Teil
der Aufgaben sehr kurze Rechenzeiten haben. In der Näherung haben
diese Rechenzeiten die Dauer Null. Die Restrechenzeit-Verteilung einer schon die Zeit $t(t \geq 0)$ gerechneten Aufgabe ist eine Exponenti-
alverteilung mit dem Erwartungswert

$$E(T_R \mid T_R > 0) = 1/\mu_R . \qquad (2.5)$$

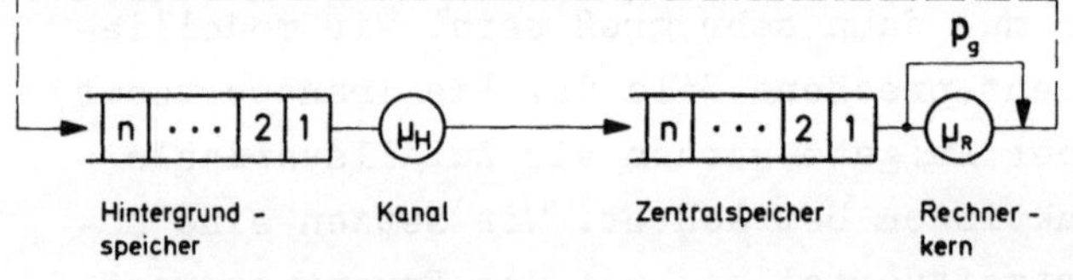

Bild 3:

Zyklisches Modell
zur Durchsatzbe-
rechnung.

Mit der Wahrscheinlichkeit p_g ist eine Aufgabe "kurz" ($T_R = 0$) und
mit ($1-p_g$) "lang". Bild 3 zeigt das Modell zur Durchsatzberechnung.
Es ist angenommen, daß eine gegebene Zahl n(= 1,2,...) von Aufgaben
gleichzeitig vorhanden sind. Jedem Platz in den beiden Warteschlangen entspricht ein Platz für die Befehle und Daten eines Programmes.
Ist die Transportzeit T_H einer Aufgabe durch den Kanal und die Rechenzeit T_R durch den Rechnerkern abgearbeitet, dann verläßt die
Aufgabe das Modell und gleichzeitig rückt im Hintergrundspeicher eine unbearbeitete Aufgabe nach. Durch die gestrichelt gezeichnete
Rückführung ist angedeutet, daß die nachrückende Aufgabe mit der fer-
tiggestellten identisch sein darf. Dieses zyklische Modell wurde in

[2] unter Voraussetzung einer optimalen Rechnerkern-Zuteilungsstrategie (Last Come First Serve) berechnet. Dabei belasten die Aufgaben mit der Rechenzeit $T_R=0$ den Rechnerkern nicht. Der Rechnerkern des Modells wird deshalb mit der Wahrscheinlichkeit p_g umgangen.

Der maximale Durchsatz, im folgenden einfach Durchsatz D genannt, wird zweckmäßigerweise auf den Rechenzeiterwartungswert $E(T_R)$ einer Aufgabe normiert und es ergibt sich

$$D \cdot E(T_R) = (\rho^n - 1)/(\rho^{n+1} - 1) \quad \text{mit } \rho = E(T_H)/E(T_R) \tag{2.6}$$

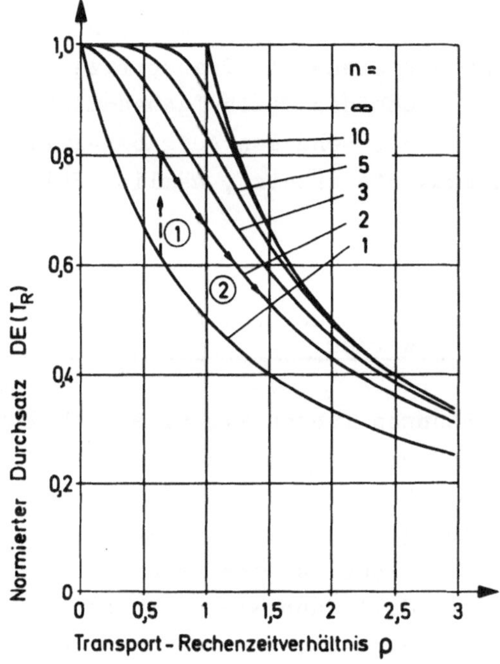

Bild 4:
Normierter Aufgabendurchsatz über dem Verhältnis der Mittelwerte von Transport- zu Rechenzeit einer Aufgabe, wenn genau n Programme im Arbeitsspeicher Platz haben.

Der Ausdruck $D \cdot E(T_R)$ ist die Wahrscheinlichkeit dafür, daß der Rechnerkern arbeitet (= Rechnerkernauslastung), Bild 4. Bei gegebenem Verhältnis ρ nimmt die Rechnerkernauslastung $D \cdot E(T_R)$ mit steigender Zahl der Plätze im Arbeitsspeicher zu, weil Kanal und Rechnerkern zunehmend gleichzeitig arbeiten können. Anstelle des Durchsatzes kann man auch die mittlere Dauer zwischen zwei aufeinanderfolgenden Aufgabenfertigstellungen betrachten. Diese "mittlere Bearbeitungszeit" ist der Kehrwert des Durchsatzes

$$E(T_B) = 1/D = (1-p_g)/(\mu_R \cdot D \cdot E(T_R)) \tag{2.7}$$

3. Zyklisches Modell mit n Plätzen im Arbeitsspeicher und vielen Teilaufgaben pro Aufgabe

Nimmt man an, daß ein Platz im Arbeitsspeicher nicht ausreicht, um den gesamten virtuellen Adressenraum eines Programmes aufzunehmen, dann zerfällt eine Aufgabe in Teilaufgaben (Bild 1b). Setzt man voraus, die Transportzeiten T_{HT} seien negativ exponentiell mit dem Erwartungswert $E(T_{HT})$ verteilt (Index T für Teilaufgabe) und die Rechenzeiten T_{RT} seien entartet negativ exponentiell verteilt mit dem Erwartungswert $E(T_{RT})$, dann kann man das zyklische Modell entsprechend Bild 3 für die Berechnung des Teilaufgaben-Durchsatzes verwenden. Nimmt man, wie bei der Durchsatzberechnung für Aufgaben, statistische Unabhängigkeit von Teilaufgabenrechen- und Transportzeiten an, dann kann man analog zu Abschnitt 2 auch den Teilaufgabendurchsatz ermitteln. Er ergibt sich aus Gl.(2.6), wenn man Aufgaben-Erwartungswerte durch Teilaufgaben-Erwartungswerte ersetzt, nämlich $E(T_R)$ durch $E(T_{RT})$ und $E(T_H)$ durch $E(T_{HT})$.

4. Aufgabendurchsatz für den Fall, daß Programme u.U. nur teilweise in den Arbeitsspeicher geladen werden

Für die nun folgenden weiteren Betrachtungen führen wir einen Arbeitsspeicher mit begrenzter Größe GR ein und unterstellen außerdem, daß ein vollständiges Programm die Größe G habe. Man kann sich nun weiterhin darauf beschränken, nur vollständige Programme zu laden und erhält ihre Anzahl dann aus $n=m=int(GR/G)$, wobei n eine natürliche ganze Zahl ist. Der zugehörige Durchsatz darf dann wie in Abschn. 2 berechnet werden. Mann kann jedoch auch zulassen, daß $n > m$ Programme unvollständig in den Arbeitsspeicher geladen werden, wobei Aufgaben in Teilaufgaben zerfallen. Aus Bild 4 entnimmt man, daß bei gegebenem Transport-Rechenzeitverhältnis ρ der Durchsatz mit der Zahl n vollständig geladener Programme zunimmt. Entsprechend ① würde bei Verdoppelung der Arbeitsspeicher-Größe (entsprechend der Verdoppelung von n) die Rechnerkern-Auslastung von 0.6 auf $\sim$ 0.8 wachsen. Ohne Arbeitsspeicher-Vergrößerung könnten n=2 Programme nur je teilweise geladen werden. Zwar würde weiterhin die Kurve für n=2 in Bild 4 gelten, aber wegen der vergrößerten Gesamttransportzeit (bei unveränderter Gesamtrechenzeit) würde man entsprechend ② in Pfeilrichtung abrutschen, so daß ein Durchsatzgewinn fraglich wird. Die Entscheidung für oder gegen teilweises Laden hängt bei gegebenem Verhältnis ρ und bekanntem Größenverhältnis GR/G davon ab, wieviele

Transporte für eine Aufgabe zusätzlich nötig werden, wenn sie nicht vollständig in den Arbeitsspeicher geladen wird.

4.1 Arbeitsspeicher-Verwaltungsstrategie

Wir führen jetzt eine Vorschrift ein, wie ein Arbeitsspeicher gegebener Größe zu unterteilen ist. Eine Arbeitsspeicher-Verwaltungsstrategie (dp,$\geq$n) soll bedeuten, daß der Arbeitsspeicher mindestens n Programme aufnehmen muß. Ist der verfügbare Arbeitsspeicher kleiner als die Programmgröße nG, dann wird jedes Programm zu gleichem Anteil x=GR/(nG) geladen. Bei streuender Programmgröße (Annahme für Abschnitt 6) ist X eine Zufallsvariable mit Werten ($0\leq x\leq 1$)

$$X = \begin{cases} GR/\sum_{i=1}^{n} & \text{bei } GR < \sum_{i=1}^{n} G_i \\ 1 & \text{sonst } (n=1,2,\ldots). \end{cases} \qquad (4.1)$$

Dabei sind die G_i Realisationen der Variablen G. Bei ausreichend großem Arbeitsspeicher dürfen auch mehr als die vorgeschriebenen n Programme -aber nur vollständig- geladen werden (n ganzzahlig).

Beispielsweise muß unter der Strategie (dp,$\geq$2) der Arbeitsspeicher so verwaltet werden, daß jederzeit zwei Programme - bei Platzmangel je teilweise - dorthin geladen werden können. Passen 3,4,... Programme vollständig hinein, dann dürfen sie geladen werden. Bei konstanter Größe vollständiger Programme und gegebener Arbeitsspeichergröße GR liegt nach einmaliger Berechnung fest, ob n=2 oder mehr Programme Platz haben. Bei streuender Programmgröße kann sich nach Fertigbearbeitung jedes Programmes die Zahl n abhängig von der Größe der nachfolgenden Programme ändern. Die Strategie (dp,$\geq$1) ist ein besonders interessanter Grenzfall: teilweises Laden tritt nur dann auf, wenn nicht einmal 1 Programm vollständig Platz hat.

4.2 Weitere Voraussetzungen

In [2] werden die gemachten Voraussetzungen mit Meßergebnissen von technisch-wissenschaftlichen Rechenanlagen verglichen und ausführlich erläutert.

1.) Die Zahl M(x) von Teilaufgaben pro Aufgabe hängt vom Ladeanteil x eines Programmes ab. M(x) ist eine Zufallsvariable, die zugehörige Zählgröße heißt m(x). Bei x=1 hat eine Aufgabe nur eine Teilaufgabe.

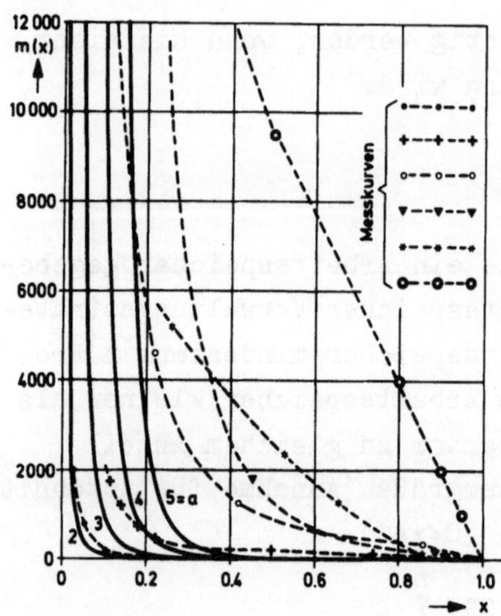

Bild 5:

Messungen für die Zahl m(x)
von Teilaufgaben pro Aufgabe
bei Laden eines Prozentsatzes
x · 100 % des virtuellen
Speichers eines Programmes
in den Arbeitsspeicher. Die
Messkurven gelten für verschiedene Programme.

Bild 5 gibt die Meßergebnisse für die Zahl m(x) von Teilaufgaben bei
bekanntem Anteil x im Arbeitsspeicher und Programmbearbeitung mit
Hilfe von demand paging wieder [2] und zeigt Näherungskurven für die
mittlere Zahl E(M(x)) von Teilaufgaben pro Aufgabe

$$E(M(x)) = x^{-a}, \qquad a > 0. \qquad (4.2)$$

Für normale Benutzerprogramme ist a $\geq$ 5 und für speziell vorbehandel-
te Programme ist a > 2 typisch.

2.) Ein nur teilweise geladenes Programm ($0 < x \leq 1$) kann nur für die
Dauer der Teilaufgabe $T_{RT}(x) \leq T_R$ (vgl. Bilder 1a,b) ununterbrochen
gerechnet werden. Teilaufgaben-Rechenzeiten seien, wie bisher für
Aufgaben-Rechenzeiten unterstellt, entartet negativ exponentiell
verteilt. Es gelte

$$E(T_R) = E(M(x)) \cdot E(T_{RT}(x)) \qquad (4.3)$$

3.) Vor der Bearbeitung einer Teilaufgabe durch den Rechnerkern ist
ein Transport der Dauer $T_{HT}(x)$ notwendig. Der Erwartungswert ist
$E(T_{HT}(x))$. Die Transportzeit einer Teilaufgabe wird –wie die Transportzeit T_H der Aufgabe- durch eine negativ exponentielle Verteilung
beschrieben. Es gelte näherungsweise (Diskussion siehe [2])

$$E(T_{HT}(x)) = g\left\{ E(T_H), x \right\} = [c + (1-c)x^b] E(T_H). \qquad (4.4)$$

Für c=1 ist $E(T_{HT}(x))=E(T_H)$. Das Bildungsgesetz für Teilaufgaben bei Platzbeschränkung für Programme streut so stark (vgl. Bild 5), daß diese Näherung im Rahmen der hier angestrebten Genauigkeit ausreicht [2].

4.) Die Größen $M(x)$, $T_{RT}(x)$, $T_{HT}(x)$, G sind statistisch vollständig unabhängig unterstellt.

4.3 <u>Aufgabendurchsatz als Funktion des Ladeanteils x von Programmen</u>

Wir betrachten fortan den Aufgabendurchsatz D, denn er ist auch im praktischen Rechenzentrumsbetrieb die interessierende Größe. Der Teilaufgabendurchsatz D_T ist um die mittlere Zahl $E(M(x))$ von Teilaufgaben pro Aufgabe größer (Gl. (4.3))

$$D_T \cdot E(T_R(x)) = D_T \cdot E(T_R)/E(M(x)) = D \cdot E(T_R) \tag{4.5}$$

Wir wissen schon aus Abschnitt 3, daß die Rechnerkernauslastung $D_T \cdot E(T_{RT}(x))$ mit Teilaufgaben analog wie die für Aufgaben berechnet werden kann. Durch die Voraussetzungen in Abschnitt 4.2 kann der Aufgabendurchsatz mit Hilfe des Ladezustands x von Programmen als Funktion der Mittelwerte für Transport- und Rechenzeit von Teilaufgaben ausgedrückt werden. Nach Gln. (4.3, 4.4) ist

$$\rho_T(x) = E(T_{HT}(x))/E(T_{RT}(x)) = g\left\{E(T_H),\ x\right\}/E(T_R) \cdot E(M(x)). \tag{4.6}$$

Für vollständig geladene Programme (x=1) ist $\rho_T(x) = \rho$ (Gl.2.6). Für den Fall c=1 in Gl.(4.4) ergibt sich mit Gl.(4.2)

$$\rho_T(x) = E(T_H)/E(T_R) \cdot E(M(x)) = \rho \cdot x^{-a} .$$

Unter Verwendung von Gl.(4.6) und den Erkenntnissen aus Abschnitt 3 kann man den in Gl.(2.6) berechneten normierten Aufgabendurchsatz für den Fall, daß n Programme nur teilweise in den Arbeitsspeicher passen (x<1), berechnen aus

$$D \cdot E(T_R) = (\rho_T^n(x)-1)/(\rho_T^{n+1}(x)-1) \tag{4.7}$$

mit $D \cdot E(T_R) = n/(n+1)$ für $\rho_T(x) = 1$.

Ist der Arbeitsspeicher genügend groß, so daß n Programme vollständig Platz haben, dann gilt weiterhin Gl.(2.6).

5. Ergebnisse für den Durchsatz bei konstanter Programmgröße und demand paging

Uns interessiert, ob oder wann es besser für den Durchsatz ist, einen Arbeitsspeicher gegebener Größe mit n vollständig oder mit > n teilweise geladenen Programmen zu füllen. Deshalb vergleichen wir Rechenergebnisse für den normierten Durchsatz bei verschiedenen Arbeitsspeicher-Verwaltungsstrategien (dp,≐n). Anstelle der Anzahl von Plätzen ist jetzt die bezogene Arbeitsspeichergröße GR/G Parameter. Die Berechnung des Durchsatzes für vollständig geladene Programme erfolgt nach Gl.(2.6) und für unvollständig geladene Programme nach Gl.(4.7). Bei der Strategie (dp,≐n) bezieht sich der Bereich $0 \leq GR/G < n$ auf unvollständig geladene Programme und der Bereich $n \leq GR \leq \infty$ auf vollständig geladene Programme.

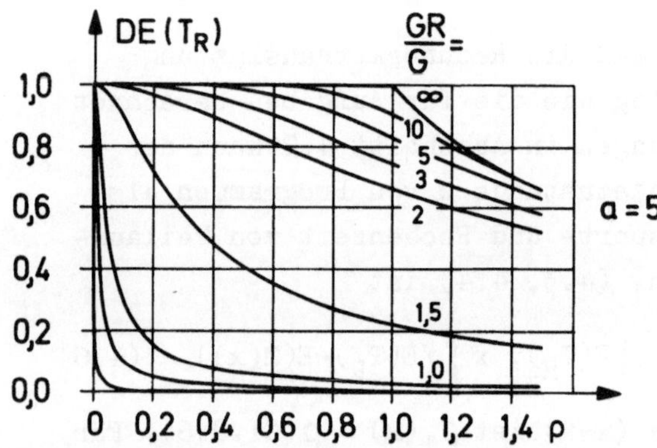

Bild 6:
Normierter Aufgabendurchsatz über dem Transport-Rechenzeitverhältnis ρ. Arbeitsspeicher-Verwaltungsstrategie (dp,≐2).

Bild 6 zeigt ein Resultat für die Belegungsstrategie (dp,≐2). Für GR/G=2,3,... stimmen die Bilder 4 und 6 überein; neu sind die Kurven für GR/G<2 (= weniger als zwei Plätze im Arbeitsspeicher). Für die Entscheidung, welche Wahl für die Zahl n zu ladender Programme durchsatzoptimal ist, benötigen wir eine Darstellung mit unterschiedlichen Werten von n=1,2,... für (dp,≐n). Um die Übersichtlichkeit zu erhalten, wird das Transport-Rechenverhältnis ρ von Aufgaben jetzt als Parameter betrachtet. Bild 7 zeigt für ρ = 0.25 die Rechnerkernauslastung D.E(T_R) über der normierten Arbeitsspeichergröße GR/G. Es sind Schaubilder für a=2,5 angegeben; in jedem ist das Ergebnis von 5 Verwaltungsstrategien (dp,≐n) mit n=1,2,3,4,5 eingetragen. Bei gegebener Konfiguration einer Rechenanlage hat ein Rechenzentrum nur begrenzten Einfluß auf den für seine Benutzeraufgaben erzielbaren Durchsatz. Eine wichtige Möglichkeit ist die Wahl der Verwaltungsstrategie des Arbeitsspeichers (dp,≥n).

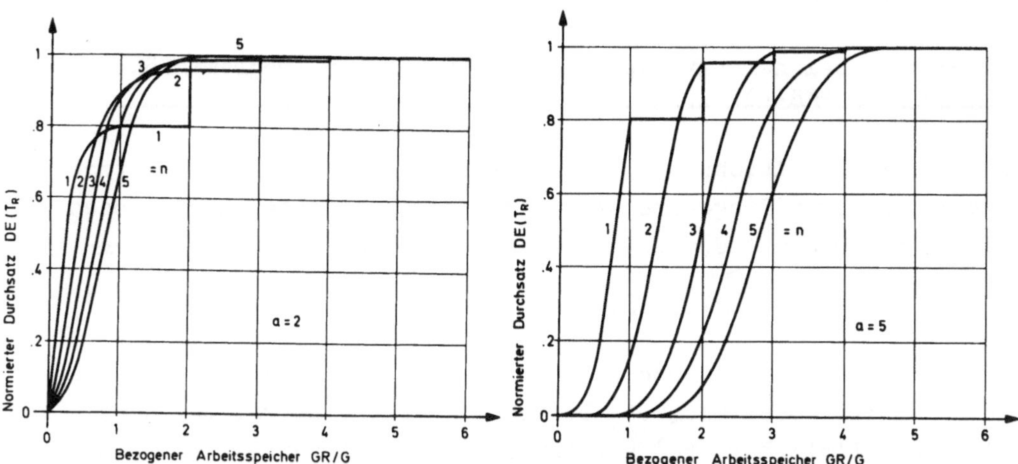

__Bild 7__: Arbeitsspeicher-Verwaltungsstrategie (dp,≥n). Transportzeitnäherung nach Gl.(4.4) mit c=0,2, b=2. Konstante Programmgröße. Für beide Bilder ist ρ = 0.25, sie unterscheiden sich im Parameter a.

Man sieht aus Bild 7, daß es abhängig von der Parameterkonstellation $\{a,\ GR/G, \rho\}$ jeweils eine durchsatzoptimale Strategie gibt, solange der Durchsatz verschiedener Strategien unterschiedlich ist. Die Sprungstellen bei GR/G = 2,3,... entstehen deshalb, weil ein weiteres Programm im Arbeitsspeicher Paltz hat und deshalb der Durchsatz steigt. Die Sprunghöhe ist für die Belegungsstrategie (dp,≥1) mit Abstand größer als für (dp,≥n), n=2,3,... . Sie nimmt außerdem für ρ von Null bis 1.0 wachsend stetig zu und für ρ >1 wachsend stetig ab. Mit zunehmendem Parameter a nimmt der Bereich GR/G, der zu einer Durchsatzsteigerung der Strategie (dp,≥2) gegenüber (dp,≥1) führt, ab.
Wählt man die Strategie (dp,≥2) und ist die Parameterkonstellation $\{a,\ GR/G\}$ ungünstig, dann erzielt man anstelle der erhofften relativ kleinen Durchsatzsteigerung unter Umständen einen großen Durchsatzverlust. Das Risiko eines Durchsatzverlustes durch Anwendung einer Verwaltungsstrategie (dp,≥n) mit n>1 gegenüber der Strategie (dp,≥1) ist umso größer, je größer a ist. Messungen an Benutzerprogrammen (Bild 5) zeigen, daß man mit Werten a≥5 rechen muß und dann ist das Risiko schon erheblich. Zusammenfassend kann man sagen, daß man bei nicht genau bekannter Parameterkombination $\{\rho, a,\ GR/G\}$ Verwaltungsstrategien (dp,≥n) mit n>2 als zu riskant ablehnen muß, denn die gegenüber (dp,≥2) mögliche Durchsatzsteigerung ist sicher

nur gering, die andernfalls zu erwartende deutliche Durchsatzeinbuße
aber bedrohlich groß.

6. Durchsatz bei negativ exponentiell verteilter Programmgröße und demand paging

Im Unterschied zu Abschnitt 5 nehmen wir jetzt an, daß der Platzbedarf vollständiger Programme streut und durch eine negativ exponentielle Verteilung mit dem Erwartungswert E(G) beschrieben werden
darf

$$P(G \leq g) = 1 - e^{-g/E(G)}. \tag{6.1}$$

Bei konstanter Programmgröße kann für jede gegebene Arbeitsspeichergröße GR entsprechend Gl.(4.1) berechnet werden, zu welchem Anteil x
ein Programm Platz hat. Bei negativ exponentiell verteilter Größe
ist -bei konstanter Arbeitsspeichergröße GR- der Anteil x für verschiedene teilweise geladene Programme unterschiedlich (nämlich eine
Zufallsgröße X). Es können jetzt für einen gegebenen Arbeitsspeicher
zu einem Zeitpunkt mehrere Programme, je vollständig, gleichzeitig
Platz haben, während zu einem anderen Zeitpunkt nicht einmal ein
Programm vollständig hineinpasst.

Eine exakte Durchsatzberechnung ist hier nicht möglich [2]. Deshalb
wählen wir ein Näherungsverfahren. Dabei werden die mittleren Bear-
beitungszeiten zyklischer Modelle mit genau n zirkulierenden Programmen, wie in Abschnitt 2 (Gln.2.6, 2.7) und Abschnitt 4.3 (Gl.4.7),
exakt berechnet. Bei vollständig geladenen Programmen wird mit der
Wahrscheinlichkeit p_n des Auftretens des Falles "n Programme haben
vollständig Platz" gewichtet. Bei teilweise geladenen Programmen
wird mit der Wahrscheinlichkeitsdichte gewichtet, daß n Programme
je zum Anteil x(0<x≤1) Platz haben und über x intergriert.

Die Wahrscheinlichkeit p_n, daß n(=1,2,...) Programme mit dem Größen-
erwartungswert E(G) vollständig in den Arbeitsspeicher der Größe GR
passen, ist nach [2] eine Poisson-Verteilung

$$p_n = \gamma^n/n! \cdot e^{-\gamma} \quad , \quad \gamma = GR/E(G) \tag{6.2}$$

Die bedingte Wahrscheinlichkeitsverteilung des Platzbedarfs Gn von
zusammen n Programmen P(xGn<GR|Gn≥GR) berechnet man aus der Restver-
teilung für Gn<g, bezogen auf die Wahrscheinlichkeit P(Gn≥GR). Daraus erhält man die bedingte Wahrscheinlichkeitsdichte dafür, daß n
Programme zusammen größer als g=GR/x sind, aus [2] zu

$$p(x) = \gamma^n / \left\{ x^{n+1} \left[(n-1)! \sum_{j=0}^{n-1} \gamma^j / j! \right] e^{-\gamma(1/x-1)} \right\} \qquad (6.3)$$

$$(x \leq 1).$$

Die benötigte Wahrscheinlichkeit p_n und die erforderliche Dichte
können also exakt berechnet werden. Der Näherungscharakter der Rechnung ergibt sich daraus, daß stationäre Bedingungen unterstellt werden, während sich in Wirklichkeit durch die Übergänge von n nach mehr
oder weniger vollständig, bzw. unvollständig ladbaren Programmen Einschwingvorgänge ergeben. Diese Einschwingvorgänge bleiben unberücksichtigt.

6.1 Ergebnisse für die Strategie (dp,≥1)

Die Berechnung des Durchsatzes bei zufällig streuender Programmgröße
wurde nur näherungsweise durchgeführt. Die Näherungsrechnung wurde durch
Simulation kontrolliert, Bild 8. Die eingetragenen Meßpunkte sind
mit 95 % statistischer Sicherheit auf ≤ ± 3 % genau bestimmt worden,
wenn nicht ein größeres Vertrauensintervall eingezeichnet ist. Die
Übereinstimmung von Simulation und Rechnung ist gut.

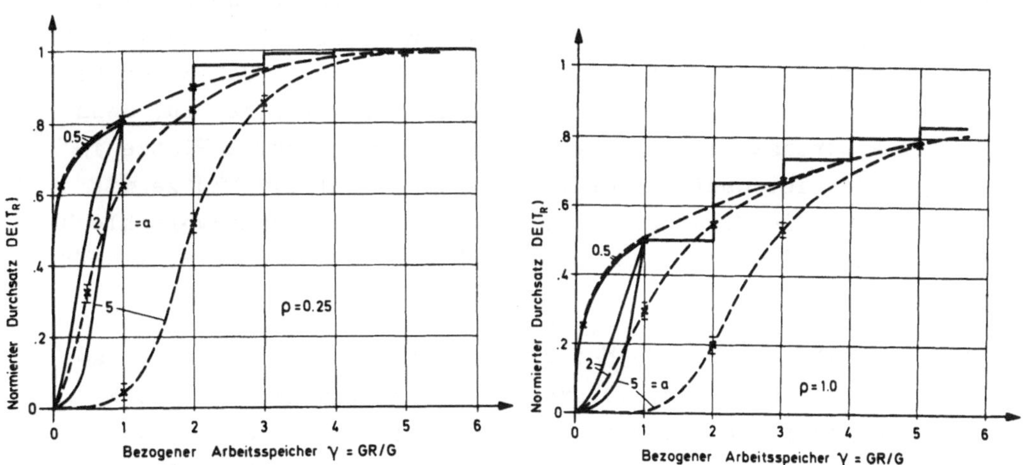

Bild 8: Verwaltungsstrategie (dp,≥1). Konstante (ausgezogene Kurven)
und negativ exponentiell verteilte (gestrichelt) Programmgröße. Transportnäherung (Gl.4.4) mit c = 1.
Die Bilder unterscheiden sich im Parameter ρ.

Neben dem Rechenergebnis bei negativ exponentiell verteilter Programmgröße ist insbesondere ein Vergleich des Einflußes der Programmgrößen
Streuung (bei ρ = konst.) auf den Durchsatz interessant. Der Durchsatz ist bei konstanter Programmgröße meistens, aber nicht immer,
höher. Das hat folgenden Grund: Bei konstanter Programmgröße ist ein
Teil des Arbeitsspeichers ungenutzt, weil kein weiteres Programm
vollständig Platz hat. Im Grenzfall hat dort beinahe ein ganzes Programm Platz. Bei streuender Programmgröße zeigt sich, daß dann genügend oft mehr Programme, als bei konstanter Größe, geladen werden
können, so daß der Durchsatz durch Parallelarbeit wächst. Für Arbeitsspeichergrößen, die gerade für n vollständig geladene Programme
konstanter Größe ausreichen, liest man ab, daß die Streuung der Programmgröße den Durchsatz verkleinert. Je größer a ist, umso größer
ist der Abszissenbereich, in dem der Durchsatz bei konstanter Programmgröße am größten ist.

6.2 Ergebnisse für die Strategie (dp,$\geq$n)

Ein Hauptziel dieser Arbeit ist, zu klären, ob und unter welchen Umständen bei streuender Programmgröße der Durchsatz durch eine Strategie (dp,$\geq$n) mit n>1 gegenüber der Strategie (dp,$\geq$1) verbessert
werden kann. Wir wollen also wissen, ob der Durchsatz durch -mit
Hilfe teilweisen Ladens von Programmen- ermöglichte Parallelarbeit
verbessert werden kann. Entscheidene Bedeutung kommt dabei dem Vergleich der Durchsätze der Strategien (dp,$\geq$1) und (dp,$\geq$2) zu, denn
der absolute Durchsatzzuwachs beim Übergang von 1 auf 2 Plätze im
Arbeitsspeicher ist deutlich größer als von i auf i+1 Plätze mit
i<1. Führt also die Strategie (dp,$\geq$2) zu einer Durchsatzverschlechterung gegenüber (dp,$\geq$1), dann sind auch Strategien (dp,$\geq$n) mit n>2
ungünstig.

Aus Bild 9 liest man ab, daß bei a=2 und genügend großem Arbeitsspeicher die Strategie (dp,$\geq$2) spürbar durchsatzgünstiger ist als
(dp,$\geq$1). Dagegen ist bei a=5 durchweg die Strategie (dp,$\geq$1) am günstigsten. Eingehende Untersuchungen [2] zeigen, daß für a$\geq$3 die Strategie (dp,$\geq$1) vorzuziehen ist. Nach Messungen ist für Benutzerprogramme a>3 typisch. Die Rechnung ergibt, daß eine nur durch teilweises Laden erreichbare Parallelbearbeitung solcher Programme unterbleiben sollte, d.h. sie sollten vollständig geladen werden.
Aus dem Vergleich der Ergebnisse in den Bildern 8 und 9 sieht man,
daß die Wahl der Transportzeitnäherung einen großen Einfluß auf das

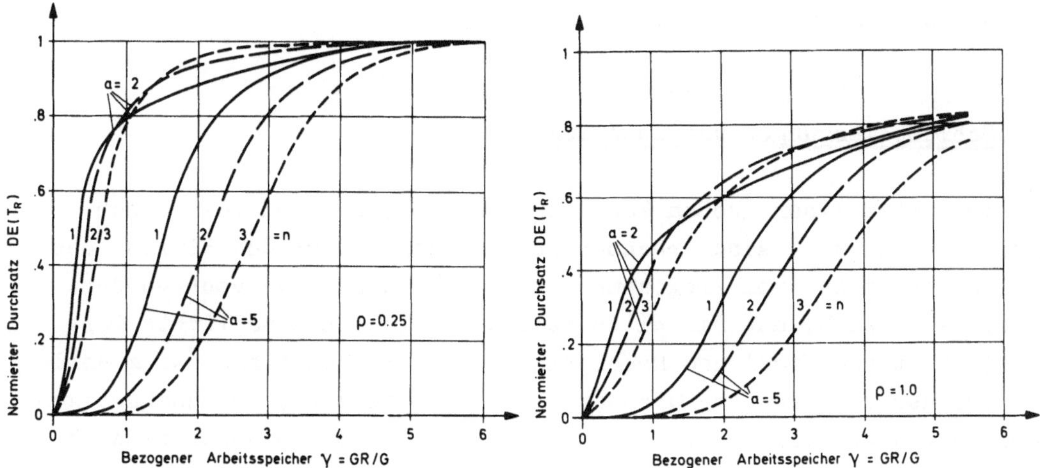

<u>Bild 9</u>: Arbeitsspeicher-Verwaltungsstrategie (dp,≥n) mit n=1,2,3. Transportnäherung (Gl.4.4) mit c=0.2, b=2. Negativ exponentiell verteilte Programmgröße. Die Bilder unterscheiden sich im Parameter ρ.

zahlenmäßige Ergebnis für den Durchsatz hat. Die Näherung hat aber (was in [2] gezeigt ist) nur einen geringen Einfluß auf die Auswahl der günstigsten Arbeitsspeicher-Verwaltungsstrategie. Für Arbeitsspeicher-Größenbereiche,in denenbei festen Parametern$\{\rho$, a$\}$ die Strategie (dp,≥2) einen kleineren Durchsatz als die Strategie (dp,≥1) erzielt, schneiden Strategien (dp,≥n) mit n>2 noch schlechter ab.

Bemerkenswert ist, daß der -nur bei kleinen Werten von a (z.B. a=2)- erreichbare maximale Durchsatzgewinn der Strategie (dp,≥2) gegenüber (dp,≥1) bei streuender Programmgröße (Bild 9) deutlich kleiner ist als bei konstanter Programmgröße (Bild 8). Die Resultate für die Strategie (dp,≥2) sind durch Simulation geprüft worden. Die Übereinstimmung von Simulations- und Rechenergebnissen ist gut, außerdem ergibt sich eine gute Übereinstimmung mit Meßwerten für die mittlere Bearbeitungszeit eines realen Systems [2].

Zum Schluß noch eine anwendungsorientierte Bemerkung: In realen Rechenanlagen wären bei Änderung des Ladeanteils x eines Programmes zusätzliche Transporte (Belegen des vergrößerten bzw. Räumen des beschlagnahmten Arbeitsspeicherbereichs des geladenen Programmes) nötig. Solche Transporte verkleinern den Durchsatz weiter. Die Durchsatzberechnung für Strategien (dp,≥n) mit n>1 berücksichtigt keine solchen Transporte, ergibt also eine obere Abschätzung für den erreichbaren Durchsatz realer Systeme.

8. Schlußbemerkungen und Ausblick

Es sind unter einer großen Zahl von Annahmen, die zum Teil durch Messungen gestützt sind, rechnerische Aussagen über den Einfluß des teilweisen Ladens von Programmen auf den Durchsatz gemacht worden. Dabei zeigt sich, daß mit Hilfe teilweisen Ladens ermöglichte Parallelarbeit von Kanal und Rechnerkern einer Rechenanlage bei günstigen Voraussetzungen den Durchsatz begrenzt steigern, bei ungünstigen Voraussetzungen aber stark verkleinern kann. Die Schlüsselrolle für die Entscheidung gegen oder für teilweises Laden zur Durchsatzsteigerung spielt das Programmverhalten selbst. Je mehr Transporte bei teilweisem Laden nötig werden, umso mehr muß abgeraten werden. Die hier verwendete Arbeitsspeicher-Verwaltungsstrategie geht von einem fest vorgegebenen minimalen Multiprogramming-Grad n aus. Es läßt sich zeigen, daß entsprechende Strategien, bei denen sich aber die Anzahl n von teilweise geladenen Programmen dynamisch, abhängig vom individuellen Platzbedarf jedes Programmes, selbst einstellt, Vorteile bieten [3]. Die resultierende Rechnerkernauslastungs-Kurve ergibt sich als Einhüllende "von oben" für die Kurven n=1,2,3... .

Das Berechnungsverfahren für den Durchsatz läßt sich durch Einführung von Kostenfunktionen (z.B. Preis als Funktion der Leistung bei Bedieneinheiten, oder Preis als Funktion der Größe beim Arbeitsspeicher) zur Bestimmung von preisgünstigen Konfigurationen aus Transportkanal, Arbeitsspeicher und Rechnerkern einer Rechenanlage bei gefordertem Durchsatz heranziehen. Das entwickelte Verfahren zur Durchsatzberechnung bei teilweise geladenen Programmen läßt sich analog auf alle Modelle anwenden, für die der Durchsatz berechenbar ist.

Literatur

[1]   Dennig,P.J., Virtual Memory. Computing Surveys, Vol.2, No.3, Sept. 1970, S.153-189

[2]   Walke, B., Durchsatzberechnung für Rechenanlagen bei wählbarer Aufteilung des Arbeitsspeichers unter mehrere Programme unterschiedlichen Platzbedarfs. Dissertationsschrift, Universität Stuttgart, 1975.

[3]   Walke, B., Multiprogrammed memory management for random-sized programs. Contribution to the 1. ECI Conference, Aug.76, Amsterdam, The Netherlands, Lecture Notes Comp. Science, Springer, Berlin, Heidelberg, New York.

Zeitgerechte Prozessorzuteilung in einer harten Realzeitumgebung

R. Henn

Institut für Informatik der Technischen Universität München

1. Modell

Für eine harte Realzeitumgebung sind die Verarbeitungsergebnisse eines Rechensystems nur dann brauchbar, wenn nach Übertragung einer Aufgabe an das Rechensystem sie innerhalb einer vorgegebenen Antwortzeit verfügbar sind. Die Zuteilung von Aufgaben (Tasks) an die _m Prozessoren_, die in dieser Arbeit gleichartig sein sollen, nimmt in diesem Zusammenhang eine zentrale Stellung ein, ebenso die Frage nach einer möglichen oder unmöglichen zeitgerechten Verarbeitung von Tasks bzw. Tasksystemen durch das Prozessorsystem.

Eine _Task_ T einer harten Realzeitumgebung wird durch folgende 2 Größen charakterisiert :

- _Zeitbedingung_ t_Z, die den Zeitpunkt angibt, zu dem die Task T beendet
   sein muß (Zeitbedingung wird erfüllt)

- _Laufzeit_ $\ell(t)$, die angibt, wielange die Task T zum Zeitpunkt t einen
   Prozessor für ihre (restliche) Ausführung beansprucht.

Da die Laufzeit einer Task von der Zeit t abhängt, schreiben wir für eine Task T genauer $T(t) = (t_Z, \ell(t))$.

Im folgenden wird anstelle von Zeitbedingung meistens der Begriff _Antwortzeit_ einer Task zum Zeitpunkt t $a(t) := t_Z - t$ $(0 \leq t < \infty)$ verwendet, und wir schreiben $T(t) = (a(t), \ell(t))$. Die Differenz aus Antwortzeit und Laufzeit heißt _Spielraum_ $s(t) := a(t) - \ell(t)$. Er gibt an, wielange eine Task vor ihrer Ausführung noch maximal verzögert werden darf, ohne daß sie ihre Zeitbedingung verletzt.

Es ist vernünftig, die Tasks nach aufsteigenden Antwortzeiten zu ordnen und zu indizieren. Wir schreiben im folgenden für die Daten einer Task $T_i(t)$ t_{iZ}, $a_i(t)$, $\ell_i(t)$ usw.

Es werden 3 Arten von Taskmengen betrachtet :

- Taskmengen
- Präzedenzsysteme
- Wälder

Bei Taskmengen sind sämtliche Tasks des Tasksystems voneinander unabhängig und sofort (d.h. zum Zeitpunkt 0) einem Prozessor zuteilbar. Wir schreiben

$M(t) = \{T_1(t), T_2(t), \ldots, T_n(t)\}$

Ein Präzedendzsystem ist eine Taskmenge, deren Tasks in einer Präzedenzrelation $<\!\cdot$ zueinander stehen können, d.h. es gibt Vorgänger-Nachfolger-Beziehungen. Eine Task darf erst gestartet werden, wenn sämtliche Vorgänger beendet sind. Wir schreiben

$G(t) = (M(t), <\!\cdot).$

Ein Wald ist ein Präzedenzsystem mit einer Präzedenzrelation, bei der eine Task höchstens einen unmittelbaren Nachfolger haben darf.

Bei der Verarbeitung eines Tasksystems wird eine <u>Prozessorbelegung</u> (schedule) definiert, welche die Belegung der Prozessoren durch Tasks zu jedem Zeitpunkt angibt. Einer Prozessorbelegung können wir den Zeitpunkt t_S der erstmaligen Prozessorzuweisung einer Task (<u>Startzeit</u>) und dem Beendigungdzeitpunkt t_E einer Task (<u>Endzeit</u>) entnehmen, ebenso den Zeitpunkt V, zu dem das Tasksystem vollständig ausgeführt ist. Das Zeitintervall $[0,V)$ wird mit <u>Verarbeitungsspanne</u> bezeichnet.

Die Zeitbedingung einer Task wird erfüllt, wenn $t_E \leq t_Z$ gilt; ebenso wird eine Antwortzeit eingehalten, wenn $a(t_E) \leq 0$ erfüllt ist. Halten sämtliche Tasks eines Tasksystems ihre Antwortzeiten ein (die Präzedenzen natürlich auch), so liegt eine zeitgerechte <u>Prozessorbelgung</u> vor.

Die Vorgänger-Nachfolger-Beziehung in einem Präzedenzsystem bewirkt, daß zu einem Zeitpunkt Teilsysteme den Prozessoren wegen noch nicht beendeter Vorgänger nicht zugeteilt werden dürfen. Die Menge der zu einem Zeitpunkt t zuteilbaren Tasks wird <u>freie Taskmenge</u> $F(t)$ genannt. Die Menge der Tasks, die zu einem Zeitpunkt einen Prozessor (ganz oder teilweise bei "processor sharing") belegen, wird mit <u>Belegmenge</u> $B(t)$ bezeichnet. Eine Strategie ist ein Prozessorzuteilungsalgorithmus, der den folgenden beiden Eigenschaften genügt :

- $B(t) \subseteq F(t)$ $(0 \leq t < V)$
- $B(t)$ erfüllt eine (zeitunabhängige) Eigenschaft für $0 \leq t < V$.

Ein Tasksystem T ist <u>zeitgerecht verarbeitbar</u>, wenn eine zeitgerechte Prozessorbelegung für T existiert, und eine <u>Strategie</u> ist <u>zeitgerecht</u>, wenn sie für jedes zeitgerecht verarbeitbare Tasssystem eine zeitgerechte Prozessorbelegung erzeugt.

Das Ziel dieser Arbeit besteht darin
- Kriterien für die zeitgerechte Verarbeitbarkeit von Tasksystemen und
- zeitgerechte Strategien für Tasksysteme
anzugeben.

2. Zeitgerechte Verarbeitbarkeit

2.1. Taskmengen

In [He 73] wurde gezeigt, daß eine Taskmenge M d.u.n.d. auf einem Einprozessorsystem zeitgerecht verarbeitbar ist, wenn bei einer Indizierung nach aufsteigenden
Antwortzeiten auf M die folgende Bedingung erfüllt ist *)

$$a_k \geq \sum_{i=1}^{k} \ell_i \qquad 1 \leq k \leq n \tag{1}$$

Bei Mehrprozessorsystemen sind die Verhältnisse wegen der Bedingung, daß eine Task
zu einem Zeitpunkt höchstens einen Prozessor belegen darf, wesentlich schwieriger.
Eine vernünftig erscheinende Erweiterung von (1) für Mehrprozessorsysteme könnte
folgende Formel sein [He 75] :

$$\sum_{i=u}^{k} a_i \geq \sum_{i=1}^{k} \ell_i \qquad 1 \leq k \leq n \qquad u = \max(1, k-m+1) \tag{2}$$

Bedingung (2) ist zwar für die zeitgerechte Verarbeitbarkeit einer Taskmenge durch
ein m-Prozessorsystem notwendig, aber nicht hinreichend. Das wird sofort an dem
folgenden Beispiel deutlich :

$$T_1 = (1,1), \quad T_2 = (2,1), \quad T_3 = (3,3), \quad T_4 = (6,1), \quad T_5 = (7,7) \qquad m=2$$

Die Bedingung (2) wird erfüllt. Die 3 Tasks T_1, T_3 und T_5 weisen einen
Spielraum von 0 auf, d.h. aber, daß T_1, T_3, T_5 niemals auf einem 2-Prozes-
sorsystem zeitgerecht beendet werden können.

In [Jo 74] wurde eine Bedingung für die zeitgerechte Verarbeitbarkeit einer Taskmenge vorgestellt, die sowohl notwendig als auch hinreichend ist. Es wird dabei die
Vorhaltung einer Task T_i vor eine Task T_k berücksichtigt. T_i hat <u>Vorhaltung</u>
vor T_k, wenn $s_i < a_k$ erfüllt ist. T_i muß bei einer zeitgerechten Verarbeitung
von T_i vor Ablauf der Antwortzeit von T_k bereits begonnen und $a_k - s_i$ Zeitein-
heiten bearbeitet werden. Die Berücksichtigung der Vorhaltung ermöglicht eine notwendige und hinreichende Bedingung für die zeitgerechte Verarbeitbarkeit einer Taskmenge auf einem m-Prozessorsystem in Gestalt der folgenden 3 Ungleichungen.

$$a_k \geq \frac{1}{m} \left[\sum_{i=1}^{k} \ell_i + \sum_{i=k+1}^{n} \max(o, a_k - s_i) \right] \qquad m \leq k \leq n-m+1 \tag{3}$$

$$a_k \geq \frac{1}{n-k+1} \left[\sum_{i=1}^{k} \ell_i + \sum_{i=k+1}^{n} \max(o, a_k - s_i) - \sum_{i=n-m+1}^{k-1} a_i \right] \qquad n-m+1 < k \leq n \tag{4}$$

---

*) T_i, a_k, s_i, ℓ_i, M, steht für $T_i(0)$, $a_k(o)$ $s_i(0)$, $\ell_i(o)$, $M(0)$

Für k < m genügt in den meisten Fällen (3), lediglich wenn es j Tasks mit
$a_k > s_i$ und k < i ≤ n und j + k < m gibt, muß gelten

$$a_k \geq \frac{1}{k+j} \left[\sum_{i=1}^{k} \ell_i + \sum_{i=k+1}^{n} \max(0, a_k - s_i) \right] \tag{5}$$

2.2. Präzedenzsysteme

In diesem Abschnitt wird gezeigt, wie die Antwortzeiten von Tasks eines Präzedenzsystems "vernünftig" gemacht werden können, ohne daß dabei die zeitgerechte Verarbeitbarkeit des Präzedenzsystems verloren geht. Der Algorithmus wird zunächst an
einem Beispiel mit einer Vorgängertask T_V = (3,1) und einer Nachfolgertask
T_N = (5,3) durchgeführt

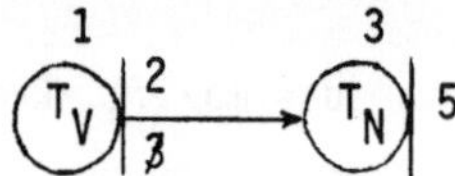

Wir erkennen sofort, daß die Antwortzeit a_V = 3 nicht sinnvoll ist. T_V gilt als
zeitgerecht verarbeitet, wenn sie zum Zeitpunkt 3 beendet wird. T_N wird dann zum
Zeitpunkt 6 beendet und verletzt ihre Zeitbedingung zum Zeitpunkt 5. Die Antwortzeit von T_V war nicht vernünftig. T_V muß zum Zeitpunkt 2 beendet sein, wenn auch
für T_N eine zeitgerechte Verarbeitung möglich sein soll. Die Verkürzung der Antwortzeit eines Vorgängers erfolgt nach dem folgenden Normalisierungsverfahren :

$$a_V' := \max(0, \min(a_V, a_N - \ell_N)) \tag{6}$$

Ist das Normalisierungsverfahren solange auf ein Präzedenzsystem angewendet worden,
bis keine Antwortzeit einer Task weiter reduziert werden kann, so liegt das eindeutig
definierte <u>normalisierte Präzedenzsystem</u> zu einem Präzendenzsystem vor. Ein nor-
malisiertes Präzedenzsystem erfüllt die Bedingung $a_V \leq a_N - \ell_N$ für alle Vorgänger
und Nachfolger im Präzendenzsystem.

<u>Satz 1</u> : Ein Präzedenzsystem (M, <·) ist d.u.n.d. zeitgerecht
            verarbeitbar. wenn sein normalisiertes Präzendenzsystem (M', <·)
            zeitgerecht verarbeitbar ist.

Der Beweis ist einfach durchzuführen und steht in [He 75]. Aufgrund der Aussage in
Satz 1 können wir die weiteren Betrachtungen über Präzedenzsysteme auf normalisierte Präzedenzsysteme beschränken.

3.   Zeitgerechte Strategien

3.1.   Kriterien für zeitgerechte Strategien

3.1.1.   Gültigkeit der zeitgerechten Verarbeitbarkeit in der Verarbeitungsspanne

Eine Strategie ist mit Sicherheit zeitgerecht, wenn sie während der Verarbeitungsspanne ein zeitgerecht verarbeitbares Tasksystem wieder in ein zeitgerecht verarbeitbares Tasksystem überführt. Die Bedingungen (1) bzw. (3) (4) (5), bieten sich zum Nachweis von zeitgerechten Strategien für Taskmengen geradezu an, da durch ihre Erfüllung zum Zeitpunkt 0 die zeitgerechte Verarbeitbarkeit der Taskmenge auf einem Einprozessorsystem bzw. auf einem m-Prozessorsystem gesichert ist. In [He 75] wurde gezeigt, daß die Gültigkeit von (2) auf den relevanten Taskmengen (leere Tasks sind hier ausgenommen) während der Verarbeitungsspanne ebenfalls eine zeitgerechte Prozessorbelegung für ein m-Prozessorsystem charakterisiert. Für Präzedenzsysteme versagt diese Methode, da wir bisher nur Bedingungen für die zeitgerechte Verarbeitbarkeit von Taskmengen kennen. Wir benötigen Mechanismen, wie sie im folgenden Abschnitt vorgestellt werden.

3.1.2.   Ablaufmatrix

Der zeitliche Verlauf der Verarbeitung eines Tasksystems wird üblicherweise in einem Gantt-Diagramm dargestellt, in dem jedem Prozessor eine Zeitachse zugeordnet ist. Auf der Zeitachse werden die Tasks eingetragen, die zum jeweiligen Zeitpunkt den Prozessor ganz oder teilweise belegen.

Ordnen wir jeder Task eine Zeitachse zu, auf welcher der Prozessor eingetragen wird, den die Task belegt, so haben wir eine dem Gantt-Diagramm dual gegenüber stehende Darstellung. Wir sagen, es liegt eine <u>Ablaufmatrix</u> vor, wenn jeder Taks eine Zeitachse zugeordent ist, kein "processor-sharing" auftritt und jede Eintragung auf den Zeitachsen sich als ganzzahliges Vielfaches einer reellen Zahl h darstellen läßt, d.h. sämtliche Eintragungen sind kommensurabel. Die Forderung nach kommensurablen Abläufen und der Verzicht auf "processor-sharing" bedeuten für den praktischen Einsatz keine Einschränkung, da die Prozessoren getaktet arbeiten und sich Abläufe in "processor sharing" durch sehr kleine h (h→0) approximieren lassen. Die Einschränkung auf kommensurable Abläufe ermöglicht eine Darstellung in Matrixform, bei welcher der i-ten Zeile die Task T_i zugeordnet ist. Die j-te Spalte hält die Belegung des Prozessorsystems zum Zeitpunkt j·h fest. Wir führen folgende Bezeichnungen ein :

$$v_i := \frac{t_{iE}}{h} - 1 \qquad \overline{v}_i := \frac{t_{iZ}}{h} - 1 \qquad 1 \le i \le n$$

$$a_{ij} := a_i(j \cdot h) \qquad o \le j \le \overline{v}_i + 1 \qquad \text{(Antwortzeit)}$$

$$\ell_{ij} := \ell_i(j \cdot h) \qquad o \le j \le v_i + 1 \qquad \text{(Laufzeit)}$$

$$s_{ij} := s_i(j \cdot h) \qquad o \leq j \leq \overline{v}_i + 1 \qquad \text{(Spielraum)}$$

$$v := \max_{1 \leq i \leq n} \{v_i\} \qquad \overline{v} := \max_{1 \leq i \leq n} \{\overline{v}_i\} \qquad \text{(Verarbeitungsspanne, Betrachtungsspanne)}$$

$$B_j := B(j \cdot h) \qquad o \leq j \leq \overline{v} \qquad \text{(Belegmenge)}$$

$$F_j := F(j \cdot h) \qquad o \leq j \leq \overline{v} \qquad \text{(freie Taskmenge)}$$

$$\underline{v} := \max_{1 \leq j \leq v} \{j : |F_j| \geq m\} \qquad \text{(Vollbeschäftigungsspanne)}$$

Im folgenden werden 2 Darstellungen für die Ablaufmatrix A verwendet.

a) Binärdarstellung

b) Normaldarstellung

In Binärdarstellung wird geschrieben :

$$A_{ij} = + \qquad \text{falls} \qquad T_i \in B_j$$

$$A_{ij} = - \qquad \text{falls} \qquad T_i \notin B_j$$

In der i-ten Zeile befinden sich bei zeitgerechter Verarbeitung von T_i genau ℓ_i/h + Zeichen und s_i/h - Zeichen.

In Normaldarstellung wird geschrieben :

$$A_{ij} = (a_{ij}, s_{ij}) \qquad \text{für} \qquad 0 \leq j \leq \overline{v}_i + 1$$

$$A_{ij} = \text{leer} \qquad \qquad \text{sonst}$$

Aufgrund der Definition von Antwortzeit und Spielraum gilt dann auf A :

$$a_{i,j+1} = a_{ij} - h \qquad 0 \leq j \leq \overline{v}_i$$

$$s_{i,j+1} = \begin{cases} s_{ij} & \text{falls} \quad T_i \in B_j \\ s_{ij} - h & \text{falls} \quad T_i \notin B_j \quad \text{und} \quad j \leq \overline{v}_i \end{cases}$$

Eine Ablaufmatrix beschreibt eine zeitgerechte Prozessorbelegung, wenn gilt :

$$s_{ij} \geq 0 \quad 0 \leq j \leq \overline{v}_i + 1 \qquad 1 \leq i \leq n$$

Voraussetzung für eine gültige Prozessorbelegung ist $|B_j| \leq m \qquad 0 \leq j \leq \overline{v}$

<u>Beispiel 1</u>

$M = \{T_1, T_2, T_3\} = \{(3,3),(4,3),(5,3)\}$ (in (a_i, ℓ_i)-Darstellung) m=2

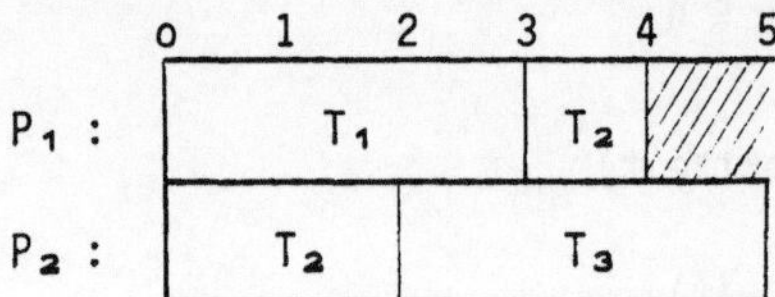

Gantt-Diagramm mit zeitgerechter Prozessorbelegung für M

```
       o   1   2   3   4

T₁ :   +   +   +
T₂ :   +   +   -   +
T₃ :   -   -   +   +   +
```

Ablaufmatrix in Binärdarstellung
mit demselben Ablauf wie im
Gantt-Diagramm

```
        o    1    2    3    4    5

T₁ :  (3,0)(2,0)(1,0)(0,0)

T₂ :  (4,1)(3,1)(2,1)(1,0)(0,0)

T₃ :  (5,2)(4,1)(3,0)(2,0)(1,0)(0,0)
```

Ablaufmatrix in Normaldarstellung mit demselben Ablauf wie
im Gantt-Diagramm

Sei $W = \{T_1, \ldots, T_w\}$ ein Weg in einem Präzendenzsystem. Zu einem Zeitpunkt kann nur eine Task aus W einen Prozessor belegen. Wir sagen

$$W \in \cdot B_j \quad \text{falls} \quad \exists! \, T_i \in W : T_i \in B_j \quad \text{mit} \quad t_{kE} \leq t_{iS} \quad 1 \leq k < i \quad 1 \leq i \leq w \quad *)$$

$$W \notin \cdot B_j \quad \text{falls} \quad \nexists T \in W : T \in B_j$$

Die folgenden beiden Operationen auf der Ablaufmatrix überführen eine zeitgerechte Prozessorbelegung in eine andere zeitgerechte Prozessorbelegung [He 75] :

1) Austauschschritt (T_x, j, W, j')

Ausführbar, wenn auf Ablaufmatrix A gilt :

$$\exists T_x, \, j, \, W, \, j', \quad 0 \leq j < v_x, \quad 0 \leq j' < \overline{v}_w, \quad j < j' :$$

$$\begin{array}{ll} T_x \notin B_j & T_x \in B_{j'} \\ W \in \cdot B_j & W \notin \cdot B_{j'} \end{array} \quad T_x \notin W \quad T_x \in F_j \quad \text{und}$$

W um h in $[j \cdot h, (j'+1) \cdot h]$ verzögerbar ohne Präzedenzverletzung.

Der Austauschschritt (T_x, j, W, j') liefert folgende Prozessorbelegung in A' :

$$\begin{array}{ll} T_x \in B_j' & T_x \notin B_{j'}' \\ W \notin \cdot B_j' & W \in \cdot B_{j'}' \end{array} \quad B_q' = B_q \;\; j < q < j', \quad B_j' \backslash T_x = B_j \backslash (W \cap B_j), \quad B_{j'} \backslash T_x = B_{j'}' \backslash (W \cap B_j)$$

Der Austauschschritt liefert eine zyklische Vertauschung in der Prozessorbelegung
auf A zwischen T_x und W in den Spalten j und j'. Dies wird in der Binärdarstellung besonders deutlich :

$*)$ $\exists!$ steht für "es gibt genau ein"

$$
\begin{array}{c}
\begin{array}{cc} j & j' \end{array} \\
\begin{array}{l}
T_x : \\
W :
\end{array}
\boxed{
\begin{array}{cc}
- & + \\
+ & -
\end{array}
}
\end{array}
\quad \rightarrow \quad
\begin{array}{c}
\begin{array}{cc} j & j' \end{array} \\
\begin{array}{l}
T_x : \\
W :
\end{array}
\boxed{
\begin{array}{cc}
+ & - \\
- & +
\end{array}
}
\end{array}
\qquad \text{*)}
$$

$$A \qquad\qquad A'$$

2) Verschiebeoperation (T_x, j, W)

Ausführbar, wenn auf Ablaufmatrix A die gesamte Ausführung von W ab Spalte j um h verzögert, und die gesamte Ausführung von T_x ab Spalte $j+1$ um h beschleunigt werden kann. d.h.

$$\exists T_x, j, W \qquad 0 \le j \le \min(v_x, v_w) :$$

$$T_x \notin B_j, \quad W \in \cdot B_j, \quad s_{w v_w} > 0, \quad |B_{v_w+1}| < m, \quad T_x \in F_j \quad \text{und}$$

$$W \text{ um } h \text{ in } [j \cdot h, (v_w+1) \cdot h] \text{ ohne Präzedenzverletzung verzögerbar.}$$

Die Verschiebeoperation (T_x, j, W) liefert folgende Prozessorbelegung auf A' :

$$
\begin{array}{ll}
T_x \in B'_j & T_x \notin B'_{v_x} \\
W \notin \cdot B'_j & W \in \cdot B'_{v_w+1}
\end{array}
\qquad B'_q = B_q \quad j < q < \overline{v}_x \quad q \ne v_x \quad q \ne v_w + 1
$$

Die Verschiebeoperation wird immer dann eingesetzt, wenn kein geeignetes j' für einen Austauschschritt gefunden werden kann. Das ist häufig nach der Vollbeschäftigungsspanne der Fall, wie in dem folgenden Beispiel für $m=2$

$$
\begin{array}{c}
\begin{array}{cccc} j & v_x & v_w & \overline{v}_w \end{array} \\
\begin{array}{l}
T_x : \\[6pt]
W :
\end{array}
\boxed{
\begin{array}{cccc}
- & + & & \\
+ & + & + & -
\end{array}
}
\end{array}
\quad \rightarrow \quad
\begin{array}{c}
\begin{array}{cccc} j & v_x & v_w & \overline{v}_w \end{array} \\
\begin{array}{l}
T_x : \\[6pt]
W :
\end{array}
\boxed{
\begin{array}{cccc}
+ & - & & \\
- & + & + & +
\end{array}
}
\end{array}
$$

$$A \qquad\qquad A'$$

Die beiden Operationen Austauschschritt und Verschiebeoperation verzögern die Ausführung eines (Teil-) Weges. Dies kann bei Präzedenzsystemen zu Präzedenzverletzungen führen. In dieser Arbeit werden diese beiden Operationen nur auf Wälder angesetzt, da bei ihnen durch die verzögerte Ausführung eines (Teil-) Weges keine Präzedenzverletzung auftreten kann.

---

*) Das +Zeichen in der W-Zeile und j-Spalte bedeutet $W \in \cdot B_j$, das -Zeichen bedeutet $W \notin \cdot B_j$.

3.2. Strategie nächste ablaufende Antwortzeit (n.a.A.)

3.2.1. Einprozessorsystem

Bei der Strategie n.a.A. belegt immer eine Task aus der freien Taskmenge mit der kürzesten Antwortzeit den Prozessor, d.h. $B(t) := T_1(t)$, wobei die Tasks von $F(t)$ nach aufsteigenden Antwortzeiten indiziert sind. Wir sehen, daß die Strategie n.a.A. eine nichtpreemptive Prozessorzuteilung liefert.

<u>Satz 2</u> : Die Strategie n.a.A. liefert für auf 1-Prozessorsystemen zeitgerecht verarbeitbare Taskmengen eine zeitgerechte Prozessorbelegung.

<u>Beweis</u> : Eine zeitgerecht verarbeitbare Taskmenge M erfüllt zum Zeitpunkt 0 die Bedingung (1). Wir zeigen, daß die Gültigkeit von (1) bei Verarbeitung nach der Strategie n.a.A. in der Verarbeitungsspanne erhalten bleibt. Sei t $(0 \leq t \leq V)$ ein Zeitpunkt, zu dem auf $M(t)$ (1) erfüllt ist, und Δt ein Zeitintervall mit $t + \Delta t \leq t_{1E}$. Dann gilt unter Berücksichtigung von $a_k(t+\Delta t) = a_k(t) - \Delta t$ $(1 \leq k \leq n)$ bzw. $\ell_1(t+\Delta t) = \ell_1(t) - \Delta t$ und $\ell_i(t+\Delta t) = \ell_i(t)$ $(2 \leq i \leq n)$ entsprechend der Strategie n.a.A.

$$a_k(t+\Delta t) = a_k(t) - \Delta t \geq \sum_{i=1}^{k} \ell_i(t) - \Delta t = \sum_{i=1}^{k} \ell_i(t+\Delta t) \quad 1 \leq k \leq n \quad t + \Delta t \leq t_{1E}$$

Damit bleibt bis zur Beendigung von T_1 (1) gültig, d.h. $\tilde{M}(t_{1E}) = M(t_{1E}) \backslash T_1(t_{1E})$ ist zeitgerecht verabeitbar und auf $\tilde{M}(t_{1E})$ ist ebenfalls (1) erfüllt. Die rekursive Fortsetzung über $\tilde{M}$ hinaus zeigt, daß während der Verarbeitung von M die Bedingung (1) auf den relevanten Taskmengen erhalten bleibt, d.h. die Strategie n.a.A. erzeugt eine zeitgerechte Prozessorbelegung und ist damit zeitgerecht. $\qquad$ q.e.d.

<u>Satz 3</u> : Die Strategie n.a.A. ist für normalisierte Präzedenzsysteme $G = (M, <\cdot)$ bei Einprozessorsystemen eine zeitgerechte Strategie.

<u>Beweis</u> Bei einem normalisierten Präzedenzsystem befinden sich die Tasks mit der kürzesten Antwortzeit immer in der freien Taskmenge. Damit liefert die Strategie n.a.A. bei Verarbeitung des Präzedenzsystems G und bei Verarbeitung der zugehörigen Taskmenge M auf einem 1-Prozessorsystem dieselbe Prozessorbelegung. Da G nur dann zeitgerecht verarbeitbar sein kann, wenn M zeitgerecht verarbeitbar ist, folgt mit Satz 2 unmittelbar die Behauptung. $\qquad$ q.e.d.

Für Einprozessorsysteme haben wir unser Ziel erreicht.

3.2.2. Mehrprozessorsystem

Bei Mehrprozessorsystemen ist die Strategie n.a.A. bei einer Indizierung nach aufsteigenden Antwortzeiten der Tasks in $F(t)$ durch $B(t) = \{T_1(t), \ldots , T_r\}$ mit

$r = \min(m, |F(t)|)$ und $T_i(t) \in F(t)$ $(1 \leq i \leq r)$ definiert.

Für die in Beispiel 1 angegebene zeitgerecht verarbeitbare Taskmenge liefert die Strategie n.a.A. folgende nicht zeitgerechte Prozessorbelegung und ist damit <u>keine</u> zeitgerechte Strategie.

P_1 : T_1 T_3

P_2 : T_2

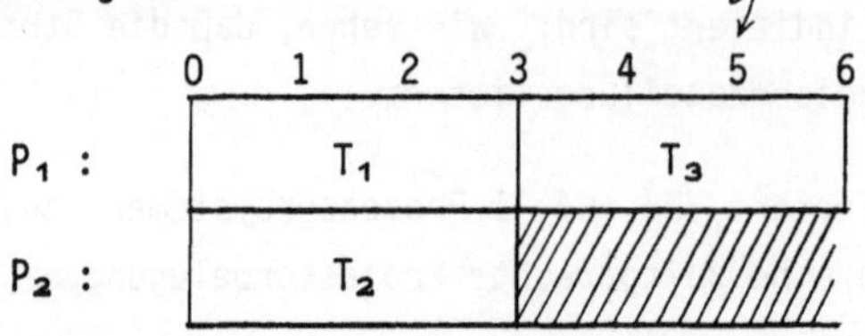

Für die folgenden Betrachtungen führen wir eine Einheitsmenge E ein, die charakterisiert ist durch

- e Einheitslaufzeit für alle Tasks in E
- $t_Z = a = r \cdot e$ mit r aus den natürlichen Zahlen.

Ein <u>Einheitswald</u> $G = (E, <\cdot)$, ist ein Wald über einer Einheitsmenge. Es wird nun gezeigt, daß die Strategie n.a.A. für Einheitswälder eine zeitgerechte Strategie darstellt. Dazu werden die Operationen auf der Ablaufmatrix eingesetzt.

<u>Lemma 1</u> : Es liege eine zeitgerechte Prozessorbelegung in Form einer Ablauf-
matrix A für einen normalisierten Wald vor und auf Spalte j gilt

$$\exists T_i, T_k : T_i \notin B_j \quad T_k \in B_j \quad T_i \in F_j \quad s_{ij} < s_{kj}$$

Dann gibt es eine zeitgerechte Prozessorbelegung mit $T_i \in B_j$
$T_k \notin B_j$, in der $A_{xy}(1 \leq x \leq n,\ 0 \leq y < j)$ unverändert bleiben.

<u>Beweis</u> : Da ein Wald vorliegt, gibt es genau einen Weg von T_k zu einem Endknoten des Waldes. Dieser Weg wird mit W_k bezeichnet.

1. $\exists \beta \quad j < \beta \leq v_i : T_i \in B_\beta \quad W_k \notin \cdot B_\beta$. Der Austauschschritt (T_i, j, W_k, β)
   liefert die Belegung $T_i \in B_j \quad T_k \notin B_j$.

2. $\nexists \beta \quad j < \beta \leq v_i : T_i \in B_\beta \quad W_k \notin \cdot B_\beta$. Das bedeutet, daß für $j < \beta \leq v_i$ gilt :
   $T_i \in B_\beta \quad W_k \in \cdot B_\beta$ oder $T_i \notin B_\beta \quad W_k \in \cdot B_\beta$ oder $T_i \notin B_\beta \quad W_k \notin \cdot B_\beta$

Für $j < \beta \leq v_i$ wird der Spielraum von T_i in stärkerem oder gleichem Maße reduziert, als dies bei W_k der Fall ist, d.h. es gilt $0 \leq s_{i\beta} < s_{y\beta} \quad j < \beta \leq v_i$ und $T_y \in W_k$ mit $t_{yA} \leq \beta \cdot h \leq t_{yE}$. Daraus folgt $\exists \gamma \quad v_i < \gamma \leq \overline{v} : W_y \notin \cdot B_\gamma$ bzw. $W_k \notin \cdot B_\gamma$.

a) $\gamma \leq \underline{v}$. Wir wählen $W_k \in \cdot B_\alpha$ in $v_i \leq \alpha < \gamma$, d.h. es gilt $W_k \in \cdot B_{\gamma-1} \quad W_k \notin \cdot B_\gamma$.
Daraus folgt wegen $\gamma \leq \underline{v} \quad \exists T_r(1 \leq r \leq n) : T_r \notin B_{\gamma-1} \quad T_r \in B_\gamma$ mit $T_r \in F_{\gamma-1}$.

Der Austauschschritt $(T_r, \gamma-1, W_k, \gamma)$ liefert

$$W_k \notin B_{\gamma-1} \qquad W_k \in \cdot B_\gamma$$
$$T_r \in B_{\gamma-1} \qquad T_r \notin B_\gamma$$

Durch fortgesetzte Anwendung dieser Konstruktion erhalten wir

$$T_i \notin B_j \qquad T_i \in B_{v_i}$$
$$W_k \in \cdot B_j \qquad W_k \in \cdot B_{v_i} \qquad W_k \in\!\!\!\!\!/\ \cdot B_{v_i+1}$$
$$T_r' \notin B_{v_i} \qquad T_r' \in B_{v_i+1}$$

Der Austauschschritt (T_r', v_i, W_k, v_i+1) liefert

$$T_i \notin B_j \qquad T_i \in B_{v_i}$$
$$W_k \in \cdot B_j \qquad W_k \in\!\!\!\!\!/\ \cdot B_{v_i} \qquad W_k \in \cdot B_{v_i+1}$$
$$T_r' \in B_{v_i} \qquad T_r' \notin B_{v_i+1}.$$

Der Austauschschritt (T_i, j, W_k, v_i) liefert $T_i \in B_j \quad T_k \notin B_j$.

b) $\gamma > \underline{v}$. Die Verschiebeoperation (T_i, j, W_k) liefert $T_i \in B_j \quad T_k \notin B_j$.

Damit kann $T_i \in B_j \quad T_k \notin B_j$ immer erzeugt werden. $\hfill$ q.e.d.

<u>Satz 4</u> : Die Strategie n.a.A. ist für normalisierte Einheitswälder zeitgerecht.

<u>Beweis</u> : Es wird von einer Ablaufmatrix A mit einer zeitgerechten Prozessorbelegung ausgegangen und in jeder Spalte von A von links nach rechts geprüft, ob die Eigenschaft der Strategie n.a.A. erfüllt ist. In Spalte j sei dies erstmals nicht der Fall, d.h. es gilt $\exists T_i, T_k : T_i \notin B_j \quad T_k \in B_j \quad T_i \in F_j \quad a_{ij} < a_{kj} \quad l_{ij} > 0$. Da die Antwortzeiten ganzzahlige Vielfache der Einheitslaufzeit e sind, gilt wegen $a_{ij} < a_{kj}$ auch $a_{ij} \leq a_{kj} - e$. Wegen $\ell_{kj} \leq e$ gilt auch $a_{ij} \leq a_{kj} - \ell_{kj} = s_{kj}$ und wegen $\ell_{ij} > 0$ gilt $s_{ij} < a_{ij}$. Daraus folgt $s_{ij} < s_{kj}$. Die Voraussetzungen für Lemma 1 sind erfüllt. Lemma 1 liefert die gewünschte Prozessorbelegung $T_i \in B_j$ $T_k \notin B_j$. Die rekursive Fortsetzung liefert eine zeitgerechte Prozessorbelegung, die der Eigenschaft von Strategie n.a.A. entspricht. $\hfill$ q.e.d.

Die in dem Beweis erzeugte preemptive Prozessorbehandlung kann durch Austauschschritte auf einfache Art und Weise in eine nichtpreemptive Prozessorbelegung überführt werden.

In [He 75] ist Satz 4 mit Hilfe von Bedingung (2) bewiesen. Dabei wird gleichzeitig gezeigt, daß Bedingung (2) für die zeitgerechte Verarbeitbarkeit von normalisierten Einheitswäldern nicht nur notwendig sondern auch hinreichend ist.

Für Bäume (Wald mit nur einem Endknoten, der Wurzel des Baumes) über einer Einheitsmenge, wobei den Tasks nur die Einheitslaufzeit e und keine Antwortzeit zugeordnet ist, wird in [Hu 61] eine nichtpreemptive Strategie angegeben, die einem freiwerdenden Prozessor genau eine Task mit der größten Weglänge zur Wurzel zuweist. Dieser sogenannte Hu-Algorithmus liefert die kürzeste Verarbeitungsspanne [0,V). Geben wir der Wurzel eine Antwortzeit $a_n \geq V$ vor, so liefert die Normalisierung für alle Tasks des Baumes "vernünftige" Antwortzeiten. Die Strategie n.a.A. erzeugt für den normalisierten Einheitsbaum dieselbe Prozessorbelegung wie der Hu-Algorithmus bei Verarbeitung des Baumes ohne Antwortzeiten. Dieses Ergebnis zeigt, daß die Minimierung der Verarbeitungsspanne ein Teilproblem der Aufgabenstellung in dieser Arbeit darstellt.

3.3. Strategie minimaler Spielraum (m.Sp.)

Die Tasks in $F(t)$ weisen entweder gleiche oder verschiedene Spielräume auf. Die verschiedenen Spielräume in $F(t)$ werden mit $\hat{s}_1(t) < \hat{s}_2(t) < \ldots < \hat{s}_r(t)$ bezeichnet. Es gilt damit $\hat{s}_1(t) \leq s(t) \; \forall T(t) \in F(t)$. Wir definieren

$$S_i(t) := \{T(t) \in F(t) : \hat{s}_i(t) = s(t)\} \quad (1 \leq i \leq r). \text{ Außerdem gilt } F(t) = \bigcup_{i=1}^{r} s_i.$$

3.3.1. Einprozessorsystem

Bei der Strategie m.Sp. belegen sämtliche Tasks aus $F(t)$ mit minimalem Spielraum den Prozessor, d.h. $B(t) = S_1(t)$. Die Tasks aus $S_1(t)$ teilen sich den Prozessor zu gleichen Teilen.

<u>Satz 5</u> : Die Strategie m.Sp. ist für normalisierte Präzedenzsysteme
und Einprozessorsysteme eine zeitgerechte Strategie.

Der Beweis wird auf ähnliche Weise wie bei Satz 2 und Satz 3 geführt, er steht in [He 75].

3.3.2. Mehrprozessorsystem

Bei Mehrprozessorsystemen ist die Strategie m.Sp. durch

$$B(t) = \bigcup_{i=1}^{b} S_i(t) \text{ mit } \sum_{i=1}^{b-1} |S_i(t)| < m \leq \sum_{i=1}^{b} |S_i(t)|$$

definiert. Dabei wird allen Tasks aus $S_1(t), \ldots, S_{b-1}(t)$ genau ein Prozessor zugewiesen, die Tasks aus $S_b(t)$ teilen sich die restlichen freien Prozessoren zu gleichen Teilen auf.

Die Taskmenge aus Beispiel 1 liefert für die Strategie m.Sp. folgenden zeitgerechten Ablauf :

	o	1	2	3	4	5
P_1 :	T_1			T_2		
P_2 :	T_2	T_2/T_3		T_3		

<u>Satz 6</u> : Die Strategie m.Sp. ist für normalisierte Wälder zeitgerecht.

<u>Beweis</u> : Es wird eine Ablaufmatrix mit einer zeitgerechten Prozessorbelegung zugrunde-
gelegt und von links nach rechts geprüft, ob in jeder Spalte die Eigenschaft der Strategie m.Sp. erfüllt ist. In Spalte j werde sie erstmals verletzt, d.h. :

$\exists T_i, T_k : T_i \notin B_j \quad T_k \in B_j \quad T_i \in F_j \quad s_{ij} < s_{kj}.$

Die Voraussetzungen für Lemma 1 sind erfüllt. Lemma 1 liefert die gewünschte Prozessorbelegung $T_i \in B_j \quad T_k \notin B_j$. Die rekursive Fortsetzung liefert eine Ablaufmatrix nach der Strategie m.Sp.   q.e.d.

Für Bäume über einer Taskmenge, deren Tasks keinen Zeitbedingungen unterliegen, ist
in [Mu 70] für m-Prozessorsysteme eine eine die Verarbeitungsspanne minimierende Strategie angegeben, nach der zu jedem Zeitpunkt der Verabeitungsspanne die Tasks mit der
größten Weglänge (Summe der Laufzeiten auf dem Weg) zur Wurzel die m-Prozessoren
belegen. Dabei findet "processor sharing" statt. Gibt man der Wurzel des Baumes
eine beliebige Antwortzeit $a_n \geq V$ vor, so liefert die Strategie m.Sp. für den
normalisierten Baum dieselbe Prozessorbelegung, da der minimale Spielraum bei normalisierten Bäumen immer auf den längsten Wegen angenommen wird. Auch hier stellt die
Minimierung der Verarbeitungsspanne ein Teilproblem der Aufgabenstellung dieser Arbeit dar.

3.4. Vorhaltestrategie (V-Strat)

Der in [Jo 74] veröffentlichte Prozessorzuteilungsalgorithmus für Taskmengen wird
im folgenden mit Vorhaltestrategie bezeichnet.

Bei der Vorhaltestrategie wird eine Liste von Tasks zugrundegelegt, die nach aufsteigenden Antwortzeiten geordnet und indiziert sind. Die Zuordnung von Tasks zu Prozessoren erfolgt nach folgender Regel :

1) T_1 wird immer zugewiesen.

2)   Alle Tasks mit Vorhaltung (s.2.) vor T_1 werden ausgewählt und belegen bis
     zu maximal m-1 Prozessoren; dabei werden die Tasks mit einem Spielraum von
     Null zuerst und anschließend die restlichen Tasks in der Reihenfolge aufstei-
     gender Antwortzeit jeweils einem Prozssor zugewiesen. Belegen $k_1 <$ m-1 sol-
     cher Tasks einen Prozessor, so werden die noch freien Prozessoren nach 3) und
     4) belegt.

3)   Der ersten, noch nicht zugewiesenen Task T_x in der Liste wird ein Prozessor
     zugewiesen.

4)   Alle Tasks mit Vorhaltung vor T_x werden bis zu einem Maximum von $m-k_i-i$ aus-
     gewählt; es gibt in der Liste keine Tasks mehr mit einem Spielraum von Null.
     Die ausgewählten Tasks werden nach aufsteigenden Antwortzeiten zugewiesen. Wenn
     noch nicht alle Prozessoren belegt sind, wird mit 3) und 4) fortgefahren.

Nach [Jo 74] wird dieser Algorithmus durchlaufen, wenn eine Task beendet wird oder der Spielraum einer nichtzugewiesenen Task Null wird. In dem folgenden Beispiel wird gezeigt, daß auch dann der obige Algorithmus durchlaufen werden muß, wenn eine nach 2) bzw. 3) zugewiesene Task ihre Vorhaltung vor eine nach 1) bzw. 4) zugewiesene Taks verliert (Vorhaltungsprüfung).

Beispiel 2 :

$$T_1 = (4,4), \quad T_2 = (4,4), \quad T_3 = (6,3), \quad T_4 = (8,6), \quad T_5 = (8,5), \quad m = 3$$

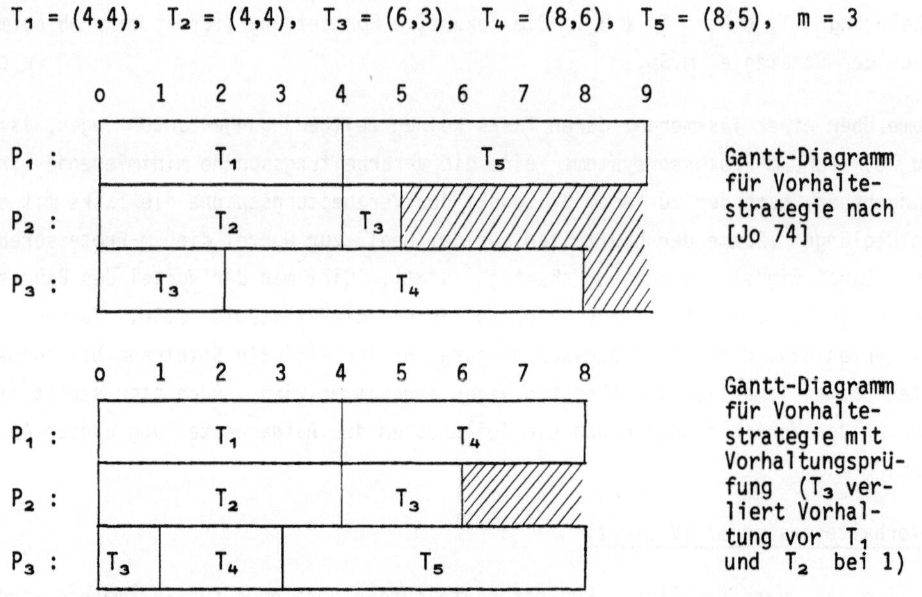

<u>Satz 7</u> : Die Vorhaltestrategie mit Vorhalteprüfung ist für Taskmengen eine zeitgerechte Strategie.

<u>Beweisskizze</u> : Es wird gezeigt, daß die Bedingungen (3), (4), (5) bei Verarbeitung der Vorhaltestrategie in der Verarbeitungsspanne erfüllt werden, wenn sie für $M(0)$ erfüllt sind. Sei Δt ein Zeitintervall, in dem keine Task beendet wird, und sei $M(t)$ eine relevante Taskmenge, die (3), (4) und (5) erfüllt. Für (3) gilt dann

$$m \cdot a_k(t) \geq \sum_{i=1}^{k} \ell_i(t) + \sum_{i=k+1}^{n} \max (0, a_k(t) - s_i(t))$$

In Δt wird die linke Seite um $m \cdot \Delta t$ reduziert, ebenso ergibt sich auf der rechten Seite $m \cdot \Delta t$ als Summe aus den Laufzeit- und Vorhaltungsreduzierungen, d.h. (3) ist bei $t + \Delta t$ erfüllt. Auf analoge Weise bleibt in Δt die Gültigkeit von (4) und (5) erhalten. Sei nun $\overline{t}_E$ der Zeitpunkt, zu dem eine Task $\overline{T}$ leer wird, d.h. $t + \Delta t = \overline{t}_E$, so gilt auf $M(\overline{t}_E)$ ebenfalls (3), (4), (5). Da $M(\overline{t}_E)$ zeitgerecht verarbeitbar ist, ist es $\overline{M}(\overline{t}_E) = M(t)\setminus\{\overline{T}(\overline{t}_E)\}$ ebenfalls. $\overline{M}(\overline{t}_E)$ erfüllt damit ebenfalls die Bedingungen (3), (4), (5). Die rekursive Fortsetzung zeigt, daß in der Verarbeitungsspanne auf den relevanten Taskmengen die Bedingungen (3), (4), (5) erfüllt bleiben.   q.e.d.

3.5. Strategie preemptive Antwortzeit (p.A.)

Dieser Strategie liegt als Basis die Strategie n.a.A. zugrunde. Es tritt eine Preemption ein, wenn der Spielraum einer Task, die keinen Prozessor besitzt, Null wird, d.h. eine wartende Task mit Spielraum Null verdrängt eine arbeitende Task mit einem Spielraum größer Null von ihrem Prozessor.

Sei $Y(t) = \{T(t) \in M(t) : s(t) = 0\}$ und sei $M(t) \backslash Y(t)$ nach aufsteigenden Antwortzeiten indiziert, so ist die Strategie p.A. definiert durch

$$B(t) = Y(t) \cup \{T_i(t) \in M(t) \backslash Y(t) : 1 \leq i \leq m - |Y(t)|\}$$

Das Gantt-Diagramm in Beispiel 1 entspricht der Prozessorbelegung nach der Strategie p.A.

<u>Satz 7</u> : Die Strategie p.A. ist für normalisierte Wälder und 2-Prozessorsysteme
zeitgerecht.

<u>Beweis</u> : Es wird von einer Ablaufmatrix A mit einer zeitgerechten Prozessorbelegung ausgegangen. Bis zur Spalte $j-1$ erfüllt A die Eigenschaft der Strategie p.A. Ab Spalte j sei dies nicht mehr der Fall, d.h.

$$\exists T_i, \ T_k : T_i \notin B_j \quad T_k \in B_j \quad T_i \in F_j \quad a_{ij} < a_{kj} \quad s_{kj} > 0 \quad \ell_{ij} > 0$$

O.E.d.A. können wir $a_{ij} \leq a_{rj}$ $(1 \leq r \leq n)$ mit $T_r \notin B_j$ und $T_r \in F_j$ wählen. Bei einem Wald gibt es nur einen Weg von T_k zu einem Endknoten. Er wird mit W_k bezeichnet. Mit Hilfe von Austauschschritt und Verschiebeoperation wird nun die p.A.-konforme Prozessorbelegung $T_i \in B_j$ $T_k \notin B_j$ erzeugt.

1. $\exists \beta \ \ j < \beta \leq v_i : T_i \in B_\beta \quad W_k \notin\cdot B_\beta.$
   Der Austauschschritt (T_i, j, W_k, β) liefert die gewünschte Belegung.

2. $\nexists \beta \ \ j < \beta \leq v_i : T_i \in B_\beta \quad W_k \notin\cdot B_\beta.$ Wegen 1. gilt $T_i \in B_{v_i} \quad W_k \notin\cdot B_{v_i}$.
   Wegen $s_{kj} > 0 \ \ \exists \gamma \ \ j < \gamma < \overline{v}_k : W_k \notin\cdot B\gamma.$

   a) $j < \gamma < v_i.$ Es liegt folgende Situation auf A vor.

   $$T_i \notin B_j \quad T_i \notin B_\gamma \quad T_i \in B_{v_i}$$
   $$T_k \in B_j \quad W_k \notin\cdot B_\gamma \quad W_k \notin\cdot B_{v_i}$$

   Wegen $m=2$ gilt $v_i \leq \underline{v}.$ Damit $\exists T_r : T_r \notin B_j \quad W_r \notin\cdot B_\gamma$ und wegen

$$a_{ij} \leq a_{rj} \quad W_r \in\kern-1.1ex{\cdot}\ B_{v_i}$$

<u>Fall 1</u> : $v_i \leq v_k$.   Es gilt

$$T_i \notin B_j \quad T_i \notin B_\gamma \quad T_i \in B_{v_i}$$
$$T_k \in B_j \quad T_k \notin B_\gamma \quad T_k \in B_{v_i}$$
$$T_r \notin B_j \quad W_r \in\kern-1.1ex{\cdot}\ B_\gamma \quad W_r \in\kern-1.1ex{\cdot}\ B_{v_i}$$

Der Austauschschritt $(T_i,\gamma,\ W_r,v_i)$ ermöglicht 1.

<u>Fall 2</u> : $v_i > v_k$.   Wegen $a_{ij} < a_{kj}$ gilt $0 \leq a_{iv_i} < a_{kv_i} = s_{kv_i}$,   d.h.

$$\exists\gamma \quad v_i < \gamma < \bar{v} : W_k \in\kern-1.1ex{\cdot}\ B_\gamma \qquad \text{siehe unter b) und c).}$$

b) $v_i < \gamma \leq \underline{v}$ Es liegt folgende Situation vor

$$T_i \notin B_j \quad T_i \in B_{v_i}$$
$$T_k \in B_j \quad W_k \in\kern-1.1ex{\cdot}\ B_{v_i} \quad W_k \in\kern-1.1ex{\cdot}\ B_\gamma$$

Wegen $\gamma \leq \underline{v}$ $\exists T_r, T_r' : T_r \in B_\gamma$ $T_r' \in B_\gamma$. O.E.d.A. können wir γ so wählen, daß $W_k \in\kern-1.1ex{\cdot}\ B_{\gamma-1}$ gilt. Daraus folgt, daß wegen m=2 $T_r \notin B_{\gamma-1}$, mit $T_r \in F_{\gamma-1}$ oder $T' \notin B_{\gamma-1}$ mit $T_r' \in F_{\gamma-1}$ gilt. O.E.d.A. wählen wir $T_r \notin B_{\gamma-1}$, d.h. es gilt

$$T_i \notin B_j \quad T_i \in B_{v_i}$$
$$T_k \in B_j \quad W_k \in\kern-1.1ex{\cdot}\ B_{v_i} \quad W_k \in\kern-1.1ex{\cdot}\ B_{\gamma-1} \quad W_k \in\kern-1.1ex{\cdot}\ B_\gamma$$
$$\qquad\qquad\qquad\qquad\qquad T_r \notin B_{\gamma-1} \quad T_r \in B_\gamma$$

Der Austauschschritt $(T_r,\gamma-1,W_k,\gamma)$ liefert $W_k \notin B_{\gamma-1}$ $W_k \in B_\gamma$ $T_r \in B_{\gamma-1}$ $T_r \notin B_\gamma$. Die Fortsetzung dieser Konstruktion liefert schießlich

$$T_i \notin B_j \quad T_i \in B_{v_i}$$
$$T_k \in B_j \quad W_k \in\kern-1.1ex{\cdot}\ B_{v_i} \quad W_k \in\kern-1.1ex{\cdot}\ B_{v_i+1}$$
$$\qquad\qquad\quad T_r' \notin B_{v_i} \quad T_r' \in B_{v_i+1}$$

Der Austauschschritt (T_r',v_i,W_k,v_i+1) ermöglicht 1.

c) $\gamma > \underline{v}$. Die Verschiebeoperation (T_i,j,W_k) liefert die gewünschte Prozessorbelegung in Spalte j.   q.e.d.

<u>Zusammenfassung</u>

Die Frage nach der zeitgerechten Verarbeitbarkeit einer Taskmenge kann beim 1-Prozessorsystem über (1) und beim Mehrprozessorsystem über (3), (4), (5)

beantwortet werden. Beim 1-Prozessorsystem reicht für die zeitgerechte Verarbeitbarkeit eines Präzedenzsystems die zeitgerechte Verarbeitbarkeit der Taksmenge über
dem normalisierten Präzedenzsystem aus. (In [He 75] ist sogar gezeigt, daß für
Wälder und Mehrprozessorsysteme die analoge Aussage gilt.)

Zeitgerechte Strategien :

	Einprozessorsystem	Mehrprozessorsystem
n.a.A.	Präzedenzsysteme	Einheitswälder
m.Sp.	Präzedenzsysteme	Wälder
V-Strat.	./.	Taskmengen
p.A.	./.	2-Prozessorsysteme und Wälder

<u>Literatur</u>

[Co 73]   E.G. Coffmann, jr., P.J. Denning :
            Operating system theory; Prentice Hall, Inc., Englewood
            Cliffs, N.J. 1973

[Ei 75]   B. Eichenauer :
            Dynamische Prioritätsvergabe an Tasks in Prozeßrechensystemen
            Dissert. Universität Stuttgart 1975

[He 73]   R.Henn, S. Lehnhoff :
            Strategien zur pseudo-kollateralen Verbeitung von Programmen
            unter Berücksichtigung vorgegebener Antwortzeiten;
            TUM - Math. Bericht Nr. 7307, 1973

[He 75]   R. Henn :
            Deterministische Modelle für die Prozessorzuteilung in einer
            harten Realzeitumgebung; Dissert. TU München 1975

[Hu 61]   T.C. Hu :
            Parallel sequencing and assembly line problems;
            Operating Research 8, No. 6, S. 841-848, Nov. 1961

[Jo 74]   H.H. Johnson, M. Maddison :
            Deadline scheduling for a real-time multiprocessor;
            Eurocomp. Conference Proceedings, S. 139-153, 1974

[Li 73]   C.L. Liu, J.W. Layland :
            Scheduling algorithms for multiprogramming in a hard-real-
            time environment; JACM, Vol. 20, No 1, S. 46-61, 1973

Mu 70   R.R. Muntz, E.G. Coffmann, jr. :
            Preemptive scheduling of real-time tasks on multiprocessor-
            systems; JACM, Vol. 17, No. 2, S. 324-338, 1970

ON THE RELATIONSHIP OF SECTOR REFERENCES, SECTOR PLACEMENT
AND PAGING PERFORMANCE.

Donald R. Innes
The Computer Laboratory,
University of Liverpool,
Liverpool L69 3BX, England.

ABSTRACT

The performance of a program in a paged virtual memory environment is significantly
influenced by the placement of its relocatable sectors. Considerable effort is currently being invested in optimising the paging performance of frequently used programs.
This paper examines the relationship of a program's sector reference behaviour to its
page reference behaviour. Lower bounds for a program's paging performance with optimum
placement of its relocatable sectors are obtained for the independent reference model
and for the least recently used and the working set page replacement policies. These
bounds are based upon the theoretically optimum sector fetch and replacement policies.
The reasons for rejecting alternative sector replacement policies are discussed. It
is shown how the shape of a lower bound can be used to estimate the page allocation or
working set size necessary to obtain a required paging performance. Results of applying the technique to a fairly well structured compiler are given to illustrate the
tightness of the lower bounds in a realistic situation. The algorithms can be applied
to a program's reference trace before pagination to obtain an estimate of the gain
which might be realised by improving the placement of its relocatable sectors in virtual
memory.

INTRODUCTION

The advantage of a virtual memory system is that is relieves the programmer of the
burden of storage management. Despite the fact that their effectiveness and overhead
leave much to be desired, this advantage has led to the widespread use of, particularly, paged memory systems. Thus it is important to minimise the additional cost
of these systems and, if possible, to make them more efficient than the equivalent
static memory allocation systems. Virtual memory systems only perform effectively
because of an inherent property of program behaviour known as locality. This property
of a program is that, during any interval of execution, its references favour a subset
of its information. The way in which program sectors are combined in pages significantly influences the locality of reference and hence the paging behaviour of a program.
The operation of assigning the sectors of a program to pages is called pagination.
An accepted measure of a program's paging behaviour is the distribution of page fault
frequency with real memory allocation. The purpose of this paper is threefold. First
to show that, in many frequently encountered situations, intuitively good procedures
for pagination often do not produce good results. The second purpose is to develop

methods for finding lower bounds for the paging performance from the sector reference
pattern. Finally we show how a lower bound can be used to estimate the real memory
allocation necessary to obtain a required paging performance.

An alternative measure of a program's performance in a paged virtual memory system
is the space-time produce. With most practical paging policies the space-time product
and the page fault rate are related, although it is not possible to specify a general
algebraic relationship. However, it is possible to state that
(a)   with "stack" paging policies the page fault rate is a monotonically decreasing
function with increasing stack size[1],
(b)   with the working set policy the page fault rate is a monotonically decreasing
function with increasing window size[2].

It has been established that a similar relationship does not exist with the first-in
first-out replacement policy[3]. Given page reference frequencies or a page reference
trace we can extract the particular relationship between space-time product and page
fault rate for that data. We could state that a pagination is optimum if it produces
fewer page faults than any other pagination for all possible memory allocations. It
is unlikely that such an optimum pagination exists. There is more likely to be a
family of sub-optimum paginations each of which is optimum over a particular range of
memory allocations.

We shall determine lower bounds for the number of page faults for any pagination for
the independent reference model, the least recently used stack policy, and the working
set policy. These bounds are derived from the sector reference behaviour of the program.
For the independent reference model we assume that the sector reference probabilities
and the sector sizes are known. For the least recently used policy and the working
set policy we assume that we have the sector sizes and a "characteristic" sector reference trace. There is experimental evidence to show that, for many programs, sector
reference traces are fairly data independent[4]. The shape of the bound indicates the
variation of page fault rate with memory allocation. Thus we can estimate, before
pagination, the amount of real memory which should be allocated to produce a required
page fault rate. This estimate can be given to the procedure which assigns sectors
to virtual memory so that it clusters for that page allocation, rather than for a
single page allocation[5].

INDEPENDENT REFERENCE MODEL

The independent reference model has been analysed for the purposes of pagination[6] and
of paging policy[7]. The probability of a reference to sector i at time t is given by
$$P_r[r_t = i] = p_i \quad \text{for } 1 \leq t, \ 1 \leq i \leq n$$
where the set of all p_i is fixed and sum to 1. Consider the following problem:

given a set of equal size sectors and their reference probabilities, how should we
partition the sectors into equal size pages. Assume that there are nV sectors $s_1,\ldots,$
s_{nV}, and that at each discrete time unit exactly one sector is referenced; sector i
is referenced at time t with probability p_i ($1 \le i \le nV$), independent of previous references. We wish to distribute the nV sectors among V virtual memory pages, with exactly
n sectors to a page. Assume that the sectors can be labelled so that $p_1 \ge p_2 \ge \ldots$
p_{nV}. Intuitively the optimum organisation is obtained by placing $s_1,\ldots,s_n$ on one
page $s_{n+1},\ldots,s_{2n}$ on another page and so on. This particular allocation of sectors
to pages has been called the frequency order organisation. It has been shown that
the frequency order organisation is best under two criteria of optimality: minimum
expected working set size, and minimum expected least recently used stack distance[6].
However, it has also been shown that the frequency order organisation does not necessarily minimise the page fault rate with the least recently used paging policy[8].

We can show that with frequency order pagination, the optimum paging policy minimises
the page fault rate. The sectors of a program are assigned to V virtual memory pages
in decreasing frequency order. Assume that the program is executed with an allocation
of N page frames. While there are free page frames no page is replaced. When there
is no free page frame the highest numbered page is the one to be replaced. The steady
state result is that the first N-1 pages have been referenced and are effectively
locked in store leaving 1 page frame into which each of the remaining V-N+1 pages can
be loaded when it is referenced. The pagination is optimum since it attempts to load
the most frequently accessed sectors as early as possible. The paging policy is
optimum since it ensures that the sectors most likely to be referenced next are retained
in store. The probability of a page fault is

$$\sum_{I=N}^{V} P_r \left[r_{t-1} \neq I \text{ and } r_t = I \right] \qquad \text{for } t \gg N$$

When the sectors are of different sizes, to obtain the optimum result the value of N
must be known before pagination is carried out. The weighted probability is obtained
by dividing the sector reference probability by the size of the sector. The sectors
are assigned to the first N pages in decreasing order of weighted probability. If
the last sector assigned is smaller than one page but cannot be contained in the Nth
page it is moved to the $N+1^{th}$ page and the gap in the Nth page is filled from the
unassigned sectors to maximise the probability of reference to page N. The remaining
sectors are assigned in decreasing order of weighted probability to further pages.
The same procedure is applied if the last sector of a page is not completely contained
by the page. The same paging policy as before is used to ensure that the most frequently accessed sectors are retained in store.

Although the independent reference model can exhibit a locality of reference, when
the probability that certain sectors will be referenced is greater than the probability

for others, it does not reflect normal program behaviour. Normally the locality of a program is not static and the probability that a sector is referenced at time t depends upon the sequence of references prior to t. This dynamic probability is much more difficult to characterise and is most concisely represented by a "characteristic" reference trace of the program. A reference trace contains the addresses of the basic instruction and data elements of the program in the order in which they were accessed during an execution of the program. For the purposes of pagination a reference trace is transformed into a sector reference trace where a sector is a relocatable block of instruction or data elements. A paging policy can be looked upon as a machine for processing either a sector reference trace or a particular page reference trace derived from the sector reference trace. We can measure the efficiency of such a machine processing a sector reference trace. We will determine in what circumstances the sector processing efficiency of a machine is a lower bound of the paging processing efficiency of the same or a different machine. Before we consider the least recently used and working set paging policies we must introduce some base terminology and the OPT algorithm. In fact the OPT algorithm was implicitly introduced as the optimum paging policy for the independent reference model.

OPT ALGORITHM

In a reference string the backward reference distance $b_t(s)$ at time t to sector s is the distance to the most recent reference to s:

$$b_t(s) = \begin{cases} k & \text{if } r_{t-k} \text{ is the last reference to s in } r_1, \ldots, r_t \\ \infty & \text{if s is not reference in } r_1, \ldots, r_t \end{cases}$$

Similarly, the forward reference distance $d_t(s)$ to the first reference to s after time t is:

$$d_t(s) = \begin{cases} k & \text{if } r_{t+k} \text{ is the first reference to s in } r_{t+1}, r_{t+2}, \ldots \\ \infty & \text{if s is not referenced in } r_{t+1}, r_{t+2}, \ldots \end{cases}$$

A sector stack is identical to a page stack except that the elements of the stack are variable size sectors rather than fixed size pages. Thus a sector stack of size N will hold any combination of up to N sectors.

The OPT, or MIN, algorithm[9] is a stack management algorithm which, in the case of a sector stack, causes the minimum number of sector faults to occur when a sector reference trace is processed with a fixed stack size. The OPT stack state transition function satisfies the following conditions for $r_{t+1} \in X$

$$S_{t+1} = \begin{cases} S_t & \text{if } X \subseteq S_t \\ S_t + X & \text{if } X \not\subseteq S_t, \ |S_t| < N \\ S_t + X - Y & \text{if } X \not\subseteq S_t, \ |S_t| = N \end{cases}$$

where $d_{t+1}(Y) = \max d_{t+1}(Z)$ for all $Z \in S_t$, and $S_o = \emptyset$. Although the OPT algorithm is unrealistic as a paging policy it is useful for our purposes since it has been proved to be the optimum paging policy. A form of the algorithm can produce, in a single pass of a reference string, the number of stack faults which occur for all stack sizes[10].

LEAST RECENTLY USED POLICY

The least recently used (LRU) policy is by far the most widely used paging policy. It is a stack algorithm with the following stack state transition function for $r_{t+1} \in X$

$$S_{t+1} = \begin{cases} S_t & \text{if } X \subseteq S_t \\ S_t + X & \text{if } X \not\subseteq S_t, \ |S_t| < N \\ S_t + X\text{-}Y & \text{if } X \not\subseteq S_t, \ |S_t| = N \end{cases}$$

where $b_{t+1}(Y) = \max b_{t+1}(Z)$ for all $Z \in S_t$, and $S_o = \emptyset$.

LRU sector bound

We wish to obtain a lower bound for the page fault rate as a function of the sector fault rate. Sector fault rates can be produced by processing a sector reference trace for various stack sizes. The page fault rate must be related to the sector fault rate by the particular pagination of sectors. We will assume that

$$\Pi_{LRU} = f_i(\pi_{LRU})$$

where Π_{LRU} is the page fault rate, π_{LRU} is the sector fault rate and f_i is some function related to the particular pagination i. We will further assume that for a given stack size there is an optimum pagination with a related function F such that

$$\Pi_{LRU} \geq F(\pi_{LRU})$$

where Π_{LRU} is the page fault rate for any pagination with that stack size. We must specify F in order to establish the bound. If the only advantage of pagination is that a number of sectors are fetched at each page fault then the maximum advantage is gained when the greatest number of sectors are fetched, assuming that each sector will be referenced before it is removed from the page stack. From the sector sizes we can determine n, the maximum number of sectors which may occur in any page. This leads us to hypothesis that for a particular stack size the lower bound on the page fault rate for any pagination can be expressed as

$$\Pi_{LRU} \geq \pi_{LRU}/n$$

However, when a number of sectors occupy the same page, if one sector is referenced, for the purposes of replacement, the backward reference distance of all the sectors in the page is set to zero. This may cause a sector to be removed from the sector stack while it remains in the page stack even when the sector stack is expanded to contain n times the number of elements in the page stack. Consider the following:

$$\text{sectors} - a,b,c,d,e,f$$
$$\text{pagination} - (a,b),(c,d),(e,f)$$
$$\text{sector reference string} - acdbefa$$

Process this reference string with a page stack of size 2 and a sector stack of size 4:

$$7 \text{ sector faults occur at } \underline{a} \ \underline{c} \ \underline{d} \ \underline{b} \ \underline{e} \ \underline{f} \ \underline{a}$$
$$3 \text{ page faults occur at } \quad \underline{a} \ \underline{c} \qquad \underline{e}$$

Thus for this example

$$\Pi_{LRU} < \pi_{LRU}/n$$

The LRU policy replaces the stack element with the greatest backward reference distance. This is an effective practical policy when, of necessity, we are unaware of the forward reference distance of elements. However, we have found a counter-example to our hypothesis that

$$\Pi_{LRU} \geq \pi_{LRU}/n$$

This is not an end point effect which can be compensated for by adding a constant to the right hand side. If the reference string acdbef is repeated x times it produces 6x sector stack faults and 2x+1 page stack faults. Since we are unaware of the actual pagination we are unable to alter the backward reference distances of sectors in the sector stack to match their alteration in the page stack. We conclude that there is no satisfactory function which, applied to the LRU sector fault rate, produces a lower bound for the LRU page fault rate.

OPT sector bound

The LRU sector bound failed because its replacement policy was not optimal. This is true of any replacement policy except that employed by the OPT algorithm. With the same conditions as for the LRU sector bound, particularly that the sector stack contains n times the number of elements as are in the page stack, we express the following theorem.

Theorem 1: $\qquad \Pi_{LRU} \geq \pi_{OPT}/n$

Proof: Allowing that the page fetch model can be up to n times more efficient than the sector fetch model, the correctness of this lower bound is established from consideration of their replacement policies.

If a sector which has been referenced is retained in the page stack then, since there are at least as many sectors in the sector stack as are in the page stack, either it will be retained in the sector stack or another sector with a smaller forward reference distance, which is not in the page stack, will be retained in the sector stack. Thus the replacement policy of sector OPT will cause no more sector faults than would occur if the sectors were replaced by the LRU page policy.

Since each unreferenced sector in the page stack corresponds to at most one reference fault in the sector model, which is fully compensated by the n factor, the theorem is proved $\square$

The weakness of this bound is in the specification of the sector stack size. For a page stack of size N we can determine, from the sector sizes, the maximum number of sectors N_s which can reside in this space. The problem is simple if we allow sectors to overlap page boundaries but more difficult if each sector must be contained in one page.

Corollary 1a: $\quad \Pi_{LRU} \geq \pi_{OPTa}/n \geq \pi_{OPT}/n$

where the size of the page stack is N and the size of the sector stack is N_s.

Proof: The necessary conditions for the proof of Theorem 1 have not changed. The characteristic of stack algorithms is that reducing the stack size will leave unchanged or increase the number of stack faults $\square$

Even with the stack size of one it is impossible to demand fetch the most recently fetched stack element. Thus two adjacent page faults must be to different pages. Let m be the maximum number of sectors which can be contained in two pages. Having determined the number of sector faults we can find integers x and y such that

$$\pi_{OPTa} = xm + y$$

Since we wish to express the inequalities in terms of the sector packing factor we shall define

$$n_b = \begin{cases} \pi_{OPTa}/2x & \text{if } y = 0 \text{ since } \pi_{OPTa} = xm \\ \pi_{OPTa}/(2x + 1) & \text{if } y \leq n \text{ since } \pi_{OPTa} \leq xm + 1n \\ \pi_{OPTa}/2(x + 1) & \text{if } y > n \text{ since } \pi_{OPTa} < (x + 1)m \end{cases}$$

where, as before, n is the maximum number of sectors which can be contained in one page.

Corollary 1b: $\quad \Pi_{LRU} \geq \pi_{OPTa}/n_b \geq \pi_{OPTa}/n \geq \pi_{OPT}/n$

Proof: The necessary conditions for the proof of Theorem 1 have not changed. With the sector packing factor n_b the lower bound has been tightened, since $n_b \leq n$ $\square$

Dynamic OPT bound

The OPT sector bound is an indirect evaluator of the effect of pagination in limiting the page fault rate for a given stack size. Since it is indirect it makes four assumptions which effect the closeness of the bound:

(a) any two consecutive page fetches will fetch the greatest number of sectors which can be contained in two pages,

(b) every sector which is fetched into the page stack will be referenced at least once before it is removed from the page stack,

(c) if a page is removed from the page stack it will contain those sectors in the stack which have the greatest forward reference distance,

(d) each page in the stack is completely filled with sector information.

The contradiction of assumption (d) is that each sector must be completely contained in a page. This is very reasonable and may in fact be the case in practice. However, determining the maximum number of sectors which can be fitted into a number of pages without any sector overlapping two pages, or alternatively bounding the expansion factor caused by this pagination policy, is a non-trivial combinatorial problem in itself. Assumptions (b) and (c) are the fundamental assumptions which support the optimality of the OPT sector bound. Rejecting either assumption should lead to inconsistency which will manifest itself in exceptions to whatever bounds are derived without both. Assumption (a) is thus the only one which we may easily and safely reject bcause we have the sector reference trace.

The dynamic OPT (DOPT) bound algorithm processes the sector reference trace in much the same way as the OPT sector bound algorithm but it uses a sector stack with an identical information capacity to the page stack for which we wish to establish the bound. Sectors are assumed to be packed into pages with possible overlap of pages by some sectors. Whenever a sector fault occurs it is treated as a page fault. A page of sectors, composed of those with the greatest forward distance, are removed from the stack. When a sector is fetched it is brought in with a sufficient number of other sectors to constitute a page. These other sectors are those sectors not currently in the stack, but possibly just removed, with the smallest forward reference distance. At any time a number of sectors, only one being fetched but several being replaced, can be partially in the stack. Reference to such a sector will cause a fault which will fetch a page of information, containing the remainder of this sector, into the stack. This bound is called dynamic OPT because a sector may occur with any number of distinct combinations of other sectors in pages being fetched or replaced. We may therefore declare the bound.

Theorem 2: $\Pi_{LRU} \geq \pi_{DOPT} \geq \pi_{OPTa}/n_b$

Proof: The dynamic OPT policy ensures that when a sector fault is serviced the new stack state is such that, with the constraint of only replacing one page of information, the forward reference distance to the next sector fault is maximised. Thus the LRU page fault rate is lower bounded by the DOPT sector fault rate. The dynamic OPT algorithm determines the actual sector packing factor from the sizes of the sectors as they are fetched. The average of the packing factor must be less than or equal to the n_b factor which is derived from the maximum possible packing of two pages.

WORKING SET POLICY

The working set (WS) policy, which allows the allocation of page framces to adapt to variation in the locality of a program during execution, has been proposed by Denning[2]. A program's working page set at time t is

$$W(t,\tau) = \{ Z \mid Z \in V \text{ and } b_t(Z) < \tau \}$$

WS sector bound

We might expect, as we did with the LRU policy, that we can construct a WS page fault rate bound for a given reference string as a function of the WS sector fault rate. Thus we might hypothesis that for a given window size τ and any pagination of the sectors of the program

$$\Pi_{WS} \geq \pi_{WS}/n$$

where Π_{WS} is the page fault rate, π_{WS} is the sector fault rate, and n is the maximum number of sectors that will fit into a page. However, since the contents of a working set are determined by the history of previous references, the sector working set at time t is

$$W_s(t,\tau) = \{ z \mid z \in v \text{ and } b_t(z) < \tau \}$$

where v is the set of program sectors. The significant difference between WS and LRU is that the WS "stack" dynamically adjusts its size to accommodate the elements refer- enced within the time window. This implies that

$$w_p(t,\tau) \geq w_s(t,\tau)$$

where $w_p(t,\tau)$ is the size of the page working set and $w_s(t,\tau)$ is the size of the sector working set. Thus the sectors contained in the sector working set must be contained in the page working set but the sectors in the page working set which have not been referenced or have been referenced, but have a backward reference distance greater than τ, cannot be in the sector working set. Although the unreferenced sectors in the page working set have been compensated for by the n factor, the effect of those with a backward reference distance greater than τ cannot be bounded as the following example will demonstrate.

Consider a program with a double loop structure. The inner loop contains statements which refer to a set of sectors A. The outer loop contains the inner loop as well as statements which refer to a set of sectors B, where $A \cap B = \emptyset$. The reference string gen- erated by the program has the form

$$(\alpha^m \beta)^n$$

where m and n are the number of iterations of the inner and outer loops respectively and α and β are sequences of references to the sectors of A and B respectively. For simplicity we may consider that the working set window τ is greater than the time required to execute all the statements of the program once. Clearly for a large enough value of m, the number of sector faults is a function of n. The reason is that during the execution of the inner loop the sectors of B are released from the working set as $b_s(z) \geq \tau$ for all $z \in B$. However, if the sectors of A and B are assigned to pages so that at least one sectors from A is in each page which contains sectors from B there will only be one page fault for each page referenced by the program. Clearly the value of m can be increased so that $b_t(z) \geq \tau$, for all $z \in B$, for any fixed value of τ. Since the number of sector faults is a function of n there is no constant factor which will compensate in the page fault bound. Once again we must reject all lower bounds which do not use the forward reference distance as the criteria for retaining sectors in the sector stack.

OPT sector bound

To apply the OPT algorithm in a WS environment it is necessary to relate the size of the sector stack to the size of the sector working set which itself depends on the size of the window τ. Although we are able to characterise the relation between the average page working set size and the page fault rate we are unable to use the average sector working set size to determine the OPT sector stack size. To apply the OPT algorithm directly the sector stack size must be static and is thus a function of the maximum sector working set size. If the maximum sector working set size is N then we will use a sector stack size of N_s as defined for Corollary 1a. Similarly we will use n_b as defined for Corollary 1b.

Theorem 3: $\Pi_{WS} \geq \pi_{OPTa}/n_b$

Proof: The paged LRU policy is a static version of the paged WS policy. If the LRU stack is the same size as the maximum page working set then the LRU policy must have the same number, or fewer, page faults as the WS policy. The π_{OPTa}/n_b bound has been established for LRU therefore it also holds for WS $\square$

variable OPT sector bound

The OPT sector bound for WS is more difficult to determine than its LRU counterpart since the maximum size of the sector working set must be found for each value of τ. More important, the bound is inherently looser than the LRU bound since it is based on the maximum working set size rather than the actual sizes. We could divide the sector reference trace into a number of shorter sequences and determine the maximum sector working set size for each sequence. The OPT sector bound could then be obtained by applying the algorithm with a different stack size for each sequence. The generalisation of this procedure is to determine the sector working set size at each reference. We can obtain a tighter bound by modifying the OPT algorithm to operate with a variable stack size.

A fault occurs because at some point between the last reference and the current reference the stack became smaller than the minimum necessary depth required to hold the sector in memory. If the size of the working set at time t is N^t, the size of the OPT sector stack at time t is N^t_s.

Theorem 4: $\quad \Pi_{WS} \geq \pi_{VOPT}/n_b \geq \pi_{OPTa}/n_b$

Proof: Any sector which is retained in the page working set will also be retained in the variable OPT sector stack or, in preference, a sector with a smaller forward reference distance which is not in the page working set will be retained in the variable OPT sector stack. Varying the size of the OPT stack will cause the same number, or more, sector faults as would occur if its size was static at the maximum size $\quad \square$

<u>EXPERIMENTAL RESULTS</u>

The algorithms for obtaining the lower bounds were applied to a reference string obtained from the syntax analysis phase of the ALGOLW compiler running under MTS on the IBM 370/168 at the University of Newcastle upon Tyne. The reference string was obtained from the compilation of a "typical" ALGOLW program. The ALGOLW compiler is structured for the page size of 4096 bytes and exhibits a high degree of locality in its execution so that we would expect the lower bounds to be fairly tight.

The lower bounds for least recently used and working set replacement are shown in figures 1 and 2 respectively. The bounds are given for the ranges of page stack allocations and window sizes. As the page stack and working set sizes decrease the ratio of sector faults to page faults decreases since the sector management makes more efficient use of the available memory. With the least recently used policy both the OPT and DOPT bounds are fairly tight. The compiler is not particularly modular and the presence of a number of large sectors favours the DOPT approach. With the working set policy the OPT algorithm based on the maximum working set size gives a much looser bound than the VOPT algorithm.

<u>CONCLUSION</u>

A quantification of the maximum performance improvement which may be gained by the improved pagination of the relocatable sectors of a program should precede any restructuring. A number of methods of estimating optimum paging performance, with the most commonly available paging disciplines, have been developed in this paper. It has been

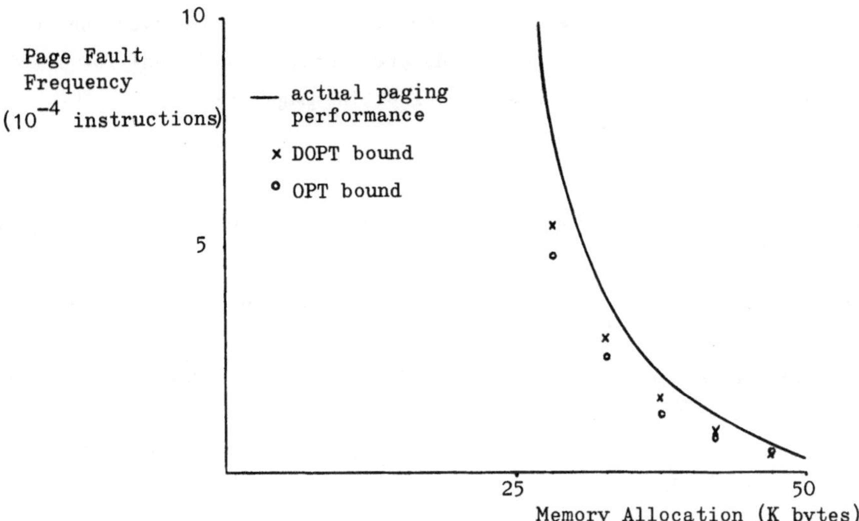

figure 1: <u>lower bounds for LRU replacement</u>

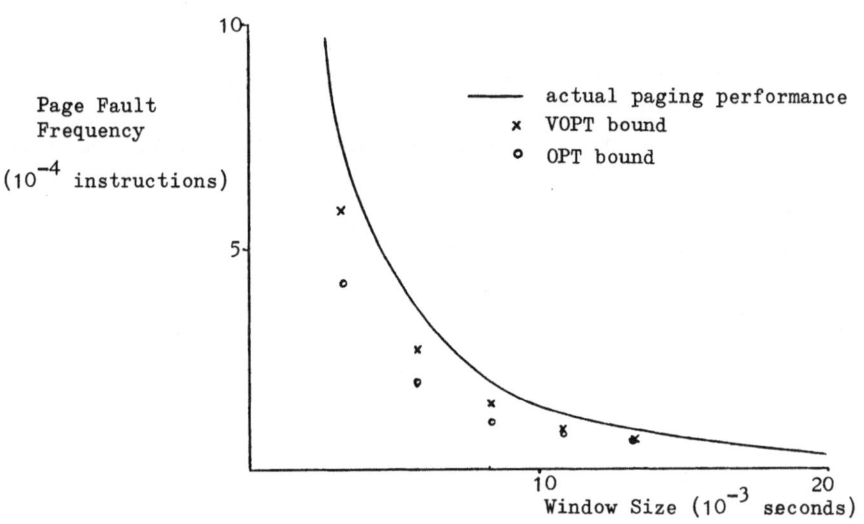

figure 2: <u>lower bounds for working set replacement</u>

shown that, for our example program, close bounds can be obtained over the operational range of page fault frequencies. The methods are likely to work best for a modular program with sector sizes of about one quarter of the page size.

REFERENCES

1.   Mattson, R., Gecsei, J., Sluty, D., and Traiger, I., "Evaluation Techniques for Storage Hierarchies", IBM Syst. J. 9,2 (1970), 78-117.

2.   Denning, P.J. and Schwartz, S.C., "Properties of the Working Set Model", Comm. ACM 15, 3 (Mar. 1972), 191-198.

3.   Belady, L.A. and Kuehner, C.J., "Dynamic Space Sharing in Computer Systems", Comm. ACM 12, 5 (May 1969), 282-288.

4.   Ferrari, D., "Improving Locality of Critical Working Sets", Comm. ACM 17, 1 (Nov. 1974), 614-620.

5.   Hatfield, D.J. and Gerald, J., "Program Restructuring for Virtual Memory", IBM Syst. J. 10, 3 (1971), 168-192.

6.   Yue, P.C. and Wang, C.K., "On the Optimality of the Probability Ranking Scheme in Storage Applications", J.ACM. 20, 4 (Oct. 1973), 624-633.

7.   Aho, A.V., Denning, P.J. and Ullman, J.D., "Principles of Optimum Page Replacement", J.ACM 18, 1 (Jan. 1971), 80-93.

8.   Fagin, R., "A Counter intuitive Example of Computer Paging", IBM Research Report RC5021, Yorktown Heights, NY 10598.

9.   Belady, L.A., "A Study of Replacement Algorithms for a Virtual Storage Computer", IBM Syst. J. 5, 2 (1966), 78-101.

10.   Belady, L.A. and Palermo, F.P., "On-line Measurement of Paging Behaviour by the Multivalued MIN Algorithm", IBM J.R.D. (Jan. 1974), 2-19.

ÜBER EINE KOSTENFUNKTION FÜR DEN SEITENWECHSEL UNTER BERÜCKSICHTIGUNG VON DATENÜBERTRAGUNG UND HAUPTSPEICHERBELEGUNG

Günther Weber
Fachbereich Informatik
Technische Hochschule
6100 Darmstadt

Übersicht:

EINLEITUNG

In den Veröffentlichungen über die Leistung von Seitenwechselalgorithmen
wird als Vergleichskriterium die Anzahl der bei der Verarbeitung eines
Programmes auftretenden Fehlseitenunterbrechungen - page fault interrupts - benutzt.
Dabei bleibt die Tatsache unberücksichtigt, daß im Mehrprogrammbetrieb
die von einem Programm belegten Hauptspeicherteile - Rahmen genannt -
anderen Programmen vorenthalten werden.
Da sich hieraus jedoch oft eine spürbare Einschränkung ergibt, sollen
hier neben den Kosten, die durch Übertragung von Seiten zwischen Hilfs-
und Hauptspeicher entstehen, auch diejenigen Kosten berücksichtigt werden, welche auf die Belegung von Rahmen zurückzuführen sind; die betrachtete Kostenfunktion wird eine lineare Kombination von Speicher - und
Übertragungskosten sein.

GRUNDLAGEN

Die folgenden Betrachtungen beschränken sich auf das einfachste Modell
eines virtuellen Speichers, d.h. es wird von der Existenz eines Haupt-
und eines Hilfsspeichers ausgegangen; von diesem Hilfsspeicher wird angenommen, daß er durch eine Magnettrommel realisiert wird. Diese Annahmen bedeuten keine ernsthafte Einschränkung, da sie in leicht ersicht-
licher Weise aufgehoben bzw. verallgemeinert werden können.

Im Laufe der 15 Jahre seit der ersten Veröffentlichung über die Idee
eines virtuellen Speichers wurden verschiedene Algorithmen zur Verwaltung eines solchen virtuellen Speichers entwickelt; diese Algorithmen
lassen sich im allgemeinen Fall in drei Teile aufspalten:

        die Hol-Strategie ,

        die Ersetzungs-Strategie und

        die Platzierungs-Strategie.

Man unterscheidet virtuelle Speicher mit fester Einteilung von Programmen und Speichermedien von solchen mit variabler Einteilung und spricht
von Seitenwechsel- und Segmentverfahren.
Wegen der Normierung der Programmstücke auf einheitliche Größe ist beim
Seitenwechsel-Verfahren im Gegensatz zum Segment-Verfahren die Platzie-
rungsstrategie uninteressant.

Von den Ersetzungs-Strategien, von denen inzwischen eine Vielzahl ver-
öffentlicht wurde, werden im folgenden drei betrachtet, die aus verschie-

denen Gründen zu den bekanntesten zählen:

FIFO   besonders einfach zu implementieren,

LRU   erzeugt für verschiedene Programmverhaltens-Modelle
         eine geringere Fehlseitenrate

und Beladys optimale Strategie (BOS abgekürzt); sie ist nicht zu reali-
         sieren, aber als Vergleichsbasis interessant.

Drei Holstrategien werden betrachtet:
SWBf   Seitenwechsel nach Bedarf mit festem Hauptspeicheranteil,
SWBv   Seitenwechsel nach Bedarf mit variablem Hauptspeicheranteil und
SWiv   Seitenwechsel im voraus.

Zur Erläuterung dieser Hol-Strategien wird der Begriff des Speicherzu-
standes eingeführt: darunter soll diejenige Teilmenge der Seiten eines
Programmes verstanden werden, die sich zu einem gegebenen Zeitpunkt im
Hauptspeicher befindet.
SWBf ist die aus dem Englischen als "demand-paging" bekannte Strategie
mit fest vorgegebener Rahmenanzahl; d.h. hier erfolgt Einlagern und Entfernen von Seiten nur bei einer Fehlseitenunterbrechung.
Bei SWBv treten die gleichen Speicherzustände wie bei SWBf auf, der Unterschied besteht darin, daß die dem einzelnen Programm zur Verfügung
stehende Rahmenanzahl nicht immer voll ausgeschöpft werden muß; d.h. es
können auch Rahmen freigegeben werden, ohne von einer Seite des betreffenden Programmes belegt zu werden. Die Entscheidung darüber, in welchem
Fall bei der Verarbeitung einer Referenzenfolge Rahmen tatsächlich freigegeben werden, bleibt hier zunächst offen; bei SWBv treten daher mehr
Möglichkeiten als bei SWBf auf. Eingelagert wird aber auch hier nur bei
Bedarf.
Unter SWiv schließlich wird hier diejenige Holstrategie verstanden, bei
der darüberhinaus jeder Speicherzustand bereits zum frühestmöglichen
Zeitpunkt ohne weitere Fehlseitenunterbrechung zugelassen wird.

An einem Beispiel sollen die drei Holstrategien erläutert werden. Zu den
einzelnen Referenzen werden hier alle zulässigen Speicherzustände angegeben; die Zeilen unter den Referenzen entsprechen den alternativen
Möglichkeiten:

Referenzenfolge   : ω = 1 2 3 4 1 2 5 1 2 3 4 5
Ersetzungsstrategie: LRU
Rahmenanzahl   : m = 4

Seitenwechsel nach Bedarf, feste Hauptspeichergröße (SWBf):

Referenzen :	1	2	3	4	1	2	5	1	2	3	4	5
Speicherzust.:	1											
		12										
			123									
				1234	1234	1234	1254	1254	1254	1253	1243	5243

Seitenwechsel nach Bedarf, var. Hauptspeichergröße (SWBv):

Referenzen :	1	2	3	4	1	2	5	1	2	3	4	5
Speicherzust.:	1	2	3	4	1	2	5	1	2	3	4	5
		12	32	34	14	12	52	51	21	23	43	45
			123	423	413	412	512	512	512	312	342	345
				1234	1234	1234	1254	1254	1254	1253	1243	5243

Seitenwechsel im voraus (SWiv):

Referenzen :	1	2	3	4	1	2	5	1	2	3	4	5
Speicherzust.:	1	2	3	4	1	2	5	1	2	3	4	5
	12	12	32	34	14	12	52	51	21	23	43	45
		32	34	14	12	52	51	21	23	43	45	
	123	123	123	423	413	412	512	512	512	312	342	345
		423	423	413	412	512		312	312	342	345	
			413	412	512				342	345		
	1234	1234	1234	1234	1234	1234	1254	1254	1254	1253	1243	5243
			1254	1254	1254	1253	1253	1253	1243	5243		
			1253	1253			1243	1243	5243			
								5243				

Beispiel: Speicherzustände bei verschiedenen Holstrategien.

Die Kostenfunktion

1. Ansatz

Es wurden bereits die zwei Kostenarten erwähnt, die in die Funtion eingehen sollen: Übertragungskosten und Speicherkosten.
Übertragungskosten entstehen bei einer Fehlseitenunterbrechung durch die
Seitenübertragungszeit selbst wie auch durch die Wartezeit unmittelbar
davor, z.B. durch die Rotationsverzögerung bei einer Trommel als Hilfsspeicher beim Lesen.
Daher soll sowohl die Anzahl der Übertragungen $n_{\ddot{u}}$ - gleich ob eine oder
mehrere Seiten übertragen werden - als auch die Anzahl der übertragenen
Seiten $n_{\ddot{u}s}$ in die Kostenfunktion für die Verarbeitung eines Programmes
ω eingehen.
Werden von diesem Programm während eines Zeitintervalles z_i zwischen
zwei Referenzen auf verschiedene Seiten b_i Rahmen belegt, so entstehen
daraus Speicherkosten, da ja im Mehrprogrammbetrieb diese Rahmen anderen
Programmen vorenthalten werden.
Die Summe über die Anzahl T der Referenzen wird mit einer Kosteneinheit
k_{sp} gewichtet - ebenso bei den Übertragungskosten ($k_{\ddot{u}}$, $k_{\ddot{u}s}$).
Diese Kosteneinheit kann z.B. dazu verwendet werden, den Multiprogram-
ming-Grad in die Kostenfunktion mit eingehen zu lassen.
Bei den Übertragungskosten kommen noch die durch Zurückübertragung zu
ersetzender, veränderter Seiten entstehenden Anteile $n_{\ddot{u}z}$ und $n_{\ddot{u}sz}$ hinzu.
Diese Kosten sind natürlich von der Holstrategie HS, der Ersetzungsstra-
tegie ES und der Rahmenanzahl m abhängig.
Aus diesen Überlegungen ergibt sich der Ansatz:

$$K_{HS,ES}(\omega,m) = k_{\ddot{u}} \cdot (n_{\ddot{u}} + n_{\ddot{u}z}) + k_{\ddot{u}s} \cdot (n_{\ddot{u}s} + n_{\ddot{u}sz}) + k_{sp} \cdot \sum_{i=1}^{T} b_i \cdot z_i$$

2. Modell zur Auswertung

Diese Kostenfunktion wird nun mit Hilfe des folgenden Modells ausgewertet:
Die Speicherzustände werden als Knoten und die Übergänge zwischen diesen
als Kanten eines gerichteten, bewerteten Graphen aufgefaßt, wobei die
Bewertung jeder Kante analog zur oben angegebenen Kostenfunktion erfolgt.

Mit Hilfe eines Kürzesten-Wege-Algorithmus werden die minimalen Kosten
der Verarbeitung einer gegebenen Referenzenfolge unter vorgegebenen Parametern bestimmt; die zugehörige Folge von Speicherzuständen wird als
optimale Lösung des Seitenwechsel-Problems bezeichnet.
Der Vergleich von Seitenwechsel-Algorithmen wird so auf den Vergleich
von minimalen Werten der Kostenfunktion zurückgeführt.
Bei SWBv und SWiv ergibt sich für das Aufsuchen der optimalen Lösung
eine Analogie zum Lagerhaltungsproblem: es gibt einerseits Lager-Kosten
(Speicher-Kosten), andererseits Transportkosten, die sich aufteilen lassen in feste und variable Kosten. Das Aufsuchen der optimalen Lösung
entspricht einem Abwägen der beiden Kostenarten gegeneinander:
Hat man langsame Hilfsspeicher und langsame Kanäle, so daß die Verzöge-
rung und damit die Transportkosten als groß anzusehen sind, können die
Gesamtkosten durch Vergrößerung des von Programm- und Datenseiten belegten Hauptspeicherplatzes gesenkt werden, wenn so die Anzahl der Seiten-
übertragungen verringert wird. Werden umgekehrt die Speicherkosten als
groß angesehen, weil z.B. insgesamt wenig Hauptspeicherplatz vorhanden
ist, so wird eine Erhöhung der Datenübertragungsrate bei Verringerung
der Hauptspeicherbelegung in Kauf genommen.

ERGEBNISSE

Mit dieser Kostenfunktion als Kriterium werden nun einige Ergebnisse
gezeigt, die verschiedene, die Leistung eines virtuellen Speicher-Systems beeinflussende Größen wie Holstrategien, Ersetzungs-Strategien
usw. betreffen.
Dabei wird mit zwei Methoden vorgegangen, die in der Rechnerverkehrs-
theorie üblich sind:
1. die analytische Methode, bei der mit mathematischen Mitteln Aussagen
   hergeleitet werden und
2. die Simulation, bei der für Einzelfälle Ergebnisse berechnet werden,
die dann wiederum statistisch ausgewertet werden können.

1. ANALYTISCHE ERGEBNISSE

Es können folgende Monotonie-Eigenschaften der Kostenfunktion gezeigt
werden:

1. Monotonie-Eigenschaft (betr. Holstrategien):

$$K_{SWBf,ES}(\omega,m) \geqslant K_{SWBv,ES}(\omega,m) \geqslant K_{SWiv,ES}(\omega,m)$$

$K_{HS,ES}(\omega,m)$ bezeichne die minimalen Kosten der Verarbeitung der Referenzenfolge bei m zur Verfügung stehenden Rahmen mit der Holstrategie HS und der Ersetzungs-Strategie ES.

Beim Beweis geht man von der Definition der Holstrategien aus: die Folge der bei SWBf durchlaufenen Speicherzustände ist unter SWBv eine mögliche Lösung, ebenso ist jede unter SWBv zulässige Lösung - und insbesondere die optimale - unter SWiv möglich. Daher können die minimalen Kosten unter SWBv nicht größer als bei SWBf und die minimalen Kosten unter SWiv nicht größer als die minimalen Kosten unter SWBv sein.

Bezüglich der zur Verfügung stehenden Rahmenanzahlen erhält man sowohl unter SWBv wie unter SWiv monoton fallende Kosten der optimalen Lösung bei wachsender Rahmenanzahl:

2. Monotonie-Eigenschaft (betr. Rahmenanzahlen):

$$K_{SWBv,ES}(\omega,m+1) \leqq K_{SWBv,ES}(\omega,m)$$

$$K_{SWiv,ES}(\omega,m+1) \leqq K_{SWiv,ES}(\omega,m)$$

Zum Beweis betrachtet man wieder die zugehörigen Speicherzustände: sie erfüllen bei wachsender Rahmenanzahl eine Obermengen-Relation; die bei m zur Verfügung stehenden Rahmen optimale Lösung ist daher auch bei m+1 Rahmen möglich.

Für SWBf gilt diese Monotonie nicht, da die Einschließungs-Eigenschaft nicht vorliegt. Es lassen sich daher leicht Beispiele mit nicht monoton fallenden Werten der Kostenfunktion bei wachsender Rahmenanzahl finden:

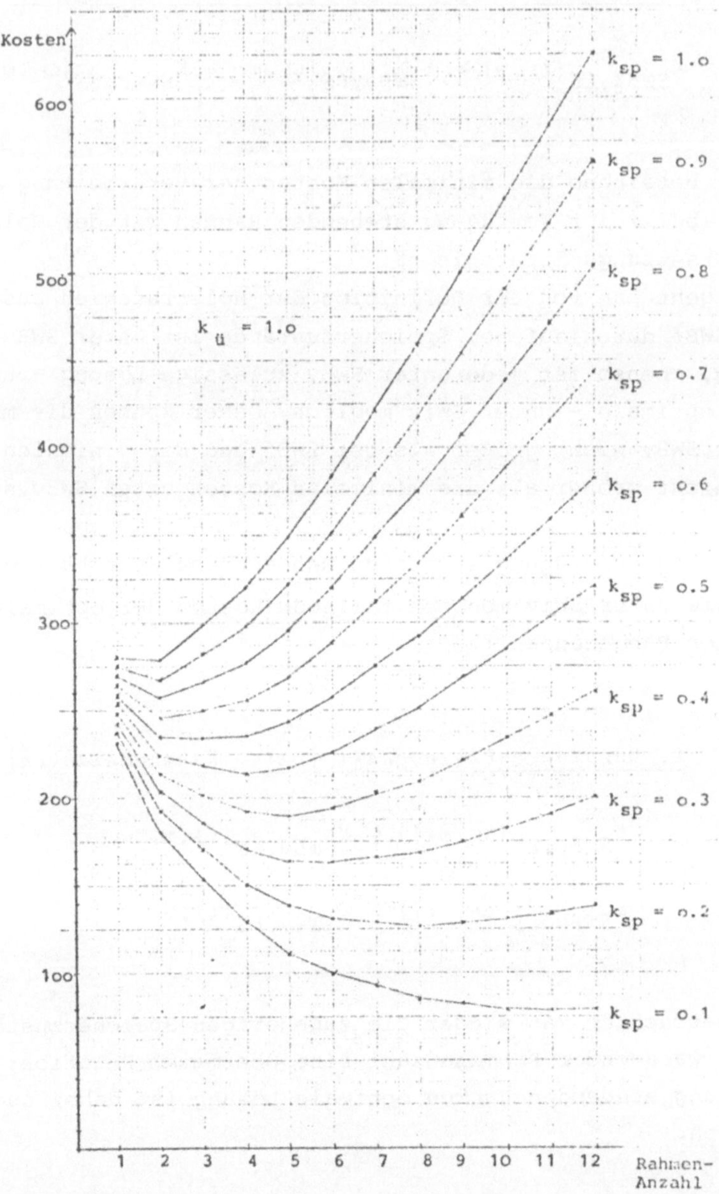

Werte der Kostenfunktion bei SWBf, Ersetzungs-Strategie: BOS.
Aufgetragen wurden die Werte für ein nach dem "Simple LRU Model" (siehe
z.B. Denning/Spirn/Savage) erzeugtes Programm mit 12 Seiten bei gleich-
verteilten Zugriffswahrscheinlichkeiten für die Keller-Positionen für
verschiedene Werte der Speicherkosten-Einheit k_{sp} bei $k_ü$ = 1.0.

2. SIMULATIONS-ERGEBNISSE

Da mit Hilfe der Simulationsmethode anstelle eines geschlossenen Ausdrucks numerische Resultate für Einzelfälle bestimmt werden, muß man vor der Durchführung von Simulationen durch geeignete Auswahl der Eingabedaten für die Aussagefähigkeit der Ergebnisse sorgen; später müssen die Ergebnisse wiederum auf den Einfluß der Eingabedaten hin überprüft und gegebenenfalls neue Simulationen durchgeführt werden.

Hier bietet sich für die Bereitstellung von Referenzenfolgen als Eingabedaten für die Simulation die Verwendung von Modellen für das Verhalten von Programmen an.
Drei der bekanntesten und meistüberprüften Modelle von Denning u.a. wurden für diesen Teil der Auswertung als Grundlage genommen. Mit den erzeugten Referenzenfolgen wurden umfangreiche Rechnungen durchgeführt. Aufschluß über den Einfluß der einzelnen Faktoren - wie Holstrategie, Ersetzungs-Strategie, Rahmenanzahl usw. - auf die Mittelwerte der minimalen Kostenfunktions-Werte erhält man mittels statistischer Verfahren. So ergibt eine Varianzanalyse folgende mittlere quadratische Mittelwertabweichungen:

Ergebnisse einer Varianzanalyse (aus 486 Werten):

Faktor:	*mittl. quadr. Mittelwert-Abweichung:*
Holstrategie	$899.7 \cdot 10^3$
Kosteneinheiten	$627.8 \cdot 10^3$
Rahmenanzahl	$61.7 \cdot 10^3$
Programmgröße	$11.3 \cdot 10^3$
Ersetzungs-Str.	$6.9 \cdot 10^3$
Referenzen-Modell	$0.2 \cdot 10^3$

Man sieht hieraus, daß bei den zugrundegelegten Werten die Wahl des Referenzen-Modells den weitaus geringsten Einfluß auf die minimalen Werte der Kostenfunktion hat. Für die Ausführung weiterer Simulationsläufe bedeutet diese Tatsache, daß man auf eine Variation der Werte dieses Parameters verzichten kann.

Über einige für die Gestaltung eines virtuellen Speicher-Systems wichtige Punkte erhält man durch die Auswertung numerischer Ergebnisse folgende Aussagen:

Beim <u>Vergleich der drei Ersetzungs-Strategien</u> fällt zunächst auf, daß der Unterschied zwischen LRU und FIFO in jedem Fall geringer ist als der Unterschied einer dieser Strategien zur Beladyschen Strategie. (Die graphische Darstellung soll dies für die Mittelwerte aus 405 experimentell ermittelten minimalen Kostenwerten verdeutlichen.)

Zum Vergleich von <u>Ersetzungs-Strategien</u>:

(Grundlage: Mittelwerte aus 405 minimalen Kostenwerten)

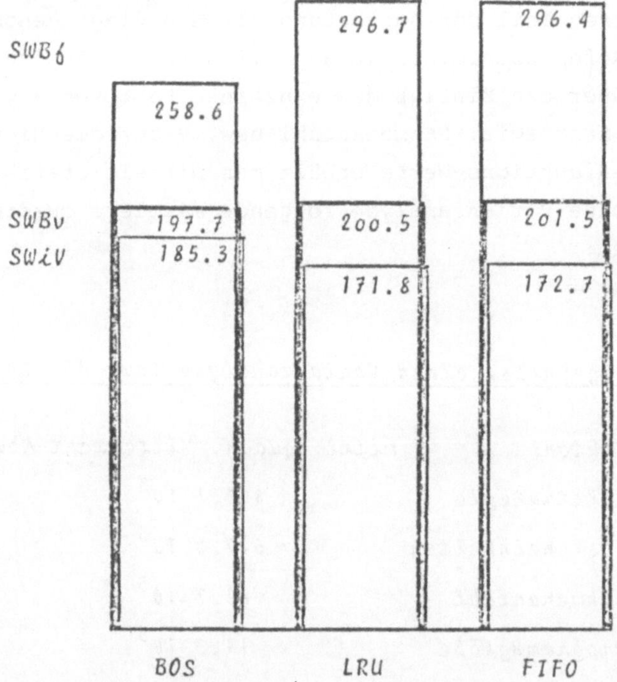

Bezüglich der Beladyschen Strategie wird deutlich, daß diese gemessen an den minimalen Werten dieser Kostenfunktion nur unter derjenigen Hol-Strategie optimal ist, für die sie konstruiert wurde (hier SWBf genannt); bei SWBv sind die minimalen Kosten unter BOS hier im Mittel niedriger als unter FIFO und LRU, es gibt aber einzelne Fälle, in denen diese realisierbaren Ersetzungs-Strategien günstiger abschneiden.
Bei Seitenwechsel im voraus ist die Beladysche Strategie schlechter als FIFO und LRU.

Vergleicht man die Simulations-Ergebnisse nach den drei <u>Holstrategien</u>
getrennt, so ergibt sich - neben der bewiesenen Relation für die minimalen Kosten -, daß diese beim Übergang von SWBv zu SWiv nicht mehr in
dem Maße fallen wie zwischen SWBf und SWBv. Dies ist für die Praxis von
besonderer Bedeutung, da SWiv nur in seltenen Fällen und dann mit erheb-
lichem Mehraufwand zu realisieren ist.
Ein großer Einfluß geht hier von der Wahl der Kosten-Einheiten aus: der
Übergang von SWBf zu SWBv lohnt sich um so mehr, je geringer die Über-
tragungseinheiten relativ zu der Speicherkosteneinheit sind.
Ein Vergleich der Simulations-Ergebnisse nach den verschiedenen Kosten-
einheiten ergibt, daß bei SWBf die Halbierung der Übertragungskosten-
Einheiten auf etwa die gleiche Verringerung der minimalen Kosten führt
wie die Halbierung der Speicherkosten-Einheit.
Bei den anderen Holstrategien ist dagegen die Verringerung der Kosten
bei Halbierung der Übertragungs-Kosten-Einheiten deutlich größer als
bei Halbierung der Speicherkosten-Einheit.

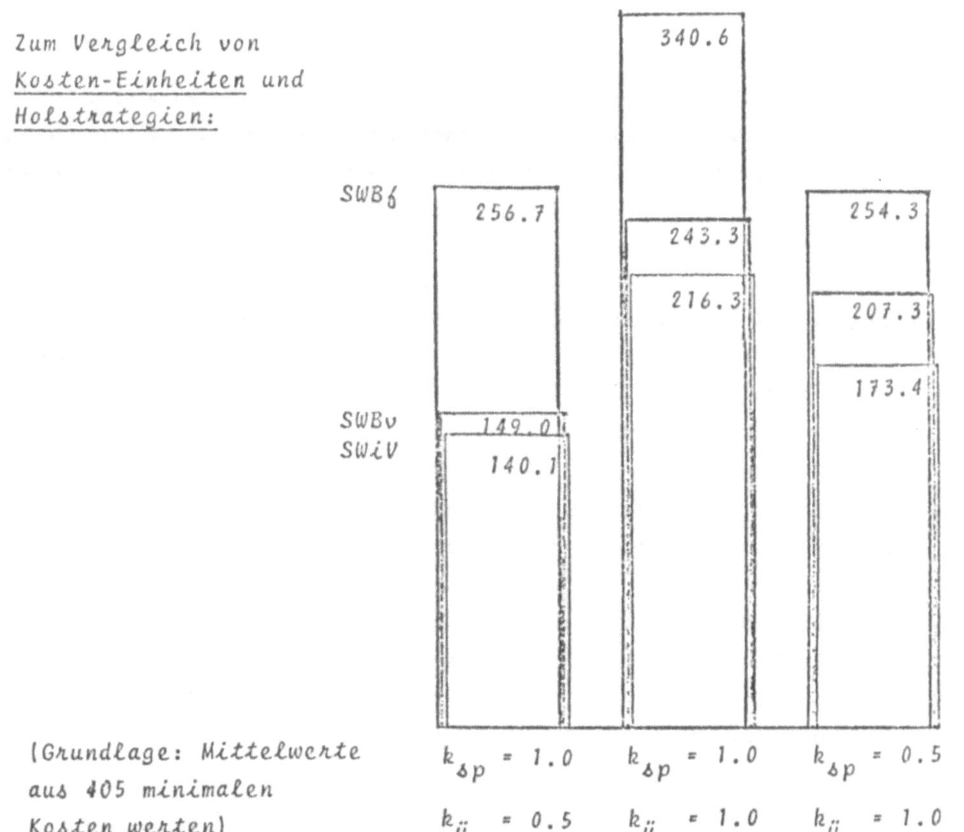

Interpretiert man die Änderung der Kosten-Einheiten als Änderung der
Konfiguration einer Datenverarbeitungs-Anlage, so bedeuten diese Ergebnisse:
bei SWBf wird etwa die gleiche Verbesserung erzielt, wenn entweder die
Hauptspeichergröße oder die Übertragungs-Kapazität zwischen Hilfs- und
Hauptspeicher verdoppelt wird;
mit SWBv oder SWiv als Holstrategie ist die Verdoppelung der Übertra-
gungskapazität einträglicher als die Verdoppelung der Hauptspeichergröße.

WERTUNG DER AUSSAGEN

Die angeführten Ergebnisse beziehen sich auf die optimale Verarbeitung
von Referenzenfolgen in virtuellen Speichern. Beim Einsatz der betreffenden Strategien wird dieses Optimum nicht immer erreichbar sein. Die
Aussagen sind daher als bestmögliche Kostenverminderungen z.B. beim
Übergang von Seitenwechsel nach Bedarf zu Seitenwechsel im voraus anzusehen.
Die Ergebnisse sollten insbesondere bei häufig benutzten Programmen
und Programmteilen angewendet werden können. Zum Beispiel sollte wegen
der großen Kosteneinsparung die Änderung der Holstrategie vom strikten
Seitenwechsel nach Bedarf weg bei denjenigen Teilen von Betriebssystemen,
Sprachübersetzern, Datenbanksystemen, Benutzerprozeduren usw. untersucht
werden, die immer wieder in der gleichen Reihenfolge ausgeführt werden.
Weitere Anwendungsmöglichkeiten der angegebenen Kostenfunktion sind in
der Bestimmung günstiger Seitengrößen und eines günstigen Multiprogram-
ming-Grades in Abhängigkeit von Parametern wie Hol- und Ersetzungs-Strategie zu sehen. Im Zusammenhang mit der Seitengröße sollten auch Probleme der internen Fragmentierung und Packungstechniken bei Matrixoperationen
und Speicher- und Suchvorgängen untersucht werden. Ferner ließen sich
anhand der angegebenen Kostenfunktion Seitenwechsel- und Segmentverfahren
gegenüberstellen.
Bei entsprechender Modifizierung der Kostenfunktion könnten Probleme
wie die optimale Lastverteilung bei Rechnernetzwerken untersucht werden. In diesem Fall ständen die Lagerkosten für die Rechnerbelegung,
während die Übertragung von Prozessen zwischen den Rechnern durch die
Transportkosten dargestellt würden.

LITERATURHINWEISE:

Zur Einführung und Übersicht:

Coffmann, E.G., Denning, P.J.:
Operating Systems Theory,
Prentice-Hall 1973

Krayl, H., Neuhold, E.J., Unger, C.:
Grundlagen der Betriebssysteme,
Sammlung Goeschen 1975 Verlag de Gruyter

Aho, A.V., P.J. Denning, J.D. Ullmann:
Principles of optimal page replacement,
J.ACM, V18,1 (1971) pp. 80-93

Denning,P.J.:
Virtual memory,
Comp. Surv. V2,3 (1970) pp. 153-189

Zur Bewertung von Seitenwechsel-Algorithmen:

Franaszek, P.A., T.J. Wagner:
Some distribution-free aspects of paging algorithm
performance,
J.ACM V21,1 (1974) pp. 31-39

Gelenbe, E.:
A unified approach to the evaluation of a class of
replacement algorithms,
IEEE T-C V22,6 (1973) pp. 611-618

Herzog, U., W. Krämer, P. Kühn, M. Wizgall:
Analyse von Betriebssystem-Modellen für Rechnersysteme
mit Multiprogramming und Paging,
Fachtagung Struktur und Betrieb von Rechensystemen
Lecture Notes in Computer Science 8 pp. 266-288

Ingargiola, G., J.F. Korsh:
Finding optimal demand paging algorithms,
J. ACM V21,1 (1974) pp. 40-53

Joseph, M.:
An analysis of paging and program behavior,
Comp. J. V13,1 (1970) pp. 48-54

King III, W.F.:
Analysis of demand paging algorithms,
IFIP Cong. Proc. 1971 pp. 485-490

Mattson, R.L., J. Gecsei, D.R. Slutz, I.L. Traiger:
Evaluation techniques for storage hierarchies,
IBM Sys.J. V9,2 (1970) pp. 78-117

Pomeranz, J.E.:
Paging with fewest expected replacements,
IFIP Cong. Proc. 1971 pp. 491-493

Experimentelle Untersuchungen und Simulationen:

Belady, L.A.:
A study of replacement algorithms for a virtual-
storage computer,
IBM Sys.J. V5,2 (1966) pp. 78-101

Boyse, J.W.:
Execution characteristics of programms in a page-on-demand
system,
C.ACM V17,4 (1974) pp. 192-196

Coffman, E.G., L.C. Varian:
Further experimental data on the behavior of programs
in a paging environment,
C.ACM V11,7 (1968) pp. 471-474

Hatfield, D.J.:
Experiments on page size, program access patterns and
virtual memory performance,
IBM J.Res.Develop. V16,1 (1972) pp. 58-66

Lenfant, J., P. Burgevin:
Empirical data on program behavior,
ICS Proc. 1975 preprints pp. 163-169

Oliver,N.A.:
Experimental data on page replacement algorithm,
Nat. Comp. Conf. 1974 pp. 179-184

Rodriguenz-Rosell, J.:
Empirical working set behavior,
C. ACM V16,9 (1973) pp. 556-560

Rodriguez-Rosell, J.:
The working set behavior of some programs,
Royal Institute of Technology, Stockholm, Dept. of
Inf. Proc., Comp. Sc., NA 72.51

Tsao, R.F., L.W. Comeau, B.H. Margolin:
A multi-factor paging experiment in W. Freiberger:
Statistical computer performance evaluation,
Academic Press New York, London 1972

Zu den verwendeten Modellen für Programmverhalten:

Denning, P.J.:
On modeling program behavior,
AFIPS Conf.Proc. 40 SJCC 1972 pp. 937-944

Denning, P.J., J.R. Spirn, J.E. Savage:
Some thoughts about locality in program behavior,
MRI Symposium proceedings Vol. XXII, Polytechnic Press pp. 101-112

Spirn, J.R., P.J. Denning:
Experiments with program locality,
AFIPS Conf.Proc. 41,I FJCC 1972 pp. 611-621

Eine ausführliche Beschreibung der Kostenfunktion
einschließlich weiterer Ergebnisse findet sich in

Weber, G.:
Eine Kostenfunktion für den Seitenwechsel unter Berücksichtigung
von Datenübertragung und Hauptspeicherbelegung,
Dissertation im Fachbereich Informatik der Technischen Hochschule
Darmstadt,1976

<u>Eine Diskussion verschiedener Zugänge zum</u>
<u>Deterministischen Scheduling Problem</u>

Sigram Schindler und Harald Lüdtke
Technische Universität Berlin

<u>Einleitung</u>

Die Informatik-Literatur der letzten Jahre enthält eine Fülle von Arbeiten aus dem
Scheduling Bereich. Während die früheren Arbeiten stets von einer ausführlichen Dar-
legung der zugrundeliegenden praktischen Fragestellungen ausgehen, vermißt man in vielen jüngeren Arbeiten eine solche Darstellung des Hintergrundes; ein im allgemeinen
recht abstraktes Modell wird von Anfang an als gegeben betrachtet. Die Problematik
derartig starker Idealisierungen dieser Modelle gegenüber der Realität wird im nächsten Abschnitt anhand von Beispielen erläutert; diese Beispiele dienen dann auch zu
Diskussionen der Frage nach von der Praxis tatsächlich benötigten Hilfsmitteln und
von Methoden zu deren Herleitung.

Zunächst jedoch einige informelle Bemerkungen zum Entstehen und zur gegenwärtigen
Stellung von Scheduling Problemen im Informatik Bereich. Das Scheduling Problem in
all seinen verschiedenen Erscheinungsformen wird im Operations Research Bereich seit
langem untersucht (eine elementare Darstellung der wichtigsten Aspekte findet man in
[1]). Diese klassischen Zugänge zum Scheduling Problem entsprechen primär aus zwei
Gründen nicht den technischen Gegebenheiten im Bereich der Rechner- bzw. Softwareor-
ganisation:

a) Der Einsatz der Betriebsmittel (Prozessoren aller Art) kann häufig (jedoch nicht
    beliebig oft) kurzfristig und "ohne" Rüstzeit geändert werden ("multiplexing",
    "preempting", etc.).

b) Die benutzten Algorithmen müssen zum "realtime"-Einsatz tauglich sein, d.h. ihre
    Laufdauer muß in allen Fällen unter vorgegebenen Schranken liegen.

Die Voraussetzung a) dürfte außerhalb des Computerbereichs kaum erfüllt sein. Die Forderung b) tritt in schwächerer Form zwar bei allen Problemen auf, jedoch selten in
der Schärfe wie in diesem Bereich. Man beachte, daß über Forderung b) nicht nur ein
quantitativer Aspekt - der der kurzen Laufzeit der Algorithmen bzw. der guten Ausnutzung der Betriebsmittel - sondern auch ein qualitativer Aspekt angesprochen wird, nämlich das Problem der Zuverlässigkeit von Softwaresystemen. Auf diesen Aspekt werden
wir im letzten Kapitel zurückkommen.

Beispiele

Die folgenden drei elementaren Beispiele sind keinesfalls repräsentativ für den gesamten Scheduling Bereich - ihre Auswahl erfolgte vielmehr mit dem Ziel, auf möglichst einfache Weise aufzuzeigen, was vom Standpunkt des Ingenieurs aus als angemessene Lösung eines Scheduling Problems betrachtet werden kann. Wir beschränken uns also auf

a) den Bereich deterministischer Voraussetzungen - im probabilistischen Bereich lassen sich Analogien dazu leicht angeben

b) drei der bekanntesten Algorithmen in diesem Bereich, nämlich von Hu [2], Muntz/ Coffman [3] und Liu [4].

1. Beispiel

Wir gehen aus von einem Computer, der aus drei unabhängig einsetzbaren Prozessoren gleicher Leistung und einem Arbeitsspeicher aus K unabhängig einsetzbaren Blöcken gleicher Größe besteht. Verarbeitet werden soll ein "paralleles" Programm, dessen von einem einzelnen Prozessor auszuführende (d.h. sequentielle) Abschnitte durch die Knoten des Graphen in Abb. 1a dargestellt werden; eine Kante zwischen zwei Knoten legt die Reihenfolge der Ausführung dieser zwei Knoten fest. Alle Knoten haben die gleiche Laufzeit, jedoch individuell unterschiedliche Speicheranforderungen, die durch die Zahlen neben den Knoten angegeben sind. Ein Abschnitt kann nur ausgeführt werden, nachdem er einen der drei Prozessoren und alle benötigten Blöcke Arbeitsspeicher erhalten hat; die Rüstzeiten (bestehend aus Prozessorumschaltzeit und Ladezeit des Abschnittes) werden als vernachlässigbar angesehen. Natürlich steht ein Prozessor bzw. ein Block zu einem Zeitpunkt nur einem Abschnitt zur Verfügung; außerdem wird ein Abschnitt nach Ausführungsbeginn ohne Unterbrechung zu Ende geführt. Das Problem des gegenseitigen Ausschlusses bleibt hier unberücksichtigt.

Vernachlässigt man die Speicheranforderungen der Abschnitte, so kann man Hu's Algorithmus zur Bestimmung eines Schedules für die Ausführung des Programms in minimaler Zeit benutzen. Abb. 1b ist das entsprechende Prozessorenbelegungs-Diagramm. Für K = 30 ist dieser Schedule mit den Speicheranforderungen nicht verträglich. Ein mit diesen Speicheranforderungen verträglicher Schedule - siehe Abb. 1c - der die gleiche minimale Verarbeitungszeit für das gesamte Programm bewirkt, kann mittels des Hu'schen Scheduling Algorithmus offensichtlich nicht gefunden werden.

2. Beispiel

Wir gehen nun aus von einer 2-Prozessor-Anlage und einem Programm der Struktur, wie sie aus Abb. 2a ersichtlich ist. D.h. wir haben nun zwei Knotengewichte, die Laufzeit eines Knotens (rechts neben dem Knoten notiert) und den Speicherbedarf (links der Knoten). Im Gegensatz zum vorigen Beispiel seien nun Unterbrechungen bei der Ausführung eines Abschnittes zu jedem beliebigen Zeitpunkt erlaubt.

Vernachlässigt man wiederum die Speicheranforderungen der Abschnitte, so kann man den Muntz/Coffman-Algorithmus zur Bestimmung eines Schedules für die Ausführung in minimaler Zeit benutzen. Abb. 2b ist das entsprechende Prozessorenbelegungs-Diagramm. Für K = 30 ist dieser Schedule mit den Speicheranforderungen nicht verträglich. Ein mit diesen Speicheranforderungen verträglicher Schedule - siehe Abb. 2c - der die gleiche minimale Verarbeitungszeit für das gesamte Programm bewirkt, kann mittels des Muntz/Coffman-Algorithmus offensichtlich nicht gefunden werden.

An diesem Beispiel wird darüber hinaus ein grundsätzliches Problem von preemptiven Scheduling Algorithmen deutlich - die Gefahr viel mehr Unterbrechungen der einzelnen Abschnitte zu erzeugen als zur Erreichung des angestrebten Zieles notwendig sind.

Für hinreichend großes L ist der Schedule aus Abb. 2b in jedem Fall unbefriedigend, auch wenn man die Speicheranforderungen beiseite läßt. Die Idealisierung der vernachlässigbaren Rüstzeiten ist nur haltbar, solange sie tatsächlich hinreichend selten auftreten bzw. die Phasen ununterbrochener Programmausführung um Größenordnungen länger sind als die Umrüstzeiten.

3. Beispiel

Um klarzustellen, daß dieser zuletzt erwähnte mögliche Defekt von preemptiven Scheduling Algorithmen nichst zu tun hat mit der Anzahl der Prozessoren oder einer Vorrangstruktur für die Verarbeitung der einzelnen Programmabschnitte, beschränken wir uns nun auf eine Einprozessor-Anlage und ein Programmsystem ohne Vorrangstruktur. Die einzelnen Abschnitte sind nun jedoch in vorgegebenen Zeitintervallen - die natürlich größer sind als die vorgegebene Laufdauer des jeweiligen Abschnittes - auszuführen. Auf das Beispiel in Abb. 3a angewandt, liefert Liu's Algorithmus den in Abb. 3b dargestellten Schedule. Sowohl das Problem mit eventuellen Speicheranforderungen als auch mit zu vielen Unterbrechungen (siehe Abb. 3c als Beispiel für eine vernünftige Lösung) liegt hier wie im vorherigen Beispiel.

Folgerungen

Der Bestand an Literatur über Scheduling Algortihmen ist in den letzten Jahren geradezu explodiert; recht vollständige zusammenfassende Darstellungen der bekanntesten
Einzelergebnisse findet man in [5,6]. In beiden Arbeiten werden ausschließlich Untersuchungen referiert, die ein Scheduling Problem als gelöst betrachten, sobald ein
effektiver Scheduling Algorithmus angegeben ist, mit dessen Hilfe irgendein Schedule
gefunden werden kann, der einer fest vorgegebenen Kostenfunktion genügt. Dabei bleiben irgendwelche Eigenarten der mittels dieses Scheduling Algorithmus konstruierten
Schedules außer Betracht. Dies bewirkt in vielen Fällen und jedenfalls unbeabsichtig-
terweise, daß Schedules ganz spezieller Beschaffenheit entstehen.

Die potentielle Unverträglichkeit solcher spezieller Eigenarten mit anderen an die
Schedules zu stellenden Anforderungen wurde im vorigen Abschnitt an drei elementaren
Beispielen verdeutlicht.

In welchem Ausmaß diese Unverträglichkeiten bei realen Problemen "im Durchschnitt"
zu Tage treten, kann gegenwärtig nicht abgeschätzt werden. So gibt es an anderer Stelle Hinweise darauf, daß theoretisch nachgewiesene Unzulänglichkeiten von Algorithmen
in der Anwendung auf realistische Probleme kaum zu beobachten sind. Kohler berichtet
zum Beispiel in [7], daß die bekannte polynomiale Vollständigkeit des Rucksack-Algo-
rithmus bei Anwendung auf praktische Probleme nicht zu Ineffektivitäten führte. In
vielen Situationen kommt der Ausführung von Programmabschnitten vor dem Erreichen un-
verrückbarer "deadlines" jedoch zentrale Bedeutung zu, z.B. bei der Steuerung zeit-
kritischer Prozesse: Eine Unverträglichkeit des vom Scheduling Algorithmus erzeugten
Schedules (aufgrund dessen spezieller Struktur) mit unerwarteten Werten anderer Parameter des Programmes oder Computers kann hier nicht akzeptiert werden.

Um der Realität Rechnung zu tragen, wird man versuchen, den Scheduling Algorithmus so
flexibel zu belassen, daß andere technische Parameter berücksichtigt werden können,
um solche Unverträglichkeiten zu vermeiden. In der Parnas'schen Entwurfs-Ideologie
ausgedrückt: Der Scheduling Algorithmus sollte nur die für die Lösung des Scheduling
Problems unbedingt notwendigen Entscheidungen festlegen und keine darüber hinausgehen-
den Festlegungen treffen. In Dijkstra's Terminologie: Anstelle nach einer speziellen
Lösung eines Scheduling Problems durch einen korrekten Scheduling Algorithmus zu suchen, sollte die allgemeine Lösung des Problems in Form eines korrekten und weitestgehend nichtdeterminierten (u.U. auch nichtsequentiellen) Prädikatentransformers gesucht werden. Alle möglichen Determinierungen dieses Transformers sind dann alle möglichen Scheduling Algorithmen (die wiederum alle möglichen Schedules liefern). Diese
Determinierung kann zur Laufzeit geschehen und unter Berücksichtigung der übrigen technischen Parameter (wie zum Beispiel Speicheranforderungen, Kanalbelastung). Es sei

darauf hingewiesen, daß diesem Zugang ein grundsätzlicher Vorteil innewohnt, nämlich
die verbesserte Zuverlässigkeit bzw. Modifizierbarkeit des so spezifizierten Systems:
Während beim konventionellen Zugang die Funktionsfähigkeit des Systems von der Ver-
wendbarkeit eines als korrekt bewiesenen speziellen Algorithmus abhängt, ist hier die
Menge aller korrekten Algorithmen, genauer ihr "Erzeugendensystem" oder "Schema" zu
implementieren und damit die Möglichkeit, unvorhersehbare Werte technischer Parameter
zur "Laufzeit" zu berücksichtigen. Insgesamt handelt es sich um den von Parnas im
Softwarebereich eingeführten "Program Family Approach".

Die Verfasser dieser Arbeit und andere haben mit einem völlig anderen formalen Zugang
- jedoch mit gleicher Zielsetzung - in vorangehenden Arbeiten mehrere einer erfolgreichen Untersuchung zugänglich scheinende Scheduling Probleme gelöst und die algo-
rithmische Komplexität ihrer Lösungen diskutiert. In allen untersuchten Fällen wurden
die aus der Literatur bekannten Scheduling Algorithmen als Spezialfälle (keineswegs
immer niedrigster Komplexität) eingebettet (siehe z B. [10-15]). Als erheblicher Nachteil dieser - im übrigen recht einheitlichen - Untersuchungen gegenüber den - ganz
und gar unterschiedlichen, völlig auf die jeweilige spezielle Problematik ausgerich-
teten - Einzeluntersuchungen anderer Autoren muß ihr wesentlich größerer formaler Aufwand betrachtet werden. Dieser formale Aufwand in der Analyse des Problems und der
Beschreibung der allgemeinen Lösung (d.h. des weitestgehend nichtdeterminierten korrekten Transformers) führt allerdings nicht auf eine hohe Komplexität aller implizierten Scheduling Algorithmen. Ganz im Gegenteil umfaßt die allgemeine Lösung ja neben
den Scheduling Algorithmen hoher Komplexität auch alle Scheduling Algorithmen niedriger Komplexität. In allen untersuchten Fällen gelang es - unseres Wissens zum Teil
erstmals - Scheduling Algorithmen anzugeben, deren Komplexität eine in N lineare
Schranke besitzt (wobei N die Anzahl der in den Beispielen erwähnten Programmabschnitte
angibt), abgesehen von einem anfänglichen Sortiervorgang, der $N \cdot \ln N$ Schritte erfordert. Trivialerweise hätten die in Abb. 1c, 2c und 3c angegebenen Lösungen auf die
hier erläuterte Weise konstruiert werden können.

Es sollte jedoch klar sein, daß im Zuge dieser Diskussion die Speicheranforderungen
der Programmabschnitte in den Beispielen jeweils ad hoc als technische Parameter bei
der Determinierung der allgemeinen Lösung des Scheduling Problems berücksichtigt wurden. Wir haben dagegen nicht das Scheduling Problem durch Hinzunahme eines weiteren
Parameters (Speicheranforderung) verallgemeinert und eine Lösung dieses allgemeinen
Problems systematisch herbeigeführt.

Abschließend sei daran erinnert, daß es höchst unwahrscheinlich ist, daß die allge-
meine optimale Lösung komplizierterer Scheduling Probleme immer effektive Scheduling
Algorithmen enthält, [16]. Will man ohne eine Klärung dieser Grundsatzfrage weitere
Ergebnisse erzielen, so muß man sich mit "suboptimalen" allgemeinen Lösungen, bzw.

Scheduling Algorithmen begnügen. Ganz allgemein stellt sich dann die Frage nach der Güte von allgemeinen Lösungen vorgegebener Komplexität. Unter Güte wären hier nicht nur Aussagen über die Laufzeit der dadurch implizierten Schedules - verglichen mit optimalen Schedules - zu erfassen, sondern auch Aussagen über den Grad der Nichtdeterminiertheit der allgemeinen Lösung, d.h. über die Mächtigkeit der Menge der erhaltenen Scheduling Algorithmen.

Literatur

[1]   Weber, H.H.: Einführung in Operations Research,
      Akademischer Verlag Frankfurt

[2]   Hu, T.C.: Parallel Sequencing and Assembly Line Problems,
      Operations Research 9, 6, November 1961, pp. 841-848

[3]   Muntz, R.R. and Coffman, E.G.: Preemptive Scheduling of Real Time Tasks on
      Multiprocessor Systems,
      Journal of the ACM, 17, 2 (1970), pp. 324-338

[4]   Liu, C.L.; Layland, G.W.: Scheduling Algorithms for Multiprogramming in a
      Real-Time Environment,
      JACM, Vol. 20, No. 1, 46-71 (1973)

[5]   Coffman, E.G., Editor: Computer and Job-Shop Scheduling Theory ,
      John Wiley

[6]   Liu, C.L.: Deterministic Job Scheduling in Computing Systems,
      to appear

[7]   Kohler, W.H.: Computational Experience with Efficient Exact and Approximate
      Algorithms for an NP-Complete Scheduling Problem,
      9th Hawaii International Conference on System Science, Honolulu, January 8-10,
      1976

[8]   Parnas, D.L.: On the Design and Development of Program Families,
      Forschungsbericht BS I 75/2, Fachbereich Informatik, Technische Hochschule
      Darmstadt

[9]   Dijkstra, E.W.: Guarded Commands, Nondeterminacy and Formal Derivation of Pro-
      grams,
      Comm. ACM 18, 8 (August 1975)

[10] Schindler, S.: Quantitative Aspects of Optimal Schedules for Multiprocessor
      Systems,
      Technical Report 73-10, Fachbereich 20, Technische Universität Berlin

[11] Schindler, S.; Simonsmeier, W.: Scheduling Independent Tasks on Different
      Processors,
      Technical Report 74-05, Fachbereich 20, Technische Universität Berlin

[12] Schindler, S.: Scheduling a Multiprocessor System on Anti-Forests,
      Technical Report 73-15, Fachbereich 20, Technische Universität Berlin

[13] Schindler, S.; Lüdtke, H.: The Complexity of Scheduling Algorithms for Three-
      Processor Systems,
      to appear

[14] Schindler, S.: Scheduling General Monitor Systems,
      9th Hawaii International Conference on System Sciences, Honolulu, January 8-10,
      1976

[15] Hennings, D.; Schindler, S.; Steinacker, M.: The Complexity of Preemptive
      Scheduling Algorithms for Multiprocessor Systems, TR 74-20, FB 20, TU Berlin

[16] Karp, R.M.: Reducibility Among Conbinatorial Problems,
      Complexity of Computer Computation, Plenum Press, NY 72

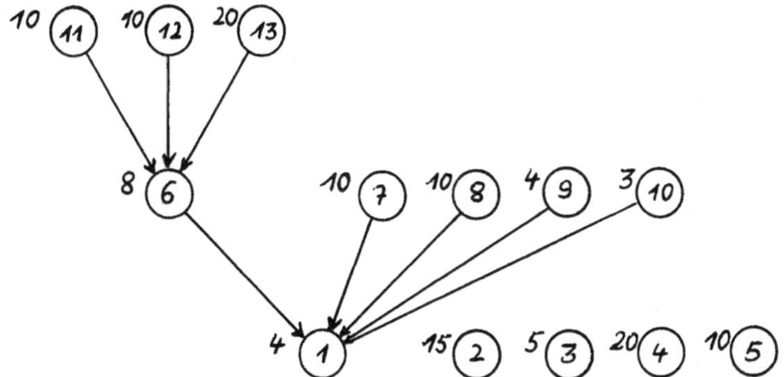

Abbildung 1a – Beispiel für ein paralleles, aus 13 Abschnitten bestehendes Programm; Unterbrechungen sind nicht erlaubt. Die Zahlen links neben den Knoten geben die Speicheranforderungen der einzelnen Abschnitte in Blöcken an. Alle Abschnitte haben gleiche Laufzeit.

Abbildung 1b – Das Prozessorenbelegungs-Diagramm für einen zeitoptimalen Schedule, der vom Hu'schen Scheduling Algorithmus erzeugt worden ist. Dieser Schedule ist nicht verträglich mit der Arbeitsspeichergröße K, wenn K < 40 Blöcke gewählt wird.

Abbildung 1c – Ein zeitoptimaler Schedule für das Programm aus Abbildung 1a, der zusätzlich die Speicheranforderungen der einzelnen Abschnitte berücksichtigt (z.B. Arbeitsspeichergröße K = 30 Blöcke).

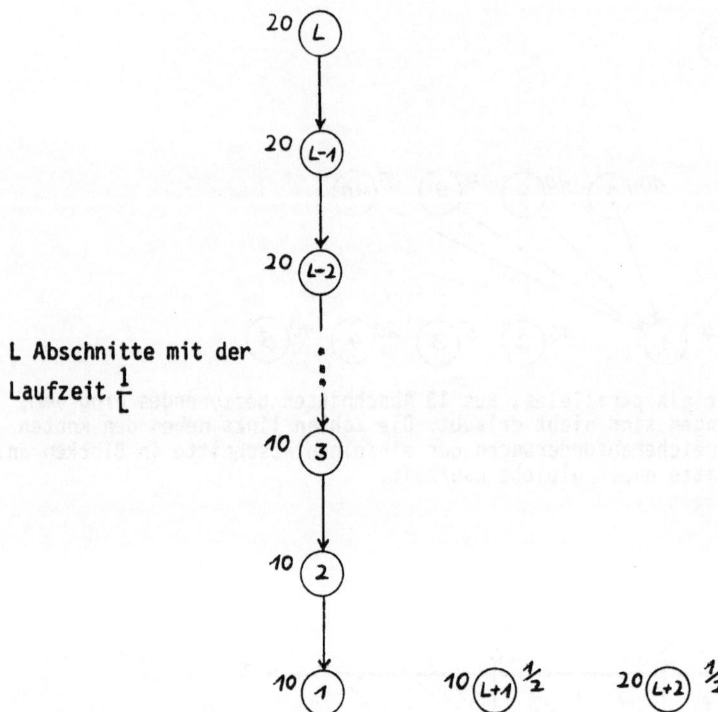

<u>Abbildung 2a</u> - Ein Programmbeispiel mit einfacher Vorrangstruktur; Unterbrechungen
sind erlaubt.

<u>Abbildung 2b</u> - Das Prozessorenbelegungs-Diagramm für einen zeitoptimalen Schedule,
der vom Muntz-Coffman Scheduling Algorithmus erzeugt worden ist. Es
gibt insgesamt 2 · (L - 1) Unterbrechungen.

<u>Abbildung 2c</u> - Beispiel für einen zeitoptimalen Schedule, in dem es keine Unterbre-
chungen der einzelnen Abschnitte gibt.

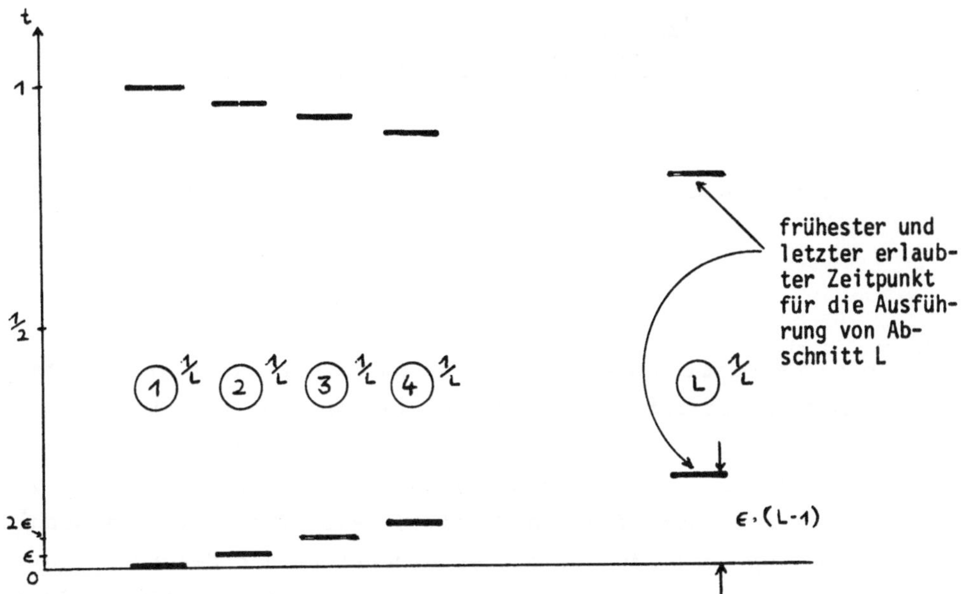

Abbildung 3a - Ein Monitor-System bestehend aus L unabhängigen Abschnitten der Laufzeit $\frac{1}{L}$; es sei $\varepsilon \ll \frac{1}{L}$ gewählt.

Abbildung 3b - Ein Schedule, erzeugt von Liu's Scheduling Algorithmus, der das Monitor-Problem löst, allerdings für große L eine unakzeptable Anzahl von Unterbrechungen erzeugt.

Abbildung 3c - Eine Lösung des Monitor-Problems mit lediglich einer Unterbrechung.

<u>A MODEL OF PROCESS COORDINATION IN</u>
<u>DISTRIBUTED COMPUTER SYSTEMS</u>

P. Ancilotti
Istituto di Elaborazione della Informazione del C.N.R.
via S.Maria, 46
56100 Pisa, ITALY

<u>ABSTRACT</u>
In this paper a formal model of process coordination in distributed
computer systems is introduced. Properties of a message-transfer mechanism are analized from a graph theoretical viewpoint. In particular deadlock conditions, that can arise owing to message-transfer activity, are
analized and a procedure for statically detect if a system is deadlock
free is given. Optimal message-buffer dimensions are determined with
respect to the system computational speed and to the message-buffer cost.

1. INTRODUCTION

The advent of *Large Scale Integration* (LSI) has made memories and
processors primitive components from which systems are designed.

The implementation of new computer system architectures has now become
actual both as local network systems and as multiprocessor systems. In
both cases the use of microprocessors makes pratical the construction of
systems with ten to hundred of processors. Any system constructed as a
set of interconnected microprocessors will be referred to as a multimicroprocessor system. Here the term microprocessor will be used, generally,
to refer to an L.S.I. chip (or set of chips) which perform as small processors.

A basic concept underlying all multimicroprocessor systems is that, at
any time, a set of asynchronous sequential processes is present in the
system.All processes run in parallel on different microprocessors. They
interact among them by exchanging messages through message-buffers. Then
the study of properties of synchronization mechanisms and message-transfer
mechanisms, is a problem of primary importance for understanding system
behaviour and then for constructing correct and efficient systems.

Thus motivated, the control of a set of communicating processes is
examined from a graph theoretical viewpoint.

This work is a part of a research on control properties of a set of
parallel asynchronous processes. In particular some results, obtained in
previous works [1-3] , are used.

First of all the class of systems with which this work is concerned,

is defined. The more important characteristic is that such systems are
constructed by a set of microprocessors. A cyclic sequential process
runs on each microprocessor. Processes exchange messages through message-buffers.

The purpose of this work is to analyze some properties of deadlock
conditions that can arise in such systems owing to the message-transfer
activity. Then a procedure is given to determine optimal message-buffer
dimensions from the point of view both of system computational speed and
of message-buffer cost.

In a paper of this length, all details of this research cannot be
presented. The purpose of this paper is to motivate and illustrate the
results, while full details can be found in [4].

2. THE MODEL

The class of systems analyzed in this paper is characterized by:
  i) Systems composed by sets of asynchronous sequential processes.
 ii) Each component process is cyclic and has a unique execution
     sequence.
iii) Component processes exchange information between each other by
     means of *send* and *receive* operations. Processes are linked
     through message-buffers.

The topological structure of a system can be represented by means of
a directed graph, called *connection graph*. In the connection graph nodes
represent processes and directed arcs represent message-buffers linking
processes.

For instance fig. 2.1 represents the connection graph of a system
composed by five processes connected by means of four message-buffers.
Process P_1 sends messages to process P_2 through message-buffer m_1 and
so on.

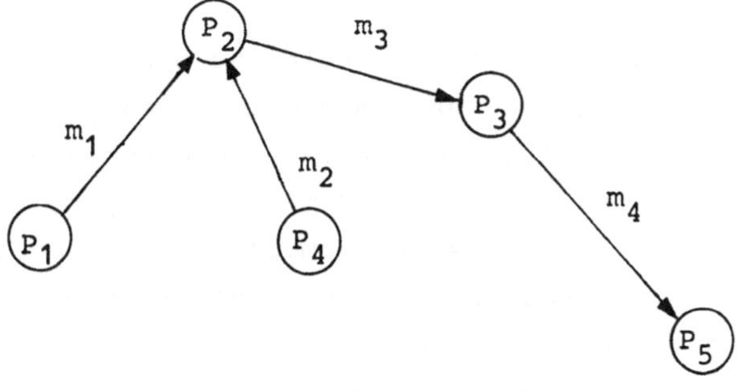

fig. 2.1

Only systems whose connection graphs are connected will be considered
in this paper.

The control structure of each process can be modeled with a precedence graph called *occurrence graph*.

Given a system of communicating processes, the occurrence graph of
each component process is characterized (see the above points i and ii)
by an infinite "chain" of nodes (fig. 2.2)

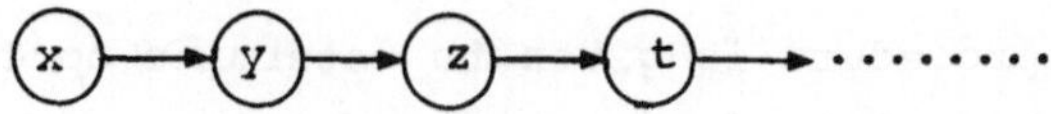

fig. 2.2

Each node represents a process operation and each directed arc x→y
represents the precedence constraint in the execution of x and y operations. The sequence of process operations, executed in the order specified by the occurrence graph, represents the process execution sequence.

Only one node in the occurrence graph has no ingoing arcs. This node
represents the first operation the process executes and is named the
initial node.

Since each process is cyclic, its occurrence graph is characterized
by the concatenation of an infinite number of equal subgraphs. Each of
them is called the *execution period* of the process. It can be looked at
the occurrence graph as a *multiply labelled marked graph* [5-6] where no
arcs contain tokens. Then only the initial node can fire initially since
it has no ingoing arcs. When the initial node is fired in its outgoing
arc there is one token and then the successor of the initial node can
fire, and so on. In this way the firing sequence of the occurrence graph
represents the execution sequence of the process.

In a similar way the occurrence graph of a system can be defined in
order to identify the set of all possible system computations. That is
each computation corresponds to a possible firing sequence of the occurrence graph and viceversa.

A procedure can be stated in order to obtain the occurrence graph of
a system given the occurrence graphs of component processes. For this
purpose it is necessary to formalize the precedence constraints the communication mechanism introduces between operations belonging to different
processes. For instance let P and Q be two communicating processes where
process P sends messages to process Q through message-buffer m. Obviously
process Q can not terminate the operation *receive* when the message-buffer
is empty. Analogously process P cannot terminate the operation *send* when
m is full. Then, for each message-buffer m, the following relations must
hold at any time:

$$(\text{number of } send \text{ operations executed}) \leq$$
$$\leq (\text{number of } receive \text{ operations executed}) + B_m \qquad (2.1)$$

(number of *receive* operations executed) $\leq$

$\leq$ (number of *send* operations executed)   (2.2)

where B_m represents the dimension of m (as the number of message frames). Relations (2.1) and (2.2) are called *synchronization constraints*.

The occurrence graph of a system is composed by the occurrence graphs of component processes plus a certain number of arcs linking nodes that belong to different processes. These new arcs represent the synchronization constraints.

Procedure 2.1 Given a system Σ of n communicating processes $P_1, P_2, \ldots P_n$, the occurrence graph of Σ can be obtained as follows:

  i) Take the n occurrence graphs of component processes;

  ii) For each pair of processes (P_i, P_j) such that the arc $P_i \rightarrow P_j$ exists in the connection graph of Σ, let m be the message-buffer that links P_i to P_j. Denoting by s_m and r_m the *send* and *receive* operations that P_i and P_j execute respectively on m:

    a) The arc a$\rightarrow$b must be introduced in the occurrence graph of Σ if a is the node corresponding to the h_{th} instance of s_m in P_i and b is the node corresponding to the h_{th} instance of r_m in P_j (for any integer h>0).

    b) The arc c$\rightarrow$d must be introduced in the occurrence graph of Σ if c is the node corresponding to the h_{th} instance of r_m in P_j and d is the node corresponding to the $(h+B_m)_{th}$ instance of s_m in P_i. (For any integer h>0). B_m denotes the dimension of m.

It can be easily proved that the occurrence graph, obtained with the procedure 2.1, models all possible system computations. In fact synchronization constraints are satisfied for all message-buffers at any point of any firing sequence of the occurrence graph.

3. DEADLOCK PROPERTIES

In systems of communicating processes deadlock conditions can arise owing to synchronization constraints.

In connection to the class of systems considered in this paper, some deadlock properties were shown in a previous work [1-2] :

Property 3.1: If a deadlock condition arise in a particular system computation, then this condition is a total deadlock (that is all the component processes are blocked). Furthermore the some deadlock condition is present in any system computation

Property 3.2: A deadlock condition can arise in system computations *only if* the system connection graph contains at least one closed path, indipendently of arc orientations in the path.

If a system computation is deadlocked then any component process is blocked, that is the process execution is suspended since a particular process operation can not terminate. Since deadlocks can arise only owing to synchronization constraints, the above operations can only be *send* or *receive* and will be referred to as *blocking operations*.

For a system whose computations are deadlocked, all firing sequences of the occurrence graph are finite, that is the occurrence graph is not live. Commoner, Holt, Even and Pnueli [5] have proved that, for a marked graph, a marking is live *if and only if* the number of tokens in every directed circuit is positive. Since the occurrence graph is a marked graph whose initial marking is such that no token exists in any arc, it follows that:

Theorem 3.1 Given a system of communicating processes, its computations are deadlocked *if and only if* at least a directed circuit exists in the occurrence graph.

First of all a particular subclass of systems will be considered, that is systems whose connection graphs are directed circuits of n processes (see fig. 3.1)

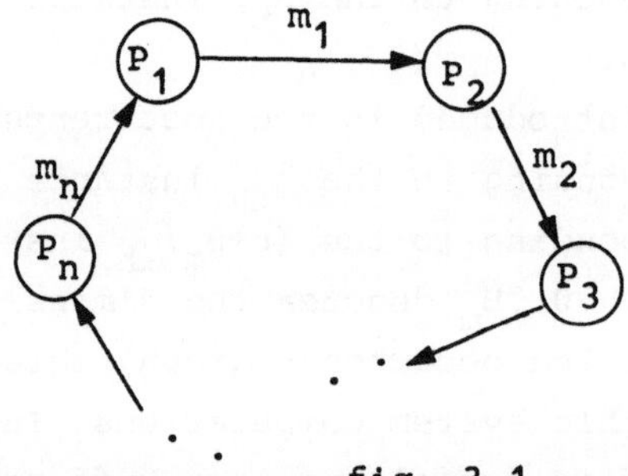

fig. 3.1

Notation: System component processes will be denoted by $P_1, P_2, \ldots, P_n$ while $m_1, m_2, \ldots, m_n$ will denote message-buffers to which $P_1 \ldots P_n$ send messages and from which $P_2, P_3 \ldots P_n, P_1$ receive them. Furthermore S_i and R_i denote the numbers of *send* and *receive* operations processes P_i and P_{i+1} execute respectively in their execution periods (i=1,...,n and i+1=1 if i=n).

For systems with cyclic connection graphs the following theorem holds:

Theorem 3.2 Given a system Σ with a connection graph characterized by a directed circuit of n processes, if system computations are deadlocked, then each computation terminate with all message-buffers ampty, or with all message-buffers full.

Proof: In fact, let a computation terminate with some message-buffers empty and some message-buffers full. Then at least two consecutive message-buffers m_i and m_{i+1} must exist, where m_i is full and m_{i+1} is empty (with $1 \leq i \leq n$ and i+1=1 if i=n). If m_i is full, the blocking operation of P_{i+1} is not a *receive* operation; then the blocking operation of P_{i+1} is a

send operation, but in such a case m_{i+1} can not be empty. Therefore message-buffers full and empty at the same time can not exist at the end of
a computation.

Q.E.D.

If a computation is deadlocked with all message-buffers empty the
deadlock condition is called a *sendless deadlock condition*. On the contrary a *receiveless deadlock condition* is present if a computation is
deadlocked with all message-buffers full.

It can be easily shown that a sendless (receiveless) deadlock condi-
tioncorresponds, in the occurrence graph, to a directed circuit where
all arcs, connecting nodes belonging to different processes, come out of
send (*receive*) nodes and enter *receive* (*send*) nodes.

A system with a cyclic connection graph is *balanced* if the following
relation holds:

$$\prod_{i=1}^{n} R_i = \prod_{i=1}^{n} S_i \qquad (3.1)$$

It can be proved that the validity of the balancing relation (3.1) is
a necessary condition for the absence of deadlocks:

Theorem 3.3 Given a system Σ with a connection graph characterized by a
directed circuit of n processes, if Σ is not balanced, then
its computations are deadlocked.

The proof of this theorem is shown in [3] .

Another important characteristic connected to the balance property is
the system periodicity. In fact the following theorem can be proved:

Theorem 3.4 Given a system Σ with a connection graph characterized by a
directed circuit of n processes , if Σ is balanced n integers
$k_1, k_2, \ldots, k_n$ can be found such that the number of *send* operations process P_i executes in its first k_i execution periods
is equal to the number of *receive* operations process P_{i+1}
executes in its first k_{i+1} execution periods (i=1,....,n and
i+1=1 if i=n).

Proof: To prove that $k_1, \ldots, k_n$ exist it is sufficient to show that an
integer non-zero solution exists for the system of simultaneous equations
(where all the coefficients are integers):

$$\begin{cases} x_1 S_1 - x_2 R_1 & = 0 \\ \quad\ x_2 S_2 - x_3 R_2 & = 0 \\ \qquad\qquad \vdots & \\ - x_1 R_n \qquad\qquad\qquad\qquad + x_n S_n & = 0 \end{cases}$$

called *Characteristic System of Equations* of Σ. Since the system is homo-
geneus, it has a non-zero solution if and only if its determinant is

equal to zero, i.e. :

$$\prod_{i=1}^{n} S_i - \prod_{i=1}^{n} R_i = 0$$

That is true because Σ is balanced (see relation 3.1).

Q.E.D.

Notation: The minimal integer solution of the characteristic system of equations will be denoted by $K_1, K_2, \ldots K_n$. Furthermore S'_i denotes the number of *send* operations process P_i executes in its first K_i execution periods ($S'_i = K_i S_i$). Analogously R'_i denotes the number of *receive* operations process P_{i+1} executes in its first K_{i+1} execution periods ($i=1, \ldots \ldots, n$ and $i+1=1$ if $i=n$).

The subgraph of the occurrence graph characterized by the first K_i execution periods of each process P_i ($i=1 \ldots \ldots n$) will be called the *generating graph*.

Unfortunately the validity of the balance property is not sufficient to avoid deadlock conditions. On the other hand theorem 3.1 does not provide a finite test since it requires the analysis of an infinite graph. However it can be proved that:

Theorem 3.5 Given a system Σ with a connection graph characterized by a directed circuit of n processes, if Σ is balanced, the system computations are deadlock free *if and only if* in the generating graph of Σ there are not directed circuits.

For simplicity the proof of this theorem is not reported here. Details of the proof can be found in [4]. Anyhow this theorem is a direct consequence of theorem 5.4 from which follows that, with respect to deadlock conditions, the occurrence graph of a balanced system, is periodic, where the generating graph represents the repetition period.

Theorem 3.5 provides, now, a finite test since the generating graph is finite.

As an example the particular case of systems with only two processes P_1 and P_2, is now considered (see fig. 3.2).

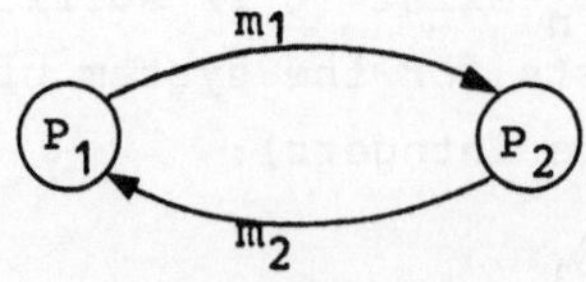

fig. 3.2

Definition 3.1: The integer t is the generic *send* operation of process P_1 in the generating graph ($0 < t \leq S'_1$).
The integer $u(t)$ is the number of *receive* operations that precede the t_{th} *send* in P_1.

The integer $w(t)$ is the number of *receive* operations of P_2 that precede the u_{th} *send* in P_2.

The *predicate* P_s is defined such that: P_s is true if and only if $(t-w)>0$ for all t such that $0<t\leq S_1'$.

Theorem 3.6 Given a balanced system Σ with a connection graph characterized by a directed circuit of two processes P_1 and P_2, sendless deadlock conditions are not present in the computations of Σ , if and only if P_s is true.

Proof: Only if: In fact if P_s is false an integer t exists such that $t-w\leq 0$ (see definition 3.1). Let a be the node of the occurrence graph corresponding to the t_{th} *send* operation of P_1 and b the node corresponding to the u_{th} *receive* operation of P_1. Then the path b→...→a exists in the occurrence graph by definition 3.1

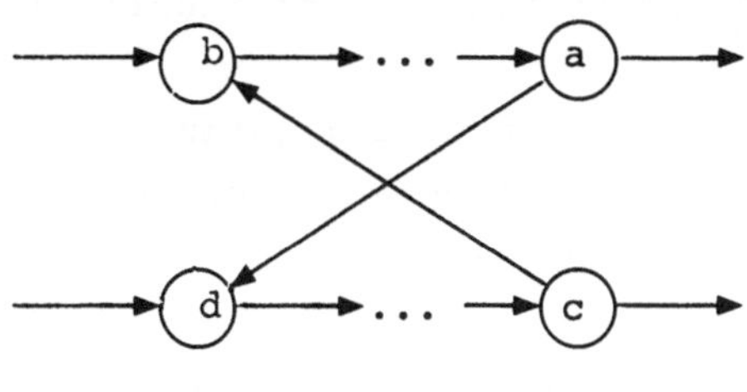

fig. 3.3

If c is the node corresponding to the u_{th} *send* operation of P_2, the arc c→b exists in the occurrence graph by procedure 2.1. Analogously the path d→...→c exists if d denotes the node corresponding to the w_{th} *receive* operation of P_2 (see fig. 3.3). By procedure 2.1 in the occurrence graph there is the arc a→d if $t-w=0$, while there is the path a→...→d if $t<w$. In both cases a directed circuit exists in the occurrence graph that corresponds to a sendless deadlock condition.

If: If a sendless deadlock condition exists, then in the occurrence graph there is a directed circuit a→d→...→c→b→...→a (see fig. 3.3) where a and c correspond to *send* operations. For instance let a be the t_{th} *send* operation of P_1, then b corresponds to the p_{th} *receive* of P_1, where $p\leq u$ (see definition 3.1) and c corresponds to the p_{th} *send* of P_2. Analogously d corresponds to the q_{th} *receive* of P_2 where $q\leq w$. Since there is the arc a→d, by procedure 2.1 $t=q$, that is $t-w\leq 0$ and then P_s is false.

Definitio 3.2: The integer $\underline{t}$ is the index of the generic *receive* operation of P_1 in the generating graph $(0<\underline{t}\leq R_2')$.

The integer $\underline{u}(\underline{t})$ is the number of *send* operations that precede the $\underline{t}_{th}$ *receive* in P_1.

Let $\underline{v}(\underline{t})$ be the integer $\underline{v}=\underline{u}-B_1$ where B_1 is the dimension of the message-buffer m_1 that links P_1 to P_2.

The integer $\underline{w}(\underline{t})$ is the number of *send* operations of P_2

that precede the $\underline{v}_{th}$ *receive* in P_2.

The *predicate* P_h is defined such that: P_h is true if and only if $(\underline{w}-\underline{t}) < B_2$ for all $\underline{t}$ such that $0 < \underline{t} \leq R_2'$ and where B_2 is the dimension of message-buffer m_2.

Theorem 3.7 Given a balanced system Σ with a connection graph characterized by a directed circuit of two processes P_1 and P_2, receiveless deadlock conditions are not present in the computations
of Σ , if and only if P_h is true.
The proof is analogue to that of theorem 3.6.

By theorems 3.2, 3.6, and 3.7 the following corollary can be deduced:
Corollary 3.1: Given a balanced system Σ with a connection graph characterized by a directed circuit of two processes P_1 and P_2,
Σ is deadlock-free if and only if P_s and P_h are true.

Corollary 3.1 provides a finite test for statically detect deadlock
conditions.

The definition of P_s and P_h can be easily extended to systems with
connection graphs characterized by directed circuits of n processes P_1.
..P_n. Then corollary 3.1 can be applaied to such systems to detect deadlock conditions.

The above results can be now extended to systems with arbitrary connection graphs. For simplicity proofs of such extensions are not given
in this paper [4]. A system is balanced if the balance relation (3.1) is
valid for each directed circuit of the connection graph. Theorem 3.4
becomes now:

Theorem 3.8: Given a system Σ of n communicating processes if Σ is balanced n integers $K_1....K_n$ can be found such that if the arc
$P_i \rightarrow P_j$ exists in the connection graph of Σ , then the number
of *send* operations process P_i executes in its first K_i execution periods, is equal to the number of *receive* operations
process P_j executes in its first K_j execution periods.
Theorem 3.5 holds also for systems with arbitrary connection graphs
and corollary 3.1 must be applaied to any directed circuit of the connection graph in order to detect deadlock conditions.

4. OPTIMAL MESSAGE-BUFFER DIMENSIONS

Let system processes run in different processors at different speeds.
Process activities evolve indipendently from each other unless two processes must interact for exchange data. During such interactions process
activities must be synchronized and then it can happen that the quicker
process must wait the slower process. In other words system computational
speed depends not only on speeds of processes but also on the number of

process interactions. Looking at occurrence graph of a system it can be seen that synchronizing constraints give rise to some arcs which impose precedence constraints among operations and then among evolution of processes. Since a synchronizing constraint (see relation 2.1) depends on dimensions of message-buffers, for each message-buffer the optimal dimension is looked for with respect to system computational speed. In fact, with greater message-buffer dimensions a more loose process coupling is obtained and then lower constraints among processes activities. On the other hand the cost of message-buffer increases with their dimensions.

With respect to the analysis of the system computational speed the occurrence graph can be modified by deleting all arcs $a \rightarrow b$ where a path $a \rightarrow a_1 \rightarrow a_2 \rightarrow \ldots \rightarrow a_n \rightarrow b$ exists in the occurrence graph. The resulting graph will be called the *reduced occurrence graph*. The precedence constraints are the same both in the occurrence graph and in the reduced occurrence graph. Then the last is more convenient for analyzing the system computational speed, since it is more simple.

The synchronizing constraint (2.1) for a message-buffer m gives rise, in the occurrence graph, to arcs coming out of nodes corresponding to the i_{th} *receive* from m (for all integer $i > 0$) and entering nodes corresponding to the $(i+B_m)_{th}$ *send* to m, where B_m is the dimension of m (see proc. 2.1).

For each message-buffer m, a dimension B_m^+ can be found such that if $B_m \geq B_m^+$ the arcs, the synchronizing constraint (2.1) introduce in the occurrence graph, are not present in the reduced occurrence graph.

A balanced system with a connection graph characterized by a directed circuit of two processes P_1 and P_2 (see fig. 3.2), is initially considered. Given such a system, for each message-buffer m_i $(i=1,2)$ the following integers are defined.

Definition 4.1: Let the integer u be the index of the generic *receive* operation of P_i.

The integer $t(u)$ is the maximum number of *send* operations of P_i that precede the $(u+1)_{th}$ *receive* of P_i.

The integer $w(u)$ is the number of *receive* operations of $P_{|i|_2+1}$ that precede the u_{th} *send* of $P_{|i|_2+1}$.

The integer $b_i(u)$ is the difference $t(u) - w(u)$ and B_i^+ is the maximum among integers $b_i(u)$ for all $u \geq 0$.

It can be proved that B_i^+ is the optimal dimension for the message-buffer m_i $(i=1,2)$.

Theorem 4.1: Given a balanced system with a connection graph characterized by a directed circuit of two processes P_1 and P_2, B_i^+ is the optimal dimension for the message-buffer m_i $(i=1,2)$.

Proof: First of all it can be proved that if $B_i \geq B_i^+$, the arcs the synchronizing constraint (2.1) introduce in the occurrence graph, are not present in the reduced occurrence graph. Let a$\to$b be an arc of the occurrence graph where a is the n_{th} *receive* operation of process $P_{|i|_2+1}$, b is the $(n+B_i)_{th}$ *send* operation of P_i, and B_i is the dimension of m_i. There is , at least, a *receive* that precede the $(n+B_i)_{th}$ *send* in P_i, since $B_i \geq B_i^+$ that is $B_i \geq$ to the number of *send* operations that precede the first *receive* in P_i. Let u be the number of *receive* that precede the $(n+B_i)_{th}$ *send* in P_i, and d the node corresponding to the u_{th} *receive* of P_i. Then the path d$\to$...$\to$b exists in the occurrence graph. Furthermore there exists the arc c$\to$d if c denotes the u_{th} *send* of $P_{|i|_2+1}$. Finally if e denotes the node corresponding to the w_{th} *receive* of $P_{|i|_2+1}$, then the path e$\to$...$\to$c exists in the occurrence graph by definition 4.1. Since $B_i \geq B_i^+$ it follows that $B_i \geq (n+B_i)-w$ that is $n-w \leq 0$. If n=w nodes e and a coincide, otherwise if n<w the path a$\to$...$\to$e exists in the occurrence graph. In both cases there is the path a$\to$...$\to$b.

On the other hand it can be proved that if $B_i < B_i^+$ there is at least an arc a$\to$b that is present also in the reduced occurrence graph, that is no path a$\to$..$\to$c$\to$d$\to$..$\to$b exists in the occurrence graph. For this purpose it is sufficient to prove that no arc c$\to$d is present in the occurrence graph together to paths a$\to$...$\to$c and d$\to$...$\to$b, where c denotes the m_{th} *send* operation of $P_{|i|_2+1}$ and d denotes the m_{th} *receive* of P_i. In fact, since $B_i < B_i^+$ there exists an integer $\bar{u}$ such that $t(\bar{u})-w(\bar{u}) > B_i$. Let b denote the node corresponding to the $t(\bar{u})_{th}$ *send* of P_i and a denote the node corresponding to the $(t(\bar{u})-B_i)_{th}$ *receive* of $P_{|i|_2+1}$. If the path d$\to$...$\to$b exists, then (see definition 4.1):

$$m \leq u \qquad\qquad (4.1)$$

Let e be the node corresponding to the $w(\bar{u})$ *receive* of $P_{|i|_2+1}$. Since a is the $(t-B_i)_{th}$ *receive* of $P_{|i|_2+1}$ and $B_i < t-w$, the node e precedes the node a. If the path a$\to$...$\to$c exists in the occurrence graph, then also the path e$\to$...$\to$a$\to$...$\to$c exists. That implies (by definition of integers u and w):

$$m > u \qquad\qquad (4.2)$$

By relations (4.1) and (4.2) it follows that the arc c$\to$d can not exist. Then the arc a$\to$b is present in the reduced occurrence graph.

Q.E.D.

Theorem 4.1, together with definition 4.1, specify a procedure to determine the optimal message-buffer dimensions. This procedure is not finite since B_i^+ is the maximum among all infinite integers $b_i(u)$ $(u \geq 0)$. However it can be easily proved that for $u > R_{|i|_2+1}$ all integers $b_i(u)$ are less than, or equal to, B_i^+. That is true owing to the periodic nature of the occurrence graph. Then the above procedure is finite since it is sufficient to determine the maximum among integers $b_i(u)$ for $0 \leq u \leq R_{|i|_2+1}$.

Furthermore the definition 4.1 can be extended to systems with connection graphs characterized by directed circuits of n processes.

Finally, given a system with an arbitrary connection graph, for each message-buffer, belonging to a directed circuit of the connection graph, the optimal message-buffer dimension can be determined following the above procedure. On the countrary, if a message-buffer does not belong to any directed circuit, a finite optimal dimension does not exist.

5. CONCLUSIONS

This paper is concerned with properties of a synchronization mechanism in a class of systems characterized by a set of parallel asynchronous processes and where each process runs on a different processor. In particular the synchronization mechanism analyzed is a message-transfer mechanism. Properties of deadlock conditions are analyzed and a procedure, for statically detect if a system is deadlock-free, is given.

Finally, optimal message-buffer dimensions are determined, with respect to the system computational speed and to the message-buffer cost.

This work is particularly oriented to distributed computer systems where these results acquire more interest.

REFERENCES

[1] P. Ancilotti, M. Fusani, N.Lijtmaer - Deadlock conditions in well structured modular systems - G.I. 4 Jaherstagung, Berlin 9-12 october 1974 - *Lectures Notes in Computer Science* - Vol. n.26, pp. 289-298, Springer Verlag.

[2] P. Ancilotti, M. Fusani, N. Lijtmaer - Interprocess Communications: Deadlock Conditions - *Internal Report B75-11* Istituto di Elaborazione della Informazione, Pisa - August 1975.

[3] P. Ancilotti, M. Fusani, N. Lijtmaer - Systems of Asynchronous Sequential Processes : The Balance Property in the Analysis of Deadlock Conditions - *Internal report B76-3* Istituto di Elaborazione della Informazione, Pisa - March 1976. (Also in proceedings of the AICA congress 1975, 30-31 october 1975 Genova Italy).

[4] P. Ancilotti - Control Properties of a set of asynchronous sequential processes - *Internal Report* Istituto di Elaborazione della Informazione, Pisa - (in preparation).

[5] F. Commoner, A.W. Holt, S. Even, A. Pnueli - Marked Directed Graphs- *JCSS* 5,1971 pp. 511-523.

[6] C. Ramchandani - Analysis of Asynchronous Concurrent Systems by Petri Nets - *MAC TR 120* MIT - February 1874

<u>APPENDIX</u>

In this appendix a simple example is given in order to illustrate the application of the results of this work.

A very simple system is considered, whose connection graph is a directed circuit of two processes P_1 and P_2 linked by two message-buffers m_1 and m_2 (see fig. 3.2).

The algorithms executed by processes P_1 and P_2 are the following:

```
Process P₁: repeat forever
            begin
            A:  <preparation of message α>;
            B:  Send α;
            C:  <preparation of message β>;
            D:  Send β;
            E:  Receive γ ;
            F:  <processing of message  γ>;
            G:  Receive δ ;
            H:  <processing of message  δ>;
            I:  Receive ε;
            J:  <processing of message ε>;
            end
```

```
Process P₂: repeat forever
            begin
            K:  <preparation of message γ>;
            L:  Send γ;
            M:  <preparation of message δ>;
            N:  Send δ;
            O:  Receive α;
            P:  <processing of message α>;
            Q:  <preparation of message ε>;
            R:  Send ε;
            S:  Receive β;
            T:  <processing of message β>;
            end
```

The system is balanced since (see the previous notation):

$$S_1=2 \quad S_2=3 \quad R_1=2 \quad R_2=3$$

then

$$S_1 \cdot S_2 = R_1 \cdot R_2$$

The minimal integer solution of the characteristic system of equations is:

$$K_1=K_2=1$$

Therefore $R_1'=R_1$, $S_1'=S_1$, $R_2'=R_2$, $S_2'=S_2$, that is the generating graph of the occurrance graph is characterized only by the first execution period of each process.

By definition 3.1, for all integers t such that $0<t\leq S_1'=2$ the difference $t-w>0$ ($t-w=1$ for $t=1$ and $t-w=2$ for $t=2$), than the predicate P_Δ is true and, therefore, by theorem 3.6, no sendless deadlock condition will be present in the system computations.

Let $B_1=2$ and $B_2=2$ be the dimensions of message-buffers m_1 and m_2 respectively. By definition 3.2 for all integers t such that $0<t\leq R_2'=3$ the difference $w-t<B_2$, that is the predicate P_n is true. (for $t=1$, $u=2$, $v=0$, $w=0$ then $w-t=-1<2$; for $t=2$, $u=2$, $v=0$, $w=0$ then $w-t=-2<2$; for $t=3$, $u=2$, $v=0,w=0$ then $w-t=-3<2$). Therefore, by theorem 3.7, no receiveless deadlock condition will be present in the system computations.

Note that if $B_1=B_2=1$ for $t=1$, $u=2$, $v=1$ and $w=2$ then $w-t=1=B_2$ that is the predicate P_n is false. That implies a receiveless deadlock condition in all system computations. In fact, in this case, a closed path $D\rightarrow E\rightarrow N\rightarrow \rightarrow O\rightarrow D$ is present in the occurrence graph of the system. Here D,E,N and O denote nodes of the occurrence graph corresponding to the operations of P_1 and P_2 with labels D,E,N and O respectively.

That is obvious because if message-buffers m_1 and m_2 can only contain a single message, P_1 and P_2 will be deadlocked after the execution of their first *send* operations. (labelled with B and L respectively). In fact no other *send* operation can terminate and the first *receive* operation, in each process, follows a second *send* operation.

By definition 4.1 for the message-buffer m_1, for all integers u such that $0\leq u\leq R_2'=3$ the integers $b_1(u)$ are the following:

$$2,\ 2,\ 2\ \text{and}\ 3$$

(for $u=0$, $t=2$, $w=0$ and $b_1(0)=2$; for $u=1$, $t=2$, $w=0$ and $b_1(1)=2$; for $u=2$, $t=2$, $w=0$ and $b_i(2)=2$; for $u=3$, $t=4$, $w=1$ and $b_i(3)=3$). Then the optimal message-buffer dimension for m_1 is $B_1^+=3$.

Analogously, for the message-buffer m_2, for all integers $0\leq u\leq R_1'=2$ the integers $b_2(u)$ are the following:

$$2,\ 3,\ 5$$

Then the optimal message-buffer dimension for m_2 is $B_2^+=5$.

SYSTEMATIC INSTALLATION MANAGEMENT

(Towards a Process of Continuous Observation and Control of Computer Performance)

H.Beilner
Abteilung Informatik, Universität Dortmund

P.S.Kritzinger
Department of Computing and Control, Imperial College, London

Abstract: Certain inadequacies are pointed out in present performance evaluation
approaches with respect to their potential usefulness for the managing of
computing installations. An alternate methodology is suggested which is
tailored to installation management's need of a continuous, systematic performance evaluation process and a corresponding research project, IMMT, is
reported on. The paper includes a selection of first results of this project
in the areas of analysing and modelling load and load dynamics as well as
performance and performance dynamics.

1. About certain inadequacies of present performance evaluation approaches

Managing a computing installation is, commonplace to say, a difficult task. It aims at
organising and controlling a complex and sophisticated system comprising a considerable
number of intricately interwoven hardware, software and operations components. It is
concerned with various, at times conflicting objectives originating from the organisation in which the computing facility is embedded and from a multitude of user individuals.

Performance evaluation, a sub-discipline of Computer Science, addresses, amongst other
questions, the technical problems of installation management. In numerous approaches,
relevant subproblems have been attacked and valuable models developed for certain parts
of computing installations, employing empirical/statistical, analytical/probabilistic
and procedural/simulation-type techniques, to name just the most important directions.
Support of a quite different nature is provided for installation management through the
instrumentation of modern computing systems: As an (almost) standard feature, so-called
software monitors are available which allow for the measuring and recording of a vast
number of system load and performance characteristics.

Installation management is still not in too good a position: The various performance
evaluation efforts have yielded numerous results which, however, do not yet combine into
a comprehensive, or even consistent, picture of computing system behaviour. It is

virtually impossible for the management of any specific installation to select the particular set of submodels which might be of assistance in controlling its very system. Software monitors, on the other hand, normally lack any additional tools for comprehending the large masses of recorded data and utilising them systematically for improving system performance. As a consequence, system performance evaluations are usually special purpose activities triggered by some observed performance insufficiency and with a rather restricted scope of problem in mind. Being devoted to different problems, even consecutive evaluations are essentially unrelated. As a result, all recommendations from these analyses cannot help but assume that system load does not change.

In reality, user needs and behaviour do develop over time. In view of the usual, considerable delay between the decision about some system alteration and the actual realisation of the corresponding change, a neglect of the medium to long term evolution of computing facilities is both unrealistic and inadequate. Moreover, the availability of at least partial system models on the one hand and of repeated system measurements on the other hand makes a systematic and continuous performance evaluation process look feasible which would more adequately serve the needs of installation management and improve its position drastically: From a mere <u>reacting to degradations of system performance</u> (which can even be expected to deteriorate further before any relief becomes effective) to an <u>acting in good time which avoids any foreseeable performance degradations.</u>

2. An approach towards overcoming these inadequacies.

For the purpose of effectively organising and controlling a computing installation, installation management has to assess present and estimate future performance of the system in terms of

- the requirements of the surrounding main organisation as given in the form of specified scope and level of services;

- the quality of service and the degree of service benefits as experienced by the user community.

The causes of any detected insufficiencies have to be identified and appropriate activities initiated which will eventually improve system performance or at least keep it from deteriorating.

These objectives demand a systematic, continuous performance analysis and evaluation process which will, almost necessarily, involve the following methodological steps:

- measuring and analysing past and present user demands as well as corresponding system performance;

- forecasting future user demands and predicting the consequent response of the unchanged system;

- relating predicted system performance and service benefits to specified service levels and to obtainable, better service quality;

- identifying the causes of any foreseeable service degradations and of any deviations from a higher service quality which should be achievable;

- suggesting changes to the system that would enable it to comply better with future demands and predicting the corresponding performance in the future environment.

In a sense, this methodology amounts to the adjusting of (a model of) a future computing system to (a model of) a future usage environment. All known performance improvement methods, if proven effective, are of course candidates for being incorporated in the described framework. Various subfields of the methodology, however, have not yet been covered (like, e.g., the modelling of load evolution). These areas will require particular attention where major assistance can be expected from the wide field of established statistical methods and models.

In an attempt to set the outlined ideas to work, and combining two precedent, similar research proposals (1,5), a corresponding research project was established in the Department of Computing and Control, Imperial College, London, in July 1974. This project, named "Installation Management Methodology and Techniques" (IMMT), aims at developing a facility for continuous, systematic performance evaluation. To ensure IMMT's effectiveness and applicability, it was decided that extensive use would be made of actual load and performance data continuously gathered for long enough time intervals and from several installations.

This paper reports on a selected subset of first results some of which have been described in much more detail in (2). During the period covered by the report, the members of the project were: H.Beilner, J.Jacobson, P.S.Kritzinger, M.M.Lehman and D.H.Simmons. The computing system load and performance data made available to us by the Rutherford High Energy Physics Laboratory have been invaluable to the project. In particular, we should like to thank Drs. M.M.Curtis and R.Taylor for their co-operation. The project is supported in part by Grant No. B/RG/9722.8 from the SRC. The necessary computations were performed at the Computer Science Computing Laboratory, Imperial College, London; the Computing Center, University College, London; the Informatik Rechenzentrum, Universität Stuttgart; the Rechenzentrum, Universität Dortmund.

3. Results to date.

The development of a methodology as described in the previous section would quite clearly require a sizeable effort which easily surpasses the limited resources of an University environment. Realistic research goals must necessarily be more modest. The eventual results of any smaller scale research attempts can, however, be expected to acquire greater practical usefulness if research targets are set in the context of a general, comprehensive framework.

As a consequence, the project IMMT was tentatively structured into a series of stages which could one day satisfy the whole of the methodology, yet actual work was started with respect to a first stage only. Stage I is to concentrate on the development of a

gross, yet effective, tool for predicting the performance of a computing system during
some future period of time while

- assuming that the computing installation (i.e., the union of hardware, software and
  operations components) stays unchanged; yet

- taking into account any foreseeable load developments (which represent the evolution
  of user needs and behaviour).

i.e., prime emphasis during this stage is on the first two steps of the methodology.

Investigating the possibilities for selecting an operational computing system as a
realistic source of load and performance data, we were very pleased to be granted access
to the corresponding records of the well-managed and well-monitored computing installation at the Rutherford High Energy Laboratory (RHEL), Didcot, England. Their system comprises an IBM 370/195 central processor unit with, at first, 2 megabytes, later, 3 megabytes of main core storage. Peripheral equipment includes a large number of remote work
stations and keyboard terminals. The operating system used is HASP/OS-MVT but with certain
MFT type modifications. Embedded in this operating system is a conversational terminal
system, ELECTRIC, and a real time experimental support system, MAST. The installation
is operated on a 24-hours-per-day, 7-days-a-week basis. The workload is mainly scientific with FORTRAN as the main programming language.

Detailed load and performance data is collected automatically in the RHEL central computer via the IBM System Management Facility (SMF; for further detail cf. IBM Publication GC 28-6712). SMF records include in particular:

- accounting information, such as CPU time and device and storage usage;

- dataset activity, such as EXCP count;

- system use information, such as step start time and device allocation time.

In a series of transformations, partially performed at RHEL and partially by us, this
SMF data is cleaned, condensed and recoded such as to be directly acceptable to an
available statistical software package, the "Statistical Package for the Social Sciences"
(SPSS). This package allows for a convenient execution of a large number of standard
statistical analyses.

The data now available to us cover a period of about 3 years of operation of the RHEL
system. It is obviously impractical, if at all feasible, to analyse the long term trends
of load and performance evolution directly from this large amount of low level data.
Consequently, we have embarked on a process of aggregating the information and character-
ising suitably selected intervals of time (e.g., hours, days, weeks) by corresponding
load and performance descriptors. The determination of these descriptors, in turn,
necessitates the detailed study of individual intervals of the selected duration. Such
studies can be performed for each interval separately and thus on a manageable body of
data. Moreover, since all inner details of the intervals become uninteresting, on the

next level of aggregation, it is sufficient to regard this innermost as homogeneous over time, i.e., static.

The course of studies, then, for Stage I will include the following steps:

- the analysis of system load for individual intervals (weeks, say) and the compact description of load by a suitable <u>load model</u>;

- the analysis of any possible changes of this load model over longer periods of time and the description of such load evolutions, as it were, by a corresponding <u>load dynamics model</u>;

- the analysis of system performance viewed as a response of the computing installation to the load submitted and the representation of these relationships via a <u>performance model</u>;

- the analysis of performance evolution due to load evolution (and possibly also to system changes) and the eventual formulation of a <u>performance dynamics model</u>.

For our first studies, we chose two intervals of one week each and about one year apart (the week beginning on 14 January 1974 and that beginning on 10 February 1975). One of the reasons why these particular two intervals were chosen is that in the interim the core memory of the system was upgraded to 3 megabytes and we expected the load characteristics of these two periods to differ noticeably.

The development of a <u>load model</u> will consist of selecting a suitable load element and describing, for any one week, the number of such elements submitted as well as all their characteristics. In more specific terms, if jobs are chosen as load elements, the weekly number of jobs must be measured and the joint distribution determined of all variables describing a single job, in particular, its CPU-, I/O- and core requirements. Far from having completed our work towards formalising the load model, we should like to present here some of our observations of the corresponding real world data. Table 1 depicts the first two sample moments of the CPU time and the number of Start I/O's of jobs, of the number of job steps per job as well as of the core requirements and the number of external data sets of job steps. Unfortunately, a proper measure of I/O time is not available. Histograms for all job and step characteristics were plotted to exhibit the various distributional forms. A major difficulty was encountered when realising that for certain characteristics the (commonly assumed) exponential/hyperexponential type distribution can, at best, serve as a gross approximation only while closer inspection reveals additional structure of a multimodal kind with unevenly spaced extrema (a histogram of the number of Start I/O's per job, Fig. 1, substatiates this statement). All load characteristics are statistically interdependent. An attempt to quantify the degree of dependence in the form of product-moment and rank-order correlation coefficients results in moderately positive values, for all pairs. A visual impression of these interrelationships can be obtained from scattergrams like that in Fig. 2 where CPUTME is plotted versus NTOTEXCP. Although the largest outliers have already been excluded from this plot, a striking observation is still the large concentration of small jobs. In fact, over 50% of the jobs have CPU times up to 10 sec and a number of Start I/O's of up to 1000. Of immediate interest is the conclusion that, at least at this installation, the frequently assumed dichotomy of CPU bound and I/O bound jobs does not appear to exist.

As a second area of concern, the development of <u>load dynamics models</u> is being prepared by investigating suitable modelling techniques. In an initial step, the evolution of a measure of load intensity, namely the number of jobs processed per week, was addressed. A 2 1/2 years plot of weekly observations of this variable (Fig. 3) reveals:

- an overall steady increase amounting to a doubling of the number of jobs, during the period covered;

- sharp lows of activity at points which can in general be linked to certain exogeneous events, some of them calender related (Christmas, bank holidays etc.), others caused by scheduled service interruptions (yearly shutdown for maintenance of the aircon-ditioning system etc.);

- a yearly cyclicity, in particular at the summer holidays;

- a remainder of unexplained variation.

The course of our modelling attempt was, omitting all details:

(a) excluding from the analysis all points which coincide with exogeneously caused service anomalities;

(b) fitting, via regression analysis, a polynomial to the remainder of the series to take care of the deterministic, nonlinear trend;

(c) fitting a time-series model to the residuals from the regression analysis (time-series analysis is a statistical technique which attempts to explain any one observation, in a series of observations, as a function of past observations and of past and present, superimposed random disturbances - cf., e.g., Box/Jenkins (4)).

The results obtained:

(a) 23 weeks (out of a total of 139 weeks) were excluded from further analysis;

(b) regression analysis step:
Model assumed, on the basis of a visual inspection of a plot of the number of jobs, n_t, per week, t (Fig. 3):

$$n_t = p^2(t) + res_t^{RA}$$

$$\text{with} \quad p^2(t) = a_o + a_1 t + a_2 t^2 \qquad \text{trend polynomial}$$

$$res_t^{RA} \qquad \text{residual from the regression analysis, at week, t}$$

estimation yields:

$a_0 = 5995.0$

$a_1 = 81.78$

$a_2 = -0.2867$

measures of the goodness of fit:

$\text{MEAN}(\text{res}_t^{RA}) = 0.0009$

$\text{STD DEV}(\text{res}_t^{RA}) = 855.8$

(c) time series analysis step:

Model assumed, on the basis of the autocorrelation function and the partial autocorrelation function of res_t^{RA}:

$$\emptyset^2(B)\,\text{res}_t^{RA} = \Theta_0 + \text{res}_t^{TSA}$$

with   B   backward shift operator

$\emptyset^2(B) = 1 - \emptyset_1 B - \emptyset_2 B^2$ second order autoregressive operator

res_t^{TSA} residual   from the time series analysis, at week, t

estimation yields:

$\Theta_0 = 107.9$

$\emptyset_1 = 0.258$

$\emptyset_2 = 0.254$

measures of the goodness of fit:

$\text{MEAN}(\text{res}_t^{TSA}) = 5 \cdot 10^{-10}$

$\text{STD DEV}(\text{res}_t^{TSA}) = 676.5$

Figure 3 depicts the original series, number of jobs processed per week, the one week ahead forecasts derived from employing the composite model and the 90% confidence area for these estimates.

As an initial step towards cause-effect __performance models__, we calculated a number of linear regression models a subset of which is given in Table 2. These models, of the form

     duration of processing a load element

     = L(characteristics of the load element)

are, by definition, not capable of explicitly reflecting the additional dependency of processing durations on the resource contention situations encountered. Since performance prediction in situations of varying and changing load (and the implied potential varia-tion in the degree of contention) is the main objective of this, the Stage I, performance model, standard regression models appear inadequate for this purpose. Regression models are, however, a useful means for obtaining an indication as to which load characteristics are influential on processing durations and which are not. In this sense, it is worth-while noting that CPU time and number of Start I/O's have a significant influence on job elapsed time while the inclusion of other available load characteristics, like amount of core requested and number of steps, does not significantly improve the goodness of fit (R^2 value). Another interesting observation is that, contrary to our expectations, the incorporation of a measure of contention (DEGREEMP, the time-weighted average of the multiprogramming level, during the job's stay on the system) as an independent variable does not improve the models either. Finally, we should like to point out how much better the variation of elapsed time is explained for large jobs as compared with that for small jobs (R^2 values of .22/.30 versus .74/.92).

We continue our overview over the first IMMT results with an observation concerning
performance evolution which was unexpected to us. Performance considerations at the
RHEL computing centre have placed prime emphasis on a high utilisation of the CPU. Consequently, it is not surprising that CPU utilisation improved markedly during the observation period (Fig. 4) from about 70%, in 1972, to about 90%, in 1975. CPU utilisation
by user jobs, however, seems to fluctuate around a constant value of just over 60% or,
in other words, CPU utilisation by the system increased at just the same rate as total
CPU utilisation improved. The users, in spite of being left with a constant power CPU,
submit an increasing number of jobs (as we know from Fig. 3). These two observations
can only be consistent if, at the same time,CPU time required per job decreases. This
suggestion can in fact be verified: Average CPU time per job shrinks from over 40 sec,
in 1972, to about 30 sec, in 1975. More precisely: The number of "short" jobs (up to
90 sec CPU time) grows at the expense of the "long" jobs (over 5 min CPU time).

As a case study of an analysis of combined system, load and performance changes, a
retrospective evaluation was attempted of the 1 MByte core upgrading at the RHEL system.
Turning again to Table 1, a comparison of the load characteristics exhibits:

- approximately unchanged CPU requirements;
- decreased I/O activities (as measured by number of Start I/O's) in spite of the larger
  number of data sets used;
- larger core requirements.

While the I/O related observations call for a separate analysis, the increase in core
requests may well be attributed to the users adapting to the larger core available.
On the system side, we notice the higher multiprogramming level attained. The waiting
for core decreased substantially - a joint effect of larger core and higher multiprogramming level. Elapsed time, made up of wait for core and incore time, improved due to
this shortened wait for core time with the incore time about unchanged. The latter fact
arises from, simultaneously, an increase in the waiting for the CPU (explainable by the
larger number of processes competing for the constant power CPU) and a decrease in the
I/O related times (caused by the smaller number of I/O requests; possibly also by a
better channel utilisation with the higher multiprogramming level). Altogether, a higher
number of jobs could be processed and a better throughput obtained.

4. Conclusion

Quite noticeably, our work has only just started to yield useful observations and
results. A rather tiresome initial period had to be completed involving a large number
of important yet not very exciting activities (such as familiarising with system and
data, writing transformation programs, creating a data base etc.). Now that the data
are more readily accessible, we hope to be able to advance somewhat faster - in particular in the following directions:

- an explanation (and eventually a model) has to be found for the multimodal distributions of certain load characteristics; this as a prerequisite for developing a load
  model in the form of a multidimensional distribution;
- measures like WAITME (I/O + wait for I/O time) and NTOTEXCP (number of Start I/O's)
  have to be further analysed in order to possibly derive a proper measure of I/O time;
- the load dynamics modelling will have to be refined by taking the seasonal regulari-
  ties explicitly into account and by turning to multidimensional models incorporating
  several load characteristics simultaneously;
- more emphasis has to be placed on constructing useful performance models; our attempts
  presently concentrate on a highly aggregated simulator and a transfer function model
  on time series basis.

Additionally, work has started towards broadening our data base by incorporating data
from an additional, operational computing facility.

References

(1) H.Beilner
    Methodik der Planung und Verwaltung von Rechensystemen
    Institut für Informatik, Universität Stuttgart
    Internal document, 1973

(2) H.Beilner, P.S.Kritzinger
    Computer Installation Management Methodology and Techniques
    Department of Computing and Control, Imperial College, London
    Publication no. 75/21 (Research Report), 1975

(3) H.Beilner, P.S.Kritzinger
    A Computer Installation Management Methodology
    Accepted for the European Computing Conference on Computer Systems Evaluation
    14-16 September 1976, London

(4) G.E.P.Box, G.M.Jenkins
    Time Series Analysis - Forecasting and Control
    Holden-Day, 1970

(5) M.M.Lehman
    Installation Management Tool
    Department of Computing and Control, Imperial College, London
    Internal document, 1974

Description of variable (Variable name)		Mean (Std. Error) 1974 week | 1975 week		Std. Deviation 1974 | 1975	
CPU time (CPUTME)	job	341 (15)	325 (16)	1546	1790
Number of Start I/O's (NTOTEXCP)	job	3781 (84)	3012 (60)	8532	6662
Core allocated/KBytes (ALLOCORE)	step	160 (1.6)	169 (9)	86	96
Core used/KBytes (USEDCORE)	step	122 (0.5)	128 (0.5)	80	85
Number of steps completed (NSTEPRCD)	job	2.38 (.01)	2.36 (.01)	1.4	1.4
Number of data sets (NDEVICES)	step	7.8 (.03)	8.2 (.03)	4.07	4.42
Elapsed time (ELAPSTME)	job	2922 (100)	2478 (59)	10262	6602
Incore time (INCORTME)	job	2132 (61)	2219 (49)	6218	5428
Wait for core time (WAITCORE)	job	790 (70)	259 (26)	7155	2939
Wait for CPU time (READYTME)	job	829 (43)	1204 (38)	4434	4202
I/O + wait for I/O time (WAITME)	job	1303 (54)	1015 (25)	5514	2761
Multiprogramming index (DEGREEMP)	job step	6.92 (.02) 6.82 (.01)	7.62 (.02) 7.52 (.01)	2.0 2.0	2.2 2.2
User CPU utilisation		62.6%	68.4%		
Throughput/jobs per hour		63.4	75.6		

<u>TABLE 1</u>: Descriptive statistics for load and performance variables of jobs and job steps for two one week intervals.

Sample sizes: jobs 1974   steps 1974   jobs 1975   steps 1975
          10429   24784   12424   29318

All times in 1/10 sec.

Dependent Variable: Job elapsed time

Unit: 1/10 sec

Independent Variables	B Coeff's		Beta Coeff's		Std. Error B		F Value	
Job CPU time Unit: 1/10 sec	2.88	2.84	0.43	0.77	0.05	0.02	2807	26865
	4.23	4.73	0.22	0.28	0.19	0.15	515	1043
	1.92	2.84	0.67	0.90	0.18	0.07	113	1855
Number of Start I/O's per job	0.39	0.24	0.33	0.25	0.01	0.005	1598	2760
	0.21	0.21	0.33	0.37	0.01	0.005	1179	1818
	0.36	0.23	0.27	0.14	0.08	0.03	18	45

Sample Sizes			R Square			ANOVA F		
	10429	12424		0.40	0.74		3544	17879
	9738	11351		0.22	0.30		1345	2391
	115	226		0.74	0.92		157	1231

TABLE 2: Regression analyses

Legend:	
All jobs of week starting 14 Jan 74	All jobs of week starting 10 Feb 75
small jobs of 1974 week	small jobs of 1975 week
large jobs of 1974 week	large jobs of 1975 week

Small jobs defined as requiring up to 100 sec CPU time and up to 300 kBytes

Large jobs defined as requiring more than 100 sec CPU time and more than 300 kBytes of core

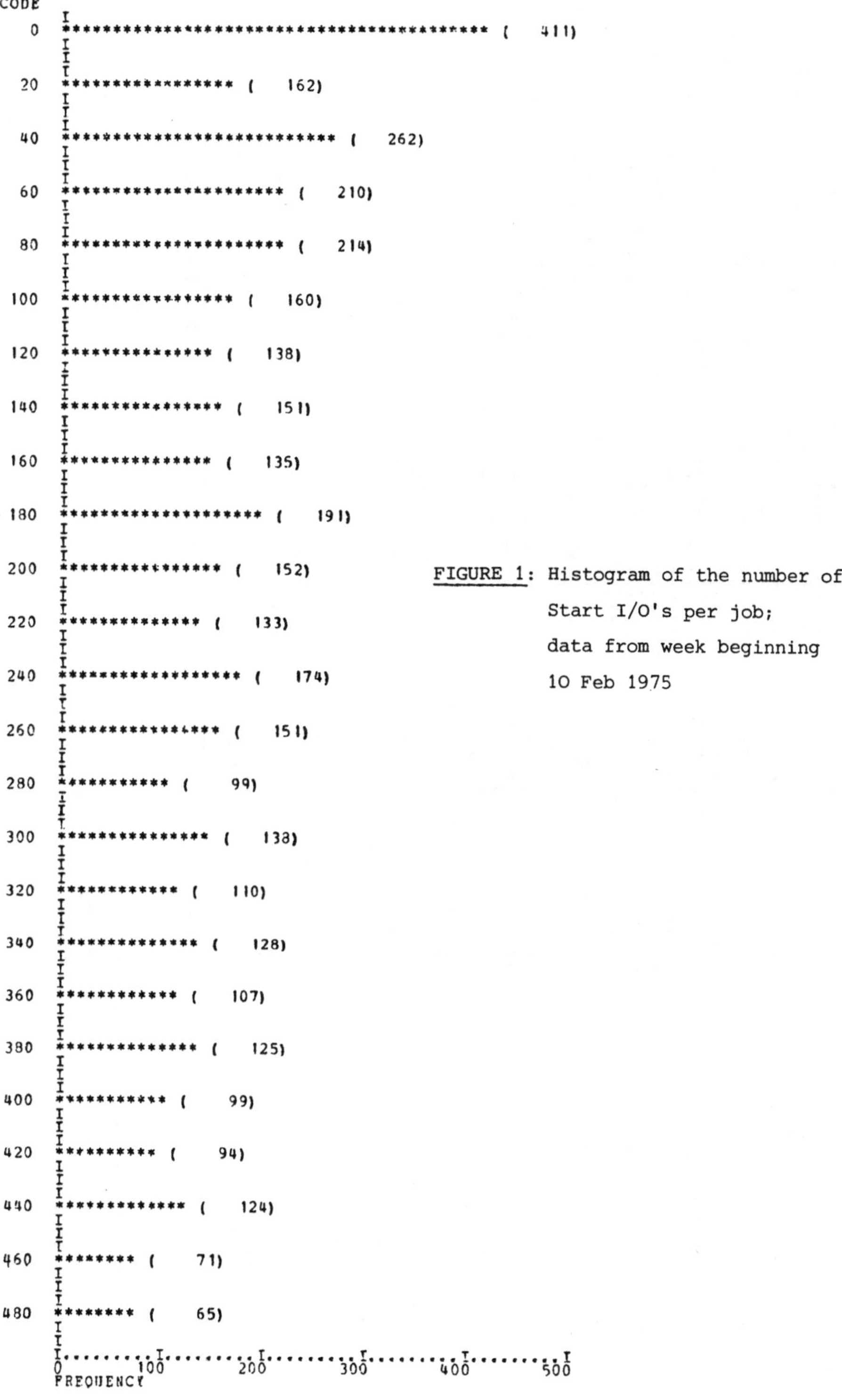

FIGURE 1: Histogram of the number of Start I/O's per job; data from week beginning 10 Feb 1975

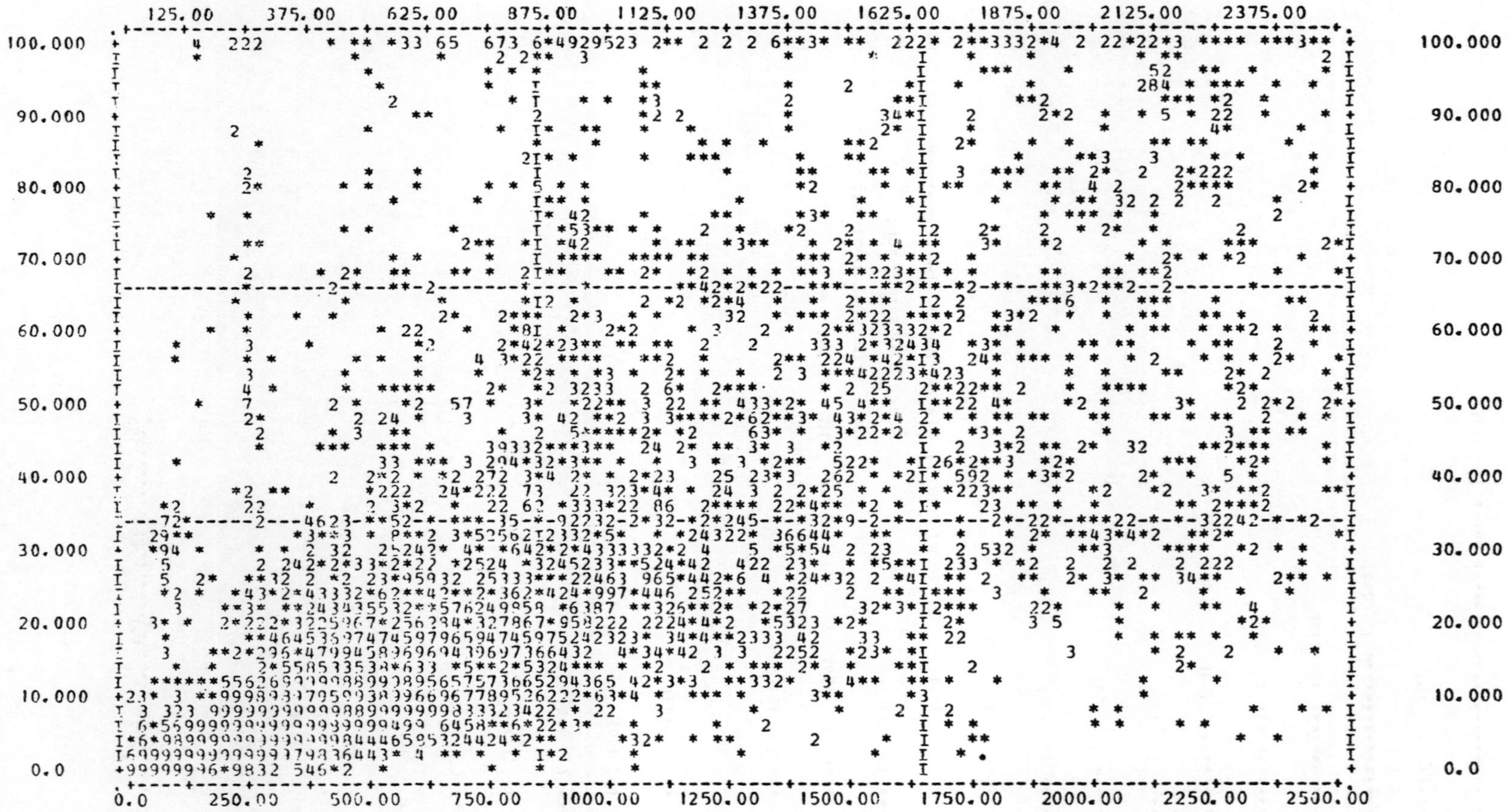

FIGURE 2: Scattergram of

job CPU time (down), unit 1/10 sec
number of Start I/O's per job (across)

data from week beginning 10 Feb 1975

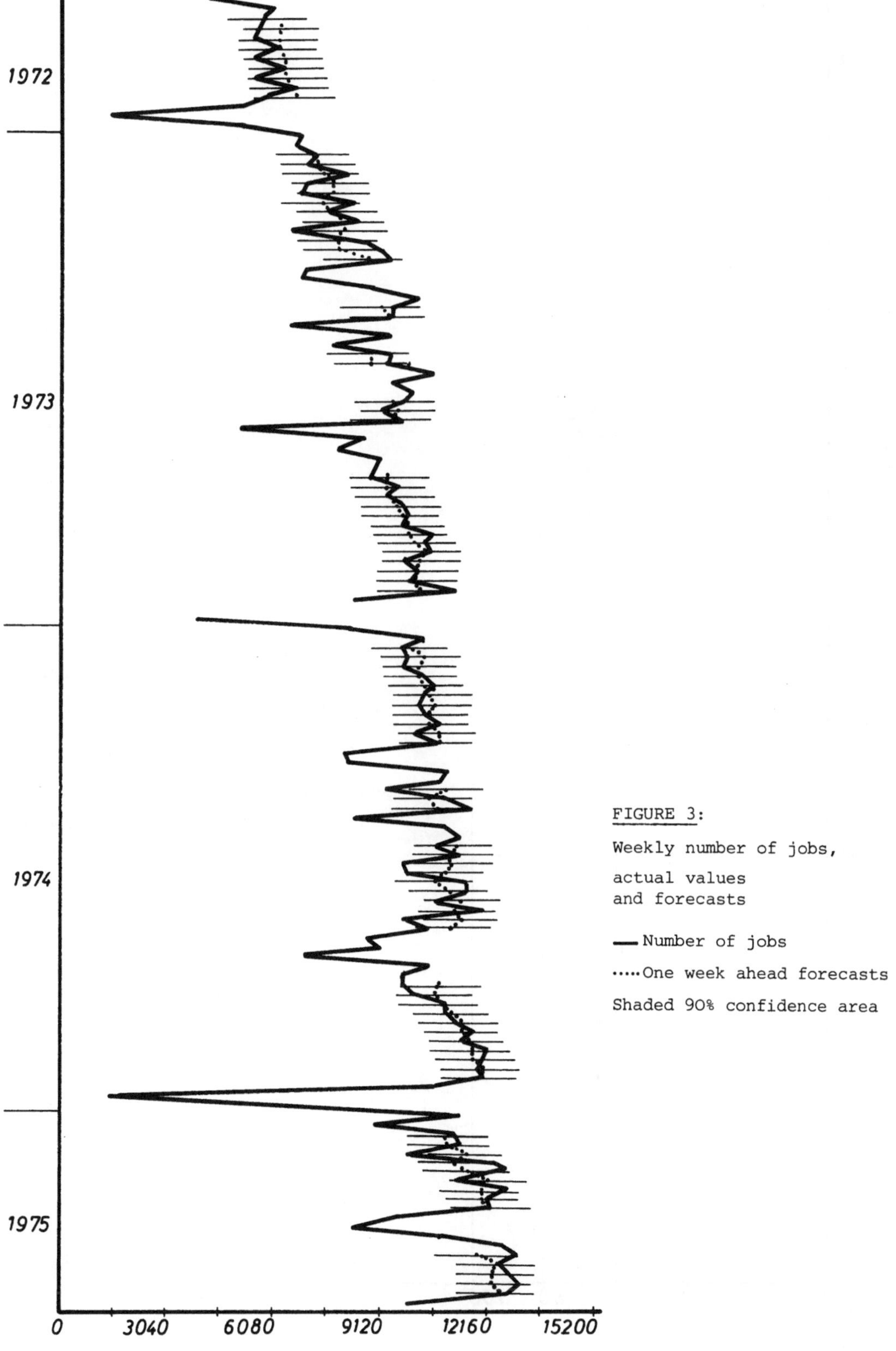

FIGURE 3:

Weekly number of jobs,
actual values
and forecasts

—— Number of jobs

·····One week ahead forecasts

Shaded 90% confidence area

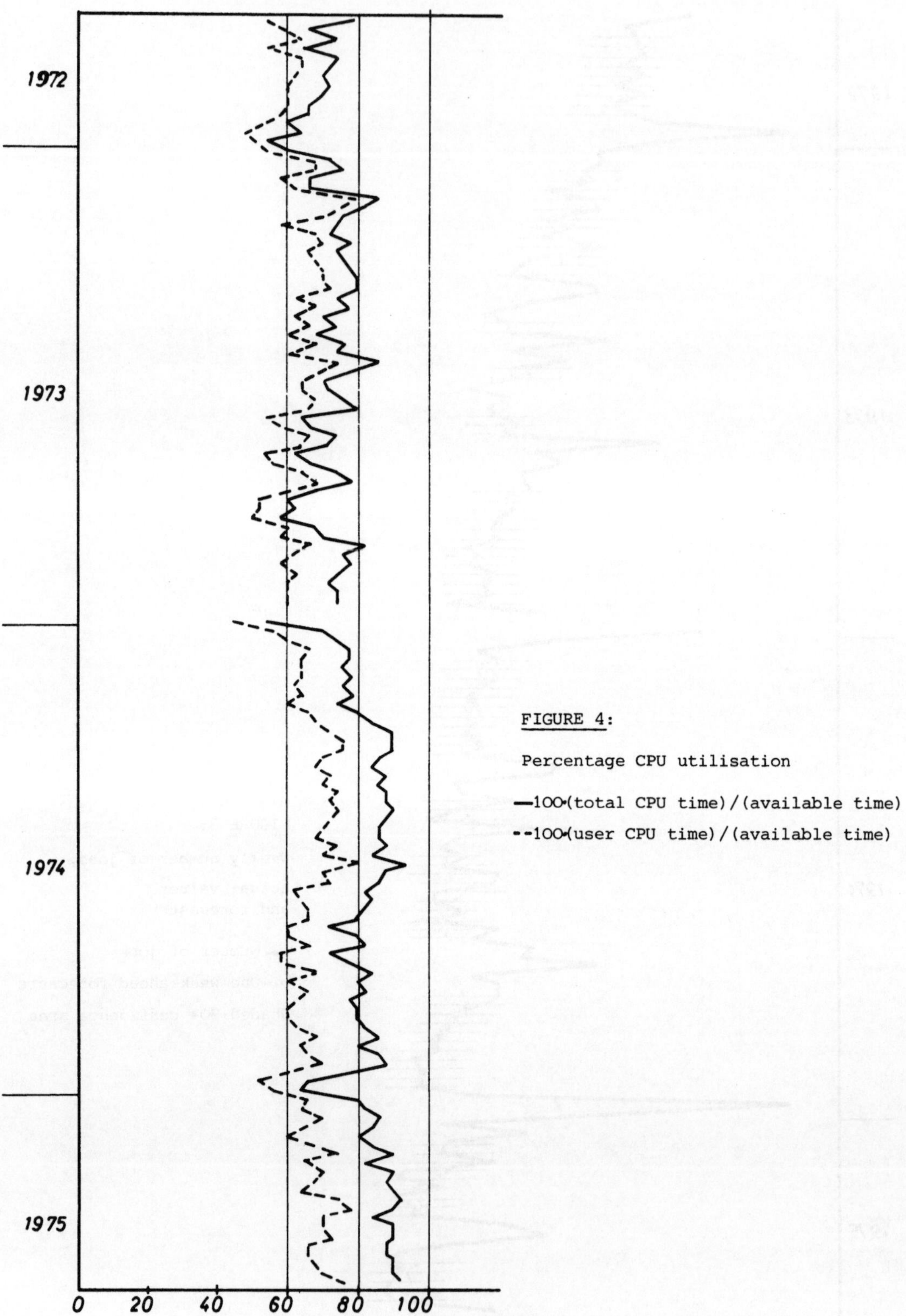

FIGURE 4:

Percentage CPU utilisation

—100×(total CPU time)/(available time)

--100×(user CPU time)/(available time)

<u>UNDERSTANDING LISP PROGRAMS IS IMPROVING LISP PROGRAMS</u>

H. WERTZ
U.E.R. Informatique & Linguistique
Université Paris 8
75571 PARIS CEDEX 12

1 - INTRODUCTION

In this paper we describe the knowledge and reasoning processes of a special LISP
system. In this system completely automatic improvements of both syntactic and semantic features of LISP programs are performed. It is defined as an ordinary LISP system
with the following restrictions :
    - exclusion of functional arguments
    - partitioning of variable- ,function- and label-names.
I call programs written in such a system : *first order LISP programs.*

Tactics and knowledge needed will be expressed both procedurally (by programs) and
structurally (by choice of representations). We consider the reasoning ability as a
central issue in the process of automatic improving and understanding of programs.

However,symbolic reasoning alone is not sufficient to understand programs efficiently.
In addition we need other methods such as :
    - use of model-programs (RUTH 1973)
    - meta-evaluation (HEWITT 1973, 1975, 1975a)
    - use of current methods in automatic program-verification : generation of asser-
      tions, theorem proving, etc. (FLOYD 1967, MANNA 1974, BOYER & MOORE 1973).

Our system, PHENARETE, detects and eliminates a great number of various errors : sometimes PHENARETE finds it necessary to modify entirely the structure of the proposed
program. But the errors are mostly quite naive : ill-located or absent statements,
spelling errors, and so on. Our system yields a number of comments and gives an informal justification of all the improvements.

When beginning this work, I had the idea to verify that one can build a program-understanding system, which is completely ignorent of the intentions of the programmer,
and which - in addition - would have the practical advantage of giving help to human
or non-human programming apprentices in the debugging process.

I regard the problem of automatic program improving as part of artificial intelligence.
A system to debug and comment programs must have some abilities common with natural
language understanding systems or robot problem solvers. Those abilities are : representation of knowledge and drawing of common sense conclusions from given facts. The
system may be considered as an artificial language understanding system.

The system PHENARETE was written in VLISP-10 (CHAILLOUX 1976, GREUSSAY 1976) and is
currently implemented on the PDP-10 at the Departement d'Informatique of the Université de Paris 8 (Vincennes). Beginners in LISP use it to debug their programs.

As a second part I will give some examples of the actual running of the system, then
describe the internal organisation, both static and dynamic. Finally I shall expose
the actual limitations and give some hints for further developments. As a conclusion
I shall compare our system with related works.

2 - A USER'S VIEW OF PHENARETE : SOME COMMENTED EXAMPLES

In this section some examples will be given that display the ability in understanding
and improvment of the actual system.

2.1 - Spelling errors

Let us suppose one has submitted the following function definition to the system :

```
(DE FACT (N)
    (COND
        ((ZEROPP N) 1)
        (T (TIMS N (FACCT (UB1 N)) )) ))
```

This is a recursive function definition which computes the factorial of any number N.
Note that this definition of FACT contains several spelling mistakes :
- ZEROP is written ZEROPP
- TIMES is written TIMS
- FACT is in the recursive call written FACCT and
- SUB1 is written UB1

PHENARETE proposes	actions undertaken
ERREUR NOM : ?ZEROPP → ZEROP	she does not know any function called ZEROPP, so PHENARETE supposes that the user intended to write ZEROP
ERREUR NOM : ?TIMS → TIMES	she does not know TIMS either, so she replaces it by TIMES
ERREUR NOM : ?FACCT → FACT	she replaces FACCT by FACT : FACT in effect is the unique function she knows of and which resembles FACCT
ERREUR NOM : ?UB1 → SUB1	the same

PROPOSITION :
(DE FACT (N)
  (COND
  ((ZEROP N) 1)
  (T (TIMES N (FACT (SUB1 N))))))))
	PHENARETE proposes her improvement of the program. Here it is purely orthographic

2.2 - Parentheses errors

Let's give PHENARETE another program :

```
(DE (FACT (N
    (COND
        (ZERO (N (1
        (T (TIMES (NN (FACT (SUB1 (N))) ))) ))) ))) )
```

It is the same recursive function but with a very strange grouping of parentheses.

PHENARETE proposes	actions undertaken
(DE FACT (N)	she has recognized that FACT is the function and N the variable
(COND ((ZEROP N) 1)	recognition of the first clause of the COND and replacement of ZERO by ZEROP
.(T (TIMES N (FACT (SUB1 N)))))))	recognition of the second clause of the COND.Since she does not know the variable NN she replaces it by N

PHENARETE could manage and rectify this unusual syntax, and she has produced a definition of FACT quite well.

2.3 - Semantic verification of control-functions

Example with COND

```
(DE (FACT) (N
    COND
        (T TIMES N FACT SUB1 N))
        (ZEROP N 1)
```

Really this definition is no better :
- very bad grouping of parentheses
- the clauses of the COND are inversed

PHENARETE proposes	actions undertaken

`(DE FACT (N)` }
`   (COND`
`     ((ZEROP N) 1)`
`     (T (TIMES N (FACT (SUB1 N))`
`   )) ))`
	correction of parentheses-errors
	
	replacement of the clauses of the COND and correction of the parenthesis-errors

2.4 - Loop improvments

Let's give our system a fourth version of FACT :

```
(DE FACT N RES
    (SETQ RES 1)
    (WHILE ((GT N 1))  (1)
           (SETQ RES (TIMES N RES)))
RES)
```

There are two errors :
- parentheses-errors
- the loop control variable is not modified inside the loop which happens to be infinite.

PHENARETE proposes	actions undertaken

`(DE FACT (N RES)` }
`  (SETQ RES 1)`
`  (WHILE (GT N 1)`
`      (SETQ RES (TIMES N RES))`
`      (SETQ N (SUB1 N)) )`
`RES)`
	correction of parentheses-errors
	
	introduction of a modification of the loop-control variable : the program terminates

2.5 - Semantic improving of a user function

A last example (the comment is within the text)

```
(DE INVERSER (L1 L2)
    (COND
        ((NULL L2) L1)
        (T
          (INVERSER
               (CDR L1)
               (CONS (CAR L1) L2))) ))
```

(1) WHILE is an idiosyncratie of VLISP, it has the general form :
       (WHILE predicate statement1 ... statementn)
and executes sequentially statement1 thru statementn as long as the predicate is true.

The reader is invited to enjoy the subtle performance of PHENARETE :

```
(DE INVERSER (L1 L2)
    (COND
        ((NULL L1) L2)
        (T
            (INVERSER
                    (CDR L1)
                    (CONS (CAR L1) L2))) ))
```

3 - DESCRIPTION OF THE SYSTEM

PHENARETE is written in VLISP. By the power of its standard control structures this language is particulary well suited for the writing of such programs.

3.1 - Control structure of PHENARETE

PHENARETE reads the programs from left to right collecting information for future readings. Every time she meets a standard LISP function, she activates a so-called *specialist*, which can use special knowledge about this function.

A specialist is defined by :
- the treatment it will apply to the message *(1)* received (use-of-the-message)
- the form of the message it sends (form-of-the-message)
- every other specialist from which it can ask, then receive informations (information-agency)

Every specialist can have access at two data bases :
1) HELP
2) AUX

When invoked each of the specialist finds the message destinated to him as the first element of HELP. It processes the message, then, the work finished, erases the first message in HELP and delivers a message, which happens to be the result of the processing, into AUX. These specialists will be activated automatically by *data driven function invocation* (SANDEWALL 1975) as soon as their name appears in the source-program.

3.2 - Data structure : the cognitive atoms

By a *COGNITIVE ATOM* we mean a LISP atom which has a private knowledge-P-list. Every bit of knowledge PHENARETE uses is currently implemented as a knowledge-P-list. Dependant on their knowledge we distinguish three classes of cognitive atoms :
- 1) atoms with knowledge about variables
- 2) atoms with knowledge about labels
- 3) atoms with knowledge about functions.

To make the writing (hence the work) of the system easier we impose that these three classes be disjoint. In fact, this restriction corresponds to the second part of our definition of first-order LISP programs.

4 - DESCRIPTION OF THE SYSTEM'S BEHAVIOUR

What the system does with the help of the exemple 2.4 will now be described.

---

(1) A message is defined as the set of information a specialist may receive from or send to another specialist.

4.1 - <u>First reading - surface-error detection and first improvements</u>

Since the source program begins with a call to the LISP definition function DE,
PHENARETE gives the control immediatly to the specialist *function-DE* which begins
the analysis. Its knowledge could be expressed as following :

<u>Specialist function-DE</u>

```
[Function-DE (X) ≡>
                & atom (car X)
                & list-of-variables (cadr X)
                & list-of-statements (cddr X)
          else :
                modify X until
                        Function-DE (X) = T]
```

which means :

> To be sure that the message received by the specialist Function-DE is a message
> superficially correct, it is necessary
>> and that the first element of the message is an atom
>> and that the second element of the message is a list of variables
>> and that the message without the first two elements is a list of statements
> If this does not happen, it is necessary to
>> modify the message until
>>> the first three clauses are satisfied.

Hence the function expects an atome as the first element.This is indeed the case
(DE <u>FACT</u> N ...)
Assuming that this is the name of the function to be defined it puts it immediately
at the beginning of the list F-N-SUBR, a list which contains the names of every func-
tion already known to PHENARETE. The following element has to be a list of variables.
So control is given to a variable list recognition specialist.

<u>Variable list recognition specialist</u>

```
[List-of-variables (X) ≡>
                    & atom (car X)
                    & ¬ name-of-function (car X)
                    & ¬ ((car X) ε (cdr X))
                    & list-of-variables (cdr X)
              else :
                    modify X until
                    list-of-variables (X) = T]
```

But this one, in spite of receiving a list - that was expected - it receives the atom
N as a message, in effect, we have :
(DE FACT <u>N</u> RES ...)
As every other specialist there is a component to complain to, and which will do **its**
best to eliminate the causes of the complaints. *(1)* This component will propose,after
having verified that N is not the name of a known function, to consider this atom as
the first element of the variable list. The same procedure is applied to the following
element, and RES is considered as the second element of the list. The following message is the list (SETQ RES 1). The specialist of variable lists, while recognising
that this list begins with the name of a function, does not accept it, and sends a
message, the newly constructed variable list, to the specialist Function-DE. From
now on PHENARETE can use that newly acquired knowledge :

---

(1) this is equivalent to the "complaint-department" of HEWITT's actors (HEWITT 1973)

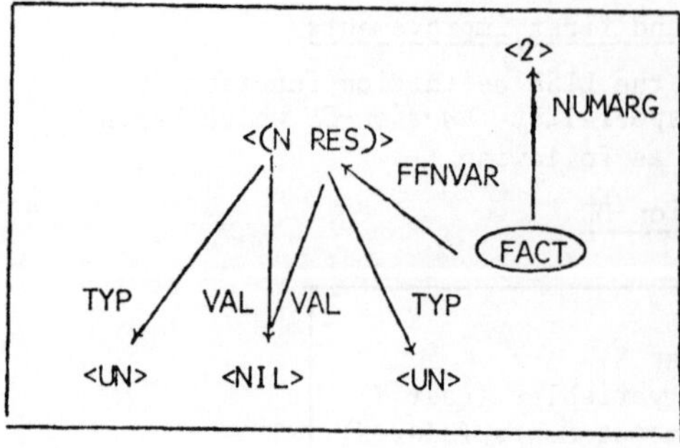

```
AUX ← (DE FACT (N RES))
HELP ← ((SETQ RES 1)
          (WHILE ((GT N 1))
              (SETQ RES
                  (TIMES N RES)))
          RES)
```

The following message is adressed to the specialist *assignment-SETQ*. The following is known :

<u>Spécialist assignment-SETQ</u>

```
[assignment-SETQ (X) ≡>
                & name-of-variable (car X)
                & S-expression (cadr X)
        else : if S-expression (car X)
                  send X to the specialist-SET
        else : modify X until
                    assignment-SETQ (X) = T]
```

There is no particular difficulty : the first element is a variable and the second is a constant. The invocation of the specialist-SETQ has a result :

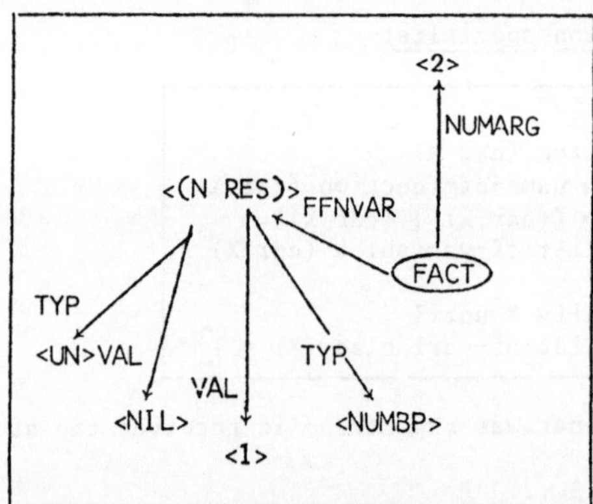

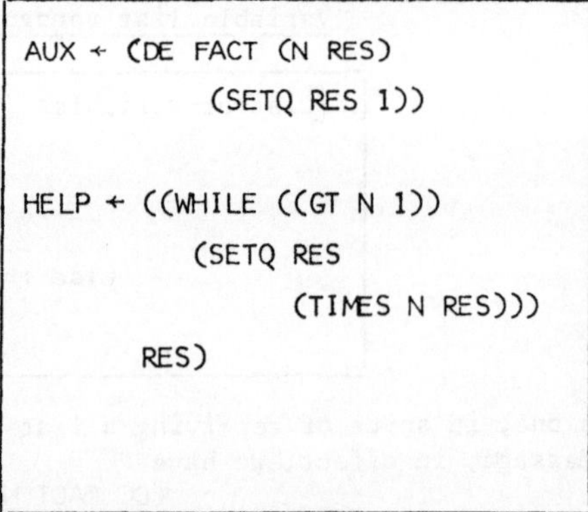

The knowledge is very limited at the first reading of the specialist of loops-WHILE to whom will be sent the following message :

<u>Specialist loop-WHILE</u>

```
[loop-WHILE (X) ≡>
              v (& atom (car X)
                 & name-of-variable (car X)
                 & list-of-statements (cdr X)
                 v list-of-statements (X)
          else :
                 modify X until
                          loop-WHILE (X) = T]
```

Since the atom is not found at the head of the message he will transform the message
                  (WHILE (GT N 1)
                          (SETQ RES (TIMES N RES)))
with the help of the specialists GT, SETQ and TIMES and concatenates this list to
AUX. The assignment of RES has given rise to a modification : now on the P-list of
RES is :
                  (TYP NUMBP VAL 1 MODIF GREATER)
and because the specialist GT expects the arguments to be numerical values, the P-
list of N is now of the form :
                  (TYP NUMBP VAL UN)
It is the specialist function-DE which is responsible for the analysis of RES, the
last element to analyse. He introduces it at the end of AUX, and because this is the
last expression of the function, the extra indication
                  (VAL NUMBP)
can be put on the P-list of FACT. HELP being empty now, PHENARETE can proceed at a
first proposition :
                  (DE FACT (N RES)
                      (SETQ RES 1)
                      (WHILE (GT N 1)
                              (SETQ RES (TIMES N RES)))
                      RES)
The knowledge collected about FACT is :

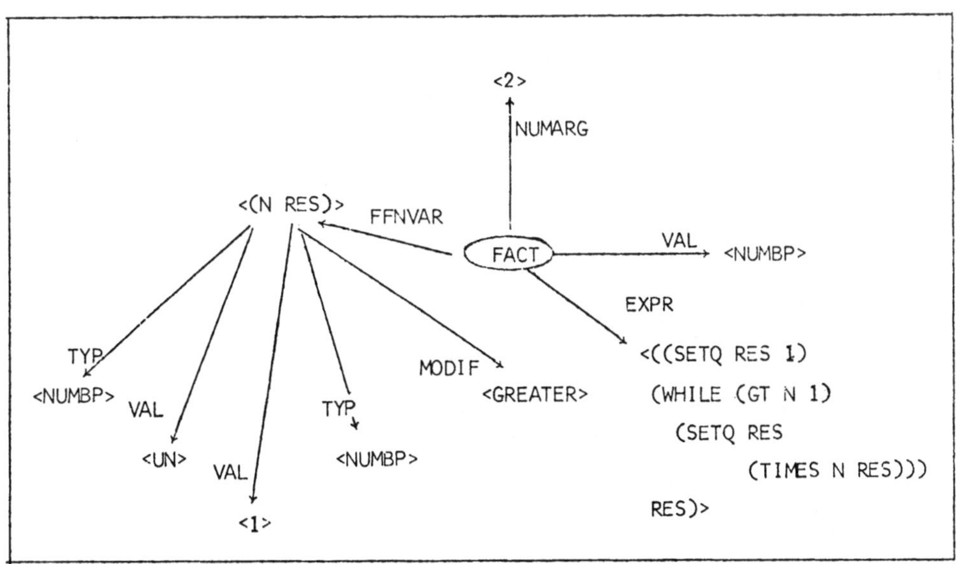

There are no more surface errors. However PHENARETE is not really satisfied :

4.2 - Readings 2 to n - semantic improvements

At the first reading, PHENARETE only collects the maximum amount of information about
the program to understand and to eliminate the surface errors which are detectable
by local analysis. PHENARETE reads and rereads the entire program as many times as
new improvements are possible (that is until the application of PHENARETE to the
program behaves like the identy function)*(1)*.

4.3 - Continuation of the example 2.4 (FACT)

Remembering what PHENARETE knows now about FACT :
- 1) it is a function with two variables
- 2) the variable RES is initialized to the value 1
- 3) N has to be a number
- 4) RES is modified in a manner which incresses its value and
- 5) the final value of RES is the value of the function.

Now she is operating on a program considered syntactically correct :

```
.1.   (DE FACT (N RES)
.2.       (SETQ RES 1)
.3.       (WHILE (GT N 1)
.4.           (SETQ RES (TIMES N RES)))
.5.       RES)
```

In analysing lines .1. and .2. PHENARETE does not learn anything new and cannot
effect any new improvement. It is a second specialist-WHILE which carries on the
analysis within the loop. This one has some more precise knowledge about the structure of a loop than his partner of the first reading.

Specialist loop-WHILE-2

```
[Loop-WHILE-2 (X) ≡>
              v (& atom (car X)
                 & list-of-statements (cdr X)
                 & (v [(NEXTL (car X))] ⊂ (cdr X)    (2)
                      v [(SETQ (car X) (CD...DR (car X)))] ⊂ (cdr X)))
              v (& predicate (caar X)
                 & list-of-statements (cdr X)
                 & [(get (caar X) 'WHT)] ⊂ (cdr X))
        else :
              modify X until
                  loop-WHILE-2 (X) = T]
```

This means :
      To be sure that the message X is a loop which terminates, it is necessary that
         or and (car X) is a atom
            and (cdr X) is a list of statements
            and that there is somewhere a modification of (car X)
                or by a (NEXTL (car X))
                or by a (SETQ (car X) (CD...DR (car X)))
         or and (caar X) is a predicate
            and (cdr X) is a list of statements
            and that there is somewhere the statement such that the predicate (caar X)
                    yields, if asked for the value of his WHT (WERTZ 1976)
      if this is not the case it is necessary to
         modify the message until the
                    first clauses are satisfied.

*(1) the method of successives approximations is widely used in the system of BOYER &
MOORE (BOYER & MOORE 1973).*

*(2) NEXTL too is an idiosyncratie of VLISP, its general form is (NEXTL arg1) where
arg1 has to be a list. NEXTL has as its value the CAR of the list and executes an
implicit (SETQ arg1 (CDR arg1)) as side-effect.*

Here (line .3.) the loop begins with the test if N>1 (hence with an invocation of the
specialiste-GT), the specialist-WHILE-2 tells every other specialist that he is for
the moment responsible for positionning the indicator WHT and giving the control to
the specialist-GT. This one, not finding any new information about N, claims that N
must have a numerical value and sends to the specialist-WHILE-2 a list of statements,
of which at least one must be within the loop. Thus the list :

```
(       (SETQ N (SUB1 N))
        (SETQ N (DIFFER N <qqc>))       )   (1)
```

The specialist-WHILE-2 not finding any of these instructions inside the loop, inserts
in the program line :

```
.4a.    (SETQ N (SUB1 N))
```

Not finding any more improvements of the program, neither during the rest of the
second reading nor during the third reading, PHENARETE finally gives the proposition
of the improved program which is :

```
(DE FACT (N RES)
        (SETQ RES 1)
        (WHILE (GT N 1)
                (SETQ RES (TIMES N RES))
                (SETQ N (SUB1 N)) )
        RES)
```

5 - UNDERSTANDING AND IMPROVING OF A RECURSIVE PROGRAM

PHENARETE considers a function as recursive when the name of the function has at
least one occurence in the body of the function specified by its definition.
To improve the recursive program INVERSER, it will be necessary to examine it global-
ly. This process will be illustrated with the example 2.5 (the numbers are for
references in the text).

```
.1.     (DE INVERSER (L1 L2)
.2.          (COND
.3.              ((NULL L2) L1)
.4.              (T
.5.                (INVERSER
.6.                    (CDR L1)
.7.                    (CONS (CAR L1) L2))) ))
```

The function is expected to reverse a list on its toplevel. We remember that in VLISP
at the call of a function the variables which have no value are initialized to NIL,
hence (INVERSER '(A B C)) is equivalent to (INVERSER '(A B C) NIL). Knowing that L2
will always have the value NIL at the first call of INVERSER,the mistake is perfectly
clear : the value of the function will always be the list L1.

5.1 - Behaviour of the system

Let us examine how PHENARETE proceeds. After a first reading - where she did not find
any possible improvement - she owns the following informations about INVERSER :

-1) it is a function with 2 arguments
-2) the names of the arguments are respectively L1 and L2
-3) it is a recursive function
-4) the value of L1 at the recursive call is (CDR L1)
-5) the value of L2 at the recursive call is (CONS (CAR L1) L2)
-6) the more recursive calls, the more L1 shrinks
-7) the more recursive calls, the more L2 grows
-8) L1 has to be a list (because the specialist-CDR expects a list as his argument)
-9) L2 has to be a list too (because the specialist-CONS expects a list as his
    second argument)
-10) nothing is known about the values of L1 nor L2

---

(1) <qqc> *can be any S-expression. It is the responsibility of future readings to
verify if* N *decreases or not.*

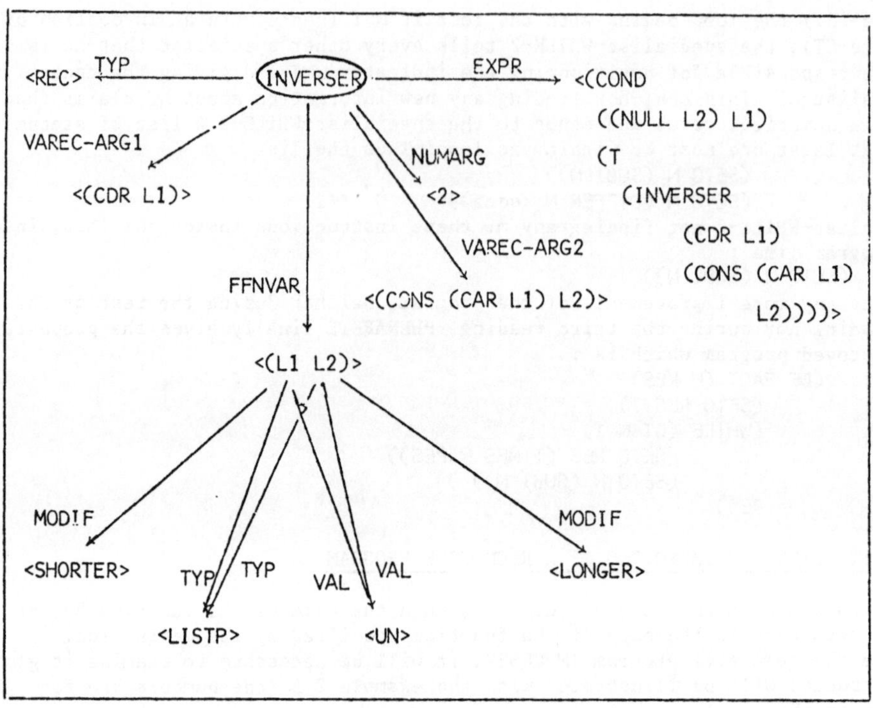

During the second reading the specialist-COND will split the world (MANNA & WALDINGER 1975, WALDINGER & LEWITT 1974) into as many hypothetical worlds as there are clauses. Here, he first supposes L2 to be NIL and continues the analysis in this case, after he will suppose L2 to be different from NIL and continue the analysis with this second hypothesis.

When supposing the value of L2 to be NIL, he knows that the value of the COND will be the current value of L1. He remembers this in a special list and PHENARETE looks for an application of this value outside the COND. Finding nothing more, because the body of the function is constituted by the COND, she puts on the P-list of INVERSER under the indicator VAL the information that one possible result of the function is L1.

After that, supposing that L2≠NIL, the specialist-COND looks for the second clause. Line .4. informs him that this will be the last one. He advances and finds (line .5.) the recursive call of INVERSER. There he stops the reading and considers once more the first clause, this time supposing that it must be the stop-clause for the recursion.

5.2 – <u>Digression : PHENARETE's knowledge of the halting of recursive calls</u>

Generally all recursive functions have the same structure : at the recursive call at least one of its arguments will be transformed in such a manner that in the run of the successive calls this argument will converge to a limit. This limit will constitute at least one of the possible tests of recursion-end.

For example : here in the function INVERSER (see example 2.5), L1 will have at the recursive call the value (cdr L1), and if L1 would be the variable of recursion, PHENARETE would expect to find a stop test having the form :

    (NULL L1)   since L1 converges to NIL (line .6.)

or

$(\begin{Bmatrix} LT \\ EQ \\ LE \end{Bmatrix}$ (LENGTH L1) numerical-value)   since L1 retracts (line .6.)

or

$$\left(\begin{bmatrix}EQ\\EQUAL\end{bmatrix}(C\begin{bmatrix}A\\D\end{bmatrix}_1^{*}R\ L1)\ qqc\right)\ \textit{(1)}$$

        if one advances in L1 until a specific element is a certain position

or

    (EQUAL L1 qqc)

        if one advances until the list is identical to another one

if the recursive variable would be L2, and here (line .7.) L2 grows longer in the run of the successive calls, she would expect a halt-test of one of these forms

$$\left(\begin{bmatrix}GT\\GE\\EQ\end{bmatrix}(LENGTH\ L2)\ numerical\text{-}value\right)$$

or

$$\left(\begin{bmatrix}EQ\\EQUAL\end{bmatrix}(C\begin{bmatrix}A\\D\end{bmatrix}_1^{*}R\ L2)\ qqc\right)$$

If the recursive function works on numbers a similar reasonning will give PHENARETE appropriate forms for the stop-test of recursion in these cases.

5.3 - Continuation of the analysis of INVERSER

Let us return to the function INVERSER ; the system, having knowledge of the values of L1 and L2 at the recursive call, will look for a test of the form :

    (NULL L1)

or

$$\left(\begin{bmatrix}LT\\LE\\EQ\end{bmatrix}(LENGTH\ L1)\ numerical\text{-}value\right)$$

or

    (EQUAL L1 qqc)

or

$$\left(\begin{bmatrix}EQ\\EQUAL\end{bmatrix}(C\begin{bmatrix}A\\D\end{bmatrix}_1^{*}R\begin{bmatrix}L1\\L2\end{bmatrix})\ qqc\right)$$

or

$$\left(\begin{bmatrix}GT\\GE\\EQ\end{bmatrix}(LENGTH\ L2)\ numerical\text{-}value\right)$$

But all he finds is the line .3. :

    (NULL L2) L1)

This cannot be correct, except when L2 would be bound to the value NIL at the first call, because PHENARETE knows that L2 will grow longer, hence will never converge to NIL. All other tests being absent PHENARETE tries to replace *(2)* (NULL L2) by a test which is as close as possible to the form (NULL L2) but which would be more adequate: she replaces line .3. by ((NULL L1) L1). However the result of the function will now in all cases be NIL, this because there is no physical modification (side effect) of global variables within the body of the function. She searches for further improvement.She looks more closely and notes that there is a construction of a list in the recursive call of the list L1. But this list is never used again. The reasonning is

---

(1) qqc *can be any S-expression.*

(2) this decision to replace one test by another one is quite arbitrary. One could also decide to add another test to those already existing, especially in the example of INVERSER *where there is no reason to think that L2 is always NIL. To remedy at this we are studying the possibility of PHENARETE making several propositions, that is : at every ambiguous point PHENARETE would have to consider all possible improvements and would have to develop each of the possible versions of the program.*

very simple : one of the elements of general knowledge (of PHENARETE) about programming is that if there is construction of a list, or computation of a numerical value
in a program , this has to be re-used inside the program or has to be its value :
otherwise improvement is possible : or to delete this part of the program or to modify the program such that the results are re-used.

Now, it is time for PHENARETE to use her whole knowledge ; if she eliminates the
construction-part enough arguments do not remain. Otherwise, if she does not change
anything, the value of the COND (and the function) will always be NIL, hence there
would be no more need for the whole function. So finally she decides to make this
list just constructed the value of the COND. Consequently, she changes once more
line .3., this gives : ((NULL L1) L2)

Another reading of this newly modified function does not permit her to proceed to
any other modification. So PHENARETE eventually proposes the function :

```
(DE INVERSER (L1 L2)
    (COND
      ((NULL L1) L2)
      (T
        (INVERSER
              (CDR L1)
              (CONS (CAR L1) L2))) ))
```

This example shows the power and the capacity of analytic reasonning of our system
very well.

6 - CONCLUSION

A slight weakness of the present system is its inability to understand functions
which call other user functions not already known to the system. To submit to PHENA-
RETE a program composed of several functions, one first must reorder the program in
such a manner that there is never a call to a function before its definition has
been encountered : this makes impossible the reading of functions which mutually
call themselves, i.e. which have a structure like :

```
(DE FOO ...                        (DE FOO1 ...
    ...                                ...
      (FOO1 ...)        and            (FOO ...)
    ...)                               ...)
```

That is no attempt has been yet made to submit massive programs, for example the
system itself. One evident solution permitting elimination of these difficulties
would be to make an initial reading.
The present system is not yet very competent in semantic understanding of programs
with side effects. Here we have an open problem, particulary for large programs with
common data bases. One possible approach would be to introduce a part of meta-evalua-
tion (HEWITT 1973, 1975, 1975a) in the actual system.
An example, suggested by P. GREUSSAY, which PHENARETE does not yet resolve, is the
following :

```
(WHILE L
       (SETQ X L)
       (SETQ RES (CONS (NEXTL L) RES))
       (SETQ L X))
```

The problem here is inverse to that of HACKER (SUSSMAN 1972, 1973), where one has to
protect variables. In our case, one has to *unprotect* variables, hence to recognise a
protection to be useful or not. Here too, one possible solution would be to meta-
evaluate the source-program.
Eventually it would be also advantageous not only to analyse the code of the program
or the function, but also a call of the function with actual arguments. PHENARETE
could gain very useful information about the type of the arguments, to say nothing
of their particular values. It is very satisfying indeed to note that PHENARETE has
never modified a correct first-order-LISP program in such a way as to introduce errors.

7 - COMPARISON WITH RELATED PROGRAMS

We will now conclude with a comparison of PHENARETE with five other related systems, each of them being quite characteristic to represent a whole class of such systems.

7.1 - DWIM

A system very close to the first reading of PHENARETE is DWIM (TEITELMAN 1974) while PHENARETE is completely automatic, DWIM works essentially in conversationnal mode.In DWIM the correction of spelling errors is more developped than in our system, but DWIM cannot perform any deep analysis of programs like PHENARETE can after the first reading.

7.2 - The analyser of RUTH

The system of RUTH (RUTH 1974) is extremely powerful for a certain class of well determined programs (especially sort-programs) but it pays attention to the intentions of the programmer in giving a library of model-programs. The system tries to unify the programs to analyse with one of these models and if this is not possible, it concludes that there is an error in the source program and it generates the necessary modifications.This technic gives a considerable power to the system but limits its generality.

7.3 - FLAVIGNY's system

B. FLAVIGNY (FLAVIGNY 1975) has written a program which detects logic errors in FORTRAN programs. We agree with him when he says that a good deal of errors can be detected without knowing the intentions of the human programmer. His method is to translate the control-flow of the program to analyse in a graph which later he examines. His system still experimental, is limited to the loop-error-research.

7.4 - DRAWL

Like PHENARETE, DRAWL (SIKLOSSY 1973) is designed to be used by inexperienced programmers. DRAWL is very efficient in the detection of surface errors - it detects about 60 different types - but it does not give any diagnosis and does not perform any modification.

7.5 - The system of DARLINGTON and BURSTALL

DARLINGTON & BURSTALL (DARLINGTON & BURSTALL 1972) have written a really powerful system to improve the implementation of LISP programs. This approach is another one : they improve *correct* programs in such a manner as to decrease execution time, in applying such technics as recursion-removal, elimination of redundant computations, etc., while PHENARETE tries to improve *incorrect* programs such that the improved program can be executed.

ACKNOWLEDGEMENT

The idea of specialists was influenced on the one hand by the BEINGS (LENAT 1975) and on the other hand by the ACTORS'system (HEWITT 1973, 1975, 1975a).
Many good ideas used in the writting of PHENARETE are results of research on the automatic program generation (GREEN, WALDINGER, BARSTOW and others 1974, GREEN & BARSTOW 1975, WALDINGER & LEVITT 1974, MANNA & WALDINGER 1975) and on program verification (LUCKHAM & SUZUKI 1975, FLOYD 1967).
The realisation of the system would have been impossible without the numerous and helpful discussions inside the Department of Computer Science of the University of PARIS 8, especially with MM. P. GREUSSAY, D. GOOSSENS, J. CHAILLOUX and Mrs. V. VON HAGEN.

REFERENCES

BOYER R.S. & MOORE J.S., (1973), *Proving Theorems about LISP Functions,* Proc. 3rd
IJCAI, Standford University, Stanford Ca., pp. 486-493.

CHAILLOUX J., (1976), *VLISP-10 Manuel de références,* Département d'Informatique,
Université de Paris 8, Février 1976, RT-17-76.

DARLINGTON J. & BURSTALL R.M., (1973), *A system which automatically improves programs,*
Proc. 3rd IJCAI, Stanford University, Stanford Ca., pp. 479-485.

FLAVIGNY B.,(1975), *Un programme détecteur d'erreurs de logique dans les programmes,*
Revue Française d'Automatique, Informatique et Recherche Operationnelle, n°
juil. 1975 B-2, pp. 43-59.

FLOYD R.W., (1967), *Assigning meanings to programs,* Proc. Amer. Math. Soc. Symposium
in Applied Mathematics, vol. 19, Providence, Rhodes Island, pp. 19-32.

GREEN, WALDINGER, BARSTOW, ELSCHLAGER, LENAT, McCUNE, SHAW & STEINBERG, (1974),
Progress Report on Program-Understanding Systems, AIM-MEMO 240, Stanford University, Stanford Ca.

GREEN C. & BARSTOW D., (1975), *A Hypothetical Dialogue Exhibiting a Knowledge Base
for a Program-Understanding System,* AIM-MEMO 258, Stanford University, Stanford

GREUSSAY P., (1976), *Descriptions compactes d'interprètes implémentables,* 2ème Colloque International sur la Programmation, B. ROBINET, avril 1976, Paris, pp. 281-
297 (to appear at Springer-Verlag).

HEWITT C., (1971), *Procedural Embedding of Knowledge in PLANNER,* Proc. 2nd IJCAI,
London, pp. 167-182.

HEWITT C., BISHOP P., GREIF I., SMITH B., MATSON T. & STEIGER R., (1973), *Actor Induction & Meta Evaluation,* ACM Symposium of Programming Languages, Boston, pp. 153-
167.

HEWITT C., (1975), *Stereotypes as an Actor Approach towards Solving the Problem of
Procedural Attachment in FRAME Theories,* in Theoretical Issues in Natural Language Processing, an interdisciplinary Workshop, Cambridge, Mass., pp. 108-117.

HEWITT C., (1975a), *How to use what you know,* proc. 4th IJCAI, Tbilisi, Georgia,
USSR, pp. 189-198.

LENAT D.C., (1975), *Synthesis of large Programs from specific Dialogues,* Actes du
Colloque IRIA : "Construction, Amélioration et Vérification de Programmes",
G. Huet, G. Kahn, Arc & Senan, pp. 225-241.

LUCKHAM D.C. & SUZUKI N., (1975), *Automatic Program Verification IV : Proof of Termination within a weak Logic of Programs,* AIM-MEMO 269, Stanford University,
Stanford Ca.

MANNA Z. (1974), *Introduction to Mathematical Theory of Computation,* McGraw Hill,N.Y.

MANNA Z. & WALDINGER R., (1975), *Knowledge and Reasoning in Program Synthesis,* Artificial Intelligence, vol. 6, n°2, North-Holland, Amsterdam, pp. 175-208.

PLATON, *Théètète,* H. Stéphanus, Paris, 1578, pp. 148E à 150D.

RUTH G.R., (1973), *Analysis of Algorithm Implementations,* Ph.D Thesis, Project Mac,
M.I.T., Cambridge, Mass.

SANDEWALL E., (1975), *Ideas about Management of LISP Data Bases*, Memo n° 332, A.I. Lab., M.I.T., Cambridge, Mass.

SIKLOSSY L., (1973), *The Case for, and some Experience with, automated Consultants*, Proc. 2nd Texas Conf. on Computing Systems, Austin, Texas, pp. 23-1 à 23-4.

SUSSMAN G.J., (1972), *Teaching of Procedures - Progress Report*, Memo n° 270, A.I. Lab., M.I.T., Cambridge, Mass.

SUSSMAN G.J., (1973), *A Computational Model of Skill Acquisition*, Ph.D. Thesis, AI-TR-297, A.I. Lab., M.I.T., Cambridge, Mass.

TEITELMAN W., (1974), *INTERLISP Reference Manual*, Xerox, Palo Alto, Ca.

WALDINGER R. & LEVITT K.N., (1974), *Reasoning about Programs*, Artificial Intelligence vol. 5, n°3, North-Holland, Amsterdam, pp. 235-316.

WERTZ H., (1976), *Sur la compréhension des programmes LISP améliorables*, Département d'Informatique, Université de Paris 8, RT 18-76.

SYMBOLISCHE LÖSUNG VON DIFFERENTIALGLEICHUNGEN
1. ORDNUNG UND 1. GRADES
DURCH HEURISTISCHE PROGRAMMIERUNG

Peter Schmidt

Institut für Informatik, Universität Bonn

Abstract: The problem of solving first order, first degree differential equations symbolically is characterized as a heuristic search process. An investigation into the problem of automatically solving such differential equations has resulted in a heuristic program, called EULE. The selection and the realization of the methods for EULE are based on a detailed analysis of the problem domain: the standard work of Kamke (1961), which is representative of the state of the knowledge of differential equations, was examined in three different respects: the collected methods of solution, the methods utilized for the collection of differential equations and the structure of these differential equations. The realization of the methods is based on this result and on defined principles which ensure the effectiveness of the program. The effectiveness of EULE can be characterized by the fact that EULE achieved a 'rate of solution' of 90% for Kamke's representative collection of first order, first degree differential equations and a rate of 95% for Murphy's (1960) representative collection. For two collections for training students EULE achieved a rate of 100%.

1. Einleitung

In der Theorie der Differentialgleichungen[+] existiert zum gegenwärtigen Zeitpunkt keine allgemeine Methode, um symbolische Lösungen von DGLen 1. Ordnung und 1. Grades, also Gleichungen der Art

(1.1) $f(x,y)y' + g(x,y) = 0$

bestimmen zu können. Die gebräuchlichsten Lösungsmethoden beruhen darauf, eine vorgelegte DGL durch Variablentransformation oder Multiplikation mit einem Ausdruck in eine der direkt lösbaren Formen zu überführen, nämlich in eine separable bzw. lineare bzw. exakte DGL, die von der Form $y'=f(x)g(y)$ bzw. $y'=f(x)y+g(x)$ bzw. $f(x,y)y'+g(x,y)=0$ mit der Bedingung $f_x-g_y=0$ sind.

Ist eine DGL vorgelegt, so empfiehlt zum Beispiel Murphy (1960) in seinem DGL-Buch folgendes Vorgehen: man solle sich den ersten Teil seines Buches vornehmen, in dem die meisten der bisher entwickelten Lösungsmethoden zusammengestellt sind; an Hand der dort gegebenen Hinweise solle man die gegebene DGL als Spezialfall eines oder mehrerer dort angegebener Typen klassifizieren und die notierten Lösungswege anwenden. Handelt man entsprechend Murphys Vorschlag, so könnte man die Erfolgsfälle wie folgt klassifizieren:

1) ein Lösungsweg wurde ohne großen Aufwand sofort gefunden,

2) ein Lösungsweg wurde durch gezieltes Probieren relativ schnell gefunden,

[+] In Anlehnung an Kamke (1961) wird das Wort "Differentialgleichung" mit DGL abgekürzt, der Plural entsprechend mit DGLen.

3) ein Lösungsweg wurde eher zufällig mit eventuell großem Arbeits-
aufwand gefunden.

Dieser Klassifizierung entsprechen etwa folgende drei Arbeits-
phasen bei der Ermittlung der Lösung.

In der <u>ersten Phase</u> werden die gebräuchlichsten, leicht nachzuprü-
fenden Muster getestet. Hierbei ist nur wichtig, Kenntnis von den bekannten Mustern und Bedingungsgleichungen zu haben.

In der <u>zweiten Phase</u> werden die durch die Betrachtung der DGL nahe-
gelegten Lösungsmethoden überprüft. In dieser Phase spielen auch Intuition und Erfahrung im Umgang mit DGLen eine beträchtliche Rolle.

In der <u>dritten Phase</u> bleibt als Möglichkeit nur die Suche auf vielen nahezu gleichberechtigten Wegen, ohne daß mathematische Theorie
oder Intuition eine allgemeine Rangfolge festlegen könnten. In dieser
Phase wird die zufällig gewählte Reihenfolge der eingeschlagenen Wege
bei der Suche mit darüber entscheiden, ob und wann eine Lösung gefunden
wird. Dem Lösungssuchenden stellt sich jederzeit die Frage, ob er mit
der Suche aufhören soll; denn bekanntlich ist nur ein verschwindend geringer Teil der DGLen elementar lösbar. Mit zunehmender Suchzeit wird
die Hoffnung auf Erfolg eher geringer als größer. Hierdurch wird eventuell auch die Fehleranfälligkeit gesteigert, so daß durch Rechenfehler
oder nicht sorgfältig bis zum Ende durchgeführte Rechnungen Lösungen
nicht gefunden werden.

Das Lösen von DGLen ist hiermit charakterisiert als ein heuristi-
scher Suchprozeß, und von daher eventuell geeignet, erfolgreich mittels
eines Computer-Programms angegangen zu werden.

Der vorliegende Text berichtet von Untersuchungen, die zum Problem
der maschinellen symbolischen Lösbarkeit von DGLen der Art (1.1) durchgeführt worden sind, und einem laufbereiten Programmsystem - genannt
EULE - das zur Auffindung von Lösungen entwickelt worden ist.

Die Motivation zu dieser Arbeit lag neben der Tatsache, daß das
Lösen von DGLen dem Autor als ein hervorragend geeignetes Gebiet für
heuristische Programmierung erschien, darin, daß ein bislang vorlie-
gendes Programm SOLDIER, das Moses (1967) im Anschluß an sein Integra-
tionsprogramm SIN geschrieben hat, als zu wenig leistungsfähig erschien. EULE übertrifft das Programm SOLDIER sicherlich darin, daß
mehr Lösungsmethoden implementiert worden sind und diese Lösungsmethoden leistungsfähiger realisiert worden sind.

Die Auswahl und Realisierung der Lösungsmethoden für EULE gründet
sich auf eine ausführliche Analyse des Problemgebiets: das bezüglich
des DGL-Wissens repräsentative Standardwerk von Kamke (1961) wurde in
Hinsicht auf existierende Lösungsmethoden, für die 367 DGLen der Sammlung benutzte Lösungsmethoden und die Struktur dieser DGLen ausgewertet.
Die aktuelle Realisierung der Lösungsmethoden orientiert sich an diesem
Ergebnis und an -auch formulierten - Prinzipien, die die Wirksamkeit
des Programms sicherstellen sollen. Die Leistungsfähigkeit von EULE
wird an Testergebnissen gemessen, die EULE für mehrere (darunter zwei
repräsentative) DGL-Sammlungen erzielt hat.

In den zuletzt genannten Punkten unterscheidet sich EULE auch wesentlich von früheren heuristischen Programmen, die mit Mitteln der
Formelmanipulation Aufgaben in komplexen Teilgebieten der Analysis lösen können, wie etwa die Programme SAINT (Slagle (1963)) und SIN
(Moses (1967), Moses (1971a)) zur unbestimmten Integration, das schon
erwähnte Programm SOLDIER zur Lösung von DGLen 1. Ordnung und 1. Grades und das Programm WANDERER (Wang (1971)) zur bestimmten Integration: der Konzeption von EULE liegt eine Analyse des Gesamtgebietes
(hier speziell der DGLen 1. Ordnung und 1. Grades) zugrunde und die
Leistungsfähigkeit wird ermittelt durch Tests an für das Gebiet repräsentativen Daten.

Der folgende Text gibt eine Beschreibung der Konzepte und Analysen
(Kapitel 2), eine sehr kurz gehaltene Beschreibung des Programmsystems
EULE (Kapitel 3), eine Auswahl der Testergebnisse, die mit EULE erzielt
worden sind (Kapitel 4) und einige Überlegungen zu EULE (Kapitel 5).

2. Zur Konzipierung

2.1 Präzisierung der Aufgabenstellung

Es wird hier die Aufgabenstellung präziser formuliert, die der Entwicklung des Programmsystems EULE zugrundeliegt.

EULE soll für vorgelegte DGLen 1. Ordnung und 1. Grades der Form

$$(2.1) \qquad f(x,y)y' + g(x,y) = 0$$

die allgemeine Lösung bestimmen können.

Dabei bezeichnet man eine von einem Parameter C abhängige Gleichung $L(x,y;C)$ als "allgemeine Lösung" von (2.1), wenn sich nach
Einsetzen von numerischen Werten für C und Auflösung dieser Gleichung
nach y Partikulärlösungen von (2.1) ergeben. Und man sagt, eine
Funktion $y=p(x)$ ist "Partikulärlösung" von (2.1), wenn $p(x)$ diffe-
renzierbar ist und die Gleichung (2.1) identisch erfüllt.

Da im folgenden die Auffindung von allgemeinen Lösungen von DGLen
1. Ordnung und 1. Grades im Vordergrund steht, wird aus Gründen der Ab-
kürzung zum einen nur noch von DGLen gesprochen und zum anderen in der
Regel von Lösung statt von allgemeiner Lösung.

Als Lösungsmethoden sind für EULE die im ersten Kapitel kurz skiz-
zierten Methoden zugelassen: dies sind Erkennung der Zugehörigkeit einer
DGL zu einem der elementaren DGL-Typen separabel, linear oder exakt bzw.
Überführung von DGLen durch Variablentransformationen oder Multiplikation mit Eulerschen Multiplikatoren in einen solchen Typ. Als Variablentransformationen sollen nur solche zugelassen sein, die nicht aus der
betrachteten Klasse der DGLen 1. Ordnung und 1. Grades herausführen.
Mit den für EULE zugelassenen Lösungsmethoden können also nur DGLen
gelöst werden, die durch Quadraturen und die elementaren Funktionen in
'geschlossener' Form lösbar sind. Dies ist insbesondere zum Beispiel für
die bekannte Spezielle Riccatische DGL $y'+ay^2=bx^\alpha$ nicht möglich.

Im Sinne der Theorie der DGLen soll eine DGL als gelöst betrachtet
werden, wenn eine Lösung in Integralform vorliegt, ohne daß die Integra-
le ausgewertet werden müßten; da bei bekanntem Lösungsweg die Herstellung einer solchen Lösung ein rein formaler Prozeß ist, wird noch auf
die Herstellung der Lösung in Integralform verzichtet, und es wird nur
der Lösungsweg angegeben.

Von EULE können DGLen bearbeitet werden, wie sie üblicherweise vorkommen. Folgende Elemente dürfen in den DGLen enthalten sein:

- Veränderliche: die unabhängige und die abhängige Veränderliche,

- Konstanten: ganze Zahlen, allgemeine Konstanten, π und e ,

- Funktionen: sin cos tan cot sec csc exp log abs arcsin arccos
  arctan arccot sinh cosh tanh coth,
  allgemeine Funktionen einer Veränderlichen,

- Ableitungen der abhängigen Veränderlichen und der allgemeinen
  Funktionen,

- die üblichen arithmetischen Operationen.

2.2 Analysen und Prinzipien zur Auswahl und Realisierung der Lösungs- methoden

Das bezüglich des DGL-Wissens repräsentative Standardwerk von Kamke
wurde für die Analyse des Problemgebietes herangezogen. Um die Frage

beantworten zu können, welche mathematischen Lösungsmethoden in dem System vertreten sein sollten, wurde die Sammlung der 367 Kamke-DGLen (1.1-1.367) daraufhin untersucht, welche Lösungswege beschritten wurden und wie häufig gleiche Lösungsmethoden auftraten. Tabelle 2.1 enthält die Ergebnisse; die in Klammern aufgeführte Zahl bezieht sich auf die Anzahl der Fälle, in denen die Lösungsmethode erst nach erfolgter Variablentransformation zum Ziel führt.

	Lösungsmethode	Häufigkeit in %
I	Typ separabel	10% (10%)
	Typ homogen	8% (1%)
	Typ lineare Koeffizienten	4%
	Typ linear	8% (6%)
	Typ Bernoulli[+]	5% (4%)
	Typ exakt	5% (1%)
II	Angabe eines Eulerschen Multiplikators	7%
	Typ Riccati und Angabe einer Partikulärlösung	4%
	Angabe einer Variablentransformation zur Überführung in eine DGL 2. Ordnung	5%
	Verweis auf andere DGL in der Sammlung	4% (5%)
	Angabe der Lösung ohne den Weg	4%
	Verweis auf die Literatur	3% (2%)
	verschiedene	4%

Tab. 2.1: Häufigkeit der für die Kamke-Sammlung
1.1-1.367 angegebenen Lösungsmethoden

Die Daten der Tabelle 2.1 geben einen ersten groben Hinweis, welche Lösungsmethoden unbedingt in dem Programmsystem vertreten sein sollten, nämlich

1) die Erkennung der elementaren Typen der Gruppe I ,

2) Methoden zur Bestimmung von Partikulärlösungen von Riccatischen DGLen und Eulerschen Multiplikatoren,

3) Methoden bezüglich Variablentransformationen.

Im folgenden werden die Grundlagen diskutiert, die maßgeblich für die Entwicklung des Programmsystems EULE zu dem vorliegenden Stand verantwortlich sind.

Zu 1): in der Gruppe I der Tabelle 2.1 finden sich die Lösungsmethoden wieder, die übereinstimmend in den DGL-Lehrbüchern als die grundlegendsten dargestellt werden. Die DGLen, die in Kamke und auch in anderen Sammlungen mit diesen Methoden behandelt werden können, zeichnen sich dadurch aus, daß ihre Typzugehörigkeit von einem mit den Typmustern vertrauten menschlichen DGL-Löser in der Regel sofort oder mit geringfügigem Rechenaufwand erkannt wird. Um sicherzustellen, daß mittels EULE auch zu diesen Typen gehörende DGLen anderer Sammlungen oder nach Variablentransformationen auftretende DGLen gelöst werden können, wurde die folgende Forderung (F1) an die Realisierung dieser Lösungsmethoden gestellt:

[+] In vielen Fällen wurde bei Bernoullischen DGLen der Typ fastlinear als Lösungsweg angegeben.

<u>Forderung (F1):</u>

> die Realisierung der Methoden zur Erkennung der Typen der Gruppe I
> sollte so leistungsstark sein, daß im Rahmen der Struktur von DGLen
> möglichst alle zu diesen Typen vorkommenden DGLen auch gelöst werden
> können; dies unabhängig davon, wie kompliziert die Beispiele für die-
> se Methoden in der Kamke-Sammlung sind.

Die Problematik, die mit der Erfüllung dieser Forderung verbunden
ist, sei stellvertretend an dem Problem der Erkennung von DGLen als
exakt erörtert. – Eine in der Form (2.1) gegebene DGL wird als exakt
erkannt, falls der Ausdruck f_x-g_y als identisch 0 nachgewiesen ist.

Richardson (1968) hat gezeigt, daß für hinreichend umfangreiche
Klassen von Ausdrücken das Problem, ob ein Element der Klasse in einem
vorgegebenen Bereich identisch 0 ist, rekursiv unentscheidbar ist.
Eine solche Klasse wird zum Beispiel erzeugt durch i) die rationalen
Zahlen und die beiden reellen Zahlen π und log(2) , ii) die Variable x , iii) die Operationen der Addition, Multiplikation und Kom-
position, und iv) die Funktionen sin, exp und abs.

Da Ausdrücke dieser so definierten Ausdrucksklasse durchaus als
Funktionen f oder g der DGLen der Form (2.1) zugelassen sind, ist
zunächst eine vollständige Erkennung der Klasse der exakten DGLen nicht
möglich. Um im Sinne der Forderung (F1) noch befriedigende Ergebnisse
zu erzielen, können zwei Wege eingeschlagen werden.

Der eine Weg besteht darin, auf Ausdrucksklassen auszuweichen, für
die ein Algorithmus existiert, der entscheiden kann, ob ein Ausdruck
identisch 0 ist. Moses (1971b) gibt eine Zusammenstellung solcher Algorithmen. Zum Beispiel gibt Brown (1969) einen Vereinfachungsalgorith-
mus für Ausdrücke, die aus folgenden Elementen bestehen: den rationalen
Zahlen, i und π , den Variablen x1,x2,...,xn, den Operationen der
Addition, Multiplikation und Division, der Funktion exp und der Kompo-
sition von Funktionen. Einen Algorithmus für Radikalausdrücke gibt zum
Beispiel Fateman (1972).

Der andere Weg besteht darin, von einem Verfahren zur Überprüfung
auf identisch 0 auszugehen, das diese Eigenschaft in Fällen, die in
irgendeinem Sinne einfach sind, feststellen kann, und dieses Verfahren
gegebenenfalls anzureichern mit speziellen Fähigkeiten.

Der zweitgenannte Weg hat gegenüber dem erstgenannten nicht nur den
Vorteil, daß er leichter zu realisieren ist und daß Erweiterungen leichter vorgenommen werden können, sondern auch daß bei erfolgreicher Realisierung ein Einblick gewonnen ist, von welcher Struktur vorkommende
exakte DGLen wirklich sind. Als Nachteil ergibt sich, daß keine Sicherheit der Erkennung gegeben ist.

Zur Prüfung der Frage, ob der zweitgenannte Weg unter Wahrung der
Forderung (F1) gangbar ist, wurde eine Analyse der Struktur der DGLen
der Kamke-Sammlung durchgeführt. Danach gilt für die 367 Kamke-DGLen,
nachdem Produkte von Summen und Potenzen von Produkten aufgelöst sind:

- die DGLen bestehen im Durchschnitt aus 4 Summanden (1.Stufe) und
  weniger als 4% der DGLen haben mehr als 6 Summanden;

- diese durchschnittlich vier Summanden haben insgesamt durchschnittlich
  9 Faktoren (1. Stufe) und nur ca. 6% haben mehr als 14 Faktoren;

- ca. 70% der DGLen sind frei von Funktionsausdrücken;
  kommen Funktionsausdrücke vor, so sind die Argumente der vorkommenden
  Funktionen von einer der Formen ax^b+cy^d oder x^ay^b , wo a,b,c,d
  für Buchstabenkonstanten oder rationale Zahlen stehen, oder von der
  Form einer Folge ineinandergeschachtelter Funktionen mit x oder y
  als innerstem Argument; in mehr als der Hälfte der Fälle treten als
  Argumente nur x oder y auf;

- ca. 90% der DGLen sind frei von Potenzen von Summen und Summenausdrücken im Nenner; kommen solche Teilausdrücke vor, so handelt es sich bei ca. 80% dieser Fälle nur um rationale Potenzen (meist Wurzeln) von Polynomen in x und y , wovon wieder in ca. 70% der Fälle diese Polynome entweder nur von x oder nur von y abhängen;

- fast 90% der DGLen enthalten als Faktoren (1. Stufe) der Summanden (1. Stufe) nur Ausdrücke der Art

$$x^a \quad \text{oder} \quad y^a \quad \text{oder} \quad a \quad \text{oder} \quad f^a(x) \quad \text{oder} \quad f^a(y) \ ,$$

wo a für eine Buchstabenkonstante oder rationale Zahl steht, oder höchstens einen Ausdruck, der nicht von dieser Art ist; in über 70% der Fälle, wo dies nicht erfüllt ist, treten nur zwei solcher Ausdrücke auf, wo diese dann spezielles Aussehen haben:

$$\text{entweder:} \quad f(A) \quad \text{und} \quad g(A) \ ,$$

$$\text{oder:} \quad P^r \quad \text{und} \quad Q^s \ ,$$

$$\text{oder:} \quad x^A \quad \text{und} \quad x^B \ ,$$

wo f und g für einen beliebigen Funktionsbezeichner stehen, A und B für beliebige Ausdrücke stehen, P und Q für Polynome in x oder y stehen, und r uns s für rationale Zahlen stehen.

Studiert man die DGLen, die nach Variablentransformationen im Verlauf des Lösungswegs entstehen, so stellt man fest, daß diese DGLen in ähnlichem Sinne einfach sind.

Nach diesen Angaben erweist sich die überwiegende Mehrzahl der DGLen als von so einfacher Struktur, daß der oben zweitgenannte Weg zur Erkennung exakter DGLen deutlich vorgezogen werden kann.

Zur Erfüllung der Forderung (F1) bei der Realisierung der Methoden der Gruppe I wurde praktisch wie folgt vorgegangen: es wurde nach Verfahren gesucht, die in erster Linie den zu erkennenden Mustern und der allgemeinen Struktur der DGLen gerecht werden, und erst in zweiter Linie den speziellen Beispielen in der Literatur angepaßt sind. Um für eine Leistungsreserve zu sorgen, sollten die Verfahren zusätzlich möglichst in sich geschlossen sein.

Zu 2): für die in der Gruppe II der Tabelle 2.1 zusammengefaßten Lösungsmethoden finden sich nicht nur in der Literatur viele Vorschläge, wie man vorgehen könnte, um entsprechende Lösungswege zu ermitteln; es lassen sich auch mit mehr oder weniger großem Aufwand weitere Vorschläge angeben. Die Partikulärlösungen für die Riccatischen DGLen oder die Eulerschen Multiplikatoren, die als Lösungsweg für manche DGLen in der Kamke-Sammlung angegeben sind, lassen sich in der Regel nach völlig verschiedenen Vorgehensweisen ermitteln. Die Auffindung solcher Lösungswege ist auch für den Menschen kein triviales Problem mehr, da sich ihm eine Vielfalt von Möglichkeiten ohne ein Endekriterium bietet.

Auf Grund dieser Charakteristik kann ein Programmsystem wohl durch geeignete Realisierung dieser Lösungsmethoden für manche DGLen andersartige Lösungswege finden, als sie in der Literatur angegeben sind. Dieses Ziel ist zur Erhöhung der Leistungsfähigkeit eines Programms unter anderem deswegen erstrebenswert, weil damit Möglichkeiten gegeben werden, auch eventuell solche DGLen zu lösen, für die in der Literatur ein nicht im Programm implementierter Lösungsweg angegeben ist. Deshalb wurde die Forderung (F2) gestellt:

Forderung (F2):

die Auswahl und die Realisierung von Verfahren zu den Methoden unter II sollten die Forderung erfüllen, daß möglichst alle mit einer der Methoden II gelösten Kamke-DGLen durch möglichst wenige und möglichst einheitliche Heuristiken oder Algorithmen erfaßt sind.

Durch diese Forderung sollten die gewählten Algorithmen oder Heuristiken so leistungsstark werden, daß ihr Anwendungsbereich deutlich über die einzelnen Exemplare der Kamke-Sammlung hinausgeht.

Zur Erfüllung der Forderung (F2) wurde praktisch so vorgegangen: es wurden zunächst die für die Kamke-DGLen notierten Eulerschen Multiplikatoren bzw. Partikulärlösungen für die Riccatischen DGLen zusammengestellt. Danach wurde versucht, anhand der in der Literatur genannten Methoden oder anhand eigener Ansätze Verfahrensweisen zu finden, die die aufgeführten Fälle abdecken.

Zu 3): Wie die Werte der Tabelle 2.1 nahelegen, sollte ein leistungsfähiges DGL-Lösesystem auch über Methoden zur Variablentransformation verfügen. Bei der Auswahl der Methoden wurde das Ziel verfolgt, die Anzahl der durch das Programm lösbaren DGLen zu erhöhen, ohne allerdings allzu spezielle Verfahrensweisen zu implementieren. Zur Erreichung des Ziels wurde die folgende Forderung (F3) gestellt:

Forderung (F3):

> die Auswahl und die Realisierung der Methoden bezüglich Variablentransformationen sollten die Forderung erfüllen, daß mit Hilfe dieser Verfahren 'viele' Kamke-DGLen erfolgreich behandelt werden können und insbesondere 'einige' Kamke-DGLen, für die durch die Methoden der Gruppen I und II von EULE noch kein Lösungsweg ermittelt werden konnte.

Durch diese Forderung sollte auch sichergestellt werden, daß diese Methoden so häufig anwendbar und so leistungsstark realisiert sind, daß zu erwarten ist, daß mit ihrer Hilfe auch nicht in der Literatur genannte Lösungswege gefunden werden können.

Die für EULE ausgewählten Methoden wurden unter Berücksichtigung der Forderung (F3) auf Grund folgender maschinell oder von Hand durchgeführter Untersuchungen (U1) - (U4) bestimmt:

(U1) sind Lösungsvorschläge für Riccatische oder Abelsche DGLen im Textteil von Kamke anwendbar auf die DGLen der Kamke-Sammlung?

(U2) Kommen in der Sammlung Muster von DGLen vor, die auch andere DGLen der Sammlung subsumieren?

(U3) Kommen gewisse Variablentransformationen häufiger vor?

(U4) Lassen sich Heuristiken finden, die in den DGLen vorkommende Teilausdrücke mit erfolgreichen Variablentransformationen verbinden?

3. Das Programmsystem EULE

Das Programmsystem EULE baut auf keinem vorhandenen algebraischen Manipulationssystem auf. EULE ist einzig zu dem Zweck entwickelt worden, gewöhnliche DGLen zu lösen. Die wesentlichen Entscheidungen bezüglich Darstellung und Vereinfachung orientieren sich an diesem Ziel.

EULE kann beliebig komplexe Ausdrücke verarbeiten, die aus den in Abschnitt 2.1 genannten Elementen bestehen. Diese können mittels eines zentralen Vereinfachers in verschiedene Standardformen überführt werden. Eine Darstellung in einer dieser Formen ist Ausgangspunkt für die Anwendung einer Lösungsmethode. Von dieser allgemeinen Darstellung wird bei manchen Lösungsmethoden zu einer spezielleren Darstellung übergegangen, um effizientere Algorithmen für DGLen, die in spezielleren Ausdrucksklassen liegen, zu ermöglichen.

EULE ist in PL/I programmiert und besteht zur Zeit aus ca. 8500 Statements.

EULE erwartet als Eingabe DGLen in einer Form, die der üblichen Notation entspricht; die wesentlichsten Einschränkungen sind:
i) alle Terme ungleich 0 müssen auf der linken Seite stehen und
ii) es müssen spezielle Namen verwandt werden, nämlich:
X bzw. Y für die unabhängig bzw. abhängig Veränderliche,

AO,A1,A2,... für allgemeine Konstanten; PI $f\ddot{u}r$ π ; E $f\ddot{u}r$ e;
FO,F1,F2,... für allgemeine Funktionen.
Wie DGLen eingegeben werden, zeigen etwa die folgenden Beispiele:

$y'+ay=ce^{bx}$ (Kamke 1.2) : Y'+AO*Y-A2*EXP(A1*X)=0

$y'+f'(x)y=f(x)f'(x)$ (Kamke 1.10) : Y'+FO'(X)*Y-FO(X)*FO'(X)=0

$x^4(y'+y^2)+a=0$ (Kamke 1.181) : X**4*(Y'+Y**2)+AO=0 .

Im folgenden wird eine sehr knappe Beschreibung des zentralen Vereinfachers (Abschnitt 3.1) und der realisierten Lösungsmethoden (Abschnitt 3.2) gegeben und die zur Lösung verwandte Strategie (Abschnitt
3.3) diskutiert. Eine ausführlichere Beschreibung in englischer Sprache
findet sich in (Schmidt (1976a)). Detaillierte Information ist dem
vollständigen Bericht (Schmidt (1976b)) zu entnehmen.

3.1 Zum zentralen Vereinfacher von EULE

Gemäß der Klassifikation von Moses (1971b) handelt es sich bei dem
zentralen Vereinfacher von EULE um einen 'liberalen' Vereinfacher.

Für eine gegebene oder im Verlauf der Lösung entstandene DGL können
fünf Standardformen, hier bezeichnet mit (ST1) bis (ST5) von Bedeutung sein. Diese Standardformen sind wie folgt zu kennzeichnen.

(ST1) Ausführung sämtlicher Standardtransformationen.

(ST2) Zusätzlich zu (ST1) Entklammerung mittels des Distributiv-
gesetzes bezüglich + und * .

(ST3) Zusätzlich zu (ST2) Auflösung von positiv ganzzahligen Potenzen
von Summen (bis zu einer durch Parameter gegebenen Größe).

(ST4) Zusätzlich zu (ST1) Faktorisierung von Summen, die als Basis
einer Potenz auftreten, in ein Produkt, dessen Faktoren entweder
nur von x oder nur von y abhängen (es wird hierzu die Faktorisierungsroutine verwendet, die auch zur Erkennung separabler DGLen
benutzt wird).

(ST5) Zusätzlich zu (ST1) Bringen des Ausdrucks auf den Hauptnenner
und Weglassen dieses Hauptnenners.

Standardtransformationen sind das Ersetzen gewisser Operatoren
(z.B. Division und binäres Minus), Normierung der Aufeinanderfolge von
Operatoren (z.B. Anwendung des Associativgesetzes), Anwendung der üblichen Vereinfachungsregeln bezüglich 0 und 1 , Entklammerungen (z.B.
Potenzen von Produkten), Sortierung der Terme in Summen und Produkten,
Zusammenfassen von sich höchstens um einen rationalen Faktor unterschei-
denden Summanden, Zusammenfassen von Faktoren mit gleicher Basis, gewisse einfache Umformungen bei Funktionsausdrücken (z.B. Übergang zum Argument, falls eine Funktion von einer Umkehrfunktion auftritt).

Über die Herstellung der fünf Standardformen hinaus können noch die
Handhabung der Funktionalgleichungen von log und exp, die Anwendung
des Additionstheorems von sin und cos und die Ersetzung von tan
und cot durch andere trigonometrische Funktionen gesteuert werden.

3.2 Implementierte Lösungsmethoden

3.2.1 Erkennung elementarer Typen

Die hier genannten Methoden zur Erkennung der Typen separabel, homogen, lineare Koeffizienten, linear, Bernoulli, fastlinear,exakt
sind entsprechend dem in Abschnitt 2.2 ausgeführten Konzept sehr leistungsstark realisiert. Ob eine DGL zu einem dieser Typen gehört, ist
einem Menschen in der Regel auf den ersten Blick oder mit ein wenig
Rechnung erkennbar. Die vorliegenden Erkennungsverfahren sind bezüglich
ihrer Leistungsfähigkeit so realisiert, daß sie wohl erst dann versagen,
wenn auch der eingeübte Mensch die Zugehörigkeit einer DGL zu einer
solchen Klasse nicht mehr 'ohne weiteres' erkennt.

<u>Separable</u> DGLen sind von der Form $f0(x)g0(y)y'+f1(x)g1(y)=0$.
Zur Erkennung dieses Typs liegt eine Faktorisierungsroutine vor, die gewisse von x und y abhängige Ausdrücke in ein Produkt zerlegen kann, dessen einer Faktor nur von y und dessen anderer Faktor nur von x abhängt. Die Wirksamkeit dieser Routine ist eng mit dem Vereinfachungssystem verflochten. Der folgende Ausdruck würde in entklammerter Schreibweise faktorisiert werden können:

$$(2/\sin(y)+y^2/a+(y+4)^{-2})(x^2\cos(x)+3/x+4a^2) \ .$$

Die Faktorisierbarkeit des Ausdrucks $yxa^2+yxa2+yx+ya+y+xa+x+1$ würde nicht erkannt, da eine Faktorisierung der konstanten Faktoren nicht mehr vorgenommen wird.

Beispiele für von EULE als separabel erkannte DGLen sind:

$$y'=((y^2-1)/(x^2-1))^{1/2} \quad \text{(Kamke 1.60) und } y'-\exp(x-y)+\exp(x)=0 \quad \text{(K. 1.75).}$$

DGLen der Form (1.1) sind <u>homogen</u>, wenn die Funktionen f und g homogene Funktionen des gleichen Grades sind. Zur Erkennung dieses Typs liegt eine einfache rekursive Prozedur vor, die den Homogenitätsgrad von beliebigen Ausdrücken liefert.

Beispiele für von EULE als homogen erkannte DGLen sind:

$$xy'+a(y^2+x^2)^{1/2}-y=0 \quad \text{(Kamke 1.113)} \quad \text{und}$$

$$xy'\cosh(y/x)+2x*\sinh(y/x)-y*\cosh(y/x)=0 \quad \text{(Kamke 1.349)} \ .$$

DGLen vom Typ <u>lineare Koeffizienten</u> sind von der Form $y'=f(\frac{Ax+By+C}{ax+by+c})$.
Zur Erkennung dieses Typs liegt neben der Erkennung von in x und y linearen Ausdrücken die Möglichkeit vor, einen in entklammerter Form gegebenen Ausdruck als Quadrat oder 3. Potenz zu erkennen.

Beispiele für von EULE erkannte DGLen dieses Typs sind:

$$(ay+bx+c)^2y'+(Ay+Bx+C)^2=0 \quad \text{(Kamke 1.292) und} \quad y'-(y+x)^a*(y-x)^{-a}=0 \quad \text{und}$$

$$y'+\sin(f((x-y+2)^2))+a=0 \quad \text{und} \quad (3x+ay+b+1)^2y'+y^2+x^2-2xy=0 \ .$$

<u>Lineare</u> DGLen sind von der Form $f0(x)y'+f1(x)y+f2(x)=0$ und
<u>Bernoullische</u> DGLen sind von der Form $f0(x)y'+f1(x)y+f2(x)y^C=0$ (C≠1).
Diese Muster werden durch einfache Zerlegungsprozesse erkannt.

<u>Fastlineare</u> DGLen sind von der Form $f0(x)h'(y)y'=f1(x)h(y)+f2(x)$.
Zu ihrer Erkennung wird die oben genannte Faktorisierungsroutine benutzt.

Ein Beispiel, das EULE als Bernoullisch und fastlinear erkannte:

$$2x^2yy'+y^2=2x^3+x^2 \quad \text{(Kamke 1.258)} \ .$$

DGLen von der Form (1.1) sind <u>exakt</u>, falls der Ausdruck f_x-g_y identisch O ist. Zur Erkennung dieses Typs wird die übliche Standardvereinfachung eingesetzt.

Ein Beispiel einer von EULE als exakt erkannten DGL ist:

$$(x*\cosh(y)+\sinh(x))y'+y*\cosh(x)+\sinh(y)=0 \quad \text{(Kamke 1.348)} \ .$$

3.2.2 Bestimmung von Partikulärlösungen von Riccatischen DGLen und
Bestimmung von Eulerschen Multiplikatoren

Für diese Methoden besteht ein sehr weiter Spielraum bezüglich der Konzipierung von Algorithmen und Heuristiken. Für eine Diskussion der Auswahl muß auf den vollständigen Bericht verwiesen werden.

Riccatische DGLen sind von der Form $f0(x)y'=f1(x)y^2+f2(x)y+f3(x)$.
Bei bekannter Partikulärlösung ist eine Transformation in eine lineare DGL möglich. Zur Bestimmung von <u>Partikulärlösungen von Riccatischen DGLen</u> liegen zwei verschiedene Wege vor.

Für DGLen, in denen als Faktoren von y^i (i=2,1,0) und y' nur rationale Zahlen und rationale Potenzen von x vorkommen, ist ein Algorithmus entwickelt worden, der vorhandene Lösungen der Form $r_1 x^{s_1} + r_2 x^{s_2} + \ldots + r_n x^{s_n}$ (r_i, s_i rational für i=1,2,...,n) ermitteln kann. Ein derartiger Algorithmus war bisher nicht bekannt. Der Algorithmus beruht darauf, daß aus der DGL Aussagen über den Leitterm von möglichen derartigen Lösungen abgeleitet werden können und Nachfolge-DGLen gebildet werden können, deren Lösungen bis auf das Fehlen des Leitterms mit den Lösungen der ursprünglichen DGL übereinstimmen. Der Algorithmus kann auch auf andere als die genannten Riccati DGLen angewandt werden, sofern nicht Potenzen von x auftreten, die keine rationalen Zahlen sind. EULE berechnete zum Beispiel die Partikulärlösungen

$\pm ax^{1/2} - x/2$ für die DGL $2x^2 y' - 2y^2 - 3xy + 2a^2 x = 0$ (Kamke 1.164) .

Für beliebige Riccatische DGLen liegt eine Heuristik zur Bestimmung von Partikulärlösungen vor, die wie folgt arbeitet: es wird für jeden Summanden der DGL, der als Faktor $y**2$ oder y oder y' hat, versucht eine Testlösung so zu bestimmen, daß der höchstwertige Summand, der frei von y ist, gelöscht wird. Diese Testlösung wird, versehen noch mit einer Konstante, in die DGL eingesetzt und aus dieser Gleichung die eventuell bestimmbare Konstante berechnet. EULE berechnete z.B die Partikulärlösung $sin(x)/cos(x)$ für die DGL

$y' - y^2 - y*sin(2x) - cos(2x) = 0$ (Kamke 1.22) und die Partikulärlösung

$-g(x)/f(x)$ für die DGL $y' = f'(x)/g(x)y^2 - g'(x)/f(x)$ (Kamke 1.33).

Zur Bestimmung von Eulerschen Multiplikatoren liegen folgende Methoden vor (DGLen werden exakt, wenn man sie mit einem zugehörigen Eulerschen Multiplikator multipliziert ; siehe auch Nachtrag).

Es können beliebige DGLen daraufhin untersucht werden, ob ein Multiplikator vorliegt, der eine Funktion von $w=w(x,y)$ ist, wobei für $w=w(x,y)$ folgende Funktionen vorkommen dürfen:

x oder y oder $x^i y^j$ oder $x^i + y^j$ oder $x^i - y^j$ (i,j natürlich); das Hauptproblem bei der Realisierung der Methode ist die Vereinfachung eines im Verlauf der Rechnung auftretenden Bruches, der zur Erkennung eines Multiplikators in der Regel auch gekürzt werden muß. Hierzu wurde eine einfache, doch sehr leistungsfähige Kürzungsheuristik gefunden, die in allen bisher studierten Fällen einwandfrei gearbeitet hat. Die Kürzungsheurustik ist: gemeinsame Faktoren werden jeweils aus Zähler und Nenner ausgeklammert und die verbleibenden Ausdrücke werden, sofern möglich durcheinander dividiert. Zu der Relevanz einer solchen Heuristik sei bemerkt, daß die Vereinfachung eines Bruches selbst für den Fall, daß Zähler und Nenner Polynome mit ganzzahligen Koeffizienten sind, aus der Sicht des Formelmanipulierers nicht unproblematisch ist (siehe hierzu etwa Moses (1974)).

EULE berechnete den Multiplikator $(x+y)^{-2}$ für die DGL

$(2ay^3 + 3axy^2 - bx^3 + cx^2)y' - ay^3 + cy^2 + 3bx^2 y + 2bx^3 = 0$ (Kamke 1.313).

Der Bruch $\dfrac{6ay^2 - 2cy - 6bx^2 + 2cx}{-3ay^3 - 3axy^2 + cy^2 + 3bx^2 y + 3bx^3 - cx^2}$ mußte dabei vereinfacht

werden zu $-2/(x+y)$, ehe der Bruch als eine Funktion von $x+y$ erkannt werden konnte und damit der Multiplikator bestimmt werden konnte.

Zur Bestimmung von Eulerschen Multiplikatoren liegt außerdem ein Algorithmus vor, der auf DGLen angewandt werden kann, bei denen als Faktoren 1. Stufe der Summanden 1. Stufe außer y' nur rationale Zahlen und rationale Potenzen von x und y auftreten. Durch diesen Algorithmus können durch Lösen eines linearen Gleichungssystems für m und n Multiplikatoren der Form $x^m y^n$ (m,n rational) bestimmt werden.

EULE berechnete zum Beispiel den Multiplikator $x^{-27}y^{-16}$ für die DGL
$x(y^2-3x)y'+2y^3-5xy=0$ (Kamke 1.293) .

3.2.3 Methoden bezüglich Variablentransformationen

Für Fälle, in denen eine vorgelegte DGL 'charakteristische' Teilausdrücke enthält, existiert eine Heuristik, die Variablentransformationen empfiehlt. Bei Auftreten von Teilausdrücken der Art $A(x,y)**C$
oder $F(A(x,y))$, wobei $A(x,y)$ für einen von x und y abhängigen Ausdruck steht, C für einen konstanten Ausdruck und F für einen beliebigen Funktionsbezeichner steht, wird die Variablentransformation

$\bar{y}=A(x,y)$, $\bar{x}=x$ vorgeschlagen.

Bei Auftreten von Ausdrücken der Art $F(A(y))$, wobei $A(y)$ entsprechend für einen von y nicht aber von x abhängigen Ausdruck steht,
wird die Variablentransformation $\bar{y}=F(A(y))$, $\bar{x}=x$ vorgeschlagen;
handelt es sich bei F um eine der trigonometrischen Funktionen, so
werden weitere Transformationen vorgeschlagen. Ist F zum Beispiel die
sin-Funktion, so wird als neue abhängig Veränderliche zusätzlich noch
$cos(A(y))$ und $tan(A(y))$ und $tan(A(y)/2)$ vorgeschlagen. Analog für
die anderen trigonometrischen Funktionen.

EULE substituierte $\bar{y}=x^2/y$ bzw. $\bar{y}=tan(y)$ in den DGLen

$xy'-y(x*log(x^2/y)+2)=0$ (Kamke 1.120) bzw.
$(x^2+1)y'+x*sin(y)cos(y)-x(x^2+1)*cos^2(y)=0$ (Kamke 1.152)
und erhielt so eine separable bzw. lineare DGL.

Von den in der Kamke-Sammlung aufgeführten parameter-abhängigen
DGLen erwiesen sich die DGLen

$y'=ay^n+bx^{n/(1-n)}$ (Kamke 1.52)   und

$y'=\dfrac{f^{1-n}g'}{(ag+b)^n}y^n+\dfrac{f'}{f}y+fg'$ $(f=f(x),g=g(x))$ (Kamke 1.53)

als so häufig anwendbar, daß eine Implementierung zur Erkennung dieser
Muster vorgenommen wurde.

3.3 Zur Strategie von EULE

Der Hauptgesichtspunkt für die Festlegung einer Strategie für EULE
war, daß unter Ausnutzung der vorhandenen implementierten Lösungsmethoden die Lösbarkeit möglichst vieler Kamke-DGLen durch EULE sichergestellt
sein sollte, wobei allerdings nur Methoden mit einem breiteren Anwendungsbereich - siehe Forderung (F3) in Abschnitt 2.2 - berücksichtigt
werden sollten. Zur Festlegung der Strategie wurden verschiedene Computer Tests durchgeführt.
a) Es hat sich gezeigt, daß das Berechnen von Partikulärlösungen
ein hinreichend schneller Prozeß ist. Besondere Steuerungen zur Unterbrechung und eventuellen Wiederaufnahme der Suche erwiesen sich damit
als überflüssig.
b) Ein systematischer Test der Kamke-DGLen hat gezeigt, daß Euler-
sche Multiplikatoren, die Funktionen sind von $x**i+y**j$ oder $x**i*y**j$
(i,j natürlich) nur ganz selten vorkommen, wenn i oder j größer 2 ist.
c) Verschiedene Variablentransformationen wurden an einer großen
Menge von Kamke-DGLen durchgeführt. Es zeigte sich, daß nur die Substi-
tutionen $\bar{y}=yx,\bar{x}=x$ und $\bar{y}=y/x,\bar{x}=x$ und $\bar{y}=x,\bar{x}=y$ die Forderung (F3) erfüllen. Die Substitutionen $\bar{y}=1/y$ und $\bar{y}=y^2$ und $\bar{y}=y^2+x^2$ jeweils mit
$\bar{x}=x$ entfielen.
d) Die Standardform (ST3) in Verbindung mit einer festen Wahl der
steuerbaren Transformationen bezüglich Funktionen erwies sich für die
meisten Anwendungen als geeignet.

Aufbauend auf diesen Ergebnissen wurde die Strategie wie folgt festgelegt. Nacheinander werden die Untersuchungen A)-D) durchgeführt.

A1) EULE prüft die DGL nacheinander in den Formen (ST1), (ST2) und (ST3), ob sie vom Typ separabel, homogen oder lineare Koeffizienten ist.
A2) EULE prüft die DGL in der Form (ST3), ob sie vom Typ linear, Bernoulli, Riccati, fastlinear, Kamke 1.52 oder Kamke 1.53 ist. Liegt eine Riccati DGL vor, so versucht EULE zunächst mit dem Algorithmus und dann mit der Heuristik Partikulärlösungen zu bestimmen.
A3) EULE prüft die DGL in der Form (ST3), ob sie exakt ist. Falls nicht, versucht EULE Multiplikatoren der Form $x^m y^n$ oder Multiplikatoren, die Funktionen sind von x oder y, zu finden.
A4) EULE vertauscht in der Form (ST3) die Variablen x und y und führt die Untersuchungen unter A2) durch.

B) EULE führt die Variablentransformationen durch, die auf Grund charakteristischer Teilausdrücke in der DGL vorgeschlagen werden. Nach jeder Transformation werden die Untersuchungen A1)-A4) durchgeführt.

C) Die Substitutionen $\bar{y}=yx$ und $\bar{y}=y/x$ werden durchgeführt. Nach jeder Substitution werden die Untersuchungen A1)-A4) durchgeführt.

D) EULE sucht nach Multiplikatoren, die Funktionen sind von $x^i \pm y^j$, $x^i y^j$ $(i,j=1,2,3)$.

4. Testergebnisse mit EULE

EULE wurde an vier verschiedenen DGL-Sammlungen getestet: den repräsentativen Sammlungen von Kamke (1961) und Murphy(1960) ('repräsentativ', d.h. die Autoren sammelten die DGLen, die ihnen als die wichtigsten erschienen) und den zu Übungszwecken zusammengestellten Sammlungen von Ince (1956) und Spiegel(1958). Da EULE auf der Basis der Kamke-DGLen entwickelt worden ist, kommt den Testergebnissen mit der repräsentativen Sammlung von Murphy besondere Bedeutung zu.

4.1 Lösungsrate

Die Leistungsfähigkeit von EULE läßt sich am besten charakterisieren durch die für verschiedene DGL-Sammlungen erzielte Lösungsrate. 'Lösungsrate', das ist die Prozentzahl der gelösten DGLen einer Sammlung, nachdem 'nicht zugelassene' DGLen (das sind DGLen, die von EULE nicht bearbeitet werden können) und 'nicht elementar lösbare' DGLen (das sind DGLen, für die keine Lösung in Form von Integralen und den üblichen Funktionen existiert) entfernt worden sind.

EULE erzielte eine Lösungsrate von 90% für die repräsentative Sammlung von Kamke, eine Lösungsrate von 95% für die repräsentative Sammlung von Murphy und für die Übungs-DGLen von Spiegel und Ince eine Lösungsrate von 100% (siehe Tabelle 4.1).

Sammlung	Anzahl der DGLen	nicht zugelassene DGLen	nicht elem. lösb. DGLen	Lösungsrate von EULE
Kamke	376	3	39	90%
Murphy	751	1	35	95%
Ince	122	1	–	100%
Spiegel	80	4	–	100%

Tab. 4.1: Lösungsrate von DGL-Sammlungen, erzielt von EULE

Moses' Programm SOLDIER erzielte für die ganz leicht zu lösenden 76 Spiegel DGLen eine Lösungsrate von 89%; dieses Ergebnis wird von EULE schon erreicht, wenn nur die Exaktheitsprüfung durchgeführt wird und nach Multiplikatoren gesucht wird (siehe Tabelle 4.2) .

4.2 Zur Leistungsfähigkeit einzelner Methoden

Kamke bzw. Murphy löst 171 bzw. 505 DGLen durch Angabe eines elementaren Typs (separabel,...). EULE erkannte diese Typen in 100% bzw. 99,4% der Fälle.

Kamke bzw. Murphy löst 18 bzw. 23 Riccati DGLen durch Angabe einer Partikulärlösung. EULE berechnete in 100% bzw. 100% die gleiche Lösung.

Kamke bzw. Murphy löst 25 bzw. 71 DGLen durch Angabe eines Multiplikators. EULE berechnete in 92% bzw. 90% der Fälle den gleichen Multiplikator.

Die obengenannten Ergebnisse, insbesondere diejenigen für die Murphy-Sammlung, zeigen, daß die Forderungen (F1) und (F2) (siehe Abschnitt 2.2) für die Realisierung der Lösungsmethoden geeignet sind.

4.3 Zusätzlich gefundene Lösungswege

EULE hat für viele DGLen einen zusätzlichen Lösungsweg gefunden, der nicht in der Literatur genannt war. Der Bericht (Schmidt (1976b)) enthält eine Liste von ungefähr 125 Kamke-DGLen, für die EULE noch einen anderen Lösungsweg gefunden hat.

Kamke bzw. Murphy notiert für 45% bzw. 43% der 40 bzw. 54 elementar lösbaren Riccati DGLen eine Partikulärlösung. EULE fand einen solchen Lösungsweg in 83% bzw. 76% der Fälle.

EULE konnte einen großen Anteil der Sammlungen nur durch die Exaktheitsprüfung und die Anwendung der Multiplikatormethoden lösen; die Ergebnisse sind in Tabelle 4.2 notiert.

Sammlung	Anzahl der getesteten DGLen	als exakt erkannt (in %)	Multiplik. gefunden (in %)	insgesamt durch diese Methoden gelöst (in %)
Kamke	333	16%	40%	56%
Ince	121	9%	71%	80%
Spiegel	76	18%	71%	89%

Tab. 4.2: Ergebnisse bei Exaktheits- und Multiplikatorprüfung

Im folgenden werden einige Beispiele gegeben, für die EULE einen zusätzlichen (manchmal wohl auch 'naheliegenderen') Lösungsweg gefunden hat.

Für die Riccatische DGL $x^4(y'+y^2)+a=0$ (Kamke 1.181) berechnete EULE die Partikulärlösungen $\pm(-a)^{1/2}x^{-2}+x^{-1}$. Kamke schlägt die Transformationen $u(x)=x^2y$ und $v(x)=u(x)-x$ vor, womit sich eine separable DGL ergibt.

Für die Riccatische DGL $x^3y'-x^6y^2-(2x-3)x^2y+3=0$ (Kamke 1.173) berechnete EULE die Partikulärlösungen x^{-3} und $-3x^{-3}$. Kamke schlägt die Transformation $y=x^{-3}u'u^{-1}$ vor, womit sich eine DGL 2. Ordnung ergibt.

Für die Riccatische DGL $xy'\log(x)-y^2\log(x)-(2\log^2(x)+1)y-\log^3(x)=0$ (Kamke 1.194) berechnete EULE die Partikulärlösung $-\log(x)$. Kamke schlägt die Substitutionen $y=u(s),s=\log(x)$ und $v'(s)=-vu$ vor, womit sich eine DGL 2. Ordnung ergibt.

Für die DGL $x(y^2+x^2-a)y'-y(y^2+x^2+a)=0$ (Kamke 1.294) fand EULE die Multiplikatoren $M1=(y^2-x^2+a)^{-2}$ und $M2=(xy)^{-1}$, woraus sofort die allgemeine Lösung $M1/M2=constans$ resultiert. Kamke schlägt die Substitution $u(x)=xy,v(x)=y/x$ vor, womit sich zwei separable DGLen ergeben.

Für die DGL $(10x^3y^2+x^2y+2x)y'+5x^2y^3+xy^2-3y=0$ (Kamke 1.304)
fand EULE die Substitution $\bar{y}=yx$, die zu einer separablen DGL führt.
Kamke notiert ein spezielles Muster, das zu einem Multiplikator führt.

Für die DGL $(y-x^2)y'+4xy=0$ (Kamke 1.218) fand EULE fünf verschiedene Lösungswege: die Substitutionen $\bar{y}=y/x$ oder $y=\bar{y}^2$, die zu einer homogenen DGL führen; Vertauschung der Variablen, womit sich eine Bernoulli DGL ergibt; die Multiplikatoren $(y+x^2)^{-3}$ und $y^{-3/2}$. Kamke notiert die Substitution $y=x^2u(x)$, womit sich eine separable DGL ergibt.

4.4 Rechenzeiten

Die Tests mit EULE wurden auf einer IBM 370/168 durchgeführt.

Wenn EULE eine DGL lösen kann, so wird diese Lösung in der Regel innerhalb von 15 Sekunden (CPU-Zeit) gefunden. Wird die Lösung in einem der Schritte A1)-A4) oder B) (siehe Abschnitt 3.3) gefunden, so sind in der Regel 5 Sekunden hinreichend. Eine halbe Sekunde ist in der Regel genug, falls die DGL von einem der elementaren Typen ist.

Für einige, in Kapitel 3 notierte, DGLen sind die Rechenzeiten notiert, die bei Verwendung der Strategie (siehe Abschnitt 3.3) benötigt wurden:

Kamke 1.348	(exakt)	0.5 sec
Kamke 1.164	(Riccati)	2.5 sec
Kamke 1.33	(Riccati)	3.2 sec
Kamke 1.313	(Multiplikator)	27.0 sec
Kamke 1.293	(Multiplikator)	1.0 sec
Kamke 1.120	(Substitution)	1.5 sec .

EULE stoppte nach einer Minute und 20 Sekunden , ohne die DGL
$(3x+2)(y-2x-1)y'=y^2-xy+7x^2+9x+3$ (Kamke 1.247) gelöst zu haben.

5. Schlußbemerkungen

Die Kamke-DGLen, die EULE nicht lösen konnte, können wie folgt klassifiziert werden:
i) Kamke löst die DGL durch eine Substitution, die EULE nicht finden konnte. Ein Beispiel hierfür ist die in Abschnitt 4.4 notierte DGL Kamke 1.247, die Kamke durch die Substitution $x=u-2/3, y=v(u)-1/3$ in eine homogene DGL überführt.
ii) Kamke löst die DGL durch eine Folge von Substitutionen. Z. B. schlägt Kamke die drei nacheinander auszuführenden Substitutionen
$u(x)=1/y$, $xv(x)=x^3u+1$ und Vertauschung der Variablen für die DGL
$x^7y'+2(x^2+1)y^3+5x^3y^2=0$ (Kamke 1.185) vor, um eine lineare DGL zu erhalten.
iii) Kamke löst die DGL durch eine Methode, die in EULE nicht implementiert ist. Hierunter fallen zum Beispiel Transformationen, die zu einer DGL 2. Ordnung führen.

Ein Programm wie EULE kann dazu beitragen Leuten, die Sammlungen von DGLen veröffentlichen, die Arbeit zu erleichtern. Murphy sprach in dem Vorwort zu seinem Buch von 'einigen tausend Seiten Notizen'.

Darüber hinaus könnte ein Programm wie EULE dazu beitragen, die Angaben über Lösungswege zu vervollständigen oder auch zu vereinheitlichen, die in DGL-Sammlungen vorgeschlagen werden. Zum Beispiel sind die vier Kamke-DGLen 1.314, 1.210, 1.207, 1.258 alle von dem Typ
$f(x)y^iy'+g(x)y^{i+1}+h(x)=0$. Dies ist gleichzeitig eine fastlineare und Bernoullische DGL. Kamke schlägt die folgenden Lösungswege vor:
Bernoulli (1.314), fast linear (1.210), Bernoulli und fastlinear (1.207),

Substitution zur Überführung in eine separable DGL (1.258) .

Literaturverzeichnis

Brown, W.S. (1969): "Rational Exponential Expressions and a Conjecture Concerning π and e", Amer. Math. Monthly, vol. 76, S. 28-34

Fateman, R.J. (1972): "Essays in Algebraic Simplification", Report MAC TR-95, Project MAC, MIT, Cambridge, Mass.

Ince, E.L. (1956): "Die Integration gewöhnlicher DGLen", Bibliograph. Inst., Mannheim, HTB Nr. 67.

Kamke, E. (1961): "Differentialgleichungen-Lösungsmethoden und Lösungen, 1. Gewöhnliche Differentialgleichungen", Akad. Verl. Ges. Geest&Portig K.G., Leipzig, 7. Auflage.

Moses, J. (1967): "Symbolic Integration", Report MAC TR-47, Project MAC, MIT, Cambridge, Mass.

Moses, J. (1971a): "Symbolic Integration: The Stormy Decade", Comm. of the ACM, vol. 14, S. 548-560.

Moses, J. (1971b): "Algebraic Simplification: A Guide for the Perplexed", Comm. of the ACM, vol. 14, S. 527-537.

Moses, J. (1974): "The Evolution of Algebraic Manipulation Algorithms", Information Processing 1974, North Holland Publ. Comp., S. 483-488.

Murphy, G.M. (1960): "Ordinary Differential Equations", D. van Nostrand Comp., Inc., Princeton, New Jersey.

Richardson, D. (1968): "Some Undecidable Problems Involving Elementary Functions of a Real Variable", The J. of Symb. Logic, vol. 33, S. 514-520.

Schmidt, P. (1976a): "Automatic Symbolic Solution of Differential Equations of First Order and First Degree", Proc. of the ACM Symp. on Symbolic and Algebraic Computation, Yorktown Heights, New York, 10-12 Aug. 1976.

Schmidt, P. (1976b): "Maschinelle symbolische Lösung von Differential-gleichungen 1. Ordnung und 1. Grades", Informatik Berichte, Universität Bonn, wird erscheinen.

Slagle, J.R. (1963): "A Heuristic Program that Solves Symbolic Integration Problems in Freshman Calculus", J. of the ACM, vol. 10, S. 507-520.

Spiegel, M.R. (1958): "Applied Differential Equations", Englewood Cliffs, N.J., Prentice Hall, Inc.

Wang, P.S. (1971): "Evaluation of Definite Integrals by Symbolic Manipulation", Report MAC TR-92, Project MAC, MIT, Cambridge, Mass.

Nachtrag:

Eine DGL der Form (1.1) hat einen Eulerschen Multiplikator, der eine Funktion einer vorgegebenen Funktion $w=w(x,y)$ ist, falls der Bruch $(g_y-f_x)/(fw_x-gw_y)$ eine Funktion von $w=w(x,y)$ ist.

Eine DGL der Form (1.1) hat einen Eulerschen Multiplikator der Form $x^m y^n$ (m,n rational), falls gilt: $nxg-myf=xy(f_x-g_y)$.

<u>ASYNCHRONOUS INTERLOCK UNITS FOR SPEED-INDEPENDENT</u>

<u>MULTIPROCESSOR SYSTEMS</u>

Paolo Corsini

Dipartimento Sperimentale di
Elettrotecnica ed Elettronica,
Università di Pisa, Pisa, Italy.

<u>Abstract</u>. In a hardware asynchronous parallel system, two or more processors may require simultaneously the use of a common functional unit, and conflicts may arise. In order to resolve these conflicts, an interlock unit is employed. Two asynchronous interlock units that can be used in asynchronous speed-independent systems are presented in this paper. Both interlock units have high modularity. They differ in the priority rule, according to which (if there are several requests) the common functional unit is assigned.

1. Introduction.

Let us consider an asynchronous system in which n "concurrent processors" $P_1, P_2, \ldots, P_n$ want to enter simultaneously their "critical section", (i.e., want to use simultaneously a common functional unit) so that conflicts arise. In order to resolve this problem ("mutual exclusion problem") a control mechanism must be used, assuring that the processors enter their critical section one after the other.

Most of the classical solutions of the mutual exclusion problem [1,2,3] postulate the existence of special "indivisible instructions" to being executed from a processor whenever it wants to enter its critical section. The execution of an indivisible instruction itself becomes the critical section so that, after all, the mutual exclusion problem must be solved by an independent hardware control mechanism (*interlock unit*) [4,5,6] to which the processors require to enter their critical section, and from which the processors are allowed to do so. The interlock units must assure that:

i)   at most one processor may be in critical section at any time
ii) if one or more processors want to enter their critical section, and no processor is in its critical section, one processor must be allowed to enter its critical section in a finite time.

Other constraints can be imposed in resolving the mutual exclusion problem, in addition to those specified at points i) and ii). Let us impose the constraint:

iii) if processors P_v and $P_{v+\alpha}$, $1 \leqslant v < n$, $1 \leqslant \alpha \leqslant n-v$, have been required to enter their critical section, P_v is allowed to enter.

In this case the interlock unit will be called *wired priority exchange* or simply *exchange*.

Let us impose the different constraint:

iii) if a processor wants to enter its critical section, it must be allowed to enter in a finite time.

In this case the interlock unit will be called *arbiter*.

The system configuration for the mutual exclusion problem is given in Fig. 1. It is assumed that the reaction time of the system units and the time for signals to propagate from a unit output to a unit input is neither constant, nor bounded, but finite. Such a system is called *speed-independent* and no master clock can synchronize its units [7,8,9].

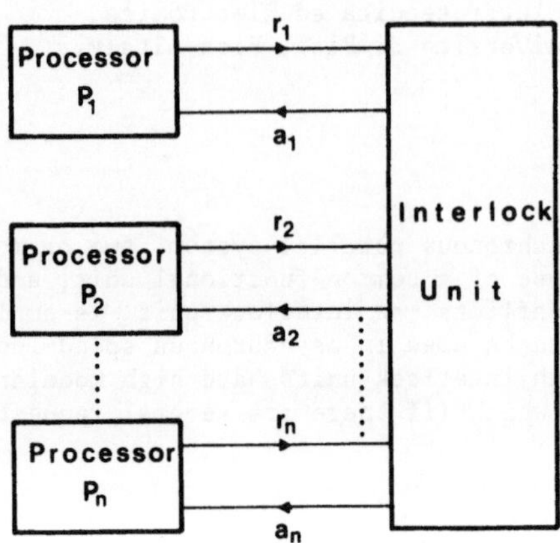

Fig. 1 System configuration for mutual exclusion problem.

Hardware interlock units have been presented in [9,10,11,12,13] . The main difficulty in the implementation of an asynchronous interlock unit is due to the fact that the classical design approaches are inadequate. In fact, let us suppose that the interlock unit has been implemented as "level asynchronous sequential circuit" [14]. Logical errors may be present since an input variable may switch at any time, i.e., even if the interlock unit is not in a stable internal state. Let us now suppose that the interlock unit has been implemented as "clocked sequential circuit" [14]. Logical errors may be present since an input variable may switch when the clock pulse is present, such that the memory element may enter they "metastable state" [12,13,15,16,17].

In [12,13], Patil presents a very simple asynchronous arbiter that resolves, without logical failures, the mutual exclusion problem in an asynchronous speed-independent system, having two councurrent processors (see Appendix). In this paper a wired priority exchange and an arbiter, without logical failures, are presented for n asynchronous concurrent processors. These interlock units utilize the two-user arbiter of Patil, have a high modularity and are usable in a speed-independent system.

Referring to the discipline according to which a processor P_i, i=1,2,...,n communicates with an interlock unit, we suppose that this communication takes place by means of a wire r_i (*request wire*) and a wire a_i (*acknowledge wire*) using "reset signalling" [8]. That is, starting from the condition $r_i=0$, $a_i=0$, when (see Fig. 1) the processor P_i wants to enter its critical section, it sends a request signal (i.e. a logical level 1) to the interlock unit on the request wire r_i. The processor P_i may enter its critical section only when an acknowledge signal (i.e. a logical level 1) is sent to it by the interlock unit on the acknowledge wire a_i. When processor P_i leaves its critical section, it resets the request wire r_i. The processor P_i may once again indicate that it wants to re-enter its critical section only upon receiving a reset signal from the interlock unit on acknowledge wire a_i.

2. Wired priority exchange.

A simple asynchronous wired priority exchange, having a high modularity, is obtained by starting from the two-user arbiter of Patil[13]. The exchange consists of n modules, one for each processor, interconnected as shown in Fig. 2a. The structure of the i-th module, i=1,2,...,n, is given in Fig. 2b. The elements I are identity elements, used to perform the "wired-or" connections of Fig. 2a. The exchange is not internally speed-independent, but its two-user arbiters are not required to resolve possible conflicts within a fixed lenght of time. Moreover, the exchange is connectible, in a speed-independent way, with the other system units. The behaviour of the exchange is now described.

Let t_o be the time in which every output of every element of every module of the exchange is at level 0, and let us suppose that, at a time t_1, a request signal arrives from a processor P_m at input r_m of the module M_m. This request signal, after y_m has switched at level 1, is accepted by M_m, i.e. produces the switch of z_m at level 1. Then w_m switches, and the level 1 is carried to the input p of the "and gate" G (in Fig. 2a). As the input q of G is also at level 1, it follows that the variable x_o switches at level 1 (*testing cycle start*). If no request signal has been sent from p_1 to the input r_1, the variable x_1 (see Fig. 2b) switches at level 1 and M_1 is disabled from accepting a possibie request signal arriving from P_1. Reasons equal to those holding for M_1, hold for $M_2,M_3,...$ and so on, until the input variable x_{e-1} of a module M_e, to which a request signal has arrived from the pertinent processor P_e, switches at level 1. Two cases may occur: (a) the request signal from P_e has been accepted, i.e., z_e is at level 1 when x_{e-1} switches, or (b) the request signal from P_e is *simultaneous* with the switching of x_{e-1}. In the first case, an acknowledge signal is sent on a_e to P_e so that P_e enters its critical section. When P_e leaves its critical section and sends a reset signal to r_e, the variable h_e switches at level 1 (the variable y_e remains at level 1 because f_e is at level 1). Therefore the variables q and x_o (see Fig. 2a) switch at level 0 (*resetting cycle start*). In the second case, the two-user arbiter of M_e must resolve the conflict, in order that either z_e switches at level 1, i.e., everything happens as in the previous case, or x_e switches at level 1, i.e. the request signal from P_e is not accepted and M_e behaves as $M_1,M_2,...,M_{e-1}$. So, in a finite time, one module M_k ($M_k=M_e$ or $M_k=M_{e+\beta}$, $k\leqslant m$) is found, that has accepted a request signal. Then, the pertinent processor first enters and then leaves its critical section, so that a reset cycle starts. In the reset cycle, the variables $x_1,x_2,...,x_{k-1}$ switch successively at level 0. Every module M_j, j=1,2,...,k-1, is enabled to accept a possible request signal arriving from the pertinent processor, but every variable a_j remains firmly at level 0, as no hazard is present at point f_j. In fact, let us consider the "and gate" G_j and its two inputs. The upper input switches at level 0 before that, possibly, the lower input switches at level 1, since in the lower path there is the delay introduced by the two-user arbiter. When x_{k-1} switches at level 0, the variables f_k and y_k switch at level 0. The delay Δ assures that a_k and h_k remain at level 1 until z_k and w_k have switched at level 0 and every transient related to the switch of w_k is put out. At this point a_k and h_k switch at level 0, so that a condition equal to the condition at time t_o or at time t_1 is reached. Note that during a test cycle, only one processor enters its critical section. This processor is the upper among those having a request signal accepted by the pertinent module.

3. Asynchronous arbiter.

The overall structure of the asynchronous arbiter and the detailed structure of the i-th module (i=1,2,...,n) are shown in Figs. 3a and 3b. The C-element is a device [18] whose output x_o, starting from p=0, q=0, x_o=0, switches every time both inputs have switched. The arbiter is not internally speed-independent, but its two-user arbiters are not required to resolve possible conflicts within a fixed lenght of time. Moreover, the arbiter can be connected in a speed-independent way, with the other system units.

In order to state precisely the arbiter behaviour, we point out the fact that a test cycle, starting when one or more processors want to enter their critical section, must not end when one processor leaves, after having entered, its critical section.

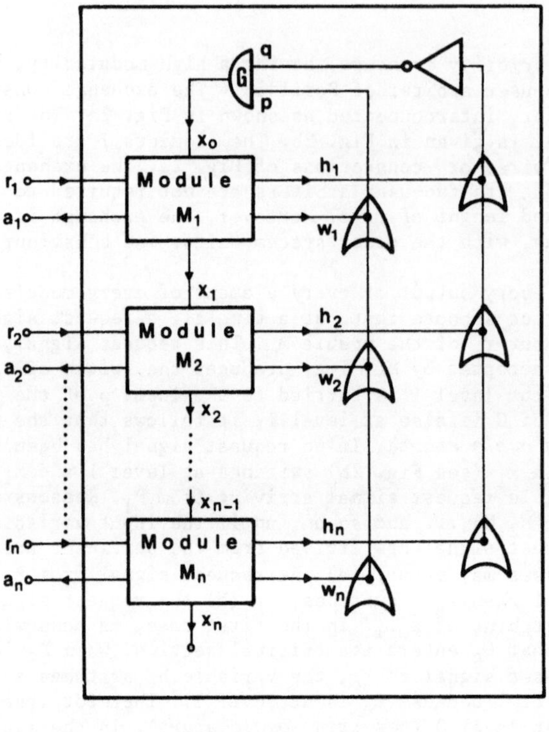

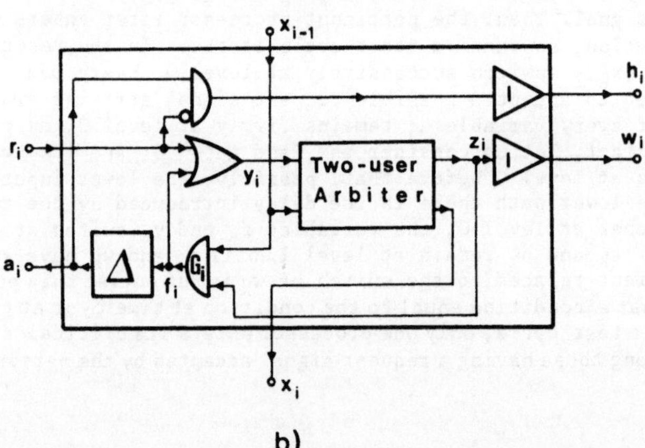

Fig. 2 a) Overall structure of the exchange
b) Detailed structure of a module M_i of the exchange, $i=1,2,\ldots,n$.

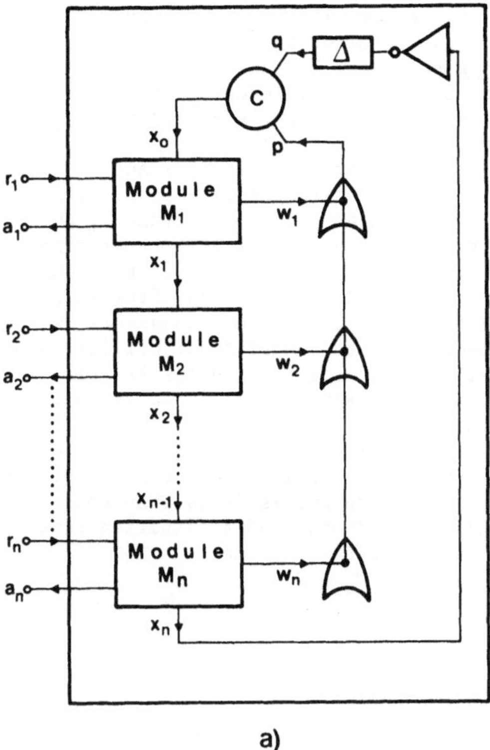

a)

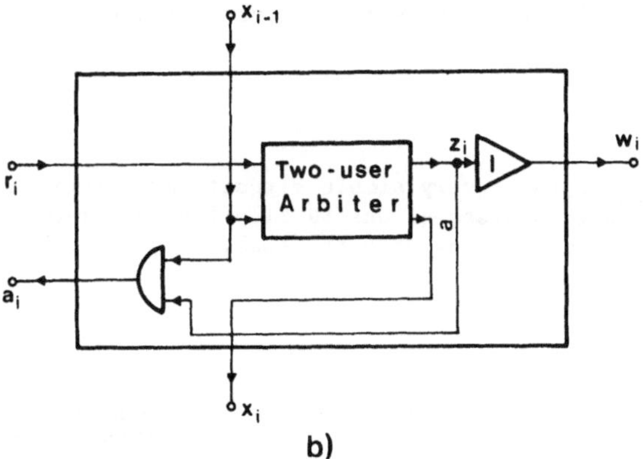

b)

Fig. 3 a) Overall structure of the arbiter
b) Detailed structure of a module M_i of the arbiter, $i=1,2,\ldots,n$.

To be precise (see Fig. 3), let t_o be the time in which every input and every output of every module of the arbiter is at level 0. Let us suppose that, at a time t_1, a request signal has arrived from a processor P_m and has been accepted by the module M_m so that the two input variables of C are at level 1. Therefore the variable x_o switches at level 1 and a test cycle starts. Let us consider a variable x_{i-1} that switches at level 1. If in M_i no request signal has been accepted, M_i is disabled from accepting a possible request signal arriving from P_i and x_i switches at level 1. If in M_i a request signal has been accepted (a possible conflict is resolved from the two-user arbiter of M_i), a_i switches at level 1, so that P_i enters its critical section. When P_i leaves its critical section and sends a reset signal to r_i, the variable z_i switches at level 0 (so that a reset signal is sent on a_i to P_i) and the variable x_i switches at level 1 (so that M_i is disabled from accepting a new request signal from P_i). Therefore in a finite time, all the processors, whose request signals have been accepted by the pertinent modules, enter their critical section, one at a time, and a situation is reached in which all the modules are disabled in accepting request signals from the pertinent processors. Level 0 is carried to the input p of the C-element, and level 1 is carried from x_n to the input of the inverter preceding the C-element. The delay Δ assures that q switches at level 0 when p has been stabilized at level 0. At this point, the variable x_o switches at level 0 and the reset cycle starts. The modules $M_1, M_2, \ldots, M_n$ are successively enabled in accepting the request signals from the pertinent processors, and a situation equal to the situation at time t_o or at time t_1 is reached in a finite time.

4. Conclusion.

Two asynchronous interlock units, without logical failures, are presented in order to resolve the mutual exclusion problem in an asynchronous speed-independent system having n concurrent processors.

The interlock units differ in the priority rule, according to which (if there are several requests) the processors are allowed to enter their critical section. Both the interlock units have a high modularity and are very simple.

Appendix.

Patil has presented in [12,13] a very simple circuit for a two-user perfect asynchronous arbiter. The circuit consists of one SR flip-flop and two threshold NOT gates. Referring to Fig. 4 and starting from the stable configuration $r_1=0$, $r_2=0$,

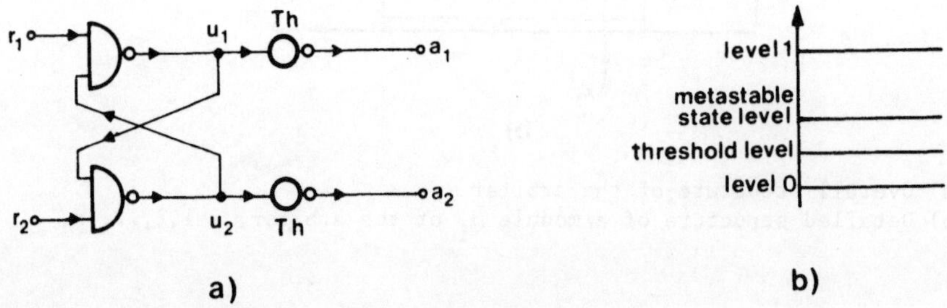

Fig. 4   a) Two-user perfect asynchronous arbiter of Patil.
b) Levels at points u_1 and u_2 of Fig. 4a.

$u_1=1$, $u_2=1$, $a_1=0$, $a_2=0$, let us suppose that a request signal arrives at input r_1 (r_2). The circuit enters an unstable state. If no request signal arrives at input r_2 (r_1), the circuit reaches the stable state $S_1=\{u_1=0, u_2=1, a_1=1, a_2=0\}$ ($S_2=\{u_1=1, u_2=0,$ $a_1=0, a_2=1\}$). A request signal arriving after this time at input r_2 (r_1) cannot be accepted, i.e. cannot produce a state change, until a reset signal is sent to r_1 (r_2). If a request signal arrives at r_1 (r_2) before the circuit is in the state S_1 (S_2) the flip-flop may enter its metastable state, but, owing to threshold gates, no acknowledge signal appears at the arbiter output terminals, until the flip-flop has definitely left the metastable state and has reached one of the two stable states.

References.

[1] E.W. Dijkstra, Solution of a problem in concurrent programming control, Comm. of the ACM, Vol. 8, p. 569, September 1965.

[2] J.B. Dennis and E.C. Van Horn, Programming semantics for multiprogrammed computations, Comm. of the ACM, Vol. 9, pp. 143-155, March 1966.

[3] D.E. Knuth, Additional comments on a problem in concurrent programming control, Comm. of the ACM, Vol. 9, pp. 321-322, May 1966.

[4] S.M. Ornestein, M.J. Stucki and W.A. Clark, A functional description of macromodules, AFIPS Conference Proceedings, Vol. 30, pp. 337-355, Spring 1967.

[5] N. Wirth, A note on "program structures for parallel processing", Comm. of the ACM, Vol. 9, pp. 320-321, May 1966.

[6] T.H. Bredt and E.J. McCluskey, Analysis and synthesis of control mechanisms for parallel processes, in Parallel Processor Systems, Technologies and Applications, L.C. Hobbs et al. (Eds.), Spartan, New York, pp. 287-295, 1970.

[7] J.B. Dennis and S.S. Patil, Speed independent asynchronous circuits, Fourth Hawaii Int. Conf. on System Sciences, pp. 55-58, January 1971.

[8] S.S. Patil and J.B. Dennis, The description and realization of digital systems, Sixth Annual IEEE Computer Society Int. Conf., pp. 223-226, September 1971.

[9] R.M. Keller, Towards a theory of universal speed-independent modules, IEEE Trans. Comput., Vol. C-23, pp. 21-23, January 1974.

[10] W.W. Plummer, Asynchronous arbiters, IEEE Trans. Comput., Vol. C-21, pp. 37-42, January 1972.

[11] P. Corsini, Self-synchronizing asynchronous arbiter, Digital Processes, Vol. 1, pp. 67-73, 1975.

[12] M.I.T. Project MAC Progress Report X, pp. 24-27, July 1973.

[13] S.S. Patil, Bounded and unbounded delay synchronizers and arbiters, Computation Structures Group Memo 103, Project MAC, M.I.T., June 1974.

[14] P.E. Wood, Switching theory, McGraw-Hill Book Company, New York, 1968.

[15] T.J. Chaney and C.E. Molnar, Anomalous behaviour of synchronizer and arbiter circuits, IEEE Trans. Comput., Vol. C-22, pp. 421-422, April 1973.

[16] I. Catt, Time loss through gatin of asynchronous logic signal pulses, IEEE Trans. Comput., Vol. EC-15, pp. 108-111, February 1966.

[17] G.R. Couranz and D.F. Wann, Theoretical and experimental behaviour of synchronizers operating in the metastable region, IEEE Trans. Comput., Vol. C-24, pp. 604-616, June 1975.

[18] D.E. Muller and W.S. Bartky, A theory of asynchronous circuits, _Proceedings of an Int. Symp. on the Theory of Switching_, pp. 204-243, Harvard University Press 1959.

EINE METHODE ZUM ENTWURF VON DIGITALRECHNERN
MIT DER PROGRAMMIERSPRACHE M I M O L A

G. Zimmermann

Zusammenfassung:

Es wird eine Methode angegeben, Digitalrechner mit Hilfe einer Programmiersprache systematisch zu entwerfen. Ausgangspunkt ist die Problemmenge, die mit
Hilfe des Zielrechners bearbeitet werden soll. Der Entwurf erfolgt durch sequentielle Übersetzung dieser Menge auf verschiedene Niveaus der Sprache. Nach jedem
Übersetzungsschritt erfolgt eine engere Definition des Zielrechners durch den
Entwerfer, der von der Sprache Entscheidungshilfen erhält. Am Ende des Prozesses
ist der Entwurf vollständig durch Deklarationen in der Sprache definiert, und
die Problemmenge liegt in Form von Mikroprogrammen vor. Die Methode wird an
einem Beispiel demonstriert.

1. Einleitung

Besteht die Aufgabe, ein Tonfrequenzfilter mit bestimmten Eigenschaften zu entwerfen, so kann man aus wenigen technischen Möglichkeiten eine auswählen und
die Schaltung dafür vollständig berechnen. Hier haben wir eine präzise Aufgabenstellung und eine präzise Methode. Für den Entwurf von Zentraleinheiten von
Digitalrechnern fehlt dagegen bisher beides. Mit dieser Arbeit soll deshalb ein
Versuch unternommen werden, diesen Entwurf zu systematisieren.

Befassen wir uns zunächst mit der Aufgabenstellung. Es ist sicher nicht die
Aufgabe eines Rechners, einen Befehl " load register from memory and skip if
zero " auszuführen. Auch die Ausführung eines ALGOL - Statements " a := a x b "
ist nicht die ursprüngliche Aufgabe, sondern die Lösung von Problemen, die für
eine digitale Verarbeitung geeignet sind. Leider ist es sehr schwierig, das Wort
" Probleme " so zu präzisieren, daß eine exakte Beschreibung der Aufgabe eines
Digitalrechners herauskäme, mit Ausnahme von Spezialprozessoren für einen sehr
kleinen Problemkreis. Man kann aber versuchen, die Menge aller Probleme in Klassen einzuteilen, z.B. in numerische und nichtnumerische Probleme. Wenn die
Klassen klein genug sind, sollten sich Repräsentanten finden lassen mit folgender
Eigenschaft: kann eine Maschine einen Repäsentanten effektiv bearbeiten, so gilt
das auch für die anderen Elemente der Klasse.

Nun muß nicht jede Maschine für alle Probleme gleich gut geeignet sein. Zur
Beurteilung der Leistung können wir deshalb die Klassen mit Gewichten versehen.
Die Aufgabe besteht dann darin, eine Maschine zu entwerfen, die für die Menge
der Repräsentanten unter Berücksichtigung der Gewichte die maximale Leistung
erreicht mit technologischen und wirtschaftlichen Einschränkungen.

Die Darstellung der Probleme kann in verschiedener Weise erfolgen. Sinnvoll
erscheint eine Angabe von Programmen in einer passenden problemorientierten
Programmiersprache. Uns ist keine Methode bekannt, ausgehend von einer solchen
Definition der Aufgabe, Digitalrechner systematisch zu entwickeln. Die Entwurfs-
methoden, wie sie z.B. in /1/ dargestellt sind, eignen sich für Details. Die in
/2/ beschriebenen Methoden beziehen sich auf Steuerwerke, hier geht es aber um
den Entwurf von Operationswerken. Sprachen wie CDL /3/ erlauben zwar die Beschreibung und Simulation von Digitalrechnern auf einem Register-Transfer-Level, bieten aber keine Entwurfsmethode.

2. Die Entwurfsmethode

Hier soll eine Methode vorgestellt werden, um ausgehend von der oben definierten
Aufgabenstellung in systematischer Weise Zentraleinheiten zu entwerfen. Wir
haben dazu eine Programmiersprache entwickelt, die einerseits den problemorientierten Sprachen nahesteht, damit Probleme hardwareunabhängig formuliert
werden können. Andererseits ist sie aber auch eine sehr detaillierte Maschinensprache in folgendem Sinne:

a.   Sprachelemente entsprechen direkt Hardware-Moduln. Durch Attribute können
diese Moduln genau spezifiziert werden.

b.   Der syntaktische Aufbau eines Satzes spiegelt den Datenfluß und damit die
Verbindungen der Moduln wieder.

c.   Die Steuerwerksfunktionen und damit die Mikroprogrammelemente werden mit
jedem Modul angegeben.

d.   Geht man von einem synchronen Automaten aus, so stellt ein <statement>
eine durch einen Taktschritt abschließbare Handlung dar. Alle <statement>,
die zur gleichen Taktzeit ausgeführt werden, sind in einem <elementary
statement block> zusammengefaßt.

Die Sprache befindet sich damit auf der Mikroprogramm- oder Register-Transfer-
Ebene eines Digitalrechners. Wir nennen sie deshalb " <u>M</u>aschine <u>I</u>ndependant
<u>M</u>icro<u>p</u>rogramming <u>L</u>anguage " M I M O L A .

Die Sprache hat verschiedene Niveaus. Ein Programm wird durch Compiler von
einem Niveau auf ein niedrigeres übersetzt. Das höchste Niveau - MIMOLA $\emptyset$ -
besitzt im Prinzip keine Einschränkungen in Bezug auf die Hardware, nur unser
Vorstellungsvermögen von möglichen Moduln setzt Grenzen. Jede weitergehende
Einschränkung führt zu einem niedrigeren Niveau und bestimmt die Übersetzungs-
handlung des Compilers.

Die Hardware der zu entwerfenden Maschine besteht zum einen aus den Moduln wie
z.B. adressierbaren Speichern, Registern, arithmetischen Einheiten. Die Moduln
können Zuordner ohne Gedächtnis sein. Die Speicher sollen beim Lesen wie Zuordner
arbeiten, d.h. daß nach Anliegen der Adresse ohne Takt der Inhalt der adressier-
ten Zelle am Ausgang anliegt. Im Innern notwendige Takte sollen nach außen nicht
sichtbar sein. Der von der Sprache definierte Takt bewirkt nur das Schreiben
in die speichernden Moduln. Diese Forderung ist ideal bei schnellen Halbleiterspeichern erfüllt. Sie läßt sich aber auch durch die Einführung von Adress-
und Datenregistern bei Kernspeichern erfüllen. Zum anderen besteht die Hardware
aus den Verbindungen der Moduln untereinander. Dabei werden Multiplexer und
Bus-Tore mit zu den Verbindungen gerechnet.

Ein Entwurf läuft nun folgendermaßen ab:

Schritt 1: Zusammenstellung und Gewichtung der Repräsentanten der Problemmenge

Schritt 2: Formulierung der Probleme in MIMOLA $\emptyset$ oder in einer höheren Programmiersprache und Übersetzung in MIMOLA $\emptyset$

Schritt 3: Aufstellung der Statistik über die zur direkten Ausführung der
Programmenge notwendigen Moduln bei Erhaltung der Parallelität

Schritt 4: Auswahl einer aufwandsmäßig vertretbaren Modul-Menge und Deklarieren
dieser Moduln in MIMOLA

Schritt 5: Übersetzung der MIMOLA $\emptyset$ - Programmenge mit dieser Deklaration in
MIMOLA 1

Schritt 6: Aufstellung der Statistik der in den MIMOLA 1 - Programmen verwendeten Verbindungen

Schritt 7: Auswahl der zu erstellenden Verbindungen nach den Kriterien:
Notwendigkeit, Häufigkeit, Ersetzbarkeit und Deklarierung derselben

Schritt 8: Übersetzung von MIMOLA 1 nach MIMOLA 2

Wenn jetzt die gesamte Hardware definiert ist, stellen alle so übersetzten
oder in MIMOLA 2 syntaktisch richtigen <elementary statement block> in einer

Taktzeit ausführbare Mikroprogrammschritte dar, die nur noch kodiert werden müssen. Werden einige Einzelheiten noch offen gelassen, wie z.B. die Länge des Mikroprogrammwortes oder die Ein-Ausgabe, so schließen sich weitere Schritte an. Fehler bei der Auswahl der Hardware führen zu Fehlermeldungen durch den Compiler und zur Wiederholung einzelner Schritte. Die Leistung der entworfenen Maschine kann nach der Anzahl der notwendigen Mikroprogrammschritte oder bei Angabe der Ausführungszeiten der Moduln nach der Rechenzeit beurteilt werden. Durch eine Veränderung der Deklarationen und Wiederholung der Prozedur vom 4. Schritt an kann der Entwurf interaktiv optimiert werden.

3. Sprachelemente

MIMOLA kann hier nicht vollständig beschrieben werden. Eine erste syntaktische Beschreibung ist in /4/ zu finden. Hier sollen nur einige charakteristische Eigenschaften gezeigt werden.

Grundelemente sind Operanden und Operatoren. Operanden sind alle speichernden Moduln und Festwerte, Operatoren die Zuordner wie Addierwerke, Demultiplexer, Schiebenetze. Die Trennung dient im wesentlichen der Übersichtlichkeit, da die Ausgänge von Operatoren wieder Operanden und Festwertspeicher auch Operatoren sein können. Die Operanden und Operatoren sind in Klassen eingeteilt, deren Elemente durch gleiche Anfangsbuchstaben gekennzeichnet sind. So ist A der Anfangsbuchstabe monadischer Operatoren, B der dyadischer, S für adressierbare Speicher, R für Register, K für Kellerspeicher.

Deklarierte Moduln werden durch angehängte alphanumerische Zeichen identifiziert, z.B.   RH6   Hilfsregister 6
Weitere Angaben werden in Klammern ohne Trennung angehängt:

      S2(116)   Speicher 2, Zelle 116
      B4(-)   arithm. Einheit 4, Funktion Subtraktion

Die möglichen Funktionen der Moduln werden in der Deklaration spezifiziert. Attribute können durch " . " getrennt angehängt werden. Die Standart-Informationseinheit ist das Wort. Seine Breite und Bitnummerierung wird in der Deklaration angegeben:

      S1($\emptyset$: 255).BIT($\emptyset$: 15)   Speicher 1 mit 256 Worten à 16 bit
Im Programmteil können auf diese Weise einzelne bit oder Teile von Worten bezeichnet werden:

      RH6.BIT(3)   bit 3 von Hilfsregister 6

Die Notation der Ausdrücke soll möglichst anschaulich die Schaltung repräsentieren, die den Ausdruck in einem Takt abarbeiten kann. Am besten wären Blockschaltbilder, z.B. Abb.1 für den Ausdruck

$$a := b + a \times c$$

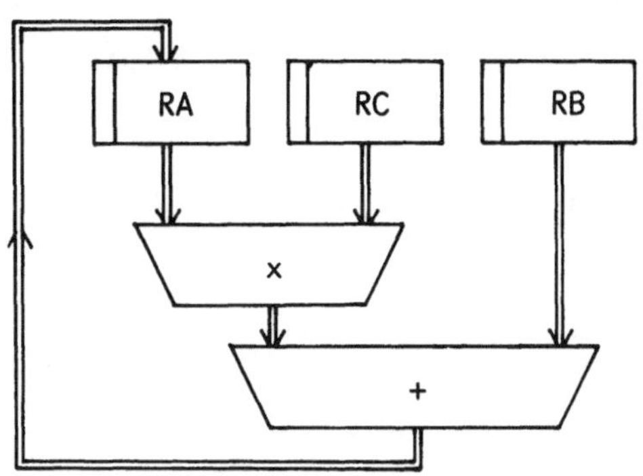

Abb. 1   Blockschaltbild für die Funktion   a := b + a x c

Symbolisch könnte man auch schreiben:

$$RA \longrightarrow B(x) \longrightarrow B(+) \longrightarrow RA$$
$$RC \nearrow \quad RB \nearrow$$

Diese Schreibweise ist nicht direkt als Eingabesprache für einen Digitalrechner geeignet. Wir benutzen deshalb die Postfix-Notation:

$$RB/RA/RC \rightarrow B(x) \rightarrow B(+) \;=: \; RA \qquad\qquad (3.1)$$

Operanden werden durch " / " getrennt, Operatoren durch " -> " hervorgehoben. Da die Zahl der Eingänge eines Operators durch den Anfangsbuchstaben festgelegt ist, ist die Schreibweise eindeutig. Das umgekehrte ALGOL-Symbol " =: " bedeutet, daß mit dem Takt das Ergebnis der linken Seite in den rechts stehenden Speicher übernommen wird. Diese Vertauschung der üblichen Schreibweise wurde vorgenommen, um den Datenfluß und Zeitablauf von links nach rechts zu demonstrieren. Der Takt ist der Abschluß der Operation.

Der Ausdruck (3.1) stellt ein <statement> dar. In MIMOLA Ø können alle <statement> gleichzeitig ausgeführt werden, für die es der Algorithmus erlaubt. Sie werden durch " , " getrennt. Eine Vertauschungsoperation schreiben wir:

$$R1 \;=: \; R2, \quad R2 \;=: \; R1$$

Ein <elementary statement block> umfaßt alle gleichzeitig ausgeführten <statement>. Er beginnt mit einem <label> , der aus L und einer Zahl

besteht. Beim Übergang von einem Niveau auf ein tieferes werden weitere durch
" . " getrennte Zahlen angehängt. Ein < elementary statement block > wird durch
" ; " abgeschlossen. Ein Beispiel in MIMOLA 1:

            L1.3   R1 =: R2,   R2 =: R1 ;

Wo es möglich und auch sinnvoll erscheint, Konstruktionen höherer Programmiersprachen hardwaremäßig zu realisieren, sind diese direkt als Sprachelemente
in MIMOLA übernommen worden, z.B.:

            L1   FOR j FROM 3 BY a TO 1ØØ ;
            L2   WHILE b DO
                      S(sum) / S(feld[j]) -> B(+) =: S(sum) , FI ;
            ....
            L6   IF S(max) / S(feld[j]) -> B(<):
                      THEN S(feld[j]) =: S(max), FI,
                      OD ;

Kleine Buchstaben bezeichnen Identifikatoren, die in Ausdrücken Adressen darstellen. Durch "[ ]" wird dereferenziert.

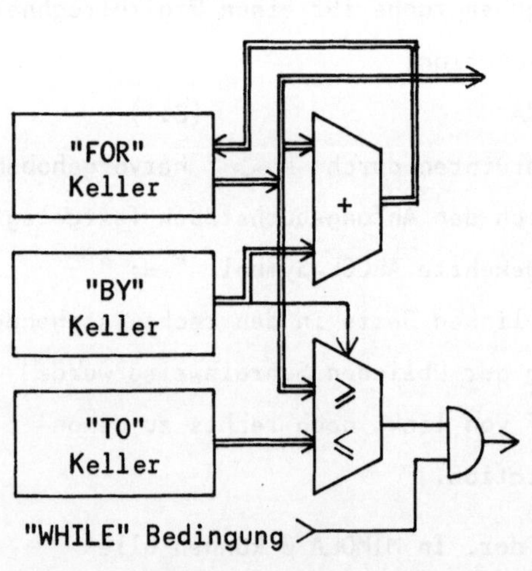

Abb.2   Modul für Wiederholungs-
         anweisungen

Abb.2 zeigt ein Beispiel für einen
Modul, der Wiederholungsanweisungen
mit 3 Kellerspeichern ausführen kann.
Die Schachtelungstiefe ist nur durch
die Tiefe der Keller bestimmt. Der
" FOR "-Keller hat im allgemeinen
einen 2. freiadressierbaren Ausgang,
um auch an die Indizes äußerer Schleifen heranzukommen.

Es konnte hier nur ein kleiner Aus-
schnitt der Sprache gezeigt werden.
Die Programmbeispiele sollten aber
trotzdem verständlich sein. Die Sprache soll lebendig bleiben, um neue
Ideen zur Rechnerorganisation standart-
mäßig aufnehmen zu können. Sie ist so
flexibel, daß neue Elemente und Moduln durch Deklarationen ohne Sprachänderungen

eingeführt werden können.

4. Entwurfsbeispiel

Im folgenden soll die Methode an einem kurzen Beispiel demonstriert werden. Die z_i sind sequentiell und rekursiv zu berechnen, damit Wiederholungsanweisungen auftreten. Ein so kurzes Problem kann natürlich nicht zu einem Universalrechner führen. Deshalb werden auch keine statistischen Untersuchungen durchgeführt. Dafür lassen sich alle Schritte von Hand nachvollziehen.

Schritt 1

Es sollen die Funktionen z_i für $i = 1 \ldots m$ nach folgenden Formeln berechnet werden, wobei die a_{ij} und y_k vorgegeben sind für $j = 1 \ldots n$, $k = 1 \ldots 2m$.

$$z_i = b_n \quad \text{mit}$$
$$b_o = 0 , \qquad b_j = b_{j-1} + a_{ij} c_j ,$$
$$c_o = y_{m+i} , \quad c_j = c_{j-1} y_i / y_{m+i} .$$

Schritt 2

Ein entsprechendes ALGOL - Programm lautet:

```
BEGIN REAL ARRAY a[1:m, 1:n] , y[1:2m], z[1:m];   INTEGER m, n;
    ( Eingabe von a, y, m, n )
  BEGIN INTEGER i,j;
      FOR i := 1 UNTIL m DO
      BEGIN REAL b,c;   b := ∅ ;
      IF y m+i  ≠ ∅  THEN
         BEGIN c := y[m+i] ↑ n ;
         FOR j := 1 UNTIL n DO
            BEGIN c := c × y[i] / y[m+i] ;
                  b := b + a[i,j] × c ;
            END ;
         END ;  z[i] := b ;
      END;
  END;  .........
END;
```

Programm 1

Der angestrichene Teil von Programm 1 läßt sich leicht in MIMOLA ∅ übersetzen:

```
L1      FOR i TO m ;
L2      DO FØ. =: S(b) ,
        IF S(y[m+i]) -> A(=Ø.): THEN GOTO L5,
        ELSE S(y[m+i]) / S(n) -> B(↑ ) =: S(c),
        FOR j TO n, FI,
        FI;
L3      DO S(c) /S(y[i]) -> B(*) / S(y[m+i]) -> B(/) =: S(c),  FI;
L4      S(b) / S(a[i, j]) / S(c) -> B(*) -> B(+) =: S(b),
        OD;
L5      S(b) =: S(z[i]),
        OD;
```

Programm 2

Mit dem in Schritt 3 aufgelisteten Aufwand ließen sich diese 5 $<$ elementary statement block$>$ in je einem Mikroprogrammschritt ausführen. Unter Berücksichtigung der Schleifen wären es 1+2m+2mn Takte.

Schritt 3

Da das Beispiel sehr kurz ist, werden nur die wichtigsten Maximalwerte angegeben:

3	Seicherausgänge
1	Speichereingang
1	Rechenwerk ↑ , *, REAL
1	Rechenwerk +, /, REAL
1	Vergleicher =, REAL
1	Rechenwerk +, INT
2	1-dim. Array-Adressierungen
1	2-dim. Array-Adressierung
2	FOR-Schleifen

Schritt 4

Wir wollen einen Speicher für REAL mit 1 Eingang und 2 Ausgängen und 2 Adressen realisieren. Für den fehlenden Ausgang stehen 2 Hilfsregister zur Verfügung. Die Deklaration dafür lautet:

```
S( Ø : 16k ).BIT( Ø : 31 )REAL ;
S :=: S1.IN, S1.OUT, S2.OUT ;
RH;.BIT( Ø : 31 )REAL ;
```

```
        RH2.BIT( Ø : 31 )REAL ;
```

Es wird 1 Rechenwerk für REAL vorgesehen:

```
        B1( +, -, *, / ).REAL, B1( = ).OUT BIT( 32 ) ;
```

Da kein Potenzieren vorgesehen ist, treten Zahlen vom Typ INT nur für Adress-
und Zählzwecke auf. Dafür sind 1 Speicher und 2 Rechenwerke vorgesehen:

```
        SI( Ø : 31 ).BIT( Ø : 15)INT ;
        SI :=: SI1.OUT, SI2.IN, SI3.OUT ;
        B2( +, -, *, / ).INT ;
        B3( +, - ).INT ;
```

Weiter sei ein FOR-Schleifen-Werk nach Abb.2 vorhanden mit den Kellern:

```
        KF( 16 ).BIT( Ø : 15 ), KF1( -1 : -15 ).OUT ;
        KB( 16 ).BIT( Ø : 15 ) ;
        KT( 16 ).BIT( Ø : 15 ) ;
        K :=: KF, KB, KT ;
        K( pop ).PUSH ;
```

Die letzte Zeile bedeutet, daß PUSH automatisch beim Kellern erfolgt, POP aber
programmiert werden muß.

```
        F1 ;  FØ. ;              CO Konstanten        CO
        I ;                      CO Befehlsregister CO
        P ;                      CO Programmzähler  CO
```

Schritt 5

Mit dieser Modul-Wahl ist das nächste Sprachniveau - MIMOLA 1 - festgelegt.
Die Übersetzung von Programm 2 ergibt:

```
L1.1    FOR i   F1 =: KF ,  F1 =: KB ,  SI1(I(m)) =: KT ;
L2.1    DO      FØ. =: S1(I(b)) ,
        IF      S1(I(y-1) / SI1(I(m)) -> B2(+) / KF -> B3(+)) / FØ.
                -> B1(=).BIT(32):
        THEN    I(L5.1) =: P , FI ,
        ELSE    I(L6.1) =: P , K(pop) =: K , FI ;
L2.2            S2(I(y-1) / SI1(I(m)) -> B2(+) / KF -> B3(+)) = V =: RH1 ,
                V =: RH2 ,
        FOR k   SI3(I(zwei)) =: KF ,  F1 =: KB ;
```

```
L2.3                SI1(I(n)) =: KT ;
L2.4      DO        RH1 / RH2 -> B1(*) =: RH1 ,
          OD ,      I(L2.4) =: P ,
          ELSE      K(pop) =: K , FI ;
L2.5      FOR j     F1 =: KF ,   F1 =: KB , SI1(I(n)) =: KT ;
L3.1      DO        RH1 / S1(I(y-1) / KF1(-1) -> B2(+)) '  B1(*) =: RH2 ,
          ELSE      I(L5.1) =: P , K(pop) =: K , FI ;
L3.2                RH2 / S1(I(y-1) / SI1(I(m)) -> B2(+) / KF1(-1) -> B3(+))
                    -> B1(/) =: RH1 ;
L4.1                I(a-n-1) / KF1(-1) / SI1(I(n)) -> B2(*) -> B3(+) =: SI2(I(h)) ;
L4.2                S1(SI1(I(h)) / KF -> B2(+)) / RH1 ->B1(*) =: RH2 ;
L4.3                S1(I(b)) / RH2 -> B1(+) =: S1(I(b)) ,
          OD ,      I(L3.1) =: P ;
L5.1                S2(I(b)) =: S1(I(z-1) / KF -> B3(+)) ,
          OD ,      I(L2.1) =: P ;
```

Programm 3

Schritt 6

Die Häufigkeit der in Programm 3 auftretenden Daten- und Adresswege zeigt
Tabelle 1. Mit einer größeren Programmenge würden sich die Häufigkeiten und
auch die Zahl der verschiedenen Verbindungen erhöhen. Letztere strebt aber
schnell gegen einen Grenzwert, der weit unter der Zahl der möglichen Verbindungen liegt. Aus Tabelle 1 lesen wir ab, daß das Programm 3 mit 39 Verbindungen
direkt ausgeführt werden kann. Wir wollen das Verfahren hier abbrechen und
annehmen, daß wir alle Verbindungen realisieren und durch Multiplexer schalten.
Die notwendigen 12 Multiplexer können durch 18 Adressbits (Zeile M.A. in Tabelle 1) gesteuert werden. Auf weitere Einzelheiten des Rechners wollen wir hier
verzichten.

Das Ergebnis des Entwurfs ist eine Zentraleinheit, deren Blockschaltbild Abb. 3
zeigt. Es sind alle Daten- und Adresswege eingezeichnet. Es fehlen die Steuer-
leitungen vom Befehlsregister I zu den Multiplexern und Moduln.

Wir wollen nun den Aufwand und die Leistung dieser Zentraleinheit mit der eines
Universalrechners vergleichen und nehmen dazu einen MODCOMP II, einen 16-bit-
Rechner. Dieser Rechner hat eine getrennte REAL-Hardware-Recheneinheit, die mit

Ausgänge	Eingänge													Adressen						
	S1	RH1	RH2	B1 links	B1 rechts	SI2	B2 l.	B2 r.	B3 l.	B3 r.	KF	KB	KT	S1	S2	SI1	SI2	SI3	KF1	P
S1				3	2															
S2	1	1	1																	
RH1				2	1															
RH2				1	2															
FØ.					1															
B1	1	2	2																	
SI1							1	4					3							
SI3											1									
F1											2	3								
B2									3	1				2						
B3						1								3	1					
KF								1		3										
KF1							1	1		1										
I							4		2					1	1	7	1	1	3	6
SUMME	2	2	2	3	4	1	3	3	2	3	2	1	1	3	2	1	1	1	1	1
M.A.	1	1	1	2	2	0	2	2	1	2	1	0	0	2	1	0	0	0	0	0

SUMME: 39 Verbind. — M.A.: 18

<u>Tabelle 1</u>

B1 vergleichbar ist und die eigene Register hat, entsprechend RH1 und RH2. Das
Hauptrechenwerk ist mit B2 vergleichbar. Der 16-Wort-Registersatz entspricht
nicht ganz SI, da er nur 1 Adresse hat. Das gleiche gilt für den Hauptspeicher
des MODCOMP und S. Der MODCOMP ist mikroprogrammiert und hat einen umfangreichen Maschinenbefehlssatz. Die in Abb.3 gezeigte Zentraleinheit hat im wesentlichen im Vergleich zum MODCOMP zusätzliche Speicherausgänge, ein Addierwerk
und einen Modul für Wiederholungsanweisungen.

5. <u>Ergebnis</u>

Der MODCOMP-FORTRAN-Compiler benutzt hauptsächlich die offene Unterprogramm-
technik, so daß die übersetzten Programme mit den in MIMOLA geschriebenen verglichen werden können. Für das in FORTRAN umkodierte Programm 1 benötigt der
MODCOMP 86 Maschinenbefehle, die auf 140 Speicherplätzen à 16 bit stehen. Das
gleiche Programm in MIMOLA 1 übersetzt - Programm 3 - hat 12 Befehle, die

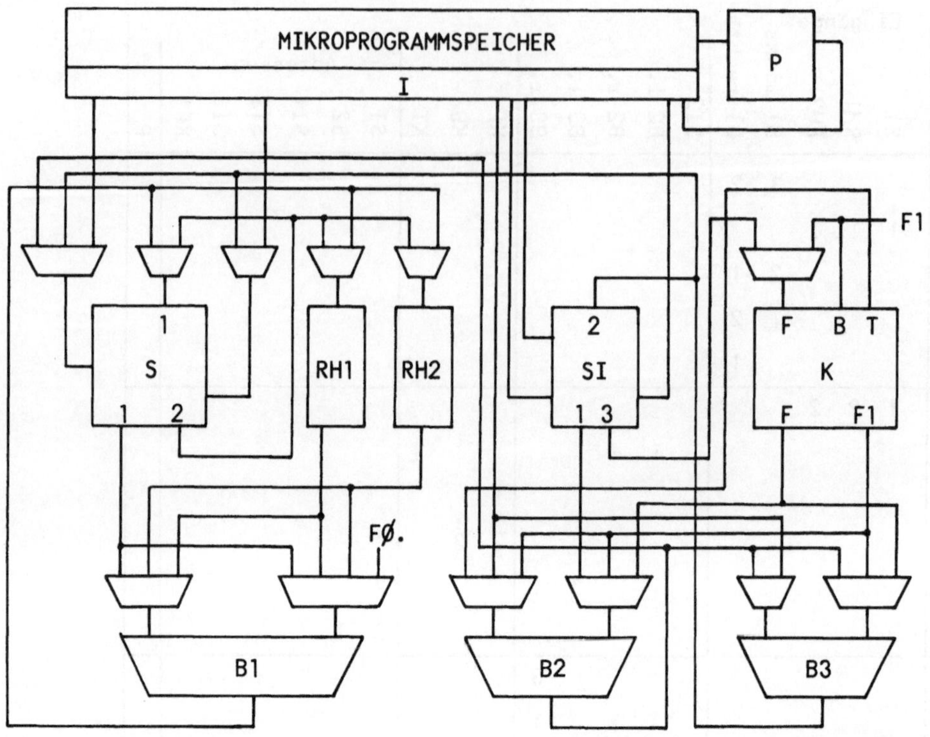

Abb. 3   Zentraleinheit

12 Mikroprogrammspeicherplätze einnehmen. Jedes Befehlswort umfaßt im Beispiel etwa 100 bit.Selbst wenn wir für einen Rechner mit allen Funktionen eine Befehlswortlänge von 160 bit annehmen, brauchten wir bei voll horizontaler Mikroprogrammierung immer noch etwas weniger Speicherraum für das Programm als beim MODCOMP. Die große Wortlänge ist bei Halbleiterspeichern kein technisches Problem.

Der Erfolg der Methode zeigt sich darin, daß z.B. der hier entwickelte Rechner um einen Faktor 7 weniger Programmschritte braucht als ein als schnell zu bezeichnender Rechner wie der MODCOMP II. Der Aufwand ist dabei nicht einmal doppelt so groß. Wenn man von gleichen Speicherzykluszeiten ausgeht, so bedeutet das auch eine Geschwindigkeitssteigerung um einen Faktor 7. Bei getrennten schnellen Daten- und Programmspeichern wird dieser Faktor bedeutend größer, da ein MODCOMP-Befehl im Mittel noch in 6 Mikroprogrammschritte zerfällt. Der Faktor 7

wurde für etwa die gleiche Modulmenge auch bei einer größeren Anzahl längerer
Programme als Mittelwert gefunden.

6. Zusammenfassung

Es wurde an einem kurzen Beispiel gezeigt, wie mit Hilfe der Sprache MIMOLA
aus einem Problem ein Prozessor entwickelt wird, dessen Organisation schrittweise durch direkt aus dem Problem abgeleitete Anforderungen und durch von der
Wirtschaftlichkeit vorgegebene Grenzen gewonnen wurde. Der Entwerfer hat auf
diese Schritte großen Einfluß, bekommt aber durch die statistische Erfaßbarkeit
der idealen Anforderungen präzise Entscheidungshilfen. Die Auswirkung der von
ihm getroffenen Entscheidungen kann er direkt nach dem wieder maschinell durch-
führbaren Übersetzungsschritt erkennen. Die Zahl der dabei erzeugten < elementary
statement block > ist in erster Näherung der Laufzeit proportional.

Es kann ein Simulator geschaffen werden, der die deklarierte Maschine exakt
simuliert und MIMOLA-Programme ausführen kann. Damit kann das Maschinenkozept
überprüft werden, was aber durch den Entwurfsformalismus nicht notwendig ist,
da Fehler bereits von dem Compiler gemeldet werden. Deshalb kann ein solcher
Simulator nur die Korrektheit der ursprünglichen Programme und der Compiler
selbst überprüfen. Er kann aber sinnvoll für Leistungsmessungen eingesetzt
werden.

Alle Schritte des Entwurfs bis auf das Auswählen der Programmenge und die Deklaration der Hardware können maschinell durchgeführt werden. Die Syntax von
MIMOLA ist durch ein Produktionssystem definiert. Die Deklarationen bestimmen
die Übersetzerhandlungen bei der Übersetzung auf ein tieferes Niveau der Sprache.
Aus syntaktisch richtigen Programmen entstehen durch die Übersetzung wieder
syntaktisch richtige, so daß die Syntax nur auf dem höchsten Niveau geprüft
werden muß. Die Übersetzung ist einfach, solange nicht optimiert wird. Während
der Entwurfsphase ist eine Optimierung aber nicht notwendig.

Die Übersetzung wird im wesentlichen so vorgenommen, daß in einem < elementary
statement block > mit Hilfe der Syntaxanalyse von links nach rechts executierbare Ausdrücke gesucht und die Moduln vergeben werden. Sind diese erschöpft, so
wird der executierbare Teil zu einem neuen < elementary statement block > ,
wobei die Syntax im Prinzip bis auf Einschränkungen gleich bleibt. Eine einfache
Optimierung kann Mehrfachberechnungen der gleichen Größe durch Zwischenspeiche-
rung vermindern, wenn dadurch < elementary statement block > gespart werden.

Für einen mit dieser Methode erstellten Prozessor stellt ein Übersetzer, der alle Deklarationen enthält, einen Compiler für beliebige Benutzerprogramme dar, der direkt von MIMOLA $\emptyset$ auf das Maschinenniveau übersetzt. Ein einfacher Assembler erzeugt dann den Mikroprogrammcode.

Auch für andere mikroprogrammierbare Maschinen kann die Sprache zur Beschreibung, Simulation und als Mikroprogrammcompiler benutzt werden. Durch die Einführung von Makros ließe sich sogar jede Maschine auf der Ebene ihrer Maschinensprache darstellen. Damit könnte MIMOLA als universelle Schnittstelle zwischen höheren Programmiersprachen und der Hardware dienen. Über die Effektivität der darauf beruhenden Compiler kann hier aber noch nichts ausgesagt werden. Es ist aber gezeigt worden, daß die Sprache MIMOLA ihre eigentliche Aufgabe erfüllt: die bessere Ausnutzung der Hardware durch einen systematischen Rechnerentwurf, der die zu bearbeitenden Probleme als Ausgangspunkt hat.

Literatur

/1/ W. Giloi, H. Liebig: Logischer Entwurf digitaler Systeme, Springer Verlag 1973

/2/ S. Wendt: Entwurf komplexer Schaltwerke, Springer Verlag 1974

/3/ Y. Chu: Computer Organization and Microprogramming, Prentice Hall 1972

/4/ G.Zimmermann: MIMOLA - Maschine Independant Microprogramming Language, Beschreibung der Syntax, Bericht des Instituts für Informatik und Praktische Mathematik, Universität Kiel, erscheint 1976

Anschrift des Verfassers

Doz. Dr. Gerhard Zimmermann, Institut für Informatik und Praktische Mathematik, Christian-Albrechts-Universität,. Olshausenstr. 40-60
23 Kiel

<u>Adressenliste</u>

Albert, J.;   Universität Karlsruhe, Inst. f.
                      angewandte Informatik u. formale
                      Beschreibungsverfahren, Postfach 6380,
                      7500 Karlsruhe, W-Germany

Ammeraal, L.;   Stichting Mathem. Centrum,
                      2E Boerhaavestraat, 49, Amsterdam 1005,
                      The Netherlands

Ancilotti, P.;   Consig. Naz. delle Ricerche, Istit.
                      di Elaborazione della Informazione,
                      Via S. Maria, 46, 56100 Pisa, Italy

Ausiello, G.;   Istituto di Automatica, Via Eudossiana, 18,
                      00184 Roma, Italy

Beilner, H.;   Universität Dortmund, Abt. Informatik IV
                      August-Schmidt-Str., 4600 Dortmund,
                      W-Germany

Corsini, P.;   Università di Pisa, Dipartim. Sperimentale
                      di Elettrot. ed Elettronica, Via Dioti-
                      salvi, 2, 56100 Pisa, Italy

Deck, M.;   Beethovenstr. 54, 6733 Haßloch,
                      W-Germany

De Michelis, G.;   Università di Milano, Gruppo Elettro-
                      nica e Cibernetica, Via Viotti, 5,
                      20133 Milano, Italy

Diel, H.;   PS Steuerprogramme KST. 3256, 7030-14,
                      Schönaicher Str. 220, 7030 Böblingen,
                      W-Germany

Encarnacao, J.;   TH Darmstadt, FB 20 (Informatik),
                      Steubenplatz 12, 6100 Darmstadt,
                      W-Germany

Erbe, R.;

IBM Wiss. Zentrum Heidelberg, Tiergartenstr. 15, 6900 Heidelberg, W-Germany

Erni, W.;

Inst. f. Angew. Mathematik, Im Neuenheimer Feld 5, 6900 Heidelberg, W-Germany

Güttler, R.;

Univ. d. Saarlandes, Fachbereich 10, 6600 Saarbrücken, W-Germany

Härder, T.;

Beethovenstr. 7, 6101 Wixhausen, W-Germany

Hanani, M.Z.;

Ben Gurion University of the Negev, P.O.B. 2053, Beersheva 84120, Israel

Hartwig, R.

IBM Deutschland GmbH, Datenverarbeitung, Wissenschaftl. Zentrum, Tiergartenstr. 15, 6900 Heidelberg, W-Germany

Henn, R.;

Institut f. Informatik, TU München, Postfach 202420, 8000 München 2, W-Germany

Heydthausen, M.;

Universität des Saarlandes, Fachbereich 10, 6600 Saarbrücken, W-Germany

Holt, A.W.;

Mass. Computer Ass., Inc., 26, Princess Street, Wakefield, Mass. 01880, U.S.A.

Innes, D.R.;

The University of Newcastle upon Tyne, Computing Laboratory, Claremont Tower, Claremont Road, Newcastle upon Tyne NE1 7RU, Great Britain

Kantorowitz, E.;

IBM Deutschland GmbH, Niederlassung Heidelberg, Tiergartenstr. 15, 6900 Heidelberg, W-Germany

Kogon, R.;	IBM Deutschland GmbH, Heidelberg Scientific Center, Tiergartenstr. 15 6900 Heidelberg, W-Germany
Kritzinger, P.S.;	Department of Computing and Control, Imperial College, 180 Queens Gate, London, Great Britain
Lanzarone, G.A.;	University di Milano, Gruppo Elettronica e Cibernetica, Via Viotti, 5, 20133 Milano, Italy
Lattermann, D.;	IBM Deutschland GmbH, Wissenschaftl. Zentrum, Tiergartenstr. 15, 6900 Heidelberg, W-Germany
Lehmann, H.;	IBM Deutschland GmbH, Wissenschaftl. Zentrum, Tiergartenstr. 15, 6900 Heidelberg, W-Germany
Lüdtke, H.;	TU Berlin, Fachber. 20, Kybernetik, Ernst-Reuter-Platz 9, 1000 Berlin 10, W-Germany
Mayer, O.;	Fachber. Informatik, Univ. Kaiserslautern, Pfaffenbergstr., 6750 Kaiserslautern, W-Germany
Mehlhorn, K.;	Universität des Saarlandes, Fachber. 10, 6600 Saarbrücken, W-Germany
Moscarini, M.;	Centro di Studio dei Sistemi di Controllo e Calcolo Automatici del C.N.R., Via Eudossiana, 18, 00184 Roma, Italy
Österle, H.;	Universität Dortmund, Abt. Wirtschafts- u. Sozialwissenschaften Postfach 500500, 4600 Dortmund 50, W-Germany

Ott, N.;   IBM Deutschland GmbH, Wissenschaftl.
                          Zentrum, Tiergartenstr. 15,
                          6900 Heidelberg, W-Germany

Pokorny, C.;   TU Wien, Inst. f. Informationssysteme,
                          Argentinierstr. 8, A-1040 Wien,
                          Austria

Pouzin, L.;   I.R.I.A., Domaine de Voluceau,
                          Rocquencourt, 78150 Le Chesnay,
                          France

Radin, G.;   IBM Research Division, Mathematical
                          Science Dept., Box 218, Yorktown Heights,
                          N.Y. 10598, U.S.A.

Räihä, K.J.;   University of Helsinki, Dept. of
                          Computer Science, Töölönkatu 11,
                          00100 Helsinki 10, Finland

Reus, J.;   Reuterallee 44, 6100 Darmstadt,
                          W-Germany

Rozenberg, G.;   Department of Mathematics,
                          University of Antwerp U.I.A.,
                          Wilrijk, Belgium

Saarinen, M.;   University of Helsinki, Dept. of
                          Computer Science, Töölönkatu 11,
                          00100 Helsinki 10, Finland

Schindler, S.;   TU Berlin, Fachber. 20, Kyber-
                          netik, Ernst-Reuter-Platz 9,
                          1000 Berlin 10, W-Germany

Schmidt, P.;   Inst. f. angew. Mathematik u. Infor-
                          matik, Abt. Informatik I, Universi-
                          tät Bonn, Wegelerstr. 6, 5300 Bonn,
                          W-Germany

Schmitz, P.;

Lehrstuhl f. Informatik, Universität zu Köln, Robert-Koch-Str. 10, 5000 Köln 41, W-Germany

Schneider, W.;

Universität des Saarlandes, FB 10, 6600 Saarbrücken, W-Germany

Simone, C.;

Universita di Milano, Gruppo Elettronica e Cibernetica, Via Viotti, 5, 20133 Milano, Italy

Solms, S.H. von

Dept. of Computer Science, Rand Africaans University, Johannesburg 2000, South Africa

Walch, G.;

IBM Wissenschaftl. Zentrum Heidelberg, Tiergartenstr. 15, 6900 Heidelberg, W-Germany

Walke, B.;

AEG, Bereich Forschung und Entwicklung, Postfach 1730, 7900 Ulm W-Germany

Weber, G.;

TH Darmstadt, Fachbereich 20, Steubenplatz 12, 6100 Darmstadt, W-Germany

Wedekind, H.;

TH Darmstadt, FB 20 (Informatik), Hochschulstr. 1, 6100 Darmstadt, W-Germany

Wernet, N.;

Universität des Saarlandes, Fachber. 10, 6600 Saarbrücken, W-Germany

Wertz, H.;

U.E.R. Informatique et Linguistique, Univ. de Paris VIII, Paris, France

Zimmermann, G.;   Inst. f. Informatik u. prakt.
Mathematik, Chr.-Albrechts-Univer-
sität, Olshausenstr. 4060,
2300 Kiel 1, W-Germany

Zöppritz, M.;   IBM Deutschland GmbH, Wissenschaftl.
Zentrum, Tiergartenstr. 15,
6900 Heidelberg, W-Germany

Lecture Notes in Computer Science

Lecture Notes in Computer Science